# Quality Control in Fact Finding

**Morten Bergsmo and Carsten Stahn
(editors)**

**Second Edition**

**2020**
**Torkel Opsahl Academic EPublisher**
**Brussels**

*Front cover:* Mr. Renzo Scarpelli of Florence at work, one of the leading pietre dure craftsmen and artists in the world. He displays the utmost quality control in his selection of motive, types of stone, their preparation, combination, and finish. In his field, Mr. Scarpelli epitomizes the idea of quality control, as illustrated by this picture. As such, he symbolizes the craftsman-like sense of quality that should be exercised in the establishment and operation of non-criminal justice fact-finding mandates. Photograph: © TOAEP 2012.

*Back cover:* A centuries old, hand-made brick taken from the wall during the restoration of the CILRAP Bottega or office in Florence. Quality control entails immediate engagement with the matter before us, seeking to alleviate hollowness or weak foundation through a hands-on approach. Photograph: © TOAEP 2020.

*Dedicated to the memory of Professor Frits Kalshoven,*
*the first Chair of the UNSC Commission of Experts*
*for the former Yugoslavia*

# PREFACE TO THE SECOND EDITION BY THE CO-EDITORS

We are pleased to release this Second Edition of *Quality Control in Fact-Finding*, with updated Chapters 1, 2, 7, 8, 11, 14 and 15; a new foreword by Professor Mads Andenæs; and three additional chapters: by Geoffrey Robertson QC ("17. Human Rights Fact-Finding: Some Legal and Ethical Dilemmas"), Dr. Emma Irving ("18. Finding Facts on Facebook: Social Media in the Work of Human Rights Fact-Finding Bodies"), and Dr. William H. Wiley ("19. International(ised) Criminal Justice at a Crossroads: The Role of Civil Society in the Investigation of Core International Crimes and the 'CIJA Model'"). The new chapters not only represent a one-fifth increase of the book's contents, but they introduce topical subjects like ethics in fact-finding, social media and fact-finding, and private fact-finding into the work. We expect that future editions will similarly expand the scope of the book, ensuring that it continues to add value to the field of fact-finding and documentation.

The First Edition was well received, with favourable reviews in the *European Journal of International Law* and the *Nordic Journal of Human Rights*, and positive feedback from professionals in the United Nations human rights system and leading non-governmental organisations. It was decided to make a Second Edition for three reasons. First, the publisher received three additional chapters that enrich the book. Secondly, the publisher is generally committed to publishing new, improved editions of its books, which is made possible by the non-profit, golden open-access approach it has adopted.

Thirdly, the Centre for International Law Research and Policy (CILRAP) is about to complete the third leg of the trilogy that is born out of its Quality Control Project, namely *Quality Control in Criminal Investigation*. In 2018, *Quality Control in Preliminary Examination: Volumes 1 and 2* were published. *Quality Control in Fact-Finding*, first published in 2013, was the first leg of the trilogy, and it was felt that the completion of this multi-year project (2013-2020) is a suitable occasion for this Second Edition to appear.

i

Whereas the second and third legs – preliminary examination and criminal investigation – both concern fact-work undertaken within criminal justice systems, *Quality Control in Fact-Finding* deals with fact-finding and documentation *outside* criminal justice, typically in United Nations human rights mandates or the documentation work undertaken by non-governmental organisations. This latter work can obviously be improved. Creating better synergies with insights that can be gleaned from the generous investments in international criminal justice since 1994 is one avenue that should be further explored.

But at the end of the road, quality control in fact-finding is about nourishing a *mindset* that encourages constant questioning of the way fact-finding is undertaken, by those who are engaged in it. This requires courage, commitment and analysis. Managers of fact-finding mandates should take active steps to facilitate a *culture* of quality control within their organisations, whereby they reward those who question their fact-finding work and ask whether something could be done better, rather than sanctioning or otherwise silencing such colleagues.

We would like to thank the publisher, in particular Mr. CHAN Icarus and Mr. Antonio Angotti, as well as Mr. Devasheesh Bais of CILRAP. We also thank the authors, both old and new.

Morten Bergsmo and Carsten Stahn
Co-Editors

# FOREWORD TO THE SECOND EDITION
## BY MADS ANDENÆS

The first edition of *Quality Control in Fact-Finding* appeared in 2013. It has influenced the discourse on and practice of international fact-finding, making 'quality control' an emerging mainstream term in this context, if not yet a rallying cry. Dealing with international human rights and criminal law monitoring and enforcement, it may seem much less important to address the primarily procedural and work-process issues of the kind this book addresses. The only problem is that good intentions and a burning heart only take you so far. It is through policy formulation and substantive law, supported by institutions, procedures and practices, that an international system gets the bite it needs. Without fact-finding, there can be no international monitoring or enforcement – it is also necessary for policy formulation and substantive law. For fact-finding to serve its purpose, it must be subjected to rigorous quality control. There are early signs that some relevant international organisations are starting to actively foster both mindsets and cultures of quality control in their fact-finding work. The book covers a broad spectrum of issues in human rights fact-finding, from the formulation of the mandate, to the use of information technology. It also includes authors of diverse backgrounds, including four Chinese scholars.

The second edition should have a further and even more penetrating impact. Human rights fact-finding can still learn from the very significant investment in international criminal justice fact-work since 1994. Synergies should be more fully utilised, and this book can help that process along. More fundamentally, the volume concerns a next-generation challenge of the international human rights and criminal law monitoring and enforcement systems. It is vital that this challenge be properly embraced in the coming years, given the broader political developments in countries such as China, India, Russia and the United States. Errors in human rights fact-finding reports can undermine not only the mandate in question, but trust in international monitoring and accountability in general. Powerful states do not fail to notice such errors, and can make use of them at will. Quality control as it is developed in the international monitoring processes also has direct consequences for domestic law and the minimum standards for its requirements for inquiries or directly for court review.

The Centre for International Law Research and Policy (CILRAP) has worked consistently on its Quality Control Project since 2013, leading to the publication of several volumes on the topic. *Quality Control in Fact-Finding* is the first of these volumes. It looks at fact-finding outside criminal justice agencies, typically in United Nations ('UN') human rights mandates or the documentation work of non-governmental organisations. The subsequent volumes in the trilogy produced by the project consider fact-finding within criminal justice agencies, at the preliminary examination and investigation stages.

The theme of quality control is consistently relevant in fact-finding, which can, by its very nature, almost always be further improved or professionalised. It is neither negative nor pointed against specific mandates or organisations. Rather, its neutral, universal character helps fact-finders not to feel defensive when confronted by this approach. This contributes to making the approach convincing at the conceptual level, and helpful at the practical and applied level. It is not about providing a handbook, but *Quality Control in Fact-Finding* and the other volumes in the trilogy may be used as such. It is just very useful to have at hand for anyone involved in a fact-finding mission or other fact-work.

Improving quality control in human rights fact-finding is not only important for victims, but also for states that feel that human rights are being used selectively against themselves, sometimes without proper grounding in facts. I know this is a feature of China's criticisms of the UN human rights machinery. The quality-control approach does not take any side in such discussions, but simply says that it is vital that all human rights fact-finding be undertaken according to the highest professional standards. This approach can serve as a bridge-builder. Through the highest procedural standards, one may achieve a higher level of legitimacy. The quality-control approach does not stop or hold back fact-finding inquiries. It provides the concepts for a discourse around, and the tools for, the inquiry. Admittedly, procedural and evidentiary requirements may be raised to such a level that they become difficult to instrumentalise and apply in practice. Quality control could become such a demanding set of requirements that they would paralyse. However, quality control must build on some absolute standards but mostly a proportionality requirement which will counter such paralysing effects. The improvement in quality control in human rights fact-finding that this book develops is empowering, because it shows why and how, and also because it increases the legitimacy and the acceptance that procedural standards and quality control can endow.

The fact-finding processes, in UN human rights mandates or the documentation work of non-governmental organisations, have different outputs. UN human rights mandates would rule in individual complaints, adopt country reports according different reporting periods or other criteria, report on themes or broader issues, or on specific incidents. Their reports may go to states directly, to the UN Human Rights Council or the General Assembly. They may require or lead to different kinds of actions from UN bodies or states. But they are used in different other contexts, and one such context is before the International Court of Justice or other courts and tribunals. In the years 1999-2005, I directed the project on 'Evidence before the International Court of Justice' at the British Institute of International and Comparative Law. I also wrote the first report from the project. It was one of the most interesting projects in my time as the Director of the British Institute. Anna Riddell and Brendan Plant's *Evidence before the International Court of Justice*[1] is the most recent publication in this project published some ten years after I left the Institute.

Already in my time directing the British Institute's evidence project, the International Court of Justice placed reliance on the fact-finding by UN Special Rapporteurs in two judgments. *The Legal Consequences of the Construction of a Wall in the Occupied Palestinian Territory* (the Israeli Wall advisory opinion) of 2004[2] relied both on the legal assessment and fact-finding of different Special Rapporteurs. In *Armed Activities on the Territory of the Congo (Democratic Republic of the Congo v. Uganda)* of 2005[3] the International Court placed even more reliance on such fact-finding. James Gerard Devaney's very important *Fact-Finding before the International Court of Justice*[4] analyses this practice, and its impact on the

---

[1]   Anna Riddell and Brendan Plant, *Evidence before the International Court of Justice*, British Institute of International and Comparative Law, London, 2016.

[2]   International Court of Justice ('ICJ'), *Legal Consequences cf the Construction of a Wall in the Occupied Palestinian Territory*, Advisory Opinion, 9 July 2004, No. 131, *I.C.J. Reports 2004*, p. 136 (https://www.legal-tools.org/doc/e5231b/).

[3]   ICJ, *Armed Activities on the Territory of the Congo (Democratic Republic of the Congo v. Uganda)*, Judgment, 19 December 2005, No. 116, *I.C.J. Reports 2005*, p. 168 (https://www.legal-tools.org/doc/8f7fa3/).

[4]   James Gerard Devaney, *Fact-Finding before the International Court of Justice*, Oxford University Press, 2016.

process before the International Court. This has been dealt with by other authors, including A. Mark Weisburd.[5]

More recently, Michael A. Becker has discussed the challenges for the Court when a party relies heavily on information not obtained through an adversarial or similarly quality-controlled fact-finding process, with particular emphasis on The Gambia's use of the UN Fact-Finding Mission's report in the case against Myanmar.[6] This problem is further highlighted by Eva Buzo, who describes how refugees in camps in Cox's Bazar in Bangladesh have been subjected to multiple interviews, that witness fatigue has set in, and that there has been active facilitation in the camps of which refugees fact-finders would be introduced to.[7] In his new chapter in this second edition, Geoffrey Robertson QC observes wisely that refugees should be interviewed

> before they come under the sway of local camp leaders who will indoctrinate them with the approved 'line' about political events back home, and will in certain cases coach them as to what to say. It may or may not be the truth, but because it is designed, for instance, to support the political line of the faction, or to support a case for asylum rather than economic migration, such coached stories must be discounted.[8]

Over years, I had encountered the varying and variable practices on fact-finding processes in NGO work, from the highest standards to something less. One early experience is writing a national report on political free speech which Interights submitted to the European Court of Human Rights in the *Lingens* case (1986). In my own work, I continued casting around for models. When I was engaged by the Council of Europe, the World Bank, the Asian Development Bank or states and their development agencies, there was no critical discourse to speak of, and no text in any way fulfilling the functions of *Quality Control in Fact-Finding*. In 2009, I was appointed a UN Special Human Rights Mandate Holder, and as *President-Rapporteur* for arbitrary detention, the methodology of fact-finding became an even more of a pressing problem. That applied to re-

---

[5]  A. Mark Weisburd, *Failings of the International Court of Justice*, Oxford University Press, 2016.

[6]  Michael A. Becker, "The Challenges for the ICJ in the Reliance on UN Fact-Finding Reports in the Case against Myanmar", *EJIL:Talk!*, 14 December 2019.

[7]  Eva Buzo, "Capturing a Crisis: What Lessons Can We Learn from the 'Overdocumentation' of the Rohingya Crisis?", *Justice in Conflict*, 20 May 2020.

[8]  See Geoffrey Robertson, "Human Rights Fact-Finding: Some Legal and Ethical Dilemmas", chap. 17 below, sub-section 17.2.6.1.

ports after country visits inspecting police stations, prisons, mental health institutions, and other places of detention, and discussing the issues with the government and civil society. It also applied to the opinions based on individual complaints, and the broader thematic reports. We developed an extensive practice on fact-finding, and tried to establish standards of quality-control.[9] There was a discourse beyond the different bodies, but it was limited.

Writing this Foreword allows me to share my appreciation of the importance of improving practice. This is a practice-oriented project. Habitual reductionism among lawyers may seek to reduce the significance of the project as merely being practice-oriented, and by that overlooking the vision that has guided the project and its discourse and scholarship value. Forgive me for stating the obvious, but while this project has been and will continue to be of great practical assistance, it goes far beyond that. Quality control has become a mainstream term in the context of fact-finding. The conceptualisation and critical discourse that the field requires has in practice been provided by the project.

Professor Mads Andenæs QC
University of Oslo

---

[9]   Jared Genser, *The UN Working Group on Arbitrary Detention*, Cambridge University Press, 2019, who writes, generally approvingly, of the procedures and fact-finding of the UN Working Group on Arbitrary Detention.

# PREFACE TO THE FIRST EDITION
## BY SERGE BRAMMERTZ

In tandem with the rise of international criminal justice since the early 1990s, we have seen a significant increase in international fact-finding outside criminal justice. Whereas many articles, books and blogs have been written on the international criminal jurisdictions, the discussion on other fact-finding mechanisms is only now beginning to attract the same level of attention. This anthology is therefore very welcome, not only for being timely, but more importantly for the creative way it frames the topic as "Quality Control in Fact-Finding" and the rich content this entails.

In criminal justice, the consequences of poor quality control may be an acquittal or an erroneous conviction. The former challenges victims. The latter can challenge the very legitimacy of a court. Weak quality control in criminal justice is therefore very visible and potentially dramatic.

But quality control is not less serious in fact-finding outside criminal justice, be it within the United Nations human rights system, international commissions of inquiry, national truth and reconciliation commissions, or by non-governmental organisations. Poor quality in their fact-finding directly affects the legitimate expectations of victims. And whereas international criminal justice is based on the principle of individual criminal responsibility, the international and regional human rights systems are centred on the principle of state responsibility. Although state responsibility does not point to individual perpetrators, but to the failures of more anonymous states, it is not less real or important than individual criminal responsibility. Rather, the two principles complement each other, as two pillars of the broader international system of reaction against serious violations of international law. Inadequate quality control in fact-finding can therefore impede the corrective role which state responsibility can play.

Quality control is in other words a common challenge in both criminal justice for core international crimes and other forms of fact-finding. I know this from my own professional experience in both areas of work. Criminal justice and fact-finding should therefore learn from each other. Neither can afford to become complacent and stop asking how the work on facts could be further improved. The process of migration of experienced professionals between the two areas should continue wherever useful. Non-criminal justice fact-finders should be willing to learn from international criminal justice to enhance quality in some work processes, even if their horizon is possible state responsibility rather than a criminal trial. And those of us who work in international criminal justice should be open to what other fact-finders have to offer. Mutual openness and respect is called for.

This book can assist us in these processes by laying out a common ground for reflection and discussion around technical and neutral terms such as quality control and professionalisation. These terms do not offend anyone and they capture a challenge facing all who serve in criminal justice or other forms of fact-finding. The book makes substantial contributions to the consideration of how fact-finding can be improved. I welcome the innovative conceptualisation of its topic, the composition of an impressive and diverse group of authors, and their texts. This is a comprehensive and useful book for which the Torkel Opsahl Academic EPublisher and the editor should be commended.

Serge Brammertz
Chief Prosecutor,
International Criminal Tribunal for the former Yugoslavia

# FOREWORD TO THE FIRST EDITION
## BY THE EDITOR

The idea to prepare this book was conceived in 1993 when I worked at the Palais des Nations in Geneva as a Legal Adviser to the Commission of Experts for the former Yugoslavia, a fact-finding mechanism established pursuant to United Nations Security Council resolution 780 (1992) on 6 October 1992. While the late Professor Torkel Opsahl was one of the five distinguished members of the Commission, I was a young international lawyer seconded by the Norwegian Foreign Ministry to assist the Commission and its small secretariat in its work. When I arrived in Geneva, Professor Frits Kalshoven was the Commission Chairman. His reception of the Norwegian secondee was attentive and warm, albeit measured. I quickly came to value this third quality of reserve most of all.

Every day, the Commission received large quantities of information on the armed conflicts raging at the time in the former Yugoslavia, including that relating to possible core international crimes. We were included in the circulation lists for a number of situation and operational reports developed in the field by various international and state actors. It was a veritable flood of information, with many sources containing graphic and gruesome descriptions of alleged violations. Despite the fact-richness, I tried to read and absorb all this information, so as to develop a deeper understanding of the complex realities of modern armed conflict through the lens of the ex-Yugoslavia wars. It made a strong impact on me and shaped my motivation to continue working with international criminal law.

Interestingly, while always displaying appropriate humanity when confronted with this material, I never witnessed Professor Kalshoven lowering his professional guard. He repeatedly asked questions about the authenticity of the source, its credibility, whether there was corroboration by other sources, the chain of transmission of any documents, the quality of translations, or the potential to verify what a source claimed. He displayed an uncompromising respect for the complexity of factual narration and reconstruction about and related to armed conflicts, and for fact-work[1]

---

[1]  The term 'fact-work' was coined in preparation of the 2013 LI Haopei Seminar held at the European University Institute in Florence on 20 May 2013, to capture work processes in

that is dependent on the exigencies of war or war-like situations. However shaken I was by what I read and heard, I sensed that Professor Kalshoven expected self-discipline in the relevant work processes, born out of a recognition of the fine balancing of interests on which international humanitarian law is based, the extent of the persistent politicisation of war, the pervasive emotions generated by war crimes, and the limits to what we can precisely know about certain incidents in armed conflicts.

From this example, I came to appreciate that the consistent fact-sensitivity required in order to have quality fact-finding cannot be turned on and off like electricity or simply prescribed normatively. It depends on the culture of fact-finding within a mechanism which is largely determined by the degree of responsible personal leadership. The abilities and qualities of those entrusted with leading fact-finding mandates cannot be replaced by large budgets, checks and balances, accountability mechanisms, or judicial review – the latter are necessary safeguards that supplement proper decisions on who should lead fact-finding. I do not think the jury is still deliberating this question.

Similarly, the commitment to professionalisation among the rank and file of individual fact-finders or fact-workers cannot be replaced by standard operating procedures, universal methodologies, or systemic approaches. The pursuit of best practices in fact-finding, when undertaken in isolation, can easily fall prey to the generalisation that Justice Richard J. Goldstone warns against in his Chapter 2: "It is folly to generalise about fact-finding missions". As the more systematic study of fact-finding now opens before us, it would be prudent for aspiring discourse actors to give effect to the considerable factual and legal diversity in fact-finding mandates and processes. This diversity is not random. It is dictated by the mandating bodies – that is, by states in execution of their foreign or domestic policies, as the case may be. This will continue to be a practice-led field, with new measures being tried out by mechanisms as varied as UN and regional human rights mandates, international fact-finding inquiries, national truth and reconciliation commissions, a myriad of fact-finding efforts of non-governmental organisations, and, hopefully, the Interna-

---

fact-finding that exceed 'finding facts' *stricto sensu*, such as analysing, assessing, corroborating or reporting facts. 'Fact-work' and 'fact-workers' are concise and more descriptive terms than many of the customary alternatives. Fact-workers should perhaps unite efforts to develop their professional terminology further. In my experience, there sometimes seems to be more resistence in the English language community than, for example, the German language space to the creation and use of new terms that lift the ability of language to reflect a greater measure of factual or other nuance.

tional Humanitarian Fact-Finding Commission. There are international, internationalised and domestic processes diversifying the picture further. This anthology illustrates how perspectives embedded in either of these non-criminal justice platforms differ and sometimes contradict one another. Compare, for example, the chapters by Professor Martin Scheinin, Judge David Re, Professor Lyal S. Sunga, Mr. Wolfgang Kaleck and Dr. Carolijn Terwindt. These constructive variations should inform those who may be tempted to advance new standard-setting to fact-finding of the inherent, naked limitations of such tools, which cannot replace the individual will to professionalise and improve the quality of fact-finding.

From the dynamics within the Commission of Experts for the former Yugoslavia and its Secretariat (as well as from the extensive informal interaction I had in 1993–1994 with the International Conference for the former Yugoslavia which had its offices in the same Palais des Nations), I came to realise that Professor Kalshoven's caution was not only a result of his intelligence and long experience with the armed forces of the Netherlands. It also reflected an acute awareness that propositions of specific violations of international humanitarian or criminal law throw shadows of incrimination on individuals and groups of individuals. The mandate of the Commission of Experts included the power to make such factual propositions. It had to be exercised responsibly. The Commission was also to be cautious in its statements on international law *de lege lata*. This disposition on the part of Professor Kalshoven revealed an awareness about the outer limits of the Commission's mandate, and how this mandate fundamentally differed from criminal justice mandates or the roles of national truth and reconciliation commissions or fact-work undertaken by non-governmental organisations. From this, I derived the lesson that good fact-finders should know the limits of their mandate as well as its centre. The scope of the mandate should guide their daily work as much as its core. Even when facing tearful victims, fact-finders should not try to be something they are not. If a fact-finding mechanism lacks the power to produce evidence in criminal trials, then there is no need to pretend otherwise. This is a common challenge for all fact-finders, regardless of the differences between their mandates.

My best supervisors have all been reluctant leaders. And so Professor Kalshoven was a very reluctant Chairman of the Commission of Experts for the former Yugoslavia. In the end, he resigned both as Chair and Member. Professor Torkel Opsahl was asked by the United Nations Office of Legal Affairs to take over. Suffering from serious, diagnosed heart weakness, he hesitated but nevertheless accepted to act as Chairman of the

Commission. He continued unabated his predecessor's line on factual accuracy and restraint. He pushed the work forward until his heart failed on 16 September 1993, when I was updating him in his Palais des Nations office on the progress of a Commission-convened meeting for non-governmental organisations on sexual violence in the former Yugoslavia. To honour his example and that of Professor Kalshoven, I decided that I would try to lead a group of experts to give more careful thought to quality control in fact-finding. It took 19 years to find the experts, opportunity and time to fulfil my pledge. I tried to use the experience gained in the meantime to fine-tune the approach eventually taken to the overall topic and sub-topics in this anthology, and the preceding 2013 LI Haopei Seminar held at the European University Institute in Florence on 20 May 2013, during which several of the book's chapters were first presented as papers.

As I transferred from the Commission of Experts to the Office of the Prosecutor of the International Criminal Tribunal for the former Yugoslavia in May 1994, I was gratified to see the extent to which the Commission's work had influenced the direction of the first investigations of the Office. As Judge David Re emphatically records in his excellent Chapter 11 below, hardly any of the Commission's factual material has been relied upon as evidence by Tribunal judges. This is not only in conformity with the thinking of the Members of the Commission with whom I worked at the time, but it reiterates the importance of knowing and sticking to one's mandate. I recall the interest with which I observed the Tribunal's investigators and prosecutors seeking to inform themselves of the alleged crimes, the patterns of crimes, the chains of authority in which suspects operated, and the power structures and decision-making processes that made up the hinterland to the harrowing landscape of crimes that arrested their professional energies. Parts of the Commission's work quite obviously set the stage for the Office of the Prosecutor's investigations and case preparation to an extent which may not yet be fully recognised. It would be useful if this interaction between a fact-finding commission and an international criminal jurisdiction were subjected to further study, drawing, *inter alia*, on the chapters below by Judge Re, Professor Dov Jacobs and Ms. Catherine Harwood. For example, the process of tapping into the wealth of information provided by one key insider used by the Tribunal until the publication of this book, had already started at the time of the Commission. Spending several hundred hours speaking with this person over a few years after I joined the Tribunal sensitised me to the multiple roles, plight, and integrity of victims, as well as the importance of their protection as a key feature of quality control strategies in fact-finding, as thoroughly demonstrated by Mr. Chris Mahony in his Chapter 10 below.

Curiously, after two years at the Tribunal, I found myself wondering how it could be that such a comprehensive criminal justice apparatus as its Office of the Prosecutor had not yet brought the substantive factual analysis as far forward since the Commission's completion of its work in 1994. I recalled the resistance I met from some investigators and prosecutors when I had suggested to introduce historical and statistical analysis to the centre of the fact-work of the Office. Quite apart from the resource demanding factual corroboration efforts underway, I came to realise that – absent contemporary precedents and models of international war crimes prosecutions – there were multi-layered educational processes going on within my Office, and that I was in the midst of that. This realisation consolidated my sense that the fact-finding arm of the Tribunal was, and would continue to be for years, its weaker limb and the one most in need of strengthening. This conclusion made me stay on at the Office of the Prosecutor much longer than I had planned, and drove me in August 2002 to move on to co-ordinate the establishment of the ICC's Office of the Prosecutor. I sought to make my modest contribution where I thought it most needed.

There were moments of frustration, such as when I witnessed how, against my persistent advice, some Tribunal investigators deconstructed the Commission of Expert's comprehensive paper archive prior to the arrival of the first Chief Prosecutor in the summer of 1994, thereby destroying the logic and drastically reducing the value of an archive that I had painstakingly helped to build into the late hours of the night, when serving at the Palais des Nations in Geneva. The best knowledge-base on war crimes in the former Yugoslavia at the time was rendered inoperational within a few hours.

Such exceptional episodes are dwarfed when contemplating how the ex-Yugoslavia Tribunal and subsequent international criminal jurisdictions have revolutionised international fact-work with regard to violations of international humanitarian and criminal law. In the course of my service to the Tribunal, it became clear to me that this rapidly accumulating experience would have to be digested and made available appropriately to those who undertake fact-work relevant to human rights violations outside criminal justice jurisdictions. The donors of international criminal justice should expect such spill-over of knowledge and expertise. The legacy of international criminal justice will be a tremendous resource for both national criminal justice and non-criminal justice fact-work for years into the future. Many professionals who have worked in international criminal justice would like to contribute to non-criminal justice fact-work. None of this is in dispute. Rather, the opposite could also be the case, namely, that towering lessons of international criminal justice and the resources it has wielded could intimidate non-criminal justice fact-work (as well as national criminal justice). A sense that "all roads lead to The Hague" can be detected, with the needs of international prosecution services being put forward as an exclusive or superior yardstick when assessing the quality of fact-finding efforts. The co-operative tone adopted by Chief Prosecutor Serge Brammertz in the Preface to this book suggests a mature leadership on this question. As Professor Martin Scheinin points out in his clear and important statement on the role and distinct characteristics of fact-finding within the United Nations human rights system in Chapter 3 below, there is no need to remake non-criminal justice fact-finding in the image of criminal justice. The former serves several purposes, by mandate and law, not shared by criminal justice. Much human rights fact-finding is ultimately geared towards considering state responsibility for human rights violations, not individual criminal responsibility for core international crimes. Such fact-finding can also have inherent advantages over criminal justice fact-work: it can be more flexible, focused, better led, and less expensive.

This book seeks to make a contribution to the emerging discourse on fact-finding mechanisms. It does so by focusing specifically on quality awareness and quality improvement in non-criminal justice fact-work. This quality control approach recognises the importance of leadership in fact-finding mandates, the responsibility of individual fact-finders to continuously professionalise, and the need for fact-finders to be mandate-centred, as discussed above. It is an approach that invites consideration of how the quality of every functional aspect of fact-finding can be improved, including work processes to identify, locate, obtain, verify, analyse, corroborate, summarise, synthesise, structure, organise, present, and disseminate facts. It is a state of mind characterised by a will to professionalise, and not just by the *ad hoc* development and adoption of standard procedures or universal methodologies that come so easily to lawyers.

As such, a quality control approach seeks to empower professional fact-finders as much as to regulate their work. This shows how the emerging discourse on fact-finding mechanisms is closely related to the discourse on knowledge transfer and capacity development in the field of criminal justice for core international crimes. One of the main challenges in fact-finding today is how to strengthen the capacity, particularly within civil society, to do relevant fact-finding in territorial states where the bulk of violations occur or are likely to take place. This is difficult, but of critical importance. It is not the responsibility of donors alone to contribute to such capacity development. Rather, resourceful human rights non-governmental organisations have a distinct responsibility, which they are discharging with varying degrees of success. It is very encouraging to see how the European Center for Constitutional and Human Rights is setting an example for larger, more resource-consuming organisations. It is noteworthy that a German-European organisation is taking the lead internationally, in a responsible and focused manner. Chapter 14 by Mr. Wolfgang Kaleck and Dr. Carolijn Terwindt is therefore particularly valuable.

It is inescapable that the quality of fact-finding will, to some extent, reflect the amount of resources available to the fact-finder. Fact-finding resources are not unlimited, but they are very unevenly distributed. Some fact-finding actors – such as the international criminal tribunals or Human Rights Watch – consume a very high percentage of the total amount of available resources. The Office of the UN High Commissioner for Human Rights and national truth and reconciliation commissions may consume less, whereas commissions of inquiry and organisations such as the European Center for Constitutional and Human Rights may be very cost-effective. This is an area which necessarily invites further analysis.

This anthology also draws our attention to the importance of utilising intelligently the remarkable capacity of the United Nations system to absorb facts widely as well as in a timely and in-depth manner, as elaborated by Professor Lyal S. Sunga in his Chapter 13 below. He asks whether we can afford to not use this unique resource better in fact-finding processes. We are left with a similar question about the International Humanitarian Fact-Finding Commission, the role of which is eloquently discussed by its Vice-President, Professor Charles Garraway, in Chapter 15.

By dissecting the overall topic of "Quality Control in Fact-Finding" into specific sub-topics in this way, it is hoped that this book will not only take the discussion forward in ways that invite broader participation and deeper contributions, but also be worthy of its dedication to the example set by Professor Emeritus Frits Kalshoven through his long life of service to international humanitarian law. It is striking how the diversity of perspectives, experience and knowledge of 19 authors exceeds what one author can reasonably contribute alone. Seeing this again reinforces my belief in open, inclusive, communicative scholarship, with appropriate conceptualisation and quality control. It may be indicative of how international law scholarship will evolve as the international community slowly but inevitably becomes a society.

Finally, let me thank Ms. Kiki A. Japutra for invaluable and indefatigable assistance in formatting this book; Ms. Kisha Krishna with English language washing and proofreading; Ms. FAN Yuwen and Ms. ZHANG Xin with assistance to make the Index; Professor CHEAH Wui Ling for her comments on this Foreword; and Mr. Alf Butenschøn Skre for incisive assistance with the dust jacket and processing of the manuscript. They have formed part of the publisher's quality control team for this book, for which I am solely responsible as editor.

Morten Bergsmo
Editor

# FOREWORD TO THE FIRST EDITION
# BY LING YAN

This anthology compiles academic papers presented at the 2013 LI Haopei Seminar on the topic "Quality Control in International Fact-Finding Outside Criminal Justice for Core International Crimes". The seminar was co-organised by the Centre for International Law Research and Policy, the European University Institute and the Peking University International Law Institute.

The LI Haopei Lecture Series was established by the Forum for International Criminal and Humanitarian Law (a department in the Centre for International Law Research and Policy) to honour the service and contribution to national and international law by the late Judge LI Haopei. Judge LI was a diplomat, academic and the first elected Chinese judge of the International Criminal Tribunals for the former Yugoslavia and Rwanda.

The Series has a number of objectives: to bring together prominent actors in the field, researchers, and interested individuals from around the world; to exchange views on key issues in international criminal and humanitarian law; to promote international criminal justice and other forms of transitional justice; and to make contributions to the public interest.

The inaugural LI Haopei Seminar was held in Oslo on 8 February 2011, eight months after the agreement on the crime of aggression was reached at the Kampala review conference. Judge Hans-Peter Kaul, the then Vice-President of the International Criminal Court, delivered a lecture on the criminalisation of aggression in the context of the Rome Statute. Judge LIU Daqun, Appeals Judge of the ICTY and ICTR, commented on Judge Kaul's lecture.

In November 2012, chapters prepared for the second seminar in the Series were published as the anthology "State Sovereignty and International Criminal Law", in separate Chinese and English editions. The successful book launch took place as a side event during the 11th Session of the Assembly of States Parties of the International Criminal Court.

In May 2013, the third LI Haopei Seminar, on which this volume is based, was held in Florence and proved to be highly successful. This book brings the chapters presented there and some additional contributions to a broader audience, giving effect to a topic of growing importance. The three institutions that organised the seminar and thus made the book possible deserve our thanks. The seminar and book are a good example of valuable academic co-operation between international law institutions and experts in China and Europe, in particular the European University Institute, a well-known institution where the late Judge Antonio Cassese served as professor before he became an international judge. It would be good if the LI Haopei Lecture Series could contribute to the increased awareness of the importance of such co-operation in the years to come.

The 2013 LI Haopei Lecture was given by Justice Richard J. Goldstone, the first Chief Prosecutor of the ICTY and ICTR, who worked with Judge LI between 1995 and 1997. He has distinguished experience in both domestic and international fact-finding inquiries. He chaired the Goldstone Commission to investigate political violence and intimidation that occurred between July 1991 and the 1994 general election that ended Apartheid in South Africa. He also led United Nations fact-finding missions or inquiries on Gaza and Kosovo.

Following his chapter, other experts from a variety of backgrounds address sub-topics such as the mandate, membership, function, operation and oversight of the relevant fact-finding missions and inquiries; their work processes; and issues pertaining to finding, reporting and submitting facts.

Fact-finding bodies and missions established to investigate serious violations of humanitarian law and human rights law can greatly impact subsequent criminal prosecutions for war crimes and other international crimes. This will, in turn, ultimately have an impact on the victims of these crimes. It is hoped that the knowledge, experiences and insights shared in this volume will be a step towards refining quality control mechanisms in future fact-finding missions, thereby making them more independent, effective and successful.

LING Yan
Professor, China University of Political Science and Law
Co-Director, LI Haopei Lecture Series

# TABLE OF CONTENTS

# 1

---

# Non-Criminal Justice Fact-Work
# in the Age of Accountability

**Marina Aksenova, Morten Bergsmo and Carsten Stahn**[*]

## 1.1. Quality Control in Fact-Finding: Questions and Definitions

The recent years have seen an increase in the number of international fact-finding commissions and other mandates that look into allegations of serious violations of international criminal, humanitarian or human rights law.[1] In 2012, the United Nations ('UN') Secretary-General stressed the growing importance of international commissions of inquiry or fact-finding missions to enhance human rights protection and combat impunity.[2] The same point was reiterated by the UN High Commissioner for Human Rights in 2015.[3]

The mounting reliance on fact-finding in international law can be explained by several factors, including generally increased expectations of

---

[*] **Marina Aksenova** is a CILRAP Research Fellow, Professor of Comparative and International Criminal Law at IE Law School and Director of the Art and International Justice Initiative. **Morten Bergsmo** is Director, Centre for International Law Research and Policy. **Carsten Stahn** is Professor of International Criminal Law and Global Justice at the Leiden Law School and Queen's University Belfast.

[1] See, for example, the International Fact-Finding Mission on the Israeli Settlements in the Occupied Palestinian Territory, (UN Human Rights Council, Israeli Settlements in the Occupied Palestinian Territory, Including East Jerusalem, and in the Occupied Syrian Golan, UN Doc. A/HRC/RES/19/17, 10 April 2012 (https://www.legal-tools.org/doc/c23d72/); the Fact-Finding Mission on Syria, UN Human Rights Council, The Current Human Rights Situation in the Syrian Arab Republic in the Context of Recent Events, UN Doc. A/HRC/RES/S-16/1, 4 May 2011 (https://www.legal-tools.org/doc/37fa81/); and the Independent International Fact-Finding Mission on the Conflict in Georgia, Council of the European Union, Council Decision 2008/901/CFSP, 2 December 2008 (Report, vol. 1: https://www.legal-tools.org/doc/b6be61/; vol. 2: https://www.legal-tools.org/doc/d0e020/; vol. 3: https://www.legal-tools.org/doc/c273c2/).

[2] UN General Assembly, Strengthening and Coordinating United Nations Rule of Law Activities, UN Doc. A/67/290, 10 August 2012, para. 19.

[3] OHCHR, "Commissions of Inquiry and Fact-finding Missions on International Human Rights and Humanitarian Law: Guidance and Practice", HR/PUB/14/7, 11 February 2015.

accountability and some limitations in the existing international criminal justice system.[4] International adjudication focuses primarily on individual criminal responsibility on the basis of charges in specific indictments. Adjudication tends to take considerably longer than non-criminal justice fact-finding, so the latter may therefore serve advocacy needs better in some situations. Furthermore, there is an inherent selectivity in international prosecutions insofar as they may only reveal parts of the story and not necessarily the whole pattern of violations. This leaves space for other mechanisms designed to ensure accountability and compliance with international obligations, non-criminal justice fact-finding being one of them.[5]

For our purposes, the terms 'fact-finding' and 'inquiry' refer to the methods of ascertaining facts used in international relations for differing purposes.[6] These methods include several types of work on facts or alleged facts, including work-processes to identify, locate, obtain, verify, analyse, corroborate, summarise, synthesise, structure, organise, present and disseminate these facts. The novel term 'fact-work' is used in this chapter and throughout the book to capture all such work-processes.[7] This term was coined in the conceptualisation of the 2013 LI Haopei Seminar on which this anthology is based, and it has been used in CILRAP's Quality Control Project more widely.

Traditionally, there are three main purposes of establishing facts in international law: to create the basis for peaceful settlement of disputes between two or more States; to supervise the execution of international agreements; and to supply the information required for the making of de-

---

[4]  Antonio Cassese, "Fostering Increased Conformity with International Standards: Monitoring and Institutional Fact-Finding", in Antonio Cassese (ed.), *Realizing Utopia: The Future of International Law*, Oxford University Press, 2012, p. 295.

[5]  Antonio Cassese mentions fact-finding and monitoring as such mechanisms (*ibid.*). The report prepared as a result of the workshop co-organised by the Permanent Mission of Portugal to the United Nations and the United Nations Office for the Coordination of Humanitarian Affairs mentions, in addition to individual criminal responsibility, fact-finding and reparations as methods of ensuring accountability for violations of humanitarian and human rights law ("Accountability and Fact-finding Mechanisms for Violations of International Humanitarian Law and Human Rights Law: The Role of the Security Council – Past and Future", 1 November 2011).

[6]  Karl Josef Partsch, "Fact-Finding and Inquiry", in Rudolf Bernhardt (ed.), *Encyclopedia of Public International Law*, North-Holland, Amsterdam-London, 1981, vol. 1, p. 61.

[7]  Unless otherwise indicated by the contributors.

cisions at an international level pursuant to Article 34 of the United Nations Charter.[8]

The first purpose is a narrow one, and refers to the inquiry as a specific procedure in cases where differences of opinion on factual matters underlie a dispute between parties.[9] Provisions for such inquiries were first elaborated in the 1899 Hague Conference, and were subsequently developed by the 1907 Hague Conference.[10] The mechanism was designed to address relationships between States. It is based on the notions of sovereignty and reciprocity – the features that hindered the following use of this dispute settlement mechanism.[11] In 1967, the UN General Assembly rejected a proposal by the Netherlands to establish a permanent commission of inquiry, and instead requested the Secretary-General to prepare a list of experts.[12] In the same vein, as expounded by Professor Charles Garraway in Chapter 15 below, the International Fact-Finding Commission established under Article 90 of Additional Protocol I of 1977 has only been activated once by States, despite its formal existence.[13]

The second function of fact-finding – supervising the execution of international agreements – serves to secure the performance of international obligations. The UN Specialized Agencies as well other global or regional bodies engage in this type of fact-finding.[14] This function has grown in the past decades to include more general fact-finding aimed at

---

[8] Karl Josef Partsch, 1981, p. 61, *supra* note 6. See also Larissa van den Herik, "An Inquiry into the Role of Commissions of Inquiry in International Law: Navigating the Tensions between Fact-Finding and Application of International Law", in *Chinese Journal of International Law*, 2014, vol. 13, p. 507.

[9] Malcolm Shaw, *International Law*, Cambridge University Press, 2008, pp. 1019–1020.

[10] *Ibid.*

[11] Cassese, 2012, p. 297, *supra* note 4.

[12] UN General Assembly, Question of Methods of Fact-Finding, UN Doc. A/RES/2329(XXII), 18 December 1967 (https://www.legal-tools.org/doc/0d9e66/); Cassese, 2012, p. 298, *supra* note 4.

[13] *Ibid.*

[14] Karl Josef Partsch, 1981, p. 61, *supra* note 6. For example, fact-finding activity by the World Trade Organization in the context of dispute resolution. For more on this topic, see Michelle T. Grando, *Evidence, Proof, and Fact-Finding in WTO Dispute Settlement*, Oxford University Press, 2009.

establishing the violations of human rights and humanitarian law con-tained in multiple treaties and customary international law.[15]

Finally, there is fact-finding for the purposes of Article 34 of the UN Charter – the provision confirming the power of the Security Council to investigate any situation or dispute that may endanger international peace and security. In reality, the Security Council is reluctant to use this provision explicitly and, instead, relies heavily on its implied powers of investigation.[16] Moreover, the Security Council is not the only UN organ sanctioning fact-finding inquiries.[17] The UN General Assembly and the UN Secretary-General sometimes exercise fact-finding powers, despite the UN Charter's silence on the matter.[18] Consequently, instead of a single specialised fact-finding body within the UN system, the practice has evolved in the direction of a plethora of different fact-finding strategies originating from the variety of sources.[19]

The establishment of the Commission of Experts for the former Yu-goslavia pursuant to United Nations Security Council Resolution 780 (1992) served as a catalyst for later developments. It denoted the begin-ning of an era, in which fact-finding is used in a broader context as a

---

[15] For example, African Commission on Human and Peoples' Rights, Resolution on Darfur, ACHPR/Res.68 (XXXV) 04, 4 June 2004, to deploy a fact-finding mission in Sudan; and Council of the European Union, Decision 2008/901/CFSP, 2 December 2008, concerning an independent international fact-finding mission on the conflict in Georgia, *supra* note 1.

[16] Bruno Simma *et al.* (eds.), *The Charter of the United Nations: A Commentary*, second edition, Oxford University Press, 2002, p. 516; James G. Devaney, "Killing Two Birds with One Stone: Can Increased use of Article 34(2) of the ICJ Statute Improve the Legiti-macy of UN Commissions of Inquiry & the Court's Fact-finding Procedure?", *STALS Re-search Paper N. 2/2013*, p. 5. For the examples of the mandates authorised by the Security Council, see *infra* Section 1.2.1.

[17] Devaney, p. 5, *ibid.*

[18] For example, UN General Assembly, Situation of Human Rights in Cambodia, UN Doc. A/RES/52/135, 27 February 1998 (https://www.legal-tools.org/doc/6e9a5f/); Letter Dated 4 May 2009 from the Secretary-General Addressed to the President of the Security Council, UN Doc. A/63/855-S/2009/250, 15 May 2009, establishing United Nations Headquarters Board of Inquiry to review and investigate nine incidents in the Gaza Strip and southern Is-rael that occurred between 27 December 2008 and 19 January 2009; Letter Dated 18 De-cember 2009 Addressed to the President of the Security Council by the Secretary-General, UN Doc. S/2009/693, 18 December 2009 (https://www.legal-tools.org/doc/c5939f/), re-garding the establishment of an international Commission of Inquiry to investigate the vio-lence that took place in Conakry on 28 September 2009.

[19] Richard B. Lillich *et al.* (eds.), *International Human Rights: Problems of Law, Policy, and Practice (Casebook)*, Aspen Publishers, 2006, p. 981.

mechanism for securing better compliance with international standards – a structure that is divorced from the will of particular States.[20] This trend includes extensive truth-seeking at the international level through international commissions of inquiry and fact-finding missions.[21]

Over the past two decades, there has been a strong turn towards the establishment of accountability through fact-finding mandates.[22] The UN has created more than 20 international commissions of inquiry ('COI') with mandates to investigate serious violations of human rights, of international humanitarian law and of international criminal law.[23] These commissions have a hybrid nature. They are neither classical fact-finders nor formal criminal bodies. Their role is not only to establish the facts and circumstances underlying human rights violations, but also to provide legal characterisations of facts and to explore possible avenues of responsibility of States and individuals. They serve as a forum to collect information and material underlying crimes and violations, or at times even as a gateway to formal criminal investigation or prosecution. Some commissions provide a frame of reference to determine what the relevant facts are in relation to early warning or mapping of violations. Others have a more investigative focus, mandating them to look at incidents, specific categories of crime, or even individual perpetrators of crime.[24] Certain commissions (for instance, COI Myanmar) have decided to publicly list suspects by name, while others have provided them in a confidential annex to the report (for instance, COI Darfur). In 2018, the Conference of States Parties of the Organization for the Prohibition of Chemical Weapons ('OPCW') took an unprecedented decision to "put in place arrangements to identify the perpetrators of the use of chemical weapons in the Syrian

---

[20]  Cassese, 2012, p. 303, *supra* note 4.

[21]  UN Human Rights Council, Report of the Special Rapporteur on the Promotion of Truth, Justice, Reparation and Guarantees of Non-Recurrence, UN Doc. A/HRC/24/42, 28 August 2013, para. 21 (https://www.legal-tools.org/doc/209022/).

[22]  See generally Christian Henderson (ed.), *Commissions of Inquiry: Problems and Prospects*, Hart/Bloomsbury, 2017.

[23]  See Catherine Harwood, *The Roles and Functions of Atrocity-Related United Nations Commissions of Inquiry in the International Legal Order*, Martinus Nijhoff, 2019.

[24]  For a typology, see Carsten Stahn and Dov Jacobs, "The Interaction Between Human Rights Fact-Finding and International Criminal Proceedings", in Philip Alston and Sarah Knuckey (eds.), *The Transformation of Human Rights Fact-Finding*, Oxford University Press, 2016, p. 255, pp. 258-259.

Arab Republic".[25] The point is thus no longer to find facts *per se*, but to frame and qualify them, or to make findings on individual responsibility.

The turn towards accountability and individualisation comes with a juridification of working methods.[26] It is necessary to identify investigative standards, thresholds of proof, protective mechanisms for witnesses and victims, or fairness protection for suspects, in particular when commissions 'name and shame' individuals publicly. Commissions may need to offer suspects an opportunity to reply when determinations on individual responsibility are made in a public report.[27] This may conflict with the short time span for which commissions are established.

Difficult questions also arise in relation to the application and interpretation of international law. Not every serious human rights violation qualifies as an international crime. The Rome Statute has become a standard point of reference in practice. However, human rights accountability mechanisms may interpret notions and elements of crimes differently than criminal courts. This may cause risks of fragmentation. A number of commissions have adopted extensive readings of crimes in order to bring violations within their mandate (for instance, COI Democratic People's Republic of Korea). Other commissions (for instance, COI South Sudan) have focused particularly on crimes that are subject to universal jurisdiction, such as torture or enforced disappearance, in order to strengthen the prospects of enforcement. In this way, choices on enforcement guide the focus of inquiry.

The relationship with criminal investigations is complex. In more and more contexts, UN fact-finding intersects with the International Criminal Court's ('ICC') situations (for instance, the Central African Republic, Libya, Guinea and Myanmar).[28] While accountability-related fact-finding

---

25 See OPCW, Conference of the States Parties, Decision Addressing the Threat from Chemical Weapons Use, C-SS-4/DEC.3, 27 June 2018, para. 10 (https://www.legal-tools.org/doc/lmqyd4/).

26 Christine Schwöbel-Patel, "Commissions of Inquiry: Courting International Criminal Courts and Tribunals", in Henderson, 2017, p. 145, *supra* note 22.

27 Ilya Nuzov and Mark Freeman, "Principle 7", in Frank Haldemann and Thomas Unger, *The United Nations Principles to Combat Impunity: A Commentary*, Oxford University Press, 2018, p. 114.

28 Mutoy Mubiala, "The ICC's Interplay with UN Fact-Finding Commissions in Preliminary Examinations", in Morten Bergsmo and Carsten Stahn (eds.), *Quality Control in Preliminary Examination: Volume 2*, Torkel Opsahl Academic EPublisher, Brussels, 2018, p. 411 (http://www.toaep.org/ps-pdf/33-bergsmo-stahn).

work may provide useful leads for international criminal courts and tribunals, or feed into analysis of preliminary examinations at the ICC, it cannot replace independent investigations. International courts often have to start from scratch, in light of the different methodologies and standards in formal criminal proceedings. Findings on context, patterns of violations or organisational structures in the work of the commissions of inquiry may be more useful for international or domestic courts than perpetrator-specific material. In some cases, the work of human rights fact-finders may complicate witness statements and evidence-gathering by formal criminal bodies. It is thus essential to avoid harm to criminal investigations in the documentation and collection of information for accountability purposes ('no harm principle').

The focus on accountability in inquiry may have structural drawbacks. The strength of less judicialized fact-finding lies in its ability to understand accountability in a broader sense than criminal prosecution. It may provide a broader historical context, trace structural violence, or identify socio-economic violations. An atrocity crime-based orientation may marginalise these dimensions. Cynically, the establishment of a commission of inquiry with an accountability mandate may be used by States as an excuse to avoid more burdensome investigations and prosecution or the establishment of an international criminal court or tribunal.

These developments pose novel issues from the perspective of quality control. Is quality control only a matter of enhanced work-processes, or does it also bear on issues such as the formulation of mandates, personnel composition of fact-finding mechanisms, independence and impartiality, and public relations? Should non-criminal justice fact-work be made more similar to the work-processes in criminal jurisdictions? To which extent do resource constraints affect quality control in non-criminal justice fact-work? Can information technology enhance quality control in non-criminal justice fact-work? Is there a need to strengthen legal capacity in such fact-work? Would increased transparency about the human resources involved in relevant fact-work reinforce a sense of accountability and, by that, quality in the work-processes?

The need for greater quality control has led to new initiatives to provide guidance on mandating and working methods of fact-finding bodies. In 2015, the Office of the High Commissioner for Human Rights ('OHCHR') issued a "Guidance and Practice" document for UN fact-finding and investigative bodies, which shares existing experiences and

UN practices. It identifies nine core principles (no harm, independence, impartiality, transparency, objectivity, confidentiality, credibility, visibility and integrity) and elaborates working methods, including different standards of proof used by commissions in UN practice.[29] The Siracusa Guidelines for International, Regional and National Fact-Finding Bodies, established through an expert process under the guidance of the late M. Cherif Bassiouni, provide a framework to ensure greater clarity and consistency in the framing of mandates, working practices, standards and reporting.[30] The Harvard Program on Humanitarian Policy and Conflict Research ('HRCR') established a HPCR Practitioner's Handbook on Monitoring, Reporting and Fact-Finding, which addresses key methodological issues and practical guidance.[31] These soft law instruments signal a shift in attitude in the professional community, namely a move from an *ad hoc* culture in fact-finding towards a more systemic framework, grounded in principle, pragmatism and bounded discretion.

Generally, there have been at least two important institutional trends since the First Edition, which change the broader context in which fact-finding takes place. They are, first, the increased role of private actors in investigations,[32] and, second, the establishment of novel investigative mechanisms, which complement fact-finding initiatives.

The documentation and tracing of violations by non-State actors, including through open source information[33] and methods of investigative journalism, has become an important part of the accountability architecture. This is not only done by non-governmental organisations ('NGOs'), but also by professional bodies. Mechanisms like the Commission for International Justice and Accountability ('CIJA') in Syria highlight a turn to privatised investigative models, sponsored by States, in cases where classical multilateral options fail to reach support, and public institutions are unable or unwilling to investigate. Such types of private investigation can

---

[29]  OHCHR, 2015, pp. 33 ff., *supra* note 3.

[30]  M. Cherif Bassiouni and Christina Abraham, *Siracusa Guidelines for International, Regional and National Fact-finding Bodies*, Intersentia, 2013.

[31]  See Rob Grace and Claude Bruderlein (eds.), *HPCR Practitioner's Handbook on Monitoring, Reporting and Fact-Finding*, Cambridge University Press, 2017.

[32]  Alexander Heinze, "Private International Criminal Investigations", in *Zeitschrift für Internationale Strafrechtsdogmatik*, 2019, vol. 2, p. 169.

[33]  See generally Sam Dubberly, Alexa Koenig and Daragh Murray, *Digital Witness*, Oxford University Press, 2020.

be attractive to States, because they may be less costly, less formalised, and more flexible in their operations. They can get the 'dirty work done', as some would say. CIJA provided, *inter alia*, documentary evidence relating to the arrest of Anwar Raslan and Eyad Ghareeb in Germany.[34] However, at the same time, private international criminal investigations pose novel ethical and legal dilemmas. They raise challenges in relation to impartiality (for example, donor-driven approach towards investigative targets), admissibility of evidence, accountability, or the protection of information-providers or staff. For instance, CIJA has been criticised for its exclusive focus on regime crimes in Syria.

In some cases, private investigative methods are faster than investigations by public bodies. A good example is Bellingcat's online investigation in the context of the aerial incident of the flight MH17. Bellingcat used open source information, including geolocation techniques, links on Facebook and other social media to identify the missile launcher that downed the aircraft and trace members of the organisations involved in the attack.[35] This method may have innovated fact-finding. The material was used by the Dutch Prosecution in the MH17 proceedings after verification of Bellingcat's investigative processes.[36]

Visual evidence, gained from open sources, is transforming the culture of investigations and prosecutions. This makes international courts and tribunals even more dependent on collaboration by private actors, such as NGOs or social media providers. For instance, in the *Al-Werfalli* case, the evidence collected through social media supported the issuance of an arrest warrant by the ICC which relied strongly on video footage.[37] This opens new opportunities. Open source derived material can be used to corroborate evidence, provide leads or establish context. As Emma Irving has noted, it may be the "beginning of what will be a long, and likely

---

[34] Alexander Heinze, "Private Investigators Helped Germany Arrest Two Former Syrian Secret Service Officers", *EJIL Talk!*, 26 February 2019. See his comprehensive chapter "Private International Criminal Investigations and Integrity", in Morten Bergsmo and Viviane Dittrich (eds.), *Integrity in International Justice*, Torkel Opsahl Academic EPublisher, Brussels, 2020 (forthcoming).

[35] See Bellingcat Investigation Team, "MH17: The Open Source Investigation Three Years Later", 17 July 2017 (available on its web site).

[36] Netherlands Public Prosecution Service, "Status of the Investigation and Position on the Progress of the Trial – Part 1 (10-3-2020)" (available on its web site).

[37] See ICC, *Prosecutor v. Al-Werfalli*, Warrant of Arrest, 15 August 2017, ICC-01/11-01/17-2 (https://www.legal-tools.org/doc/881fb6/).

complex, relationship between open source evidence and international criminal justice",[38] as further elaborated in her chapter in this Second Edition. But it also creates risks. Visual evidence remains highly dependent on the narratives that surround the images.[39] It may affect the equality of arms to the detriment of the defence. For example, the first cognitive or affective impression created through the production of images is often difficult to reverse.

Classical fact-finding has been supported by new types of investigative mechanisms. The lack of agreement on international justice in Syria has prompted the establishment of the International, Impartial and Independent Mechanism to Assist in the Investigation and Prosecution of Crimes in Syria ('IIIM') by the UN General Assembly. This mechanism fills in an important gap, namely a missing link in the accountability landscape between human rights investigations and domestic criminal jurisdiction. It bridges fact-finding and prosecution. It is vested with the formal legal mandate to collect and preserve evidence as well as to prepare files for trials in national and/or international courts. As such, it must abide by international criminal law standards.[40] It is not a criminal jurisdiction *per se*, but has a 'quasi-prosecutorial' function. It serves as a central repository of potential evidence and information and as a gateway towards domestic jurisdictions, including States exercising universal jurisdiction, or towards a future criminal body.[41] It has placed the emphasis on structural investigation, in order to support and encourage the exercise of universal

---

[38] Emma Irving, "And So It Begins… Social Media Evidence in an ICC Arrest Warrant", *Opinio Juris*, 17 August 2017.

[39] Keith Hiatt, "Open Source Evidence on Trial", in *Yale Law Journal Forum*, 2016, vol. 125.

[40] See UN General Assembly, International, Impartial and Independent Mechanism to Assist in the Investigation and Prosecution of Persons Responsible for the Most Serious Crimes under International Law Committed in the Syrian Arab Republic since March 2011, UN Doc. A/RES/71/248, 11 January 2017, para. 4 (https://www.legal-tools.org/doc/fecaf0/). See Christian Wenaweser and James Cockayne, "Justice for Syria? The International, Impartial and Independent Mechanism and the Emergence of the UN General Assembly in the Realm of International Criminal Justice", in *Journal of International Criminal Justice*, 2015, vol. 15, p. 211.

[41] See Report of the International, Impartial and Independent Mechanism to Assist in the Investigation and Prosecution of Persons Responsible for the Most Serious Crimes under International Law Committed in the Syrian Arab Republic since March 2011, A/72/764, 28 February 2018, para. 7 (https://www.legal-tools.org/doc/42c191/).

jurisdiction by States, as evidenced by the trial of Anwar Raslan and Eyad Ghareeb before the Higher Regional Court in Koblenz.[42]

The IIIM was followed by the lesser known Independent Investigative Mechanism for Myanmar, established by the Human Rights Council.[43] It is, *inter alia*, mandated to prepare case files, based on the information collected by the Independent International Fact-Finding Mission on Myanmar. It has an open-ended mandate. The replication marks a structural move towards a multi-layered fact-finding structure, in which non-criminal investigation work becomes, at least institutionally, more clearly distinguishable from formal criminal investigations. This may provide a healthy safeguard against judicial overreach by commissions of inquiry or classical fact-finding missions. As Nicholas Koumjian, the Head of the Mechanism, stated, the mere presence of investigative mechanisms is intended to provide a message on deterrence and prevention: "We are watching and will work to ensure that those who commit crimes will be brought to account".[44] However, it is still an open question to what extent investigative mechanisms do successfully strengthen domestic investigations and prosecutions or the exercise of international justice. They rely heavily on State co-operation and the work of other information-providers, and need to build trust in their work, in order to serve as a gateway to prosecutions. One challenge is the prevailing uncertainty about the 'end user':

> [B]uilding a prosecutable criminal case requires presenting credible evidence that proves each element of the crime to the high evidentiary standards required in various jurisdictions for a criminal conviction.[45]

Overall, international criminal justice thus appears to move towards a multi-layered system of fact-finding and investigation. In situations of

---

[42] See Caroline Fehl, "The Partial Return of Universal Jurisdiction: Syrian Torturers on Trial in Germany", *Global Policy*, 12 May 2020.

[43] UN Human Rights Council, Situation of Human Rights of Rohingya Muslims and Other Minorities in Myanmar, UN Doc. A/HRC/RES/39/2, 3 October 2018 (https://www.legal-tools.org/doc/0917d7/).

[44] Statement to the Human Rights Council by Mr. Nicholas Koumjian, Head of the Independent Investigative Mechanism for Myanmar, 9 September 2019 (available on the UN's web site). On the role of messaging and communication in international criminal justice more generally, see Carsten Stahn, *Justice as Message*, Oxford University Press, 2020.

[45] Report of the Independent Investigative Mechanism for Myanmar, UN Doc. A/HRC/42/66, 7 August 2019, para. 46.

ongoing conflict, where justice is hampered by politics, developments point towards a dual structure, according to which 'public' inquiry and investigation is complemented by different forms of privatised inquiry, fact-finding or criminal investigation. This 'public-private' model is followed by the exercise of criminal jurisdiction, either internationally, in a hybrid form, or through universal jurisdiction.[46]

We must, however, remain cognizant at all times that the international criminal justice system is based on the principle of complementarity, so no stone should be left unturned in trying to strengthen ability and will to national investigation and prosecution in the jurisdiction where alleged violations have occurred. Those concerned with building international criminal justice should also endeavour to contribute to national criminal justice – the former cannot be detached from the latter.

But this anthology focuses on quality control in international fact-finding. Such fact-finding may be undertaken within the UN human rights system, in the context of truth and reconciliation processes, through international or regional organisations in connection with challenges to international peace and security; or through non-governmental organisations.[47] To orient the reader through a large number of international fact-finding commissions and mandates, the next section of this chapter (Section 1.2.) provides their brief overview and classification. The list of the mandates presented in Section 1.6. at the end of the chapter supplements the description. Section 1.3. summarises individual contributions to this anthology, and Section 1.4. indicates challenges for further research and analysis in the area of international fact-finding.

---

[46] Caroline Fehl and Eliška Mocková, "Chasing Justice for Syria: Roadblocks and Detours on the Path to Accountability", Peace Research Institute Frankfurt Spotlight 5/2017, 28 September 2017.

[47] For the purposes of this chapter, the term 'core international crimes' is used for the categories war crimes, crimes against humanity, acts of genocide, and crimes of aggression. As such, the term includes all serious violations of international human rights law which may amount to core international crimes, not only violations against life, physical integrity and personal liberty, but also non-physical violations that can constitute, for example, persecution as a crime against humanity. 'Criminal justice for core international crimes' is used – rather than 'international criminal justice' – in order not to exclude internationalised or national criminal justice for core international crimes from the discussion. The frequently inflated term 'international criminal justice' is narrower and therefore not used here.

## 1.2. Overview of Fact-Finding Mandates

The annex in Section 1.6. contains a list of the international fact-finding mandates from the last decades.[48] This record is not exhaustive, but provides a good overview of the events happening in international fact-finding between 1992 and 2020. A brief glance at the list is sufficient to see that the fact-finding missions are diverse, plentiful, geographically dispersed, and established by different bodies and under different circumstances. One may catalogue the mandates according to different criteria, including the body that authorised its establishment, the scope of the mandate, and the result of the fact-finding mission. The present section provides a short description of the mandates according to these classifications.

### 1.2.1. Sanctioning Body

The organs of the United Nations remain the main source of international fact-finding processes. The UN Security Council engages in fact-finding through the exercise of its implied powers. Investigations into the situations in the former Yugoslavia,[49] Burundi,[50] Rwanda,[51] Somalia,[52] Sierra Leone,[53] and Darfur[54] are examples of this activity by the Security Council. The Security Council also occasionally requests the UN Secretary-General to initiate fact-finding. The Secretary-General appointed the Commission of Experts to review the prosecution of serious violations of human rights in Timor-Leste;[55] the international commission to investi-

---

[48] See *Annex: International fact-finding mandates 1992–2020.*

[49] UN Security Council, Resolution 780 (1992), UN Doc. S/RES/780 (1992), 6 October 1992 (https://www.legal-tools.org/doc/cdc5ad/).

[50] UN Security Council, Resolution 1012 (1995), UN Doc. S/RES/1012 (1995), 28 August 1995 (https://www.legal-tools.org/doc/80c1a0/).

[51] UN Security Council, Resolution 935 (1994), UN Doc. S/RES/935 (1994), 1 July 1994 (https://www.legal-tools.org/doc/1594bd/).

[52] UN Security Council, Resolution 885 (1993), UN Doc. S/RES/885 (1993), 16 November 1993 (https://www.legal-tools.org/doc/6e9cc7/).

[53] UN Security Council, Resolution 1306 (2000), UN Doc. S/RES/1306 (2000), 5 July 2000 (https://www.legal-tools.org/doc/c9aea8/).

[54] UN Security Council, Resolution 1564 (2004), UN Doc. S/RES/1564 (2004), 18 September 2004 (https://www.legal-tools.org/doc/1ba770/).

[55] Letter Dated 24 June 2005 from the Secretary-General Addressed to the President of the Security Council, UN Doc. S/2005/458, 24 June 2005 (https://www.legal-tools.org/doc/e0807f/).

gate the assassination of the former Prime Minister of Pakistan, Mohtarma Benazir Bhutto;[56] an expert panel on the illegal exploitation of natural resources in Congo;[57] and a Panel of Inquiry on the flotilla incident that occurred in 2010 outside Gaza.[58] The UN Secretary-General may rely on other international organisations in conducting its fact-finding activities. For instance, the Secretary-General deployed the mission to Syria to investigate the alleged use of chemical weapons after consultations with the World Health Organization and the Organization for the Prohibition of Chemical Weapons.[59] The Security Council and the Secretary-General sometimes undertake joint fact-finding activities such as the inquiry into the management of the UN Oil-for-Food Programme.[60] Despite being less active than the Security Council or the Secretary-General in fact-finding, the UN General Assembly may still request an appointment of a fact-finding mission. It did so in respect of the past serious violations of national and international law in Cambodia.[61]

The UN Commission on Human Rights and, subsequently, the UN Human Rights Council are responsible for a large number of fact-finding initiatives. The former body, for instance, led the establishment of the independent Fact-Finding Commission for Post-Ballot Human Rights Violations in East Timor,[62] and prepared a report as a result of the official visit to Chile by the Special Rapporteur on the situation of human rights and fundamental freedoms of indigenous people;[63] while the latter established

---

[56] Letter Dated 24 March 2005 from the Secretary-General to the President of the Security Council, UN Doc. S/2005/203, 24 March 2005.

[57] Statement by the President of the Security Council, UN Doc. S/PRST/2000/20, 2 June 2000.

[58] Statement by the President of the Security Council, UN Doc. S/PRST/2010/9, 1 June 2010 (https://www.legal-tools.org/doc/356fb8/).

[59] Letter Dated 22 March 2013 from the Secretary-General Addressed to the President of the Security Council, UN Doc. S/2013/184, 25 March 2013.

[60] UN Security Council, Resolution 1538 (2004), UN Doc. S/RES/1538 (2004), 21 April 2004 (https://www.legal-tools.org/doc/89711b/).

[61] UN General Assembly, Situation of Human Rights in Cambodia, para. 16, *supra* note 18.

[62] UN Commission on Human Rights, Situation of Human Rights in East Timor, UN Doc. 1999/S-4/1, 27 September 1999 (https://www.legal-tools.org/doc/653b45/).

[63] UN Commission on Human Rights, Human Rights and Indigenous Issues, UN Doc. E/CN.4/RES/2003/56, 24 April 2003.

---

the Commission of Inquiry on Lebanon,[64] the UN Fact-Finding Mission on the Gaza Conflict,[65] the Fact-Finding Mission for the Syrian Arab Republic,[66] and the Independent Investigative Mechanism for Myanmar.[67] It is common for the Office of the UN High Commissioner for Human Rights to undertake fact-finding missions as a part of its mandate. This was the case with the visit of Mary Robinson to Chechnya in 2000 to investigate the situation of human rights.[68]

Organisations of a regional character – in particular those specialising in the protection of human rights and the promotion of peace and security – also play an important role in modern fact-finding. The African Commission on Human and Peoples' Rights takes up an active role in the region. Among its initiatives are the fact-finding missions to Zimbabwe and Sudan.[69] Another regional body conducting fact-finding missions in the region is the Economic Community of West African States that dispatched the fact-finding mission to Mali.[70] In Europe, the Council of the European Union and the Organization for Security and Cooperation in Europe are among the organizations that initiate fact-finding. The former was responsible for the mission to investigate the conflict in Georgia in 2008,[71] and the latter for the fact-finding mission to the occupied territo-

---

[64] UN Human Rights Council, The Grave Situation of Human Rights in Lebanon Caused by Israeli Military Operations, UN Doc. A/HRC/RES/S-2/1, 11 August 2006 (https://www.legal-tools.org/doc/9e7f9b/).

[65] UN Human Rights Council, Report of the United Nations High Commissioner for Human Rights on the Implementation of Human Rights Council Resolutions S-9/1 and S-12/1, Addendum: Concerns Related to Adherence to International Human Rights and International Humanitarian Law in the Context of the Escalation between the State of Israel, the de Facto Authorities in Gaza and Palestinian Armed Groups in Gaza that Occurred from 14 to 21 November 2012, UN Doc. A/HRC/22/35/Add.1, 6 March 2013.

[66] UN Human Rights Council, Report of the United Nations High Commissioner for Human Rights on the Situation of Human Rights in the Syrian Arab Republic, UN Doc. A/HRC/18/53, 15 September 2011 (https://www.legal-tools.org/doc/5bf068/).

[67] UN Human Rights Council, Situation of Human Rights of Rohingya Muslims and Other Minorities in Myanmar, UN Doc. A/HRC/RES/39/2, 3 October 2018.

[68] UN High Commissioner for Human Rights, Statement on Chechnya, 4 April 2000.

[69] African Union, Decision on 17th Annual Activity Report of the African Commission on Human and Peoples' Rights, Assembly/AU/Dec.56 (IV), 30–31 January 2005 (https://www.legal-tools.org/doc/92fe98/); Resolution on Darfur, 2004, *supra* note 15.

[70] ECOWAS, Statement on the Situation in the North of Mali, Communiqué N°: 065/2012, 19 March 2012.

[71] Council of the European Union, Council Decision 2008/901/CFSP, 2 December 2008 concerning an independent international fact-finding mission on the conflict in Georgia.

---

ries of Azerbaijan surrounding Nagorno-Karabakh in 2005.[72] The Union of South American Nations is the Latin American regional organisation that conducts fact-finding activities in the region.

Fact-finding by non-governmental organisations becomes more and more widespread. The International Federation for Human Rights ('FIDH'), for example, is a Paris-based NGO that specialises in human rights fact-finding. One of its missions was to Angola to analyse the context in which human rights defenders were operating in the country.[73] Another example of NGO work is the Independent Civil Society Fact-Finding Mission to Libya, established by the Arab Organization for Human Rights in co-operation with the Palestinian Centre for Human Rights.[74] This undertaking served as an alternative to the UN Fact-Finding Mission in investigating allegations of the widespread violations of international law committed in Libya since 15 February 2011.[75] CIJA, mentioned in the previous section, is yet another illustration of a privately led investigative initiative. It was established in May 2012 as an NGO listed in the Netherlands.[76]

Finally, fact-finding missions may originate from within the State. This is usually the case with truth and reconciliation commissions established by domestic parliaments.[77] There are other instances when domestic organs sanction fact-finding. The King of Bahrain, for example, set up the Bahrain Independent Commission of Inquiry to report on the violations of human rights law during the protests that occurred in Bahrain

---

[72] Report of the OSCE Fact-Finding Mission to the Occupied Territories of Azerbaijan Surrounding Nagorno-Karabakh, 28 February 2005 (https://www.legal-tools.org/doc/b08893/).

[73] Lillich *et al.* (eds.), p. 981, *supra* note 19; FIDH, "ANGOLA: From Theory to Practice It's Time to Guarantee the Capacity of Human Rights Defenders to Act" (available on its web site).

[74] Report of the Independent Civil Society Fact-Finding Mission to Libya, 31 January 2012 (https://www.legal-tools.org/doc/c4f71a/).

[75] UN Human Rights Council, Report of the International Commission of Inquiry on Libya, UN Doc. A/HRC/19/68, 8 March 2012 (https://www.legal-tools.org/doc/a7b7ee/).

[76] Michelle Burgis-Kasthala, "Entrepreneurial Justice: Syria, the Commission for International Justice and Accountability and the Renewal of International Criminal Justice", in *European Journal of International Law*, 2019, vol. 30, no. 4.

[77] For example, see Truth and Reconciliation Commission of South Africa established by The Promotion of National Unity and Reconciliation Act, No. 34 of 1995 (assented to 19 July 1995) (https://www.legal-tools.org/doc/42cdab/).

from February-March 2011.[78] The President of Kyrgyzstan initiated the creation of the Independent International Commission of Inquiry into the Events in southern Kyrgyzstan in 2010.[79] The Danish Immigration Service dispatched a fact-finding mission to Colombo to investigate the human rights and security situation for Tamils in Sri Lanka.[80]

### 1.2.2. Scope of the Mandate

The diversity of fact-finding missions manifests itself not only in the variety of the bodies that sanction such missions, but also in the scope of their mandates, which can be formulated in very broad or very narrow terms. There are fact-finding endeavours aiming at monitoring the fulfilment of a particular international obligation such as compliance by Iraq with its disarmament obligations imposed after the Gulf War,[81] or non-violation by Syria of the prohibition to use chemical weapons.[82] The scope of the mandate can be even narrower and focus on the investigation of a particular event – such as the assassination of a political leader (Rafiq Hariri or Benazir Bhutto),[83] or specific attacks on UN personnel.[84] Some other missions are temporarily, rather than substantively, limited. This is usually the case with the reports prepared by the Office of the UN High Commissioner for Human Rights as part of its investigative mandate. For example, the mission of Mary Robinson to look into the situation of human rights in Chechnya lasted only five days.[85] These types of missions are not focused

---

[78]  See the Royal Order No. 28 of 2011 attached as annex to the Report of the Bahrain Independent Commission of Inquiry, 23 November 2011.

[79]  Report of the Independent International Commission of Inquiry into the Events in Southern Kyrgyzstan, 4 May 2011 (https://www.legal-tools.org/doc/5e0afc/).

[80]  Danish Immigration Service, "Human Rights and Security Issues concerning Tamils in Sri Lanka", 6/2010 ENG, October 2010.

[81]  UN, Security Council, Resolution 1284 (1999), UN Doc. S/RES/1284 (1999), 17 December 1999 (https://www.legal-tools.org/doc/92dfbe/).

[82]  Letter Dated 22 March 2013 from the Secretary-General Addressed to the President of the Security Council, UN Doc. S/2013/184, 25 March 2013.

[83]  UN Security Council, Resolution 1595 (2005), UN Doc. S/RES/1595 (2005), 7 April 2005 (https://www.legal-tools.org/doc/4a0623/); and Letter Dated 2 February 2009 from the Secretary-General to the President of the Security Council, UN Doc. S/2009/67, 2 February 2009.

[84]  UN Security Council, Resolution 885 (1993), *supra* note 52.

[85]  Report of the UN High Commissioner for Human Rights and Follow up to the World Conference on Human Rights: Situation of Human Rights in Chechnya in the Russian Federation, 5 April 2000 (https://www.legal-tools.org/doc/68d31e/). See also Report of the High

on collecting facts as much as they serve to show the responsiveness of the international community to the situations that require its immediate attention.[86] The scope of the mission's mandate may be limited to the establishment of particular facts. For example, the OSCE's Fact-Finding Mission to the Occupied Territories of Azerbaijan Surrounding Nagorno-Karabakh aimed at determining the existence of settlements in the area.[87]

However, it is often the case that the mandate of the mission is broad and requires its members to make normative assessments of the violations of human rights and humanitarian law in the region. For example, the UN Human Rights Council dispatched a mission to Syria to investigate "*all* alleged violations of international human rights law".[88] Likewise, the mandate of the Independent Investigative Mechanism for Myanmar is to "collect, consolidate, preserve and analyse evidence of the most serious international crimes and violations of international law committed in Myanmar since 2011".[89] The Independent International Fact-Finding Mission on the Conflict in Georgia sanctioned by the EU Council in Georgia investigated "the origins and the course of the conflict in Georgia, including with regard to international law, humanitarian law and human rights, and the accusations made in that context".[90] The report of the Fact-Finding Mission on the Gaza Conflict conducted by the UN Human Rights Council considered "any actions by all parties that might have constituted violations of international human rights law or international humanitarian law".[91] However, this report explicitly stated that the mission did not attempt to identify the individuals responsible for the commission of offences.[92] This is in contrast with the work of the UN Commission of Ex-

---

Commissioner for Human Rights on the Situation of Human Rights in Kosovo, UN Doc. E/CN.4/2000/32, 31 May 1999.

[86] M. Cherif Bassiouni, "Appraising UN Justice-Related Fact-Finding Missions", in *Journal of Law and Policy*, 2001, vol. 5, no. 35, p. 45.

[87] Report of the OSCE Fact-Finding Mission to the Occupied Territories of Azerbaijan Surrounding Nagorno-Karabakh, *supra* note 72.

[88] UN Human Rights Council, Report of the United Nations High Commissioner for Human Rights on the Situation of Human Rights in the Syrian Arab Republic, para. 4 (emphasis added), *supra* note 66.

[89] OHCHR, "Independent Investigative Mechanism for Myanmar" (available on its web site).

[90] Council Decision 2008/901/CFSP, *supra* note 71.

[91] Report of the United Nations Fact-Finding Mission on the Gaza Conflict, UN Doc. A/HRC/12/48, 25 September 2009, para. 11 (https://www.legal-tools.org/doc/ca9992/).

[92] *Ibid.*, para. 25.

---

perts for the former Yugoslavia, which collected information regarding the persons individually responsible for crimes against humanity and grave breaches of international humanitarian law.[93]

There are also missions with a narrowly framed mandate, which still engage in normative assessments of the violations of human rights and humanitarian law. For instance, the FIDH organised a mission to analyse the human rights situation in the Mapuche communities in Chile as related to forest exploitation and the Ralco project.[94] Another example is the UN Board of Inquiry to review and investigate nine incidents in the Gaza Strip and southern Israel that occurred between 27 December 2008 and 19 January 2009. It assessed the deaths of civilians in accordance with the rules and principles of international humanitarian law.[95]

### 1.2.3. Outcome of the Mission

The classification of fact-finding missions based on their outcome is a less straightforward exercise than categorising on the basis of the sanctioning body or the scope of their mandates. The result of the mission may not always be easily foreseeable. This is because fact-finding missions operate in a highly politicised context, and the outcome depends, among other things, on the degree of political support from the Security Council, as well as the authority that established the mission.[96] The other reason for the lack of predictability is the fact that the mandates operate on an *ad hoc* basis, without proper continuity or institutional memory.[97]

There are a number of potential outcomes of the fact-finding missions, depending on the scope of their respective mandates and political will. First, factual investigations conducted by the relevant body may result in the establishment of a court or tribunal. This strategy allows for the initiation of individual prosecutions of those responsible on the basis of

---

[93] Final Report of the Commission of Experts Established Pursuant to Security Council Resolution 780 (1992), UN Doc. S/1994/674, 27 May 2004, para. 4 (https://www.legal-tools.org/doc/3a3ae2/).

[94] FIDH, Report on International Investigative Mission in Chile – The Mapuche People: Between Oblivion and Exclusion, No. 358/2, 22 August 2003.

[95] Letter dated 4 May 2009 from the Secretary-General Addressed to the President of the Security Council, para. 28, *supra* note 18.

[96] Bassiouni, 2001, p. 38, *supra* note 86.

[97] *Ibid.*, p. 48.

the information collected by the fact-finding mission.[98] Examples of such missions are the Commission of Experts for the former Yugoslavia,[99] the International Commission of Inquiry concerning Rwanda,[100] the Group of Experts for Cambodia,[101] and the International Independent Investigation Commission to assist in investigation of all aspects of the assassination of the former Prime Minister of Lebanon, Rafiq Hariri.[102]

Secondly, some missions, short of providing the basis for international prosecutions, may come up with a list of recommendations of a humanitarian character addressed to the State concerned or the international community as a whole. For example, the Commission of Inquiry on Lebanon advised the UN Human Rights Council to enhance humanitarian assistance and reconstruction, to assess the legality of some weapons and to address and promote legal means for individuals to redress.[103] The Independent International Fact-Finding Mission to investigate the implications of the Israeli settlements on the civil, political, economic, social and cultural rights of the Palestinian people throughout the Occupied Palestinian Territory called upon Israel to cease all settlement activities without preconditions, initiate a process of withdrawal of all settlers from the Occupied Palestinian Territory, and put an end to the human rights violations that are linked to the presence of settlements.[104]

---

[98] There are fact-finding limitations in the work of international tribunals which fall outside the scope of this chapter. For the treatment of the topic, see Nancy Amoury Combs, *Fact-Finding Without Facts: The Uncertain Evidentiary Foundations of International Criminal Convictions*, Cambridge University Press, 2010.

[99] Final Report of the Commission of Experts Established Pursuant to Security Council Resolution 780 (1992), UN Doc. S/1994/674, 27 May 1994, para. 3.

[100] Final Report of the Commission of Experts established pursuant to Security Council Resolution 935 (1994), UN Doc. S/1994/1405), 9 December 1994, para. 3 (https://www.legal-tools.org/doc/361096/).

[101] Report of the Group of Experts for Cambodia Established Pursuant to General Assembly Resolution 52/135, 15 March 1999 (https://www.legal-tools.org/doc/7dbb86/).

[102] Report of the Secretary-General on the Establishment of a Special Tribunal for Lebanon, UN Doc. S/2006/893, 15 November 2006 (https://www.legal-tools.org/doc/0bf8d5/).

[103] Report of the Commission of Inquiry on Lebanon pursuant to Human Rights Council Resolution S-2/1, UN Doc. A/HRC/3/2, 23 November 2006, para. 31 (https://www.legal-tools.org/doc/c58b38/).

[104] Report of the Independent International Fact-Finding Mission to Investigate the Implications of the Israeli Settlements on the Civil, Political, Economic, Social and Cultural Rights of the Palestinian People throughout the Occupied Palestinian Territory, including East Jerusalem, UN Doc. A/HRC/22/63, 7 February 2013, paras. 112–113 (https://www.legal-tools.org/doc/4047e2/).

---

Thirdly, the fact-finding mission may lead to further institutional developments, such as the establishment of a more permanent body with a wider mandate. The conclusions of the Human Rights Council fact-finding mission for the Syrian Arab Republic about the existence of patterns of human rights violations in the country resulted in the establishment of a body with a wider mandate and an additional task of identifying those responsible with a view of holding them accountable – an independent international commission of inquiry.[105]

Fourthly, the deployment of the fact-finding mission may result in the expression of public outcry and concern in response to the security and humanitarian situation in a certain region. The ECOWAS Fact-Finding Mission in Northern Mali in 2012 resulted in the call for cease-fire.[106] This particular outcome corresponds to the public outreach role of human rights organisations.

Fifthly, the missions may aim at broader goals such as contributing to truth, justice and reconciliation in the respective region. This is usually the case with truth and reconciliation commissions ('TRCs').[107] Finally, the mission may be context-based and strive to achieve a particular political aim. This was the case with the Security Council's fact-finding mission to Kosovo prior to its declaration of independence.[108]

## 1.3. Chapter Contributions

Chapters 2 and 3 open this anthology with the analysis and observations based on the professional experience of the authors. Chapter 2 by Richard J. Goldstone offers an insider's look into the fact-finding missions and inquiries in South Africa and internationally. Goldstone participated, *inter alia*, in the Standing Commission on Political Violence and Intimidation in South Africa (the Goldstone Commission), the Oil-for-Food Inquiry, and the UN Fact-Finding Mission on Gaza. He provides an authoritative

---

[105] Report of the Independent International Commission of Inquiry on the Syrian Arab Republic, UN Doc. A/HRC/S-17/2/Add.1, 23 November 2011, paras. 1, 4 (https://www.legal-tools.org/doc/925e44/).

[106] ECOWAS, Statement on the Situation in the North of Mali, Communiqué, *supra* note 70.

[107] See, for example, Final Report of the Truth and Reconciliation Commission for the Republic of Liberia, vol. I: Findings and Determinations, 30 June 2009, p. 6 (https://www.legal-tools.org/doc/306448/).

[108] UN News Centre, "Security Council Told that Kosovo Remains Calm but Tense", 10 May 2007.

and insightful account of the challenges inherent in fact-finding missions and the lessons that he has learned with regard to the quality control of such missions. Goldstone's particular recommendations on how to improve the quality control of fact-finding missions include enhancing its actual and perceived independence, clearly stipulating the terms of reference, paying attention to the language of the report, and ensuring the security of the mission members.

In Chapter 3, Martin Scheinin draws on his experience as a member of the UN Human Rights Committee and as Special Rapporteur of the Human Rights Council in his critical assessment of the independent fact-finding by the UN human rights machinery. Scheinin contends that not all 'fact-finding' shares the same purpose or should be guided by the same standards. In particular, the procedures aiming at establishing the responsibility of a State for human rights violations should not be subjected to evidence requirements typical for determining individual criminal accountability. Scheinin also encourages applying caution when using the material obtained through fact-finding in criminal investigation.

In Chapter 4, the author Simon De Smet focuses on quality control and the theory of fact-finding. He points out that modern international fact-finding is unsatisfactory due to the lack of awareness of the basic epistemic principles that are at play. De Smet discusses a few epistemological concepts relevant to international fact-finding in an attempt to sharpen the understanding of the process of fact-finding and its limitations. In particular, he emphasises the relevance to international fact-finding of the two different methods of justifying beliefs: the probabilistic method and the relative plausibility theory.

Chapter 5 by LIU Daqun discusses quality control in truth and reconciliation processes, recognising truth-seeking as an important post-conflict goal in its own right, which exists either alongside trials or as an alternative. He explores various aspects that are vital for the functioning of the truth and reconciliation commissions: composition of the commission, applicable standard of proof, resources, and the production of the final report. He stresses the significance of having a clear mandate for conducting the investigations in conformity with four principles: fairness, credibility, impartiality and independence. He maintains that the ability of commissioners to shape policy and resolve ambiguity in the commission's mandate is another vital consideration for effective truth-seeking.

Chapters 6 and 7 look into the specific issue of the formulation of the mandates of international fact-finding commissions. In Chapter 6 FAN Yuwen aspires to contribute to the improvement of the quality of fact-finding by formulating criteria for the mandates. The author proposes a layered approach to the formulation and implementation of the mandates, whereby the best result is achieved by balancing conflicting considerations on a step-by-step basis. Among these issues are the tension between accuracy and flexibility, breadth and specificity, and impartiality and neutrality. Isabelle Lassée argues in Chapter 7 for a new approach to the design and implementation of the mandates of international fact-finding missions. She identifies two main problems with the mandates: first, they are not always timely or contextually relevant; and second, the work of the missions often lacks methodology. Lassée offers a solution to these problems through the enhancement of the external and internal coherence of the mandates. External coherence refers to the formulation of the mandate in precise terms by the sanctioning body, while the internal coherence denotes the overall methodology adopted by the commission itself.

Chapter 8 explores another crucial aspect of international fact-finding: the selection of the members of the mission. In this chapter, WU Xiaodan reflects on the importance of the composition of the mission for the credibility, legitimacy and effectiveness of the mandate. She outlines some concerns stemming from the lack of a uniform procedure for selecting the members of UN-mandated fact-finding missions. In particular, WU focuses on the questions of impartiality, legal expertise and management skills of mission members. She concludes that the UN needs to develop and standardise a uniform set of rules for fact-finder selection to further legitimise the process of international fact-finding.

In the following Chapter 9, Dan Saxon proceeds with the quest for improvement of the quality of fact-finding endeavours. Saxon argues that it is of utmost importance to clarify the purposes of international fact-finding missions. He points out that while the missions are often set up to report on the violations of international human rights and humanitarian law, the legal perspective may ignore the political context in which the mandate operates. This confusion leads to the lack of clear understanding of the objectives of international fact-finding missions. Saxon recommends de-coupling mission activities from politics to the greatest extent possible.

Chapters 10 and 11 offer two distinct case studies of fact-finding missions, one in Nepal, and one in the former Yugoslavia. Christopher B. Mahony, in Chapter 10, considers security implications linked to the establishment of the Commission on Investigation of Disappeared Persons, Truth and Reconciliation in Nepal in the spring of 2013. Mahony focuses on the commission's anticipated inability to provide adequate protection to the witnesses; which may lead, in turn, to the delay (and potential denial) of truth and justice. The author identifies a number of areas where the work on witness protection can be improved. These fields include funding allocation, personnel training, and the management of the programme.

In Chapter 11, David Re ponders reasons why the reports prepared by the fact-finding missions in the former Yugoslavia had comparatively little effect on either the evidence presented at trial or the factual findings of the judgements themselves. Re concludes that there is an overlap in gathering material (or 'evidence' if it gets to the court) for the purposes of fact-finding and international criminal justice, and the credibility of the courts and fact-finding missions increases only with improving the accuracy and reliability of the information on which they rely. In this regard, the fact-finding organisations should learn from how criminal courts scrutinise their reports.

Chapter 12 provides a different perspective on the same subject matter. It questions the impact of international criminal law on international fact-finding. Dov Jacobs and Catherine Harwood reflect on the ambiguity of the international criminal law-focused fact-finding: on the one hand, it improves the quality of the final product by requiring rigorous methodology that enhances the credibility of the reports, but on the other hand, it unnecessarily reduces the scope and the outcome of the fact-finding mission. The authors track the migration of international criminal law concepts from the courtroom into fact-finding commissions, while questioning the use of these concepts as a point of reference. They conclude that international criminal law outside the courtroom might not actually be international criminal law.

The discussion about the interplay between international criminal law and international fact-finding continues in Chapter 13, where Lyal Sunga offers his view as to whether the information from the UN human rights sources could be admitted as direct evidence in an international criminal trial. He answers the question in the positive, suggesting that the urgency of international criminal justice for victims, survivors, and affected communities demands that international criminal investigators and prosecutors take into account the information available to them despite the obstacles posed by the different standards of proof and *modus operandi* of various fact-finding missions.

Wolfgang Kaleck and Carolijn Terwindt focus in Chapter 14 on the fact-finding work by NGOs. They take a step back from the general debate about the need to create a uniform standardised methodology for NGO fact-work and assess critically the role of the NGO's position *vis-à-vis* the communities with which they work. It is frequently the case that NGO fact-work plays a role in courtroom proceedings. However, this path, often adopted by the NGOs as given and without further considerations, requires more reflection.

Chapter 15 highlights the challenges specific to the humanitarian law fact-finding. In this contribution, Charles Garraway, a former Vice-President of the International Humanitarian Fact-Finding Commission, identifies different legal regimes that shape the process of modern fact-finding and determine its parameters. Garraway reflects on the future of the Commission that, despite having been called into action only once in the past, offers some distinct advantages for the future. Among these benefits are its legitimacy as a permanent institution established pursuant to an international mandate and its efficiency in processing confidential enquiries.

Chapter 16 by Ilia Utmelidze contains reflections on methodological challenges involved in processing large quantities of information in the context of international fact-finding and possibilities of using information technology. The author discusses the quantitative and qualitative challenges involved in international fact-finding, with the primary focus on methodology-based technological tools that could make fact-work more effective and accurate as well as support knowledge-based technology and methodology.

The new Chapter 17 by Geoffrey Robertson examines key ethical and legal dilemmas of fact-finding, based on his rich experience in human rights practice. He stresses the important need to ensure accuracy and impartiality in working practices and to protect sources. He argues that courts should respect the confidentiality obligations of human rights fact-finders and their commitment not to expose informants, when summoned to testify in court. He shows that the House of Lords has developed a "public interest defence" for the media against libel actions, which "should cover the publication of most human rights reports".

The new contribution by Emma Irving (Chapter 18) analyses the opportunities and challenges of the turn to social media in inquiry and investigation processes. She clarifies both the vulnerabilities and the contributions of digital-derived evidence to the work of human rights fact-finding bodies, based on the examples of Myanmar and Palestine. She concludes that "it is too soon" to draw "broad ranging conclusions on how the quality of human rights fact-finding is affected by the turn to social media". She argues that different types of fact-finding bodies should learn from each other, in order to make fact-finding more effective.

Growing involvement of non-State actors has become part and parcel of the international justice landscape, particularly in situations of on-going atrocity as Syria. Chapter 19 by William H. Wiley addresses the trend towards a privatisation of fact-finding and investigations, based on the CIJA model. He pleads for public-private partnership in international criminal justice. He argues that public fact-finders or investigators are "untroubled by the partial shift of responsibility for criminal justice to the private sector which is implied by the CIJA model". He concludes that the absence of "private-sector participation" would entail imply a "loss of the hard-won progress made since 1993".

## 1.4. Further Research Agenda

This book shows that there are several issues pertaining to non-criminal justice fact-finding commissions and inquiries that can benefit from further research. Such analysis could contribute to increasing the quality of their fact-work. The improvements can be both substantial and procedural.

### 1.4.1. Substantive Issues

From the substantive point of view, one of the most decisive challenges in fact-finding is the formulation of the mandate. It is essential to pose realistic objectives that fact-finding missions are able to achieve. The current trend is overexpansion of the scope of the mission.[109] It appears that in many instances fact-finding drifts away from the fact-work towards defining the law.[110] In other cases, one observes an ambitious attempt to un-

---

[109] Report of the Special Rapporteur on the Promotion of Truth, Justice, Reparation and Guarantees of Non-Recurrence, para. 94, *supra* note 21.

[110] Dapo Akande and Hannah Tonkin, "International Commissions of Inquiry: A New Form of

derstand comprehensively root causes, circumstances, factors, context and motives of countrywide situations of repression or violence.[111] The fact-finding commissions with widely defined, open-ended objectives may struggle to meet the expectations, especially when funding is inadequate or the available time is limited.[112] Consequently, there is a high demand for the formulation of the discreet specific functions that have the potential of being met in practice.[113]

Another substantive research issue pertaining to international fact-finding concerns the intertangling of factual conclusions and legal assessments. Some reports prepared by the fact-finding commissions go beyond factual conclusions and make legal pronouncements. This peculiarity gives fact-finding missions a normative flavour. The task of ascertaining the facts is certainly to be performed in an impartial manner.[114] This does not mean, however, that fact-finding is a neutral activity.[115] As one of the legal commentators put it back in 1973, fact-finders "cannot afford an attitude of neutrality".[116] The solution may be to work on devising procedures separating to the largest extent possible questions of fact from questions of law, while respecting the boundaries of the mission as defined by the mandate.

Another issue for further research is defining the purposes of fact-finding. As discussed extensively in several chapters of the anthology, the commissions differ from judicial organs in that they are not bound by the 'beyond reasonable doubt' standard of proof, the principle of equality of arms, or the principle of individual criminal responsibility. The question that arises is that of procedural fairness or lack thereof in handling the information obtained by the mission.[117] If the mission's objective is to establish patters of violations as opposed to assessing individual conduct for

---

Adjudication?", *EJIL:Talk!*, 6 April 2012.

[111] Report of the Special Rapporteur on the Promotion of Truth, Justice, Reparation and Guarantees of Non-Recurrence, para. 40, *supra* note 21.

[112] *Ibid.*, para. 97.

[113] *Ibid.*, para. 102.

[114] Bertrand G. Ramcharan, *International Law and Fact-Finding in the Field of Human Rights*, Martinus Nijhoff, 1982, p. 7.

[115] *Ibid.*

[116] Theo van Boven, "Fact-Finding in the Field of Human Rights", in *Israel Yearbook on Human Rights*, 1973, vol. 3, no. 93, p. 106.

[117] Akande and Tonkin, *supra* note 110.

criminal trial purposes,[118] does it have to elaborate on the standard of proof used in the report?[119] The answer to this question has to be influenced by an additional consideration that the reports of the commissions often become authoritative statements about the situation and are frequently used to back the decisions of the political bodies.[120] There are particular difficulties attached to determining violations of norms of international humanitarian law due to their specific characteristics, such as, for example, the relevant state of mind of the attacker and his or her evaluation of the situation *before* the attack.[121]

Finally, the broader turn to private international criminal investigations requires further scrutiny. As a result of advances in technology, non-State actors play an ever-growing role in fact-finding. However, significant doubts remain as to what extent human rights actors should serve as private criminal investigators. There is an important qualitative difference between documentation, fact-finding and criminal investigation. Well-meaning civil organisations may easily underestimate the complexity of investigative processes. While standards are gradually built in the UN system, the private sector is much more diffuse and less regulated. It is important to clarify to what extent private actors should be bound by minimum standards, in order not to inflict harm or compromise the work of public bodies, and how compliance with such standards can be monitored. Risks relating to physical and digital security must be addressed. There is a need to analyse more thoroughly how private-public partnerships can ensure effective investigation and prosecution. Existing experiences at the ICC have shown that the 'outsourcing' of work by public institutions to private investigative bodies carries significant risks. A critical question is how collaborative ties may be strengthened without compromising the integrity or development of public sector institutions, and whether professional private investigative bodies should be seen as a viable model for the future, rather than as an option of last resort. Syria will be a historic test case to assess to what extent private inquiry and investigation may

---

[118] Théo Boutruche, "Credible Fact-Finding and Allegations of International Humanitarian Law Violations: Challenges in Theory and Practice", in *Journal of Conflict and Security Law*, 2011, vol. 16, no. 1, p. 114.

[119] *Ibid.*, p. 114.

[120] Akande and Tonkin, *supra* note 110.

[121] Boutruche, p. 124, *supra* note 118.

stimulate greater exercise of domestic jurisdiction, including universal jurisdiction.

### 1.4.2. Procedural Issues

In addition to the substantive challenges, there are a number of procedural issues ingrained in international fact-finding that require a closer look because they have the potential of influencing the outcome of the mission. For example, it is advisable to look into improving logistical support for fact-finding missions because practical problems such as access to the country under examination, availability of information, or security concerns for the mission's members may impede fact-finding processes. It would be beneficial to further explore ways of securing State consent to allow access to classified military information, which is essential in determinations on some questions of international humanitarian law.[122] This was the case with Israel's refusal to fully co-operate with the UN Fact-Finding Mission on the Gaza Conflict. Israel declined to provide the members of the mission with access to Gaza.[123] Fact-finding could benefit from exploring alternative mechanisms of obtaining information in the instances when the physical access of mission members to the territory in question is limited by the State under scrutiny. Open source investigation is one possible solution to this challenge, even though other problems may arise linked to collecting data from publicly available sources, such as, for instance, the reliability of evidence and its verification.[124]

Logistical issues are particularly pressing in the case of fact-finding by non-governmental organisations. The fact-finding work of the most prominent human rights NGOs tends to focus on issues of physical integrity (such as torture), extrajudicial executions, and arbitrary detention.[125] This data is often in the exclusive control of States, which are not keen on disclosure.[126] Further analysis of the nature and impact of challenges such as those described above could make a significant contribution.

---

[122] *Ibid.*, p. 121.

[123] Report of the United Nations Fact-Finding Mission on the Gaza Conflict, *supra* note 91, para. 144.

[124] Hiatt, 2016, *supra* note 39.

[125] Diane Orentlicher, "Bearing Witness: The Art and Science of Human Rights Fact-Finding", in *Harvard Human Rights Journal*, 1990, vol. 3, p. 94.

[126] *Ibid.*, p. 95.

The substantive outcome may also be affected by the mere lack of visibility of the mission. Fact-finding cannot be perceived as a process that ends with the production of a written document. It is only a part of the process whereby the mission achieves its objectives. Research into outreach activities, such as public communication in connection with the submission of the final report, is essential to increase the impact of the mission and, hence, its efficiency. It is advisable to involve different stakeholders in the discourse related to the report after it has been released. This is an area that requires further analysis.

There is also room for further study of how there could be improvement in the composition of fact-finding missions, their organisation, and the resources made available to them. The anthology contributes to this discussion in Chapters 5 and 8. These issues strongly affect the quality and impartiality of fact-finding processes. For example, the appointment of non-UN staff associated with certain political agendas as heads or members of such missions might prejudice the final outcome.[127] Structuring financial issues pertaining to fact-finding can also release undue pressure and uncertainty.

Research effort could also be directed to enhancing the key work-processes in international fact-finding, including the writing of reports and conclusions. The mediocre performance of some fact-finding missions may be explained by the lack of rigorous methodology and quality control, which may, in turn, be caused in part by the lack of continuity in international fact-finding.[128] In this regard, some consider it unfortunate that the attempts to establish a permanent commission of inquiry with its own terms of reference, composition and procedure, failed.[129] The methodology of fact-finding is a particularly serious challenge for non-governmental organisations. The credibility of NGO reports is often subjected to enhanced scrutiny by the international community, with suggestions that NGOs lack objectivity or that the output suffers from low quality. This criticism could stem in part from the lack of generally recognised methodological standards guiding substantial fact-finding endeavours by the NGOs and guarding it against distortions.[130] Given that some of the larg-

---

[127] Bassiouni, p. 39, *supra* note 86.

[128] *Ibid.*, p. 41.

[129] Partsch, 1981, p. 62, *supra* note 6.

[130] Orentlicher, p. 135, *supra* note 125.

---

est NGOs do not even have internal manuals for their fact-finding work, reaching broader agreement among such organisations would seem rather ambitious at this stage of their professionalisation. This is an area that invites critical research.

## 1.5. Conclusion

Since the 1990s, non-criminal justice international fact-finding has come to enjoy wide recognition as a corollary and, in many cases, an alternative to international criminal justice as a mechanism for achieving accountability for violations of humanitarian and human rights law. Such fact-finding often has the capacity to surpass international criminal justice in accomplishing the objectives of setting the historical record and contributing to national reconciliation. Despite its mounting importance, the topic of non-criminal justice, international fact-finding receives considerably less attention in scholarly literature than various issues related to international criminal law. The present anthology seeks to remedy this situation and contribute to a deeper understanding of the challenges inherent to non-criminal justice fact-finding. Its specific focus – quality control in fact-finding – embraces different aspects of the process. The quality of the mandate, independence, methodology, and reporting practices determine the utility, efficacy and legitimacy of fact-finding commissions and inquiries. Different legal regimes and standards of reporting make the final outcome of the mission less predictable absent proper quality control.

Increasing the awareness and understanding of quality control may enhance the value of non-criminal justice fact-finding to relevant stakeholders, including, ultimately, the victims and, indirectly, taxpayers who make it possible for the governments to support such commissions. More refined quality control mechanisms can make the success of international fact-finding less dependent on the individual composition of any given commission. The leadership of fact-finding processes remains, however, of the utmost importance to foster a culture of quality control, in which the will of individual fact-finders to professionalise is nurtured by example and not only by peers. Being mandate-centred helps fact-finders to sharpen their awareness of quality control. Quality control can contribute to the substantive independence of the fact-finders' assessment of allegations of serious violations of international criminal, humanitarian or human rights law.

## 1.6. Annex: Some International Fact-Finding Mandates 1992–2020

The data in the table below are largely taken from the International(ised) Fact-Finding Mandates Collection in the ICC Legal Tool Database, a Collection which, at the time of the release of this edition, contained 1,535 documents on fact-finding mandates concerning 37 countries.

| Name: | Date of establishment: | Legal basis/ Establishing body: |
|---|---|---|
| UN Fact-finding mission to South Vietnam | 11 October 1963 | UN General Assembly at the request of the Government of Vietnam |
| Commission of inquiry on the reported massacres in Mozambique | 12 December 1973 | General Assembly resolution 3114 (XXVIII) |
| Ad Hoc Working Group to inquire into the situation of human rights in Chile | 27 February 1977 | UN Commission on Human Rights Resolution 8 (XXXI) |
| Security Council Commission concerning Israeli settlements in Arab territories occupied since 1967, including Jerusalem | 22 March 1979 | UN Security Council Resolution 446 (1979) |
| Commission of Inquiry under Resolution 496 (1981) in connection with the Republic of the Seychelles | 15 December 1981 | UN Security Council Resolution 496 (1981) |
| Security Council Commission of Investigation established in pursuance of Resolution 571 (1985) | 20 September 1985 | UN Security Council Resolution 571 (1985) |
| Mission to Cuba to observe the human rights situation | 10 March 1988 | Commission on Human Rights Decision 1998/106 |
| Special Rapporteur on the situation of Human Rights in Iraq | 6 March 1991 | UN Commission on Human Rights Resolution 1991/74 |
| Commission of Experts for the former Yugoslavia | October 1992 | UN Security Council Resolution 780 (1992) |

| Special Rapporteur on the situation of human rights in Cambodia | 19 February 1993 | UN Commission on Human Rights Resolution 1993/6 |
|---|---|---|
| Special Rapporteur on the situation of human rights in the Palestinian territories occupied since 1967 | 19 February 1993 | UN Commission on Human Rights Resolution 1993/2 A |
| Independent Expert on the situation of human rights in Somalia | 10 March 1993 | UN Commission on Human Rights Resolution 1993/86 |
| Panel of Inquiry on Liberia to conduct a thorough and full investigation of the massacre of the civilians, which occurred near Harbel, Liberia on the morning of 6 June 1993 | 9 June 1993 | UN Security Council via Statement by President of the Security Council S/25918 |
| Fact-finding mission to investigate human rights violations in Abkhazia, Republic of Georgia | October 1993 | UN Secretary-General |
| Commission of Inquiry concerning Somalia | 16 November 1993 | UN Security Council Resolution 885 (1993) |
| Preparatory fact-finding mission to Burundi to investigate the coup d'état of 21 October 1993, the assassination of President Melchior Ndadaye, and the subsequent massacres | March 1994 | UN Secretary-General |
| Commission of Experts to investigate violations of international humanitarian law during the Rwandan Genocide | July 1994 | UN Security Council Resolution 935 (1994) |
| Truth and Reconciliation Commission of South Africa | 19 July 1995 | Parliament |
| International Commission of Inquiry concerning Burundi | 28 August 1995 | UN Security Council Resolution 1012 (1995) |

| International Commission of Inquiry concerning Rwanda to investigate reports relating to the sale or supply of arms and related material to former Rwandese Government Forces | 7 September 1995 | UN Security Council Resolution 1013 (1995) |
|---|---|---|
| Joint Mission to investigate allegations of massacres and other human rights violations occurring in Eastern Zaire (now the Democratic Republic of the Congo) since September 1996 | 15 April 1997 | UN Commission on Human Rights Resolution 1997/58 |
| UN Secretary-General's Investigative team charged with investigating serious violations of human rights and international humanitarian law in the Democratic Republic of the Congo | 15 July 1997 | UN Secretary-General |
| Group of Experts for Cambodia | 18 February 1999 | UN General Assembly Resolution 52/135 |
| Report of the High Commissioner for Human Rights on the situation of human rights in Kosovo, Federal Republic of Yugoslavia | 13 April 1999 | UN Commission on Human Rights |
| UN Inquiry into Possible Human Rights Violations in East Timor | September – November 1999 | UN Commission on Human Rights resolution 1999/S-4/1; Economic and Social Council decision 1999/293 |
| Monitoring, Verification and Inspection Commission to verify compliance by Iraq with its disarmament obligations imposed after the Gulf War | 17 December 1999 | UN Security Council Resolution 1284 (1999) |

| | | |
|---|---|---|
| Mission of Mary Robinson, High Commissioner for Human Rights to investigate the situation of human rights in Chechnya in the Russian Federation | March-April 2000 | Mandate of a High Commissioner for Human Rights |
| Panel of Experts on the Illegal Exploitation of Natural Resources and Other Forms of Wealth in the Democratic Republic of the Congo | 2 June 2000 | UN Secretary General |
| Panel of Experts appointed pursuant Security Council Resolution 1306 (2000), paragraph 19, in relation to Sierra Leone | 5 July 2000 | UN Security Council Resolution 1306 (2000) |
| Commission of inquiry to investigate violations of human rights and humanitarian law in the occupied Palestinian territories after 28 September 2000 | 19 October 2000 | UN Commission on Human Rights Resolution S-5/1 |
| La Commission d'enquête internationale pour la Côte d'Ivoire | 15 January 2001 | UN Secretary-General |
| The official visit to Chile by the Special Rapporteur on the situation of human rights and fundamental freedoms of indigenous people, which took place between 18 and 29 July 2003 | 24 April 2001 | UN Commission on Human Rights |
| African Commission on Human and Peoples' Rights Fact-Finding Mission to Zimbabwe, 24–28 June 2002 | April-May 2001 | 29th Ordinary Session of the African Commission on Human and Peoples' Rights of the African Union |

| | | |
|---|---|---|
| Truth and Reconciliation Commission/Informe Final de la Comisión de la Verdad y Reconciliación (Peru) | June 2001 | Interim President |
| International investigative mission in Chile – The Mapuche People: Between Oblivion and Exclusion | Early 2002 | International Federation for Human Rights ('FIDH') |
| The Special Rapporteur's third fact-finding mission to Myanmar undertaken in October 2002 and information received by him up to 10 December 2002 | 25 April 2002 | UN Commission on Human Rights |
| OHCHR fact-finding mission to Côte d'Ivoire | 20 December 2002 | UN Secretary-General |
| Commission of Inquiry on the events connected with the march planned for 25 March 2004 in Abidjan | 2 April 2004 | UN Secretary-General |
| Special Rapporteur on the situation of human rights in the Democratic People's Republic of Korea | 15 April 2004 | UN Commission on Human Rights Resolution 2004/13 |
| Independent Inquiry Committee into the United Nations Oil-for-Food Programme | April 2004 | UN Secretary General and Security Council |
| Mission of the African Commission on Human and Peoples' Rights to Sudan | July 2004 | African Commission on Human and Peoples' Rights Resolution, 35th Ordinary Session May-June 2004 |
| International Commission of Inquiry on Darfur | 18 September 2004 | UN Security Council Resolution 1564 (2004) |
| Commission of Experts to Review the Prosecution of Serious Violations of Human Rights in Timor-Leste (then East Timor) in 1999 | January 2005 | Letters between the Secretary-General and the President of the Security Council S/2005/96 and S/2005/97 |

| | | |
|---|---|---|
| OSCE Fact-Finding Mission to the Occupied Territories of Azerbaijan Surrounding Nagorno-Karabakh | January 2005 | Mandate of the Organization for Security and Co-operation of Europe ('OSCE') Fact-Finding Mission as agreed by the parties |
| Truth and Reconciliation Commission of Liberia | 12 May 2005 | National Transitional Legislative Assembly of the National Transitional Government of Liberia |
| International Independent Investigation Commission to assist in investigation of all aspects of the assassination of the former Prime Minister of Lebanon, Rafiq Hariri, along with 22 others in Beirut on 14 February 2005 | 7 April 2005 | UN Security Council Resolution 1595 (2005) |
| Fact-Finding Mission to Zimbabwe to assess the Scope and Impact of Operation Murambatsvina | May 2005 | UN Special Envoy on Human Settlements Issues in Zimbabwe |
| The Liberian Truth and Reconciliation Commission ('TRC') | May 2005 | National Parliament |
| United Nations Independent Special Commission of Inquiry for Timor-Leste | 12 June 2006 | UN Secretary-General |
| Commission of Inquiry on Lebanon | 11 August 2006 | UN Human Rights Council Resolution S-2/1 |
| High-Level Fact-Finding Mission to Beit Hanoun | 15 November 2006 | UN Human Rights Council Resolution S-3/1 |
| Colombia Fact-Finding Mission | March 2007 | International Bar Association's Human Rights Institute |

| | | |
|---|---|---|
| UN Security Council Kosovo Fact-Finding Mission | April 2007 | Security Council fact-finding mission to Kosovo requested by Russia to inform the vote on Kosovo's independence |
| Mapping Exercise documenting the most serious violations of human rights and international humanitarian law committed within the territory of the Democratic Republic of the Congo between March 1993 and June 2003 | 8 May 2007 | UN Secretary-General |
| The Commission of Inquiry on Post-Election Violence | 22 May 2008 | President of Kenya |
| Truth, Justice and Reconciliation Commission | 2008 | Parliament |
| African Union Fact-Finding Team for Darfur | November 2008 | African Union authorization |
| Fact-Finding Mission to Kenya | 6–28 February 2008 | OHCHR |
| Independent International Fact-Finding Mission on the Conflict in Georgia | 2 December 2008 | Council of the European Union Decision 2008/901/CFSP |
| Commission of Inquiry into the Benazir Bhutto assassination | 3 February 2009 | Letters between the Secretary-General and the President of the Security Council |
| United Nations Headquarters Board of Inquiry to review and investigate nine incidents in the Gaza Strip and southern Israel that occurred between 27 December 2008 and 19 January 2009 | 11 February 2009 | UN Secretary General |
| UN Fact-Finding Mission on the Gaza Conflict | 3 April 2009 | UN Human Rights Council Resolution S-9/1 |

| | | |
|---|---|---|
| The Independent Expert on the Situation of Human Rights in the Sudan | 18 June 2009 | UN Human Rights Council Resolution 11/10 |
| International Commission of Inquiry mandated to establish the facts and circumstances of the events of 28 September 2009 in Guinea | 28 October 2009 | UN Secretary-General |
| OHCHR monitoring mission in Guinea | 26 March 2010 | UN Human Rights Council resolution 13/21 |
| International Fact-Finding Mission to investigate violations of international law, including international humanitarian and human rights law, resulting from the Israeli attacks on the flotilla of ships carrying humanitarian assistance | 2 June 2010 | Human Rights Council in resolution 14/1 |
| Danish Immigration Service's Fact-Finding Mission to Colombo, Sri Lanka | 19 June – 3 July 2010 | Danish Immigration Service |
| Panel of Experts on Accountability in Sri Lanka | 22 June 2010 | UN Secretary-General |
| Panel of Inquiry on the 31 May 2010 Flotilla Incident (the Palmer Committee) | 2 August 2010 | UN Secretary-General |
| Fact-Finding Missions of the United Nations Joint Human Rights Office into the Mass Rapes and Other Human Rights Violations Committed by a Coalition of Armed Groups along the Kibua-Mpofi Aix in Walikale Territory, North Kivu, from 30 July to 2 August 2010 | August 2010 | United Nations Joint Human Rights Office; The United Nations Organization Stabilization Mission in the Democratic Republic of the Congo |

| | | |
|---|---|---|
| Independent International Commission of Inquiry into the Events in southern Kyrgyzstan | September 2010 | An initiative from the Nordic countries; the President of the Kyrgyz Republic; OSCE; UN |
| OSCE Minsk Group Co-Chairs conducted a Field Assessment Mission to the seven occupied territories of Azerbaijan surrounding Nagorno-Karabakh | 7–12 October 2010 | Organization for Security and Cooperation of Europe |
| African Union Fact-Finding Mission in Côte d'Ivoire | February 2011 | African Union |
| International Commission of Inquiry on Libya | 25 February 2011 | UN Human Rights Council Resolution S-15/1 |
| Special Rapporteur on the situation of human rights in the Islamic Republic of Iran | 24 March 2011 | UN Human Rights Council Resolution 16/9 |
| International Commission of Inquiry on Côte d'Ivoire | 25 March 2011 | UN Human Rights Council Resolution 16/25 |
| Fact-Finding Mission to Syria | March 2011 | International Bar Association's Human Rights Institute |
| Fact-Finding Mission for the Syrian Arab Republic | 29 April 2011 | UN Human Rights Council Resolution S-16/1 |
| Independent Expert on the situation of human rights in Côte d'Ivoire | 17 June 2011 | UN Human Rights Council resolution 17/21 |
| Bahrain Independent Commission of Inquiry | 29 June 2011 | The King of Bahrain |
| Fact-Finding Mission to Zimbabwe | June 2011 | International Bar Association's Human Rights Institute |
| OHCHR Assessment Mission to Yemen | June-July 2011 | OHCHR |

| | | |
|---|---|---|
| Independent International Commission of Inquiry on the Syrian Arab Republic | 22 August 2011 | UN Human Rights Council Resolution S-17/1 |
| Fact-finding mission in Kenya to identify perpetrators of killings and cattle raiding in a conflict-prone border region. | August 2011 | Intergovernmental Authority on Development (Conflict Early Warning and Early Response Unit) |
| UNASUR Fact-Finding Mission in Bolivia to investigate a clash in the Pando province in September 2008 | December 2011 | Union of South American Nations |
| National Truth Commission/Comissão Nacional da Verdade (Brasil) | Late 2011 | President and Senate |
| Independent Civil Society Fact-Finding Mission to Libya | 2012 | Arab Organization for Human Rights; Palestinian Centre; International Legal Assistance Consortium |
| ECOWAS Commission Fact-Finding mission to the Republic of Mali | 16–18 March 2012 | Economic Community of West African States |
| International Fact-Finding Mission on Israeli Settlements in the Occupied Palestinian Territory | 22 March 2012 | UN Human Rights Council Resolution 19/17 |
| Fact-Finding Mission to Georgia | April 2012 | International Bar Association's Human Rights Institute |
| Special Rapporteur on the situation of human rights in Belarus | 28 June 2012 | UN Human Rights Council Resolution 20/13 |
| Special Rapporteur on the situation of human rights in Eritrea | 17 July 2012 | UN Human Rights Council Resolution 20/20 |
| OAS Fact-Finding Mission to Paraguay | July 2012 | Organization of American States |

| | | |
|---|---|---|
| Commission of inquiry on human rights in the Democratic People's Republic of Korea | 21 March 2013 | UN Human Rights Council Resolution 22/13 |
| Independent Expert on the situation of human rights in Mali | 21 March 2013 | UN Human Rights Council Resolution 22/18 |
| UN Fact-Finding Mission to investigate allegations of the reported use of chemical weapons in Syria | March 2013 | UN Secretary General after the consultations with the World Health Organization and Organization for the Prohibition of Chemical Weapons |
| Fact-finding mission in Angola to analyse the context in which human rights defenders are operating in the country | April 2013 | International Federation for Human Rights and the World Organization Against Torture ('OMCT') |
| Commission on Investigation of Disappeared Persons, Truth and Reconciliation in Nepal | 2 April 2013 | Parliament |
| OHCHR Fact-finding Mission to the Central African Republic | 13 June 2013 | UN Human Rights Council Resolution 23/18 |
| Independent Expert on the human rights situation in the Central African Republic | 27 September 2013 | UN Human Rights Council Resolution 24/34 |
| International Commission of Inquiry on the Central African Republic | 5 December 2013 | UN Security Council Resolution 2127 (2013) |
| Panel of Experts on Yemen | 26 February 2014 | UN Security Council Resolution 2140 (2014) |
| OHCHR Investigation on Sri Lanka | 27 March 2014 | UN Human Rights Council Resolution 25/01 |
| OPCW Fact-Finding Mission in Syria | 29 April 2014 | Director-General of OPCW |
| Commission of Inquiry on Human Rights in Eritrea | 27 June 2014 | UN Human Rights Council Resolution 26/24 |

| Independent Commission of Inquiry on the 2014 Gaza Conflict | 23 July 2014 | UN Human Rights Council Resolution S-21/1 |
|---|---|---|
| OHCHR mission to Iraq to investigate alleged violations and abuses of international human rights law committed by the so-called Islamic State in Iraq and the Levant | 1 September 2014 | UN Human Rights Council Resolution S-22/1 |
| OHCHR Investigation on Libya | 27 March 2015 | UN Human Rights Council Resolution 28/30 |
| OHCHR Fact-finding mission to investigate atrocities committed by the terrorist group Boko Haram and its effects on human rights in the affected States | 1 April 2015 | UN Human Rights Council Resolution S-23/1 |
| OHCHR Assessment mission in South Sudan | 2 July 2015 | UN Human Rights Council Resolution 29/13 |
| OPCW-UN Joint Investigative Mechanism | 7 August 2015 | UN Security Council Resolution 2235 (2015) |
| United Nations Independent Investigation on Burundi | 17 December 2015 | UN Human Rights Council Resolution S-24 |
| Commission on Human Rights in South Sudan | 23 March 2016 | UN Human Rights Council Resolution 31/20 |
| Commission of Inquiry on Burundi | 30 September 2016 | UN Human Rights Council Resolution 33/24 |
| International, Impartial and Independent Mechanism to Assist in the Investigation and Prosecution of Persons Responsible for the Most Serious Crimes under International Law Committed in the Syrian Arab Republic since March 2011 | 21 December 2016 | UN General Assembly Resolution 71/248 |

| | | |
|---|---|---|
| OHCHR Mission to Bangladesh to interview Rohingyas fleeing from Myanmar since 9 October 2016 | January 2017 | OHCHR |
| Independent international fact-finding mission on Myanmar | 24 March 2017 | UN Human Rights Council Resolution 34/22 |
| Team of international experts on the situation in Kasaï | 23 June 2017 | UN Human Rights Council Resolution 35/33 |
| Group of Eminent Experts on Yemen | 29 September 2017 | UN Human Rights Council Resolution 36/31 |
| The United Nations Commission of Inquiry on the 2018 protests in the Occupied Palestinian Territory | 18 May 2018 | UN Human Rights Council Resolution S-28/1 |
| The Independent Investigative Mechanism for Myanmar | 27 September 2018 | UN Human Rights Council Resolution 39/2 |
| Independent International Fact-Finding Mission on the Bolivarian Republic of Venezuela | 27 September 2019 | UN Human Rights Council Resolution 42/25 |

# 2

---

# Quality Control in International Fact-Finding Outside Criminal Justice for Core International Crimes

### Richard J. Goldstone[*]

## 2.1. Introduction

It was my great privilege to work with the late Judge LI Haopei when he was one of the first 11 judges appointed to the United Nations International Criminal Tribunal for the former Yugoslavia. He served in the Appeals Chamber of both that Tribunal, as well as that of the International Criminal Tribunal for Rwanda. Judge LI was in his late 80s at the time of his appointment. He brought a vigorous mind and huge experience in international law with him to The Hague. He was mentally and physically agile. My wife, Noleen, and I accompanied a group of the judges to a game park some hours by bus from Arusha in Tanzania. It was a bumpy ride on unpaved roads, but that did not appear to be of concern to Judge LI. He was fluent in more than a dozen languages and his spoken and written English was impeccable. His judgements are models of concise analysis and elegant writing.

---

[*] **Richard J. Goldstone** is a retired Justice of the Constitutional Court of South Africa. He served as the first Chief Prosecutor of the International Criminal Tribunals for the Former Yugoslavia and Rwanda. This chapter is based on his 2013 LI Haopei Lecture presented at the European University Institute in Florence on 20 May 2013. Justice Goldstone was appointed by the UN Secretary-General to the Independent International Committee to investigate the Iraq Oil-for-Food Programme. In 2009, he led the UN Fact-Finding Mission on Gaza. Among his other professional endeavours, Goldstone served as chairperson of the Commission of Inquiry regarding Public Violence and Intimidation that came to be known as the 'Goldstone Commission'; and of the International Independent Inquiry on Kosovo. He also was co-chairperson of the International Task Force on Terrorism, which was established by the International Bar Association; director of the American Arbitration Association; a member of the International Group of Advisers of the International Committee of the Red Cross; and national president of the National Institute of Crime Prevention and the Rehabilitation of Offenders. He is a foreign member of the American Academy of Arts and Sciences and an honorary member of the Association of the Bar of the City of New York.

During Judge LI's period of office in The Hague, my wife and I also had the pleasure of making the acquaintance of his daughter, Professor LING Yan. She is a distinguished lawyer and teacher and we were able to renew our friendship on a recent visit to Beijing, where we enjoyed her friendship and hospitality.

When informed that the FICHL proposed to establish a lecture series (on which this volume is based) in the name of her father, Professor LING stated:

> I remember my father as a curious man. I hope the LI Haopei Lecture Series will consistently place on the agenda cutting-edge topics and always seek to contribute to the broadening of our understanding of international law and its role. If it does, the Series could serve as a meeting ground for open-minded international lawyers and students from East and West.[1]

The topics addressed in the LI Haopei Lecture Series certainly reflect the wish of Professor LING.

## 2.2. The Approach of this Chapter

Fact-finding missions are usually, if not invariably, established to inquire into situations that are politically fraught and in which the facts are hotly disputed. If such inquiries are to have any value, there must be general confidence by the contesting sides that the inquiry will be conducted impartially and independently. There must be a perception that those who are entrusted with the mission will not be biased in favor of or against one of the contesting parties.

Fact-finding missions might have various objectives. They might be established to calm a nation and to assist reconciliation. They might be set up to provide the basis for future criminal investigations. Alternatively, they may be intended to deter future violations of the norms of human rights or humanitarian law. Some of these objectives may overlap.

During my career, I have been involved with a number of different fact-finding missions, both domestic and international. I propose in this chapter to consider my own experiences and to approach the issue of quality control through that subjective lens.

---

[1] "Statement by Professor LING Yan" (available at http://www.fichl.org/li-haopei-lecture-series/statement-by-professor-ling-yan/).

I have been privileged to be involved in the following fact-finding missions and inquiries:

- South Africa:
  1. The death in detention of Clayton Sithole (1990);
  2. the Sebokeng Inquiry (1990); and
  3. the Standing Commission on Political Violence and Intimidation (the Goldstone Commission) (1991–1994).

- International:
  1. The Kosovo Commission (2000);
  2. the Oil-for-Food Inquiry (2004–2005);
  3. Gaza and Operation Cast Lead (2009); and
  4. the Hammarskjold Inquiry (2012–2013).

For the sake of brevity, it is not possible to consider all of them here and I have omitted the Kosovo and Hammarskjold inquiries from the analyses that follow.

## 2.3. Clayton Sithole Inquiry

During the Apartheid years, scores of South Africans, the vast majority black, died in police detention. In every case, the police put out exculpatory explanations. Regardless of those explanations, there was a widespread perception that the police were responsible for those deaths.

On 11 February 1990, Nelson Mandela was released from prison after serving 27 years of a life term for high treason. 12 days earlier, it was announced that there had been yet another death in detention. Clayton Sizwe Sithole was found hanged in a prison cell in the Johannesburg Central Police Station. Sithole was a member of the armed wing of the African National Congress. He was also the partner of Zindzi Mandela, the daughter of Nelson and Winnie Mandela, and the father of her three-month old son.

According to the police, Sithole was one of a group of men who had been arrested after having been found in possession of an arms cache that included an AK-47 automatic rifle, a revolver and 27 rounds of ammunition. Four days after his arrest, Sithole was found hanged in his cell. Much to the surprise of most South Africans, President F.W. de Klerk announced that he was establishing a judicial inquiry into the death of Sithole. I accepted the invitation from President de Klerk to conduct the inquiry. This appointment was highly unusual, as inquests into unnatural deaths were invariably held by a magistrate under legislation that regulated autopsies. The decision to appoint a judge of what was then the highest court in the land, to inquire into this matter reflected the political sensitivity of the incident.

As the evidence unfolded during five days of oral testimony, it became clear beyond any question that Sithole had in fact taken his own life; indeed, that conclusion was shared by the legal team acting for his family. I found that the probable reason for the suicide was Sithole's remorse at having informed the police of alleged criminal conduct by Winnie Mandela. Because she was not represented at the inquiry, I considered it unfair to make public the substance of the serious allegations that implicated her in serious criminal conduct. With the agreement of counsel for the Sithole family and the South African Police, these allegations were kept confidential.

The finding was broadly accepted by South Africans and, importantly, by the black majority who had no good reason to place any trust in the Apartheid police force. One of the reasons for the acceptance of the finding was the impartiality that I had demonstrated during my previous 10 years on the bench of the Transvaal Supreme Court and my rulings against the Government of the day. This was clearly present to the mind of President de Klerk in having decided to appoint me to conduct the inquiry. The transparency with which the evidence was led was also as important. I decided that I would not hold the inquiry in a court building, preferring instead a more public-friendly venue. We sat in a hearing room at the Johannesburg City Hall. There was no visible security and large numbers of people attended the five days during which the evidence was heard.

The South African Government wanted to avoid the death of Sithole casting a dark shadow over the release from prison of Nelson Mandela and the opening of a new chapter of reconciliation in South Africa. The fact-finding mission and the acceptance of its conclusion that there was no foul play in the death removed this incident from the political discourse.

## 2.4. Sebokeng

In 1990, South Africans anticipated that the transition to democracy would be a peaceful process. That expectation was shattered by the incremental escalation of public violence across the country. The vast majority of the white community referred in a demeaning fashion to the "black-on-black" violence resulting from the political rivalry between the

Nelson Mandela's African National Congress ('ANC') and Mangosuthu Buthelezi's Inkatha Freedom Party ('IFP'). Mandela ascribed much of the violence to an Apartheid-supporting "third force" as a way of destabilising the ANC and retarding the transition to democracy. Elements in the police and army were alleged to have been behind these attempts to destabilise.

On a number of occasions, the transition process was interrupted and almost derailed by some of the more serious incidents of violence, death and injury. The first of these resulted from a mass protest-march on 26 March 1990 by many thousands of black inhabitants of Sebokeng, a township near Johannesburg. A line of police officers blocked the demonstrators from advancing in the direction of a white residential area. There was a stand-off that ended with the police firing live ammunition at the demonstrators, killing 14 and injuring almost 400 of them.

I was appointed by President de Klerk to conduct a judicial fact-finding inquiry into the incident. I again decided that the inquiry should not be held in a court building, and the evidence and argument were heard in the civic centre in a town not far from Sebokeng. The public gallery was full to overflowing on most of the days on which we sat. There was no security and on one of the days of the inquiry there was a scare when a young man wearing battle fatigues walked into the public gallery carrying what turned out to be a wooden replica of an AK-47 automatic machine gun. I noticed the young man walk into the hall and, observing his relaxed manner, I was not concerned. However, when a plainclothes police officer saw the man, he requested me to adjourn the hearing. I did so for the short time it took to establish that there was no danger posed by the young man. As one might expect, the incident resulted in quite some media attention.

The families of those killed and injured were represented by leading counsel and so, too, were the South African Police. After many days of evidence, I issued a report in which I criticised the actions of the police and held that they had used force that was "immoderate and disproportionate to any lawful object to be attained". I recommended that the police officers responsible for the shooting should be prosecuted for homicide and that the State be held liable for the payment of damages to the families of those killed and to those who were injured.

Elements in the white community were scathing in their criticism of the report. I was accused of ignoring the safety and security interests of the white community and failing to appreciate the valiant efforts of the police to protect white South Africans. I received a number of death threats and much criticism from the right-wing, pro-Apartheid press.

However, the majority of South Africans, and especially black South Africans, received the report with relief and satisfaction that the wholly unnecessary loss of life and serious injuries were held to be the consequence of criminal activity by the police. Importantly, the Government of the day accepted the correctness of the findings. Nine of the police officers were charged with murder and later received amnesty from the Truth and Reconciliation Commission.

## 2.5. The Goldstone Commission

In consequence of the escalating violence in many parts of South Africa, the Government passed a new law to make provision for the President to appoint the five-person Standing Commission of Inquiry Regarding the Prevention of Public Violence and Intimidation. It was given wide powers of subpoena, and search and seizure of documents. In the second half of 1991, I was approached by the Minister of Justice with the request to chair the Commission. It was not an easy decision for me and it was obvious that the Commission would be a controversial one. The Minister informed me that my choice had been the unanimous decision of all of the parties who were negotiating a peaceful transition from white rule to democracy. I realised that my independence was crucial if the Commission was to succeed. After some initial hesitation, I agreed to accept the position on condition that I continued full-time with my duties as a judge of the Supreme Court of Appeal. I did not wish the independence that comes with judicial office to be compromised. I also preferred not to be paid for work on the Commission. The Government accepted my conditions.

There were four other members of the Commission, two black and two white. It was apparent from the outset that such an ongoing fact-finding commission could not succeed without active co-operation from all political groups in the country. Shortly after my appointment, I met with the leaders of the political groups. They all promised support and, for the ensuing three years, made good on that promise.

The Commission sat for almost three years and held over 40 discrete inquiries into specific situations of violence. It also held three thematic inquiries: the first with regard to the management of mass marches and demonstrations; the second to investigate ways and means of reducing the prospects of violence in our first democratic election; and the third, into the effects of violence on children.

The Commission required appropriately trained and experienced investigators. There appeared to be no other alternative than to recruit them from within the ranks of the South African Police. My concern was the universal distrust with which the majority of South Africans viewed the police. I adopted a few stratagems to overcome this problem. I informed the Commissioner of Police that I required 20 police officers to be seconded to the Commission. I also informed him that I planned to publish their names in every South African newspaper with a request for information concerning any one of them that would disqualify him from working with an independent commission of inquiry. That was done and elicited only one negative response concerning one of the police officers, whom I subsequently did not appoint. The Commission established three separate investigation units. I requested the European Union to appoint five senior police officers to work with those units, which they did. Finally, the South African Law Society appointed independent retired senior attorneys to work with each of the units. These measures unquestionably added to the perception of independence which these units and the Commission were generally able to establish.

Soon after we opened the Commission's offices in Johannesburg and Cape Town, allegations of politically motivated violence began to pour in. The reports came from the government, political parties, the police, non-governmental organisations and members of the public. We could not investigate all of the allegations and decided to concentrate on the most egregious incidents and especially those in which the security forces and political parties were implicated. With regard to the latter, much ill will had developed between the ANC and the IFP with countless allegations and counter-allegations. Assassinations and attacks on innocent civilians had become almost daily occurrences.

In June 1991, there was a massacre of civilians, adults and children, in an ANC-supporting village of Boipatong. I again had to convene an inquiry. This time President de Klerk suggested to me that I might consider inviting a renowned international jurist to sit with the Commission. I agreed that this was a good idea. I decided to approach Proful Bhagwati, the former Chief Justice of India. To my delight, Justice Baghwati immediately accepted my invitation and spent many weeks sitting with us in South Africa. His presence helped assure the people of South Africa of the independence of the inquiry into what was a highly politicised and contested event.

In 1992, the Commission prepared an interim report in which it listed in historical sequence the causes of political violence in South Africa. It discussed how racial oppression began in the colonial era, continued into the 20th century and became entrenched in its most egregious form during the Apartheid era. It referred to the disparity of wealth in our society and the many decades of oppression of the black majority of our people. It also discussed the political rivalry between the ANC and the IFP.

At that time, our reports were, in accordance with the relevant legislation, sent to President de Klerk to be made public by him at a time he considered appropriate. They were accompanied by a government media statement. The media briefing that accompanied the interim report stated that our Commission had ascribed the main cause of the violence in our society to the rivalry between the ANC and IFP. This skewed description of the report dominated the media headlines around the country.

That night, Nelson Mandela returned from a trip abroad and on the following morning, addressed an important meeting of the ANC. He castigated the report and accused us of bias and incompetence. His remarks were clearly based upon the official media release and the hype that had followed it. I was anguished at this unfair portrayal of the report and even more by Mandela's response to it. At about 15:00 that afternoon, I received a call from Nelson Mandela. He said that he had now read the report and agreed with most of it. He said that he was calling me for two reasons. The first was to apologise for having criticised the report. He said that he had erred in doing so without the benefit of having read it, and for relying on media reports of its contents. He went on to say that he had called a media conference for 16:00, at which he would publicly apologise to me for his remarks. The second reason for the call, he said, was to ask me whether he could say at the media conference that I had accepted his apology. Of course, I agreed.

There are a number of lessons to be learned from this incident. The first was that by holding back our reports and issuing them with their spin, the Government was undermining the independence and credibility of the Commission. I issued my own media statement, calling on the President to undertake to make public all future reports within 24 hours of his receiving them and that they would on no account be accompanied by any government media statement. President de Klerk, to his credit, immediate-

ly agreed to these requests. Nelson Mandela's call to me and his apology
are testimony to his innate integrity and dignity and, even more so, to his
political instinct that informed him that if he did not withdraw his censure
of the Commission, he would have done permanent damage to the Commission and placed its future in jeopardy. President de Klerk's reaction to
my requests concerning future reports similarly displayed his political appreciation of what was at stake.

In 1992, the Commission found conclusive evidence to support
Mandela's allegations concerning a "third force". This came about in consequence of a search and seizure operation conducted by a unit of the
Commission at what appeared to be commercial offices in Pretoria. Investigations revealed that the offices were a front for a department of Military
Intelligence and the files seized pointed to criminal conduct designed to
discredit ANC leaders and to foment violence between the ANC and the
IFP. De Klerk appointed the head of the South African Air Force to conduct a follow-up inquiry and that, in turn, led to the dismissal of 23 senior
officers of the South African Defense Force.

The work of the Commission obviously upset many in South Africa's security establishment and many white South Africans who dreaded
the transition from Apartheid to democracy. That resulted in renewed
death threats. In consequence, I was given no option but to accept police
protection, that extended into the early years of the 21st century.

The Goldstone Commission created the climate that led to the establishment in 1995 of the Truth and Reconciliation Commission. Much
of the evidence it heard confirmed important findings of our Commission.

## 2.6.   The Oil-for-Food Inquiry

In 2004, I had recently retired from the Constitutional Court of South Africa and was teaching at New York University Law School. I received a
telephone call from Kofi Annan, then Secretary-General of the United Nations. He asked me whether I would agree to serve on a three-person
Committee of Inquiry into the United Nations Iraq Oil-for-Food Programme. This programme had been set up by the Security Council in
1996 to avoid the abandonment of the oil sanctions that had been placed
on Iraq and that were causing serious hardship to the people of that country.

The Oil-for-Food Programme allowed the Government of Saddam
Hussein to sell Iraqi oil on condition that the proceeds were paid into an

escrow account controlled by the United Nations. The monies received could be used by Iraq for the purchase of humanitarian goods that were subject to inspection by the United Nations. The aim was to prevent goods being received by Iraq that could be used for the manufacture of weapons of mass destruction. The programme was in operation from 1996 to 2003. It involved approximately USD 110 billion of oil sales and purchases of humanitarian goods. It was controlled nominally by the Security Council, but in reality, by a specially established department in the UN Secretariat.

In 2003 and 2004, there were growing reports of corruption in the management and operations of the Programme. The United States Congress took up the allegations and a number Congressional Committees became seized of the issues.

In his initial phone call, Kofi Annan informed me that he had approached Paul Volcker, the former head of the US Reserve, to lead the inquiry and that the third member would be a Swiss academic, Mark Pieth, who had expertise in bank frauds. The problem, said Annan, was that Paul Volcker had not agreed to accept the appointment. He requested me to meet with Volcker and to encourage him to agree to come on board. Volcker's involvement was crucial to the inquiry having credibility in the United States.

On the following morning, I met with Paul Volcker. His problem, he explained, was that the proposed committee would have no powers of subpoena and that it would be unable to obtain crucial assistance from governments. He had prepared a resolution that he wished the Security Council to approve, in which the committee was welcomed and with which all Member States were requested to co-operate. He had sent the draft to Ambassador John Negroponte, the US Permanent Representative to the UN. Russia had threatened to veto such a resolution. The Russian Government, as the major purchaser of Iraqi oil, was not keen on such an inquiry. During my meeting with Volcker, Kofi Annan confirmed the Russian threat and, in a separate call, Negroponte added that the French were then also threatening a veto. France, too, had reasons for avoiding an inquiry in the face of allegations that senior French diplomats had accepted bribes from the Iraqi Government.

Volcker informed Negroponte that if the US wished him to lead the inquiry, then he would insist that the resolution be put to the Security Council. Should the resolution be vetoed, he would reconsider his position. The following day, I was again meeting with Paul Volcker when the news came through that the resolution had been passed unanimously. "Of course", said Volcker, "Russia and France would hardly veto a resolution welcoming an inquiry into a situation in which they were implicated in allegations of criminal conduct".

Apart from allegations of corruption on the part of officials of a number of governments, there were emerging rumours of the improper involvement of Kofi Annan's son, Kojo, with a Swiss company that had received a lucrative contract to inspect the humanitarian goods on their arrival at an Iraqi port.

The actual and perceived independence and integrity of the Oil-for-Food Inquiry Committee were essential. We also required adequate funding for what promised to be a complex exercise. Eventually the cost was USD 65 million, of which approximately USD 40 million was spent on document management – some 13 million pages of documents.

We made it clear to the Secretary-General that the inquiry was bound to be an intrusive one and that we would require access to all UN sources and databases, including his own and those of the most senior UN officials. That was promised to us and Kofi Annan fully complied with his commitment. We set up an international office in New York that was separate from the UN. We assembled a staff of over 70 people from 28 countries.

The Commission received support from the key governments, Iraq, Switzerland and Jordan. The documentation given to us provided evidence of the wholesale corruption of the UN Programme. The controls set up by the Secretariat were wholly inadequate. As a result, hundreds of millions of dollars worth of bribes were paid to Saddam Hussein. In order to 'save their necks', meticulous records were maintained by the Iraqi Oil Ministry.

The allegations implicating Kofi Annan proved to be without substance. He would have been spared much embarrassment if the UN had earlier more efficiently investigated the allegations. Our committee established that of the 4,500 companies that supplied goods under the Programme, about 2,500 of them paid bribes.

The Committee issued a number of reports in which the operations of the Programme were laid bare. They resulted in domestic investigations and prosecutions in a number of countries, some of which are still ongoing.

The work of the Committee saved the reputation and office of the Secretary-General and will hopefully make a recurrence less likely.

## 2.7. The Gaza Fact-Finding Mission

In March 2009, I was enjoying a relaxing vacation in New Zealand when I received an e-mail message from Navi Pillay, the UN High Commissioner for Human Rights. She asked if I would be willing to lead a fact-finding mission to Gaza relating to the war there, which had taken place between December 2008 and January 2009. The Israel Defense Forces ('IDF') called this Operation Cast Lead. She attached the resolution of the Human Rights Council that resolved to establish such a mission. It contained a patently one-sided mandate relating only to war crimes allegedly committed by Israel. There was no word about war crimes allegedly committed by Hamas in sending many hundreds of unguided rockets into civilian areas. I informed the High Commissioner that having considered the mandate, I was not interested. I thought that was the end to the matter. How wrong I was!

Navi Pillay followed up with a request that I visit Geneva and meet with and advise the President of the Human Rights Council and Nigerian Ambassador to Geneva, Martin Umhoimobi. I met with Ambassador Umhoimobi a couple of weeks later. He informed me that it was his prerogative as President of the HRC to set up the Fact-Finding Mission and to determine its precise mandate. He agreed that the mandate contained in the HRC resolution was a biased one. The advice he sought from me was on appropriate wording for an even-handed mandate. After a discussion, he requested me to write the terms of the mandate I suggested he should give to such a mission. I wrote the following: "[…] to investigate all violations of international human rights law and international humanitarian law that might have been committed at any time in the context of the military operations that were conducted in Gaza during the period from 27 December 2008 and 18 January 2009, whether before, during or after". He read what I had written and agreed that it would be an appropriate mandate. He said that if I agreed to chair the Mission, then that mandate would be adopted. As one might expect, it was difficult to refuse to accept a mandate that I had written. I also found it difficult to refuse to investigate alleged war crimes committed in the Middle East when I had not hesitated in the case of South Africa, the Balkans and Rwanda. Of course, being Jewish made it more difficult, but this was no reason to refuse to become involved. On a number of occasions, I had criticised the anti-Israel bias of the HRC. So, too, had Kofi Annan, who referred to the "disproportionate focus on violations by Israel" while neglecting other parts of the world such as Darfur where, he said, there were "far graver crises". He later added that Israel should not be given a free pass but that the Council should give the same attention to grave violations by other states as well. Having regard to my life-long support for Israel and the objective terms of the mandate, I was optimistic that Israel would co-operate with the Mission and would certainly allow it to visit and make inquiries in Israel. This was the first even-handed action to come from the HRC relating to Israel. It appeared to me to be an opportunity that Israel should seize, and thereby create a precedent. It was also present to my mind that the United States had just taken up a seat on the HRC and would welcome the terms of the mandate.

Before any formal announcement was made of my agreement to lead the Mission, I insisted on attempting to meet with the Israeli and Palestinian ambassadors in Geneva to discuss co-operation from their governments with the Mission. The Palestinian Ambassador immediately agreed to meet and offered me the unconditional co-operation of the Palestinian Authority. To my regret, the Israeli Ambassador informed me that he had no authority to meet with me. I immediately sent him a letter, setting out the new mandate and requesting his government's co-operation. I offered to travel to Jerusalem to meet with the appropriate Israeli officials to seek their advice on how the mandate should be implemented by the Mission. A few days later, I received a negative response that was expressly based on the mandate contained in the HRC resolution that I had previously already rejected. I responded, pointing out that I had refused the original mandate and reiterated the terms of my mandate. It took more than two months before that letter was answered. In the interim, I sent a personal letter to the Israeli Prime Minister requesting a meeting and advice. All these requests were turned down.

By the time the final refusal came from the Israeli Government, the work of the Mission had progressed and I had already made the first of two visits to Gaza.

Before commencing on the Mission, I had one other serious concern, namely that the Arab sponsors of the original resolution would renounce the mandate I had been given by Ambassador Umhoimobi. I feared that the HRC might adopt those parts of any report that dealt with Israeli violations and reject those relating to Hamas or Palestinian violations as falling outside of the mandate. To prevent that from happening, I called a meeting with the four Ambassadors who represented the sponsors of the resolution. I indicated to them that I was not prepared to proceed with the Mission unless I had their acceptance of the new mandate. Not without some reluctance, they gave me that assurance.

I was aware that the Israeli refusal of all co-operation, which included a refusal to allow our Mission into Israel, meant that we would have to proceed without having the benefit of direct and official evidence from one of the two main protagonists. We attempted to make up for this disadvantage by having regard to informal witnesses and reports from Israeli NGOs, as well as reports put out by the Israel Defense Forces. Evidence from many Israeli witnesses was obtained by telephone calls made from Geneva, by the Mission's staff.

Perhaps the most traumatic and emotional experience of my career was meeting in Gaza, at their homes, with victims of the war. Many had lost members of their families and others had been grievously injured. The most heart-rending visit was that with the al-Samouni family. The extended al-Samouni family has lived for generations in the so-called 'al-Samouni area of Zeytoun', which is situated south of Gaza City. It is a semi-rural area in which there are a number of houses, some but not all of which are occupied by members of the al-Samouni family.

On 4 January 2009, members of the Givati Brigade of the IDF ordered all of the members of the family of Saleh al-Samouni to step outside, where the father identified each member of his family. The Israeli soldiers had decided to take over the house as part of the IDF ground operation and ordered its occupants to relocate to the home of Wa'el al-Samouni that was about 35 yards away. The Israelis had satisfied themselves that there was no ammunition stored in that house. A request from the family to be allowed to go to Gaza City was refused. Consequently, there were over 100 members of the family in the single-story home of Wa'el al-Samouni. Early in the morning of 5 January 2009, three male members of the al-Samouni family went outside to gather firewood. They were in clear sight of the Israeli troops including those who had ordered the family to leave their home and relocate in the house of Wa'el al-Samouni. Within minutes, projectiles were fired (apparently from helicopter gunships) at the three members of the al-Samouni family as they returned with the firewood and, immediately after that, further projectiles hit the house. A total of 21 members of the family were killed, some of them young children and women; 19 were injured. Of those injured, another six subsequently died from their injuries.

That was the evidence, considered credible and supported by ambulance records and reports given at the time to non-governmental organisations. We came to the conclusion that, as a probability, the attack on the al-Samouni family constituted a deliberate attack on civilians. The information we had did not permit a different conclusion. The crucial consideration was that the civilians, including many women and children were instructed by Israeli troops to relocate to a house that was some 35 yards from where they had set up a command post. Members of the al-Samouni family regarded the presence of the IDF as a guarantee of their safety. It was the same Givati Brigade that fired the missiles that killed so many members of that family.

For the first time, at the end of October 2010, it was belatedly announced by Israeli Military Advocate General Mandelblit that the Israeli Military Police were investigating whether the air strike against the al-Samouni home was authorised by a senior Givati brigade commander who had been warned of the danger to civilians. At about the same time, there were reports that the attack had followed the Israeli military receiving poor quality drone photographs showing what was interpreted to be a group of men carrying rocket launchers towards a house. The order was given to bomb the men and the building. An inquiry from the soldiers on the ground could have established that the men were carrying firewood. Notwithstanding any shortcomings with regard to the Israeli investigations, it is to the credit of the IDF that investigations into a number of the allegations made against the IDF were conducted and that some adverse findings were made public. General Mandelblit, in pursuing this course, earned the wrath and strong criticisms of some elements in Israel who believe that its soldiers should be supported no matter what the facts might indicate. Following the conviction of the two Israeli soldiers who used a nine-year-old child as a human shield, a wall of the home of General Mandelblit was spray-painted with graffiti calling him a "traitor".

Another consequence of the Gaza Report is that the Israel Defense Forces announced changes in their Rules of Engagement designed for the increased protection of civilians and banned the use of white phosphorous in civilian areas. Our criticisms of the military justice system also resulted in the Turkel Commission set up by the Government of Israel being mandated to examine that system. A recent report has justified some, but not all, of those criticisms.

On the other hand, neither Hamas nor any other Gaza militant group has made any serious attempt to investigate those responsible for the firing of rockets and mortars into civilian areas of Southern Israel, conduct found by the Mission to constitute war crimes and possibly crimes against humanity. Indeed, notwithstanding that the Report placed Palestinian militants on notice that their rocket fire into Israel constituted war crimes, such criminal conduct has continued.

It was the evidence regarding the al-Samouni bombings that caused me to reconsider the finding that Israel had deliberately targeted civilians. After many sleepless nights, I came to the conclusion that had I known the responses from Israel at the time of writing the report, I would not have made that judgement. The tipping point was provided by the report from United States retired Judge Mary Davis, also appointed by the HRC, to the effect that the IDF had devoted resources to conduct some 400 investigations into allegations of war crimes committed during Operation Cast Lead.

It was in that context that I felt compelled to write the op-ed that appeared in the Washington Post on 1 April 2011. In it, I referred to some of the events which I have just outlined. I went on to state that had I been made aware of that information at the time of writing the Report, I would have reconsidered some of the findings and the Report would have read differently. In particular, I said that it would have influenced the finding that Israel intentionally targeted civilians.

## 2.8. Quality Control

In light of the foregoing experience, I turn to consider some of the lessons I have learned with regard to the quality control of fact-finding missions.

a)  There is the necessity of actual and perceived independence. The most effective way to obtain that is by consulting the parties on the choice of mission members. That is what was done in the case of the Goldstone Commission. The five members were agreed on after long debates by the political leaders of the parties to the peace negotiations and in particular, De Klerk, Mandela and Buthelezi. In such a situation, one cannot expect the members of the mission to be consulted about the identity of other members. The parties to the negotiations took some months to agree on the composition of the

Commission and it was not up to me or the other members to give input or to reject any of the other members. In the case of the Gaza Mission, too, I was not consulted on the other members of the Mission – that was in the hands of the High Commissioner for Human Rights, in consultation with the President of the HRC. I might add that, in hindsight, it is highly unlikely that consultation would have resulted in an Israeli Government agreement to a Fact-Finding Mission set up by the HRC. I was over-optimistic in believing that an even-handed and objective mandate and my chairing the Mission would have convinced the Government of Israel to lend its co-operation.

b)   The terms of reference must be clear and unbiased and in no way pre-judge any of the issues.

c)   Care should be taken in the appointment of the staff appointed to work with fact-finding missions. In the case of the Goldstone Commission, I have described the lengths to which we went to assure the people of South Africa that our work would not be compromised by having members of the South African Police serve with the Commission. In the case of the Gaza Mission, I am not aware of any criticism directed at specific members of the staff that were appointed to work with us.

d)   The manner in which a fact-finding report is written is also important. Its language should not be pejorative and its conclusions should not go beyond the facts found to be established. The conclusions and recommendations should reflect objectivity and the sources of information clearly and transparently recorded.

e)   The quality of a report will be determined by the public reaction to it. In hotly-disputed situations, that determination will reflect the views and prejudices of those who assess it. It must be accepted as inevitable that those criticised by a fact-finding report will be critical of it. Nonetheless, the purpose of fact-finding missions should not be to make people happy but rather to spur them on to take appropriate action to deter further human rights violations and, where relevant, to encourage justice mechanisms to bring acknowledgement to victims and appropriate prosecutions and punishment of those who should be held to account for violations.

f) To the extent possible, and consistent with the security of the members of the mission, witnesses and the integrity of its work, the activities of a mission should be performed in as public a manner as possible. It should be open to scrutiny by the media and, through it, by the people who are concerned with the findings.

The methodology adopted by the mission should be fully set out in the report.

## 2.9. Conclusion

It is folly to generalise about fact-finding missions. Each situation will have its unique features. What works with regard to one may well fail if applied to another. My experiences with regard to fact-finding in South Africa were facilitated by the exceptional leadership of Nelson Mandela and F.W. de Klerk. Their support for the work of the missions and, especially, their recognition of the independence given to them was crucial to their success. The support given by Kofi Annan to the work of the Oil-for-Food Inquiry Committee was similarly crucial. Without it, we would not have been able to make a positive finding with regard to his integrity and, I might add, that of his predecessor, Boutros Boutros-Ghali.

The Gaza Fact-Finding Mission was of a very different mold. The main party to be investigated, the Israel Defense Forces, refused to cooperate at all, thereby seriously weakening the efficiency and completeness of the Mission's investigations. That factor was, of course, well-publicised both in and apart from the Report. I hasten to add that no party that resorts to the use of military force should be exempted from the most careful scrutiny, both domestically and internationally. Nor should any such party hold a veto over such investigations.

Unfortunately, the number of armed conflicts continues to proliferate in many regions of the world. Ever-growing populations, global warming and increasingly scarce resources of food and energy give rise to fierce competition between people and nations, which does not augur well for world peace. Steps to protect innocent civilians from the ravages of war must be pursued with vigour and resolve.

# 3

---

# Improving Fact-Finding in Treaty-Based Human Rights Mechanisms and the Special Procedures of the United Nations Human Rights Council

**Martin Scheinin**[*]

## 3.1. Introduction

This chapter is to be seen as a complement to the other contributions included in this volume. As stated by Justice Goldstone in the previous chapter, its basic tenet is that not all 'fact-finding' serves the same purpose or should be subject to the same standards. In particular, this author defends the view that the various mechanisms of mainstream human rights bodies that seek to establish state responsibility for human rights violations should *not* be subjected to the evidence requirements typical for determining individual criminal accountability. Neither should they be subordinated to the extraneous purpose of gathering evidence for parallel or future criminal trials.[1]

This chapter will address independent fact-finding within the two main arms of the United Nations human rights machinery: the Treaty Bodies established for the purpose of monitoring state compliance with the main UN human rights treaties, and the so-called Special Procedures

---

[*] **Martin Scheinin** is Professor at the European University Institute. Before his appointment, he served for 15 years as a professor in Finland. From 1993–1998, he was Professor of Constitutional Law at the University of Helsinki, where he had also obtained his doctorate in 1991. From 1998–2008, he was Professor of Constitutional and International Law and Director of the Institute for Human Rights at Åbo Akademi University in Turku, Finland. From 1997–2004, he was a member of the United Nations Human Rights Committee, the treaty body acting under the Covenant on Civil and Political Rights. In 2005, he was appointed as the first United Nations Special Rapporteur on human rights and counter-terrorism, a position of trust he held until July 2011.

[1] Such a proposal has been made, albeit with important caveats, by Lyal S. Sunga, "How can UN human rights special procedures sharpen ICC fact-finding?", in *International Journal of Human Rights*, 2011, vol. 15, pp. 187–205.

serving the intergovernmental Human Rights Council, namely Special Rapporteurs and Working Groups. As the focus of this chapter is on fact-finding by independent expert bodies or individual independent experts, the features of fact-finding in the Universal Periodic Review conducted upon states by the intergovernmental Human Rights Council itself[2] (*id est*, a kind of peer review) will not be addressed. Neither will this chapter look into Commissions of Inquiry, established *ad hoc* by the Human Rights Council through a discretionary decision. In short, this chapter addresses only regular human rights monitoring by independent experts within the UN human rights framework.

The chapter is partly based on the author's personal experience and reflections, having served eight years (1997–2004) as a member of the Human Rights Committee, one of the treaty bodies; and six years (2005–2011) as Special Rapporteur of the Human Rights Council. The majority of the text (section 3.2.) will deal with treaty bodies, followed by a brief discussion on special procedures (section 3.3.) to complement the preceding section. A short conclusion (section 3.4.) closes the chapter.

## 3.2. Fact-Finding by UN Human Rights Treaty Bodies

After World War II, the Universal Declaration of Human Rights (1948) was adopted, not as a treaty, but in the form of a solemn declaration. However, there was a more ambitious plan of moving ahead towards a treaty (a Covenant) and an international human rights court. The Declaration was adopted first, knowing that the other steps would take some time. Early UN treaties that in substance related to human rights, such as the Convention on the Prevention and Punishment of the Crime of Genocide (1949) and the Convention Relating to the Status of Refugees (1951), did not establish any courts, other independent monitoring bodies, or even independent monitoring procedures. In 1965, the idea of a treaty-monitoring body composed of individual experts was included in the Convention for the Elimination of All Forms of Racial Discrimination. The same concept was applied by the establishment of the Human Rights Committee in the 1966 Covenant on Civil and Political Rights ('ICCPR'), and, with a modification, also in its twin sister, the Covenant on Economic, Social and Cultural Rights. In the latter Covenant, monitoring was to be in the

---

[2]    For the Universal Periodic Review, see General Assembly Resolutions A/RES/60/251 (2006), para. 9, and A/RES/65/281 (2011), Annex, Part I.

hands of an intergovernmental body, the Economic and Social Council ('ECOSOC'). In the decades that followed, ECOSOC decided to delegate its monitoring authority to an independent expert body,[3] and gradually a whole line of more specific human rights treaties were adopted, dealing with issues from torture to disability to disappearances; or with specified beneficiaries ranging from women to children to migrant workers. As of today, there are nine 'core' human rights treaties[4] monitored by 10 independent expert bodies, as the Convention against Torture ('CAT') has two separate expert committees.[5]

### 3.2.1. Typology of Monitoring Mechanisms under Human Rights Treaties

The treaty bodies are typically composed of 18 individual experts, elected by a meeting of the states that are party to the treaty in question. Even if their mandates are not clearly categorised in precise legal terms in the respective treaties, the treaty bodies are in every case entrusted with functions that are geared towards assessing and facilitating state compliance with the treaty. The exact functions differ from treaty to treaty but basically fall into five categories, so that, under each treaty, the respective body (or, in the case of CAT, the two expert bodies taken together) has from three to five of these mechanisms at its disposal. These are, as follows:

1.  The consideration of periodic reports by each state party on its implementation of the treaty.[6] The outcome is typically a set of Concluding Observations where the treaty body assesses the degree of

---

[3]  ECOSOC Resolution 1985/17 established a Committee on Economic, Social and Cultural Rights, to be elected by ECOSOC. Subsequently, the adoption of the Optional Protocol to the International Covenant on Economic, Social and Cultural Rights (2008) (http://www.legal-tools.org/doc/757da7/) created a treaty basis for the Committee, albeit technically only in respect of the new functions established by the Protocol, namely individual and inter-state complaints and inquiries.

[4]  These nine treaties, generally referred to as core human rights treaties, together with their optional and additional protocols are available on the United Nations Office of the High Commissioner for Human Rights' web site..

[5]  The Convention against Torture and Other Cruel, Inhuman or Degrading Treatment or Punishment (1984) (http://www.legal-tools.org/doc/326294/) established a Committee against Torture and the Optional Protocol to the Convention against Torture and other Cruel, Inhuman or Degrading Treatment or Punishment (2002), the Subcommittee on Prevention.

[6]  See, *e.g.*, ICCPR Article 40 (http://www.legal-tools.org/doc/2838f3/). The ICCPR is here used to illustrate the legal basis of the various monitoring mechanisms.

compliance and provides its recommendations.[7] This is the only monitoring mechanism common to all nine treaties (without their Optional Protocols) and is mandatory for all states parties.

2. The consideration of individual complaints that a state (which has accepted the optional right of individual complaint) has violated the human rights of the complainant.[8] Such complaint procedures are available to the majority of states in the world under the ICCPR and have gradually become available under the other treaties as well, with the adoption of the Optional Protocol to the Convention on the Rights of the Child being the latest addition (2011).

3. The consideration of inter-state complaints where one state party asserts that another state party has breached its treaty obligations.[9] Although included in most of the treaties, this mechanism has so far remained a dead letter in the UN human rights system.

4. Inquiry procedures triggered by an indication of particularly serious or systematic human rights violations, often entailing a country visit by the expert committee.[10] This mechanism comes closest to separate Commissions of Inquiry and it has so far mainly been utilised under the CAT, which nowadays also has a less dramatic mechanism of visits to places of detention by designated national visiting mechanisms, or by an international Subcommittee on Prevention.

5. The adoption of General Comments.[11] Following the example set by the Human Rights Committee, the treaty bodies have gradually come to adopt General Comments or General Recommendations which consolidate the findings made by the other monitoring mechanisms and produce a systematic analysis of the requirements of the treaty under a specific article or issue.

---

[7] Notably, the text of ICCPR Article 40 is silent about any state-specific outcome of the reporting procedure. The institution of Concluding Observations adopted by the monitoring body is a product of gradually evolving practice.

[8] See, Optional Protocol to the International Covenant on Civil and Political Rights (1966), Article 1. The fact that 114 states have ratified this protocol is one of the success stories of UN human rights treaty monitoring.

[9] ICCPR, Article 41.

[10] This mechanism is missing from the ICCPR.

[11] See, ICCPR Article 40, Paragraph 4, which refers to 'general comments' as an outcome of the reporting procedure. Gradually, the institution has through evolving practice obtained its own life and been adopted by the other treaty bodies.

As is evident from the above typology, the role of fact-finding is very different in the greatly diverging mechanisms available to any single treaty body. Taking the Human Rights Committee as an example once again, the Committee operates under mechanisms (1), (2) and (5), with mechanism (4) remaining so far a dead letter, and mechanism (3) not belonging to the toolbox in this particular case. The role of fact-finding is minimal when the Committee produces its General Comments (5), as they are primarily consolidations of treaty interpretations, based on the Committee's earlier practice under the other mechanisms. That leaves us with mechanisms (1) and (2) which represent the most typical forms of monitoring by UN human rights treaty bodies. A closer look at fact-finding in those two mechanisms follows.

### 3.2.2. Fact-Finding in the Reporting Procedure

The reporting procedure (1) is inquisitional in nature, in the sense that there is formally only one party, the state, appearing before the Committee. All the questioning is done by the Committee itself, in the form of an agreed List of Issues and through oral questioning by individual members. The 'facts' are largely produced by the reporting state, in its written periodic report and through answers given both to the List of Issues and to the oral questions. Those facts can be complemented by the Committee and its individual members, often relying upon 'shadow reports' or other submissions by non-governmental organisations, reports emanating from other human rights procedures, and basically any available source of information. For the methodology of the Committee's assessment, the only important limitation is that nothing goes into the Concluding Observations by the Committee without first being formulated as a question to the government and allowing it the opportunity to respond.

The Concluding Observations are produced in a standard format where, after some introductory paragraphs and, in most cases, a small number of 'positive observations', the bulk of the document lists problematic areas in the country's compliance with the ICCPR. Each paragraph contains two parts, an assessment of the situation (facts), and a recommendation for how to improve compliance. The recommendation part combines elements of law and policy without always making it clear whether some change is mandatory as a legal treaty obligation, or whether it would 'just' secure the better enjoyment of human rights, as a matter of policy. The preceding assessment portion of the paragraph includes a statement of the factual situation and an explanation, based on treaty interpretation, of why this is problematic in relation to ICCPR obligations. The default option in indicating a problem is to pronounce that the Committee is 'concerned' over the situation. This concern flows from the ICCPR provisions but does not amount to an authoritative statement that the state party is in breach of its legally binding human rights obligations. A 'concern' may equally well relate to the absence of information or the inadequacy of national mechanisms to secure compliance, even when no actual violations have been found.

During my own time on the Human Rights Committee, mere 'concern' was clearly separated from situations where the Committee used the word 'incompatible' to state that the law or practice of the country was in deviation from the legal requirements of the ICCPR. A quick look at most recent Concluding Observations by the Committee shows that while the terminology may have evolved, the basic distinction is still there. In July 2013, the Committee dealt with the Sixth periodic report by Finland and used the word 'concern' in every substantive paragraph of the Concluding Observations, except the one with positive observations and one paragraph where the Committee 'regrets' that Finland has not withdrawn its remaining reservations to the ICCPR.[12] In the same session the Committee dealt with the initial report by Indonesia, and expressed many 'concerns', but also exhibited various forms of qualified language: it stated that some laws were "inconsistent with" the ICCPR (paragraph 6), "regretted" circumstances resulting in impunity for human rights violations (paragraph 8), "regretted" the use of capital punishment for crimes "which do not meet" the ICCPR standard (paragraph 10), "regretted" the discrimination against women and laws allowing female genital mutilation (paragraphs 11–12), "regretted" the use of corporal punishment (paragraph 15), and "regretted" the law on defamation of religion which was deemed to be "incompatible" with the ICCPR (paragraph 25).[13]

### 3.2.3. Fact-Finding in the Procedure for Individual Complaints

In contrast to the consideration of periodic reports, the procedure for individual complaints (2) is accusatorial or adversarial in nature. The Human

---

[12] Human Rights Committee, 108th session, Concluding observations on the sixth periodic report of Finland (advance unedited version), para. 4.

[13] Human Rights Committee, 108th session, Concluding observations on the initial report of Indonesia (advance unedited version).

Rights Committee, through a written procedure,[14] hears the complainant and the respondent government, and provides them with the opportunity to submit comments on the other party's submission. There is no independent fact-finding or possibility of *amici curiae*, and the possibilities of the Committee to look into other sources than the submissions by the parties are very limited.[15]

Even if the 'final views' follow the format of a judicial decision, they are based on facts 'as submitted' under the limitations of a written procedure, and the main task of the Committee is to apply the law (the ICCPR) to those facts. Of course, there will be situations where the facts are in dispute between the parties. But there are no clear rules, and probably cannot be, about which party to believe. Some rules of thumb can nevertheless be derived from the Committee's practice: (a) a failure by the state party to co-operate may result in a default finding of a violation, on the basis of the facts submitted and sufficiently substantiated by the complainant;[16] (b) a state party is presumed to know its own law, so if for instance it claims that an effective domestic remedy would have existed, the Committee is likely to believe it;[17] and (c) the Committee exercises a degree of deference in relation to domestic courts, so that if facts and evidence were assessed by them, the Committee is likely to defer to that assessment, unless the complainant manages to show that the domestic procedure was tainted by arbitrariness or denial of justice.[18]

As the Committee's task is to assess whether the complainant is a victim of a violation of the negative or positive state obligations under the ICCPR, there is no requirement of *mens rea* on the side of any person.

---

[14]  See, ICCPR Optional Protocol, Article 5, Paragraph 1: "The Committee shall consider communications received under the present Protocol in the light of all written information made available to it by the individual and by the State Party concerned".

[15]  As quoted in the preceding footnote, the Committee is to look only into written information submitted by the parties. In rare cases, the Committee has referred to earlier factual findings made in the reporting procedure in respect of the same state, for example, *Polay Campos v. Peru*, Communication 577/1994 (1997), para. 8.8.

[16]  See, *e.g.*, *Diergaardt et al. v. Namibia*, Communication 760/1997 (2000), para 10.2: "In the absence of a reply from the State party, due weight must be given to the authors' allegations to the extent that they are substantiated".

[17]  As an extreme example of the (mis)application of this presumption, see, *Galina Vedeneyeva v. the Russian Federation*, Communication 918/2000 (2005), para. 7.3.

[18]  See, for example, *Moti Singh v. New Zealand*, Communication 791/1997 (2001), para. 6.11.

The mere fact that a person could not enjoy his or her human rights as guaranteed by the ICCPR, and that this situation is being attributed to the actions or omissions of the state in question, is sufficient for a finding of violation. The Committee has not applied a 'beyond reasonable doubt' standard in assessing disputed facts, but instead makes a contextual assessment through fairly soft rules of thumb, as formulated above.[19] A find-

---

[19] The European Court of Human Rights has, however, on occasion applied the standard of 'beyond reasonable doubt' when assessing conflicting factual accounts presented to it by the applicant and the respondent government. That said, the meaning of this phrase is quite different than as traditionally applied by domestic courts in criminal proceedings. Recently, the ECtHR explained at length its *sui generis* notion of beyond 'reasonable doubt' as follows: "151. In cases in which there are conflicting accounts of events, the Court is inevitably confronted when establishing the facts with the same difficulties as those faced by any first-instance court. It reiterates that, in assessing evidence, it has adopted the standard of proof 'beyond reasonable doubt'. However, it has never been its purpose to borrow the approach of the national legal systems that use that standard. Its role is not to rule on criminal guilt or civil liability but on Contracting States' responsibility under the Convention. The specificity of its task under Article 19 of the Convention – to ensure the observance by the Contracting States of their engagement to secure the fundamental rights enshrined in the Convention – conditions its approach to the issues of evidence and proof. In the proceedings before the Court, there are no procedural barriers to the admissibility of evidence or pre-determined formulae for its assessment. It adopts the conclusions that are, in its view, supported by the free evaluation of all evidence, including such inferences as may flow from the facts and the parties' submissions. According to its established case-law, proof may follow from the co-existence of sufficiently strong, clear and concordant inferences or of similar unrebutted presumptions of fact. Moreover, the level of persuasion necessary for reaching a particular conclusion and, in this connection, the distribution of the burden of proof, are intrinsically linked to the specificity of the facts, the nature of the allegation made and the Convention right at stake. The Court is also attentive to the seriousness that attaches to a ruling that a Contracting State has violated fundamental rights […]. 152. Furthermore, it is to be recalled that Convention proceedings do not in all cases lend themselves to a strict application of the principle *affirmanti incumbit probatio*. The Court reiterates its case-law under Articles 2 and 3 of the Convention to the effect that where the events in issue lie within the exclusive knowledge of the authorities, as in the case of persons under their control in custody, strong presumptions of fact will arise in respect of injuries and death occurring during that detention. The burden of proof in such a case may be regarded as resting on the authorities to provide a satisfactory and convincing explanation […]. In the absence of such explanation, the Court can draw inferences which may be unfavourable for the respondent Government […]. 153. The Court has already found that these considerations apply also to disappearances examined under Article 5 of the Convention, where, although it has not been proven that a person has been taken into custody by the authorities, it is possible to establish that he or she was officially summoned by the authorities, entered a place under their control and has not been seen since. In such circumstances, the onus is on the Government to provide a plausible and satisfactory explanation as to what happened on the premises and to show that the person concerned was not detained by the authorities, but left the premises without subsequently being deprived of

ing of a violation can be based on the state party's failure to implement its positive obligations under the ICCPR.[20] Specifically, findings of discrimination can be made with or without the demonstration of a discriminatory intent, including in situations of indirect discrimination where seemingly neutral laws produce a discriminatory outcome.[21]

### 3.2.4. Fact-Finding in Inquiry Procedures by Treaty Bodies

As there is no inquiry procedure (4) under the ICCPR, our example comes from the UN human rights treaty body that has the broadest experience of utilising such a procedure, the Committee Against Torture. The procedure is based on CAT Article 20, which is subject to an opt-out clause in Article 28. The inquiry procedure is subject to confidentiality, and the Committee is required to seek the co-operation of the state concerned, so that a visit to the country may take place only with its consent. Ultimately, the Committee may, after consultations with the state concerned, decide to include 'a summary account' of the results of the proceedings in its annual report. The threshold for launching the inquiry procedure is that the Committee has received "reliable information which appears to it to contain well-founded indications that torture is being systematically practised in the territory of a State Party".[22]

According to information in the public domain, the procedure has been utilised in respect of nine states (Brazil, Egypt, Mexico, Montenegro, Nepal, Peru, Serbia, Sri Lanka, Turkey), out of which three (Brazil, Mexico and Nepal) have resulted in a full public report and the other six in 'summary accounts'. The reports on Mexico and Brazil were both produced through a thorough process that included a visit to the countries in question and resulted in findings that indicate the occurrence of systemat-

---

his or her liberty [...]. Furthermore, the Court reiterates that, again in the context of a complaint under Article 5 § 1 of the Convention, it has required proof in the form of concordant inferences before the burden of proof is shifted to the respondent Government [...]". *El-Masri v. the former Yugoslav Republic of Macedonia*, Application no. 39630/09, Grand Chamber Judgment of 13 December 2012 (https://www.legal-tools.org/doc/3f5063/).

[20] As a classic case, see *Delgado Paez v. Colombia*, Communication 195/1985 (1990), para. 5.6: "Accordingly, while fully understanding the situation in Colombia, the Committee finds that the State party has not taken, or has been unable to take, appropriate measures to ensure Mr. Delgado's right to security of his person under Article 9, para. 1".

[21] See, *e.g.*, *Simunek et al. v. the Czech Republic*, Communication 516/1992 (1995) para. 11.7 and *Althammer et al. v. Austria*, Communication 998/2001 (2003), para. 10.2.

[22] CAT Article 20, para. 1.

ic torture.[23] The report on Nepal was drawn up without the Committee's visit to the country and also with very limited other forms of co-operation by the concerned state.[24] It is nevertheless based on multiple sources of information and contains an explicit conclusion that "torture is being systematically practised in the territory of Nepal".[25]

In making its findings, the Committee has cited its own definition of 'systematic torture':

> The Committee considers that torture is practised systematically when it is apparent that the torture cases reported have not occurred fortuitously in a particular place or at a particular time, but are seen to be habitual, widespread and deliberate in at least a considerable part of the territory of the country in question. Torture may in fact be of a systematic character without resulting from the direct intention of a Government. It may be the consequence of factors, which the Government has difficulty in controlling, and its existence may indicate a discrepancy between policy as determined by the central Government and its implementation by the local administration. Inadequate legislation which in practice allows room for the use of torture may also add to the systematic nature of this practice.

This definition makes it quite clear that even if the modalities of fact-finding in the inquiry procedure may vary from case to case and be dependent on co-operation by the government, the inquiry procedure is not geared towards proving the occurrence of the crime of torture, or the guilt of persons alleged to have committed that crime. That said, especially when there has been a visit to the country, the inquiry procedure may

---

[23] Committee Against Torture, Report on Mexico produced by the Committee under Article 20 of the Convention and reply from the Government of Mexico, UN document CAT/C/7526 (2003). For the main findings by the Committee, see paras. 218–219. Committee Against Torture, Report on Brazil produced by the Committee under Article 20 of the Convention and reply from the Government of Brazil, UN document CAT/C/39/2 (2009). For the main findings by the Committee, see para. 178.

[24] Annual report by the Committee Against Torture 2012, UN document A/67/44, Annex XIII, para. 14 (http://www.legal-tools.org/doc/bc326b/).

[25] *Ibid.*, para. 108.

provide elements of genuinely novel fact-finding that could be useful also in the context of criminal prosecution against particular individuals.[26]

### 3.2.5. Improving Fact-Finding by Treaty Bodies

The most obvious link between fact-finding for criminal procedures and the work of human rights treaty bodies is in the area of evolving inquiry procedures by the latter. Treaty bodies have a lot to learn from criminal procedures, including interview techniques, documentation and analysis of data from interviews, and the use of forensic experts as part of the inquiry. That said, treaty bodies have their own function of assessing treaty compliance by the state in question, and the success of their inquiry procedures is greatly dependent on the co-operation from the very state that is under scrutiny. Therefore, reliance on forensic and criminal law expertise by treaty bodies in their inquiry procedures must not be subordinated to their use as fact-finding mechanisms for subsequent criminal prosecutions, and should not be seen to serve any other purpose than the assessment of treaty compliance by the state. The applicable law in that assessment is the law of state responsibility,[27] which is quite different from the law of criminal responsibility, including in the issue of the role of individual or collective intent behind actions and omissions that have resulted in human rights violations.

As to fact-finding in the reporting procedures and handling of individual complaints by treaty bodies, the main common improvement needed is to upgrade the resources available to treaty bodies. Above all, it should be understood that the actual sessions of the treaty bodies need more resources and creative thinking, in order to deliver more in quantity and quality. There is a huge backlog in the consideration of both reports from states and complaints by individuals. These delays undermine the legitimacy of the whole treaty body system. A drastic improvement in the handling of reports would be obtained by the simple solution of considering the reports in two parallel chambers of each treaty body, hence doubling the capacity. The Committee of the Rights of the Child has already

---

[26] For an assessment of the CAT inquiry procedure, see Nigel Rodley, "The United Nations Human Rights Council, Its Special Procedures, and Its Relationship with the Treaty Bodies: Complementarity or Competition?", in Kevin Boyle (ed.), *New Institutions for Human Rights Protection*, Oxford, 2009, pp. 61–63.

[27] See, Articles on State Responsibility by the International Law Commission, annexed to and endorsed in General Assembly Resolution A/RES/56/83 (2002).

done this. In relation to the benefit, the cost is reasonably moderate, as it really only relates to the number of interpreters and conference room officers. Of course, for a period of time, the greater efficiency will result in a larger number of documents, until the backlog has been cleared.

When it comes to the consideration of individual complaints, the nature of the exercise should not be shifted away from the establishment of state responsibility for human rights violations through an adversarial procedure, based on the submissions of the individual victim and the respondent state. The role of the treaty body should remain in the field of treaty interpretation by producing an analysis of the 'facts as submitted' under the normative framework established by the treaty in question and fine-tuned through the institutionalised practices of interpretation, developed by the treaty body in question. This accumulates as subsequent practice under the treaty and is tacitly approved by the states parties through the consideration of the annual reports by the treaty bodies at the General Assembly.[28] The quality of the decisions, including in their treatment of facts as submitted by the parties, could nevertheless be improved by recruiting more qualified legal staff to prepare the drafts for the respective treaty body. Without deviating from the main rule of the consideration of complaints on the basis of written submissions by the parties, two improvements should be introduced through piloting on a discretionary basis: (a) In carefully selected pilot cases, the treaty bodies should invite *amicus curiae* briefs from third parties, perhaps on condition that the actual parties (the complainant and the respondent state) agree to this.[29] (b) Similarly, upon consent by the parties to carefully selected cases, the treaty bodies should allow for oral hearings in order to pose questions to the parties and enable the hearing of witnesses and expert witnesses.

A major improvement in the potential of the treaty body reporting procedure can be seen in the project for human rights indicators developed by the UN Office of the High Commissioner for Human Rights.[30]

---

[28] Reference is made to Article 31, Paragraph 3(b) of the Vienna Convention of the Law of Treaties ('subsequent practice' as a primary means of treaty interpretation) and the position elaborated in Martin Scheinin, "Impact on the law of Treaties", in Menno Kamminga and Martin Scheinin (eds.), *The Impact of Human Rights Law on General International Law*, Oxford, 2009, pp. 23–36.

[29] Notably, the Committee on Economic, Social and Cultural Rights will accept *amicus curiae* briefs under the new Optional Protocol to the respective Covenant.

[30] See *Human Rights Indicators: A Guide to Measurement and Implementation*, United Nations, 2012.

The rationale of the project is in defining standardised categories of factual information (statistics), requested from the reporting state, to assist the treaty body in assessing its compliance with treaty obligations. The methodology of the indicators project is complex, starting from the definition of three to five 'attributes' of each human right, *id est*, main substantive dimensions of a human rights treaty provision. These are derived from the institutionalised practices of interpretation under the treaty, including the General Comments by the treaty body. The next step is the selection of three types of indicators for each attribute, namely structural, process and outcome indicators. This is done by assessing the categories of statistical information that are likely to be realistically available, coupled with an assessment if they can be used for evaluating the legal and institutional framework for the implementation of a human right (structural indicators), the strategies and policies of the country towards the same goal (process indicators) , and the actual enjoyment of the human right by the people, including various segments of the population (outcome indicators). The three types of indicators, coupled with the attributes of a human right, generate an indicators chart for each treaty provision. The ultimate assessment of compliance or non-compliance will nevertheless rest with the treaty body, which, through interaction with the state party, will be able to make best possible use of the presumptions generated through the indicators. Even if ambitious and complex, the indicators project has great potential of moving the consideration of periodic state party reports from a seemingly intuitive assessment by 'experts' into a fact-based science. The facts in question will mainly comprise standardised categories of statistical information and the nature of the exercise will therefore be very different from fact-finding for criminal proceedings.

## 3.3.  Fact-Finding by the Special Procedures of the Human Rights Council

The treaty bodies discussed above represent one arm of regular human rights monitoring by independent experts within the UN human rights framework. The other arm is constituted by the special procedures serving the intergovernmental Human Rights Council. The special procedures are somewhat of a moving target, as new mandates keep emerging and old ones are reviewed, extended and sometimes discontinued. This is, of course, because of the absence of a treaty basis for the mandates, which then keep shifting according to the needs and even whims of the Human

Rights Council as a political body. The General Assembly resolution establishing the Human Rights Council contained a phrase that the Council "shall assume, review and, where necessary, improve and rationalize all mandates, mechanisms, functions and responsibilities of the Commission on Human Rights in order to maintain a system of special procedures".[31]

### 3.3.1. Basic Facts about Special Procedures

The special procedures consist of six Working Groups, each with five expert members coming from the five traditional regions in the world, and 42 one-person expert mandates, usually called Special Rapporteurs.[32] Out of the latter, the bulk of the mandates (30) are thematic and a smaller number (12) have been established for monitoring the human rights situation in a particular country. Some (nine) of the thematic or country-specific one-person mandates carry the title 'Independent Expert' (and not 'Special Rapporteur') which may entail less emphasis on fact-finding, as an independent expert may have been appointed for a short term (one year) to produce a desktop study, while Special Rapporteurs usually serve for two consecutive three-year periods and engage in a number of functions, including fact-finding through country visits.

In 2012, the special procedures taken together submitted 129 reports to the Human Rights Council, including 60 on country visits and 69 other reports (usually thematic studies), and 32 reports to the General Assembly. They carried out 80 country visits to 55 countries and sent 603 communications to 127 states.[33]

### 3.3.2. Fact-Finding by Special Procedures

For the purposes of this volume, the most interesting dimensions of the work of the special procedures are communications (letters) to governments and country visits by Special Rapporteurs. These two functions contain, or at least have the potential to contain, significant fact-finding insights. However, partly on the basis of this author's own experience from six years as Special Rapporteur, this is rarely the case with the letters sent to governments (communications). In usual UN parlance the letters are categorised as either 'urgent appeals' or 'allegation letters', with 'other

---

[31] General Assembly Resolution A/RES/60/251 (2006), para. 6.

[32] These numbers come from the publication United Nations Special Procedures: Facts and Figures 2012, UN Office of the High Commissioner for Human Rights, 2013.

[33] *Ibid.*, p. 37.

letters' recognised as a third category in 2011.[34] Usually the letters contain a caveat saying that the Special Rapporteur has made no determination of the facts. The rate of responses by governments is fairly low, and even when they do return with factual responses, the possibility of a Special Rapporteur to make any independent assessment of those assertions are very limited. 'Urgent appeals' serve a diplomatic or humanitarian purpose, by alerting the government that the respective United Nations Special Rapporteur is aware of the fact that an individual is subject to an imminent risk of a human rights violation, such as torture. 'Allegation letters', in turn, are usually based on information received from families or non-governmental organisations, and the role of the Special Rapporteur is to transmit the alleged facts to the government and to seek its response. The third category, 'other letters', typically relate to a thematic report under preparation by the Special Rapporteur and aim at clarifying the domestic law of the country concerned, rather than empirical facts. All in all, the communications function of special procedures should not be seen as a fact-finding mechanism.

That leaves us with country visits as 'true' fact-finding by the special procedures. These visits are conducted upon the invitation of the government and, in practice, require co-operation and facilitation by the hosting government. As there is no treaty basis for the special procedures, the degree of co-operation often depends on the goodwill of the government. Nevertheless, the special procedures have adopted a document called 'Standard Terms of Reference for fact-finding missions'[35] which is transmitted to the government when a Special Rapporteur accepts an invitation for a country visit. Hence, there is a degree of a contractual arrangement to guarantee the preconditions of independent fact-finding through the visit.[36]

---

[34] *Ibid.*, p. 10.

[35] The document was adopted in 1997 by an annual meeting of the special procedures under the (then) Commission on Human Rights, and it is reproduced as Annex V in the report from that meeting, UN document E/CN.4/1998/45.

[36] The Standard Terms of Reference is not to be confused with a document called "Code of Conduct for Special Procedures", adopted by the Human Rights Council (Decision 5/2) (https://www.legal-tools.org/doc/9c46e8/). This fairly vague document leaves the impression of trying to restrict the freedom of action by the independent experts but not really managing to do so because of being a watered-down text. For instance, letters of allegation sent to governments "should not be exclusively based by reports disseminated by mass media" (Article 9(e)).

The Standard Terms of Reference include freedom of movement in the whole country and freedom of inquiry, including access to places of detention, confidential and unsupervised contact with witnesses and other private persons (including persons deprived of their liberty), and full access to all documentary material relevant to the mandate. Further, the document also entails assurances that no reprisals will result from providing information to the Special Rapporteur. In practice, Special Rapporteurs do insist on, for instance, access to places of detention and go there with their own security personnel and interpreters, in order to avoid relying on any services provided by the government. For some Special Rapporteur mandates (*exempli gratia,* torture), access to places of detention is a key dimension of the whole mandate, and a country visit will simply not be undertaken without guarantees that confidential access will in fact materialise. For some other mandates, such access is just one method of fact-finding, so that a meaningful country visit can also take place without visiting places of detention but then results, of course, in a report where no assessment is made about the situation in prisons.[37]

Having served as a Special Rapporteur, my assessment of governments respecting the Standard Terms of Reference is fairly positive. In Turkey (2006), the regional prosecutor in Diyarbakir (a Kurdish area) made an unannounced visit to a maximum-security prison happen within an hour, and we were able to interview the named individuals we had wanted to see. In Tunisia, still during the Ben Ali regime (2010), we were able to interview the high-profile terrorist suspects or convicts we had asked for and could review their medical files, as well as a separate logbook at a police station, used for recording how the special forces of the Ministry of Interior brought in and took out terrorism suspects.

Clearly, there are some special procedures where the mandate overlaps with international crimes, so that the procedure in question could, in principle, produce factual information of relevance for criminal prosecution, provided the government of the country allows access to the country, in accordance with the Standard Terms of Reference. This may in particu-

---

[37] As Special Rapporteur on human rights and counter-terrorism, I usually visited prisons and other places of detention where terrorism convicts or suspects were held, to interview the detainees. However, I accepted to visit two countries without such visits, namely the United States of America (including to observe Military Commission hearings in Guantanamo Bay) and Egypt (to assess a new counter-terrorism law under preparation and coupled with a publicly expressed expectation of a second visit later).

lar be true for country-specific Special Rapporteurs, as these mandates are often established in the context of an emerging or a preceding human rights crisis in the country. That said, some of the thematic mandates, such as those of the Special Rapporteurs on torture, arbitrary executions or slavery, or the Working Group on disappearances would also have the same potential.

### 3.3.3. Improving Fact-Finding by Special Procedures

Proposals to improve the fact-finding by the special procedures of the Human Rights Council should be based on an evaluation of how these mechanisms could better serve their own objective to assess how states comply with human rights. Four proposals are made here, but a common denominator of the three first ones is the need to secure that the Human Rights Council as the main intergovernmental United Nations body in the field of human rights will provide stronger political backing to the operation of its independent expert procedures, without interfering with their independence. The proposals are as follows. First, the Human Rights Council needs to be more vocal in supporting unconditional access to any country by the special procedures, including by making it a *de facto* membership condition of the Council itself, so that a so-called standing invitation is issued for all special procedures and then also honoured in practice. Second, the Human Rights Council must insist on full respect for the Standard Terms of Reference for fact-finding missions, including by reacting strongly to every incident where it is reported that someone was subjected to reprisals after speaking to a special procedures mandate. Third, the conclusions and recommendations issued by special procedures in their reports to the Human Rights Council require unconditional and non-selective follow-up and action by the Council itself. For instance, the Universal Periodic Review (peer review) conducted by the Council should be geared towards implementing the findings by the treaty bodies and special procedures, instead of second-guessing or watering down what the independent expert procedures have produced.

The fourth proposed improvement relates to the relationship between the special procedures and the Office of the High Commissioner for Human Rights. As the special procedures are based on the work of unpaid independent external experts, they must be guaranteed a proper share of the resources of the Office, including in the form of staff assistance, so that any impression is removed that the Office might be interfering with the independence of the mandate holders, including by being selective or conditional in its day-to-day provision of resources.

## 3.4. Conclusion

The two arms of regular UN human rights mechanisms based on the work of independent experts, the treaty bodies and the special procedures of the Human Rights Council, both include a significant dimension of fact-finding. In both cases, there are obvious shortcomings in the fact-finding and also obvious available solutions for how the situation could be greatly improved. In relation to possible links between fact-finding in UN human rights expert procedures and in criminal prosecutions, two important points need to be made.

Firstly, as human rights expert procedures serve the purpose of establishing the responsibility of a state for human rights violations under the law of state responsibility, the standard is very different from that applied for individual criminal responsibility. State responsibility may flow from actions or omissions, including in relation to so-called positive obligations related to the promotion of human rights. For establishing state responsibility, there is no requirement that a crime has been committed, or more generally, that there has been any malicious intent on the side of any individual.

Secondly, even where fact-finding by human rights mechanisms has the potential of producing factual records that might be useful in a criminal case, for instance through interviews conducted by a Special Rapporteur during a country visit, great caution should be applied when trying to make use of that material for criminal prosecution. Above all, the purpose of human rights procedures to facilitate better respect for and better promotion of human rights should not be put at risk through such aspirations. In addition, there may be other practical and even legal problems in making use of the factual records in a criminal trial.[38]

---

[38] In particular, there may be pertinent issues related to the privileges and immunities of United Nations functionaries that might constitute legal obstacles to, for instance, hearing a Special Rapporteur or any assisting UN staff member as a witness by a court, unless the Secretary-General waives the immunity. During my time as Special Rapporteur this issue was repeatedly raised by the UN Secretariat when Special Rapporteurs were, for instance, asked to submit an *amicus curiae* brief to or appear as an expert witness at a court. See, Convention on the Privileges and Immunities of the United Nations (1946) (http://www.legal-tools.org/doc/f68109/).

# 4

---

# Justified Belief in the Unbelievable

## Simon De Smet[*]

## 4.1. Introduction

This chapter deals with the theory behind the practice of fact-finding.[1] All too often, fact-finding is talked about as if it were something self-evident, something that everyone is capable of doing and requiring no special skills or training. Whereas it is unquestionably so that everyone engages in some sort of fact-finding in daily life ("when does the bus leave?", "who ate the last orange?", *et cetera*), few are conscious of the mental processes involved in it. This form of fact-finding could be called 'intuitive', in the sense that the fact-finder does not consciously think about how she arrives at factual conclusions from whatever form of evidence she relies upon. To the extent that 'intuitive' fact-finding allows us to get by in our daily lives, there is nothing wrong with it. However, some people are required to engage in fact-finding as part of their profession. They make findings about facts and events that may deeply affect the lives of many other people. Lawyers, for example, are often called upon to engage in fact-finding, particularly in the context of adjudication. Similarly, journalists and NGO investigators report about facts and events that take place

---

[*]   **Simon De Smet** is a Legal Officer in the Chambers of the International Criminal Court (since 2003). He has served as a Law Clerk at the International Court of Justice (to Judges Thomas Buergenthal and Pieter Kooijmans, 2002–2003), and was a First Lieutenant (Reserve) in the Belgian Air Force (1993–2005). He holds a Ph.D. from Cambridge University, an LL.M. from Columbia University School of Law, and a Licentiaat in de Rechten from the University of Ghent.

[1]   Most of what follows is based upon the author's research for a doctoral dissertation at Cambridge University. A more fully developed treatment of the topics in the context of judicial fact-finding will appear as part of a forthcoming book by this author entitled *Rethinking Fact-Finding by International Courts* to be published by Cambridge University Press.

---

in different parts of the world. International fact-finders are situated somewhere between these two categories.[2]

This chapter starts from the assumption that most international fact-finders, like their lawyer and journalist counterparts, engage in their fact-finding tasks largely 'intuitively'. Even though they may display great care and circumspection in making their findings, they do not necessarily have a strongly developed understanding of what the underlying principles and concepts of fact-finding are. The basic point of this chapter is that this is unsatisfactory and that international fact-finders should be more aware of the basic epistemic principles that are at play, so that they may be more 'conscious' about the fact-finding process. If fact-finding is a profession, then the process should be professionalised.

This is not to suggest that international fact-finders currently often get the facts wrong or that, if they did act more 'consciously', they would get the facts right more often. However, it is suggested that a greater understanding of basic epistemic principles would improve the overall epistemic quality of international fact-finding. In particular, there is a need to be more transparent about the strength and quality of particular findings and to be more precise about the evidentiary value of the available evidence and the inferences that are drawn from it. Indeed, while many international fact-finders are clearly very diligent in their efforts, it is sometimes difficult to escape the impression that international reports lack a solid theoretical framework. Even when standards of proof are applied, it is often difficult for an observer to ascertain how 'strong' or 'reliable' the many factual claims actually are. This can be a problem when the findings inform policy-making or lead to the public condemnation of certain groups or individuals.

The purpose of this chapter is thus to shed some light on a few basic epistemological concepts that are relevant to international fact-finders. It is hoped that this will stimulate reflection on what it is that international inquirers actually do when they report on international crimes. This should allow for greater control over the quality of their findings. Indeed, it is only possible to evaluate and improve current practices if one understands the basic elements of what fact-finding actually is.

---

[2]  In what follows, I will use 'international fact-finding' and 'international fact-finders' as shorthand to cover all possible forms of IGO or NGO sanctioned fact-finding into core international crimes.

As epistemology covers a vast philosophical area, what follows will necessarily be basic and succinct. Indeed, it is not possible to do justice to the richness of the subject within the scope of a single chapter. Nevertheless, it is hoped that the introduction of some basic epistemological concepts may raise awareness among practitioners about what is involved in fact-finding from a theoretical perspective. This, in turn, will hopefully sharpen awareness about the inherent limitations of most fact-finding and encourage future international inquirers to be more precise about the nature and strength of their findings. The ultimate message of this chapter is a call for greater epistemic modesty.

## 4.2. What is Fact-Finding?

For the present purposes, there is no need to discuss complex epistemic debates about what constitutes truth. It suffices to adopt a simple definition of 'truth' as referring to 'what really happened'. It will be assumed that the truth can, in principle, be ascertained by anyone, as long as the right information is available. We therefore sidestep the thorny issues of radical cultural relativism and epistemic scepticism.

International inquiries pertain to facts that have already taken place. Factual findings in this context are thus affirmations of factual propositions about the past. Accordingly, when a fact-finder makes a 'finding', she claims knowledge about the past. Crucially, in the vast majority of cases, international inquirers will not have personally experienced or observed the events about which they report. This is important from an epistemic point of view, because most epistemologists make a fundamental distinction between perceptual knowledge and testimonial knowledge.[3] As international inquirers have no direct perceptual knowledge about the facts they report, they actually testify about evidence they have collected and analysed during the investigation and give their opinion about what this evidence demonstrates.

Putting matters more formally, fact-finders generate hypotheses about the past and confirm them on the basis of the available evidence by formulating a theory of how the evidence is an instance or a consequence of the hypotheses. Breaking down this definition, fact-finding thus involves three main elements, namely hypotheses (that is, claims about real-

---

[3] See, Noah Lemos, *An Introduction to the Theory of Knowledge*, Cambridge University Press, 2007; Robert Audi, *Epistemology, A Contemporary Introduction to the Theory of Knowledge*, 3rd ed., Routledge, 2011.

ity in the form of factual propositions), evidence, and a theory that is based on background knowledge, which explains how the evidence 'proves' the hypotheses.

It goes without saying that fact-finders should only make factual claims which they themselves believe to be true.[4] In addition, we expect fact-finders to be both objective and rational. This means that we expect fact-finders to have valid reasons for affirming the factual propositions they advance. Crucially, we expect fact-finders to be able to explain those reasons to us, so that we can form our own opinion about their quality. In epistemological terms, fact-finders are expected to be able to 'justify' their beliefs. It should be noted, however, that even if a factual proposition is justified, this does not necessarily mean it is true. Indeed, a proposition can be justified but not true, just like it can be true but not justified. Nevertheless, having justification for one's beliefs is essential from an epistemic point of view, because believing without justification is an epistemic *fault*, whereas have a justified belief in an untruth is an epistemic *mistake*.[5]

For most practical purposes, the question epistemologists pose to fact-finders is not so much whether their factual findings are true, but whether they are justified. Whether a belief is justified depends on a number of factors, the most important of which is the totality of evidence the fact-finder has at her disposal. As the evidence one has can – at least in theory – always be defeated by evidence one does not have, it follows that as long as one does not have *all* the evidence, one's beliefs remain *defeasible*.

Therefore, apart from giving us the hypotheses and the theories that underpin them, fact-finders should be able to express how confident they are of the accuracy, as well as the strength of their findings. This estimation should be based on more than intuition or guesswork on behalf of the fact-finder. Ideally, the fact-finder should be able to explain exactly what the sources of uncertainty or doubts are, and to what extent they hedge the accuracy of the findings. In order to be able to convey this information, fact-finders must have a method for determining and communicating their

---

[4] Belief in this sense could be roughly defined as a dispositional affirmative attitude towards a proposition of state of affairs. Andrew Chignell, "The Ethics of Belief", in Zalta *et al.* (eds.), *Stanford Encyclopedia of Philosophy*, Spring 2013.

[5] Hock Lai Ho, *A Philosophy of Evidence Law: Justice in the Search for Truth*, 2008, Oxford University Press.

level of confidence in the findings. If this method is also understood by the reader of the report, it will be a lot easier for her to evaluate the 'quality' of the findings and have a better understanding of their precariousness.

This links straight back to the issue of justified beliefs and how they are formed. Indeed, beliefs can be justified in different ways and it is essential to understand how a particular fact-finder has justified hers, in order to understand how the findings could be defeated. The following section offers a very brief overview of the two main strands in epistemology concerning how one can come to beliefs about the past on the basis of evidence. This is but a very brief and summary introduction to a complex field. Nevertheless, it is hoped that by providing even a rudimentary overview of major trends in modern epistemology, the reader will develop some basic awareness about the existence of different theoretical models and abandon the idea that the fact-finding process is something based purely on intuition and common sense, and cannot be conceptualised or explained.

## 4.3. Two Approaches Towards Justifying Beliefs

With the caveat that we are, for the purpose of this chapter, grossly simplifying a sophisticated debate; it is possible to identify two major strands in modern epistemology that offer fundamentally different accounts of how beliefs about factual events can be justified.[6] In essence, they represent two different 'methods' of induction.[7] The first is the probabilistic method, also referred to as Bayesian epistemology,[8] which aims at establishing the probability of factual propositions on the basis of the laws of probability. The second method centres around the concept of 'Inference

---

[6] The field is obviously much richer and more nuanced than that. L. Jonathan Cohen, for example, developed an alternative model for judicial fact-finding L. Jonathan Cohen, *The Probable and the Provable*, 1977, Oxford University Press. So did John Henry Wigmore, *The Science of Judicial Proof as Given by Logic, Psychology and General Experience and Illustrated in Judicial Trials*, 3rd ed., Little Brown, 1937. However, the goal of the present chapter is mainly to illustrate that epistemology offers more than one account of fact-finding and that fact-finders may therefore have to consider their own position in this regard.

[7] This is not to say that they are mutually exclusive and that fact-finders have to choose between one or the other. Indeed, there are even some suggestions that the two methods may be integrated. See Peter Lipton, *Inference to the Best Explanation*, 2nd ed., Cambridge University Press, 2004, pp. 103–120.

[8] William Talbot, "Bayesian Epistemology", in Zalta *et al.* (eds.), *Stanford Encyclopedia of Philosophy*, Summer 2011.

to the Best Explanation', sometimes also referred to as the relative plausibility theory.

Although neither of these schools offers ready-made reasoning models that always lead to the truth, let alone provide simple algorithms that are easy to apply in practice, there is nevertheless great benefit in being aware of them, as a better understanding of the underlying concepts may improve the way in which fact-finders approach their task.

### 4.3.1. Probabilistic Account of Fact-Finding

The basic idea behind Probability Theory is that our beliefs about the world are not categorical but come in degrees.[9] This may be counter-intuitive, as past events either did or did not happen. This is of course true from a historical perspective, but from the viewpoint of the fact-finder such absolute certainty is almost always unattainable. By convention, one's degree of belief is expressed on a scale from 0 (when one is certain that a proposition is false) to 1 (when one is certain that a proposition is true). When asked about whether one thinks a fair coin will land heads, the answer should therefore be 0.5, expressing the fact that one has no basis on which to predict which of the two sides will land up. In this case, it is easy to determine the probability, as there are only two even possibilities. However, in order to be useful for fact-finding about the past, probability theory has to offer a lot more. In particular, it must offer a way to determine the probability of claims about the past.

There are different approaches towards how to determine probability. However, once the initial probability has been determined, the basic principles of how to process them are basically the same. In the next two sections, an ultra-succinct overview of the two main approaches to determining probability will be discussed. After that, a brief introduction will be given about how Bayesian epistemology prescribes that fact-finders should determine their beliefs in light of the available evidence.

---

[9]  See, Henk Tijms, *Understanding Probability*, 3rd ed., Cambridge University Press, 2012; Ian Hacking, *An Introduction to Probability and Inductive Logic*, Cambridge University Press, 2001; John Haigh, *Probability – A very short introduction*, Oxford University Press, 2012.

### 4.3.1.1.  Frequency-Type Probability[10]

Probability theory is frequently associated with making predictions about certain types of events that are based either on logical calculation or on statistical data. An example of the first kind is the probability of throwing a six with a fair die or the probability of winning the jackpot in the lottery. Examples of probabilistic statements based on statistical data range from extrapolating the results of exit polling at elections, to calculating the likelihood of someone with a certain DNA developing a particular disease. This type of probability is usually referred to as quantitative or frequency-type probability.[11] It focuses on measuring sequences of similar events and developing an understanding of the tendency or disposition of certain events or characteristics to arise under particular conditions. As it makes little sense to speak of frequency in relation to single events,[12] it may appear that this type of probability is of little use to international fact-finders. However, although each violation of human rights or instance of an international crime constitutes a single and unique event, frequency-type probability may still be highly relevant for international fact-finders. Two examples are offered to demonstrate the point.

First, DNA or similar types of evidence may be available that can assist the fact-finder in identifying victims or perpetrators. The power of DNA evidence lies in the fact that it tells us how likely it is that a person randomly selected from a given population would match the sample. Usually this probability is very small, thereby seemingly making it highly probable that the suspect is guilty in the case of a match. However, caution is required, because some people make the mistake of assuming that, if for example the likelihood of finding a match in a randomly selected person is 0.002 this means that there is a 0.998 probability that the suspect is guilty in case of a match. However, if the relevant population from which the suspect is randomly selected is 600,000, we can expect 1,200 individuals to match the sample. This means that, if there is no other evidence implicating the suspect, the probability of him being guilty on the basis of the matching DNA is only 0.000833. This basic mistake is often

---

[10]  The terminologies 'Frequency-type probability' and 'Belief-type probability' are borrowed from Hacking, 2001, see *supra* note 9.

[11]  Sometimes the term 'objective probability' is also used, for example, Colin Aitken and Franco Taroni, *Statistics and the Evaluation of Evidence for Forensic Scientists*, 2nd ed., Wiley, 2004.

[12]  Hacking, 2001, p. 136, see *supra* note 9.

referred to as the Prosecutor's Fallacy. On the other hand, if there is other evidence that narrows the pool of potential suspects to just four individuals and only one of them matches the DNA sample, this raises the probability to 0.992. In other words, other evidence is needed to narrow the pool of suspects and DNA evidence alone cannot do all the work.

A second example of how Frequency-type probability can assist international fact-finders is if there are very large numbers of victims of mass atrocities. Frequency-type probability may help fact-finders in designing their investigation so that they can concentrate their limited resources on interviewing a statistically relevant sample of the victim population, in order to draw probabilistic inferences about the population as a whole. Space does not permit a detailed discussion of this approach, but suffice it to say that, under the right circumstances, careful sampling is a potentially very powerful tool that can vastly improve the quality of fact-finding.

### 4.3.1.2. Belief-Type Probability

A different strand of probability theory approaches the determination of probabilities from a more subjective angle. Personal probability theorists take a person's individual confidence level about an uncertain event or proposition as the starting point.[13] The classical definition of Belief-type probability states that it is "a degree of belief (as actually held by someone based on his whole knowledge, experience, information) regarding the truth of a statement or event E (a fully specified single event or statement whose truth or falsity is, for whatever reason, unknown to the person)".[14]

Belief-type probability can be relied upon when no Frequency-type probabilities are available. Recourse to Belief-type probability will be appropriate whenever the event in question cannot be considered as part of a long sequence of repetitions under identical conditions. A typical example would be the trustworthiness of a particular witness in relation to a particular part of his or her testimony. In other words, when no Frequency-type probability is available or possible, Belief-type probability can, in principle, fill the gap.

---

[13] Hacking, 2001, pp. 127–139, see *supra* note 9; Aitken and Taroni, 2004, pp. 21–23, see *supra* note 11.

[14] Bruno De Finetti, "Probability: the subjectivistic approach", in Raymond Klibansky (ed.), *La philosophie contemporaine*, vol. 2, La Nuova Italia, 1968, p. 45.

Although this approach is not as empirically exact as Frequency-type probability, it is not entirely arbitrary either. One of the main constraints in this regard is that an individual's beliefs and confidence levels must be coherent, in the sense that they must respect the basic rules of probability.[15] Most importantly, if someone considers several possible hypotheses that explain a single event, the sum of the probabilities for all of these hypotheses must be 1.[16] For example, if it is unknown which militia carried out a particular attack on a village and there are three possible culprits, it would not be possible to consider the probability for each of those militia to be 0.5, as this would amount to a total of more than 1, which is not possible. Fact-finders faced with such situations must thus fine-tune their probability estimates. Another basic rule is that the probability of a conjunction can never be higher than that of its individual conjuncts. So, for example, it would be a mistake to say that the probability that suspect A ordered an attack is 0.8, if the probability of the suspect having been the commander at the relevant time is only 0.7. This is because being a commander is a prerequisite for giving orders and the hypothesis that the suspect gave the order can thus only be true if the hypothesis that he was the commander is also true.

Although the strength of beliefs cannot be measured empirically, it can be expressed numerically. In terms of how persons are expected to determine their personal probability estimates, there is no single universal method. One approach that is popular among probability theorists is to fathom a person's degree of confidence in a particular proposition by gauging how much risk the person would be willing to take when offered a bet. Epistemologists have developed sophisticated heuristics to help individuals with determining their degree of belief.[17] For example, if someone is asked to provide her personal probability of the chance that it will rain tomorrow, one can imagine a situation where someone is offered a bet to win a prize if she chooses correctly between (a) the chance that it will rain tomorrow and (b) the chance that a fair coin will land on heads. If the person chooses (a), this means that she thinks that the chance that it will

---

[15] See references in *supra* note 9.

[16] Another constraint is a person's probability estimate about the truth of a particular proposition must be inversely proportionate to the probability of the proposition being false. Therefore, if one considers that there is a 0.7 probability that it will rain tomorrow, this implies that there is a 0.3 probability that it will remain dry.

[17] Hacking, 2001, pp. 151–162, see *supra* note 9.

rain tomorrow is greater than 0.5, as otherwise she would have chosen the coin. Although this approach may be thought of as being overly subjective, it has the great advantage of allowing the fact-finder to factor in all doubts she may have, for example, about the trustworthiness of the evidence. In the example, the person asked to bet on whether it will rain tomorrow may have heard that the weather forecast predicted rain, but she may not be confident in the reliability of this prediction. Belief-type probability thus accounts for the reality that, in many cases, there simply is no objective way to establish probability. In the absence of replicable experiments under identical conditions, reasonable people can disagree about the degree of probability certain evidence confers.[18] This is because "the probability assigned to any event must be allowed to depend not only on the specific event in question, but also on the individual whose uncertainty is being expressed, and on the state of background information in light of which this assessment is being made".[19]

It is not suggested that the approach described above provides easy solutions to all factual questions fact-finders may encounter. However, it is important to be aware of the possibility to work with probabilities, even when there are no statistical data. The fact that Belief-type probability is subjective does not mean that it is irrational. Indeed, one great benefit of approaching fact-finding in this manner is that it forces the fact-finder to be more rigorous in thinking about uncertainty. The main point here is thus not that there are unique solutions to complex evidentiary problems, but that probability theory can be a powerful tool to structure one's reasoning about such complex evidence. The next section explains how this can be done in practice.

### 4.3.1.3.  Bayesian Networks

Regardless of how one determines the initial probabilities, a key issue for all fact-finders is how to process large volumes of complex information and determine how a vast collection of evidence relates to one or more hypotheses. The main probabilistic tool for this is something called

---

[18]  Despite this so-called 'subjective vagueness', people are usually able to distinguish between reasonable and unreasonable probability assessments. See Julia Mortera and Philip Dawid, "Probability and Evidence", in Tamas Rudas (ed.), *Handbook of Probability: Theory and Applications*, Sage, 2008, p. 404.

[19]  Philip Dawid, "Probability and Proof", Appendix to Terence Anderson, David Schum and William Twining, *Analysis of Evidence*, Cambridge University Press, 2nd ed., 2005, p. 36.

'Bayesian networks', named after the 18th century probability theorist, Reverend Thomas Bayes (1702–1761). One of the great benefits of Bayesian networks is that it allows the fact-finder to break down the great complexity of a particular case into smaller and simpler parts for separate analysis, whilst preserving overall coherence by linking all parts probabilistically.[20] Another advantage of Bayesian networks is that it forces the fact-finder to analyse the evidence in much greater detail, both in terms of relevance and probative value. Arguably, this leads to greater accuracy in the overall probability assessment.[21]

Bayesian networks are structured graphical representations of probabilistic relationships between several random variables.[22] The network includes two types of variables: evidence and hypotheses, which are all represented by 'nodes'. Nodes that are probabilistically related are connected with arrows. For each node, a probability table must be made.[23] When a particular node does not receive any arrows from another node, it is called a 'parent node' and the probability will be unconditional, that is, $P(A)$. If, on the other hand, the node is a 'child' (that is, it receives arrows from other nodes), its probability will be conditional, that is, $P(A/x, y, z, [...]$ depending on how many 'parents' there are). It is important to stress

---

[20] Aitken and Taroni, 2004, p. 430, see *supra* note 11; Mortera and Dawid, 2008, p. 420, see *supra* note 18.

[21] According to research, persons come up with very different probability assessments when asked to determine the overall probability assessment of a collection of evidence as a whole, compared to when they are asked to specific prior and conditional probabilities for each of the items of evidence and hypotheses separately. See Fred Luminoso, "Bayesian Belief Network Analysis of Legal Evidence", in *Stanford Undergraduate Research Journal*, vol. 1, 2002, p. 49.

[22] See Aitken and Taroni, 2004, pp. 429–454, see *supra* note 11; A. Biedermann, F. Taroni, and S. Bozza, "Implementing statistical learning methods through Bayesian networks (Part 1: A guide to Bayesian parameter estimation using forensic science data)", in *Forensic Science International*, 2009, vol. 193, pp. 63–71; A. Biedermann, F. Taroni, S. Bozza, and W.D. Mazzella, "Implementing statistical learning methods through Bayesian networks (Part 2: Bayesian evaluations for results of black toner analysis in forensic document examination)", in *Forensic Science International*, 2011, vol. 204, pp. 58–66; P.E.M. Huygen, "Use of Bayesian Belief Networks in legal reasoning", 17th BILETA Annual Conference, 2002; Philip Dawid, David Schum and Amanda Hepler, "Inference Networks: Bayes and Wigmore", in Philip Dawid, William Twining and Mimi Vasilaki (eds.), *Evidence, Inference and Enquiry*, 2011, Oxford University Press, pp. 119–150; Mortera and Dawid, 2008, pp. 403–422, see *supra* note 18; Luminoso, 2002, pp. 46–50, *ibid.*

[23] The probability value for a node can be determined on the basis of either Frequency-type or Belief-type probability estimates.

that there is not a single way in which Bayesian networks must be constructed. Indeed, it is perfectly possible that two fact-finders come up with different probability relationships, reflecting their individual views and perceptions about the evidence and knowledge of the area of interest.[24] As such, Bayesian networks are nothing else than a snapshot of a given fact-finder's state of knowledge and understanding at a given moment in time, which is always liable to change if new information becomes available. Significantly, Bayesian networks can 'integrate' missing evidence, that is, evidence that might be expected to exist, but is not available.[25] This is very useful, because it can inform the fact-finder about the defeasibility of the available evidence, by providing an indication of the potential impact of the missing evidence on the overall probability estimate, if it were to be found.

As an example, consider an incident during which a civilian area was allegedly attacked with chemical weapons by the ruling regime of a country. According to the allegation, nerve gas was deployed by the air force. The allegation is denied by the regime. Yet, it is assumed that the regime has both chemical weapons capability and an operational air force. There is no evidence of any order or instruction from the regime to the air force to use chemical weapons. The two main questions that arise are thus whether the victims were killed by chemical weapons and, if so, whether these chemical weapons were deployed by the regime. With regard to the first issue, there is evidence that the bodies of those killed showed no signs of injuries or violence. There are also images of some bodies showing that the victims vomited and/or had foam around mouth and nose. It is known that these are the symptoms of nerve gas.[26] No autopsy was carried out on the victims and no tissue samples were taken. There is thus no chemical analysis of whether the victims were exposed to nerve gas and, if so, which type. However, investigators did find spent shells at the site of the killing and chemical analysis shows that they probably contained nerve gas. Although there are witnesses who saw planes take off from an

---

24  Aitken and Taroni, 2004, p. 431, see *supra* note 11. Reasonable people can disagree about whether/how certain evidence is relevant to a certain hypothesis as well as about the appropriate probability estimate (unless the latter is of the Frequency-type).

25  Aitken and Taroni, 2004, pp. 439–442, see *supra* note 11.

26  This is specialised information, which the fact-finder would have to obtain from an expert, such as the Organisation for the Prohibition of Chemical Weapons.

air force base on the day of the attack, there is no evidence that these planes flew over the area where the victims were killed.

This cluster of information could be represented in a Bayesian network as seen in the next page (Table 1).

Each of the boxes represents a 'node' in the network. Nodes representing hypotheses are rectangular, whereas nodes representing evidence are rounded rectangular. Missing evidence – that is, evidence which is expected to exist on the basis of the hypothesis under consideration, but that is not available – is depicted in nodes with dashed contours. It should be noted that, apart from graphical elegance and clarity, the positioning of different nodes is unimportant. What matters are the probability relationships that are made visible by the arrows, and that there is no circularity. For each of the nodes, a probability estimate must be given. It is important to note, in this regard, that it would be possible to refine the analysis for each node by adding further information. For example, the hypothesis that the regime has chemical weapons is currently a parent node, with no evidence supporting it. The probability estimate will therefore be unconditional. If evidence were available, however, it would be possible to determine the probability of the regime possessing chemical weapons conditional on the available evidence in a separate graph and simply plug the result in the main analysis.

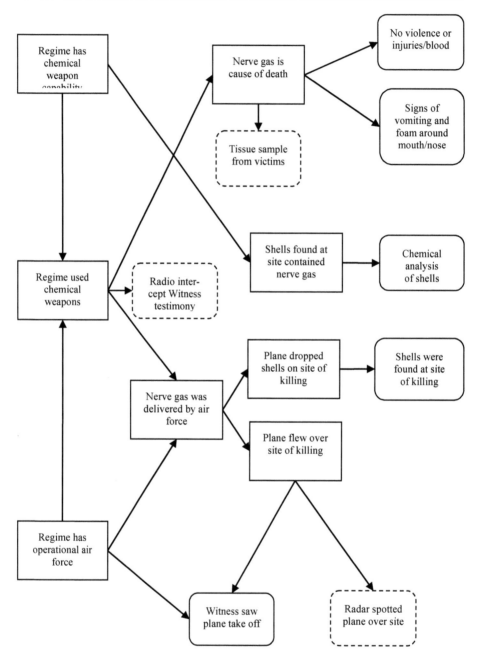

**Table 1. Bayesian Network.**

Once the relevant probability estimates have been entered, it is possible to calculate the posterior probability of the allegation that the regime used chemical weapons based on the available evidence. The main formula that does the work in calculating the overall probability of the hypothesis is Bayes' Rule, which is stated as follows:

$$Pr(H/E) = Pr(E/H).Pr(H)/Pr(E)^{27}$$

It would lead too far to explain how the overall probability of the hypothesis is calculated and how this can be updated in light of revised probability estimates for a given node or the introduction of additional evidence. However, it can easily be seen how even a fairly simple scenario can quickly engender a highly complex network of nodes and probability relationships, which is complex to create and involves challenging calculations.[28] In fact, until fairly recently, the arithmetic involved was too complex for Bayesian networks to have any real-life applicability. However, modern computers can now handle this[29] and thus, the possibility of using Bayesian networks in real fact-finding situations is no longer fanciful.[30]

---

[27] Notation: Pr: Probability; H; Hypothesis; E; Evidence, thus Pr(H/E) stands for the probability of hypothesis H given evidence E, and Pr(E/H) signifies the likelihood of evidence E given hypothesis H. Pr(H) stands for the prior probability of the hypothesis without evidence E. This prior probability can be based on previously considered evidence. Pr(E) stands for the prior probability of the evidence, that is, irrespective of any particular hypothesis. It may often be difficult to determine the prior probabilities of the hypothesis or the evidence. This is where the concepts of Frequency-type and Belief-type probability, discussed above, come into play.

[28] See, for an example, Philip Dawid and Ian Evett, "Using a Graphical Method to Assist the Evaluation of Complicated Patterns of Evidence", in *Journal of Forensic Science*, 1997, vol. 42(2), pp. 226–231.

[29] For example, *Hugin* is a programme that allows the construction of complex Bayesian networks for a variety of purposes.

[30] A powerful example of how Bayesian networks are already being used in practice today is offered by medicine. Indeed, computer programmes have been developed in which the doctor (or patient herself) enters all the symptoms displayed by the patient (as well as data about the patient herself) and the programme returns a number of possible diagnoses with corresponding probabilities for each of them. Such programmes essentially operate on the basis of Bayesian networks and offer the enormous advantage of ensuring that all the relevant and most up-to-date research is taken into consideration with every diagnosis. See, for a brief discussion of an example, John Fox, "Arguing about the Evidence: A Logical Approach", in Philip Dawid, William Twining and Mimi Vasilaki (eds.), *Evidence, Inference and Enquiry*, Oxford University Press, 2011, pp. 151–182.

By including nodes for missing evidence, the fact-finder can anticipate the potential impact of such evidence and articulate potential sources
of uncertainty. For example, if radio intercepts were found showing that
orders were given by the regime to use nerve gas against the population of
the targeted area, this would increase the probability of regime responsibility. Conversely, if tissue samples were available from the victims, but
chemical analysis would show no traces of nerve gas, the proposition that
they were killed by chemical weapons would decrease in probability. Alternative explanations, such as massive food or other forms of poisoning,
might then become more probable instead.

This brings us to an essential point about Bayesian networks: they
are a tool to express and analyse theories about evidence and events, and
nothing more. Bayesian networks do not prescribe a certain outcome or
even dictate how to construct a theory of the case. What the correct probability relationships are is always open to discussion. This is why proponents of Bayesian networks argue that even for those who do not believe
in expressing beliefs numerically, it is still useful to formalise probabilistic relationships because it forces one to think carefully about how evidence and hypotheses may be connected (or not). This may help avoid
mistakes and allow others to review and criticise the reasoning.

Although Bayesianism has many staunch supporters and offers
many benefits, it is not free from difficulties. Perhaps the greatest challenge for the use of Bayesianism in practice is that fact-finders often find
it difficult to determine the prior probabilities of the hypotheses and the
evidence. Moreover, Bayesianism assumes that fact-finders start their investigation with one or more hypotheses already formulated. Although the
hypotheses to be investigated may sometimes be given, for example when
the fact-finder is tasked to verify a certain allegation (for example, that
chemical weapons were used by the regime), in many cases fact-finders
will have to consider at least part of the evidence before any hypotheses
are formulated. However, this means that this part of the evidence has already influenced the prior probability of the hypothesis before Bayes' rule
can be applied. This evidence therefore falls outside the Bayesian calculus
because otherwise it would be counted twice (once during the formulation
and attribution of the prior probability of the hypothesis, and once as part
of the Bayesian network). Another potential difficulty with the Bayesian
method is that it may be difficult for fact-finders to fit in evidence that
supports a hypothesis that is not being considered within the Bayesian

network, because it may be more difficult to see the probabilistic relations between such evidence and the hypothesis under consideration. As long as this other hypothesis is also analysed – perhaps in a separate Bayesian network – there is no real problem, because then the hypothesis that has the greatest posterior probability will be favoured. However, if only one hypothesis is considered, there is a risk that certain evidence will simply not be counted because it stands in no obvious probabilistic relationship to that hypothesis. Finally, there is no denying that, even with the support of computers, applying the Bayesian method to intricate fact-patterns with lots of evidence is a complex and labour-intensive endeavour, requiring a fairly advanced level of familiarity with probability theory. However, it is precisely in those complex cases that working with Bayesian networks will provide most added value. It may thus be useful for international fact-finders to enlist the support of probability experts in analysing the evidence.

### 4.3.2. Inference to the Best Explanation

Inference to the Best Explanation ('IBE') offers a completely different approach towards fact-finding than Bayesianism. In a nutshell, IBE works as follows: the fact-finder is presented with a finite amount of evidence. From this evidence, it is possible to infer a number of hypotheses/scenarios/narratives, which each explain (part of) the available evidence in a different manner. The hypothesis which, if true, would best explain the available evidence should, according to IBE, be retained as the correct factual finding.[31] This process is abductive in nature to the extent that plausible explanations must be generated from the evidence. At the same time, it is also a process of elimination, or at least ranking, of explanations until only one remains as the best. From an epistemic point of view, the fact-finder is justified in believing the 'best explanation'.[32]

---

[31] It is important to understand that the limitations of the epistemic claim IBE makes. IBE is not a method that guarantees that the best actual explanation will be found. Rather, IBE states that the best of the *available* explanations is the explanation that should be retained as an actual explanation. Lipton, 2004, p. 58, see *supra* note 7.

[32] However, IBE does not claim that the best explanation is always a good enough explanation. When none of the available explanations is sufficiently good, no explanation should be retained and consequently no finding is possible. This is why Peter Lipton suggested that IBE might me more accurately called "Inference to the Best Explanation if the Best is Sufficiently Good". Lipton, 2004, p. 154, see *supra* note 7.

Before entering the question as to how the best explanation should be identified, it may be useful to briefly address the issue of how the competing explanations are generated. Indeed, when presented with a mass of evidence, it may not be very easy to recognise what needs to be explained. Useful guidance in this regard may be found in the work of Peter Lipton, who argued that fact-finders should focus their inquiry on so-called contrastive explanation.[33] Contrastive explanation focuses on finding explanations for why something is the case rather than something else. So, instead of asking "why X", the contrastive explanation model asks the question "why X rather than Y".[34] In doing so, the inquiry is focused on a more precise issue, which makes it easier to identify the potential explanations and the relevant evidence. This approach makes sense, as it is intuitively easy to understand that no single hypothesis can explain all the evidence.[35] Contrast sets can relate to any point of interest about which we are uncertain or unclear.[36] In a judicial context, the contrast sets will usually be provided by the parties, who will formulate different and usually conflicting hypotheses (the respective 'cases'), and offer different explanations of the evidence. Similar conditions will sometimes apply to non-judicial fact-finders, who may receive competing claims about what happened during a certain incident. For example, when the evidence shows that armed violence was used at a certain location, it is often the case that the inhabitants will claim that they were the innocent victims of an unprovoked aggression, whereas the attacking force will argue that they were acting against a legitimate military target that was positioned at the location in question. Within these competing hypotheses, countless further contrast sets may be distinguished (for example, "why was the location encircled prior to entry, rather than being entered from one direc-

---

[33] Lipton, 2004, see *supra* note 7.

[34] Lipton, 2004, p. 33, see *supra* note 7. It should be noted that X and Y need not be incompatible. However, to aid the explanatory exercise, it may be easier in such cases to rephrase the contrast to "why (X and not-Y) rather than (Y and not-X)", *ibid.*, p. 35.

[35] In this sense, Lipton, 2004, p. 76, see *supra* note 7. As Lipton explains, evidence that is not explained by a hypothesis is simply irrelevant to it. However, evidence that is irrelevant to one particular hypothesis may be highly relevant to another one. If this other hypothesis ends up being the better one, this would defeat the first hypothesis. In this sense the evidence *is* relevant to the first hypothesis.

[36] It should also be understood that although explanation is usually carried out in a binary fashion ("why X rather than Y?"), it will often be necessary to consider several contrast sets in relation to the same fact (*i.e.*, after resolving the question "why X rather than Y?", the fact-finder may still have to consider "why X rather than Z?", *et cetera*).

tion?", "why was one church destroyed but another left untouched?", *et cetera*). When the fact-finder is not presented with competing claims, it is her task to formulate them herself.[37] Usually the fact-finder will be guided in this respect by her own background knowledge as well as by specific information about the general situation and context.[38] However, there is a risk that this method of generating hypotheses and potential explanations will be skewed, insofar as it will yield only potential explanations that fit within the existing background beliefs of the fact-finder.[39] It is thus possible that the true explanation will not be considered because it simply did not fit with the background beliefs of those involved in generating the short list of potential explanations. This is why it is important to always consider the possibility that the true explanation may be something that the fact-finder is unfamiliar with.[40]

Assuming that all the potentially plausible explanations have been canvassed, and that the true explanation is one of them, it is important to know how to identify which one qualifies as best.[41] Unfortunately, there is no clear set of criteria on offer and different authors seem to emphasise different criteria.[42] It appears that this difference may, at least in part, be explained by the angle from which the authors are approaching the issue. Authors who approach IBE from a more formal epistemic angle and adhere to coherentism emphasise the coherentist aspect of IBE.[43] Those who put the emphasis more on the psychological workings of human fact-

---

[37] Even when competing explanations are proposed to the fact-finder, she may still add additional ones herself, when she thinks that particular potentially plausible explanations are lacking.

[38] For example, if previous attacks were not initiated by shelling, it might be a useful inquiry for the fact-finder to find out why in a particular instance the attack was preceded by shelling.

[39] Lipton, 2004, p. 151, see *supra* note 7.

[40] See discussion on NEW hypothesis, *infra*, section 4.3.2.2., "Naturalised Method for Identifying the Best Explanation".

[41] David Schum, "Species of Abductive Reasoning in Fact Investigation in Law", in *Cardozo Law Review*, 2001, vol. 22, p. 1655.

[42] Larry Laudan, "Strange Bedfellows: Inference to the Best Explanation And the Criminal Standard of Proof", in *International Journal of Evidence and Proof*, 2007, vol. 11, p. 292.

[43] See, *e.g.*, Amalia Amaya, "Inference to the Best Legal Explanation" in H. Kaptein, H. Prakken and B. Verheij, (eds.) *Legal Evidence and Proof - Statistics, Stories, Logic*, 2009, Ashgate, p. 135.

finding rely more on the process of comparing narratives in light of general background assumptions.[44]

Reflecting the two aforementioned strands in IBE, section 4.3.2.1. first considers methods that are associated with coherentist epistemology. Section 4.3.2.2. subsequently briefly discusses less formal, so-called 'naturalised', forms of IBE. It is not suggested that these two categories are exhaustive. They are merely intended to given an idea about how IBE can be implemented in different ways.

### 4.3.2.1.  A Coherentist Model for Identifying the Best Explanation

According to the 'coherentist school',[45] the best explanation coincides with the most coherent explanation.[46] There are different theories in general, and especially in scientific epistemology, about what accounts for coherence maximisation, but one that has found its way into legal epistemology is the theory of constraint satisfaction, developed by Paul Thagard.[47] Briefly summarised, this model is based on the assumption that within any given set of elements (which may include both hypotheses and evidence), each element is related to one or more others in a binary way: either the two elements cohere with each other, or they do not. For example, a photograph showing persons wearing SS uniforms in front of the Eiffel tower coheres with the hypothesis that the Third Reich invaded France. On the other hand, the testimony of Eichmann does not cohere with holocaust denial.

To summarise the main principles of coherentist IBE, as they have been developed by Thagard, and adapted specifically for (criminal) legal epistemology by Amaya:

- Principle E1: *Symmetry*. Explanatory coherence is a symmetrical relation, unlike, say, conditional probability.

---

[44]  Ronald Allen and Michael Pardo, "Juridical Proof and the Best Explanation", in Law and Philosophy, vol. 27(3), 2008.

[45]  Amaya, 2009, see *supra* note 43.

[46]  According to the coherence theory of justification, if a belief coheres with the other beliefs one holds, this makes it reasonable to hold that belief – and not when it conflicts with one's other beliefs. See Lemos, 2007, p. 66 *et seq.*, see *supra* note 3.

[47]  Paul Thagard and Karsten Verbeurgt, "Coherence as Constraint Satisfaction", in *Cognitive Science*, 1998, vol. 22, p. 1; Paul Thagard, *Coherence in Thought and Action*, MIT Press, 2000; Paul Thagard, "Evaluating Explanations in Law, Science and Everyday Life", in *Current Directions in Psychological Science*, 2006, vol. 15, p. 141.

- Principle E2: *Explanation.* (a) A hypothesis coheres with what it explains, which can either be the evidence or another hypothesis; (b) hypotheses that together explain some other proposition cohere with each other; and (c) the more hypotheses it takes to explain something, the lower the degree of coherence.[48]

- Principle E3: *Analogy.* Similar hypotheses that explain similar pieces of evidence cohere.

- Principle E4: *Priority.* (a) Propositions that describe the results of observation have a degree of acceptability on their own; (b) hypotheses that are compatible with innocence have a degree of acceptability on their own.[49]

- Principle E5: *Contradiction. Contradiction* Contradictory propositions are incoherent with each other.

- Principle E6: *Competition.* If P and Q both explain a proposition and if P and Q are not explanatorily connected, the P and Q are incoherent with each other.

- Principle E7: *Acceptance.* (a) The acceptability of a proposition in a system of propositions depends on its coherence with them; (b) the guilt hypothesis may be accepted only if it is justified to a degree sufficient to satisfy the reasonable doubt standard.[50]

Principle E4(a) is of great significance, because it ensures a link between hypotheses and (observed) reality.[51] It also obliges adjudicators to consider all the evidence that has been presented at trial before coming to any definite conclusions about the best explanation. This reduces the risk that adjudicators simply adopt their preferred explanation and find it to be

---

[48] This last principle could also be referred to as the principle of simplicity: the simpler and more elegant the explanation, the higher the probability of it being true.

[49] (b) applies specifically in the criminal law context, and is an application of the presumption of innocence, which is itself a hypothesis, but one that is given particular weight by the law.

[50] Amaya, 2009, see *supra* note 43.

[51] Thagard and Verbeurgt, 1998, see *supra* note 47:

[...] explanatory coherence theory gives priority (but not guaranteed acceptance) to elements representing the results of observation and experiment [...] assuming with the correspondence theory of truth that observation and experiment involve in part causal interaction with the world, we can have some confidence that the hypotheses adopted on the basis of explanatory coherence also correspond to the world and are not mere mind-contrivances that are only internally coherent.

the most coherent one, whilst ignoring the factual evidence.[52] However, the mere requirement to formally consider all the evidence does not exclude the possibility of bias in finding coherence; by artificially attaching low probative value to evidence which conflicts with the preferred belief, one may acquire coherence for the preferred hypothesis, while still accounting for all the evidence. It is therefore important to attribute the correct weight to evidence, independently from how well it explains certain hypotheses.

When one is confronted with a mass of evidence, the task of the fact-finder is to analyse how each potential explanation accounts for all the elements of information contained in the evidence. This is done by dividing the elements into two groups: those elements which are accepted, because they cohere with each other, and those that are rejected, because they are incoherent with the accepted elements. It should be noted, in this regard, that, according to Thagard, the more hypotheses it takes to explain something, the lower the degree of coherence.[53]

It will be clear from the above that finding the best explanation is not a straightforward and linear exercise. In the words of Thagard:

> Explanation evaluation is not simply a matter of determining which of two or more competing hypotheses fits best with the evidence. We may also need to consider how hypotheses fit with each other, particularly when one hypothesis provides an explanation of another. [...] the cognitive process of explanation evaluation must consider the fit of hypotheses with each other as well as with the evidence, so that inference involves coming up with the overall most coherent picture of what happened. [...] we should accept and reject propositions on the basis of their overall coherence with each other. Because hypotheses and evidence can be coherent and incoherent with each other in many ways [... IBE is] a high-

---

[52] Thagard, 2006, see *supra* note 47:

Explanation evaluation is often a highly emotional enterprise. A scientist with a favorite theory will react to a challenging alternative not merely with disbelief but possibly also with annoyance or even more negative emotions. In legal cases, the prosecution and the defense will have very different emotional attitudes toward the prospect of the accused being convicted, and obviously the accused and his or her supporters will react with intensely negative emotions toward the prospect of conviction. Ideally, the judge and jury are supposed to be neutral, but they are as prone as anyone else to affective biases.

[53] Amaya, 2009, see *supra* note 43; and Thagard, 2006, see *supra* note 47.

ly complex and nonlinear process. We cannot simply accept the evidence and then accept a hypothesis and then reject its competitors, because evidence and competing hypotheses must all be evaluated together with respect to how they fit with each other. This makes explanation evaluation sound like a very mysterious holistic process.[54]

Crucially, the coherentist IBE model is based on the assumption that coherence is a symmetrical relation. This allows Thagard and Verbeurgt to argue that this epistemic model is not circular,[55] because it proceeds by way of the *simultaneous* evaluation of multiple elements.[56] Like Bayesian networks, the simultaneous analysis and evaluation of large volumes of evidence and hypotheses is a daunting task. To aid the process and to make it more deliberate, Thagard (among others) has developed algorithms, which allow the whole process to be formalised.[57] Moreover, he has developed a number of computer programmes, which are capable of calculating overall coherence values.[58]

### 4.3.2.2. Naturalised Method for Identifying the Best Explanation

A more 'naturalised' method for identifying the best explanation is proposed by, among others, Allen and Pardo,[59] and Josephson.[60] When IBE is

---

[54] Thagard, 2006, see *supra* note 47.

[55] The circularity critique in essence argues that if one justifies believing A because it coheres with B and C and B because it coheres with A and C, this is a circular argument of auto-justification which has no basis other than the fact that A, B and C are subjectively believed.

[56] Thagard and Verbeurgt, 1998, see *supra* note 47.

[57] *Ibid.*:

Compared to rigorous explorations of deductive logic and probability theory, coherence approaches to epistemology and ethics have been vague and imprecise. In contrast, we have presented a mathematically exact, computationally manageable, and psychologically plausible account of how coherence judgments can be made.

[58] Thagard and Verbeurgt, 1998, see *supra* note 47. For a similar effort to formalise abductive reasoning more generally, see P. Snow, and M. Bellis, "Structured Deliberation for Dynamic Uncertain Inference", in *Cardozo Law Review*, 2001, vol. 22, p. 1747; F. Bex *et al.*, "Sense-making software for crime investigation: how to combine stories and arguments?", in *Law, Probability and Risk*, 2007, vol. 6, p. 145; D. Walton, *Witness Testimony Evidence – Argumentation, Artificial Intelligence, and Law*, Cambridge University Press, 2008.

[59] Allen and Pardo, 2008, p. 223, *supra* note 44.

[60] John Josephson, "On the Proof Dynamics of Inference to the Best Explanation", in *Cardozo Law Review*, 2001, vol. 22, p. 1621.

---

described as a form of 'naturalised' epistemology,[61] this refers to the fact that it is based on the findings by cognitive psychologists about how humans in the real world actually go about making factual determinations.[62] From these observations, a theoretical model of fact-finding was derived.[63]

The account by Allen and Pardo starts from the observation[64] that people tend to arrive at factual conclusions by comparing several plausible narratives,[65] which may all account for the evidence they were presented with, and choosing the best one from among those narratives "by applying similar criteria to those invoked in the philosophy of science".[66] The criteria identified by Allen and Pardo for selecting the best explanation are contained in a non-exhaustive list, which includes: "the extent to which [the explanation] is consistent, simpler, explains more (consilience), better accords with background beliefs (coherence), is less *ad hoc*, and so on; and is worse to the extent it betrays these criteria". Crucially, Allen and Pardo hold that "[t]here is no formula for combining such criteria; rather, each is a standard which must be weighed against the others".[67]

Josephson offers the following criteria for selecting the best explanation: (1) How decisively the leading hypothesis surpasses the alternatives; (2) how well the hypothesis stands by itself, independently of the alternatives; and (3) how thorough the search for alternative explanations was.[68] Josephson also proposes a requirement to systematically consider two 'standard' explanations in every case. The first explanation which must always be considered is what Josephson calls the 'NOISE hypothesis'. This hypothesis is based on the explanation that all or some im-

---

[61] Ronald Allen and Brian Leiter, "Naturalized Epistemology and the Law of Evidence", in *Virginia Law Review*, 2001, vol. 87(8), p. 1492.

[62] Richard Feldman, "Naturalized Epistemology", in Edward Zalta *et al.* (eds.), *Stanford Encyclopedia of Philosophy*, 2012.

[63] Although Allen and Pardo's account was developed in the context of judicial fact-finding, there is no reason why it could not apply to non-judicial inquiries as well.

[64] See Nancy Pennington, and Reid Hastie, "A Cognitive Theory of Jury Decision Making: The Story Model", in *Cardozo Law Review*, 1991, vol. 13, p. 519.

[65] Indeed, identifying the best explanation does not necessarily mean that all the other possible contenders are therefore implausible. IBE is thus a lot more than simply distinguishing the plausible from the implausible.

[66] Allen and Pardo, 2008, see *supra* note 44.

[67] *Ibid.*

[68] Josephson, 2001, see *supra* note 60.

portant part of the data one is trying to explain is simply incorrect, because it is "merely coincidence, misperception, miscategorization, fraud, perjury, experimental error, noise, or some similar phenomenon. Sometimes the data should be 'explained away' rather than explained, in which case the commitment to the givens is retracted in the interest of presenting a more satisfactory overall theory".[69] The NOISE hypothesis is of great importance, because it forces the adjudicator to factor in her confidence in the accuracy and/or credibility of the data that she is trying to explain.

A second hypothesis, which Josephson suggests should always be considered, is the NEW hypothesis. This hypothesis obliges the adjudicator to consider that there might be explanations of which he or she has not thought, simply because they are unprecedented. This hypothesis is also very important, because it obliges adjudicators to question the limitations of their background beliefs that have spawned the available explanations. A straightforward example of the NEW hypothesis would be an important scientific advance, which the adjudicator had previously never heard of and therefore did not take into consideration. The NEW hypothesis plays a very useful role because it is crucial to encourage fact-finders to actively explore the possibility of finding narratives that lie beyond their existing background knowledge.

Interestingly, Josephson also provides an exhaustive list of mistakes that can be made, which may lead to incorrect conclusions:

1. The false abductive conclusion was overrated, for example, with respect to plausibility, simplicity, explanatory power, or internal consistency. This might be due to reasoning mistakes, mistaken background beliefs, or to missing evidence.
2. The true answer was underrated. Again, this might be due to reasoning mistakes, mistaken background beliefs, or to missing evidence.
3. The true answer was not considered. The hypothesis set was not broad enough. This might be because the true answer was outside the range of past experience.[70]
4. There was something wrong with the data so that it did not really need to be explained. The true answer was some species of the NOISE hypothesis, which was not considered, or if it was considered, it was underrated. This is a special case of (3) or (2).

---

[69] *Ibid.*, p. 1628.
[70] Hence, the need to always consider the NEW hypothesis.

5. The true answer was mistakenly ruled out. This is a species of (2).
6. The false abductive conclusion was mistakenly thought to explain the data (that is, it was a mistake to judge that, if it were true, it would explain the data). This is a species of (1).
7. The true answer was mistakenly thought not to explain important findings. This is a species of (2).

Regardless of whether they adhere to IBE or not, international fact-finders are well-advised to take note of these points as it may help them to critically review their own analysis.

Finally, it should be stressed that fact-finders should resist the urge to identify a 'best' explanation in the face of weak or insufficient evidence (or the fact-finder's understanding thereof). Indeed, sometimes the best is simply not good enough.[71] For example, if the best of the available explanations would have a probability of only 0.1, it may be better for the fact-finder to abstain from making any finding at all and to simply conclude that no conclusions are possible on the basis of the available evidence.

## 4.4. Three Building Blocks of Fact-Finding

Regardless of which fact-finding method is adopted, there are three key 'ingredients' in any form of fact-finding. Together, they determine the quality of the output of the fact-finding process. In the words of Susan Haack: "the degree to which evidence warrants a conclusion depends on three factors: (i) how strong the connection is between the evidence and the conclusion (supportiveness); (ii) how solid each of the elements of the evidence is, independent of the conclusion (independent security), and (iii) how much of the relevant evidence the evidence includes (comprehensiveness)".[72]

Each of these epistemic building blocks will be discussed in turn, albeit in the inverse order from Haack's. First, the question of 'how much' evidence is required for accurate fact-finding will be addressed. Second, an overview of the most relevant issues relating to the assessment of the credibility of evidence will be presented. Third, an analysis of what Haack describes as 'supportiveness' will be offered under the more generic heading of how to draw correct inferences from evidence. As will be seen,

---

[71] See Lipton, 2004, p. 56, see *supra* note 7.
[72] Susan Haack, "Warrant, Causation, and the Atomism of Evidence Law", in *Episteme*, vol. 5(3), 2008.

specific problems arise in relation to each of these building blocks in the context of international fact-finding.

### 4.4.1. Optimal Evidential Dataset

Both Bayesianism and IBE provide epistemic models for generating justified beliefs on the basis of the available evidence. Therefore, even if there are legal or practical obstacles to compiling a comprehensive evidential dataset, Bayesianism and IBE can still be applied and justify the fact-finder's beliefs on the basis of the available evidence. Whether or not it is appropriate to rely on findings made on such a basis is a different question, to which neither Bayesianism nor IBE offer an answer. For a response, we must thus look at other epistemic theories. However, before doing so, it is useful to consider two different conceptions of evidentiary weight.

### 4.4.1.1. Two Conceptions of Evidentiary Weight

Regardless of which conception about fact-finding one adheres to, it is important to introduce a critical distinction between two conceptions of weight that are associated with (collections of) evidence. The first weight concept is probably the one that is most familiar to lawyers and is concerned with the inferential power, or probative value, of an item (or collection of items) of evidence. Evidence is 'strong' in this sense when it makes a particular proposition a lot more probable or is an important factor in favouring a particular explanation. In theory, a single item of evidence can achieve this result.[73]

A finding that is supported by only one item of evidence may be entirely convincing and accurate. But whether it is epistemically appropriate to justify one's belief in the historical accuracy of a proposition on a single exhibit depends on whether other evidence exists that is relevant to the proposition. This is the second way in which weight plays a role, namely as an expression of the comprehensiveness of the evidential dataset upon which a factual finding is based. This second sense of weight can be re-

---

[73] When one adheres to IBE, the single item of evidence may allow for only one plausible explanation. For example, in a theft case where the stolen goods are found in possession of the accused a short moment after they were removed, the adjudicator may attach so much weight to this fact that no other evidence is required to convince the adjudicator of guilt. Comparable dynamics operate when one adheres to the probabilistic school of legal epistemology: if one item of evidence makes the ultimate probandum probable to the required degree, the adjudicator is justified in believing it.

traced to the work on probability by John Maynard Keynes.[74] According to Keynes,

> [a]s the relevant evidence at our disposal increases, the magnitude of the probability of the argument may decrease or increase, according as the new knowledge strengthens the unfavourable or the favourable evidence; but something seems to have increased in either case, – we have a more substantial basis upon which to rest our conclusion.[75]

If the evidential dataset is complete, the fact-finder should, in theory, have all the elements to identify the true explanation. If, on the other hand, the evidential dataset is incomplete, it is less likely that the fact-finder will consider all plausible explanations or determine the correct probability. This is because the plausibility and/or probability of a hypothesis may hinge on a single item of evidence. As long as not all the evidence has been analysed, it is difficult to rule out the possibility that an item of evidence that has yet to be discovered could defeat the conclusions reached on the basis of the available evidence. Therefore, the more comprehensive the evidential dataset, the more Keynesian weight it has and the greater the justification of the fact-finder in having a strong belief in a particular finding.

Nevertheless, there is no direct correlation between the weight of an evidential dataset and the accuracy of any findings that are based on it.[76] Indeed, a fact-finder may – by sheer coincidence – get everything right on the basis of very thin evidence, just like a fact-finder may draw the wrong conclusions from an optimal evidential dataset. Yet, in principle, the more information is available to the fact-finder, the more confidence she can have in her beliefs. This is because with each additional item of evidence, the level of uncertainty about the defeasibility of the hypothesis or proposition under consideration is reduced.[77]

---

[74]   John Maynard Keynes, *A Treatise on Probability*, MacMillan Press, 1921; Dale Nance, "The Weights of Evidence", in *Episteme*, vol. 5(3), 2008, p. 267.

[75]   Keynes, 1921, p. 71, *ibid.*

[76]   L. Jonathan Cohen, "Twelve Questions about Keynes's Concept of Weight", in *British Journal for the Philosophy of Science*, 1985, vol. 37, p. 264 Although, according to Michael and Adler "if we had all of the relevant knowledge, our knowledge would be adequate and we could assert the proposition to be true or false". 'Knowledge' is used here as synonymous for evidence. Jerome Michael, and Mortimer Jerome Adler, "The Trial of an Issue of Fact I", in *Columbia Law Review*, 1934, vol. 34, p. 1288.

[77]   In slightly outdated probabilistic terms:

It should be stressed, however, that increasing the number of items of evidence does not necessarily increase the likelihood that a certain proposition will be proven (or negated).[78] Indeed, the more evidence becomes available, the less certain an adjudicator may become about the facts of a case. More evidence may generate more potential plausible explanations, which may make it harder to identify which one warrants being believed. Accordingly, the fact-finder may become increasingly less confident about which way her factual judgment should go as more additional evidence becomes available. With only a slight touch of irony, one might say that from an epistemic point of view, the fact-finder's doubts are more accurate.

The concept of weight of the evidential dataset is thus of great importance and it is vital to understand its implications. First, it is crucial that the process of adding new evidence is not skewed. If there is bias in the collection process that systematically selects evidence that favours a particular proposition, the fact of augmenting the available evidence will have little epistemic merit.[79] Building an optimal evidentiary dataset is thus not a matter of simply increasing the volume of evidence. The additions must, to the maximum extent, fairly reflect all the available evidence. The optimal evidential dataset must thus consist of all the "information practically derivable from all extant sources that can reasonably be made available to and considered by the decision-maker".[80]

Second, evidence only adds weight when it is relevant[81] to the inquiry. However, this condition should be interpreted broadly in the sense

---

The worth of probability values always increases with successive proofs and disproofs, since it is a measure of the total amount of knowledge without any regard to the differential amounts of favorable and unfavorable knowledge. Michael and Adler, 1934, p. 1288, *supra* note 76.

[78] As Cohen observes,

[…] the quantity of evidence relevant to a certain argument is independent of the probability of the evidence given the conclusion. A great quantity of evidence might have been collected in a murder trial, with most of it tending to incriminate the accused, but it might also include and unshakable alibi. In such a case the evidence available might have relatively low probability, given the innocence of the accused, but it would have a heavy Keynesian weight.

See Cohen, 1985, p. 272, see *supra* note 76.

[79] Nance, 2008, p. 272, see *supra* note 74.

[80] Cohen, 1985, p. 265, see *supra* note 76.

[81] Relevance is used here in the epistemic sense:

that everything that is relevant to any of the different hypotheses that are being considered, as well as the ones that will ultimately be rejected, should be included. As long as the issue to which the evidence is relevant potentially helps the fact-finder to attain a more informed decision, adding it will increase the weight of the evidential dataset. Perhaps counter-intuitively, the probative value of an item of evidence is not determinative of the amount of weight it adds to the evidential dataset.[82] This raises the question of so-called cumulative evidence. Evidence is cumulative when it proves a proposition that is already proven by another item of evidence. If the available evidence has already given the adjudicator such a strong categorical belief in the proposition that she considers further evidence could not change that belief (that is, she thinks the new evidence cannot defeat the old), adding additional evidence will not advance the fact-finding process. Under such conditions, cumulative evidence may thus safely be left out of the evidential dataset.

Third, evidence will only add weight when it is deemed credible. Simply adding evidence without information about its credibility has little epistemic merit. This is because it is not possible to determine whether evidence has any inferential value when it is not determined to be credible. This raises an important question about Keynesian weight which is rarely addressed in this context, namely what to do with evidence about which essential information concerning its credibility is lacking. This question is particularly salient if the evidence in question is the only information that is available in relation to a particular proposition. The question is whether, in such circumstances, it is better to add evidence of uncertain credibility or to suppose that the evidence has no value and therefore to consider that there is a gap in the evidential dataset. Although it might be argued that it is better to keep evidence of uncertain credibility out of the evidential da-taset because it may confuse or mislead the fact-finder, in some cases evidence of indeterminate trustworthiness may still corroborate a proposition.

---

[...] a true proposition $R$ is non-conversationally relevant to an askable question $Q$ if and only if there is a proposition $A$ such that the truth of $R$ is or would be some reason, though not necessarily a complete or conclusive reason, for anyone's accepting or rejecting $A$ as an answer to $Q$.

See L. Jonathan Cohen, "Some Steps Towards a General Theory of Relevance", in *Synthese*, vol. 101, 1994, p. 178.

[82] This is because the degree of relevance varies, depending on the proposition for which it is used in support and on the order in which it is presented. See Cohen, 1985, p. 271, see *supra* note 76.

---

The better view is thus that even evidence of uncertain reliability should be part of the evidential dataset, as long as the necessary caveats are made.

Finally, it is crucial that if certain evidence is missing (that is, evidence known to exist but not obtainable), this information – that is, the existence of a gap in the evidential dataset – should be 'included' in the evidential dataset.[83] This is because weight is measured in function of the totality of theoretically relevant evidence, not in function of the total amount of actually obtainable evidence.[84] Therefore, even if the evidential dataset contains all the available evidence, it might still not have maximal (or even sufficient) Keynesian weight.[85] The great challenge for fact-finders is thus to know the full extent of the theoretically relevant evidence. Compiling a comprehensive evidential dataset thus requires carefully surveying of the theoretical totality of the evidence in light of all plausible hypotheses of the case. This is an iterative process: as more evidence is found, new hypotheses may become plausible and old ones may be abandoned. For every plausible hypothesis, efforts must be made to locate the available evidence and to identify which items are missing.

In some instances, predicting the theoretical existence of evidence will be relatively easy: for example, if someone was killed there must have been a corpse. However, in many other cases, predicting the existence of evidence is a lot more speculative. A lot depends on the details of the propositions under consideration. For example, if the proposition to be proved is that two persons entered into a common plan to do a certain deed, they may have reached this agreement in many different ways. There may or may not be a document containing the plan; the two persons may have met in person, or they may have negotiated through intermediaries; any meeting during which the plan was discussed may have been attended by other individuals (potential witnesses) or not; *et cetera*. If the fact-finder has no idea about how the plan came into existence, she cannot make a reasonable estimation about the theoretically total evidential dataset. If the correct explanation of how the plan came into being involves a scenario that the fact-finder does not even contemplate, she may not even realise that there is a gap in the evidential dataset. It is thus far from fanciful to imagine situations where fact-finders do not know about the

---

[83] Perhaps it is more accurate to speak of metadata about the evidential dataset in this regard.
[84] Cohen, 1985, p. 273, see *supra* note 76.
[85] *Ibid.*

existence of evidence, without being aware of their ignorance. These are the infamous "facts we don't know we don't know". This implies that the theoretical totality of evidence often remains indeterminate. Under such circumstances, it is difficult to make definitive evaluations of the Keynesian weight of the available evidence and, therefore, of the strength of any findings that are based on this evidence. It is important to always be alert to this possibility.

### 4.4.1.2.   When is the Evidential Dataset Optimal?

Armed with these insights about evidentiary weight, the next, more difficult, question of when the fact-finder has gathered enough evidence can be tackled. The answer to this question depends to a large extent on whether the objective of the investigation is to establish the truth. This may appear like a rhetorical question, as it seems hard to imagine that international investigations would ever not aspire to establish the truth. However, pragmatic considerations may often make this goal difficult to reach, which is why international fact-finders are sometimes recommended to rely on standards of proof.[86] Whilst this is an understandable suggestion, it should be clearly understood that when standards of proof are applied, especially when they are relatively low (for example, the balance of probabilities),[87] it is difficult to maintain that any findings made on this basis should be accepted as establishing the definitive truth. When, for example, a finding is made on the balance of probabilities, this means that there potentially is up to a 0.49 probability that the finding may be defeated. It may well be that this is sufficient for many practical purposes or that it is the best that can be attained. However, assuming that the goal of an investigation is to establish the truth, it is important to understand the implications with regard to the collection of evidence.

---

[86]   Indeed, this is one of the recommendations of a report sponsored by the Geneva Academy of International Humanitarian Law and Human Rights Law. See, Stephen Wilkinson, *Standards of Proof in International Humanitarian and Human Rights Fact-Finding and Inquiry Missions*, Geneva Academy of International Humanitarian Law and Human Rights Law, 2012; the report observes that:

> [a] failure to report behaviour (for example, as a result og applying an exaggeratedly demanding standard of proof or deliberately avoiding clear determinations), even for honourable reasons, may delegitimize the fact-finding process as well as the sponsoring institution and is an affront to victims of abuse.

[87]   Wilkinson concludes, "balance of probabilities [which is defined as "sufficient evidence – more evidence supports the finding than contradicts it (51%)"] is likely to be the most coherent standard of proof to apply in most circumstances", *ibid*.

The leading epistemic theory in this regard is Evidentialism. According to strict Evidentialist theory, forming beliefs about facts on the basis of insufficient evidence is an epistemic failure.[88] Indeed, from an Evidentialist point of view, it is better to withhold belief in a proposition than to accept it on the basis of an incomplete evidential dataset. This position is perhaps best epitomised by Clifford's Principle, which holds that "It is wrong always, everywhere, and for anyone to believe anything on insufficient evidence".[89] This raises the question of when the available amount of evidence is sufficient. Indeed, many Evidentialists, including Locke, Hume and Clifford, insist that one should adjust one's degree of belief in a proposition in proportion to the amount of evidence one possesses and that one should only *firmly* believe when one has sufficient evidence.[90] Hall and Johnson argue that, if one's goal is to believe only true propositions, then one has a duty to keep looking for more evidence until one is certain about the proposition.[91] Evidentialism thus links the *ethical* duty[92] to gather more evidence to the *subjective* certainty of the fact-finder. When this level cannot be reached and no further evidence can be found, the fact-finder should abstain from making any finding.

It thus becomes important to define when subjective certainty is reached. This brings us back to the question of which epistemological model the fact-finder relies upon. Whereas Bayesianism and IBE involve a synchronic duty – that is, the obligation to responsibly determine the

---

[88] Chignell, 2013, see *supra* note 4; Richard Feldman and Earl Conee, "Evidentialism", in *Philosophical Studies*, 1985, vol. 48, pp. 15–34.

[89] William Clifford, "The Ethics of Belief", in Tim Madigan (ed.), *The Ethics of Belief and Other Essays*, Prometheus, Amherst, MA, 1877 (reprinted 1999), pp. 70–96. Based on Clifford's own writings, this phrase was recently updated and reformulated as *Clifford's Other Principle*. "It is wrong always, everywhere, and for anyone to ignore evidence that is relevant to his beliefs, or to dismiss relevant evidence in a facile way". Peter Van Inwagen, "It is wrong, everywhere, always, and for anyone, to believe anything upon insufficient evidence", in Jeff Jordan and Daniel Howard-Snyder (eds.), *Faith, freedom and rationality*, Rowman and Littlefield, 1996, p. 145.

[90] Chignell, 2013, p. 20, see *supra* note 4, who defines 'sufficient' as "strong enough for the belief to count as knowledge if true".

[91] Richard Hall and Charles Johnson, "The Epistemic Duty to Seek More Evidence", in *American Philosophical Quarterly*, 1998, vol. 35, no. 2, p. 133: "For every proposition p about which S is not subjectively certain, S has a subjective epistemic duty to seek more evidence about p".

[92] Even if accurate fact-finding is the goal there can be no obligation of result, only an ethical duty of the fact-finder is to do everything possible to achieve that goal. Chignell, 2013, see *supra* note 4.

probability of an hypothesis or select the best explanation on the basis of the *available* evidence and background knowledge – Evidentialism imposes a diachronic obligation to continue searching for additional evidence until the fact-finder reaches a point where she believes that her findings are so strong that she is – subjectively – certain about them. For our present purposes, subjective certainty can be defined as the fact-finder's belief that based on the epistemic method she has applied, the findings are so strong that they cannot be defeated by further evidence. When applied to Bayesianism, Evidentialism would thus require both a finding of fact of high probability (for example, above 0.95) as well as a firm belief on the part of the fact-finder that this probability is not liable to decrease as a result of the presentation of further evidence. In terms of IBE, Evidentialism implies that the fact-finder would have to be confident that no new evidence could make another explanation better than the one currently being considered as superior. This requires that the fact-finder has seriously considered and rejected the NEW hypothesis, taking into consideration the possibility of new evidence.

In short, it is when Bayesianism or IBE are combined with Evidentialism that fact-finders have to worry about optimal Keynesian weight, for it is only an optimal evidential dataset that can justify a fact-finder's belief in the non-defeasibility of her findings. It will be noted, in this regard, that whether an evidential dataset has reached optimal Keynesian weight may be evaluated differently by different people. This is because the ability to imagine alternative explanations and making the corresponding predictions about the (theoretical) existence of evidence depends to a large extent on the prior knowledge and background beliefs of the fact-finder. This conforms with Evidentialist principles, which require only that the fact-finder attains *subjective* certainty. However, this once again demonstrates the limitations of our epistemic abilities; limitations that should be acknowledged and factored into any factual findings that are made.

### 4.4.1.3.  Particular Challenges for Investigations Concerning Core International Crimes

It is important to consider the implications of the theory summarised above for international fact-finding in the context of massive violations of human rights and humanitarian law. Indeed, the question must be asked whether it is realistic to apply Evidentialist precepts to the type of situations that are routinely the subject of international investigations. Even assuming that all theoretically relevant evidence is available, the cost of obtaining and processing it may be prohibitive. This chapter will not address the practical and political problems international investigators routinely face. Instead, attention is drawn to two particular evidentiary challenges that typically arise in the context of core international crimes. First, a lot of international cases involve multiple evidential datasets. Second, international investigators are frequently presented with compound facts, which involve vast amounts of evidence.

#### 4.4.1.3.1. Multiple Layers of Facts

Unlike investigations into 'ordinary' crimes, which usually centre around facts that are concentrated in time and space, international fact-finders routinely have to deal with several factual layers. First, there are historic and contextual circumstances, which are necessary for a proper understanding of the case or which may be a constitutive element in the definition of particular crimes (hereafter referred to as 'contextual elements'). Second, there are the underlying events and incidents for which a state or an individual is claimed to be responsible (hereafter referred to as 'principal events').[93] Finally, there are the facts which link states or persons to the principal events (hereafter referred to as 'responsibility indicators'). Which facts qualify as responsibility factors depends on the applicable principles of state responsibility or mode of criminal responsibility being applied by the international fact-finder.

#### 4.4.1.3.2. Contextual Elements

Contextual elements embrace a wide range of factual issues. For the present purposes, a distinction is made between the historical and sociopolitical context and the more specific contextual elements that must be established according to the legal definition of certain international crimes. With regard to the former, there is no denying that the social, political and historical context plays a very prominent role in international fact-finding. This is true even for relatively small cases, which involve fairly discrete and isolated events. International fact-finders cannot fulfil their role without obtaining an understanding of the historical contexts in which cases are situated. This idea was cogently expressed by former ICJ Judge Pieter Kooijmans, who pointed out in *Armed Activities*:

---

[93] In international criminal law parlance, those facts are often referred to as the 'crime base'.

> [A] court should make clear in its reasoning that it is fully aware of the wider context and the complexity of the issues involved. A judgment which is not seen as logical and fair in its historical, political and social dimensions runs the risk of being one compliance with which will be difficult for the parties.[94]

He therefore insisted that:

> A two-dimensional picture may correctly depict the object shown but it lacks depth and therefore does not reflect reality in full.[95]

The same is undoubtedly true for non-judicial fact-finders, perhaps even more so, as they cannot fall back on their institutional authority and depend only on the quality of their factual findings to inspire trust and compliance. Moreover, as will be discussed in more detail later, history and context are epistemically highly relevant.[96] This implies that historical context must be part of the evidentiary process. A mere 'awareness' of historical, political and social dimensions is insufficient.

The situation in relation to the contextual elements of international crimes presents similar challenges. However, fact-finders will be under even greater pressure, in this regard, as making a positive finding about the contextual elements is a prerequisite for any claim that a particular international crime has been committed. The contextual element for crimes against humanity, for example, is a requirement that every instance of the crime was committed as part of a widespread or systematic attack directed against a civilian population. According to Article 7(2)(a) of the Rome Statute, an attack against a civilian population means "a course of conduct involving multiple commission of acts referred to [...] against any civilian population, pursuant to or in furtherance of a State or organizational policy to commit such an attack". Thus, even in a case involving a single incident (for example, one massacre) the fact-finder must also investigate whether it took place as part of a widespread or systematic at-

---

[94] International Court of Justice, *Armed Activities on the Territory of the Congo (Democratic Republic of the Congo v. Uganda)*, Judgment of 19 December 2005, *ICJ Reports 2005*, p. 168 (http://www.legal-tools.org/doc/e31ae7/), Separate Opinion Judge Kooijmans, para. 4 (https://www.legal-tools.org/doc/5b8384/).

[95] *Ibid.*, para. 14.

[96] See Section 4.4.3. below, "Correct Inferences".

tack.[97] The requirement that an attack against a civilian population was widespread implies that the fact-finder must, in principle, collect evidence on several incidents, even though the inquiry may be focused on a single event. In the case of war crimes, findings must be entered about the nature of the armed conflict as being either international or non-international in character. As is well-known, this issue involves complex questions about the level of control exercised by third states over internal armed groups.[98]

It can easily be understood that if fact-finders want to comply with Evidentialist precepts in relation to contextual elements, the amount of evidence required will be enormous. The time and resources required for making even the most rudimentary findings about history and context can easily eclipse the evidentiary effort involved in determining the principal events and responsibility indicators. Yet, in many cases the function of an international inquiry is precisely to signal that serious international crimes are being committed. In such circumstances, the international fact-finder is faced with a difficult choice: either she can adjust her epistemic ambitions, thereby potentially jeopardising the credibility and epistemic integrity of her factual and legal findings; or she must accept the risk of not being able to come to any conclusion at all.

### 4.4.1.3.3. Principal Events

Regardless of the historical and socio-political context, international fact-finders are usually expected to make findings about particular principal events. Rather than a singular fact, such as the killing of a person or a car crash, principal events in international cases are usually compound facts; that is, events that consist of a pattern or amalgamation of a number of incidents of the same or similar nature. Principal events are usually captured under summary headings, for example, "the persecution of the Kurds", "the killing of 7,000 civilians at Srebrenica", *et cetera*; yet it is clear that these are not singular facts. Unless the deaths were the consequence of one action, for example, the explosion of a single bomb, the killing of 7,000 civilians by different perpetrators can hardly be seen as one single fact. Even if individual killings are interlinked because they

---

[97]  See *ICC Elements of Crimes*, Introduction to Article 7 (http://www.legal-tools.org/doc/3c0e2d/).

[98]  ICTY Appeals Chamber, *Prosecutor v. Duško Tadić (Appeal Judgement)*, 15 July 1999, IT-94-1-A, para. 137 (http://www.legal-tools.org/doc/8efc3a/); *Nicaragua*, para. 115 (http://www.legal-tools.org/doc/046698/).

result from a co-ordinated plan and operation, each killing stands alone as a unique event.

In principle, evidence needs to be presented for each single case of murder that is alleged to have taken place. This raises serious epistemic problems. First, if only evidence of one or two killings is available, fact-finders cannot enter a finding in relation to the deaths of all the other alleged victims. Second, gathering evidence on each and every killing would consume enormous amounts of time and resources. An alternative approach may be to focus on a number of specific cases as anecdotal evidence for a wider allegation. However, apart from supporting "where there is smoke there must be fire-arguments", this method cannot claim to support an actual factual finding about the principal event – including all its composites – as a whole.

#### 4.4.1.3.4. Responsibility Indicators

Lastly, international fact-finders will often be expected to link a state/regime or individual to the principal events. Findings in this regard usually require additional evidence about specific facts. Typical responsibility factors include authority, control, intent and knowledge. Grossly oversimplifying, the attribution of responsibility usually hinges on questions of "who knew what when" and "who said what to whom". The kind of evidence pertaining to such facts will usually be qualitatively different from the witnesses who give evidence about contextual elements and principal events.

International investigations into core international crimes will thus generally involve several layers of evidence. Each category of facts typically requires its own separate evidential dataset. Moreover, if compound facts are alleged, each constitutive incident will also require its own separate evidential dataset. Typically, the different evidential datasets are only tangentially related to each other and there usually is relatively little overlap in terms of items of evidence that appear in more than one dataset. This implies that international fact-finders must go through the Bayesian/IBE process separately for each evidential dataset. It further implies that the issue of optimal Keynesian weight arises for each evidential dataset separately.

### 4.4.2. Correct Credibility Assessments

Having an optimal evidential dataset is a precondition for accurate fact-finding, but it is not sufficient. Whatever fact-finding method is being used, if it is applied to false or otherwise incorrect evidence, it will yield inaccurate outcomes. Evidence can only serve as proof if it is safe for the fact-finder to rely on the information contained in it. It is essential, therefore, to weed out unreliable evidence from the evidential dataset.

Assessing the credibility of evidence is a core function for any fact-finder. If it is not done carefully, this severely jeopardises fact-finding accuracy. Yet, legal epistemology is surprisingly underdeveloped on the subject. A ready explanation for this theoretical underdevelopment is that each item of evidence is unique and it is thus difficult to come up with general rules on the subject. Moreover, it is commonly assumed that assessing credibility is something one does on the basis of common sense.[99] Even in a judicial context, the law by and large seems to entrust credibility assessments to the good sense of adjudicators, which in jurisdictions that have the jury are lay persons. Nevertheless, there are a number of important considerations that can be made from an epistemological point of view. There is also an important body of research in the field of cognitive psychology that is highly relevant. It is useful to consider these points at a theoretical level, because they provide important insights into the particular challenges facing international fact-finders. A first fundamental point in this regard is that the credibility of evidence is evaluated differently depending on the type of evidence concerned.

### 4.4.2.1. Categorising Evidence

Evidence comes in many shapes and forms and it may be categorised according to different criteria. For example, evidence may be categorised according to its proximity to the facts in issue. The two main categories here are 'direct' evidence versus 'indirect' or 'circumstantial' evidence.[100] Another way of categorising evidence is based on the nature of the evi-

---

[99] Daniel Blinka, "Why Modern Evidence Law Lacks Credibility", in *Buffalo Law Review*, 2010, vol. 58, p. 357.

[100] Paul Roberts and Adrian Zuckerman, *Criminal Evidence*, Oxford University Press, 2004, p. 182 *et seq.*:

Opportunity, motive, previous conduct, possession of incriminating articles, and physical proof of identity (including fingerprints and DNA samples) are all standard forms of circumstantial evidence [in the criminal context].

dence. Familiar categories in this respect are 'documentary evidence', 'physical' or 'real' evidence and 'testimonial' evidence. Within these broad categories, further categorisation is possible. For example, testimonial evidence may be categorised according to whether it is first-hand, derivative (hearsay) or opinion evidence.

For the purposes of discussing credibility, it is helpful to employ a more abstract categorisation of evidence, based on the inherent nature and characteristics of the information-carrier. This categorisation by and large reflects the two major sources of knowledge as traditionally recognised by epistemologists: perception and testimony.

Evidence is perceptual when the relevant information it contains can be ascertained by the fact-finder herself in person. As there is no one who stands between the fact-finder and the information contained in the evidence, perceptual evidence provides adjudicators with knowledge through their own powers of perception. By perceiving the evidence, the fact-finder (or the expert on her behalf) obtains the information it contains. As mainstream epistemology considers perception to be a warrant for justified belief,[101] assessing the evidentiary value of perceptual evidence is relatively straightforward.

Because perceptual evidence provides adjudicators with perceptual knowledge, it need not be tested for credibility.[102] All that is needed to give perceptual evidence probative value is relevant information about its origin. Two questions must be answered in this respect: First, whether the evidence is genuine and not tampered with and, second, who retrieved it from where and when? Indeed, often the real significance of perceptual evidence turns on the testimonial evidence that authenticates it and explains the context in which it was retrieved. This leads us to the other category of evidence: testimonial evidence.

Testimonial evidence is information about a fact or event that is transmitted to the fact-finder *via* another source. Testimonial evidence is thus an indirect source of information. It is information 'about something' rather than the 'something' itself. The source is a conduit for information

---

[101] See, for example, Robert Audi, *Epistemology – A Contemporary Introduction to the Theory of Knowledge*, 3rd ed., Routledge, 2011, p. 16 *et seq.*

[102] This is not to say that the fact-finder may not misinterpret the objective evidence, through perceptual defects, inattention or bias, for example. However, these are all problems with the fact-finder, not with the evidence itself.

about something that happened or existed externally to the source. The paradigmatic example of testimonial evidence is witness testimony. Testimony forms one of the main bases for any form of fact-finding.[103]

The line between perceptual and testimonial evidence is not always easy to draw. For example, when intangible physical evidence (for example, blood type) is involved, it will usually be necessary to rely on an expert to 'extract' the information from the perceptual evidence, that is, the blood sample. The blood type of a person cannot be 'seen' by everyone; this requires someone with the relevant medical knowledge and the right equipment. The fact that an expert is needed to determine the blood type does not change the perceptual nature of the blood sample. Nevertheless, strictly speaking, the expert's report is not perceptual evidence because what it contains is an account of what the expert observed when investigating the blood sample. In other words, the probative value of perceptual evidence is conditional upon the reliability of the conduit (in this case the expert) and it is important to test her competence and credibility, even though, ostensibly, one is dealing with perceptual evidence.

Another type of evidence that might be thought to straddle the two categories is written testimonial evidence. A written record of testimony is perceptual evidence in the sense that the words are perceived by the reader directly, but the content of the words, that is, the information asserted, is testimonial.[104] When faced with such 'dual' evidence it will be necessary to apply both the tests for perceptual and testimonial evidence, that is, verify the authenticity and chain of custody of the document and, to the extent possible, assess the trustworthiness of the author in relation to the assertions made in the text.

It will be clear from the above that testimonial evidence plays a pivotal role in fact-finding. This raises the question about what warrant we have for justifying our beliefs on the basis of testimonial evidence. This constitutes yet another delicate epistemic question.

---

[103] John Vickers, "The Problem of Induction", in Edward Zalta (ed.), *The Stanford Encyclopedia of Philosophy*, Fall 2010:

> Although testimony is not a form of induction, induction would be all but paralysed were it not nourished by testimony. Scientific inductions depend upon data transmitted and supported by testimony and even our everyday inductive inferences typically rest upon premises that come to us indirectly.

[104] Roberts and Zuckerman, 2004, p. 185, see *supra* note 100.

### 4.4.2.2. The Epistemology of Testimony

Testimony in its different manifestations is by far the most complex form of evidence with which fact-finders are routinely presented. Since fact-finding missions almost by definition take place after events have taken place, testimonial evidence is often the only source of information about those events. There are two main strands in general epistemology when it comes to testimony.[105] Both deal with the question of whether it is possible to acquire justified belief or knowledge on the basis of testimony and, if so, under what conditions. The so-called 'reductionists', starting with Hume, argue that testimony as such, that is, the simple fact that someone asserts a factual proposition, does not provide a warrant for believing what is asserted. They claim that, before testimony can be believed, the trustworthiness of the speaker must be established and each proposition contained in the testimony must be retraced to someone's perception, memory or inference. 'Non-reductionists', on the other hand, claim that unless contrary evidence is available, testimony is essentially reliable. The latter view is based on the assumption that in the large majority of instances in our daily lives, testimony *is* trustworthy and that it would be impossible for people to function if we did not, as a default rule, accept most testimony as true. Moreover, non-reductionists argue that it is impossible to assess the reliability of testimony without relying on knowledge (especially background information) that was itself obtained through other testimony, thereby creating a problem of infinite regress.

For the purpose of international fact-finding, it seems uncontroversial that the fact-finder should adopt a 'local reductionist' stance,[106] as the type of testimony that is relied upon as evidence by international fact-finders is qualitatively different from the type of day-to-day testimony with which non-reductionist theory is mostly concerned.[107]

According to Elizabeth Fricker, one of modern epistemology's main proponents of reductionism, the basic idea behind Reductionism is that

---

[105] The following short introduction draws mainly upon Jonathan Adler, "Epistemological Problems of Testimony", in Edward Zalta (ed.), *Stanford Encyclopedia of Philosophy* 2010.

[106] Contrary to so-called 'global reductionism', which requires that all testimonial evidence must be retraced to perception, memory or inference, local reductionism only requires that the testimony of a specific witness must be reliable and grounded in perception, memory or inference of that witness. For a criticism of this position, Axel Gelfert, "Indefensible Middle Ground for Local Reductionism about Testimony", in *Ratio*, 2009, vol. 22, p. 170.

[107] For example, giving of the time or confirming that the children were brought to school.

belief in a witness's trustworthiness needs to be empirically grounded. There is no general epistemic entitlement to trust any witness, just because one has no evidence of her untrustworthiness.[108] To believe what a speaker testifies without engaging in some assessment of the latter's trustworthiness is to believe blindly and uncritically.[109]

In essence, reductionism requires that fact-finders have "empirically grounded knowledge of the trustworthiness of the teller".[110] However, trustworthiness is not a blanket quality of witnesses. Reductionism does not require the hearer of testimony to form an opinion about whether everything that a particular witness might testify about would be trustworthy. It is necessary and sufficient that the hearer has a basis for believing that a specific assertion by the witness – the actual testimony – is trustworthy.[111] A witness may be trustworthy when asserting factual proposition A, but untrustworthy when asserting factual proposition B. As a matter of principle, the trustworthiness of each factual proposition contained in testimony must be assessed separately. Thus, it is possible to accept testimony from a witness with a general reputation of mendacity, so long as the witness is considered trustworthy with respect to the assertion of interest.

When assessing trustworthiness, adjudicators need to consider as much relevant information as possible about a particular witness.[112] The main purpose is to ascertain the reasons for which a witness makes a particular statement. According to Fricker,

> [t]he primary task for the hearer is to construct enough of a theory of the speaker, and relevant portions of her past and present environment, to explain her utterance: to render it comprehensible why she made that assertion on that occasion. Whether the speaker's assertion is to be trusted will, generally speaking, be fall-out from this theory which ex-

---

[108] Elizabeth Fricker, "Second-Hand Knowledge", in *Philosophy and Phenomenological Research*, vol. LXXIII (3), 2006, p. 599.

[109] Elizabeth Fricker, "Against Gullibility", in Bumal Matilal and Arudan Chakrabarti (eds.), *Knowing from Words*, Kluwer, 1994, pp. 125–161.

[110] Fricker, 2006, p. 615, see *supra* note 108.

[111] Fricker, 1994, p. 146, see *supra* note 109.

[112] Swift makes a similar argument in relation to hearsay evidence, which she argues should be excluded, because adjudicators do not have "sufficient information about foundation facts about the four testimonial qualities of perception, memory, sincerity and language use". Eleanor Swift, "A Foundation Fact Approach to Hearsay", in *California Law Review*, 1987, vol. 75, p. 1341.

plains why she made it; and it is difficult to see how sincerity and competence could be evaluated other than through the construction of such an explanation.[113]

This is reminiscent of IBE, which holds that testimony should be given credence on the basis of an abductive theory about what best explains why the witness is making certain assertions in the context of an investigation.[114] If the best explanation for why witness X declared *that p* is that she observed *p* first-hand and is testifying truthfully and accurately, then the adjudicator is entitled to base her beliefs fully on the testimony.[115]

### 4.4.2.3. Assessing Trustworthiness in the Context of International Investigations

Assessing the trustworthiness of testimony is without doubt one of the most complex and challenging task fact-finders face. If done properly, it is a labour-intensive exercise, which involves the systematic and meticulous evaluation of several 'credibility factors'. Two factors play a key role in the evaluation of trustworthiness, namely competence and credibility.[116] By assessing those factors, fact-finders aim to gain insights about the perceptual origin and quality of the information transmitted by the testimony of a witness as well as her motivation for providing it. The main difficulty in this regard is the availability of adequate information about the witness and the circumstances under which she has acquired perceptual or other knowledge about the event or fact about which she testifies.

This is one reason why, before evaluating a witness's trustworthiness, it is useful to first analyse the content of the testimony as such. The main factor that fact-finders consider in this regard is coherence.[117] Coherence is a substantive credibility factor, as it relates to the information contained in the testimony rather than to the witness per se. Nevertheless,

---

[113] Fricker, 1994, p. 149, see *supra* note 109.

[114] Allen and Pardo, 2008, see *supra* note 44.

[115] Jonathan Adler, "Testimony, Trust, Knowing", in *Journal of Philosophy*, 1994, p. 274.

[116] David Schum and Jon Morris, "Assessing the competence and credibility of human sources of intelligence evidence: contributions from law and probability", in *Law, Probability and Risk*, 2007, vol. 6, p. 254.

[117] As Uviller remarked, "coherence is probably the central cognitive mechanism for ascribing credence". Richard Uviller, "Credence, Character, and the Rules of Evidence: Seeing Through the Liar's Tale", in *Duke Law Journal*, 1993, vol. 42, p. 783.

coherence is often a key indicator about potential problems with a witness's trustworthiness.

Coherence operates at two levels. First, coherence can be assessed 'internally'. Is everything a witness says consistent? Are there internal contradictions or missing links in the narrative? As a high degree of coherence is the norm, finding that testimony is internally coherent will not significantly increase its trustworthiness.[118] However, if there are blatant and unexplained inconsistencies in a witness's story, this will put a negative light on her trustworthiness.

The second level at which coherence operates relates to how the facts/events asserted in testimony fit in with the general background beliefs of the fact-finder. If the witness asserts something that is physically or logically impossible, this will in all likelihood reduce the adjudicator's credence in the testimony. A lesser form is when testimony simply seems implausible. Something is implausible when it does not match with the expectations of the fact-finder. This aspect of coherence is complex and potentially dangerous, because fact-finders may be unfamiliar with the socio-cultural context from which witnesses speak and may therefore be missing the correct frame of reference to evaluate their testimony fairly.[119] This problem is very much related to the issue of cognitive consensus discussed later in relation to the problem of correct inferences.[120] Nevertheless, coherence in this sense can still serve as a warning signal.[121] When testimony appears outlandish, fact-finders must be extra careful in assessing the trustworthiness of the witness in regard to this particular aspect of the testimony. In this sense, incoherence serves as what Paul Thagard describes as a 'reflection-trigger': if testimony is incoherent with

---

[118] Peter Kosso, "Historical Evidence and Epistemic Justification: Thucydides as a Case Study", in *History and Theory*, vol. 32(1), 1993, p. 5: "coherence is only to be expected and is therefore not impressive verification".

[119] Uviller, 1993, p. 783, see *supra* note 117

[120] Section 4.4.3.3. on Cognitive Consensus.

[121] Combs argues that "[i]nconsistencies are probably the most prevalent testimonial problem at the international tribunals [ICTR, SC-SL and Special Panels for East Timor] and perhaps the most worrisome, for although inconsistencies are particularly easy to explain by means of 'innocent' explanations [...] they are also particularly likely to reflect perjury". Nancy Combs, *Fact-Finding Without Facts*, Cambridge University Press, 2011, p. 105.

prevailing background beliefs, the need to verify the witness' trustworthiness becomes extra important.[122]

### 4.4.2.3.1.  Competence

Competence concerns the question of whether a witness has the necessary credentials for giving the information she testifies about. When we are dealing with expert testimony, the question is whether the expert is indeed qualified in the relevant scientific discipline. However, when an eyewitness is simply reporting perceptual knowledge, the question is whether she actually made the observation to which she testifies. Before relying on testimony, the fact-finder will thus have to be convinced, first, that this witness was at the relevant place at the relevant time and, second, that the witness accurately observed, remembered and recounted the event. The first aspect can be referred to as material competence, whereas the second aspect may be called substantive competence. A few remarks about the second category are warranted because particular issues may arise in this regard in the context of international investigations.

In essence, substantive competence determines whether the witness has the required mental or intellectual ability to understand the events or facts she perceived and to provide an intelligible account about them.[123] In general, the intelligence, maturity, education and life experience of witnesses are important factors in evaluating substantive competence. Moreover, the witness must be able to communicate the relevant information in a manner that is intelligible for the fact-finder. This may be less than self-evident in an international context, as the vocabulary, concepts and references used by a witness may be to a large extent foreign to the fact-finder. In addition, the capacity to transfer information intelligibly may be influenced by the physical, psychological, intellectual and cultural faculties of the witness.

According to certain epistemologists, competence with respect to those subject matters about which common sense tells us that people are nearly always right can be assumed, unless there are indications to the contrary.[124] For example, barring particular situations, it would seem pointless to spend time investigating whether a witness is competent to

---

[122]  Thagard, 2006, see *supra* note 47.

[123]  Schum and Morris, 2007, p. 254, see *supra* note 116.

[124]  Fricker, 1994, p. 151, see *supra* note 109.

distinguish between day and night. For all other topics, there is no default presumption of competence. [125] In such cases, competence must be demonstrated by providing information about the relevant cognitive capacities of the witness and the circumstances in which the information was perceived by the witness.[126]

This raises an important first point about the assessment of competence of certain witnesses by international fact-finders. As Nancy Combs has demonstrated in her study about fact-finding by a number of international criminal tribunals, certain categories of witnesses who regularly appear in international criminal trials have great difficulty providing information about such basic issues as time, duration, distance and other numerical estimations in general.[127] It appears that witnesses from rural societies with low education levels are often incompetent to answer questions that would be considered as utterly basic in a Western domestic court.[128] Considering the importance of such information for fact-finding (including verification of trustworthiness), this may cause important problems.

In some cases, witnesses also have tremendous difficulty communicating whatever information they may have. This may be due to linguistic problems,[129] but it can also be a consequence of fundamental misunderstandings owing to a lack of shared background knowledge and a different socio-cultural belief system.[130] The resulting miscommunication may impede witnesses from transmitting their testimony, or fact-finders from receiving the information correctly. More psychological and socio-anthropological research may be needed to see whether it is possible to bridge the gaps between witnesses and fact-finders in this respect. Until that time, fact-finders are well-advised to question seriously whether they have fully understood the information that a witness actually tried to convey. This will often add a layer of uncertainty to the fact-finding process,

---

[125] *Ibid.*, p. 152.

[126] *Ibid.*, p. 151.

[127] Combs, 2011, p. 21 *et seq.*, see *supra* note 121.

[128] Combs gives examples of witnesses who are unable to provide even an approximate date of key events and of witnesses giving totally unrealistic estimations of distances between places of the duration of events.

[129] In some cases, the witness's language may lack the vocabulary necessary to accurately describe concepts; Combs, 2011, p. 76, see *supra* note 121.

[130] *Ibid.*, p. 56.

which requires delicate treatment, as the source of doubt or confusion may be the fact-finder herself, at least from the perspective of the witness and her community.

Even if communication and comprehension pose no particular problems, in many cases there is little or no external information to verify a witness's claims of competence. Most information about a witness's competence generally comes from the witness herself. Under those circumstances, determining competence to a large extent boils down to evaluating credibility, to which we will briefly turn our attention now.

### 4.4.2.3.2. Credibility

Witnesses may lack credibility for two reasons. First, they may mistakenly believe that they know something about an event. Second, witnesses may give testimony about facts that they know to be untrue or about which they have no knowledge.[131]

Witnesses may be mistaken about the facts they testify to for a wide variety of reasons. Most psychologists agree that testimony involves three stages. First is the moment where the information about an event is observed. Second, there is the retention phase, during which the information is stored in the witness' memory. Finally, there is the actual testimony, during which information is retrieved from memory and asserted to an audience. At all three stages, many things can go wrong. There is no space to discuss the many ways in which testimony can be mistaken,[132] but attention should be drawn to two factors, bias and time lapse, which are of particular importance in international investigations.

Witnesses are biased when they have certain expectations about an event they are perceiving, remembering or recounting. It should be stressed that bias is often unintentional. A technically competent witness may therefore in all sincerity believe and testify *that p* – even though she

---

[131] An important question in this regard is whether witnesses should testify only about facts/events that they perceived themselves or whether they should also be allowed to transmit information they have obtained from other persons. This is the infamous hearsay problem. Unfortunately, space does not permit to deal with this fundamental challenge here.

[132] For a brief overview of the main factors affecting perception, memory and retrieval, see Elizabeth Loftus, David Wolchover and Douglas Page, "Witness Testimony: Psychological investigative and evidential perspectives", in Anthony Heaton-Armstrong, Eric Shepherd, Gisli Gudjonsson and David Wolchover (eds.), *Witness Testimony: Psychological, Investigative and Evidential Perspectives*, Oxford University Press, 2006, pp. 7–22.

did not actually observe $p$ – because her observation or recollection is biased. As bias is often specific to particular ethnic or social groups, fact-finders may not be aware of its existence. Moreover, witnesses can have so-called 'temporary biases', which are expectations that are specific to a particular context. This type of bias is caused by an active expectation on the part of the witness that is linked to the situation she is in.[133] Another very powerful type of bias is the witness's self-interest. Concern about the consequences of making a certain observation may considerably affect the perception of reality, as well as the way in which it is recounted during testimony. Belief in the goodness and integrity of a particular person may also severely bias the way in which that person's behaviour is perceived by witnesses.

Another important factor influencing the trustworthiness of testimony is the amount of time that has passed since the event was observed. There is ample psychological evidence that people add, change or delete information from their memories under influence of a wide range of factors. Memory loss is greatest shortly after the observation was made.[134] The longer the time-lapse between perception and the giving of testimony, the greater the chance that what witnesses say does not reflect their original perception. In addition, as more time passes, witnesses may integrate the accounts of others into their memory. Frequently, such extraneous information about events gets mixed up with the witness's own perceptions. The witness may thus end up believing that she made certain observations – which, in reality, she did not.

Both time lapse and bias pose great problems for international fact-finders. International investigations often start several months or even years after the relevant events took place. The expected deterioration of memory will thus usually already have taken place. The witness's memory will generally also be contaminated by others' stories and cultural biases will have had their full effect as well. There is very little international fact-finders can do to remedy this problem. In some cases, the witnesses' memories will have deteriorated so much that their testimony no longer carries much evidential weight. This is an unfortunate but inescapable reality, which must be fully acknowledged by international fact-

---

[133] An extreme example of this form of bias is offered by hunters who mistakenly shoot a fellow hunter, believing that they are seeing the game they were looking for.

[134] Loftus, Wolchover and Page, 2006, p. 12, see *supra* note 132.

finders. Simply wishing the problem away or pretending that it does not affect the quality of testimony is epistemically irresponsible and undermines the confidence in the factual findings that are based upon such evidence.

As if it were not enough that it may be exceedingly hard to evaluate the competence of international witnesses to core international crimes, research suggests that it may be equally difficult for international investigators to detect when witnesses are trying to deceive them.

Deception can take many forms. The most obvious cases are when witnesses testify to something that they know to be wrong. However, it is also appropriate to speak of deception when witnesses state facts about which they have no information (that is, the witness is speculating about something that could be true or contrives something). And although it is perhaps not correct to qualify it as lying, withholding information known by the witness to be relevant is also a form of deception.

Deception is not usually a black or white matter. One of the key insights from deception-detection psychology is that people usually deceive for a specific reason. The motivation to deceive may thus be present in one situation (or in relation to a particular subject) but not in another. Sincerity and deception should thus probably be conceived of as aligned along a continuum, rather than as categorical concepts.[135] Moreover, mendacious witnesses rarely, if ever, make exclusively deceptive statements. It is therefore senseless to speak of witnesses as being truthful or deceptive *per se*, as if everything they say is either sincere or deceptive. This is sometimes called the Fundamental Attribution Error. Fact-finders often appear to have the tendency to overestimate the importance of the truthful/mendacious 'character' of witnesses and underestimate the context in which particular statements are made.[136] Even if a witness is caught lying about a particular issue or at a particular time, this does not necessarily imply that she is therefore insincere on other matters or at a different moment in time (and *vice versa*). Similarly, when a witness gives two incompatible accounts about an event, one must necessarily be deceptive. However, this does not mean that the other one cannot be sincere and if the

---

[135] Bella DePaulo, Brian Malone, James Lindsay, Laura Muhlenbruck, Kelly Charlton, and Harris Cooper, "Cues to Deception", in *Psychological Bulletin*, 2003, vol. 129, p. 106.

[136] Maureen O'Sullivan, "The fundamental attribution error in detecting deception: The-boy-who-cried-wolf-effect", in *Personality and Social Psychology Bulletin*, 2003, vol. 29, pp. 1316–1327.

fact-finder is able to determine which version is trustworthy (which will normally also involve finding an explanation as to why the witness lied on a different occasion), there is no impediment to relying on it.

Detecting deception is a challenging under any circumstances, but cognitive psychology suggests that the challenge is even greater at the international level. First, cultural and linguistic barriers often stand in the way of a meaningful examination dialogue.[137] Witnesses often seem to consider that the wrong questions are being asked or that they have to explain many things before being able to answer a question intelligibly. This is sometimes perceived as unwillingness on the part of the witness to answer 'straightforward' questions.[138] Whether or not this is the case is often extremely difficult to determine for international fact-finders.

To make matters even more difficult, international fact-finders, contrary to what they themselves may believe,[139] cannot rely on their impressions about the trustworthiness of witnesses by observing their demeanour. There is no space to give even a succinct overview of the cognitive psychology of deception detection, which is a discipline in its own right. One of the key lessons from extensive psychological research is that we are much less able to ascertain deception on this basis than is generally assumed.[140] Second, research clearly demonstrates that deception cues are to

---

[137] In an examination dialogue,

> [...] the questioner seeks information on whether the answerer has the information. [...] On this view, examination dialogue seeks information about information. It seeks information about whether another party has that information. So it is not just seeking the information".

See Walton, 2008, p. 211, see *supra* note 58.

[138] Cultural sensitivities and taboos may have a similar effect.

[139] The ICC Appeals Chamber, for example, stated that:

> The importance of in-court testimony is that the witness giving evidence under oath does so under the observation and general oversight of the Chamber. The Chamber hears the evidence directly from the witness and is able to observe his or her demeanour and composure [...].

See ICC-01/05-01/08-1386, para. 76 (https://www.legal-tools.org/doc/7b62af/).

[140] DePaulo *et al.*, 2003, p. 75, see *supra* note 135, referring to Zuckerman *et al.* (1981): "no one behavior or set of behaviours would ever be found that always occurs when people are lying and never occurs any other time". See also Aldert Vrij, "Why professionals fail to catch liars and how they can improve", in *Legal and Criminological Psychology*, 2004, vol. 9, no. 2, p. 159; S. Porter, and L. ten Brinke, "The truth about lies: What works in detecting high-stakes deception?", in *Legal and Criminological Psychology*, 2010, vol. 15, p. 57.

a large extent culturally determined.[141] In plain words, liars behave differently depending on their cultural origin. Cues that may be helpful in detecting deception in Caucasians may not be prevalent among Africans or Asians. This implies that international fact-finders cannot rely on their personal understanding of 'how liars behave' (a policy that is discredited even within one cultural group) when they must assess witnesses from other regions of the world.[142] Finally and crucially, in many international investigations witnesses testify *via* an interpreter, which completely annihilates any useful verbal or linguistic cues.[143]

The lessons from all this are that, first, credibility assessments should to the maximum extent be individualised for each proposition contained in the testimony. Fact-finders should thus not stop at forming a general impression about the truthful/mendacious character of a witness. Instead, testimony should be dissected into separate (clusters of) propositions, which should each be scrutinised for truthfulness. Second, categorical credibility evaluations are generally unachievable. All we can do is to ask whether, on balance, the available evidence about a witness favours or disfavours her competence in providing this testimony, keeping in mind the number of relevant questions that remain unanswered; and whether the available evidence favours or disfavours trustworthiness, again keeping in

---

[141] Charles Bond, Adnan Omar, Mahmoud Adnan and Richard Bonser, "Lie Detection Across Cultures", in *Journal of nonverbal behavior*, 1990, vol. 14, no. 3, p. 189. For example, several studies have shown that Africans generally make less eye contact, smile more, display greater variation in pitch and pause more in their speech. See Robin Engel and Richard Johnson, "Toward a better understanding of racial and ethnic disparities in search and seizure rates", in *Journal of Criminal Justice*, vol. 34, 2006, p. 612.

[142] This applies in the first place to non-verbal cues. In addition, there is extensive research demonstrating that emotion-recognition is to a considerable degree culture-specific, see Hillary Elfenbein, and Nalini Ambady, "On the Universality and Cultural Specificity of Emotion Recognition: A Meta-Analysis", in *Psychological Bulletin*, 2002, vol. 128, p. 203. As many deception-cues are driven by emotions (for example, the fear of being found out, embarrassment about lying, *et cetera*), the fact that it is more difficult for observers to recognise emotions cross-culturally makes it even less likely that deception will be accurately detected.

[143] Moreover, recent research suggests that deception detection is influenced by whether a statement is made in the speaker's mother tongue or second language and whether that language is the hearer's mother tongue or not. See Keens Hiu Wan Cheng and Roderic Broadhurst, "Detection of Deception: The Effects of First and Second Language on Lie Detection Ability", in *Psychiatry, Psychology and Law*, 2005, vol. 12, no. 1, p. 107.

---

mind the number of questions that remain unanswered.[144] This does not necessarily give us a firm grip on trustworthiness. Even after thorough testing, testimony therefore remains essentially defeasible evidence.[145]

### 4.4.3. Correct Inferences

At its most basic level, fact-finding is about assessing relationships between evidence and hypotheses. Unless there is direct and trustworthy evidence for every relevant part of the event under consideration, fact-finders have to rely on inferences to come to a complete picture about what happened. Inferences from evidence are by definition based on generalisations.[146] Indeed, the very process of inferring hypotheses from evidence is inductive in nature.[147] According to Bex *et al.*, explanations come in a causal story structure.[148] Essentially, this means that a story is a (mostly) chronological sequence of causally linked events. Evaluating an explanation therefore involves analysing two levels of generalisations: first, the internal causal links within the story must conform to the background knowledge of the adjudicator (so-called '*causal* generalisations'); second, the story must be linked to the available evidence by plausible *evidential* generalisations.[149] Moreover, credibility assessments depend in large part on background knowledge and other forms of generalisations. Generalisations are thus essential to every aspect of fact-finding, regardless of which method is being applied. Accordingly, it is crucial that the limitations and pitfalls of reasoning on the basis of generalisations are understood.

### 4.4.3.1. Categories of Generalisations

To evaluate the validity of an inference it is necessary to analyse the soundness of the generalisation upon which it relies. It is extremely rare

---

[144] Schum and Morris, 2007, p. 264, see *supra* note 116. They go on to propose a Bayesian algorithm for calculating a subjective probability assessment for how credible the testimony is.

[145] Walton, 2008, p. 32, see *supra* note 58.

[146] Terence Anderson, David Schum, William Twining, *Analysis of Evidence*, Cambridge University Press, 2005, p. 263; Terence Anderson, "Generalisations and Evidential Reasoning", in Philip Dawid, William Twining and Mimi Vasilaki (eds.), *Evidence, Inference and Enquiry*, Oxford University Press, 2011, pp. 225–244.

[147] Anderson *et al.*, 2005, p. 82, see *supra* note 146.

[148] Bex *et al.*, 2006, p. 2, see *supra* note 58.

[149] *Ibid.*, p. 3.

for the applicable generalisations to be universally true. Moreover, there is the even more basic problem that the wrong generalisation may be applied. To unpack these problems about generalisations, it is useful to briefly analyse the different types of generalisations that are at play in the legal context.

Generalisations can be case-specific or generic. Case-specific generalisations refer to information about the immediate context with which the fact-finder is concerned. An example of a case-specific generalisation might be: "On most Sundays X goes to church" or "Regime Y does not tolerate opposition and systematically incarcerates those who oppose it".

Generic generalisations, often referred to as background knowledge, relate to the state of the world more generally and may be based on the personal experience of the fact-finder, scientific evidence, common/general knowledge (as inculcated by education, media, popular fiction, *et cetera*), and synthetic-intuitive generalisations (that is, commonly held beliefs, based on intuitions about how the world around us functions).[150]

Examples of the background generalisations might be:

a) the population of New York City consists of many different ethnic groups ('general knowledge');
b) weaker states do not attack much stronger states ('synthetic-intuitive generalisation');
c) chemical agent type X will kill all fish stock in a river if released in Y quantity ('scientific generalisation'); and
d) during the rainy season in geographical region A, visibility is often reduced because of haze ('personal experience')

Generalisations vary in strength and degree of universality. Strong generalisations are posited with certainty, whereas weak generalisations are expressed in a tentative manner. For example, "elephants weigh more than mice" would be a strong and universal generalisation. This generalisation is true under all circumstances. It therefore provides maximum inferential support. "On average, women live longer than men" is not a very strong generalisation, because it is qualified. It is also not universal because not every woman will grow older than every man.

---

[150] Anderson *et al.*, 2005, see *supra* note 146; Deirdre Dwyer, *The Judicial Assessment of Expert Evidence*, Cambridge University Press, 2008.

Strong universal generalisations are rare in the context of human rights fact-finding. Most generalisations can, at best, provide inferential support for a possibility. Any finding reached on such basis will therefore remain defeasible, even if the evidence remains the same.

### 4.4.3.2.    Reference-Class Problem

One problem with generalisations is knowing which one to apply.[151] Sometimes, several generalisations may appear to be relevant to interpreting an item of evidence or evaluating a hypothesis. Different generalisations may lead to different inferences. Scientific generalisations offer a good example of this. For example,

> Generalisation $A^1$: 'People who have been exposed to chemical agent X have between 5%-10% higher chance of developing heart disease than people who have not been exposed this agent'

If founded on reliable empirical research, this generalisation applies universally, but it will hardly prove a damage claim from a person who purports to have developed heart disease as a consequence of exposure to the chemical agent. However, when the reference class becomes more specific, the numbers sometimes change dramatically. For example, specialised research may show that:

> Generalisation $A^2$: 'Male persons over 50 who have been exposed to chemical agent X on a daily basis through inhaling (as opposed to skin contact), for more than 2 years, have a 65% higher chance of developing heart disease than an average male person.'

The numbers have gone up, but the generalisation has become much narrower and can be applied only in very particular cases. This example illustrates a central danger of generalisations: if the wrong reference class is used, the applied generalisation may lead to incorrect conclusions, *even though the generalisation itself is accurate.*

The problem is that fact-finders are not always aware of all relevant generalisations and reference classes. If the fact-finder is only aware of the wrong generalisation, there is no reason why she should have any hesitation in applying it. For a lay fact-finder, highly specialised studies that

---

[151] Paul Roberts, "From theory into practice: introducing the reference class problem", in *International Journal of Evidence and Proof*, 1997, vol. 11, p. 243.

underpin more specific generalisations may not be readily available or indeed comprehensible. This is why fact-finders frequently refer to the specialised knowledge of experts when dealing with technical or scientific matters. Without such specialised advice, it may be exceedingly difficult for fact-finders to know the correct reference class.

The reference class problem is not limited to scientific generalisations. It also applies to generalisations that are not expressed in statistical terms. For example, "People carrying a loaded weapon are more likely to commit violent crime" may not be the correct reference class for a police officer. Moreover, reference classes are often socially and culturally relative. To give a trite example, "most people usually have dinner between six and seven o'clock" may be broadly accurate in the Netherlands, but it is probably not applicable in Spain.

As a general matter, almost any generalisation can be challenged in two ways: the generalisation can be refined, by adding new conditions for its application, or it can be shown that an exception to the generalisation applies. Anderson *et al.* suggest the following protocol for assessing the plausibility and validity of generalisations in the context of a legal argument, formulated as a list of questions to be asked about the applicable generalisation:[152]

- Is the generalisation precise?
- Is the generalisation ambiguous?
- Is the generalisation stated as a universal or is it qualified by a hedge as to its frequency?
- Is the generalisation empirical (capable of being shown to be true or false)?
- Is the generalisation expressed in value laden or emotive terms?
- What is the empirical basis for the generalisation: scientific evidence/general experience/common sense/speculation/prejudice?
- Can the truth of the generalisation be reasonably disputed?
- Can a rival generalisation that points in the opposite direction/supports a different conclusion be articulated?

---

[152] Anderson *et al.*, 2005, p. 279, see *supra* note 146 [slightly adapted].

- Does the least vulnerable/most plausible version of the generalisation offer strong/moderate/weak/negligible support to the inference?

As this list of questions clearly demonstrates, generalisations must be handled with extreme care. It is therefore crucial for fact-finders to understand the foundations as well as the limitations of the generalisations they rely on. To summarise, the following can go wrong:

- First, the generalisation may be factually wrong (for example, the generalisation is informed by bias).

- Second, the wrong generalisation may be applied (for example, the wrong reference-class may be applied).

- Third, no relevant and/or reliable generalisation may be known to the adjudicator.

- Fourth, the correct generalisation may be applied wrongly (for example, logical mistakes or wrong application of exceptions).

- Fifth, the generalisation may be too hedged to provide a warrant for definite conclusions.

Considering the central role of generalisations in fact-finding, it is useful to pause a little longer on the subject to consider the specific challenges international fact-finders face when applying generalisations.

### 4.4.3.3. Cognitive Consensus

It is trite to state that fact-finders usually do not have exhaustive knowledge of all the factual issues that can potentially come up during an investigation. Yet, it is generally assumed that international fact-finders are capable of making accurate findings about the facts of most cases. This assumption implies that we are generally confident that international fact-finders are able to apply the right generalisations in a correct manner. This confidence is in part based on the further assumption that when a fact-finder is faced with a factual issue she is totally unfamiliar with, she will get assistance from someone who is knowledgeable about that topic. The standard example of such assistance is scientific evidence. When the fact-finder is faced with a question of scientific proof, she will usually invoke the help of an expert. In essence, through experts, fact-finders are able to draw upon specific generalisations of specialised areas of knowledge that would otherwise be unavailable to them.

However, leaving specialised knowledge aside, one might reasonably ask what gives us such confidence that fact-finders can always discern the appropriate generalisations for making correct inferences from evidence about international events. As was seen above, apart from case-specific generalisations that have been established by evidence, and scientific generalisations that have been tested empirically, most generalisations have no precise or verified empirical basis. Instead, they are based on what is alternatively described as 'common knowledge', 'general experience', 'background knowledge', 'shared beliefs', or 'society's stock of knowledge'.[153] What renders these generalisations legitimate is the assumption that they are commonly shared by all members of society. In other words, regardless of whether they are empirically accurate, they are accepted as such by society and it is therefore acceptable for the fact-finder to rely upon them. This idea has been advanced by Cohen, who spoke about there being a 'cognitive consensus' within a given society, which makes it legitimate for fact-finders to draw upon 'common knowledge' in order to make inferences about facts and evidence.[154]

Although this may be a defensible proposition for investigations at the national level, involving local events,[155] it is much more problematic at the international level. This is because many generalisations are culture-specific, in the sense that what is generally accepted as true in one society may be greeted with great scepticism in another.[156] For example, in certain communities particular persons (for example, witch doctors or priests) are believed to be able to wield great, supernatural, powers. This proposition, which is of great importance to the members of the relevant community, may be derided by others who deny the existence of anything supernatural. Whether one sees an argument in this for cultural relativism or not, it is clearly problematic to speak of an 'international cognitive consensus' in cases that involve such elements of disagreement.

If Cohen is right, there is no such thing as an 'international stock of knowledge' and therefore no 'international cognitive consensus' to legiti-

---

[153] Anderson *et al.*, 2005, p. 269, see *supra* note 146.

[154] Cohen, 1977, see *supra* note 6.

[155] But see Anderson *et al.*, 2005, p. 274, see *supra* note 146, for a summary of the different criticisms that have been voiced of this suggestion.

[156] As was noted, even within one culture generalisations may differ, depending upon factors such as the social group, age, gender and education of the one who believes the generalisation.

mate fact-finding by international fact-finders. Even if the international fact-finder in all honesty tries to understand the evidence before her, there is a very real chance that she will apply a different generalisation from what a person steeped in local culture and society would accept as correct. This conclusion is deeply troubling, because it potentially invalidates the epistemic legitimacy of international investigations, at least in the eyes of the local population. While this may not necessarily affect the accuracy of the findings – after all, the locally prevalent generalisation may be empirically wrong – it may make acceptance of the findings by the local population more difficult.

It is important not to overstate the problem. As with case-specific generalisations, culture-specific generalisations can be argued about and may be verifiable on the basis of evidence. With the appropriate information and explanation, international fact-finders may well be able to internalise previously unfamiliar generalisations and draw upon them when making inferences. In other words, there is nothing inherently mystical about many culturally-specific generalisations and it is possible to explain their inferential implications to international fact-finders. Nevertheless, it may well be that in certain cases the international fact-finder will simply refuse to accept the validity of particular 'local' generalisations (for example, supernatural powers of witch doctors), which may make it difficult to connect with the 'reality' of the people who are most concerned with the findings. In such situations the fact-finder is faced with a dilemma: either to 'impose' her own view of reality and risk alienating the very persons about whose lives the findings are made, or to accept the local views despite her own conviction that they are incorrect or implausible.

Nevertheless, there are generalisations which are arguably universal. Most scientific generalisations, for example, apply regardless of the cultural context of the case.[157] Moreover, some generalisations may simply be uncontroversial or can be objectively verified. For example, the generalisation that 'the United States systematically blocks every proposed resolution in the Security Council that would impose sanctions upon Israel'

---

[157] This is not to say that any generalisation that claims to be 'scientific' must therefore be accepted at face value. Indeed, scientific evidence has received a lot of academic attention recently, precisely because it is not so universally valid and reliable as might be popularly thought. As with any form of evidence, scientific evidence requires careful interpretation and explanation. See, *e.g.*, Dwyer, 2008, see *supra* note 150; Mike Redmayne, *Expert Evidence and Criminal Justice*, Oxford University Press, 2001.

is not very controversial. It suffices to check the voting record of the United States over a statistically relevant period to demonstrate that it is historically correct.[158] Even when it is not possible to prove the accuracy of a generalisation, the possibility cannot be excluded that there may be generalisations that are so widely accepted that they can be considered as the shared beliefs of the international community as a whole. However, demonstrating the existence of such 'international cognitive consensus' may be even harder than proving the existence of *opinio juris* in relation to a rule of customary international law. In fact, it is not immediately obvious which criteria should be applied for determining when a particular *opinio factis* has matured into a part of the international cognitive consensus. As with *opinio juris*, there is thus a risk that fact-finders will take their personal background beliefs for universally accepted truths. Indeed, it is quite possible that those who formulate the supposed 'international cognitive consensus' may well be influenced by their own moral aspirations about how they would like the world to be.

The above arguments have not been raised to cast doubt on the possibility of legitimate international fact-finding. This chapter does not defend a cultural relativist position. Rather, it is argued that the lack of universal acceptance of many generalisations is a genuine problem and that conscious efforts must be made to mitigate the specific difficulties of cross-cultural fact-finding. A solid understanding of the local context seems to be a key requirement in this regard. Paradoxically, the general requirement that international fact-finders must be impartial and independent naturally leads towards the selection of fact-finders who have no special link with the communities implicated in the cases they are investigating. This understandable reflex has the effect, however, that fact-finders will lack any profound knowledge and understanding about the local circumstances. It may be a good idea, therefore, to include someone from the region among the fact-finders because, as Combs observed "although [local fact-finders] too can be fooled, [they] at least bring to the table a basic understanding of the culture that renders them more willing – and more able – to reject implausible cultural invocations".[159] Another

---

[158] But see Amit Pundik, "Statistical evidence and individual litigants: a reconsideration of Wasserman's argument from autonomy", in *International Journal of Evidence and Proof*, 2008, vol. 12, p. 303. The past does not predetermine the future and the US can at any time decide to change its policy of decades.

[159] Combs, 2011, p. 369, see *supra* note 121.

possible measure that may be available to international fact-finders is to obtain expert advice on the relevant anthropological and historical background.

However, no procedural measure can fully remedy the lack of universal cognitive consensus. It is therefore important that international fact-finders are constantly alert to this issue and recognise the limitations of their personal 'stock of common knowledge'. In addition, it is important to be transparent about the degree of inferential support that the applied generalisations afford. To the extent that the applied generalisations lack strength or universality, this should be clearly indicated and the fact-finder should explain how this may affect the reliability of the findings.

## 4.5. Conclusion

With this necessarily condensed *tour d'horizon* of the main epistemic aspects of fact-finding, the reader should now have the basic elements for a structural analysis of the strengths and weaknesses of current fact-finding practices. As stated at the outset, the main purpose for providing this short overview is twofold. On the one hand, it is hoped that being more aware of basic epistemic principles will allow international fact-finders to go about their business in a more conscious and deliberate manner. Although it is not suggested that fact-finding in the international context can ever be hard science, it is important to recognise that it is possible to rationalise the process much more than is commonly thought. Once this is accepted, it also becomes possible for fact-finders to be much more explicit and transparent about how they arrive at their findings.

The second purpose behind this chapter is to alert fact-finders, as well as those who rely on their findings, to the many challenges and intrinsic limitations involved in international investigations. As has hopefully become clear, international fact-finders face considerable epistemic limitations at almost every level of the fact-finding process. Each of these limitations increases the degree of uncertainty and corresponding risk of error.

First, the ability to collect and process very large volumes of evidence is inherently limited. International fact-finders frequently operate under considerable time pressure and usually have less than adequate resources. As time and/or resources run out, fact-finders have to be selective in the collection of evidence. The resulting evidential dataset will thus usually be far below the Keynesian optimal weight that Evidentialism prescribes. As was seen, if the evidential dataset is incomplete, any conclusions that are based on it are inherently defeasible.

Second, the ability of international fact-finders to evaluate the trustworthiness of the available evidence is severely limited. Even if only part of the above observations were valid, the prospects for international fact-finders to make assess the trustworthiness of testimonial evidence look very bleak indeed. This can create a serious epistemic dilemma, as reductionism requires that fact-finders have affirmative reasons for believing that witnesses are trustworthy. However, if international fact-finders are not habitually in a position to form a knowledgeable opinion about a witness's trustworthiness, they have no basis on which to rely on the testimony as proof. In such cases, the epistemically prudent thing to do would be to ignore the testimony.[160] However, the consequences of such a rigorous position may be too drastic and devastating for international investigations, as they often depend heavily on testimonial evidence. The pragmatic solution, which consists of relying on testimony despite having insufficient information about its trustworthiness, while defensible on the basis of necessity (that is, the need to avoid epistemic paralysis), should acknowledge the extent to which this weakens the reliability of any findings that are based on such evidence.

Third, the all-pervading limitations of the fact-finders' background knowledge and lack of universal cognitive consensus deeply affect the inferential process at every level, including the generation of hypotheses, the assessment of coherence, trustworthiness and plausibility of the evidence, as well as the evaluation of probabilistic relations and/or relative explanatory power of different hypotheses. This issue touches upon the inherent limitations of all fact-finders' epistemic abilities. Indeed, uncertainty is caused as much by the lack of good evidence as by the fact-finders' own epistemic limitations. This is perhaps the most testing problem of them all, because it requires fact-finders to – openly – acknowledge their limited epistemic competence.

Unfortunately, international fact-finders are systematically under considerable pressure caused by the expectation that they will be able – in a short amount of time and with minimal resources – to come up with ac-

---

[160] Combs goes so far as to state that "[t]he testimonial deficiencies plaguing the international tribunals impair their fact-finding competence to such a degree as to render international criminal proceedings a form of show trial", Combs, 2011, p. 172, see *supra* note 121.

curate and reliable findings. No one has much use for ambivalent and highly tentative findings. Yet, this is sometimes all that may be reasonably achievable on the basis of the available evidence and the fact-finder's cognitive limitations. From an epistemic viewpoint, international fact-finders are well-advised to resist the natural urge to present unequivocal and categorical findings. Instead, it is arguably better to strive for greater precision and transparency about the doubts and uncertainties that are left after the investigation has been closed. Crucially, the reasons for those doubts and uncertainties should be identified. This implies that the fact-finder should give details about the limitations of her investigation and how this has affected the Keynesian weight of her evidential dataset. Any glaring gaps in the evidence should be identified and the potential impact on the findings acknowledged. The same openness should be displayed with regard to the questions that may still remain concerning the trustworthiness of the evidence. Finally, the report should be transparent about its potential inferential weaknesses and clearly expose potentially problematic generalisations that were relied upon.

The ultimate aim of so much epistemic self-chastisement is to give the receiver of the report a clear and candid picture of the justification for each of the findings, as well as the potential grounds of defeasibility. Rather than relying on artificial decision tools like standards of proof or other forms of classification of factual findings, this chapter advocates for a much more nuanced and transparent description of the strengths and weaknesses of every finding. By providing more information about the information, the receiver of the report is given maximal insight in the justifications for each of the findings and is thereby able to critically evaluate them.

Ultimately, in fact-finding, as in other human endeavours aimed at truth and understanding, the classical paradox still holds: often knowing how little one actually knows is the only path to wisdom. Accordingly, if we really want to improve the quality of international fact-finding, we are well-advised to take Socrates' lesson to heart and show some humility about our epistemic abilities. Insisting on better quality in international fact-finding may thus result in fewer and more tentative findings. This may not be a very satisfying prospect from several points of view, but if it is quality and not quantity we are after, it is the only way forward.

# 5

---

# Quality Control in
# Truth and Reconciliation Processes

## LIU Daqun[*]

## 5.1. Introduction

This chapter seeks to address how the quality of post-conflict truth and reconciliation processes can be enhanced. It has become a widespread expectation that there will be a truth and reconciliation commission ('TRC') as part of transitions from armed conflict to peace, or from military to civilian rule.

In the past decade or two, along with the establishment of the various international criminal jurisdictions, truth-seeking commissions and other investigative bodies have flourished as a means of post-conflict justice, to investigate social problems, inquire into episodes of human rights violation, address international crimes, and provide recommendations for the rebuilding of peace and justice. Truth-seeking has become an important post-conflict objective in its own right, while criminal trials occur more often in conflicts where one side emerges victorious. Truth-seeking commissions have gained momentum alongside the global trend of democratisation after the Cold War, starting in Latin America by addressing the issue of disappearances of persons[1]; continuing in Africa, for national reconciliation in South Africa; and finally in Asia, to deal with the serious violations of human rights following conflicts.[2] Up until now, more than

---

[*] **LIU Daqun** is a Judge of the International Residual Mechanism for Criminal Tribunals in The Hague. The views expressed in this chapter do not necessarily reflect the views of any organisation or governments.

[1] In 1982, Bolivia set up the National Commission of Inquiry into Disappearances, which is believed to be the first truth commission after the Cold War. See Priscilla B. Hayner, *Unspeakable Truths: Confronting State Terror and Atrocity*, Routledge, New York, 2001, p. 14.

[2] In March 2005, the Presidents of Indonesian and East Timor signed an agreement to set up the Commission on Truth and Friendship ('CTF') to investigate human rights violations when East Timor voted for independence and to seek reconciliation between the two states.

50 States in the world have utilised such methods to resolve social problems and to address human rights violations.

Such TRCs come with both political and material costs, since they engage victims and their traumatisation, expose violations, and generate incriminations. They may also destabilise a society and inadvertently undermine the rebuilding of peace. It is therefore essential that TRCs operate as professionally as possible. Increasing the awareness of quality control in the creation and operation of TRCs is of fundamental importance.

The theme of this anthology is relevant at every stage of the work of TRCs, including the definition of the mandate, selection of the composition of the commission, definition of standards of proof, creation of standard procedures of interview, management of resources, engagement of individuals and the public, and the production of the final report. This chapter seeks to address how the quality of post-conflict truth and reconciliation processes can be enhanced.

## 5.2. Definition and Mandate

Various investigative commissions may have different names, mandates, compositions, procedures, ways of engaging the public, and forms of final reports. In one international document defining fact-finding – the *Declaration on Fact-finding by the United Nations in the Field of the Maintenance of International Peace and Security* – it is stated that fact-finding under the auspices of the United Nations is:

> [a]ny activity designed to obtain detailed knowledge of the relevant facts of any dispute or situation which the competent United Nations organs need in order to exercise effectively their functions in relation to the maintenance of international peace and security.[3]

This definition assumes the perspective of the United Nations and may not be detailed and specific enough to cover all situations. One scholar rightly recapitulates the term as follows:

---

See Priyambudi Sulistiyanto, "Politics of Justice and Reconciliation in Post-Suharto Indonesia", in *Journal of Contemporary Asia*, 2007, vol. 3, no. 1.

[3]    See Declaration on Fact-finding by the United Nations in the Field of the Maintenance of International Peace and Security, General Assembly Resolution, UN Doc. A/RES/46/59, 9 December 1991; United Nations Office of Legal Affairs, *Handbook on the Peaceful Settlement of Disputes between States*, UN Doc. OLA/COD/2394, 1992, pp. 24–33.

[…] international fact-finding is deemed to refer to predomi-
nately ad hoc investigative mechanisms tasked with ascertaining relevant facts and information relating to a situation
of human right or humanitarian concern, by means of which
it is determined whether or not the relevant international
normative framework has been violated by states or non-
state actors.[4]

From the above-mentioned definition, there might be some common
characteristics for many of these investigative bodies. Firstly, they focus
on past events instead of the present situation. Secondly, they may investigate a situation or a specific case, that is, look into a pattern of abuse
over a set period of time. For instance, the National Commission for the
Disappearance of Persons ('CONADEP') in Argentina was set up in 1983
by the President to uncover incidents of human rights violations that occurred from 1976 when the military took power, to 1983 when power returned to civilian rule.[5] They may also look into a specific case. For example, Israel established the Commission of Inquiry into the Events at the
Refugee Camps in Beirut in 1982 to investigate massacres of Palestinians
from 16 to 18 September 1982.[6] Thirdly, the investigating bodies are temporary or *ad hoc* mechanisms that complete their work by submitting a
report to the relevant authority, which documents its findings and proposes recommendations for further action. Normally, the investigating bodies
will function for one or two years or less. A few of them will last for five
or six years. Some of them simply fade out because of political or financial predicaments. Fourthly, those investigating bodies are either officially
authorised, or empowered by governments or international authorities,
such as the United Nations. The advantage of governmental involvement
or official backing is that this could help with the provision of resources
and facilitate the inquiry. Strictly speaking, however, investigative bodies

---

4   Stephen Wilkinson, "Standards of Proof in International Humanitarian and Human Rights
    Fact-Finding and Inquiry Missions", *Geneva Academy of International Humanitarian Law
    and Human Rights*, 2014.

5   Priscilla B. Hayner, "Fifth Truth Commission – 1974 to 1994: A Comparative Study", in
    *Human Rights Quarterly*, 1994, vol. 16, no. 4, p. 558; see "Nunca Más: Informe de la
    Comisión Nacional sobre la Desaparición de Personas (Never Again: Report of the Na-
    tional Commission on the Disappearance of Persons)", 20 September 1984 (https://www.
    legal-tools.org/doc/0d9b6d/).

6   "Final Report of the Israeli Commission of Inquiry into the Events at the Refugee Camps
    in Beirut", in *Journal of Palestine Studies*, 1983, vol. 12, no. 3 ('Kahan Report'). The Re-
    port may also be found in *International Legal Materials*, 1983, vol. 22, no. 3.

are normally non-governmental organisations, especially in situations where the government is involved as a party to the conflict. Fifthly, the formation of the body may be a part of a broader peace or reconciliation agreement by all the parties in the conflicts, or it may be the product of actions by the executive branch of government. The latter situation has the benefit of enabling swift action to address human rights abuses.

In any case, fact-finding has become a very practical and useful way to settle disputes, both domestically and internationally. As the concept note of the 2013 LI Haopei Seminar noted, there are academic efforts underway to map and analyse the best practices of the plethora of international fact-finding commissions, which look into allegations of serious violations of international criminal law, humanitarian or human rights law. Regardless of what an investigative body is called, be it a 'truth and reconciliation commission' or an entity by any another name, its main purpose is to reach national reconciliation by inquiring into past crimes and addressing the violation of human rights. Some TRCs have listed specific tasks. For instance, the National Truth and Reconciliation Commission ('CNVR') in Chile was established in April 1990 with four primary tasks: to establish a complete picture of human rights violations that occurred between 11 September 1973 and 11 March 1990; to gather evidence that allows victims to be identified; to estimate reparations; and to recommend legal and administrative measures to prevent a repetition of similar abuse in the future.[7]

An investigative body should have a clear mandate for conducting the investigations in conformity with four principles: fairness, credibility, impartiality and independence. The mandate serves as a legal template for the investigation. Firstly, it specifies what the commission is to investigate, both in terms of the types of crimes and the time frame open to its investigation. Secondly, the mandate outlines how its work is to be conducted. Thirdly, in the interest of fairness, it sets up the protocol for conducting interviews, taking statements and admitting documents with clearly defined standards of proof. Fourthly, it provides its members with sufficient tools to do the work. Any means and practice to discover relevant information should be encouraged. The investigative body should be able to conduct its work independently and without outside interference. The

---

[7]    Mark Ensalaco, *Chile under Pinochet: Recovering the Truth*, University of Pennsylvania Press, 2000.

mandate should clearly state whether or not the commission has the power to issue subpoena to compel witnesses or evidence to appear before it; whether it has search and seizure powers; and whether the recommendation of the commission is mandatory. Fifthly, it establishes the rules of procedure and guidelines for handling evidence. The mandate may specify whether or not the testimony will provide the basis for subsequent prosecution and reparations. The power to name names or grant amnesty is another issue to be considered in drafting the mandate. As a matter of fact, a TRC is not a judicial body that can make binding judgement or grant amnesty, but it could make recommendations for the judicial bodies to take necessary action if these are deemed necessary. To date, the South African TRC is the only one to have had the power to grant blank amnesty, but others may have power to recommend that the government grant amnesty to individuals. In the case of East Timor, in order to help low-level offenders reintegrate into the society, the Commission for Reception, Truth and Reconciliation has granted amnesty to some individuals who committed minor crimes.[8]

## 5.3. Establishment and Composition

There are various ways to form a commission. If a TRC is set up immediately following a conflict, its establishment is likely to be regulated in the peace agreement signed by the parties to the conflict. Members of the commission are selected to represent the different sides of the conflict in equal numbers and a neutral person is selected by all sides. It is similar to the formation of an arbitration panel. In the case of Chile, the National Truth and Reconciliation Commission was composed of an even number of representatives from the left and the right.[9] In Ecuador, the Truth and Justice Commission was made up of seven members; one was appointed by the Ministry of Government and Police, three were named by international human rights NGOs and three were from domestic NGOs.[10]

In most situations, the TRC is established by the government of the territorial state, which also appoints the commissioners. It is the most effective way to form a commission as it ensures the full support of the

---

[8]  Wendy Lambourne, "Unfinished business: Justice and Reconciliation in East Timor", in *Centre for Peace and Conflict Studies of the University of Sydney's Peace Writes Newsletter*, December 2004.

[9]  Ensalaco, 2000, *supra* note 7.

[10]  Hayner, 2001, p. 14, *supra* note 1.

government, thereby implying that resources and facilities are more easily provided. However, the disadvantage is that the commission's impartiality and fairness might be put in doubt, particularly if the government has been involved in the investigated crimes. In some cases, we have seen that different branches of the government have been involved in the formation of the commission. In 1999, the Presidential Truth Commission on Suspicious Deaths in South Korea was established. The Commission is made up of 15 members, eight recommended by the Nations Assembly, four appointed by the President, and three nominated by the Chief Justice of the Supreme Court.[11]

In some countries, the legislative body is able to establish an investigative body. The parliamentary basis of a commission will probably increase its legitimacy if the legislative body votes for well-respected members of society, such as religious leaders, artists, academics, and dignitaries from civil society and the legal community. Selecting commissioners who are broadly representative in ethnicity, religion, political views and gender, will provide the investigation with greater influence and legitimacy.

In some instances, an international organisation, such as the UN Security Council or the Office of the UN High Commissioner for Human Rights, is also able to establish an investigative body. Normally, the investigative body is established by adopting a resolution. There have been significant developments in international practice in this area since the Commission of Experts for the former Yugoslavia established, pursuant to the UN Security Council Resolution 780 (1992),an institution which served as a model for later developments.12 On 18 September 2004, the Security Council adopted Resolution 1564 to establish the International Commission of Inquiry on Darfur, Sudan. Based on its report, the situation of Darfur was referred to the International Criminal Court by the Security Council.13

Foreign commissioners may also be considered as they are not involved in the conflicts and are generally regarded as impartial. However,

---

[11] Kuk Cho, "The Transitional Justice in Korea: Legally Coping with Past Wrongs After Democratization", in *Pacific Rim Law and Policy Journal*, 2007, vol. 16, no. 3.

[12] UN Security Council, Resolution 780 (1992), UN Doc. S/RES/780 (1992), 8 October 1992 (https://www.legal-tools.org/doc/5887b3/).

[13] UN Security Council, Resolution 1564 (2004), UN Doc. S/RES/1564 (2004), 18 September 2004 (http://www.legal-tools.org/doc/1ba770/).

the drawback of this approach is that they often do not fully understand the culture and specific situation of the country. Additionally, some sovereignty-inclined persons may not like foreigners to conduct these investigations and may consider the investigations to be a private affair that should be kept purely within domestic jurisdiction. For example, in the case of El Salvador, the polarised society and extensive involvement of both sides in the conflict, led to the United Nations playing a significant role in selecting commissioners for the Truth Commission. All the commissioners were foreign dignitaries and were named by the Secretary-General of the United Nations. This turned out to be one of the reasons why the report of the commission was criticised by all sides in El Salvador.[14]

No matter how a commission is formed, commissioners need to have the vision to shape policy and resolve ambiguities in the commission's mandate. They will set the tone of the investigation, both publicly and within the commission. A team of experts (including legal, medical, psychological and forensic experts) is needed to assist the commissioners. Effective management is important. Staff must be skilled and interviewers need to be sensitive and have the necessary techniques and experience to conduct the investigation. The TRC may also set up sub-committees to carry out different tasks. In the case of South Africa, the TRC set up three committees: the Human Rights Violation Committee conducted investigations; the Amnesty Committee reviewed applications from perpetrators of human rights violations; and the Reparation and Rehabilitation Committee produced recommendations related to measures for healing.[15]

## 5.4. Standards of Proof

In the field of international criminal justice, no indictment can be issued, and no trial can take place, without credible evidence. The prosecutors of the international tribunals are required to prove these crimes by a legal standard of proof 'beyond a reasonable doubt'. Justice Robert H. Jackson,

---

[14] Paul Seils, "The Limits of Truth Commissions in the Search for Justice: An Analysis of the Truth Commission of El Salvador and Guatemala and Their Effect in Achieving Post-Conflict Justice", in M. Cherif Bassiouni (ed.), *Post-Conflict Justice*, Brill, 2002.

[15] Dorothy C. Shea, *The South African Truth Commission: The Politics of Reconciliation* Chapman and Ball, 2000; see Truth and Reconciliation Commission of South Africa, "Report Summary and Guide to Contents", 21 March 2003 (https://www.legal-tools.org/doc/586a97/). The seven volumes of the Report are available on the Legal Tools Database.

the principal American prosecutor at the Nuremberg trials and an Associate Justice of the United States Supreme Court, famously stated that the aim of the prosecutors at Nuremberg was to "establish incredible events by credible evidence".[16] He wished to set before the court the relevant evidence "with such authenticity and in such detail that there can be no responsible denial of these crimes in the future and no tradition of martyrdom of the Nazi leaders can arise among informed people".[17]

Although the standard to deal with evidence outside of criminal justice may not be as high as in international criminal tribunals; the fact remains that truth and reconciliation commissions, like international tribunals, flourish or fail depending on their ability to acquire evidence. Therefore some quality control for the admission of evidence must be in place. This is not only necessary to enhance the credibility of the truth commission itself, but also to secure the credibility of the evidence for possible use in future litigation before domestic or international criminal courts. According to their purpose and mandate, different TRCs may establish their own objective standards of proof. If the standard of proof is set too high, it will be very difficult to reach a conclusion. For instance, Geneva Call, a Geneva based non-governmental organisation, conducted a verification mission to the Philippines to assess whether an armed group had complied with the agreement reached for non-use of anti-personnel landmines. The mission adopted the standard of 'beyond reasonable doubt'. As a result, it was unable to reach a definite conclusion.[18] On the other hand, if the standard is set too low, the TRC may be burdened with piles of complaints, inviting ill-founded allegations.

In the ICTY and ICTR, the standard of proof varies at different stages of proceedings. At the investigation stage, the Prosecutor shall evaluate the information received or obtained and decide whether there is a "sufficient basis" to proceed.[19] If the Prosecutor would like to submit the indictment to a judge for confirmation, he shall be satisfied that there is

---

[16] Robert H. Jackson, "Justice Jackson's Report to the President on Atrocities and War Crimes", 7 June 1945 (https://www.legal-tools.org/doc/6504ed/).

[17] Quoted by Associate Justice of US Supreme Court Stephen G. Greyer, "Crimes Against Humanity Nuremberg, 1946", in *New York University Law Review*, 1996, vol. 71, no. 5.

[18] Wilkinson, *supra* note 4.

[19] Article 18(1) of the Statute of the International Tribunal for the Former Yugoslavia, see UN Security Council, Resolution 827 (1993), UN Doc. S/RES/827 (1993), 25 May 1993 (http://www.legal-tools.org/doc/dc079b/).

"sufficient evidence to provide reasonable grounds" for believing that a suspect has committed a crime within the jurisdiction of the Tribunal.[20] For a judge to confirm the indictment, he shall be satisfied that a *prima facie* case exists.[21] When the Prosecutor concludes his case, the defence may submit a motion of 'no case to answer'. The test to be applied at this stage is "whether there is evidence (if accepted) upon which a reasonable [trier] of fact could be satisfied beyond reasonable doubt of the guilt of the accused on the particular charge in question, not whether an accused's guilt has been established beyond reasonable doubt",[22] which is the standard for the conviction after the hearing of all evidence by a trial chamber.

It is submitted that the first two standards lend themselves best as standards of proof in the work of TRCs. If the TRC seeks to include a particular accusation in its report or submit the case to the competent authority for prosecution, it may, to be on the safe side, adopt the *prima facie* standard after affording the accused the opportunity to defend him- or herself.

## 5.5. Standard Procedure of Interview

Interviews of victims and witnesses are the most important work of TRCs. This will consume most of the time, resources, manpower and energy of the commission. The CAVR of East Timor found through its fact-finding that between 84,000 and 183,000 people might have been killed. It also found 18,600 cases of disappearance and killings, 8,500 cases of torture, and thousands of cases of rape and sexual assault.[23] The interviews should follow a standard procedure. The victims may submit their statements before, during or after the interview. The statement should be relevant and reliable, accurate, and have probative value. Normally, the interview is not conducted in public and if necessary, pseudo names or other protective measures may be applied. It should be conducted on a voluntary basis, unless the commission issues a subpoena to compel a victim to tell his or

---

[20] Rule 47(2) of the Rules of Procedure and Evidence of the ICTY, IT/32/Rev. 45, 8 December 2010 (http://www.legal-tools.org/doc/30df50/).

[21] Article 19(1) of the Statute of the International Tribunal for the Former Yugoslavia, 25 May 1993 (http://www.legal-tools.org/doc/b4f63b/).

[22] Para. 9 of the ICTY, *Prosecutor v. Radovan Karadžić*, Judgement, Appeals Chamber, IT-95-5/18-AR98*bis*.1, 11 July 2013 (https://www.legal-tools.org/doc/84001b/).

[23] "Chega! (Enough!): The Report of the Commission for Reception, Truth and Reconciliation Timor Leste", 2005.

her story. It is not uncommon that witnesses to such horrific crimes remain traumatised by their experience and are unwilling or unable to assist the investigators. They should therefore have access to medical and psychological counselling before or after the interview. They should also be informed of whether the evidence they give might be used in any future judicial proceedings. Collecting and preserving evidence in a manner consistent with trial standards could result in stronger contributions for future prosecutions. If that is the case, the evidence and document data preservation should be conducted in such a way as to be admissible in court proceedings.

## 5.6. Resources

A TRC needs adequate resources in order to carry out its mandate, which is crucial to conducting meaningful inquiries. For instance, resources are needed to recruit staff with the necessary skills and experience to conduct the investigations; and for all related field trips, interviews and trainings. Resources are also needed to assemble experts, provide the physical infrastructure for the commission's database and archives, and to draft the final report.

The majority of the resources of TRCs tend to come from governments. As post-conflict governments face many rebuilding needs, the TRCs must compete for funds. In some cases, donations from outside the country are also accepted. The amount of outside donations largely depends on the performance of the TRC. In the case of Haiti, foreign donors withdrew their support because of the malfunctioning of the Haitian National Commission for Truth and Justice ('CNVJ').[24] The commission should also have resources in place in anticipation of the secondary trauma that some staff may suffer as a result of hearing many harrowing stories.

In most cases, a lack of resources is the main reason why a TRC stops its work. On 18 March 1998, the newly elected President of the Philippines established the Presidential Committee on Human Rights to investigate human rights violations under the former President Ferdinand Marcos' rule. After functioning for only less than one year, the attempt

---

[24] Audrey R. Chapman and Patrick Ball, "The Truth of Truth Commission: Comparative Lessons from Haiti, South Africa, and Guatemala", in *Human Rights Quarterly*, 2001, vol. 23, no. 1.

was aborted, because of a shortage of staff and a lack of financial support from the Government, which was under the influence of the military.[25]

## 5.7. Engaging Individuals and the Public

It is essential to engage both individuals and the public in the process of truth seeking. Holding public hearings may be the most effective way to involve the whole society in the process, and to guarantee the transparency of the proceedings. Much information will be a matter of public record and awareness. Victims should have the choice of giving testimony in public or in camera. In order to void the risk of providing an open venue for unsubstantiated accusations, the public hearing should offer the opportunity for the defence to express his or her view and perspective of the events.

In some countries, traditional methods of community justice were employed.[26] In East Timor, the TRC ('CAVR') encouraged every village or community to conduct community-wide ceremonies, in which low-level offenders would confess their wrongdoings before the victims. In return for admitting their wrongdoings, offering reparations and committing to community service, and/or making a public apology, these offenders would receive amnesty. The whole community would take part in such ceremonies, so as to reach community reconciliation. The CAVR conducted 216 community reconciliation events involving 1,403 perpetrators.[27]

In Rwanda, in order to seek truth, justice and reconciliation, Gacaca courts were set up to reconstruct what happened during the genocide, in order to expedite legal proceedings, facilitate the reconciliation of all Rwandans and build unity. Strictly speaking, Gacaca was a semi-judicial body. It involved both plaintiffs and witnesses in interactive court proceedings against alleged criminals who took part in the genocide. The defendants were brought to trial, which were held in public, where survivors and the victims' families could confront the accused. The accused had the option to confess to their crimes or maintain their innocence. The villagers

---

[25] Priscilla B. Hayner, "Commissioning the Truth: Further Research Questions", in *Third World Quarterly*, 1996, vol. 17, no. 1.

[26] "What is Traditional Justice?", International Centre for Transitional Justice (available on its web site).

[27] Lambourne, 2004, *supra* note 8.

were involved in the process to a great extent, and could speak either for or against the defendant.[28]

The commission should not overlook outreach efforts to educate the population about the investigation. Broadcasting on television or radio can provide a way to engage the entire country in the truth-seeking process. Otherwise, the public has only press releases and news leaks by which to be informed of the process.

## 5.8. Final Report

Public hearings cannot substitute for a final report that serves as a lasting reminder of past crimes and as an outline of further measures for redress and prevention. The TRC's final report is its legacy and is therefore one of the most crucial elements in the whole process. Normally, the final report will include, but is not limited to, the purpose and mandate of the commission, the composition of the commission, a description of its work and, finally, its findings and conclusions.

The key objective of the final report is to lay out, after investigation, what the truth of the event investigated is, and who was found to be responsible for the crimes. Depending on the TRC's mandate, the final report may name names or turn over to the government or judicial bodies the names of those suspected of culpability.[29] The TRC may grant amnesty to low-level offenders who committed minor crimes, but there should never be any blanket amnesty, especially for high-level offenders who committed serious crimes, in particular international crimes such as genocide, serious war crimes and crimes against humanity.[30]

The report should also outline recommendations for the further redress and prevention of such crimes. One purpose of investigating past human rights abuses is to prevent them from occurring in the future. As such, the recommendation should concentrate on the establishment of the rule of law. The recommendation may propose possible prosecution, institutional reform, reparation, vetting and the joining of a specific international human rights convention. The final report might also recommend

---

[28] Eric Stover and Harvey Weinstein, *My Neighbor, My Enemy: Justice and Community in the Aftermath of Mass Atrocity*, Cambridge University Press, Cambridge, 2004.

[29] Jason S. Abrams and Priscilla B. Hayner, "Documenting, Acknowledging and Publishing the Truth", in Bassiouni (ed.), 2002, *supra* note 14.

[30] Principle 1.8, in M. Cherif Bassiouni *et al.*, *The Chicago Principles on Post-Conflict Justice*, International Human Rights Law Institute, 2007, pp. 35, 36.

some symbolic or cultural measures, for example, waging a campaign to educate the public, setting up a memorial monument, or fixing a national memorial day.[31]

In Chile, the final report of the National Truth and Reconciliation Commission ('CNVR') criticised the military and police for common use of illegal imprisonment, torture and summary execution during the Pinochet rule. The report also called for the concept of 'national security', which had justified the military actions, to be revisited. The report stressed the importance of education and advocated human rights training for the military and police. The report recommended reducing the scope of military jurisdiction and reforming the Code of Military Justice, and also requested the Chilean Government to sign a few international human rights conventions. With regards to reparation, about 5,000 people (the families of those killed and disappeared) received some USD 5,000 per year. Other reparations include educational scholarships, free health services, and exemption from military service.

## 5.9. Conclusion

The quality control of international fact-finding is a very important element in ensuring the success and efficiency of truth and reconciliation commissions. As the concept note of the 2013 LI Haopei Seminar highlighted, increasing the awareness and understanding of quality control may enhance the value of international fact-finding to the victims of serious violations of international law and, indirectly, to the taxpayers who make it possible for governments to create and support such commissions. Active quality control can also contribute to the real independence of those involved in TRCs, and their assessment of allegations of serious violations of international criminal, humanitarian or human rights law. Focusing on the theme of quality control can help stakeholders to create better TRCs that contribute more effectively to truth-telling and reconciliation.

This theme is neutral and technocratic – it directs the analysis towards the professionalisation of the fact-finding done by TRCs. Such fact-finding falls outside the ambits of criminal justice (which is not the subject of this book) and international human rights fact-finding (described,

---

[31] Mark Ensalaco, "Truth Commissions for Chile and El Salvador: A Report and Assessment", in *Human Rights Quarterly*, 1994, vol. 16, no. 4.

*inter alia*, in Chapter 3 by Professor Martin Scheinin). But with the growing expectation that truth and reconciliation processes will follow armed conflict or military rule, whether there are criminal investigations and trials or not, the professionalisation of such fact-work becomes increasingly important. Moreover, some TRCs entail political risks that can destabilise peace as much as criminal trials can. It is therefore essential that the quality of TRCs be enhanced to the extent possible. The collection of accumulated knowledge, insights and advice contained in this anthology should assist that process.

# 6

---

# Quality Control and the Mandate of International Fact-Finding

## FAN Yuwen[*]

## 6.1. Introduction

When it comes to international fact-finding in the field of human rights, every detail matters. The sub-topics of each chapter of this book are therefore important and need to be properly discussed. Of all the issues, the mandate of an international fact-finding commission marks the very beginning of its life. It is key to the authority, legitimacy and efficacy of international fact-finding commissions. As Confucius once said,

> [i]f something has to be put first, it is, perhaps, the rectification of names [...] When names are not correct, what is said will not sound reasonable; when what is said does not sound reasonable, affairs will not culminate in success; when affairs do not culminate in success, rites and music will not flourish; when rites and music do not flourish, punishments will not fit the crimes; when punishments do not fit the crimes, the common people will not know where to put hand and foot [...].[1]

These words from the most eminent thinker, politician and philosopher in ancient China could also serve today as a precise interpretation for the far-reaching significance of mandates on the cycle of international fact-finding commssions. In Confucius' view, the first thing to do should be to correct names. Here, "names" is meant to denote a role or function or authority proper to one's title, which has the same meaning as 'man-

---

[*] **FAN Yuwen** (LL.B., China University of Political Science and Law, and M.A. in International Law from Graduate School, Chinese Academy of Social Sciences) obtained her doctoral degree in international law from Peking University, China. During her studies, she participated in the Human Rights Master Programme of Peking University Law School and Lund University Raoul Wallenberg Institute of Human Rights and Humanitarian Law.

[1] Confucius, *The Analects*, translated with an introduction by D.C. LAU, Penguin, 1979, p. 118.

date' in the English context today. Confucius' logic predicts that if mandates (names) are not correct, the work of a fact-finding commission, such as its report on a problematic situation (what is said) will not be reasonable and acceptable to the public. Specifically, it will not achieve its purpose to disclose facts, reduce tensions, and facilitate an agreement in the debated issues (*id est*, its affairs will not culminate in success). Nor will the commission succeed in creating a culture respectful of human rights (rites and music will not flourish) or serve for international law and justice (punishments will not fit the crimes and the common people will not know "where to put hand and foot"). To translate into modern English, "[t]he success of a fact-finding mission will very much depend on the mandate".[2]

The importance of the mandate of international fact-finding commissions has been widely acknowledged and attention has been drawn to this topic. The mandate determines the scope of international fact-finding missions, as well as their political authority. It has been noted, "[d]epending on the extent to which the truth commission accomplishes what the mandate has instructed it to do, it could be considered a success".[3] A proper mandate for an international fact-finding mission can ensure that its investigations are welcomed by victims, governments as well as other practitioners; and guarantee that its reports are widely read and considered conclusive and fair.

However, the mandate of these commissions, among other issues of international fact-findings, are "still relatively under-studied".[4] This chapter will first summarise a standard model for the terms of reference of international fact-finding commission mandates, on the basis of a comparative study of different international fact-finding missions and their mandates. Then, it will discuss how this model of mandates could be adapted to various circumstances in international fact-finding. Lastly, as the design, formulation and evaluation of the mandate of a commission need clear criteria, the chapter will propose a set of criteria to assess the mandates of international fact-finding commissions.

---

[2]   Axel Berg, "The 1991 Declaration on Fact-finding by the United Nations", in *European Journal of International Law*, 1993, vol. 4, p. 110.

[3]   Eric Brahm, "Uncovering the Truth: Examining Truth Commission Success and Impact", in *International Studies Perspectives*, 2007, vol. 8, p. 17.

[4]   Priscilla B. Hayner, "Fifteen Truth Commissions – 1974 to 1994: A Comparative Study", in *Human Rights Quarterly*, 1994, vol. 16, p. 598.

## 6.2. Model of Mandates for International Fact-Finding Commissions: A Comparative Perspective

The present author has identified dozens of different international fact-finding commissions and made a comparison between the terms of reference of their mandates. Given the detailed table of international fact-finding mandates in section 1.6. above, this section will proceed directly with the analysis of the terms of reference in the mandating documents. Although the mandates of different international fact-finding missions could differ greatly due to the varied nature of the situations they deal with,[5] a mandate model can still be surmised from the practices of previous and current international fact-finding commissions.

### 6.2.1. Minimum Core Elements of a Proper Mandate

The competence of an international fact-finding commission is primarily demonstrated by the language used in its mandating instrument. The terms of reference in the commission's mandate must be formally correct irrespective of what is said. There are certain patterns in mandate language, from which some minimum core elements of a mandate can be derived.

Firstly, the mandates usually touch upon the purpose of the fact-finding commission.[6] For example, for the Commission of Experts for the former Yugoslavia, its purpose, according to its mandate, was to act "with a view to providing the Secretary-General with its conclusions on the evidence of grave breaches of the Geneva Conventions and other violations of international humanitarian law committed in the territory of the former Yugoslavia";[7] in the case of the Independent International Fact-Finding Mission on the Conflict in Georgia, its mandate makes clear that

> [t]he aim of the fact-finding mission shall be to investigate the origins and the course of the conflict in Georgia, including with regard to international law (footnote: Including the Helsinki Final Act), humanitarian law and

---

[5]  Judge Thomas Buergenthal, "Truth Commissions: Between Impunity and Prosecution", in *Case Western Reserve Journal of International Law*, 2006–2007, vol. 38, p. 220.

[6]  The purpose of international fact-finding commissions can also be stated in many commission reports.

[7]  S/RES/780 (1992), para. 2 (https://www.legal-tools.org/doc/5887b3/).

human rights, and the accusations made in that context (footnote: Including allegations of war crimes).[8]

The purpose of the fact-finding commission can also be reflected by the powers and sometimes even the methods of work elaborated in the commission's mandate. Take as an example the Commission of Inquiry on Lebanon. Although there is no explicit expression on the purpose of the commission, it sets forth the following powers of the commission, which are directed to the purpose of the commission and define the boundaries of the commission's aims and activities:

(a) To investigate the systematic targeting and killings of civilians by Israel in Lebanon;

(b) To examine the types of weapons used by Israel and their conformity with international law;

(c) To assess the extent and deadly impact of Israeli attacks on human life, property, critical infra-structure and the environment. [9]

Secondly, the terms of reference of such commissions' mandates usually focus on specific matters within a particular geographic scope during a defined period of time. In the mandate of the UN Fact-Finding Mission on the Gaza Conflict, it said,

> [...] to investigate all violations of international human rights law and international humanitarian law that might have been committed at any time in the context of the military operations that were conducted in Gaza during the period from 27 December 2008 and 18 January 2009, whether before, during or after.[10]

The geographic scope and *ad hoc* nature[11] of the mandate guarantees the commissions' work as being concrete and limits the commission's power to an extent that is more politically acceptable. Although it is argued that a commission's mandate should be broad, applying a few sig-

---

[8] Council of the European Union, Council Decision 2008/901/CFSP, Article 1.

[9] A/HRC/S-2/1 (https://www.legal-tools.org/doc/9e7f9b/).

[10] A/HRC/12/48 (https://www.legal-tools.org/doc/ca9992/).

[11] For a different opinion, it is argued that "the existence of a permanent body with a flexible mandate would ensure a more rapid investigation". See Michael P. Scharf, "The Case for a Permanent International Truth Commission", in *Duke Journal of Comparative and International Law*, 1996–1997, vol. 7, p. 382.

nificant restrictions to limit the scope of the object of investigation can sometimes make the investigation less problematic.[12]

Thirdly, the terms of reference of commission mandates also itemise the applicable law and highlight the scope of conclusions. The terms of reference usually list the applicable law as human rights and humanitarian law.[13] And the scope of the commissions' conclusions is usually limited to fact-finding. However, few commissions make the authority of their conclusions clear, which might compromise the influence of the results. Some mandates stipulate that the parties under investigation should provide their full co-operation to the commission during its investigations,[14] which could be difficult to enforce. More importantly, some commissions' mandates go beyond the purpose of fact-finding. For example, some aim to focus on legal findings or hold perpetrators accountable.[15] These go beyond the general mandate of international fact-finding commissions and may lead to confusion and concerns among the parties,[16] and thus create an extra burden for the commission.

The first conclusion based on the comparative study of different international fact-finding commissions is that there should be a core mandate for each international fact-finding commission. This should include, at a minimum, the following elements: the commission's purpose, working method, the geographic scope and time span of the fact-finding, the applicable law, and the scope of the commission's conclu-

---

[12] Brahm, 2007, p. 30, see *supra* note 3.

[13] For example, see the mandate of Commission of Experts for the Former Yugoslavia, S/RES/780 (1992); the mandate of International Commission of Inquiry for Darfur, S/RES/1564 (2004); and the mandate of UN Fact-Finding Mission on the Gaza Conflict, A/HRC/12/48.

[14] For example, see the terms of reference of International Commission of Inquiry mandated to establish the facts and circumstances of the events of 28 September 2009 in Guinea, S/2009/556.

[15] For example, see the mandates of International Commission of Inquiry for Darfur, S/RES/1564 (2004) (http://www.legal-tools.org/doc/1ba770/); the Commission of Inquiry for Guinea, S/2009/556 (https://www.legal-tools.org/doc/df9140/); and the International Commission of Inquiry to investigate all alleged violations of international human rights law in the Libyan Arab Jamahiriya, A/HRC/S-15/1 (https://www.legal-tools.org/doc/233009/).

[16] For example, persons being investigated will fear that their statements to the commission could be used against them later in court, thus compromising the will to co-operate. See Eszter Kirs, "Contours of the Mandate of Truth Commissions", in *Miskolc Journal of International Law*, 2007, vol. 4, pp. 110–111.

sions. These minimum core elements of a mandate provide the parameters of investigation to the international fact-finding commission, and thus serve as the foundation of the mandate model for international fact-finding commissions.

### 6.2.2. Implied Mandate

By reading the reports of different fact-finding commissions, it is detected that such commissions conduct their missions with the methods they have found suitable, usually not limited to the terms of reference in their mandates. For example, according to their report, the Commission of Experts for the former Yugoslavia had asked different governments to gather information on behalf of the commission, [17] which was not provided for in the terms of reference of its mandate.

Since no one can predict all the actual needs of a commission, a mandate cannot possibly be exhaustive. Besides, "there is nothing to guide, instruct or assist the heads and appointees to these missions of how to better carry out their mandates".[18] Moreover, any mandate must, in practice, be tailored to certain situations. It therefore falls to the commission itself to develop its mandate in an implied way. Fortunately, the members of international fact-finding commissions are professional and experienced experts in the field and are normally well-qualified to decide on the method of work to be used in their application of the mandate. This makes the commissions' work more flexible and efficient.

However, is it appropriate for the commission itself to extend its mandate through practice, when the parties have only agreed to a limited original mandate? Who should interpret and implement this kind of implied mandate? On the one hand, it is argued that

> [...] even in situations where states have claimed that the mandate-holder had acted outside of the given mandate, precedence was given to the mandate-holder's interpretation of his/her mandate.

---

[17] UN Security Council, Letter Dated 24 May 1994 from the Secretary-General to the President of the Security Council, S/1994/674, 27 May 1994 (https://www.legal-tools.org/doc/5887b3/).

[18] M. Cherif Bassiouni, "Appraising UN Justice-Related Fact-Finding Missions", in *Journal of Law and Policy*, 2001, vol. 5, p. 36.

On the other hand, others argue that "fact-finding commissions have an obligation to act in strict conformity with their mandate";[19] and if the commission is allowed to operate according to an implied mandate, too much power will be given to the commission members who are on a temporary, perhaps unpaid, assignment.[20] These questions remain challenging and need further study.

### 6.2.3. Extended Mandate

In reading the mandating documents systematically and thoroughly, it should be noted that there are often some follow-up resolutions that expand the mandate of certain international fact-finding commissions. For example, the mandate of the Commission of Experts for the former Yugoslavia was extended by UN Security Council resolutions twice;[21] the mandate of the Independent International Commission of Inquiry on the Syrian Arab Republic has been extended by UN Human Rights Council several times;[22] the same has been true for the International Commission of Inquiry to investigate all alleged violations of international human rights law in the Libyan Arab Jamahiriya.[23] The gradual enlargement of the mandate through resolutions by the mandating body certainly meets special needs and allows the mandate to be more flexible. On the other hand, this could also weaken the authority of the mandates. To conclude, the mandate should be, in the first place, clear and carefully formulated, yet flexible. If an extension is found to be necessary after the mandate has been determined and made public, it would be better to try to solve this problem by way of implied mandate as mentioned in section 6.1.2.2. above. However, if the original mandate was already biased in the first place, an amendment is the only option.[24]

---

[19] Berg, 1993, p. 111, see *supra* note 2.

[20] Lara Talsma, "UN Human Rights Fact-Finding: Protecting a Protection Mechanism", in *ILSA Quarterly*, 2012, vol. 20, issue 3, p. 31.

[21] Its mandate in S/RES/780 (1992) has been extended by S/RES/787 (1992) (http://www.legal-tools.org/doc/5d14b9/) and S/RES/827 (1993) (http://www.legal-tools.org/doc/dc079b/).

[22] Its mandate in A/HRC/RES/S-16/1 (http://www.legal-tools.org/doc/37fa81/) has been extended by A/HRC/S-17/1 and A/HRC/ RES/19/22.

[23] Its mandate in A/HRC/S-15/1 has been extended by A/HRC/17/L.3.

[24] Such as in the case of UN Fact-Finding Mission on the Gaza Conflict, the terms of reference which is widely considered biased in A/HRC/S-9/L.1 has been replaced by the mandate provided in the commission's report A/HRC/12/48. For further analysis, see Nigel S.

With a minimum core mandate provided by its mandating document and further developed by the implied mandate and extended mandate, an international fact-finding commission can faithfully conduct its investigation and achieve its purpose, and thus play an important role in the field of human rights protection. However, this model of mandates summarised from the comparative study of the mandates of different international fact-finding commissions suffers from two main problems. The first problem is with regard to the selection of different commissions. Most of the commissions included in this comparative study are UN-mandated commissions, but there are many more commissions in the field. As Hayner realised ten years ago, "[i]n fact there are many more examples of truth commissions than is generally realized".[25] Therefore, this model of mandates may not be able to provide an overall picture of the mandates of international fact-finding. To address this problem, it would be helpful to set up an international database compiling all the information related to the mandates of different fact-finding commissions: how they are drafted, adopted, amended, interpreted and implemented. Although much of the information in international fact-finding is confidential, the documents of mandates are available for academic study. The second problem is that the above study is based on the textual analysis of mandate documents and reports of the commissions. This textual approach may not be sufficient to fully reflect the interests and opinions of all stakeholders. Additionally, it may not accurately reflect the operational reality of the mandate, because as Professor Bassiouni observed, it "may be long on mandate but thin on substance, while others may be short on mandate and thick on substance, with everything else somewhere in between".[26]

## 6.3. Proposed Criteria for the Mandates of International Fact-Finding Missions

The above analysis provides a standard model of mandates for future development. A clear criterion to assess if a mandate is proper to the

---

Rodley, "Assessing the Goldstone Report", in *Global Governance*, 2010, vol. 16, pp. 193–194; Agnieszka Jachec Neale, "Human Rights Fact-Finding into Armed Conflict and Breaches of the Laws of War", in *American Society of International Law Proceedings*, 2011, vol. 105, p. 85.

[25] Hayner, 1994, p. 599, see *supra* note 4.

[26] Bassiouni, 2001, p. 36, see *supra* note 18.

---

mission is still needed. Efforts have been made to set up some criteria for the mandates of international fact-finding commissions, but the previous experiences were limited to specific organisations, situations or matters, and were, above all, not legally binding.

### 6.3.1. Previous Experiences on Criteria for Mandates

The earliest attempt to set up clear criteria for the establishment of mandates for fact-finding missions can be traced back to the 1980s. The 59th Conference of the International Law Association, held in Belgrade 28–23 August 1980, approved by consensus a set of minimal procedures to protect the integrity of human rights fact-finding by non-governmental organisations. Regarding the mandate, it provided that:

1. The organ of an organization establishing a fact finding mission should set forth objective terms of reference which do not prejudge the issues to be investigated. These terms should accord with the instrument establishing the organization.

2. The resolution authorizing the mission should not prejudge the mission's work and findings.

3. While terms of reference should not unduly restrict the mission in the investigation of the subject and its context, they should be so specific as to indicate the nature of the subject to be investigated.[27]

Although the Belgrade Minimal Rules were designed for the mandates of fact-finding by non-governmental organisations, they have identified several aspects that should be common to all fact-finding missions. One is the 'objective' criterion. A mandate must not pre-judge the issues and should be objective and unbiased. An objective mandate may earn the commission more political support, and directs the investigation and its conclusion in a fair way. The other is the 'specific' criterion, which could be achieved by making clear the time span, geographic scope, applicable laws and, most importantly, the issues that are under investigation.

With regard to the efforts of the UN system, the General Assembly in 1991 adopted the Declaration on Fact-Finding by the United Nations in

---

27 The Belgrade Minimal Rules of Procedure for International Human Rights Fact-Finding Missions, in *American Journal of International Law*, 1981, vol. 75, p. 163.

the Field of the Maintenance of International Peace and Security. It stipulated that:

> 3. Fact-finding should be comprehensive, objective, impartial and timely.

> 22. States should cooperate with United Nations fact-finding missions and give them, within the limits of their capabilities, the full and prompt assistance necessary for the exercise of their functions and the fulfillment of their mandate.

> 23. Fact-finding missions should be accorded all immunities and facilities needed for discharging their mandate, in particular full confidentiality in their work and access to all relevant places and persons, it being understood that no harmful consequences will result to these persons. Fact-finding missions have an obligation to respect the laws and regulations of the State in which they exercise their functions; such laws and regulations should not however be applied in such a way as to hinder missions in the proper discharge of their function.

> 25. Fact-finding missions have an obligation to act in strict conformity with their mandate and perform their task in an impartial way. Their members have an obligation not to seek or receive instructions from any Government or from any authority other than the competent United Nations organ. They should keep the information acquired in discharging their mandate confidential even after the mission has fulfilled its task.[28]

This declaration on fact-finding has raised comprehensive criteria for the mandate of the missions. It underlines that mandates of fact-finding missions should be objective, impartial, independent, and emphasises the importance of state co-operation.

Besides these general principles for NGO and UN mandated fact-finding, there have also been experiences on specific matters in the field of human rights protection. One is the Manual on the Effective Investigation and Documentation of Torture and Other Cruel, Inhuman or Degrading Treatment or Punishment ('Istanbul Protocol') , which stipulated that:

---

[28] Declaration on Fact-Finding by the United Nations in the Field of the Maintenance of International Peace and Security, 67th plenary meeting, 9 December 1991.

[…] Recommendations for defining terms of reference are as follows:

- They should be neutrally framed so that they do not suggest a predetermined outcome. To be neutral, terms of reference must not limit investigations in areas that might uncover State responsibility for torture;

- They should state precisely which events and issues are to be investigated and addressed in the commission's final report;

- They should provide flexibility in the scope of inquiry to ensure that thorough investigation by the commission is not hampered by overly restrictive or overly broad terms of reference. The necessary flexibility may be accomplished, for example, by permitting the commission to amend its terms of reference as necessary. It is important, however, that the commission keep the public informed of any amendments to its mandate.[29]

The Manual prescribed the neutral, specific and flexible nature of the mandate for fact-finding missions.

Another contribution is the Updated Set of principles for the protection and promotion of human rights through action to combat impunity by the Commission on Human Rights. It instructed that:

To avoid conflicts of jurisdiction, the commission's terms of reference must be clearly defined and must be consistent with the principle that commissions of inquiry are not intended to act as substitutes for the civil, administrative or criminal courts. In particular, criminal courts alone have jurisdiction to establish individual criminal responsibility, with a view as appropriate to passing judgment and imposing a sentence.[30]

There is also the Report of the Special Rapporteur on torture and other cruel, inhuman or degrading treatment or punishment:

A commission of inquiry should be created by way of the legal instrument that is most appropriate to its context and should reflect the high importance that States give to such

---

[29] Istanbul Protocol, submitted to the United Nations High Commissioner for Human Rights in 1999, para. 107 (http://www.legal-tools.org/doc/28b5a1/).

[30] E/CN.4/2005/102/Add.1, principle 8.

investigative bodies. The legal instrument establishing a commission of inquiry may be an act of parliament, an executive order or decree, or a decision of the highest courts in exercise of their investigatory functions. In all circumstances, the legal instrument establishing a commission of inquiry should identify clearly the terms of reference of the commission's mandate, including a clear temporal and/or geographic framework that is appropriate for the issue being investigated. The mandate should not excessively broaden the universe of violations to be investigated. The text of the authorizing instrument should also set out clearly the scope of the inquiry, citing with precision the events and issues to be addressed. The terms of reference should be stated in neutral language to avoid the impression of a predetermined outcome. A commission should have flexibility to amend its terms of reference in exceptional circumstances, as long as newly found elements warrant the amendment and the commission's decision is publicly and transparently explained.[31]

Although these previous experiences listed above have their limitations, they have to some extent reached consensus on the criteria for international fact-finding commissions' mandates. However, as these previous experiences relate to different areas of fact-finding, they have not been able to provide systematic criteria for quality control of the mandates of international fact-finding commissions.

### 6.3.2. Layered Approach of Criteria for Mandates

Based on these previous experiences, with the intent to provide clear criteria for further quality control of international fact-finding's mandates, this chapter proposes a layered approach to define the criteria for the mandates of international fact-finding missions.

This approach is displayed in the following table.

---

[31] A/HRC/19/61, para. 64.

| Table 1 | Criteria | Quality Control |
|---|---|---|
| **A Layered Approach** | Impartiality/Neutrality | Legitimacy/Credibility |
| | Accuracy ⬅➡ Flexibility | Efficacy |
| | Breadth ⬅➡ Specificity | Feasibility |
| | Political Acceptance (Digestibility) ⬆ ⬇ Power to make investigations + Power to make recommendations | Basis of Establishment |

**Table 1: Criteria for the Mandate of International Fact-Finding outside Criminal Justice for Core International Crimes.**

This table is the proposed system for the criteria for international fact-finding commissions' mandates. In the bottom, as the foundation, the mandate needs political acceptance and powers to discharge its functions. However, more power to the commission usually means less political acceptance from all parties. This therefore needs to be carefully balanced. This is the basis of the establishment of the mandate. The upper layer is broad as well as specific. Only when the commission has a broad mandate on specific matters or geographic areas or time span, can the commission actually conduct its work and ensure the feasibility of its mandate. The third level is accurate and flexible. The mandate should be as accurate as possible on the minimum core elements of mandates, yet leave enough room for the commission itself to flexibly discharge its mandate (usually with regards to the methods of work).[32] At the highest level is the requirement of impartiality.[33] The mandate should be clear and unbiased, never pre-judge the situation before its professional investigation so that every party respects the commissions' work and results. Impartiality can make

---

[32] For other similar opinions, see, for example: "Each commission's mandate should be appropriate to the situation or conflict at hand, and flexible enough to allow interpretation by the member of the commission"; Priscilla B. Hayner, in "International Guidelines for the Creation and Operation of Truth Commissions: A Preliminary Proposal", in *Law and Contemporary Problems*, 1996, vol. 53, p. 179.

[33] Neale, 2011, pp. 85–86, see *supra* note 24.

political acceptance more easily achieved. In all, this layered approach could lead to a virtuous circle of the mandate. Establishing a sound mandate needs to be approached one step at a time, with careful attention to a sense of balance along the way.

## 6.4. Conclusion

In conclusion, a proper mandate of an international fact-finding commission should consist of a core mandate in its establishing document and an implied mandate developed from the practice of the commission. However, there is no exclusive model for mandates of every commission. The mandate should be context-specific, as each commission has its own unique features. With regards to the quality control of mandates, four layers of criteria have been proposed and should be implemented. However, it should also be borne in mind that "practice is the sole criterion for testing truth",[34] a quote which was brought up in the front page of *GuangMing Daily* in China in 1978 and has become one of the most influential thoughts for contemporary China.

A proper mandate is the first line of defense for international fact-finding and we should have rules ready for the drafting, interpretation and implementation of the mandates. This will serve to prepare us on our journey to seek truth from facts, and "we are all led to the truth for which we are ready".[35]

---

[34] "Practice Is the Sole Criterion for Testing Truth", in *GuangMing Daily*, 11 May 1978.
[35] Neale Donald Walsch, *The Complete Conversation with God*, Penguin, 2005.

# 7

---

# Coherence in the Design and Implementation of the Mandates of International Fact-Finding Commissions: Internal and External Dimensions

## Isabelle Lassée[*]

In this chapter I propose an approach for the design and implementation of United Nations- mandated commissions of inquiry into grave violations of human rights and humanitarian law. The approach is aimed at increasing the impact of these commissions.

Commissions of inquiry are mandated by the United Nations ('UN') to inquire into grave violations of human rights and humanitarian law committed in the context of armed conflict or serious internal disturbances. The evolution of international law – together with the changing nature of recent conflicts – renders the need for commissions of inquiry all the more pressing, for a number of reasons. On the one hand, the development of the doctrine of the Responsibility to Protect augments the need for early and detailed information about the nature of violations being committed, in order to facilitate decision-making by UN bodies and other stakeholders. On the other hand, the recent upsurge of internal disturbances, coupled with severe state repression – sometimes escalating into civil war – has also justified the mandating of formal fact-finding missions. This is because recent conflicts have been characterised by the restricted access of international observers to the conflict zone. This results in a dire lack of objective and accurate information, which is often aggravated by sustained and elaborate propaganda from both sides of the conflict.

---

[*] **Isabelle Lassée** holds a Ph.D. from University Paris II- Panthéon Assas. She is the author of *Les missions d'établissement des faits des Nations Unies sur les violations graves du droit international humanitaire ou massives des droits de l'homme*, Livres de Institut Universitaire Varenne, 2017, and the editor of *Sri Lanka's Time to Try, Prosecuting conflict related abuses*, South Asian Centre for Legal Studies, 2019. She is a co-founder of the South Asian Centre for Legal Studies (Colombo), and served as its Head of Programmes from 2013 to 2019.

In order to adapt to these ever-increasing needs and challenges, a new approach to the design and implementation of the mandates of international fact-finding missions may be required. Indeed, the proliferation of commissions of inquiry over the last 10 years has highlighted the divergences in the creation and implementation of these bodies' mandates. Two problems may be identified with respect to the design and implementation of such commissions.

First, commissions' mandates are not always timely and contextually relevant. Commissions of inquiry are mandated in very different political and humanitarian contexts, ranging from internal disturbances to full-blown armed conflict, or even post-conflict situations. They may therefore be created as an early warning mechanism for the protection of human rights; or at the other end of the spectrum, to serve a transitional justice function. However, in designing a meaningful intervention, mandating bodies often fail to draw from the specific contexts in which commissions are created. Thus, there is a need for more targeted and contextually relevant interventions to enhance the impact of these commissions of inquiry and the efficiency of follow-up responses.

Second, with respect to the implementation of the commissions' mandates, some commentators have raised concerns regarding the lack of consistency in the methodologies adopted. This lack of consistency may be explained by the existence of several external constraints that pose challenges to the selection of a methodology for the fulfilment of these commissions' mandates. Attempts to overcome these challenges have led to a somewhat *ad hoc* development of fact-finding methodologies. While scholars outline the need for more consistent approaches, they also acknowledge that a measure of flexibility in the methodology adopted is required. This flexibility is deemed necessary to allow for adaptation to the different contexts in which commissions operate, and to the various challenges they face while carrying out their fact-finding mission, including state-imposed restrictions or prohibitions on access to territories. However, the inconsistent development of fact-finding processes undermines the credibility of these commissions and the prospects for proper implementation of their recommendations. Thus far, no comprehensive and systematic approach has been proposed to reconcile the imperatives of consistency on the one hand, and diversity on the other.

I argue that the response to problems with respect to both the mandate and the methodology of commissions of inquiry lies in the adoption of an overarching conceptual framework that uses a two-tier approach to consistency. This requires an appreciation of the external and internal dimensions of coherence.

External coherence means that the mandate of the commission meaningfully reflects the purposes for which it is created, and is suitably aligned with the context of its intervention. These purposes ought to depend on the context of the commission's intervention. I submit that the mandating body may assist the commission in carrying out its mandate by explicitly identifying these purposes. If the mandating body fails to do so, the commission ought to identify these core purposes through a contextual interpretation of its mandate. This would ensure that the commission's intervention is suitably aligned with the context in response to which it is mandated.

Internal coherence means that the overall methodology adopted by the commission is calibrated to the fulfilment of its mandate. This could be achieved by interlocking the mandate of the commission with its methods of work, applicable standards of proof and the scope of its conclusions and recommendations.

Although this approach of ensuring external and internal coherence does not depart from an intuitive understanding of the core requirements for an efficient intervention, its practical implementation blurs the line between technical and policy decisions and requires reassessment of the role of commissions in the protection of human rights. It also challenges the assumption that a uniform approach to fact-finding, devoid of contextual considerations, exists.

## 7.1. The Need for a Contextual and Purposive Intervention: Towards External Coherence

Commissions of inquiry are created by UN organs to assist in the maintenance of peace and security or the protection of human rights. The importance of fact-finding for the maintenance of peace and security is recognised in several declarations and reports. For instance, the General Assembly has long recognised that "an important contribution to the peaceful settlement of disputes and to the prevention of such disputes could be made by providing for impartial fact-finding within the framework of international organizations and in bilateral and multilateral conventions".[1] Similarly, the Declaration on Fact-Finding by the United Nations in the Field of the Maintenance of International Peace and Security recognises that "international peace and security depends to a large extent on its acquiring detailed knowledge about the factual circumstances of any dispute or situation, the continuance of which might threaten the maintenance of international peace and security".[2] This important function of international fact-finding is also emphasised by Secretary-General Boutros Boutros-Ghali in his report, "In larger freedom: towards development, security and human rights for all".[3]

The UN Charter – explicitly[4] or implicitly[5] – grants fact-finding powers for the maintenance of peace and security to the General Assembly, the Security Council and the Secretary-General. These powers may be utilised through the establishment of subsidiary organs,[6] typically commissions of inquiry. The General Assembly, the Security Council and the Secretary-General have increasingly resorted to fact-finding in order to inquire into allegations of grave violations of human rights and humani-

---

[1] United Nations General Assembly, Resolution 1967 (XVIII), Question of Methods of Fact-Finding, 18th session, 16 December 1963, UN Doc. A/RES/18/1967 (https://www.legal-tools.org/doc/37663d/).

[2] United Nations General Assembly, Resolution 46/59, Declaration on Fact-Finding by the United Nations in the Field of the Maintenance of International Peace and Security, 67th plenary meeting, 9 December 1991, UN Doc. A/RES/46/59.

[3] United Nations General Assembly, In Larger Freedom: Towards Development, Security and Human Rights for All, Report of the Secretary-General, 59th session, 21 March 2005, UN Doc. A/59/2005, § 25 (https://www.legal-tools.org/doc/5739f5/).

[4] Charter of the United Nations, 24 October 1945, 1 UNTS XVI (hereinafter 'UN Charter') (http://www.legal-tools.org/doc/6b3cd5/) Article 34: the Security Council has the power to "investigate any dispute, or any situation which might lead to international friction or give rise to a dispute, in order to determine whether the continuance of the dispute or situation is likely to endanger the maintenance of international peace and security".

[5] UN Charter, *supra* note 4, Article 11, § 2: "[the General Assembly] may discuss any questions relating to the maintenance of international peace"; Article 14: the General Assembly is also authorised to "recommend measures for the peaceful adjustment of any situation, regardless of origin, which it deems likely to impair the general welfare or friendly relations among nations"; Article 39: "[the Security Council] shall determine the existence of any threat to the peace, breach of the peace, or act of aggression and shall make recommendations, or decide what measures shall be taken in accordance with Articles 41 and 42, to maintain or restore international peace and security"; and Article 19: "[the Secretary-General] may bring to the attention of the Security Council any matter which in his opinion may threaten the maintenance of international peace and security".

[6] UN Charter, *supra* note 4, Articles 22 and 29.

tarian law. This is because the protection of human rights and combating impunity fall under the broad rubric of the maintenance of peace and security. In addition, UN organs with specific human rights mandates also resort to fact-finding, as described in Chapter 3. The UN Commission on Human Rights – and subsequently, the UN Human Rights Council – has created Working Groups and Special Rapporteurs, and has mandated *ad hoc* commissions of inquiry. Similarly, the Office of the UN High Commissioner for Human Rights also resorts to fact-finding.

UN fact-finding into grave human rights and humanitarian law violations therefore aims at furthering the protection of human rights.[7] It is a purposive activity. Professor B. Ramcharan notes that:

> [...] the task of ascertaining the facts is certainly one of a (semi)-judicial character to be performed in an impartial way with a view to disclosing the concrete and real situation. This, however, does not mean that fact-finding is a neutral and uncommitted activity. It is rather a function fulfilled in the public interest and in the light of the purposes and principles of the organization which provides the machinery for the investigation.[8]

Developments in international law over the last two decades – including the maturing of international criminal law and the development of the doctrine of the Responsibility to Protect – have diversified the varying purposes for which fact-finding may be commissioned. Commissions of inquiry may be created to achieve purposes as diverse as facilitating the international protection of populations at risk, putting an end to impunity, and supporting the transition towards peace, rule of law and democracy. They may serve these purposes by identifying relevant means for intervention by UN mechanisms,[9] examining state responsibility[10] or identify-

---

[7]  Bertrand G. Ramcharan, *International Law and Fact-Finding in the Field of Human Rights*, Nijhoff, The Hague, 1983, p. 7.

[8]  *Ibid.*

[9]  See, *e.g.*, United Nations Human Rights Council, Report of the United Nations Fact-Finding Mission on the Gaza Conflict, 12th session, 25 September 2009, UN Doc. A/HRC/12/48 (hereinafter 'Goldstone Report'), §§ 1765, 1766 and 1768 (https://www.legal-tools.org/doc/ca9992/).

[10]  See, *e.g.*, United Nations Human Rights Council, Report of the Commission of Inquiry on Lebanon pursuant to Human Rights Council Resolution S-2/1, 3rd session, 23 November 2006, UN Doc. A/HRC/3/2 (hereinafter 'Report of the Commission of Inquiry on Lebanon'), § 344.

ing alleged perpetrators,[11] recommending positive changes in domestic law,[12] contributing to truth telling,[13] and identifying reparation measures.[14] They may also operate as a 'complementarity' substitute when states fail to comply with their obligation to investigate human rights and humanitarian law violations.[15]

The underlying purposes of commissions of inquiry necessarily derive from the specific political and humanitarian contexts in response to which they are created. As emphasised by the UN Secretary-General in his report on implementing the doctrine of the Responsibility to Protect, fact-finding missions are initial steps towards timely and decisive responses tailored to the specific circumstances of each case.[16] Key factors for a contextual intervention include the existence and advancement of an armed conflict, and the nature and gravity of allegations of human rights and humanitarian law violations. Depending on these factors, commissions may be mandated to assess the need for early responses that would prevent the deterioration of the human rights situation;[17] to determine whether responses in the realm of the Responsibility to Protect – or other

---

[11] See, *e.g.*, United Nations Security Council, Report of the International Commission of Inquiry Mandated to Establish the Facts and Circumstances of the Events of 28 September 2009 in Guinea, letter dated 18 December 2009 addressed to the President of the Security Council by the Secretary-General, 18 December 2009, UN Doc. S/2009/693, § 215 (hereinafter 'Report of the Commission of Inquiry on Guinea') (https://www.legal-tools.org/doc/c5939f/).

[12] See, *e.g.*, UN Office of the High Commissioner for Human Rights, "Report from OHCHR Fact-finding Mission to Kenya, 6-28 February 2008", 28 February 2008 (hereinafter 'Report of the OHCHR Fact-Finding mission on Kenya'), p. 18 (https://www.legal-tools.org/doc/75ec55/), "the Government of Kenya should consider establishing a regulatory framework against hate-speech by drafting a law for parliament's consideration".

[13] See, *e.g.*, Goldstone Report, *supra* note 9, § 1683.

[14] See, *e.g.*, Report of the Commission of Inquiry on Guinea, *supra* note 11, § 270; Goldstone Report, *supra* note 9, § 1768.

[15] United Nations General Assembly, Report of the Special Rapporteur on the Situation of Human Rights in Myanmar, 66th session, 16 September 2011, UN Doc. A /66/635, § 74 (https://www.legal-tools.org/doc/6584f5/).

[16] United Nations General Assembly, Implementing the Responsibility to Protect, Report of the Secretary-General, 63rd session, 12 January 2009, UN Doc. A/63/677 (hereinafter 'UN Secretary-General Report on Implementing the responsibility to protect'), § 53.

[17] See, *e.g.*, United Nations Human Rights Council, Resolution S-2/1, The Grave Situation of Human Rights in Lebanon Caused by Israeli Military Operations, 2nd special session, 11 August 2006, UN Doc. A/HRC/S-2/1 (hereinafter 'UN Human Rights Council Resolution 2/1') (https://www.legal-tools.org/doc/9e7f9b/): the second extraordinary session was convened two days after the beginning of the military operations.

---

measures for the maintenance of international peace and security – are justified;[18] or to identify relevant transitional justice measures and means for their implementation.[19]

In addition, previous or ongoing responses to the situation by the UN or other stakeholders also need to be taken into account when mandating commissions of inquiry. Indeed, depending on their nature and efficacy, these other responses may influence the commissions' underlying purposes. For instance, the commission of inquiry on Libya was mandated the day before the situation was referred to the International Criminal Court ('ICC') by the UN Security Council.[20] The commission took note of this referral and decided to consider events in the light of Articles 6 to 8 of the Rome Statute, in order to support the ICC's work with respect to accountability in Libya.[21] This decision contrasts with the interpretation of its mandate by the High-Level Mission on the situation of human rights in Darfur. The High-Level Mission was mandated by the UN Human Rights Council approximately 18 months after the referral of the situation of Su-

---

[18] See, *e.g.*, United Nations Human Rights Council, Resolution S-9/1, The Grave Violations of Human Rights in the Occupied Palestinian Territory, Particularly due to the Recent Israeli Military Attacks against the occupied Gaza Strip, 9th special session, 12 January 2009, UN Doc. A/HRC/S-9/1 (hereinafter 'UN Human Rights Council, Resolution S-9/1') (http://www.legal-tools.org/doc/27fa66/), §§ 8–9, where the commission "[c]alls for urgent international action to put an immediate end to the grave violations committed by the occupying Power, Israel, in the Occupied Palestinian Territory, particularly in the occupied Gaza Strip; Also calls for immediate international protection of the Palestinian people in the Occupied Palestinian Territory, in compliance with international human rights law and international humanitarian law".

[19] See, *e.g.*, United Nations Human Rights Council, Resolution S-3/1, Human Rights Violations Emanating from Israeli Military Incursions in the Occupied Palestinian Territory, Including the Recent One in Northern Gaza and the Assault on Beit Hanoun, 3rd special session, 15 November 2006, UN Doc. A/HRC/S-3/1 (hereinafter 'UN Human Rights Council, Resolution S-3/1') (http://www.legal-tools.org/doc/9f48ff/), § 7. The commission was mandated a few days after the end of the Israeli military operations in Beit Hanoun to: (a) assess the situation of victims; (b) address the needs of survivors; and (c) make recommendations on ways and means to protect Palestinian civilians against any further Israeli assaults.

[20] United Nations Security Council, Resolution 1970 (2011), 6491st meeting, 26 February 2011, UN Doc. S/RES/1970 (2011) (http://www.legal-tools.org/doc/2316c9/).

[21] United Nations Human Rights Council, Report of the International Commission of Inquiry to Investigate All Alleged Violations of International Human Rights Law in the Libyan Arab Jamahiriya, 17th session, 1 June 2001, UN Doc. A/HRC/17/44 (hereinafter 'First Report of the Commission of Inquiry on Libya'), p. 2.

---

dan to the ICC.[22] Prior to this referral, the Security Council had mandated a commission of inquiry that dealt extensively with questions of individual criminal accountability.[23] After having detailed various efforts undertaken by the international community to put an end to the conflict and to protect human rights, the Mission interpreted its mandate in light of the responsibility to protect. It drew extensively from the nature and impact of previous responses in order to identify the remaining needs of protection.[24] In both examples, previous and ongoing responses were crucial elements in the determination of the commissions' underlying purposes. This is consistent with the idea that measures deployed by the UN or other stakeholders in pursuit of human rights protection should form part of a comprehensive and integrated policy.[25] Indeed, the efficacy of the response is enhanced when the different measures deployed complement each other.

Although the importance of a contextual intervention is emphasised in UN literature,[26] my research reveals that mandating bodies rarely locate fact-finding initiatives in their broad political and humanitarian contexts, and thus fail to frame the commissions' interventions accordingly. The contextual backgrounds giving rise to the creation of commissions of inquiry are often articulated in the declarative parts of various mandating resolutions, but are rarely integrated into the operative parts containing the mandates of the commissions. Thus, mandating resolutions include

---

[22] United Nations Security Council, Resolution 1593 (2005), 5158th meeting, 31 March 2005, UN Doc. S/RES/1593 (2005) (http://www.legal-tools.org/doc/4b208f/).

[23] United Nations Security Council, Resolution 1564 (2004), 5040th meeting, 18 September 2004, UN Doc. S/RES/1564 (2004) (hereinafter 'UN Security Council, Resolution 1564 (2004)') (http://www.legal-tools.org/doc/1ba770/).

[24] United Nations Human Rights Council, Report of the High-Level Mission on the Situation of Human Rights in Darfur Pursuant to Human Rights Council Decision S-4/101, 4th session, 9 March 2007, UN Doc. A/HRC/4/80 (hereinafter 'Report of the High-Level Mission on Darfur'), p. 3.

[25] United Nations General Assembly, Responsibility to Protect: Timely and Decisive Response, Report of the Secretary-General, 66th session, 25 July 2012, UN Doc. A/66/874 (hereinafter 'UN Secretary-General, Report on Responsibility to Protect: Timely and Decisive Response'), §§ 20, 24 and 37; United Nations General Assembly, Early Warning, Assessment and the Responsibility to Protect, Report of the Secretary-General, 64th session, 14 July 2010, UN Doc. A/64/864 (hereinafter 'UN Secretary General, Report on Early warning, assessment and the responsibility to protect'), § 9 c.

[26] UN Secretary-General, Report on Responsibility to Protect: Timely and Decisive Response, *supra* note 25, §§ 10, 20 and 48.

---

detailed accounts of allegations of violations,[27] the evolution of the humanitarian situation,[28] previous reactions and recommendations of UN organs,[29] ongoing or failed peace processes,[30] and relevant interventions by regional organisations.[31] But while mandating bodies recall, note or sometimes express concern with respect to these developments; they do not explicitly state how these contextual elements are relevant to the commissions' underlying purposes.

In addition, while mandating bodies create commissions for a wide range of purposes, they either fail to identify these purposes[32] or improperly limit the commissions' mandates to the quest for criminal accountability.[33] The systematic restriction of the scope of the commissions' mandates to criminal accountability may undermine the design of comprehensive responses to critical human rights situations. Although the focus on criminal accountability may operate as a strong deterrent to human rights violations and thereby contributes to the overall protection of human

---

[27] See, *e.g.*, United Nations Human Rights Council, Resolution S-16/1, The Current Human Rights Situation in the Syrian Arab Republic in the Context of Recent Events, 16th special session, 29 April 2011, UN Doc. A /HRC/RES/S-16/1 (hereinafter 'UN Human Rights Council, Resolution S-16/1') (http://www.legal-tools.org/doc/37fa81/); UN Human Rights Council Resolution 2/1, *supra* note 17.

[28] See, *e.g.*, United Nations Human Rights Council, Resolution 16/25, Situation of Human Rights in Côte d'Ivoire, 16th session, 25 March 2011, UN Doc. A/HRC/RES/ 16/25 (hereinafter 'UN Human Rights Council, Resolution 16/25') (http://www.legal-tools.org/doc/7b9efc/), §§ 6 and 7.

[29] See, *e.g.*, UN Human Rights Council, Resolution 16/25, *supra* note 28; United Nations Security Council, Resolution 935 (1994), 3400th meeting, 1 July 1994, UN Doc. S/RES/935 (1994) (hereinafter 'UN Security Council, Resolution 935 (1994)') (http://www.legal-tools.org/doc/1594bd/); UN Security Council, Resolution 1564 (2004), *supra* note 23.

[30] See, *e.g.*, UN Security Council, Resolution 1564 (2004), *supra* note 23.

[31] See, *e.g.*, UN Human Rights Council, Resolution 16/25, *supra* note 28, §§ 1–2; UN Security Council Resolution 1564 (2004), *supra* note 23.

[32] See, *e.g.*, UN Human Rights Council Resolution 2/1, *supra* note 17, § 7; S/RES/935 (1994), 1 July 1994, Rwanda, § 1; UN Rights Council, Resolution S-9/1, *supra* note 18, § 14.

[33] See, *e.g.*, UN Human Rights Council, Resolution S-16/1, *supra* note 27, § 7, United Nations Human Rights Council, Resolution S-15/1, Situation of human rights in the Libyan Arab Jamahiriya, 15th special session, 25 February 2011, UN Doc. A/HRC/ RES/S-15/1 (hereinafter 'UN Human Rights Council, Resolution S-15/1') (http://www.legal-tools.org/doc/6012d0/); UN Human Rights Council, Resolution 16/25, *supra* note 28, § 10.

rights,[34] fact-finding missions are primarily mandated to identify responses to a situation threatening the protection of human rights.[35] Therefore, the restriction of commissions' foci to criminal accountability at this initial stage may inhibit their ability to identify appropriate responses outside the realm of criminal accountability.

This practice also increases difficulties met by commissions in the fulfilment of their mandates. Mandates focusing on criminal accountability naturally trigger the adoption of methods of work tailored to the quest for criminal accountability. However, this restricts the scope of fact-finding and ignores approaches, facts and insights relevant to other purposes that animate the creation of these commissions in the first place. The Commission of Inquiry on Côte d'Ivoire mandated by the Human Rights Council in March 2011 exemplifies this problem. As the terms of resolution 16/25 reveal, one of the commission's underlying purposes was to promote – and contribute to – transitional justice. The text of the resolution contains several references to bringing the perpetrators to justice, as well as facilitating democracy and peace, rule of law, and reconciliation.[36] However, the mandate of the commission is limited to the quest for criminal accountability. It is therefore regrettable that the narrow focus of the commission's mandate on individual criminal accountability did not allow it to shed light on the institutional weaknesses and political practices detrimental to the transitional justice process. Besides, the adoption of a methodology tailored to the quest for criminal accountability may not adequately support recommendations made by commissions. Thus, it is not unusual that commissions issue recommendations unsupported by the fact-finding exercise, but nonetheless deemed necessary in light of the broad political and humanitarian context. Notwithstanding the inadequacies in its mandate, the conclusions and recommendations of the commission of inquiry on Côte d'Ivoire deal extensively with questions of transitional justice including justice, truth, but also vetting and lustration, thereby reflecting the underlying purpose for which it was mandated.[37] How-

---

[34] UN Secretary-General, Report on Implementing the Responsibility to Protect, *supra* note 16, § 53; UN Secretary-General, Report on Responsibility to Protect: Timely and Decisive Response, *supra* note 25, § 12.

[35] K.T. Samson, "Procedural Law", in Bertrand G. Ramcharan (ed.), *International Law and Fact-Finding in the Field of Human Rights*, Martinus Nijhoff, The Hague, 1983, p. 56.

[36] UN Human Rights Council, Resolution 16/25, *supra* note 28.

[37] United Nations Human Rights Council, Report of the International Commission of Inquiry on Côte d'Ivoire, 17th Session, 1 July 2011, UN Doc. A/HRC/17/48 (hereinafter 'Report of

ever, the fact-finding exercise geared towards the quest for criminal accountability did not allow the commission to identify factors limiting the
prospects for transitional justice. As a result, its recommendations lack
specificity and are not supported by findings of fact. A mandate crafted in
compliance with the imperative of external coherence would have enabled
the commission to avoid this disconnect and to issue more specific recommendations for the implementation of transitional justice measures,
both to the Ivorian government, and to the Office of the High Commissioner for technical support.[38]

Thus, the lack of external coherence may hinder coherent implementation of their mandates by commissions of inquiry. It may lead to
disconnects between commission's mandate, the methodology they adopt,
their findings of fact, and their conclusions and recommendations.

In practice, the drafting of the commissions' mandates is a highly
politicised exercise. Back and forth discussions between country delegations very often lead to modifications of draft resolutions. Final resolutions submitted to the vote therefore reflect the outcome of relative bargaining positions, diplomatic pressures and compromises. In light of this,
expecting mandating resolutions to reflect the underlying purposes of a
commission's intervention may seem unrealistic. Yet, a close comparison
of draft and final mandating resolutions reveals that the negotiation process generally does not affect the identification of underlying purposes, or
lack thereof.[39] Indeed, insufficient compliance with the imperative of ex-

---

the Commission of Inquiry on Côte d'Ivoire') (https://www.legal-tools.org/doc/9d910a/), §
127.

[38] *Ibid.* The recommendation to the United Nations High Commissioner for Human Rights is
framed in the following general terms:

Give technical assistance to the Ivorian authorities in all human rights initiatives, in
particular for the establishment and operation of the Dialogue, Truth and Reconciliation Commission.

[39] See, *e.g.*, United Nations Human Rights Council, Draft Resolution, The Grave Situation of
Human Rights in Lebanon Caused by Israeli Military Operations, 2nd special session, 09
August 2006, UN Doc. A/HRC/S-2/L.1, § 7: decides to "[d]ispatch, urgently, a high-level
commission of inquiry [...] to: (i) Investigate the systematic targeting and killing by Israel
of civilians in Lebanon; (ii) Examine the types of weapons used by Israel and their conformity with international law; and (iii) Assess the extent and deadly impact of Israeli attacks on human life, property, critical infrastructure and environment" and UN Human
Rights Council Resolution 2/1, *supra* note 17, §7:

[d]ecides to establish urgently and immediately dispatch a high-level commission of
inquiry comprising eminent experts on human rights law and international humanitari-

ternal coherence originates in the drafting rather than at the negotiation stage.[40] Thus, sponsoring states and other relevant stakeholders may rem-

an law [...]: (a) To investigate the systematic targeting and killings of civilians by Israel in Lebanon; (b) To examine the types of weapons used by Israel and their conformity with international law; (c) To assess the extent and deadly impact of Israeli attacks on human life, property, critical infrastructure and the environment.

United Nations Human Rights Council, Draft Resolution, The Grave Violations of Human Rights in the Occupied Palestinian Territory, Particularly due to the Recent Israeli Military Attacks against the occupied Gaza Strip, 9th special session, 12 January 2009, UN Doc. A/HRC/S 9/L.1, § 14: "[d]ecides to dispatch an urgent, independent international fact-finding mission, [...] to investigate all violations of international human rights law and international humanitarian law by the occupying Power, Israel, against the Palestinian people throughout the Occupied Palestinian Territory, particularly in the occupied Gaza Strip, due to the current aggression" and UN Human Rights Council, Resolution S-9/1, *supra* note 18, § 14:

[d]ecides to dispatch an urgent, independent international fact-finding mission, [...] to investigate all violations of international human rights law and international humanitarian law by the occupying Power, Israel, against the Palestinian people throughout the Occupied Palestinian Territory, particularly in the occupied Gaza Strip, due to the current aggression.

United Nations Human Rights Council, Draft Resolution, The Current Human Rights Situation in the Syrian Arab Republic in the Context of Recent Events, 16th special session, 28 April 2011, UN Doc. A/HRC/S-16/L.1, § 9, "[d]ecides to establish an independent, impartial and credible United Nations led international investigation into the human rights violations in Libya to ensure that there is full accountability for those responsible for violations" and UN Human Rights Council, Resolution S-16/1, *supra* note 27, § 7:

[...] dispatch urgently a mission to the Syrian Arab Republic to investigate all alleged violations of international human rights law and to establish the facts and circumstances of such violations and of the crimes perpetrated, with a view to avoiding impunity and ensuring full accountability.

United Nations Human Rights Council, Draft Resolution, Situation of human rights in the Libyan Arab Jamahiriya, 15th special session, 23 February 2011, UN Doc. A/HRC/S-15/L.1, § 9: "[d]ecides to establish an independent, impartial and credible United Nations led international investigation into the human rights violations in Libya to ensure that there is full accountability for those responsible for violations" and UN Human Rights Council, Resolution S-15/1, *supra* note 33, § 11:

[d]ecides to urgently dispatch an independent, international commission of inquiry [...] to investigate all alleged violations of international human rights law in the Libyan Arab Jamahiriya, to establish the facts and circumstances of such violations and of the crimes perpetrated and, where possible, to identify those responsible, to make recommendations, in particular, on accountability measures, all with a view to ensuring that those individuals responsible are held accountable.

40  Sometimes the negotiation process even leads to a clearer delineation of purposes. See, *e.g.*, United Nations Human Rights Council, Draft Resolution, Human Rights Violations Emanating from Israeli Military Incursions in the Occupied Palestinian Territory, Including the Recent One in Northern Gaza and the Assault on Beit Hanoun, 3rd special ses-

edy this problem at the initial drafting stage by drawing from the context of intervention to determine the commissions' underlying purposes.

If mandating bodies were to craft commissions' mandates in compliance with the principle of external coherence, this would lead to greater internal coherence in the work of commissions of inquiry. Indeed, as I will argue, if commissions' mandates are externally coherent, commissions may ensure internal coherence by focusing on the selection of relevant sets of potential recommendations and supporting those recommendations through the fact-finding exercise.

## 7.2. Increasing Internal Coherence: The Importance of Relevant and Well-Supported Recommendations

Internal coherence consists of interlocking commissions' mandates with their methodologies, conclusions and recommendations. It is ensured when commissions adopt a methodology that satisfies two conditions. First, commissions must adopt a methodology narrowly tailored to the fulfilment of their mandate and underlying purposes. Methodological elements that may vary according to commissions' underlying purposes are the necessary methodological steps required to justify conclusions of fact on the questions commissions are mandated to investigate. These include the nature and gravity of violations considered; the selection of relevant facts; the applicable law; the nature and amount of evidence considered by commissions; and the standard of proof and verification of information. Second, the methodology adopted must adequately support the commissions' conclusions and recommendations.

I contend that internal coherence is most effectively maintained if commissions focus on supporting, by their findings of fact, recommendations useful to furthering their underlying purposes. This approach of internal coherence focuses on recommendations as the cornerstone of human rights fact-finding. Indeed, recommendations are both the outcome of

---

sion, 14 November 2006, UN Doc. A/HRC/S-3/L.1, § 6: "[d]ecides to dispatch urgently a high level fact-finding mission to Beit Hanoun" and UN Human Rights Council, Resolution S-3/1, *supra* note 19, § 7:

[d]ecides to dispatch urgently a high-level fact-finding mission, to be appointed by the President of the Human Rights Council, to travel to Beit Hanoun to, *inter alia*: (a) assess the situation of victims; (b) address the needs of survivors; and (c) make recommendations on ways and means to protect Palestinian civilians against any further Israeli assaults.

fact-finding and the roadmap for subsequent intervention by various stakeholders. First, recommendations – rather than facts – are the ultimate outcome of fact-finding. Indeed, findings of fact are not absolute but relative to the methodology adopted by commissions of inquiry.[41] This explains why they cannot be read, analysed and interpreted without reference to the fact-finding methodology adopted. Therefore, efficient fact-finding should be geared towards establishing facts to the extent necessary to support the commissions' recommendations. Second, recommendations shape the roadmap for follow-up actions by various stakeholders, in order to implement UN policy with respect to the situation at hand. Therefore, the actions and measures recommended ought to constitute intermediary steps for the advancement of the very purposes animating the creation of commissions.

Although recommendations are central to the fact-finding exercise, their importance is often undervalued, by scholars and commissions alike. The relevant literature on human rights fact-finding, which pays scant attention to recommendations issued by fact-finding bodies; as well as the practice of commissions of inquiry, evidence this problem.

Follow-up actions that may be recommended by commissions include a wide array of prevention and protection instruments available to UN member states, the UN system, regional and sub-regional organisations and their civil society partners. For instance, the UN Secretary-General, in his report on the implementation of the Responsibility to Protect, notes that measures that may be deployed in pursuit of this goal include pacific measures under Chapter VI of the Charter,[42] as well as coercive ones under Chapter VII,[43] or regional and sub-regional arrangements under Chapter VIII.[44] In addition, whenever necessary in light of the con-

---

[41] Thomas M. Franck and H. Scott Fairley, "Procedural Due Process in Human Rights Fact-Finding by International Agencies", in *American Society of International Law*, 1980, p. 309 (hereinafter 'Franck and Fairley, 1980').

[42] UN Secretary-General, Report on Responsibility to Protect: Timely and Decisive Response, *supra* note 25, §§ 10 and 22.

[43] UN Secretary-General, Report on Responsibility to Protect: Timely and Decisive Response, *supra* note 25, §§ 31 and 32, UN Secretary General, Report on Implementing the Responsibility to Protect, *supra* note 16, §§ 57 and 58.

[44] UN Secretary-General, Report on Responsibility to Protect: Timely and Decisive Response, *supra* note 25, § 9; United Nations General Assembly, The Role of Regional and Sub-Regional Arrangements in Implementing the Responsibility to Protect, Report of the Secretary-General, 65th session, 27 June 2011, UN Doc. A/65/877–S/2011/393.

text, and justified by findings of fact, commissions of inquiry may also
recommend actions under the first and second pillars of the responsibility
to protect, including assistance and capacity-building. In this respect, the
United Nations Office of the High Commissioner for Human Rights, the
Emergency Relief Coordinator, its development agencies and the Bretton
Woods institutions may play a major role.[45] However, in spite of this wide
range of possible follow-up actions to advance UN goals in a given situation, recommendations issued by commissions of inquiry tend to be crafted in very general terms, and lack specificity.[46] Many recommendations
merely state international standards with respect to the protection of human rights,[47] accountability and administration of justice,[48] humanitarian
responses,[49] rule of law standards,[50] or transitional justice measures.[51]

---

[45]   UN Secretary-General, Report on Responsibility to Protect: Timely and Decisive Response, *supra* note 25, § 30.

[46]   See, *e.g.*, UN Human Rights Council, Report of the Independent International Commission
of Inquiry on the Syrian Arab Republic, 17th special session, 23 November 2011, UN Doc.
A/HRC/S-17/2/Add.1 (hereinafter cited as 'First Report of the Commission of Inquiry on
Syria') (https://www.legal-tools.org/doc/925e44/), pp. 21–22: recommend the government
to "[p]ut an immediate end to gross human rights violations" and to "[a]llow immediate
and full access for the commission and outside observers and other United Nations human
rights monitoring bodies" and recommend the international Community to "[a]ssist the
Syrian Arab Republic in addressing serious institutional weaknesses by strengthening the
independence of its judiciary and reforming its security sector through bilateral and multilateral development cooperation"; First Report of the Commission of Inquiry on Libya, *supra* note 21, p. 9: recommend the National Transitional Council to "ensure the immediate
implementation of applicable international humanitarian law and international human
rights law"; Report of the Commission of Inquiry on Côte d'Ivoire, *supra* note 37, p. 26:
recommend the international community and UN agencies to "[s]upport the governmental
authorities, particularly at the financial level, in their efforts to combat impunity and promote the rule of law". In contrast, for detailed and specific recommendations, see, *e.g.*
Goldstone Report, *supra* note 9, § 1764 onwards.

[47]   See, *e.g.*, First Report of the Commission of Inquiry on Syria, *supra* note 46, p. 23: "Provide Syrian nationals seeking protection with refuge in accordance with the provisions of
the international law governing asylum".

[48]   See, *e.g.*, Report of the Commission of Inquiry on Côte d'Ivoire, *supra* note 38, p. 25:
"Ensure that those responsible for violations of human rights and international humanitarian law are brought to justice; in this context, the investigations initiated must be conducted
in an exhaustive, impartial and transparent fashion"; First Report of the Commission of Inquiry on Libya, *supra* note 21, p. 9; First Report of the Commission of Inquiry on Syria,
*supra* note 46, p. 21.

[49]   See, *e.g.*, Report of the Commission of Inquiry on Côte d'Ivoire, *supra* note 37, pp. 25–26:
"[s]trengthen coordination between the various parties involved so as to ensure an appropriate response to the humanitarian crisis", "[p]rovide appropriate assistance to victims, in

This is symptomatic of the absence of a real effort to support recommendations by findings of fact.

The approach I propose aims at increasing the efficacy and quality of the work of commissions of inquiry by focusing primarily on relevant and well-supported recommendations. On the one hand, the efficacy of the commissions' work depends on the relevance of recommendations for follow-up actions in a given context. On the other hand, the quality of their work depends on how well findings of fact support their recommendations. Therefore, increasing the efficacy and quality of fact-finding outside criminal justice requires that specific attention be given to: first, the identification of categories of potential timely and contextually relevant recommendations; and second, to the design of work methods adapted to making findings of fact that would adequately support these recommendations. This approach also ensures internal coherence by interlocking the commission's methods of work, conclusions, recommendations and its underlying purposes as reflected in the mandate.

This approach, in practice, would first require commissions to identify the nature of potential sets of recommendations relevant to their underlying purposes. The High-Level Mission on the situation of human rights in Darfur mandated by the UN Human Rights Council exemplifies how a commission may systematically identify categories of follow-up actions relevant to a given purpose.[52] Having decided to "employ an analysis drawn from the responsibility to protect",[53] the commission determined that critical needs for improving the situation of human rights in

---

particular women, children, older persons and persons with disabilities", and "[t]ake steps to develop lasting solutions for displaced persons".

[50] See, *e.g.*, First Report of the Commission of Inquiry on Libya, *supra* note 21, p. 9: "To bring all laws and policies of the Libyan Arab Jamahiriya into conformity with international human rights standards".

[51] See, *e.g.*, Report of the Commission of Inquiry on Côte d'Ivoire, *supra* note 37, p. 25:

As part of the reform of its security institutions, ensure that the persons responsible for violations are not integrated into the national army or into any other security force and that a professional army that respects human rights is swiftly established.

First Report of the Commission of Inquiry on Libya, *supra* note 21, p. 9: "To grant adequate reparations to the victims or their families, and to take all appropriate measures to prevent the recurrence of violations".

[52] Report of the High-Level Mission on Darfur, *supra* note 24.

[53] *Ibid.*, p. 3.

Darfur – in light of previous efforts already deployed by the UN and the African Union – include needs for:

> [...] enhanced protection, renewed progress toward peace, expanded humanitarian space, increased accountability for perpetrators, programmes to address root causes, efforts to ensure the implementation of existing recommendations from authoritative human rights bodies; and compensation for the victims of violations of human rights.[54]

The commission specifies that the recommendations made are aimed at achieving these purposes.[55]

The determination of potential sets of recommendations relevant to the commissions' underlying purposes is a delicate exercise. It first requires commissions to assess the relevance of specific measures for the advancement of their underlying purposes. Commissions must thus weigh the likely impact of each measure for the protection of human rights or the advancement of transitional justice in the specific context of their intervention. Second, commissions must balance different imperatives while issuing recommendations. For instance, commissions must ensure that the measures they envisage stand a realistic chance of being implemented.[56] However, feasibility considerations should not eclipse the obligation to uphold international standards.[57] In practice, commissions must therefore balance the need to issue feasible recommendations, while at the same time encouraging UN bodies and other stakeholders to overcome political roadblocks and to intervene as appropriate to maintain peace and security and protect human rights. Each of these choices adds a layer of difficulty to carrying out the mandate of a commission. Yet, commissions ought not to evade this onerous task by issuing standardised and general recommendations. Commissions are mandated to assist mandating bodies in the decision-making process.[58] Therefore issuing contextually relevant recommendations is inherently part of their mission. Indeed, commissions should offer guidance rooted in their overall assessment of the situation.

---

[54] *Ibid.*

[55] *Ibid.*

[56] International Center for Transitional Justice, "Transitional Justice in the United Nations Human Rights Council", June 2011, p. 5 (available on its web site).

[57] Steven R. Ratner, "Accountability and the Sri Lankan Civil War", in *American Journal of International Law*, October 2012, vol. 106, no. 4, p. 802.

[58] See, *e.g.*, UN Charter, *supra* note 4, Article 34.

Next, commissions must ensure that the methodology adopted is suited to potential recommendations, furthering the commission's underlying purposes. For instance, if commissions recommend more domestic and international investigations, this ought to be supported by findings of credible allegations of human rights and humanitarian law violations. This follows because the standard of 'credible allegations' represents the threshold for the triggering of investigations into alleged violations.[59] To recommend actions falling under the third pillar of the responsibility to protect, commissions may have to prove under a higher standard of proof that genocide, war crimes, ethnic cleansing or crimes against humanity have been committed and that "national authorities are manifestly failing to protect their populations".[60] In his report on the implementation of the Responsibility to Protect, the UN Secretary-General specifies that the more robust the response, the higher the standard for authorisation.[61] Therefore, commissions should integrate this requirement – and adjust their standard of proof accordingly – when recommending measures under the third pillar of the responsibility to protect. Other methodological choices – including the selection of relevant facts, the applicable law, the nature and amount of evidence considered by commissions – ought to be governed by the same considerations.

This approach of internal coherence enables commissions to reconcile the competing demands of diversity and consistency in the design of their methodology. Though scholars recognise the need for a measure of

---

[59] European Court of Human Rights, *Brecknell v. United Kingdom and other cases* (App. Nos. 32457/04, 34575/04, 34622/04, 34640/04, 34651/04), Judgment, 27 November 2007, § 22 (https://www.legal-tools.org/doc/57ec5a/); Geneva Convention for the Amelioration of the Condition of the Wounded and Sick in Armed Forces in the Field, 12 August 1949, 6 UST 3114, 75 UNTS 31, Article 49 (http://www.legal-tools.org/doc/baf8e7/); Convention for the Amelioration of the Condition of the Wounded, Sick and Shipwrecked Members of Armed Forces at Sea, 12 August 1949, 6 UST 3217, 75 UNTS 8, Article 50 (http://www.legal-tools.org/doc/0d0216/); Geneva Convention Relative to the Treatment of Prisoners of War, 12 August 1949, 6 UST 3316, 75 UNTS 135, Article 129 (http://www.legal-tools.org/doc/365095/); Geneva Convention Relative to the Protection of Civilian Persons in Time of War, 12 August 1949, 6 UST 3516, 75 UNTS 287, Article 146 (http://www.legal-tools.org/doc/d5e260/); International Committee of the Red Cross, written by Jean Pictet *et al.*, *Commentary: Geneva Convention For The Amelioration Of The Condition Of The Wounded And Sick Armed Forces In The Field*, 1952, vol. 1, pp. 365–66.

[60] UN Secretary-General, Report on Implementing the Responsibility to Protect, *supra* note 16, § 49.

[61] *Ibid.*, § 50.

flexibility in the methodology adopted by commissions of inquiry,[62] they nonetheless critique the lack of consistency caused by *ad hoc* developments of fact-finding processes and methodologies.[63] According to the approach of internal coherence I propose, commissions ought to tailor their methodology to the different purposes for which they are created. This approach therefore satisfies the imperative of diversity. However, the absence of reference points in the assessment of procedures adopted by each commission undermines the credibility of their findings and recommendations. It also ultimately hinders their efficacy.[64] Therefore, commissions of inquiry should be assisted in the determination of purpose-based methodological approaches by a comprehensive set of guidelines gleaned from best practices. The framework that I propose does not provide clear-cut solutions for the choice of methods of work in each contextual configuration. However, the identification of best practices for purpose-based methodological approaches would lead to a more consistent development of fact-finding methodologies. This approach would also provide the necessary flexibility for commissions to adapt to contextual parameters.

## 7.3. Contours of the Teleological Approach and Justification of the Division of Labour between Mandating Bodies and Commissions of Inquiry

Mandating bodies and commissions of inquiry each have a role to play in maintaining the overall coherence of the fact-finding exercise. The distinction between internal and external dimensions of coherence suggests the need for a specific division of labour between mandating bodies and commissions of inquiry, with respect to the methodology adopted by commissions.

---

[62] Ramcharan, 1983, *supra* note 7, p. 2; Rob Grace and Claude Bruderlein, "HPCR Draft Working Paper: Building Effective Monitoring, Reporting, and Fact-finding Mechanisms", p. 25 (hereinafter 'Grace and Bruderlein, HPCR Draft Working Paper') (available on the Humanitarian Policy and Conflict Research's web site).

[63] Rob Grace and Claude Bruderlein, Program on Humanitarian Policy and Conflict Research Harvard University, ESIL Reflections, 15 July 2012, vol. 1, issue 2, "On Monitoring, Reporting, and Fact-finding Mechanisms" (available on ESIL's web site); M. Cherif Bassiouni, "Appraising UN Justice-Related Fact-Finding Missions", in *Washington University Journal of Law and Policy*, 2001, vol. 5, p. 41; Franck and Fairley, 1980, *supra* note 41, p. 310.

[64] Bassiouni, 2001, *supra* note 63, pp. 40–41; Franck and Fairley, 1980, *supra* note 41, p. 310.

---

Rule 18 of the Model Rules of Procedure for United Nations bodies dealing with violations of human rights (hereinafter 'Model Rules of Procedure') specifies that:

> Rules concerning sources of information as well as methods of work of the ad hoc body regarding the gathering of other evidence, including matters of forms, content, relevance and admissibility of such evidence shall be determined by the organs establishing the ad hoc body in the terms of reference of the ad hoc body unless the ad hoc body itself is explicitly authorized to draw up rules on such matters.[65]

This differs significantly from the Draft Model Rules of Procedure suggested by the UN Secretary-General for *ad hoc* bodies of the United Nations entrusted with studies of particular situations alleged to reveal a consistent pattern of violations of Human Rights (hereinafter 'Draft Model Rules of Procedure'). Indeed, Rules 18 and 20 of the Draft Model of Procedure provide significantly more autonomy to fact-finding bodies to determine the methods they adopt for the collection of information, as well as the admissibility, relevance and weight to be attached to evidence.[66] In addition, while the Draft Model Rules of Procedure provides procedures for the writing of the fact-finders' report, including "conclusions and recommendations",[67] references to conclusions or recommendations were removed in the final version of Rule 20.[68]

It is important to note that the Economic and Social Council in resolution 1879 ('LVI') on 'Model Rules of Procedure for United Nations Bodies dealing with violations of human rights' did not endorse the Model Rules of Procedure *per se*. Instead, it only brought reports of the working group on Model Rules of Procedure to the attention of the organs and bodies of the UN dealing with questions of human rights.[69] In addition,

---

[65] United Nations Commission on Human Rights, Report of the Working Group established under Resolution 14 (XXVII) of the Commission on Human Rights, 13th session, 1 February 1974, UN Doc. E/CN.4/1134, Rule 18.

[66] E/CN.4/1021/Rev.1, Rules 18 and 20.

[67] E/CN.4/1021/Rev.1, Rule 8.

[68] United Nations Commission on Human Rights, Report of the Working Group Established under Resolution 14 (XXVII) of the Commission on Human Rights, 13th session, 1 February 1974, UN Doc. E/CN.4/1134, Rule 20.

[69] United Nations Economic and Social Council, Resolution 1879 (LVI): Model Rules of Procedure for United Nations Bodies Dealing with Violations of Human Rights, 1899th

the concluding words specifying that the rules must be "taken into account whenever the need arises" were removed from the final version of the resolution.[70] On the other hand, the Economic and Social Council ('ECOSOC'), in its resolution, took note of the Draft Model Rules of Procedure suggested by the UN Secretary-General.[71] To be clear, neither the Model Rules of Procedure nor the Draft Model Rules of Procedure are mandatory. In addition, based on the terms of the ECOSOC resolution, rules contained in the Model Rules of Procedure do not necessarily prevail over those contained in the Draft Model Rules of Procedure.

Interestingly, the practice of mandating bodies and commissions of inquiry has been more consistent with the framework laid out in the Draft Model Rules of Procedure than with that of the Model Rules of Procedure. Mandating bodies generally refrain from determining the methodology to be adopted by fact-finding bodies.[72] Thus, in the absence of any reference to the methodology in mandates or terms of reference, the exception has become the norm and fact-finding bodies *de facto* determine their methodology.[73] Similarly – and despite the removal of provisions expressly authorising this practice in the Model Rules of Procedure – fact-finding bodies generally issue recommendations.[74] Commissions of inquiry mandated by the UN have adopted similar practices.[75]

I submit that while mandating bodies ought to determine the underlying purposes for which commissions are created, commissions should be tasked with determining their methods of work, standards of proof and

---

plenary meeting, 17 May 1974, UN Doc. E/1870 (LVI) (hereinafter 'ECOSOC, Model Rules of Procedure for United Nations Bodies dealing with violations of human rights').

[70]  United Nations Economic and Social Council, Report of the Commission on Human Rights on its 13th session UN Doc. E/5464-E/CN.4/1154, 8 March 1974, p. 35.

[71]  ECOSOC, Model Rules of Procedure for United Nations Bodies dealing with violations of human rights, *supra* note 69.

[72]  Samson, 1983, *supra* note 35, pp. 47–49.

[73]  *Ibid.*, pp. 47–48.

[74]  Theo C. van Boven, "The Reports of Fact-Finding Bodies", in Bertrand G. Ramcharan (ed.), *International Law and Fact-Finding in the Field of Human Rights*, Nijhoff, The Hague, 1983, p. 212.

[75]  See, *e.g.*, Report of the Commission of Inquiry on Lebanon, *supra* note 10; Report of the Commission of Inquiry on Guinea, *supra* note 11; Report of the OHCHR Fact-Finding mission on Kenya, *supra* note 12; First Report of the Commission of Inquiry on Libya, *supra* note 21; Report of the High-Level Mission on Darfur, *supra* note 24; Report of the Commission of Inquiry on Côte d'Ivoire, *supra* note 37; First Report of the Commission of Inquiry on Syria, *supra* note 46.

scope of their findings and recommendations. In other words, while mandating bodies ought to be responsible for external coherence, commissions of inquiry ought to be responsible for internal coherence. Several reasons could justify this division of labour.

First, this division of labour provides sufficient flexibility for commissions to adapt to constraints faced in the fulfilment of their mandate. The determination of methods of fact-finding is not exclusively a conceptual exercise, but is also contingent on various practical constraints. These constraints have a significant influence on the determination of the best-suited methods of work, and are not always foreseeable at the time commissions are mandated. Thus, although methods of work should be geared towards supporting contextually relevant sets of recommendations, a measure of flexibility is also necessary to account for the various constraints commissions may encounter in the fulfilment of their mandate. For instance, commissions are often informed of restrictions on access to the territory – likely the most compelling constraint[76] – only after requests to the receiving state have been refused,[77] or remained unanswered.[78] It is therefore important to permit commissions to adapt to these constraints in the carrying out of their mandate and allow them the space to adjust their methodology accordingly.[79]

Second, the determination by mandating bodies of the purposes for the establishment of commissions of inquiry would guide commissions in the choice of methodology and provide an external reference point against which the choice of methods of work, standards of proof and scope of commissions' findings and recommendations may be assessed. In this respect, the mandate of the commission of inquiry on Burundi provides an

---

[76] See, *e.g.*, United Nations Human Rights Council, Report of the High-Level Fact-Finding Mission to Beit Hanoun established under Resolution S-3/1, 5th session, 18 June 2007, UN Doc. A/HRC/5/20, § 13 (https://www.legal-tools.org/doc/868bb5/).

[77] See, *e.g.*, United Nations Human Rights Council, Report of the High-Level Fact-Finding Mission to Beit Hanoun established under Resolution S-3/1, 9th session, 1 September 2008, UN Doc. A/HRC/9/26, §§10 and 11 (https://www.legal-tools.org/doc/16fb5a/); Goldstone Report, *supra* note 9, § 8.

[78] See, *e.g.*, United Nations Human Rights Council, Report of the United Nations High Commissioner for Human Rights on the Situation of Human Rights in the Syrian Arab Republic, 15 September 2011, UN Doc. A/HRC/18/53, § 7 (https://www.legal-tools.org/doc/5bf068/).

[79] Grace and Bruderlein, HPCR Draft Working Paper, p. 25, *supra* note 62.

example of a useful delineation of purposes. It specifies that the commission was mandated

> [t]o establish the facts [...]. To recommend measures of a legal, political or administrative nature, as appropriate, after consultation with the Government of Burundi, and measures with regard to the bringing to justice of persons responsible for those acts, to prevent any repetition of deeds similar to those investigated by the commission and, in general, to eradicate impunity and promote national reconciliation in Burundi.[80]

Finally, this approach of a division of labour between mandating bodies and commissions of inquiry also recognises the fact that mandating bodies are political bodies empowered to issue resolutions and decisions for the maintenance of peace and security or the protection of human rights; while commissions of inquiry are technical bodies mandated to make findings of fact. The determination of the purposes of commissions of inquiry is a policy choice,[81] and therefore should remain in the hands of mandating bodies. The determination of methods of work, on the other hand, is a technical choice,[82] and should therefore be made by commissions themselves.

The justification based on the technical or policy nature of choices would, however, require that fact-finding bodies refrain from issuing recommendations. This position is reflected in the Model Rules of Procedure. Indeed, "most members of the working group felt that an *ad hoc* body should not offer policy recommendations, which would rather be the task of the parent organ".[83] The governments of France, Italy and the Netherlands also expressed similar views in their comments on the Model Rules of Procedure.[84] However, scholars increasingly agree that the issuance of

---

80  United Nations, Security Council, Resolution 1012 (1995), 3571st meeting, 28 August 1995, UN Doc. S/RES/1012 (1995) (http://www.legal-tools.org/doc/80c1a0/).

81  Robert Miller, "United Nations Fact-Finding Missions in the Field of Human Rights", in *Australian Yearbook of International Law: Annual Survey of Current Problems of Public and Private International Law with a Digest of Australian Practice*, 1975, p. 41.

82  Grace and Bruderlein, HPCR Draft Working Paper, *supra* note 62, p. 24.

83  United Nations Economic and Social Council, 56 Social Committee, 2 Summary Records, UN Doc. E/AC.7/SR.749 (1974), p. 169; United Nations Commission on Human Rights, Report of the Working Group established under Resolution 14 (XXVII) of the Commission on Human Rights, 11th session, UN Doc. E/CN.4/1086 (1972), p. 8.

84  E/CN.4/1071 add. 2; E/CN.4/1071 add. 2, pp. 5–6; E/CN.4/1071, add. 4, p. 3.

recommendations is an inherent part of UN human rights fact-finding.[85] I propose to justify this by reference to the primary purpose of human rights fact-finding. Indeed, if – as I contend – commissions of inquiry are purposive initiatives primarily mandated to identify follow-up responses best suited to advance the protection of human rights in a given situation, recommendations are the natural outcome of fact-finding. Therefore, the practice of commissions issuing recommendations based on their findings of fact would be justified, provided that the following two conditions are satisfied. First, that mandating bodies guide the recommendations by determining the underlying purposes animating the creation of commissions. This would limit the commissions' margin of appreciation with regards to policy decisions. Second, that the methodology adopted by commissions is supported by purpose-based methodological guidelines, and justified for each set of potential recommendations. This would ensure that recommendations are supported by facts on the ground and are supported by sturdy procedural rules. Professors Thomas M. Franck and H. Scott Fairley deemed these last two guarantees sufficient to justify the issuance of policy recommendations by fact-finding bodies.[86]

## 7.4. Conclusion

This chapter challenges the idea that there exists a uniform fact-finding formula that may be replicated in – or even adapted to – different contexts. I argue that the adoption of 'one-size-fits-all' mandates and methods of fact-finding undermines the efficiency of interventions for the maintenance of peace and security and the protection of human rights. Indeed, the framework adopted for the design of fact-finding methodologies must take into account the political and contextual parameters that both shape and constrain commissions' interventions. This does not mean that each commission must reinvent the wheel[87] and cannot borrow from best practices for the design of its fact-finding methodology. However, because fact-finding methods are necessarily contingent on the context of the commissions' interventions, it is difficult for scholars and practitioners to identify these best practices.

---

[85]   Ramcharan, 1983, p. 7, *supra* note 7; van Boven, 1983, *supra* note 74, p. 184.
[86]   *Ibid.*
[87]   Bassiouni, 2001, *supra* note 63, p. 41

The examination of the work of commissions of inquiry in light of the specific contexts in which they operate reveals that fact-finding mechanisms outside criminal justice are mandated for a wide range of purposes and that these purposes lead to the creation of commissions with distinctive features. I therefore propose to draw from these purposes to identify best practices in fact-finding by commissions of inquiry and submit that the selection of methodological approaches by a commission ought to be contingent on the purposes for it was established.

I go further to claim that each category of recommendations – or follow-up measures – issued by commissions requires a corresponding purpose-based methodological approach. This is because recommendations are intermediary steps for the implementation of the commissions' underlying purposes.

In practice, according to this approach, the mandating body would ideally state explicitly the purposes for the establishment of the commission. In the event that it does not, the commission ought to identify these purposes through a teleological and contextual analysis of its mandate. Next, commissions should identify the nature of potential recommendations relevant to the commission's underlying purposes. Following this, commissions should select the methodological approaches best suited to support categories of recommendations already identified. In this, they should be assisted by a set of guidelines gleaned from best practices.

In practice, the adoption of this teleological framework for the design of commissions' mandates and methods of fact-finding would require improvements in three areas. First, stakeholders' discussions leading up to the initial drafting of mandating resolutions should focus on how to maximise the commissions' intervention in a given context. This would ensure a better recognition of the commissions' underlying purposes. Second, the commissions' expertise in policy and political issues must be strengthened so as to facilitate the identification of potential sets of relevant recommendations. This may be done by ensuring that the commissions' staff includes a wide range of experts. Commissions may also benefit from more advisory meetings on policy and political issues. Third, a sustained effort should be undertaken to determine best practices for purpose-based methodological approaches. Scholarly studies on commissions of inquiry and on different international instruments that may be deployed as follow-up mechanisms may offer valuable insight to guide these choices.

By examining the purposes for which commissions of inquiry are mandated in different contexts and revealing the necessary link between these purposes and fact-finding methodologies, I attempt to identify a framework within which commissions may more effectively fulfil the purposes for which they were intended and enhance the quality and efficacy of their work. Thus, the comprehensive approach I propose seeks to remedy three current limitations of UN-mandated commissions of inquiry pointed out by scholars. First, this approach provides transparent and coherent criteria for the determination of appropriate methods of work. Second, it enhances the relevance of the conclusions and recommendations of these commissions. Third, it provides an external reference point against which the choice of their methods of work may be assessed, thereby ensuring the quality control of the commissions' work.

# 8

---

# Quality Control and the Selection of Members of International Fact-Finding Mandates

## WU Xiaodan[*]

Fact-finding missions are playing an increasingly important role in the international community's endeavour to ascertain disputed facts and investigate violations of international law, particularly human rights and humanitarian law. The recent proliferation of United Nations fact-finding bodies, especially in the case of debated events or complex situations, has highlighted the issue of member selection and triggered serious controversy about the independent, impartial and fair nature of these fact-finding bodies. Given the significance of the selection of fact-finders, the absence of relevant requirements in the UN, and the disturbing results this can lead to, this chapter argues that the professionalisation of fact-finders and better transparency and regulation of their selection are overdue, and will propose the qualifications required.

## 8.1. Introduction

Due to the lack of a centralised mandating body, international fact-finding missions have developed in an *ad hoc* manner and emerged from different institutional sources in response to serious or politicised incidents.[1] Fact-finding is not a new tool in international relations.[2] The original concept can be traced back to the 1899 Hague Convention for the Pacific Settlement of Disputes providing for the use of international inquiry commissions for disputes.[3] Currently, there are several categories of international

---

[*] **WU Xiaodan** is Associate Professor of the Law Faculty of China Central University of Finance and Economics. Her main research fields are international human rights law and outer space law. She holds a Ph.D. from University of Milan, Italy.

[1] Philip Alston, "Commissions of Inquiry as Human Rights Fact-Finding Tools", in *American Society of International Law Proceedings*, 2011, vol. 105, no. 1, p. 84.

[2] John G. Merrills. *International Dispute Settlement*, Cambridge University Press, Cambridge, 3rd edition, 1998, pp. 44–61.

[3] See Articles 9, 10, 11, 12, 13 and 14 of the Convention for the Pacific Settlement of International Disputes, 29 July 1899 (https://www.legal-tools.org/doc/b1e51f/).

fact-finding undertaken by a variety of actors, including but not limited to the parties involved; governmental organisations, both international and regional, such as the United Nations, the Council of Europe and the Inter-American Commission on Human Rights; and civil society organisations including Human Rights Watch and Amnesty International. Even within the United Nations, besides the principal organs and their subsidiaries, such as the General Assembly, the Security Council, the Human Rights Council, other organs and specialised agencies have initiated fact-finding mandates in line with their respective functions and responsibilities.

Since the end of the Cold War, the United Nations, with a renewed sense of responsibility for international legal accountability and civilian protection, has acknowledged the importance of timely and accurate knowledge of all relevant facts and has progressively employed fact-finding mechanisms when exercising its functions in relation to the maintenance of international peace and security and the protection of human rights. As an early stage peace negotiation tool, the goal of fact-finding in most cases is to examine the facts of an incident by a neutral third party, to reduce tensions and areas of disagreement in a problematic situation.[4] Increasingly, however, fact-finding has been utilised more for the implementation and enforcement of international human rights and humanitarian legal norms by establishing violations and identifying perpetrators. This can, in part, be attributed to a trend of human rights mainstreaming. Fact-finding and report writing provide a systematic and neutral analysis of human rights violations and are deemed as essential to international human rights monitoring. Without fact-finding mechanisms, the implementation of human rights norms would be baseless, like a tree without roots. It was suggested four decades ago that fact-finding lied "at the heart of human rights activities".[5]

From the 1990s, many fact-finding commissions have been established by the United Nations to assess some of the most serious situations of human rights and humanitarian law violations across the world: in the

---

[4] Peter Malanczuk, *Akehurst's Modern Introduction to International Law*, Routledge, London, 7th Edition, 1997, p. 277; Arthur Lenk, "Fact-Finding as a Peace Negotiation Tool – the Mitchell Report and the Israeli-Palestinian Peace Process", in *Loyola of Los Angeles International and Comparative Law Review*, 2002, vol. 6, no. 1, pp. 291–296.

[5] Thomas M. Franks and H. Scott Fairley, "Procedural Due Process in Human Rights Fact Finding by International Agencies", in *American Journal of International Law*, 1980, vol. 74, no. 2, p. 308.

former Yugoslavia, Darfur, Lebanon, Guinea, Georgia, Israel and the Occupied Palestinian Territories, Libya, Syria, Congo, Myanmar, South Sudan and Venezuela. Some of these reports led to the establishment of international tribunals or were conducted for the purpose of collecting information to be used as evidence in international criminal adjudication,[6] which further increased the standards of accuracy and credibility of fact-finding. For instance, the interim report of a fact-finding mission to the former Yugoslavia sent by the Security Council in 1992 to enquire about the alleged violations of international humanitarian law prompted the decision to establish the International Criminal Tribunal for the former Yugoslavia.[7] The related fact-finding report with its thorough and systematic preliminary review of the facts was the basis for the referral of the Darfur situation to the International Criminal Court.[8]

## 8.2. The Significance of Member Selection for the Credibility, Legitimacy and Effectiveness of Fact-Finding Mandates

A legitimate international fact-finding mandate should provide neutral facts to the relevant organizations and bodies to design better policies and countermeasures, or to the international courts and tribunals to adjudicate cases. In light of their crucial role, the reports of fact-finding missions require accuracy, independence and impartiality. When these qualities are absent, the international community risks relying on reports which have no clear measure of reliability, and which may be detrimental to the pursuit of human rights. Several aspects of the process are relevant to the quality control of a fact-finding mission's work and one of them is the selection of its members.[9]

The selection of members is relevant to the credibility, impartiality and accuracy of a fact-finding mission's work.[10] Selecting the right personnel can ensure the objectivity, fairness and effectiveness of the fact-finding process, guarantee the results of the related missions and ultimate-

---

[6]   David S. Weissbrodt, Fionnuala Ni Aolain, Joan Fitzpatrick, and Frank Newman, *International Human Rights: Law, Policy and Process*, 4th edition, 2009, p. 610.

[7]   UN Security Council Res. 827, UN Doc. S/RES/827 (1993), 25 May 1993 (http://www.legal-tools.org/doc/dc079b/).

[8]   UN Security Council Res. 1564, UN Doc. S/RES/1564 (2004), 18 September 2004 (http://www.legal-tools.org/doc/1ba770/).

[9]   Thomas M. Franks and H. Scott Fairley, 1980, p. 311, see *supra* note 5.

[10]   *Ibid.*

ly discover truth and achieve justice. Otherwise, it would potentially or actually jeopardise the legitimacy and credibility of the mission, make it highly politicised, increase the risk that it is manipulated for other purposes, and constitute a source of tension.

The UN fact-finding missions are gaining influence in international society and their reports are frequently referred to by international courts and tribunals, as well as by governments, NGOs and other interested actors. Nonetheless, after more than 60 years, there is a lack of rules to guarantee the quality of fact-finding missions and little consensus about the requirements and procedures for the selection of fact-finders. The only document that defines fact-finding is the Declaration on Fact-Finding in the Field of the Maintenance of International Peace and Security in 1991 (hereinafter 'the 1991 UN Declaration').[11] The focus of this document was on conflict resolution and the term 'human rights' finds no place in its lengthy provisions.[12] It says that fact-finding under the auspices of the United Nations is "any activity designed to obtain detailed knowledge of the relevant facts of any dispute or situation which the competent United Nations organs need in order to exercise effectively their functions in relation to the maintenance of international peace and security".[13] The 1991 Declaration establishes basic principles for UN fact-finding missions, including a commitment to "comprehensive, objective, impartial and timely" fact-finding, but without explicit and specific requirements for this. As a result, fact-finding bodies are differently composed with considerable variance in quality. Thus, the UN should develop better practices in order to rely on fact-finding reports as verifiable sources for decision-making, and formulate some basic rules and guidelines. This would not amount to the standardization or generalization of fact-finding missions, which warrant caution in light of the inherently context-specific nature of international fact-finding inquiries, as Richard J. Goldstone and Martin Scheinin warn in Chapters 2 and 3 respectively.

Additionally, the particularities of the UN system and some other elements make the quality control of fact-finders more important. Firstly, the UN was established as a political organisation and, as such, it is large-

---

[11] UN General Assembly Resolution, A/RES/46/59 (1991), 9 December 1991.

[12] Philip Alston, "The Darfur Commission as a Model for Future Responses to Crisis Situations", in *Journal of International Criminal Justice*, 2005, vol. 3, no. 3, p. 601.

[13] UN General Assembly Resolution, A/RES/46/59 (1991), 9 December 1991.

ly governed by political considerations. With respect to justice-related fact-finding missions, the contrast, and at times the conflict, between *realpolitik* and the values of justice is frequently an issue.[14] Secondly, in general, the purposes or tasks of UN fact-finding appear to be broader than the inquiry arrangements of the regional governmental organisations, treaty-based arrangements or NGOs. The UN fact-finding missions may be extended to the determination of legal questions, liability and even remedies, and thus go beyond fact elucidation.[15] Thirdly, within the United Nations, there is no adjudicative human rights system such as in the Council of Europe, like a UN Court of Human Rights or a World Court of Human Rights,[16] to review the reliability and accuracy of the fact-finding reports as a filtering mechanism. On the contrary, the decisions on referral to the International Criminal Court or establishment of *ad hoc* international criminal jurisdictions rely on the outcome of the fact-finding missions.

## 8.3. Concerns about the Partiality, Unfairness and Inappropriateness of Fact-finders

There are no requirements for the selection of members of UN-mandated fact-finding missions and a high degree of opaqueness seems to be the rule on how and why they are designated. They are normally nominated by UN organs establishing the related missions, sometimes based on a list. There is no further information besides the number of members, their names, their nationalities and, occasionally, their occupations. The transparency of the Human Rights Council on fact-finders is exceptional. Since the first independent investigation on the Gaza Conflict in 2009, the biographical information of the members, usually amounting to one paragraph on each member's occupation, expertise and related work experi-

---

14  M. Cherif Bassiouni, "Appraising UN Justice-Related Fact-Finding Missions", in *Journal of Law and Policy*, 2001, vol. 5, p. 37.

15  Zeray Yihdego, "The Gaza Mission: Implications for International Humanitarian Law and UN Fact-Finding", in *Melbourne Journal of International Law*, 2012, vol. 13, no. 1, p. 163.

16  For more information, see Thomas Buergenthal, "A Court and Two Consolidated Treaty Bodies", in Anne Frans Bayefsky (ed.), *The UN Human Rights Treaty System in the 21st Century*, Kluwer, 2000, p. 301; F. Viljoen, "Fact-Finding UN Human Rights Complaints Body – Analysis and Suggested Reform", in *Max Planck Yearbook of United Nations Law*, 2004, vol. 8, pp. 96–97; Martin Scheinin, "Towards a World Court of Human Rights", Research report within the framework of the Swiss Initiative to commemorate the 60th anniversary of the Universal Declaration of Human Rights, 22 June 2009 (available on the UDHR60's web site).

ence, is provided in the majority of the cases. Limited information is provided in four among the 18 missions: Israeli Settlements in the Occupied Palestinian Territory, 2012; Democratic People's Republic of Korea, 2013; Sri Lanka, 2014; and Libya, 2015.[17] As for the 2012 Mission on Occupied Palestine, the available information about the selection and the members themselves is limited. Three members would be appointed by the President of the Human Rights Council[18] among "distinguished individuals who have expertise in relevant subject areas, in particular international human rights law";[19] on 6 July 2012, the President appointed 'high-level experts' and made their names and occupations public.[20]

Generally, the members of fact-finding mandates are individuals of high moral standard and proven experience in the relevant field, most often professors of international law, former judges or prosecutors of international tribunals or UN legal officers and experts. However, the recent proliferation of fact-finding commissions into alleged human rights and humanitarian law violations during the last two decades, especially in some controversial situations, and the more active roles they are playing have triggered a severe debate about the independent, impartial and fair nature of these fact-finders.

### 8.3.1. The Commission of Experts for the Former Yugoslavia

The Commission of Experts for the former Yugoslavia was initially composed of five highly recognised experts who were well-qualified in relevant fields of international law and from various parts of the globe: Professor Frits Kalshoven of the Netherlands as Chairman; Professor M. Cherif Bassiouni of Egypt; Mr. William H. Fenrick of Canada; Judge Keba M'baye of Senegal; and Professor Torkel Opsahl of Norway (on whose

---

[17] See UN Human Rights Council, "International Commissions of Inquiry, Commissions on Human Rights, Fact-Finding missions and other Investigations" (available on its web site).

[18] UN Human Rights Council Resolution, A/HRC/RES/19/17, 10 April 2012, para. 9 (http://www.legal-tools.org/doc/bd201d/).

[19] Report of the Secretary-General on the Implementation of Human Rights Council Resolution 19/17, A/HRC/20/13, 3 August 2012, para. 9.

[20] Report of the Independent International Fact-Finding Mission to Investigate the Implications of the Israel Settlement on the Civil, Political, Economic, Social and Cultural Rights of the Palestinian People through Occupied Palestinian Territory, Including East Jerusalem, UN Human Rights Council Resolution, A/HRC/22/63, 7 February 2013, para. 2 (https://www.legal-tools.org/doc/4047e2/).

name the publisher of this volume is based).[21] However, the composition of the Commission quickly brought it under fire. There were questions about the qualifications of the Chairman and why the commissioners had been chosen from a short list of between 10 and 15 names compiled by the UN Office of Legal Affairs.[22] Almost a year later, the resignation of the Chairman, Frits Kalshoven, as a protest because the Commission did not have the full political support of major governments, such as the United Kingdom and France, was interpreted as confirmation that the Commission would amount to nothing more than a 'toothless study'.[23] The death of Professor Torkel Opsahl in mid-September 1993 rendered the future of the Commission even bleaker. The commission was re-organised: Professor Bassiouni was appointed as Chairman, and Professor Christine Cleiren of the Netherlands and Judge Hanne Sophie Greve of Norway were appointed as new members.[24] Professor Bassiouni tried to energise the Commission.[25] The Commission managed to undertake some important studies and built up a systematic archive at its headquarters in Geneva. Professor Bassiouni also sought to create a documentation database at his DePaul University's International Human Rights Law Institute with grants from civil society funds.[26] A trust fund was set up to undertake field investigations with contributions by 13 governments.[27]

---

[21] The Commission was established to examine and analyse information gathered with a view to providing its conclusions on the evidence of grave breaches of the Geneva Conventions and other violations of international humanitarian law committed in the territory of the former Yugoslavia. See Security Council Resolution 780 (1992), 6 October 1992 (http://www.legal-tools.org/doc/cdc5ad/). About the composition of the Commission, see S/24657, 14 October 1992 and para. 6 of the final report, S/1994/674, 27 May 1994 (https://www.legal-tools.org/doc/3a3ae2/).

[22] Michael P. Scharf, "The Gateway to the Era of Accountability", in Cherif Bassiouni and the 780 Commission, *An Occasional Paper of the Frederick K. Cox International Law Center*, October 2006, p. 9.

[23] Halfway Response to All-Out War, *New York Times Editorial*, 9 October 1992.

[24] See Final Report of the Commission of Experts Established pursuant to Security Council Resolution 780 (1992), UN. Doc. S/1994/674, 27 May 1994, para. 7.

[25] Michael P. Scharf, 2006, p. 9, see *supra* note 22.

[26] M. Cherif Bassiouni, "The Commission of Experts Established Pursuant to Security Council Resolution 780: Investigating Violations of International Humanitarian Law in the Former Yugoslavia", in *Occasional Paper*, no. 2, International Human Rights Law Institute, DePaul University College of Law, 1996, pp. 10–14.

[27] Michael P. Scharf, 2006, p. 9, see *supra* note 22.

## 8.3.2.  The International Commission of Inquiry Concerning Rwanda

At the request of the UN Security Council, the International Commission of Inquiry concerning Rwanda was established by the Secretary-General to investigate grave reported violations of international humanitarian law committed in the territory of Rwanda, including the evidence of possible acts of genocide.[28] It consisted of three experts,[29] who claimed no special expertise in international criminal law, international humanitarian or human rights law. Moreover, all of them were from West African countries – Togo, Mali and Guinea – rather than from a variety of regions in Africa or the world. They were less well known than the members of the Commission of Experts for the former Yugoslavia. It is argued that a more international spectrum of experience and expertise could have lent greater credibility to this important fact-finding effort.[30]

## 8.3.3.  The Fact-Finding Mission on the Gaza Conflict

The Fact-Finding Mission on the Gaza Conflict established by the President of the Human Rights Council had been embroiled in controversy ever since its creation; and its report, known as the Goldstone Report, has aroused much political, diplomatic and legal controversy.[31] The Gaza Conflict Mission raised criticisms about bias and prejudice from its mandate and composition, its method of conducting investigation, and about the style, presentation, legal interpretation, content and conclusions of the Goldstone Report.[32] Chapter 2 discusses this fact-finding process. It was

---

[28]  UN Security Council Resolution 935 (1994), 1 July 1994 (http://www.legal-tools.org/doc/1594bd/).

[29]  UN Doc. S/1994/906, 29 July 1994.

[30]  Lyal S. Sunga, "How Can UN Human Rights Special Procedure Sharpen ICC Fact-Finding?", in *International Journal of Human Rights*, 2011, vol. 15, no. 2, p. 195.

[31]  The Mission was established on 3 April 2009 with the mandate "to investigate all violations of international human rights law and international humanitarian law that might have been committed at any time in the context of the military operations that were conducted in Gaza during the period from 27 December 2008 and 18 January 2009, whether before, during or after". See United Nation Office of the High Commissioner for Human Rights, Press Release, 3 April 2009.

[32]  Chatham House, Report of An Expert Meeting Which Assessed Procedural Criticisms Made of the UN Fact-Finding Mission on the Gaza Conflict ('The Goldstone Report'), 27 November 2009 (https://www.legal-tools.org/doc/ca9992/); A. Bell, "A Critique of the Goldstone Report and Its Treatment of International Humanitarian Law", in *American Society of International Law Proceedings*, 2010, vol. 104, no. 1, pp. 79–86.

led by Richard J. Goldstone, former member of the South African Constitutional Court and former Chief Prosecutor of the International Criminal Tribunals for the former Yugoslavia and Rwanda. The three other members were Professor Christine Chinkin, professor of international law at the London School of Economics and Political Science and a member of the High Level Fact-Finding Mission to Beit Hanoun (2008); Ms. Hina Jilani, advocate of the Supreme Court of Pakistan and a member of the International Commission of Inquiry on Darfur; and Colonel Desmond Travers, a former officer in the Irish Armed Forces and member of the Board of Directors of the Institute for International Criminal Investigations. Evidently, they had the required expertise and experience in international humanitarian, human rights, and criminal law.

However, Professor Christine Chinkin was requested by UN Watch to recuse herself from the Gaza Conflict Mission on the grounds that she had already pronounced her opinion on the merits of the particular question to be decided by the Mission, thereby giving rise to actual bias or the appearance thereof.[33] There was no doubt about the personal integrity of Professor Chinkin, and there is no evidence demonstrating that her public comments regarding the conflict had affected her performance or that her participation had detrimental impact on the impartiality of the Mission's conclusions. Nonetheless, her participation created a 'perception of bias', which should be avoided by every fact-finding body.[34]

The subsequent doubt and hesitation of Judge Goldstone about the allegations against Israel concerning its alleged policy of deliberate and indiscriminate attacks against Palestinian civilians spurred further debates. Judge Goldstone's insistence on the truth and courage to admit the imperfection of the original work is admirable.[35] Nonetheless, the other three members stood firm on their findings and conclusions in the Goldstone Report and rejected the call for reconsideration because there was no UN

---

[33] A statement signed by Professor Christine Chinkin in *The Sunday Times* of 11 January 2009 declared Israel to be the aggressor and a perpetrator of war crimes. For more information, see UN Watch Request to Disqualify Christine Chinkin from UN Goldstone Mission on Gaza, 20 August 2009.

[34] Chatham House, 2009, p. 7, see *supra* note 32.

[35] In response to the follow-up reports to monitor the independence, effectiveness and genuineness of the investigations undertaken by both the Government of Israel and the Palestinian side, Judge Goldstone wrote: "If I had known what I know now, the Goldstone Report would have been a different document", Richard Goldstone, "Reconsidering the Goldstone Report on Israel and War Crimes", *The Washington Post*, 2 April 2011, p. 21.

procedure or precedent to that effect and the Goldstone Report had become an official UN document. This divergence in perspectives of the
members was unprecedented and gave rise to substantive and procedural
implications within the UN fact-finding regimes.[36] It raised questions on
the credibility and impartiality of the Goldstone Report and, more generally, on how to ensure the objectivity of a fact-finding mission, the need
for a clear procedure to select members, and how to balance the authority
of the UN, the integrity of the report, and the freedom of mission members when there are revelations of new evidence at a later stage.[37]

### 8.3.4. The Fact-Finding Mission on Israeli Settlements in the Occupied Palestinian Territory

The Human Rights Council decided to set up an independent international
fact-finding mission to investigate the implications of the Israeli settlements on the civil, political, economic, social and cultural rights of the
Palestinian people throughout the Occupied Palestinian Territory.[38] Three
experts were appointed as members of this mission: Christine Chanet
(Chairperson), Judge of the Court of Cassation of France and member of
the UN Human Rights Committee; Asma Jahangir, a Pakistani human
rights lawyer and the Trustee of the Board of the UN Voluntary Fund on
Contemporary Forms of Slavery; and Unity Dow, Commissioner of the
International Commission of Jurists and practicing lawyer in Botswana.[39]
They are all female experts in international human rights law. Two of
them are specialists in women's rights and they have no expertise in international humanitarian law or experience in armed conflicts, which naturally raised doubt about their ability to fulfil the mandate of the mission.

### 8.4. The Proposed Requirements and Procedures for Member Selection of Fact-Finding Missions

There are three sets of documents concerning the selection of fact-finders:
the Minimal Rules of Procedure for International Human Rights Fact-

---

[36] Zeray Yihdego, 2012, p. 178, see *supra* note 15.

[37] *Ibid.*, p. 205 and p. 216.

[38] Human Rights Council Resolution, A/HRC/RES/19/17, 10 April 2012.

[39] Report of the Independent International Fact-Finding Mission to Investigate the Implications of the Israeli Settlement on the Civil, Political, Economic, Social and Cultural Rights
of the Palestinian People through Occupied Palestinian Territory, Including East Jerusalem,
Human Rights Council Resolution, A/HRC/22/63, 7 February 2013, para. 2 (https://www.
legal-tools.org/doc/4047e2/).

Finding Missions approved by the 59th Conference of the International Law Association in August 1980 in Belgrade ('Belgrade Minimal Rules') ;[40] the Protocol I of 1949 Geneva Conventions and the Rules of the International Humanitarian Fact-Finding Commission ('IHFFC');[41] and the Guidelines on International Human Rights Fact-Finding Visits and Reports proposed by the International Bar Association's Human Rights Institute in conjunction with the Raoul Wallenberg Institute ('the Lund-London Guidelines') in September 2009.[42]

These rules and guidelines contain some principles and rules that can be included in future UN norms for fact-finder nomination, while bearing in mind that they were created for the fact-finding mandates of civil society or treaty-based organisations and there thus exist some delicate differences in their objectives. The Belgrade Minimal Rules were intended to curb serious abuses and departures from the fundamental norms of due process, encourage states to co-operate with fact-finding missions by non-governmental organisations, and contribute to the credibility of the facts found.[43] The Lund-London Guidelines aim at setting an agreed international standard of good practice in the conduct of fact-finding visits and in the compilation of reports.[44] The preamble clearly declared that, although primarily intended for the use of NGOs, the guidelines can provide direction to all those engaged in human rights fact-finding with a view to improving accuracy, objectivity, transparency and credibility in human rights fact-finding.[45] The purpose is improving quality and effec-

---

[40] Thomas M. Franck, "Current Development: The Belgrade Minimal Rules of Procedure for International Human Rights Fact-Finding Missions", in *American Journal of International Law*, 1981, vol. 75, no. 1, pp. 163–165.

[41] See Article 90 of Protocol I Additional to the Geneva Conventions of 12 August 1949 and relating to the Protection of Victims of International Armed Conflicts, adopted on 8 June 1977, entered into force on 7 December 1978, UN Doc. A/32/144, Annex I (http://www.legal-tools.org/doc/d9328a/); Rules of the International Humanitarian Fact-Finding Commission, as adopted by the Commission on 8 July 1992 in Berne and amended on 11 March 2003, 13 February 2009 and 11 February 2011 in Geneva (http://www.legal-tools.org/doc/3731ef/).

[42] The Guidelines on International Human Rights Fact-Finding Visits and Reports, Raoul Wallenberg Institute of Human Rights and Humanitarian Law (available on Refworld's web site).

[43] Thomas M. Franck, 1981, p. 163, see *supra* note 40.

[44] The Guidelines on International Human Rights Fact-Finding Visits and Reports, see *supra* note 42, Preamble, para. 2

[45] *Ibid.*, para. 3.

tiveness of fact-finding activities by putting a clear emphasis on the impartiality, expertise, and working skills of its members. In accordance with Article 90 of the Protocol I of 1949 Geneva Conventions, the IHFFC, a permanent enquiry Commission, composed of 15 individuals elected by the States that have recognised its obligatory competence, was constituted in 1991, primarily aiming at investigating allegations of grave violations of international humanitarian law.

The nature and tasks of fact-finding missions, the above-mentioned concerns, the three sets of documents, and the practice of regional governmental organisations all highlight the following requirements for member selection: impartiality, legal expertise, management skills, and other considerations such as geographic and gender balance.

### 8.4.1. Impartiality

Three fundamental principles that should guide fact-finding activities are neutrality, impartiality and independence.[46] The credibility and impact of fact-finding mandates and their reports depend upon the extent to which they are perceived to have been objective, fair and impartial. Fact-finding must be "as impartial and as fair to the parties as procedural and evidentiary rules can render it without making the inquiry's task impossible, not merely for ethical reasons but in order to maximize the credibility and impact of the facts found".[47] A requirement of the procedural law applicable to international fact-finding in the field of human rights "is to ensure the impartiality and objectivity of the fact-finders".[48] In the 1991 UN Declaration, impartiality is twice listed as a requirement for the missions.[49]

All three sets of documents emphasise that impartiality of the members is essential. According to the Belgrade Minimal Rules, the fact-finding mission should be composed of persons who are respected for their integrity, impartiality, and objectivity and who are serving in their

---

[46] Rob Grace, Claude Bruderlein, "Building Effective Monitoring, Reporting, and Fact-Finding Mechanisms", *Working Paper of the Program on Humanitarian Policy and Conflict Research*, Harvard University, April 2012.

[47] Thomas M. Franks and H.S. Fairley, 1980, p. 310, see *supra* note 5.

[48] Klaus Samson, "Procedural Law", in Bertrand G. Ramcharan (ed.), *International Law and Fact-finding in the Field of Human Rights*, Boston, 1982, pp. 41–42.

[49] Article 3 provides that fact-finding should be comprehensive, objective, impartial and timely. Article 25 further requires that fact-finding missions have an obligation to perform their task in an impartial way, see *supra* note 11.

personal capacities. In accordance with Article 90(1) of Additional Protocol I, each member of the IHFFC must be of "high moral standing" and "acknowledged impartiality". Rule 1 of the IHFFC Rules of the Procedure provides that members shall accept no instructions from any authority or person whatsoever and serve in their personal capacity instead of representing the States of which they are nationals in the performance of their functions. In other words, they are not acting as representatives of any governments or international organisations, but as individuals accountable for themselves. The requirements are regarded as indispensable to the credibility and effectiveness of the Commission.[50] The Lund-London Guidelines require that the NGO should ensure that all members of the delegation must, at all times, act in an independent, unbiased, objective, lawful and ethical manner.[51]

One result of impartiality is that the fact-finders must be independent from suspected perpetrators and from institutions with an interest in the outcome of the inquiry. Over the armed conflict between Georgia and Russia, the Russians themselves have conducted their own fact-finding commission of inquiry, the findings of which were not accepted by the European Court of Human Rights ('ECtHR'). The ECtHR has established that those responsible for or carrying out an investigation into unlawful killing by state agents must be independent from those implicated in the events – meaning "not only a lack of hierarchical or institutional connection, but also a practical independence".[52] This is an interesting pronouncement in light of the ICC's complementarity principle that urges national investigations and prosecutions.

There are no rules providing that a fact-finder whose impartiality is affected must recuse him- or herself, or be disqualified. UN Watch advocates that the rules and precedents of international criminal tribunals, such as the Special Court for Sierra Leone and the International Criminal Tri-

---

[50] Aly Mokhtar, "Will This Mummification Saga Come to an End? The International Humanitarian Fact-Finding Commission: Article 90 of Protocol 1", in *Penn State International Law Review*, 2003, vol. 22, no. 2, p. 252.

[51] The Guidelines on International Human Rights Fact-Finding Visits and Reports, see *supra* note 42 para. 10.

[52] European Court of Human Rights, *Hugh Jordan v. the United Kingdom*, Application No. 2474/94, Judgement, 4 May 2001, para. 107.

bunal for Rwanda, are analogous and pertinent.[53] Future UN rules could use the IHFFC Rules and the Belgrade Rules of Procedures for reference. The former provides that the members shall not engage in any occupation or make any public statement on current armed conflict that may shed a legitimate doubt on their morality and impartiality and, in case of doubt, the Commission shall decide on the proper measures to take.[54] In other words, the members are forbidden to act in a way that would damage their impartiality; otherwise, they would possibly be disqualified. They should be cautious when writing or speaking on international conflicts or systematic human rights violations that could potentially be subject to an investigation by the Commission.[55] The latter explicitly provides that in order to facilitate the task of the mission, the government(s) concerned should be consulted in regard to the composition of the mission whenever possible.[56] Clearly, the rules were intended to gain co-operation and official support from governments, which is essential for the missions to work with full authority and gain access to certain documents. This is inspiring for future UN rules when the mandate involves sensitive situations.

### 8.4.2. Legal Expertise

Are fact-finders necessarily lawyers? What specialised knowledge is required for the effective gathering and analysis of information? In other words, does a mission have to be composed of experts in international human rights law, humanitarian law or criminal law?

The nature of fact-finding mechanisms makes finding the right people who have the requisite expertise, experience and competence necessary to interpret the mandate, investigate the matter effectively, and make sound decisions, critical. A fact-finder's lack of relevant expertise and experience could reduce the precision and weight of the legal analysis. It is even regarded as virtually impossible to conduct fact-finding without knowledge of the law because it is only through legal expertise that one can select the relevant facts from the huge quantity of information around

---

[53] UN Watch Request to Disqualify Christine Chinkin from UN Goldstone Mission on Gaza, 20 August 2009, p. 25.

[54] Rule of the International Humanitarian Fact-Finding Commission, Rule 3, see *supra* note 41.

[55] Chatham House, 2009, p. 7, see *supra* note 32.

[56] Thomas M. Franck, 1981, Article 5, p. 163, see *supra* note 40.

a given incident.[57] Moreover, the academic credentials of the legal experts could lend legitimacy to the missions.[58] Therefore, fact-finders are supposed to be acquainted with various aspects of international human rights law, criminal law, humanitarian law, military law in case of armed conflict, and investigation. They should be vigilant of human rights violations and the competent authorities of the UN human rights protection mechanisms. In addition, to account for the dangers of an international military conflict, fact-finding personnel should have experience with armed conflict and fact-gathering techniques.[59]

The fate and eventual function of every fact-finding report vary, depending to a certain extent on the political dynamics in the UN. Sometimes, the fact-finding missions need to be composed of politicians so as to devise the missions to pursue the values of truth and justice without generating politically unwanted results. Yet these politicians could possibly lack expertise and experience in related international law, mechanisms and procedures. Is there a way to successfully combine legal expertise and political sense? The selection of members of the EU Inquiry Mission into the war over South Ossetia in 2008 is enlightening in this regard.[60] The team consisted of three persons led by a Swiss diplomat, Ambassador Heidi Tagliavini.[61] However, the mission contracted some 20 experts for specific written contributions on military, legal, humanitarian and historical issues to be considered under the mandate.[62] Additionally, a Senior Advisory Board was set up to review the Mission's work and provide it with counsel and guidance. This was composed of widely respected politicians and senior civil servants with special expertise in the field of inter-

---

[57] Théo Boutruche, "Credible Fact – Finding and Allegations of International Humanitarian Law Violations: Challenges in Theory and Practice", in *Journal of Conflict and Security Law*, 2011, vol. 16, no. 1, p. 7.

[58] Rob Grace, Claude Bruderlein, 2012, p. 38, see *supra* note 46.

[59] Tyler. B. Musselman, "Skirmishing for Information: The Flaws of the International Legal System as Evidence by the Russian-Georgian Conflict of 2008", in *Transnational Law and Contemporary Problems*, 2010, vol. 19, no. 1, p. 348.

[60] The Council of the European Union decision concerning an independent international fact-finding mission on the conflict in Georgia, 2008/901/CFSP, 2 December 2008.

[61] The Council of the European Union decision concerning an independent international fact-finding mission on the conflict in Georgia, 2008/901/CFSP, 2 December 2008, Article 1 and 3, see *supra* note 60.

[62] Report of the Independent International Fact-Finding Mission on the Conflict in Georgia, Report, vol. I, p. 6 (http://www.legal-tools.org/doc/b6be61/).

national relations, conflict management and humanitarian as well as human rights issues.[63] Therefore, gaining external professional assistance is a clever arrangement when the missions are led by politicians. In this case, proper training is necessary to make sure that team leaders or members have basic knowledge in international humanitarian law, criminal law and human rights law.

The requirements for the competence of members in the Lund-London Guidelines are the highest and most specific. The Geneva Protocol provides that "the contracting parties shall ensure that the persons to be elected to the Commission individually possess the qualifications required", without further specification.[64] Given the nature and competence of the Commission to enquire into any facts alleged to be a grave breach or other serious violation, it is axiomatic that some qualifications, such as being experts in humanitarian law or experienced in investigation, ought to be considered in the nomination and election of members so as to enable the Commission to function appropriately and effectively.[65] In accordance with the Lund-London Guidelines, the NGO should be confident that the members have the relevant competence, experience and expertise relevant to the matters pertaining to the terms of reference.[66] They should also have sufficient time for pre-mission briefings and/or training for the implementation of the mission and any proposed follow-up work, including contributing to the report.[67]

### 8.4.3. Management Skills

Investigating teams consisting of persons from different legal systems require 'team building' and a great deal of guidance and assistance. This also raises many questions of how to do things in truly international endeavours. Poor leadership skills or a lack of managerial experience could offset the benefits of the legitimacy given by academic credentials.[68] The

---

[63] Report of the Independent International Fact-Finding Mission on the Conflict in Georgia, Report, Volume I, p. 40, see *supra* note 62.

[64] Protocol Additional to the Geneva Conventions of 12 August 1949, Article 90(1)(d), see *supra* note 41.

[65] Aly Mokhtar, 2003, p. 253, see *supra* note 50.

[66] The Guidelines on International Human Rights Fact-Finding Visits and Reports, see *supra* note 42, para. 8.

[67] *Ibid.*, para. 9.

[68] Rob Grace, Claude Bruderlein, 2012, p. 39, see *supra* note 46.

---

US State Department explicitly criticised the composition of the Commission of Experts for the former Yugoslavia that there was too much emphasis on academic qualifications and too little on investigative or managerial skills.[69] Up until now, there has been no systematic design and no sign of taking management skills into consideration in member selection.

Without proper staff support, fact-finding missions would lose much time in administrative and logistical preparations and cut significantly into the limited period of time that they are given to undertake and complete their work. Usually, the office of the Secretary-General is responsible for providing support to the fact-finding missions, but without a specific mandate and specific persons in charge. For example, for the Gaza Mission it was only vaguely mentioned that a secretariat was established by the Office of the United Nations High Commissioner for Human Rights to provide support.[70] It is hard to tell what its specific responsibility was and whether the staff could spare sufficient time to make substantial contributions.

### 8.4.4. Geographic and Gender Considerations

The geographic representation of the mission is based on political balance and the understanding of cultural differences. The diversity of civilisations and legal systems could serve the purpose of collecting and analysing information, facilitating the fact-finding task and augmenting the effectiveness and credibility of the missions. Article 90(1)(d) of Geneva Protocol I provides that the Commission as a whole requires equitable geographical representation, but it is not clear how to achieve this. According to the Lund-London Guidelines, a variety of elements should be considered in the composition, such as gender, geographic, racial, ethnic and other types of balance and diversity, linguistic expertise and in-country knowledge.[71] Where appropriate, the members should have the relevant expertise and skills in interviewing children, women, victims of torture or other vulnerable groups, and internally-displaced persons.[72]

---

[69]  Michael P. Scharf, 2006, p. 7, see *supra* note 22.

[70]  Report of the United Nations Fact-Finding Mission on the Gaza Conflict, Human Rights Council Resolution, A/HRC/12/48, 25 September 2009, para. 3 (https://www.legal-tools. org/doc/ca9992/).

[71]  The Guidelines on International Human Rights Fact-Finding Visits and Reports, see *supra* note 42, para. 11.

[72]  *Ibid.*, para. 13.

Inadequate gender balance among staff could affect a mission's work, for example, when interviewing female witnesses or victims. Most of the missions are composed completely of males. But as mentioned earlier, a mission composed of only females is not appropriate either. According to the Lund-London Guidelines, the delegation members should be especially aware of the vulnerabilities of particular categories of potential interviewees who need to be approached with the utmost care; and only those with the relevant expertise and skill should undertake this kind of interview.[73] Particular methodological techniques should be considered in certain cases. For example, female victims of sexual abuse should be offered the choice of being interviewed by a female member of delegation.[74]

Because of the political nature of the UN, the equitable geographic and political representation of members can sometimes seem more important than competence, specific expertise and general appropriateness. Another problem is that not all UN Member States have the capability of contributing personnel with the expertise required for these missions.

## 8.5. Concluding Remarks

The UN fact-finding missions are facing a number of challenges in particular, regarding the quality control of their work. Among others, an important factor is the selection of its members. The extent to which the selection of fact-finders is in conformity with procedural fairness influences the outcome of the related missions. With the increasing need for consistent and systematic collection and analysis of information, the UN should improve and develop a uniform set of rules, including the requirements and procedures for the selection of fact-finders to make the process transparent, consistent and predictable, and to ensure the credibility and effectiveness of the mission and its work. Increased transparency about the human resources involved would also reinforce a sense of accountability and quality in the work process.

Professor Bassiouni argued for the selection of recurring appointees because it can provide for more experience and expertise, thereby contributing to the success of the mission.[75] However, with the proliferation of fact-finding mandates across a wide range of countries and situations,

---

[73] *Ibid.*, para. 45.

[74] *Ibid.*, para. 45.

[75] M. Cherif Bassiouni, 2001, p. 39, see *supra* note 14.

recurring appointees could be inadequate and might not be able to understand the particularity of every situation. Establishing a permanent fact-finding body in the UN might not be needed or feasible, but an expert list nominated by member States would be more appropriate.[76]

---

[76] This is practised in the Dispute Settlement Mechanism of the World Trade Organisation; the composition of a mandate is not decided by the concerned States.

# 9

------

# Purpose and Legitimacy
# in International Fact-Finding Bodies

## Dan Saxon[*]

> It is a terrible mass of evidence; but I feel that it ought to be
> published and widely studied by all who have the better in-
> terests of humanity at heart.[1]

Not long ago, the authors of a report by the International Law Commission observed that "normative conflict is endemic to international law".[2]
This chapter addresses the normative conflicts inherent in the purposes of
international fact-finding missions ('FFMs') and how these conflicts impact the quality of the work and the legitimacy of FFMs. I argue that the
most effective means of ensuring the quality, credibility and legitimacy of
FFMs entails clarification of the purposes of FFMs and reform of their
procedures.

## 9.1. The Purpose(s) and Mandates of FFMs: Legal or Political?

The mandates of international FFMs established during recent years (and
section 1.6. contains a detailed overview) commonly include instructions
to investigate and report on serious violations of international law, in particular, breaches of international human rights law.[3] Put very simply, fact-

------

[*] **Dan Saxon** serves as Senior Legal Advisor to the Specialist Prosecutor's Office for Koso-
vo. At the time of writing, he was Assistant Professor of Global Justice and International
Human Rights, Leiden University College. During 2011 and 2012 the author was the Legal
Adviser to the United Nations Independent International Commission of Inquiry for Syria.
The views expressed in this chapter are the author's personal views, and do not necessarily
reflect the views of the United Nations or the Commission of Inquiry for Syria.

[1] Letter from Viscount Grey of Fallodon, Secretary of State for Foreign Affairs (UK), to
Viscount Bryce, 23 August 1916, in *The Treatment of Armenians in the Ottoman Empire,
1915–16: Documents Presented to Viscount Grey of Fallodon by Viscount Bryce*, London,
His Majesty's Stationery Office, 1916, xviii.

[2] *Fragmentation of International Law: Difficulties Arising from the Diversification and
Expansion of International Law*, International Law Commission, 2006, para. 486.

[3] A/HRC/RES/22/13, Situation of Human Rights in the Democratic People's Republic of
Korea, 9 April 2013, para. 5 (https://www.legal-tools.org/doc/44666d/); A/HRC/S-17/1,

finding can be generally defined as "a method of ascertaining facts"[4] or a "systematic collection of facts"[5] about the circumstances, causes, consequences and aftermath of an event or events. Thus, on their face, FFMs are simply neutral investigative bodies intended to record and report serious contraventions of international law.

This legal perspective, however, ignores the political context in which FFMs are established and operate. Their fact-finding purpose may be subservient to political and diplomatic objectives. These may include attempts to create a 'safety-valve' through which the international community may criticise a particular regime; to facilitate the resolution of a conflict or temper its severity;[6] or, more cynically, to act as a 'place-holder' for an international community that cannot achieve consensus on a strategy for addressing a crisis.[7]

Moreover, different purposes may blend and change over time as conditions improve or worsen during fluid situations of armed conflict, civil unrest or other forms of security crises. For example, in August 2011 when the United Nations Human Rights Council voted (33 countries in favour; four against and nine abstentions) to approve the resolution that established the Independent International Commission of Inquiry for Syria ('Syria COI'), Thailand's Representative explained that Thailand supported the resolution "because of the situation on the ground and the need to turn back the tide of violence in Syria. [And] out of respect for the peo-

---

Situation of Human Rights in the Syrian Arab Republic, Resolution adopted by the Human Rights Council at its 17th special session, 22 August 2011, paras. 12 and 13; A/HRC/16/L.33, Situation of Human Rights in Côte d'Ivoire, 18 March 2011, para. 10; A/HRC/RES/S-15/1, Situation of Human Rights in the Libyan Arab Jamahiriya, 25 February 2011, para. 11 (https://www.legal-tools.org/doc/233009/).

[4] Théo Boutruche, "Credible Fact-Finding and Allegations of International Humanitarian Law Violations: Challenges in Theory and Practice", in *Journal of Conflict and Security Law*, 2011, vol. 16, p. 108, citing Karl Joseph Partsch, "Fact-Finding and Inquiry", in Rudolf Bernhardt (ed.), *Encyclopedia of Public International Law*, North-Holland, Amsterdam, 1992, p. 343.

[5] *Ibid.*

[6] Statement by Navi Pillay, High Commissioner for Human Rights to the Human Rights Council, 19th special session on "The Deteriorating Human Rights Situation in the Syrian Arab Republic and the Killings in El-Houleh", Geneva, 1 June 2012.

[7] I am grateful to Catherine Harwood for suggesting the metaphor of a 'place-holder' to describe certain FFMs.

ple of Syria *and to send a firm message to the Government of Syria*".[8] Indonesia's Representative, on the other hand, noted that the Human Rights Council's objectives with respect to Syria were to have "a concrete impact on the ground, promote and protect human rights, *and not to allow further politicization of the issue*".[9] 'Politicization' can be defined as the manipulation of factual information to reflect policy preferences.[10] At the United Nations, apparently, one state's political message may be another state's effort to re-focus attention away from politics.

To be effective, modern FFMs cannot ignore the political contexts and complexities of the events or situations under investigation. For example, at the close of World War II, Buchenwald was the first major concentration camp captured intact by the western allies. Officers from the U.S. Army's Psychological Warfare Division were sent to Buchenwald and tasked to prepare a report explaining "how a German concentration camp was organized, what role was assigned to it in the Nazi State and what happened to those who were sent to the camps by the Gestapo and detained there by the SS".[11] The team members soon realised that the complex situation within Buchenwald could only be understood with the collaboration of members of the myriad political, national, religious and social sub-groups that comprised the inmate population: Social Democrats,

---

[8]   Sihasak Phuangketeow, Human Rights Council Decides to Dispatch a Commission of Inquiry to Investigate Human Rights Violations in the Syrian Arab Republic, 23 August 2011 (available on the United Nations Office at Geneva's web site). After the massacre of civilians in the town of El-Houleh in May 2012, the United Kingdom's Representative to the Human Rights Council argued that the Council "should send a clear message to the Assad Government that its barbarity would not go unchallenged". Human Rights Council Requests Commission of Inquiry to Conduct a Special Inquiry in the Events in El Houleh, Office of the High Commissioner for Human Rights, Press Release (available on the United Nations Office of the High Commissioner for Human Rights ('OHCHR') web site).

[9]   Dian Triansyah, "Human Rights Council Decides to Dispatch a Commission of Inquiry to Investigate Human Rights Violations in the Syrian Arab Republic", 23 August 2011 (available on the OHCHR's web site).

[10]  Joshua R. Rovner, "Intelligence-Policy Relations and the Problem of Politicization", Ph.D. Dissertation, Massachusetts Institute of Technology, 2008. For example, after World War II, in order to appease Stalin's preferred view of history, the leadership of Poland's communist government directed that the official estimates of non-Jewish Polish dead and Jewish dead be increased and decreased, respectively, so that the two numbers were equal: three million each. Timothy Snyder, *Bloodlands: Europe Between Hitler and Stalin*, London, Vintage, 2011, p. 356.

[11]  Eugene Kogon, *The Theory and Practice of Hell: The German Concentration Camps and the System Behind Them*, Farrar, Straus and Co., New York, 1946, p. 8.

Communists, Socialists, Germans, Poles, Russians, French, Spanish, Jews, Jehovah's Witnesses, Jewish Political Prisoners, Special Political Prisoners, Convicts, Jewish Convicts, 'Asocial' Prisoners, Jewish 'Asocial' Prisoners, so-called 'Labor Disciplinary Prisoners' (or 'Loafers'), Jewish 'Race Defilers', Clergymen, Children, Gypsies and Homosexuals.[12]

More recently, the Chairmen of the Syria COI described the complex religious and political dynamics affecting the Syria conflict:

> There have been strong overtones of sectarianism in many of the violations committed. The Syrian conflict is extremely complex. It is vital that its sectarian dimension be placed within the broader geopolitical context. Indeed, it is politics that pushes sectarianism and that now engenders violence of a more sectarian nature, and which empowers its perpetrators.[13]

Nevertheless, efforts to *comprehend and document* complex situations and events are distinct from FFMs that attempt to *achieve* political objectives. The former reflects neutral efforts to perform an objective task; the latter weakens the institution of FFMs by colouring their results with political influences and goals.

In addition, the politicisation of FFM mandates promulgated by the United Nations Human Rights Council eviscerates the independence of fact-finders and creates a structural and ethical contradiction for Commissioners and other leaders of FFMs, who must comply with the "Code of Conduct for Special Procedures Mandate-holders of the Human Rights Council":

> Article 3 – General Principles of Conduct
>
> Mandate-holders are independent United Nations Experts. While discharging their mandate, they shall:
>
> (a) Act in an independent capacity, and exercise their functions in accordance with their mandate, through a professional, impartial assessment of facts based on internationally recognized human rights standards, and free from any kind of extraneous influence, incitement, pressure, threat or interference, either direct or indirect, on

---

[12] *Ibid.*, pp. 8–9, 39–47 and 297.

[13] Address by Paulo Sérgio Pinheiro, Chair of the Independent International Commission of Inquiry on the Syrian Arab Republic, to the United Nations General Assembly Plenary Session, New York, 29 July 2013.

the part of any party, whether stakeholder or not, for any reason whatsoever, the notion of independence being linked to the status of mandate-holders, and to their freedom to assess the human rights questions that they are called upon to examine under their mandate.[14]

The Code of Conduct also requires mandate-holders to "[f]ocus exclusively on the implementation of their mandate, constantly keeping in mind the fundamental obligations of truthfulness, loyalty and independence pertaining to their mandate".[15] It prohibits mandate-holders from seeking or accepting instructions from governments, individuals, non-governmental organisations or other groups.[16] The creation of FFMs with political goals, conversely, makes it impossible for leaders of FFMs to maintain their independence. It vitiates the duties of United Nations mandate-holders to "maintain and reinforce the trust they enjoy of all stakeholders"[17] and to "base their conclusions and recommendations on objective assessments of human rights situations".[18]

Professor M. Cherif Bassiouni, a veteran of several international FFMs, is highly critical of the system that permits FFMs to serve political ends: "It's a quagmire. It's a failed system by any standard. It's a seizure of the fact-finding process by the political process to develop a political outcome".[19] The lack of objectivity driven by political pressures and purposes can cast a long shadow over the legitimacy of the results of any fact-finding body. For example, former United Nations Special Rapporteur and FFM Commissioner John Dugard explains that the institution of fact-finding is severely harmed by the "exceptionalism" accorded to Israel by the United States and European Governments.[20] The FFMs established

---

[14] Code of Conduct for Special Procedures Mandate-holders of the Human Rights Council, Art. 3(a) (emphasis added).

[15] *Ibid.* Art. 3(d).

[16] *Ibid.* Art. 3(f). Indeed, mandate-holders must "exercise their functions in strict observance of their mandate [...]". *Ibid*, Art. 7.

[17] *Ibid.* Art. 3(h).

[18] *Ibid.* Art. 12(a).

[19] M. Cherif Bassiouni, presentation at "From Fact-Finding to Evidence: Harmonizing Multiple Investigations of International Crimes", The Hague Institute for Global Justice, 27 October 2012.

[20] John Dugard, "Experiences and Lessons Learned from Gaza", in *Human Rights Fact-Finding, Evidence and International Crimes*, Grotius Centre for Legal Studies, Summer School on Human Rights and Transitional Justice, Leiden University, 10 July 2013.

by the Human Rights Council to investigate events in the Middle East are compromised because Israel receives 'a free pass' with respect to compliance with international humanitarian law.[21] At a minimum, therefore, combining a mandate to investigate facts with political objectives and goals puts the credibility of FFMs at grave risk.

A review of the foundational documents that created the United Nations Human Rights Council (hereinafter 'Human Rights Council') indicates the intent of the members of the United Nations to emphasise "the importance of ensuring universality, objectivity and non-selectivity in the consideration of human rights issues, *and the elimination of double-standards and politicization*".[22] Furthermore, the methods of work of the Council must be "transparent, fair and impartial and shall enable genuine dialogue".[23] This language militates against the politicisation of the purposes and objectives of FFMs, and requires transparency and genuine discussion – within the Human Rights Council – prior to the modification or re-interpretation of a FFM mandate by one or more Commissioners.

One school of thought acknowledges that FFM "mandates will remain political in nature since these are mostly issued by political bodies".[24] Thus, given the "imperfect" nature of the mandates of FFMs, Commissioners or other leaders of FFMs must have the freedom to interpret their mandates "flexibly", subject to "peer review".[25] This flexible approach to determining the purposes and parameters of FFMs permits these bodies to react to changing situations. Yet, it also potentially imbues Commissioners with great power, including the power to divert from the instructions provided by the international political bodies that created the FFM. For example, in July 2013, the Chairman of the Syria Commission of Inquiry told the United Nations General Assembly that: "[T]his war is a chronicle of missed opportunities on the part of influential states and the international community". Whether this opinion is accurate is irrelevant to

---

[21]  *Ibid.*

[22]  UNGA/A/RES/60/251, 3 April 2006, 2 (emphasis added).

[23]  *Ibid.*, para. 12.

[24]  Claude Bruderlein, Director of Program on Humanitarian Policy and Conflict Research, Harvard University and Director, Harvard Group of Professionals on Monitoring, Reporting and Fact-Finding, remarks at "From Fact-Finding to Evidence: Harmonizing Multiple Investigations of International Crimes", The Hague Institute for Global Justice, 27 October 2012.

[25]  *Ibid.*

the mandate of the Commission, which says nothing about reporting or commenting on the international community's response to the Syrian crisis.[26] Moreover, by providing such comments to the United Nations General Assembly, Commissioners become political figures themselves, rather than fact-finders.

Furthermore, when members of an 'independent' FFM consider whether to stretch or reduce their given mandate, and wish to consult their 'peers' about this matter, it is not clear who constitutes a 'peer' for the purposes of such discussions. For example, does the scope of 'peer' in this context include only other Commissioners of international commissions of inquiry? Or should the term 'peer' include experts from the academic and scientific community? Will members of the diplomatic community, NGO representatives and/or officials of international institutions constitute a 'peer' for the purposes of these kinds of consultations? Each of the aforementioned professionals may have an interest in persuading a particular FFM to interpret its mandate broadly or narrowly, or even to ignore portions of the mandate altogether.

In one of the United Nations Human Rights Council's foundational documents, then UN Secretary-General Kofi Annan describes the concept of 'peer review' as a function of the new *Council* in the exercise of its review of the human rights situations in states. Annan explained that the Human Rights Council,

> [...] should have an explicitly defined function as a chamber of peer review. Its main task would be to evaluate the fulfillment by all States of all their human rights obligations. This would give concrete expression to the principle that human rights are universal and indivisible. Equal attention will have to be given to civil, political, economic, social and cultural rights, as well as the right to development. And it should be equipped to give technical assistance to States and

---

[26] When it established the Syria Commission of Inquiry, the Human Rights Council directed it to:

> [...] investigate all alleged violations of international human rights law since March 2011 in the Syrian Arab Republic, to establish the facts and circumstances that may amount to such violations and of the crimes perpetrated and, where possible, to identify those responsible with a view to ensuring that perpetrators of violations, including those that may constitute crimes against humanity, are held accountable.

A/HRC/S-17/2, Report of the Human Rights Council on its 17th special session, 22 August 2011, para. 13.

policy advice to States and United Nations bodies alike. Under such a system, every Member State could come up for review on a periodic basis. Any such rotation should not, however, impede the Council from dealing with any massive and gross violations that might occur. Indeed the Council will have to be able to bring urgent crises to the attention of the world community.[27]

The Secretary-General emphasised that transparency is crucial to peer review, reflected in the concept of 'universal scrutiny', whereby the performance of all member states with respect to their human rights obligations would be subject to assessment by other states.[28] Thus, 'peer review', by the Human Rights Council, is supposed to reduce "the politicization and selectivity"[29] that were the hallmarks of the former Commission on Human Rights. This definition of the concept of 'peer review', highlighting the importance of transparency and the dangers of politicising the evaluation of human rights conditions within states, suggests that only the Human Rights Council, the political body that creates Independent International Commissions of Inquiry, should (transparently) modify the meaning or interpretation of these FFM mandates.[30] Rather than unilateral changes to the mandates established by the political body that created them, the better practice for Commissioners of United Nations human rights FFMs would be to return to the Human Rights Council for consultation and clarification of their mandate.

## 9.2. The Marriage of Fact-Finding and Accountability

In addition to the two general purposes mentioned above, documenting human rights violations and furthering political agendas, the mandates of several recent FFMs suggest that the information gathered may, or should,

---

[27] Speech of Kofi Annan to Human Rights Commission, 7 April 2005, cited in "In Larger Freedom: Towards Development, Security and Human Rights for All, Report of the Secretary-General", UNGA/A/59/2005/Add.1, 23 May 2005, para. 6 (https://www.legal-tools. org/doc/5739f5/). The Secretary-General originally intended the Human Rights Council to be a principal body of the United Nations, allowing it to stand as a peer alongside the Security Council and the Economic and Social Council. *Ibid.*, para. 14.

[28] *Ibid.*, para. 8.

[29] *Ibid.*

[30] Indeed, Art. 6(d) of the "Code of Conduct for Special Procedures Mandate-Holders of the Human Rights Council" encourages Human Rights Council mandate-holders to "bring to the attention of the Council" suggestions that may enhance their capacity to ulfil their mandate; 18 June 2007.

be used to hold accountable those individuals who are responsible for the abuses.[31] For example, when Poland introduced the draft resolution to the Human Rights Council that resulted in the establishment of the Commission of Inquiry for Syria, its representative observed that the investigative work of the Commission of Inquiry would "ensure that perpetrators were held accountable".[32] A focus on accountability can serve several objectives. First, it puts military and civilian superiors on notice that if they continue to violate the law, they may be held responsible, thereby potentially deterring future crimes.[33] Second, accountability serves to break down established patterns of impunity and helps to restore the rule of law. Lastly, by holding accountable those who are most responsible for crimes, society may restore some measure of justice to the victims of these abuses.[34]

From one perspective, 'human rights' FFMs serve a different purpose from 'criminal' FFMs. The 'human rights' fact-finder may place more emphasis on identifying systemic problems in a particular state and then addressing these issues with State officials to ameliorate those problems. "Criminal investigators, on the other hand, search for suspects".[35] However, in the context of an investigation into gross and/or systematic human rights violations, attempts to de-couple criminal accountability

---

[31] A/HRC/RES/22/13, Situation of Human Rights in the Democratic People's Republic of Korea, 9 April 2013, para. 5; A/HRC/S-17/1, Situation of Human Rights in the Syrian Arab Republic, Resolution Adopted by the Human Rights Council at its 17th Special Session, 22 August 2011, paras. 12 and 13; A/HRC/16/L.33, Situation of Human Rights in Côte d'Ivoire, 18 March 2011, para. 10; A/HRC/RES/S-15/1, Situation of Human Rights in the Libyan Arab Jamahiriya, 25 February 2011, para. 11.

[32] Cezary Lusinski, Human Rights Council Decides to Dispatch a Commission of Inquiry to Investigate Human Rights Violations in the Syrian Arab Republic, The United Nations Office at Geneva, 23 August 2011.

[33] Navanethem Pillay, United Nations High Commissioner of Human Rights, observes that the deterrence of the most flagrant human rights abuses *via* the application of accountability measures has "been a critical component of human rights advocacy". "What Are Human Rights For?", in Daniel Moeckli, *et al.* (eds.), *International Human Rights Law*, Oxford University Press, Oxford, 2010, p. 6.

[34] When the Human Rights Council passed a resolution establishing a Commission of Inquiry for Cotê d'Ivoire, the U.S. Representative to the Council expressed her hope that through the work of the Commission of Inquiry: "all those who lost their lives during this troubled period will find a measure of justice". Statement by Ambassador Eileen Chamberlain Donahoe, 25 March 2011.

[35] Ian Urbina, "Tensions Mar Blast Inquiry In Texas as Agencies Disagree on Goals", *The New York Times*, 27 June 2013, A23.

from human rights fact-finding creates a false dichotomy. Part of the relevance of fact-finding processes – whether by national or international bodies – includes the identification of persons responsible for international crimes.[36] For example, after the killings of civilians in the town of El-Houlah, Syria in May 2012, Mexico's representative to the Human Rights Council argued that it "was the obligation of the Council to ensure an investigation that would contribute to bringing those responsible to justice".[37] Thus, to ignore the value of accountability is to reinforce and legitimise impunity for the abuses that have occurred,[38] thereby leading to more abuses, more conflict and a perverse result for FFMs.[39]

Individual state officials – concerned about their own accountability – may be less inclined to co-operate with fact-finders who are investigating crimes. Nevertheless, this is not a fatal impediment to FFMs. Persistent and creative investigators usually will be able to locate other witnesses and sources of evidence who can provide insider information about events, including admissions about policies, intentions and conduct. For example, *a century ago*, the British fact-finding body that investigated Turkey's extermination of its Armenian population discovered that in July 1915, during the deportation of the Armenian population from the Kaisaria District of Turkey, the Governor was petitioned to allow charitable Muslim families to take in Armenian infants, to save them from dying during the journey. The Governor replied: "I will not leave here so much as the odour of the Armenians; go away into the deserts of Arabia and

---

[36] Statement delivered on behalf of all Special Procedures Mandate-Holders of the United Nations Human Rights Council at the Nineteenth Special Session of the Human Rights Council on the Situation of Human Rights in the Syrian Arab Republic, Geneva, 1 June 2012 (available on the OHCHR's web site).

[37] Human Rights Council Requests Commission of Inquiry to Conduct a Special Inquiry in the Events in El Houleh, Office of the High Commissioner for Human Rights, 1 June 2012 (available on its web site).

[38] See A/HRC/RES/22/24, "Situation of Human Rights in the Syrian Arab Republic", 12 April 2013 (recalling that the issue of accountability for those responsible for international crimes deserves to be raised in a more robust manner to counter the pervasive sense of impunity in Syria),; and A/HRC/Res/ 21/26, "Situation of Human Rights in the Syrian Arab Republic", 17 October 2012, para. 10 (in which the Human Rights Council encourages the international community to ensure that there is no impunity for abuses and violations of international law in Syria) (https://www.legal-tools.org/doc/4e9c2a/).

[39] In July 2013, the Head of the Syria Commission of Inquiry told the UN General Assembly that: "[A]ccountability must form part of the [peace] negotiations if any future peace is to endure". Address by Paulo Sérgio Pinheiro, United Nations General Assembly, 29 July 2013.

---

dump your Armenians there".[40] In order to instigate the Turkish population to greater violence, the Government of Turkey published a report describing crimes committed by Christians – in particular Armenians – against Muslims.[41] When an American doctor sought permission from Turkish authorities to provide assistance to Armenian deportees languishing in inhospitable mountain and desert terrain, his request was refused. When the physician replied: "Why, they will die," the Turkish official responded: "Why do you suppose they are sent there for?".[42]

Thus, it is short-sighted to draw a distinction between fact-finding and accountability. For example, in recent comments on the Human Rights Council's work concerning the Syria crisis, the US Representative to the Council argued that "[t]he international community must continue to support documentation and other efforts to lay the groundwork for accountability for human rights violations [in Syria], even as work continues toward a political settlement [...]".[43] Thus, within the context of gross and/or systematic violations of human rights, the work of every professional fact-finding body can contribute to the process of holding accountable those most responsible for the abuses.[44]

---

[40] "Statement By a Traveller from Kaisaria", published in the Armenian Journal Balkanian Mamoul, of Roustchouk, in *The Treatment of Armenians in the Ottoman Empire, 1915–1916*, p. 328.

[41] Resumé of a Letter Dated Konia, 2/15 October 1915, from a Well-Informed Source at Bucharest, *The Treatment of Armenians in the Ottoman Empire*, 1915–16, p. 437.

[42] "Statement by Miss A., A Foreign Resident at AC, Written Subsequently to Her Departure from Turkey in September 1915, Communicated by the Rev. I.N. Camp, of Cairo", *The Treatment of Armenians in the Ottoman Empire*, 1915–16, p. 536.

[43] Statement by Ambassador Eileen Chamberlain Donahue, U.S. Representative to the UN Human Rights Council, HRC – 23rd Session, 14 June 2013.

[44] For example, after the massacre of civilians in the Syrian village of El-Houleh in May 2012, the Human Rights Council requested the Commission of Inquiry to "urgently conduct a comprehensive, independent and unfettered special inquiry, consistent with international standards, into the events in El-Houleh and, if possible, to publicly identify those who appear responsible for these atrocities, and to preserve the evidence of crimes for possible future criminal prosecutions or a future justice process, with a view to hold to account those responsible, [...]", A/HRC/S-19/2, S-19/1. "The Deteriorating Situation of Human Rights in the Syrian Arab Republic, and the Recent Killings in El-Houleh", 1 June 2012, para. 8 (https://www.legal-tools.org/doc/d3a043/).

## 9.3. Recommendations for Future Fact-Finding Bodies

In order to protect the legitimacy of international fact-finding work, their mandates and activities should be de-coupled from politics to the greatest extent possible. As a start, FFMs should be established with the purpose of solely performing 'neutral' fact-finding. They should not be conceived or viewed as political or diplomatic tools to achieve geo-political ends. Second, although mandates should be drafted with precision, when the mandates of FFMs require modification or re-interpretation, that process should involve the members of the Human Rights Council in an open dialogue. Third, FFMs should not be given, nor should they assume, the task of making recommendations for resolving or ameliorating the situations or events that they investigate.[45] Obvious recommendations, such as the need for a regime to "put an immediate end to gross human rights violations",[46] are unnecessary. The development of more nuanced recommendations, such as the possible structure(s) of post-conflict transitional justice mechanisms, inevitably layer the fact-finding process (and the members of the FFM) with a political dimension. Thus, it is more appropriate for the political bodies that create FFMs – such as the Human Rights Council or the United Nations Security Council – to design and develop such recommendations as part of the process of 'peer review'.

Fourth, where fact-finding mandates involve the investigation of allegations of violations of fundamental human rights and other crimes under international law, the possibility of holding accountable those individuals who are responsible for such abuses should be an important pillar of the work of the FFMs.

Fifth, individuals appointed to serve on international FFMs should be experienced fact-finders with expertise in international law *and* accountability, that is, judges, prosecutors, criminal defence attorneys, historians, professional analysts and others with law enforcement, military and/or forensic expertise. It is unhelpful and inefficient to appoint career

---

[45] When the UK Government published its report on the Armenian genocide in 1916, it noted that "[f]acts have only been dealt with; questions of future policy have been avoided". Letter from Viscount Bryce to Viscount Grey of Fallodon, Secretary of State for Foreign Affairs, in *The Treatment of Armenians in the Ottoman Empire*, xvi.

[46] A/HRC/S-17/2/Add.1, Report of the Independent International Commission of Inquiry on the Syrian Arab Republic, 23 November 2011, para. 112 (https://www.legal-tools.org/doc/925e44/).

administrators, diplomats, academics and other individuals whose professional expertise do not match the objectives of the FFM.

Sixth, leaders and commissioners of FFMs should be individuals with proven records of independence from the influences of states and other institutions. As trite as this may seem, FFM members must be individuals who are willing and able to make decisions based on the facts and the law, rather than on the comments of their 'friends'.

Seventh, the work of FFMs should always avoid expressions of bias, which undermine the credibility of findings and results. For example, the British Government's report about the treatment of the Armenian population in Turkey referred to the Government of Turkey in 1915-16 as "[t]he rule of the savage gang".[47] Its description of the historical record of Turkish authorities was even more one-sided, and unnecessary:

> But the record of the rulers of Turkey for the last two or three centuries, from the Sultan on his throne down to the district Muressarif, is, taken as a whole, an almost unbroken record of corruption, of injustice, of an oppression which often rises into hideous cruelty.[48]

Finally, FFMs should not hesitate to review and evaluate all credible sources of information about events that fall within their mandate. In this regard, the British report on the Armenian tragedy reflected academic and forensic expertise, creative investigative work, and sound analysis:

> They [the Docs describing the Armenian Genocide] do not, and by the nature of the case cannot, constitute what is called judicial evidence, such as a Court of Justice obtains when it puts witnesses on oath and subjects them to cross-examination. But by far the larger part [...] does constitute historical evidence of the best kind, inasmuch as the statements come from those who saw the events they describe and recorded them in writing immediately afterwards. They corroborate one another, the narratives given by different observers showing a substantial agreement, which becomes conclusive when we find the salient facts repeated with no more variations in detail than the various opportunities of the independent observers made natural. The gravest facts are those for which the evidence is most complete, [...] In this

---

[47] Preface by Viscount Bryce, in *The Treatment of Armenians in the Ottoman Empire*, p. xxii.
[48] *Ibid.*, p. xxviii.

case there are [...] admissions of the Turkish Government and of their German apologists.[49] [...] There are no discrepancies or contradictions of importance, but, on the contrary, countless scattered pieces of mutual corroboration.[50]

## 9.4. Conclusions

In his report about the structure and operations of the Buchenwald concentration camp, published shortly after World War II, Eugene Kogon argued that "[t]he world, [...] must pause for self-analysis".[51] Today, the importance and frequency of fact-finding work requires similar reflection about the purposes and procedures of FFMs. Politicised fact-finding processes are doomed to ridicule and irrelevancy. Similarly, FFMs that ignore or minimise the need for accountability for fundamental and systematic violations of human rights undermine one of the significant benefits of fact-finding work. The drafting of clear guidelines for FFMs would be an important step toward the goal of improving the legitimacy of fact-finding activities.

---

[49] *Ibid.*, pp. xxvi–xxvii.

[50] Letter from Mr. Herbert Fisher, Vice-Chancellor of Sheffield University, to Viscount Bryce, 2 August 1916, in *The Treatment of Armenians in the Ottoman Empire*, p. xxix.

[51] *The Theory and Practice of Hell*, p. 13.

# 10

---

# Witness Sensitive Practices in International Fact-Finding Outside Criminal Justice: Lessons for Nepal

### Christopher B. Mahony[*]

## 10.1. Introduction

This chapter considers the security implications of quality control in fact-finding, particularly with regard to truth commissions in transitional justice contexts. It addresses the lessons offered by variant levels of quality control in fact-finding commissions for the proposed Commission on Investigation of Disappeared Persons, Truth and Reconciliation in Nepal. In doing so, I draw on research conducted in Kenya and South Africa funded by the Institute for Security Studies and the Special Court for Sierra Leone, as well as upon my experience working at Sierra Leone's Truth and Reconciliation Commission in 2003, and Special Court in 2008. I also draw on research conducted for the International Centre for Transitional Justice in Nepal in 2011. The chapter considers the difference in threat to witnesses and to wider communities of commissions employing variant quality control in fact-finding under circumstances of uneven political, economic and social risk. I analyse in particular the impact of a commission's mandate and capacity upon the quality of fact-finding, especially

---

[*] **Christopher B. Mahony** is Senior Political Economy Specialist at the World Bank. At the time of writing, he was Deputy Director of the New Zealand Centre for Human Rights Law, Policy and Practice, Faculty of Law, University of Auckland. He obtained a D.Phil. in Politics at the University of Oxford. He holds a Bachelor of Commerce degree (B.Com.) and a Bachelor of Laws (LL.B.) degree from the University of Otago, and a Master's degree in African Studies (M.Sc.) from the University of Oxford. He was admitted to the bar of the High Court of New Zealand in 2006 where he appeared for the Crown in criminal and refugee matters. He drafted the recommendations on governance for the Sierra Leone Truth and Reconciliation Commission, and co-authored the 'Historical antecedents to the conflict' chapter. In 2008, he directed the Witness Evaluation Legacy Project at the Special Court for Sierra Leone. He has advised the International Criminal Court, the British and United States governments, the International Centre for Transitional Justice, and the Open Society Initiative, on transitional justice and justice sector reform.

practices relating to the security of persons that a commission interacts with. In doing so, I consider how a potential Nepali truth commission might balance the physical and psychological security of witnesses and sources, as well as the threat of further instability, with the imperative to find facts and to respect the rights of implicated persons to their reputations. Leading civil society elements in Nepal have called for prosecution of crimes committed during the conflict. However, they have not articulated the level of fact-finding quality control required for independent investigation and prosecution that does not jeopardise witness security.

There are a number of critical variables that inform the consideration of the need to establish a historical record, as well as the potential implications of doing so. Unlike the peace versus justice debate that considers a criminal process,[1] a fact-finding exercise may have no punitive function and does not need to accord the same level of rights to accused or implicated persons. It may therefore employ anonymity throughout and may decline to attribute individual responsibility. This chapter considers how and when a Nepali Commission might apply various investigative and reporting practices, given the lessons of commissions elsewhere – and reflects on the question: what is the appropriate level of 'quality control' for fact-finding in Nepal?

### 10.1.1. Nepal's Proposed Commission on Investigation of Disappeared Persons, Truth and Reconciliation

In July 2007, Nepal's Ministry of Peace and Reconstruction ('MoPR') proposed legislation that would establish a Truth and Reconciliation Commission ('TRC') in Nepal. The Government also proposed separate legislation calling for the establishment of a "high-level independent commission" to investigate and submit a report on disappearances during Nepal's armed conflict.[2] The then-proposed commissions constituted the proposed response to human rights abuses that occurred during Nepal's civil conflict, including 13,000 deaths at the hands of the Royal Nepal Army ('RNA'), the Armed Police Force, and the Maoist People's Libera-

---

[1]  Chandra Sriram and Suren Pillay (eds.), *Peace versus Justice? The Dilemma of Transitional Justice in Africa*, University of KwaZulu Natal Press, Scottsville, 2009.

[2]  Section 10(1), Act of Disappearing a Person (Crime and Punishment) Bill, (2066 B.S.) 2011 ('Disappearances Bill').

tion Army ('PLA').[3] Both bills were tabled before Parliament in 2010, but did not progress. In November 2011, a political agreement was reached establishing a task force comprising politicians from Nepal's three main political parties – United Communist Party of Nepal (Maoist), Nepali Congress, and United Marxist-Leninist. The task force recommended prioritising reconciliation over truth-seeking by incorporating an amnesty for crimes committed during the conflict.[4] In March 2013, the four main political parties dispensed with the separate bills and passed an Ordinance, without allowing victims or stakeholders to see it.[5] The Ordinance created a single Commission on Investigation of Disappeared Persons, Truth and Reconciliation.[6] The Ordinance provides the Commission power to grant amnesty, but also to recommend prosecution to the Attorney-General.[7]

Prominent human rights bodies and organisations criticised the Disappearances Bill and the TRC Bill for failing to comply with international law and standards, particularly pertaining to amnesty for serious crimes.[8] Similar criticism has been levelled against the Commission on Investigation of Disappeared Persons, Truth and Reconciliation Ordinance, which Nepal's Supreme Court issued an order against.[9] Civil society groups have also been dissatisfied with the extent to which the proposed fact-finding

---

[3] Human Rights Watch, "Waiting for Justice: Unpunished Crimes from Nepal's Armed Conflict", September 2008.

[4] TRIAL, "Written Information for the Adoption of the List of Issues the Human Rights Committee with Regard to Nepal's Second Periodic Report", CCPR/C/NPL/2, April 2013, p. 13 (available on the Office of the High Commissioner for Human Rights' web site).

[5] *Ibid.*, p. 14.

[6] Ordinance on Commission on Investigation of Disappeared Persons, Truth and Reconciliation, no. 2069 (2012), 14 March 2013, Nepal Gazette (Unofficial translation by ICTJ, 2 April 2013) ('TRC Ordinance').

[7] *Ibid.*, Sections 23 and 25.

[8] United Nations Office of the High Commissioner for Human Rights, "OHCHR-Nepal raises Concerns about Truth and Reconciliation Commission Bill", Press Release, 3 August 2007; Amnesty International, "Nepal Disappearances Law Must Meet International Standards", 2 September 2009; ICTJ, "Selecting Commissioners for Nepal's Truth and Reconciliation Commission", Briefing Paper, March 2011.

[9] "Nepal Court Blocks Civil War Truth Commission", *BBC News*, 1 April 2013; United Nations Office of the High Commissioner for Human Rights, "OHCHR Comments on the Nepal Commission on Investigation of Disappeared Persons, Truth and Reconciliation Ordinance – 2069 (2013)", 3 April 2013; TRIAL, 2012, *supra* note 4; Amnesty International, 2009, *ibid.*

facilitates witness protection.[10] The willingness of witnesses to co-operate with the Commission will be instructed by witness-sensitive quality control of its fact-finding, namely, its perceived independence, efficacy, capacity to affect punitive processes, and ability to provide witness protection. One victim described the anticipated inability of the previously proposed commissions to investigate abuses by stating: "if there is not protection, we cannot find the truth".[11] This comment is representative of feedback from Nepali victims, witnesses, civil servants and civil society actors. They anticipate that witnesses will be reluctant to co-operate with investigations perceived as causing more security harm than truth-seeking good. Witness apprehension is instructed by police failure to adequately investigate voluminous alleged incidents of extrajudicial killings, enforced disappearances, torture and other abuses.[12] No one has been successfully prosecuted.

## 10.1.2. Nepal's Political Background

In 2005, the PLA's political wing, the Communist Party of Nepal (Maoist) ('CPN-M'), joined anti-Government demonstrations and pro-democracy political parties in a united front of opposition to the Monarchy. The main pro-democracy parties included the Communist Party of Nepal (United Marxist-Leninist) ('CPN-UML'), and the Nepali Congress ('NC'). The conflict ended in November 2006 with the signing of the Comprehensive Peace Agreement ('CPA') by the CPN-M and the Government.[13] The CPA called for the establishment of a TRC "to probe those involved in serious violations of human rights and crimes against humanity", and to foster "reconciliation in society".[14] The CPA also placed PLA combatants in cantonment camps without their arms, dissolved parallel Maoist structures, and required the creation of an interim constitution and parliament (Constituent Assembly ('CA')) to negotiate a new constitution and government.

---

[10] The author conducted field research in Nepal in November 2011, in which he interviewed numerous civil society actors.

[11] Victim speaking at a meeting with victims and victim representatives, 22 November 2011, Kathmandu.

[12] Human Rights Watch, "Indifference to Duty: Impunity for Crimes Committed in Nepal", 2010, p. 2.

[13] The CPN-M had already agreed terms with the main political parties. Article 1(4), Comprehensive Peace Agreement Held between the Government of Nepal and Communist Party of Nepal (Maoist), 21 November 2006.

[14] *Ibid.*, Article 5(2)(5).

The CPN-M won elections in 2008. In January 2009, it formed the Unified Communist Party of Nepal – Maoist ('UCPN-M'), after joining with the CPN ('Unity Centre-Masal').

The UCPN-M held control of the Government in a coalition with the CPN-UML party until 4 May 2009. Political instability has followed. Various coalitions have been formed and collapsed after failing to agree to a new constitution and security sector reform.[15] The Madhesi parties represent groups formerly outside of government. The Madhesi parties formed a 2011 coalition government with the UCPN-M.[16] The four-point UCPN-M/Madhesi agreement provided a general amnesty to the Maoist insurgency, the Madhesi movement, and all other actors apart from the Nepal Army and the police.[17] That coalition, along with those subsequent, failed to achieve constitutional reform. The result is an ethnicised federalist system supported by the Maoists and the Madhesi parties, but opposed

---

[15] The Maoists were then in opposition until 3 February 2011 when CPN-UML led a coalition government with support from the Nepali Congress ('NC') and 21 other parties. The third government was led by CPN-UML again in coalition with Maoists. On 29 May 2011, the Parliament extended the deadline for a constitution by three months for the first time. On 28 August 2011, Maoist Vice-Chairman Baburam Bhattarai was elected Prime Minister and granted a new deadline of 30 November 2011. In January 2011, the United Nations Mission in Nepal departed without significant security implications indicating Maoist 'buy-in' to the political process. Agreement on the part of the Maoists to disarm the PLA and integrate former combatants was met with cautious optimism given the rhetoric of some Maoist figures prior to the agreement. The CPN-UML, the CPN-M and the NC formed the two-thirds majority agreement required to extend the CA but failed to form an inclusive government. The Madheshi Front also refused to participate in the government. The deal, which extended the CA by three months, required Maoist handover of arms, integration of Maoist combatants and completion of the first draft of the Nepali constitution. After the coalition failed to implement the deal, the Prime Minister resigned. A previous coalition had agreed to address Madhesi Front demands without specifying the demanded autonomous Madhesi region and a separate national army unit of 10,000 Madhesi youths. A diversity of previously excluded groups has emerged with espoused aspirations of self-determination that could provide sources of ethnicised future instability. See Anand Verma, "The Crisis of the Constituent Assembly in Nepal", *Tehelka*, 27 May 2011; International Crisis Group, "Nepal's Fitful Peace Process", *Asia Briefing*, no. 120, 7 April 2011, p. 1. Jason Miklian, "Nepal's Terai: Constructing an Ethnic Conflict", *PRIO South Asia Briefing Paper*, no. 1, 20 July 2008, p. 4; Rebecca Crozier and Zuleika Candan, "Participation and Obstruction: Justice and Security Sector Reform in Nepal", International Alert, November 2010, p. 13.

[16] Gani Ansari, "Maoists, Madhesis Ink Four-Point Deal", *Republica*, 29 August 2011.

[17] *Ibid.*

by the UML and Nepali Congress parties.[18] While parties have taken steps toward compromise and inclusivity, the extent to which internal party politicking drives compromise on substantive issues, such as security sector reform and constitutionality, remains unclear.[19] These and other disagreements may cause instability around the scheduled November 2013 Elections.[20] Any witness protection entity accompanying a commission must be completely cognisant of savvy political actors' capacity to misuse investigative and protective functions. Misuse might include implicating and marginalising political opponents. Therefore, ensuring safe and authentic testimony *via* a high level of fact-finding quality control is critical to a Nepali Commission's integrity and credibility, particularly given the historical tendencies of local actors to target witnesses.[21]

### 10.1.3. Three Key Witness-Oriented Elements Distinguishing Fact-Finding Commissions from Courts

There are three key elements regarding witnesses that distinguish fact-finding commissions from courts: (1) they do not need to have punitive consequences (directly or indirectly); (2) witnesses do not need to be cross-examined in accordance with accused rights; and (3) they are less vulnerable to the inducement of inauthentic witness testimony.

*Truth commissions are by nature not punitive bodies.* This is significant for the threat to witnesses because it is the threat posed to perpetrators of prosecution that ordinarily stimulates the greatest threat. Truth commissions can stimulate that threat. Unlike criminal trials, truth commissions enjoy discretion on whether or not to name names and/or attrib-

---

[18]  International Crisis Group, "Nepal's Constitution: The Expanding Political Matrix", *Asia Report*, no. 234, 27 August 2012, no. 234.

[19]  In an earlier Constituent Assembly coalition for example, the Nepali Congress conceded many 10-point pre-conditions, including the Prime Minister's resignation, immediate return of Maoist seized property and Young Communist League dismantling. The Maoists also conceded to handing over arms. However, local observers allege the UCPN-M and UML leadership worked together to marginalise respective internal opposition. See Verma, 2011, *supra* note 15; International Crisis Group, 2011, p. 8, *supra* note 15; Interview with justice sector donors, 23 November 2011, Kathmandu; International Crisis Group, 2012, *supra* note 18.

[20]  Hou Qiang, "News Analysis: Security still main concern in Nepal's 19. November elections", *Xinhua News Agency*, 28 August 2013.

[21]  United Nations General Assembly, Human Rights Council, Report of the Special Rapporteur on the Promotion and Protection of the Right to Freedom of Opinion and Expression, Ambeyi Ligabo, UN Doc. A/HRC/7/14/Add.1, 25 February 2008.

---

ute individual command responsibility for abuses.[22] When commissions decide to investigate command responsibility, as well as the number and nature of abuses, procuring insider testimony or statements becomes more important. Insider witnesses hold information about who ordered abuses and who knew they occurred. Insider witnesses are often sparse, and easily identified by the information within a report asserting individual command responsibility. Insider witnesses cannot be protected through provisions of anonymity (providing testimony or statements anonymously), particularly where criminal proceedings are likely to follow. Often they require formal witness protection – defined as relocation with their families (permanent or non-permanent) and, in some instances, identity change. Unless relocation is undertaken of one's own volition, these measures require a great deal of finance, institutional independence and operational sophistication. If a fact-finding commission does not exhibit these qualities, the interests of witnesses' physical and psychological security demand that commissions limit themselves to investigating the scale and nature of abuses, and not those with command responsibility for them. Ambiguity as to subsequent criminal proceedings increases the threat.

At commissions, many abuses can be established and corroborated using many different evidential sources, including anonymous witness testimony and statements. One evidential advantage over criminal processes, from the perspective of witness security, is that commissions may rely more heavily on anonymous statements. Witnesses do not have to appear to give testimony. The consequence of greater reliance on witness statements is that witness narratives are not held up to the same level of interrogation as in an adversarial or inquisitorial criminal process.

Consideration of a witness protection and witness-sensitive practices programme at Nepal's proposed Commission must plan for the possibility that punitive consequences may flow from the Commission, and that Commission witnesses may be called to testify in criminal proceedings. This chapter identifies a witness protection framework based on best practices, and a level of capacity sufficient to provide both formal witness protection and anonymity, while maintaining a credible evidential basis. The importance of protecting witnesses and ensuring the integrity of facts found is elevated by the seriousness of alleging mass human rights abuse.

---

22 Some Nepali civil society actors believed the commissions would name names. Interview with Civil Society actor, Kathmandu, 2 December 2011.

Truth commissions, by design, are devoid of adversarial parties vulnerable to inducing witness testimony that preferences one narrative over another. Unlike an adversarial criminal justice process, the systemic nature of a truth commission's investigative work is to ascertain a historical truth without pressure to implicate particular parties or persons. The material benefits of witness protection, therefore, are less likely to be misused through inducing inauthentic testimony. This does not totally dispel the potential for witnesses to pursue witness protection's material benefits by constructing false narratives that imply a significant threat. Similarly, it does not preclude the possibility that actors with interests in implicating groups or individuals may attempt to infiltrate a commission and skew fact-finding for political purposes. Balancing protection with evidential authenticity requires evaluation, not only of the protective measures available and adopted, but also of the witness-oriented practices and their inter-dependence, across all organs of the commission, and within a State's security, political and socio-economic context.

## 10.2. Nature and Scale of the Threat to Witnesses

The safety of witness participation at a truth commission is instructed by the following elements:

- The threat to witnesses:
- Prosecution threat to implicated persons (increases their interest in impeding testimony);
- Commission independence (decreases public sympathy for implicated persons);
- The threat of local or State-wide stigmatisation of implicated persons.
- Likelihood of the threat being carried out:
- Security: adherence to the rule of law of the population (particularly the armed);
- Politics, security sector reform, economic and social conditions;
- Influence or capacity of the implicated persons.
- Commission capacity to protect participants:
- Anonymity;
- Other *ad hoc* measures; and
- Formal protection.

## 10.2.1. Security Sector Reform

At the Sierra Leone TRC ('SLTRC'), the deployment of a large UN peacekeeping force, a conclusive victory for one party to the conflict, the democratic election of that party, amnesty for all but the 13 most responsible for crimes, and security sector reform diminished the threat to witnesses and its likelihood of being carried out.[23] A de-politicised and professionalised security sector poses a far smaller threat to witnesses. Although security sector reform may not dissolve the politicisation of combatants totally, it can be used to incentivise combatants in such a way as to mitigate their inclination towards intimidating witnesses. Wherever possible, security sector reform should be prioritised ahead of politically sensitive investigations.

In Nepal, the Army, the police and the PLA have proven unwilling to allow investigation of abuses, ready to intimidate those that might testify to abuses, and adept at leveraging their clout in the political class to secure impunity.[24] The PLA and the NA retain clout amongst the UCPN-M and the other political parties respectively. Despite the transfer of authority over the Nepal Army from the former King to the President, the Army retains its own independence, antipathy towards reform, and history of intimidating witnesses.[25] Making a commission the pre-eminent arbiter

---

[23] Combatant induction into the army was conditional upon combatant adherence to conditions of service.

[24] Despite 56 per cent of donor-supported security and justice sector reform focusing on State and civilian oversight, the NA and the PLA have refused to co-operate with investigations into crimes allegedly committed by their combatants. Both armed groups have argued that alleged crimes will be dealt with by transitional justice mechanisms. Victims and victim representatives cited multiple incidents of witness intimidation, including targeted killings. See Crozier and Candan, 2010, p. 7, *supra* note 15; Human Rights Watch, 2010, pp. 8–9, *supra* note 12; Victim speaking at a meeting with victims and victim representatives, 22 November 2011, Kathmandu, *supra* note 11.

[25] The Army Act, 2063, 28 September 2006 (https://www.legal-tools.org/doc/5e9c9b/) provided control over the Army to the representatives of the people and Article 114, Interim Constitution of Nepal, 15 January 2007 (https://www.legal-tools.org/doc/9624c4/) provides the President of the Republic of Nepal as Supreme Commander in Chief of a Nepal Army that is democratic, ethno-regionally inclusive and trained in human rights and democratic values. See Narahari Acharya, "The Nepalese Army", in Bishnu Sapkota (ed.), *The Nepali Security Sector: An Almanac*, 2009, Brambauer Publishers, Hungary, p. 123; International Crisis Group, 2011, p. 16, *supra* note 15. For an example of the threat posed by the Nepal Army to witnesses of its abuse, see UN Doc. A/HRC/7/14/Add.1, 2008, p. 125, *supra* note 21.

of alleged wartime criminality elevates the Army and PLA's interest in manipulating Commission investigations, including access to witnesses.

The Army's pre-eminent security position, including arbitrary discretion to clamp down on expression of civil discontent, increases its political clout.[26] Similarly, ethno-regional discontent within the Army provides ethnicised political parties with an enthusiastic instrument to deploy against witnesses depicted as ethno-regionally biased.[27] The Army's utility for non-UCPN-M parties lends it relative impunity.[28]

Like the non-UCPN-M parties with the Army, the UCPN-M has an interest in protecting PLA combatants, including its political leadership, from prosecution or public condemnation. The PLA has not been used in political action since its confinement to cantonments[29] under the 2006 peace agreement and their subsequent integration into the armed forces.[30] Demobilisation may render some disenfranchised PLA or Army elements vulnerable to actors seeking to direct them against witnesses. Perceived impunity mitigates the threat perpetrators pose.[31] Similarly, investigating abuses during the vetting of combatants for inclusion in the army heightens the threat those combatants pose to witnesses that might implicate them, and diminishes their chance of army inclusion.[32]

### 10.2.2. Potential for Further Instability (Emerging Socio-Economic and Political Threats)

A plethora of dynamics threatens Nepal's ongoing security. Outbreaks or continuation of instability provide savvy actors, particularly those within the political establishment, the means to pursue persons perceived as like-

---

[26] The Government security policy mandates the army to put down "destructive activities", "activities against the national interest", and other incidents of which engaging in political discussion or protest could be interpreted. See International Crisis Group, 2011, p. 18, *supra* note 15.

[27] *Ibid.*, p. 16.

[28] *Ibid.*, p. 17.

[29] Semi-permanent barracks.

[30] "One Step Closer: Integration of Ex-Combatants in the Army is Over, the Peace Process is Not", *Ekantipur*, 28 August 2013.

[31] Interview with Civil Society actor, 16 November 2011, Kathmandu.

[32] The national police human rights section also vets combatants for deployment to UN missions. This also constitutes a motive for combatants to impede any investigation of their own role in abuses. Interview with member, Nepal Police, 22 November 2011, Kathmandu; Interview with Civil Society actor, 20 November 2011, Kathmandu.

ly to co-operate with a commission. The police may employ heavy-handed methods already directed at armed groups, against witnesses of police abuse.[33] Similarly, inter-party violence, tempered by 2010 political inclusion, could flare again.[34] Narcotics and other organised-crime-related violence in the Terai region are allegedly linked to political parties and increasingly attractive to disenfranchised youths.[35] These youths might prove attractive as proxy instruments of intimidation for political and security sector elites. Similarly, elites may employ other political or apolitical armed groups not involved in the conflict, as disassociated instruments of witness intimidation.[36]

The Maoist threat is predominantly located in Nepal's rural geography, where they exercise monopoly control over decision-making *via* armed Maoist youths and an absent State.[37] The integration of over 1,400 PLA combatants into the Army, and the reintegration of most combatants

---

[33] Crozier and Candan, 2010, p. 16, *supra* note 15.

[34] Political violence surrounding Maoist protests predominantly involving clashes between CPN-M and UML affiliates, including indiscriminate bombings, killings and kidnappings, was particularly prevalent during the 13 months prior to Madhav Kumar Nepal's 30 June 2010 departure from the Prime Minister's office. See International Crisis Group, 2011, p. 8, *supra* note 15.

[35] A 2009 Home Ministry report noted that only 23 of the 109 armed groups active in Nepal were political or political or criminal. Victims and their representatives cite the cost of hiring someone to carry out a targeted execution along the border region with India as being 5000 rupees or USD 60. Victim speaking at a meeting with victims and victims' representatives, 22 November 2011, Kathmandu. Crozier and Candan, 2010, pp. 13–14, 20, *supra* note 15.

[36] Such groups include the Kirati Janabadi Workers Party ('KJWP') and Royalist or Hindu far-right parties. Political actors also employ Village Development Committee budgets to provide patronage for armed youth enforcement of subversive activities such as general economic shutdowns. See International Crisis Group, 2011, p. 14, *supra* note 15; Crozier and Candan, 2010, p. 16, *supra* note 15.

[37] Geographical factors, such as elevation and forest, explained 25 per cent of the conflict intensity variation, while pre-conflict poverty is also a significant predictor of conflict intensity. The rural and relatively isolated Dang district, for example, is particularly vulnerable to 30,000 Young Communist League and 10,000 Youth Force foot soldiers that have often violently clashed and are easily manipulated by political actors. Fringe political groups such as the Kirati Janabadi Workers Party ('KJWP') continue to pose a peripheral security threat in rural areas. In March 2011, the KJWP burned down a village development committee office in Udaipur in Nepal's East where public sentiment appears ripe for civil disobedience and protest. See Crozier and Candan, 2011, pp. 2, 4, *supra* note 15; Quy-Toan Do and Lakshmi Iyer, "Geography, Poverty and Conflict in Nepal", in *Journal of Peace Research*, 2010, vol. 47, no. 6, pp. 735–748, 736, 740.

into communities, significantly diminishes the threat the Maoists posed when in containment.[38]

### 10.2.3. The Role of Perceived Prosecution in Exaggerating or Mitigating the Threat to Witnesses

The increased threat posed to witnesses in a longer criminal process is further exaggerated in the instance of a preceding truth commission, particularly one with inadequate protective capacity. Those that pose a threat to witnesses are not necessarily attempting to seek revenge, but are often attempting simply to kill a process: prosecution. When the level of witness-oriented quality control in fact-finding is inadequate proportionate to the threat, the consequences for actual and perceived witnesses and sources can be severe. For example, the commission of inquiry into post-election violence in Kenya, where the threat of subsequent ICC or domestic prosecutions was clear, cited senior leaders of the two main political parties as responsible for the 1,133 people killed.[39] Exaggerating the threat further was the fact that Kenyan efforts to reform the security sector and to disarm non-State armed groups did not precede national and international fact-finding. Targeted killing of witnesses followed, before and after the Commission's presiding Judge handed the ICC the names of persons requiring criminal investigation.[40] Even after the Kenya National Commission on Human Rights and after the Waki Commission of Inquiry witnesses began to be targeted, United Nations Special Rapporteur on extrajudicial, summary or arbitrary executions, Philip Alston, visited Mt.

---

[38] Elements within UCPN-M have previously threatened to recruit in response to potential NA expansion. See Crozier and Candan, 2010, p. 12, *supra* note 15; *Ekantipur*, 2013, *supra* note 30.

[39] The inquiries were carried out by the Kenyan National Commission on Human Rights ('KNCHR') and the Commission of Inquiry into the Post-Election Violence ('CIPEV'), commonly known as 'the Waki Commission'. Report of the Commission of Inquiry into the Post-Election Violence, 15 October 2008, pp. 345-348 (https://www.legal-tools.org/doc/a1063a/).

[40] A police driver turned KNCHR insider witness provided testimony to 58 alleged murders of arrested persons by Kenyan police officers. He was murdered outside a safe house he had been placed in by the KNCHR, which had no background in protective practices. The Kenyan government passed witness protection legislation. However, remarks from Kenyan officials and the legislation's designing personnel indicated the programme's capacity, and the capacity of Kenyan criminal justice, would only facilitate protection in politically expedient cases in the short to medium term. See Chris Mahony, *The Justice Sector Afterthought: Witness Protection in Africa*, Institute for Security Studies, Pretoria, 2010, pp. 117, 121, 129 (https://www.legal-tools.org/doc/f476e7/).

Elgon, where police crimes occurred, to carry out enquiries. Police followed Special Rapporteur Alston, and witnesses were subsequently intimidated.[41] Alston's behaviour constituted a grave miscalculation of the level of witness-sensitive quality control required in the Kenyan situation. In Nepal, targeted killings of witnesses have already occurred in cases reported to the police.[42] Public denouncements have procured witness intimidation.[43]

Like the Kenyan Commission of Inquiry, South Africa's Truth and Reconciliation Commission ('SATRC') relied on prior investigative reports by local non-governmental organisations that failed to adequately protect witness anonymity.[44] However, the threat to witnesses was severely diminished with a witness protection programme and State reluctance to prosecute abuses that the SATRC reported.[45] Were prosecutions to have been pursued by the South African State, the threat to witnesses testifying before the SATRC would have been exaggerated.[46] At Sierra Leone's Truth and Reconciliation Commission ('SLTRC'), the ambiguity of the Commission's relationship with the Special Court for Sierra Leone deterred many potential witnesses, particularly perpetrators, from testifying. However, the SLTRC's amnesty for all but 13 prosecuted by the Special Court, combined with the security circumstances described above, mitigated perpetrator incentives to carry out threats to witnesses.[47]

---

[41]  Electronic communication from a civil society actor accompanying the visit to Mt. Elgon, 26 May 2010; see also Mahony, 2010, *ibid.*

[42]  Interview with Civil Society actor, 16 November 2011, Kathmandu.

[43]  *Ibid.*

[44]  Joanna R. Quinn and Mark Freeman, "Lessons Learned: Practical Lessons Gleaned from inside the Truth Commissions of Guatemala and South Africa", in *Human Rights Quarterly*, 2003, vol. 25, no. 4, pp. 1117–1149, 1123.

[45]  The SATRC was reluctant to invoke subpoena powers and the South African State was unwilling to prosecute even those not provided amnesty by the SATRC, *ibid.*, p. 1126.

[46]  At the inception of the SATRC, it was not clear if accused persons would be prosecuted or not. Witness protection availability and wide media coverage lent witness participation public legitimacy, emboldening victim and insider witness participation. At the SATRC, because of non-prosecution of perpetrators (particularly those that did not testify before the SATRC), perpetrators were threatened more commonly than witnesses, *ibid.*, p. 1123.

[47]  A last-minute reservation by the United Nations delegate stated that the UN did not recognise amnesty in cases of international criminal law allowing the Special Court's jurisdiction over these crimes. Section 7(3), Sierra Leone, Truth and Reconciliation Commission Act, 23 February 2000, Sierra Leone Gazette, vol. 131, no. 9, allows the TRC to withhold incriminating evidence from criminal processes; Article 26, Peace Agreement between the

## 10.2.4. Naming Names: Attributing Individual Responsibility

At Guatemala's Commission for Historical Clarification ('CEH'), the conflict's primary perpetrators, the State and State security forces, vehemently opposed naming names or prosecution.[48] The State also refused to provide information, documentation or other evidential co-operation. It refused to establish a witness protection programme, despite targeted killings carried out by police and criminal groups linked to State security forces.[49] Where names are not named and prosecution appears less certain, linking targeted killings to witness co-operation can be difficult.[50] This means that where investigations have already taken place, where prosecution is perceived as imminent and where witnesses are widely known, their targeted killing can more easily be attributed to their co-operation with a commission's investigations. Where conflict persists or where witness or perpetrator identities are not publicly known (as in Guatemala), drawing a connection between targeted killings and witness co-operation becomes more difficult.[51] Focusing investigations only on the scale and

---

Government of Sierra Leone and the Revolutionary United Front, 7 July 1999; United Nations Security Council, Report of the Secretary-General on the Establishment of a Special Court for Sierra Leone, UN Doc. S/2000/915, 4 October 2000, 5 (https://www.legal-tools.org/doc/4af5d2/).

[48] They committed 93 per cent of documented abuses (including 200,000 killed) during the 1960–1996 civil war. Negotiations surrounding the mandate to name perpetrators delayed the Commission's creation by three years. The rebel Unidad Revolucionaria Nacional Guatemalteca ('URNG') committed only three per cent of the abuses. See Priscilla Hayner, *Unspeakable Truths: Transitional Justice and the Challenge of Truth Commissions*, 2nd ed., Routledge, New York, 2011, pp. 32, 34; Quinn and Freeman, 2003, p. 1122, *supra* note 44.

[49] *Ibid.*, p. 35; Immigration and Refugee Board of Canada, Guatemala: Protection Available to Witnesses of Murder and for Victims of Violent Crime (1998–1999)", 22 February 2001.

[50] The incremental threat of justice sector reform and prosecution of abuses comparative to the eminence of punitive consequences in Kenya makes linking targeted killings to perceived witness co-operation in civil war cases more difficult. Guatemalan State reluctance to prosecute after the presentation of the Commission's report was evident in its refusal to extradite Guatemalan President of the Congress, Jose Efrain Rios Montt to Spain to face war crimes charges and the fact only three of the 626 documented massacres were prosecuted by 2009. Hayner, 2011, p. 35, *supra* note 48.

[51] Guatemala's ability to prosecute civil war abuses and other politically sensitive crimes required formal witness protection capacity to avoid police and other army affiliates targeting key insider witnesses. The recent prosecution of four former soldiers for a 1982 massacre and the arrest of a former General on charges of genocide and crimes against humanity signal the incremental steps toward formal criminal justice for civil war abuses in Guatemala. Immigration and Refugee Board of Canada, 2001, *supra* note 49; United States De-

nature of the abuses and not on individual responsibility (naming names) diminishes the threat, whilst making it more difficult to identify particular incidents, and therefore witnesses.

### 10.2.5. An Ambiguous Punitive Deterrent in Nepal

In Nepal, ongoing political negotiations appear to place questions surrounding investigation and prosecution of abuses at an ambiguous periphery. Because of the already overwhelmed nature of an under-resourced State prosecution (250 lawyers throughout 75 districts already dealing with over 50,000 cases), only a select few, with greatest responsibility, could feasibly be prosecuted.[52] The Ordinance provides for cases to be referred to the Attorney-General for prosecution.[53] The Ordinance does not indicate whether a special entity to investigate crimes will be established, or if the police will carry out that function (even if they are investigating police or army crimes). The Prime Minister appoints and may dismiss the Attorney-General.[54] He might use this leverage, like Nepali politicians have in the past, to impede or interfere in criminal investigations.[55] Even where the Commission does not provide amnesty, the Government may employ *de facto* amnesty by pressuring the Attorney-General to abstain from prosecuting amnestied cases. It is hoped that a new constitution will establish a State prosecution independent of the executive and the Attorney-General.[56] If the Commission provided cases to an independent prosecuting entity, a significant mode of political interference would be removed. Political interference in attempted prosecutions of Army and police personnel has proven immovable over the previous two decades.[57]

---

partment of State, Internal Cable, ID: 146476, 19 March 2008, Embassy Guatemala; Amnesty international, "Guatemalan Former Soldiers Sentenced to 6,060 Years for Massacre", 3 August 2011.

[52] The Attorney-General's office claims they are currently attempting to pursue all cases despite their limited capacity (the court system's budget is less than one percent of the budget. Interview with member Attorney-General's office, 22 November 2011, Kathmandu.

[53] Section 25(3), TRC Ordinance, *supra* note 6.

[54] Section 134(1), Interim Constitution of Nepal, 2007, *supra* note 25.

[55] Crozier and Candan, 2010, pp. 19–20, *supra* note 15.

[56] Interview with justice sector donors, 22 November 2011, Kathmandu, *supra* note 19.

[57] Both the Army and the police have historically employed targeting of witnesses as well as political interferences to impede investigations. United Nations General Assembly, Human Rights Council, Report of the Special Rapporteur on the Promotion and Protection of the

Ambiguity also surrounds the number of persons that might be cited as most responsible, were naming of names and/or prosecutions to occur. The number would instruct how senior a person liable to be prosecuted might be. If those fearing prosecution believe that they can leverage political clout to dissuade the Attorney-General from prosecuting, or the police from effectively investigating, they may well employ that more subtle manipulative option rather than target witnesses. Unless amendments to the Ordinance protect witnesses and compel prosecution, civil society actors view the likely security consequences for witnesses as outweighing the Commission's truth-seeking capacity.[58] In such a situation, some civil society actors think that names should not be named, unless a clearer prosecutorial and protective capacity and mandate is provided.[59]

## 10.3. Considering a Formal Protection Programme: Financial Security and Political Parameters

The cost of providing formal witness protection has been prohibitive for most truth commissions. Ensuring methods of investigation that maintain witness anonymity are employed is critical to procuring information without jeopardising witnesses' psychological or physical security.[60] These methods may not procure the same level of information required to establish command responsibility for alleged crimes. However, a commission's capacity to provide protection may preclude those investigations. In Nepal, restrained investigations would diminish the threat a commission poses to senior military, PLA or political figures and the threat that they, in turn, pose to witnesses.

In the event that the commission decides to name names and pursue insider witnesses, the requirements in law, structural independence, fiscal outlay and personnel need to be considered.

---

Right to Freedom of Opinion and Expression, Ambeyi Ligabo, UN Doc. A/HRC/7/14/Add.1, 25 February 2008, pp. 125–127; Mandira Sharma, "Criminal Justice System in Nepal", in Sapkota (ed.), 2009, pp. 277, 281, *supra* note 25.

[58] Interview with Civil Society actor, 16 November 2011, Kathmandu; Interview with Civil Society actors, Kathmandu, 2 December 2011.

[59] Interview with Civil Society actor, 16 November 2011, Kathmandu.

[60] For a discussion of these techniques see the section on investigation under pre-testimony protection.

---

## 10.3.1. A Legal Framework for Witness Protection

In order to evaluate the adequacy of a commission's capacity to respond to the implications of sensitive investigations for witness security, one must consider the legal framework. This includes domestic legislation, international law and the consideration of the legal mandate at other truth commissions. There is no present witness protection legislation in Nepal. Only the Human Trafficking Act provides for *ad hoc* protection.[61] However, a draft criminal code provides for unspecified and unchallengeable security 'arrangements' and a Witness Protection Bill, providing formal witness protection, has been drafted.[62] The Witness Protection Bill leaves the proposed programme vulnerable to fiscal intimidation by Parliament, provides for normative audit procedures that compromise practice and therefore security, and provides several authorities access to sensitive information.[63] Perhaps most concerning is the Bill's provision of decentralised admission authority to committees comprised of the Chief District Police Officer, District Public Attorney and a Chief District Officer designate in each district.[64] Given the extent of political interference in the criminal justice system, particularly at district level,[65] a fact-finding commission should refrain from using or co-operating with a national witness protection programme empowered by the proposed Bill. The Bill requires revision to reflect the independence and capacity of the commission-specific programme this report proposes. The Bill's decentralised nature is purportedly due to the remote and semi-autonomous nature of many Nepali districts.[66]

---

[61]  It provides for providing for security during travel, temporary police protection, access to rehabilitation centres and in camera court proceedings. It also criminalises dissemination of confidential information, allows persons reporting trafficking to "remain unnamed" and admits victims' statements as evidence without the victim appearing as a witness for cross-examination. Section 5(2), 6(3), 25–27, Human Trafficking and Transportation (Control) Act, 2064, 24 July 2007.

[62]  Sections 3(2), 5, 8, 11–16, Draft Bill Made for the Protection of Witnesses; Section 114, Draft Criminal Procedure Code and Criminal Offences (Offence and Implementation) Act 2067, as cited in Informal Sector Service Centre ('INSEC'), "Witness Protection: A Study Report", Office of the United Nations High Commissioner for Human Rights, 2011, p. 37.

[63]  Sections 61, 61(5), 45(2), Draft Bill Made for the Protection of Witnesses, *ibid.*.

[64]  *Ibid.*, Section 17.

[65]  See Section 10.4. of this chapter on State co-operation.

[66]  Interview with member, Ministry of Peace and Reconstruction, 20 November 2011, Kathmandu.

International legal obligations, while demanding more (including formal protection),[67] place an ambiguous burden on the extent to which a protection programme is required, or what constitutes adequate fulfilment of State obligations in its absence.[68] The reality is that obligations are only triggered when a threat is considered adequately serious. How that discretion should be exercised remains unclear under international law.

There also exists a need for commission-specific witness protection legislation. One critical element that distinguishes South Africa's TRC from Kenya's Waki Commission is that it had its own Witness Protection Programme and held public hearings.[69] The SATRC's 100 percent protection success rate facilitated many findings and a richer historical narrative. Kenya's Commission of Inquiry lacked witness protection capacity and mandate, despite a precarious security situation. Indiscreet investigative methods of contacting and maintaining contact with witnesses exacerbated the threat those witnesses faced.

The Nepal Commission Ordinance provides for a three-person committee, made up of a former chief justice and a civil society actor appointed by the Government and a member of the National Human Rights Commission.[70] The Committee will recommend five Commission members to the Government and those Commissioners shall have discretion to

---

[67] The specific instruments include the Organized Crime Convention (the protection of victims and/or witnesses is also explicitly addressed in the Convention's protocols on Trafficking in Persons, and Smuggling of Migrants) and the United Nations Convention against Corruption. United Nations, General Assembly, United Nations Convention against Transnational, Organized Crime, UN Doc. A/RES/55/25, 8 January 2001, Annex II, Articles 6, 7, 24, 26 (https://www.legal-tools.org/doc/33df9e/); United Nations Office on Drugs and Crime, *Good Practices for the Protection of Witnesses in Criminal Proceedings Involving Organised Crime*, United Nations, New York, 2008, p. 2, 25; Nepal ratified the Convention Against Corruption on 31 March 2011. The convention encourages States parties to sign witness protection co-operation agreements with one another. See United Nations General Assembly, United Nations Convention against Corruption, UN Doc. A/RES/58/4, 21 November 2003, Articles 32, 33, 37, para. 4 (https://www.legal-tools.org/doc/hwuihi/).

[68] Under Article 9, Paragraph 1 of the International Covenant on Civil and Political Rights (http://www.legal-tools.org/doc/2838f3/), the United Nations Human Rights Committee found that the State is obligated to take adequate action to protect witnesses where a formal protection programme is absent. United Nations, Human Rights Committee, *Lalith Rajapakse v. Sri Lanka*, Decision, UN Doc. CCPR/C/87/D/1250/2004, 26 July 2006, para. 9.7.

[69] Section 35, Promotion of National Unity and Reconciliation Act, 34 of 1995, 19 July 1995.

[70] Section 3, TRC Ordinance, *supra* note 6.

---

'make appropriate arrangements' for protection.[71] Leaving the discretion in the hands of the Commissioners will inevitably cause their capacity and independence to instruct the level of protection provided.

Historically, given political inclination to interfere in politically sensitive investigations, interpreting the Bill's provision of discretion to request Government of Nepal assistance in protecting witnesses[72] as compelling Commission/Government co-operation would be ill-advised. Rather, the terms 'the Commission shall' could be interpreted as providing the Commission sole discretion over the level of protection provided.[73] However, sole discretion requires the Commission to retain its own capacity including security and intelligence personnel.

Another concerning absence in the legislation is the weakness of whistle-blower protection. The Ordinance provides for the shifting of personnel to other agencies or regions.[74] While the Ordinance prohibits legal action against persons providing testimony or information to the Commission,[75] it does not protect the careers or work environment of whistle-blowers.[76] Whistle-blower protection is critical to procuring insider witness co-operation and identifying command responsibility. In circumstances of a high threat of political interference, fact-finding commissions should interpret their legal mandate, from both international and domestic instruments, as providing discretion to themselves to provide sovereign psychological and physical protection to witnesses.

## 10.3.2. Funding

As already stated, the cost of naming names, investigating chain of command, and protecting insider witnesses is significantly higher than that of limiting investigations to the scale and nature of abuses, particularly where threat levels are high. In Kenya, despite limited resources and a high threat level, the Waki Commission investigated the chain of command behind abuses, causing witnesses to be targeted and in some instances killed. In Sierra Leone, the same approach, despite limited means,

---

71   *Ibid.*, Section 17(1.

72   *Ibid.*, Section 17(3).

73   See the section on the protection program's location.

74   Section 17(2), TRC Ordinance, *supra* note 6.

75   *Ibid.*, Section 17(4).

76   Whistle-blower protection includes criminalisation of subtle forms of intimidation such as job loss, career stagnation or similar methods deployed against witness family members.

was adopted. The SLTRC's total budget was five million dollars. For purposes of impartiality, the Commission's funds were administered by the United Nations Development Program. It was only empowered to 'take into account' victims and witnesses' 'interests' when inviting them to give statements, including security and anonymity related concerns The SCSL was expected in 2003 to cost around USD 400 million on the basis that proceedings would conclude in 2009.[77] However, the threat level had diminished due to the detention of persons to be held criminally accountable and the reintegration and rehabilitation of other combatants. South Africa had a comparatively large budget that allowed for witness protection in an environment in which the accused still wielded influence over State security forces. Protective capacity accompanied with a low threat of prosecution, allowed the SATRC to investigate the chain of command.[78] The South African TRC was endowed with over 300 personnel and a budget of USD 18 million per year for two and a half years (and a reduced budget for its concluding three years). The financial burden of providing further protection to witnesses has been cited as one justification for the non-prosecution of cases arising from SATRC testimony. The Commission's capacity constraints left witness protection vulnerable to infiltration by former State security sector elements seeking to impede witness testimony. In the case of Guatemala, a meagre budget and a high threat level meant that the Guatemalan Commission did not name names. The success for witness security has been difficult to ascertain. The Guatemalan Commission had a USD 11 million budget and up to 200 personnel for 18 months of operation but did not have a formal protection programme, effectively prohibiting public hearings.[79]

Taking statements from witnesses is the lowest cost a fact-finding commission will bear. Employing anonymity in reporting and encourag-

---

[77] Interview with former member, Registry, Special Court for Sierra Leone, Cheltenham, United Kingdom, 19 April 2007; Interview with former member, Registry, Special Court for Sierra Leone, Freetown, 2 April 2007; Section 7(4), Truth and Reconciliation Commission Act, 2000, *supra* note 47.

[78] Quinn and Freeman, 2003, p. 1121, *supra* note 44; Interview with former prosecution member, National Prosecuting Council – KwaZulu Natal, Pretoria, South Africa, 1 April 2008; Paul van Zyl, "Dilemmas of Transitional Justice: The Case of South Africa's Truth and Reconciliation Commission", in *Journal of International Affairs*, 1999, vol. 52, no. 2, pp. 647–667, 653.

[79] Hayner, 2011, p. 33, *supra* note 48; Quinn and Freeman, 2003, p. 1122, *supra* note 44.

ing witnesses to tell of the socio-economic impact of a conflict will mini-mise the cost of identifying and approaching witnesses discreetly. This is because it will be difficult for perpetrators to ascertain who gave testimo-ny about abuses and who simply spoke of a diminished standard of living. Given the small size of Nepal's economy, such an approach may be the most fiscally sensible option.

Provision of psychosocial support is a significant cost but facilitates greater witness psychological security and openness, driving a richer his-torical narrative. This cost can be mitigated with comprehensive psycho-social training of statement takers, or (where witnesses are comfortable with their presence) collaboration with local State actors or NGOs that work with victims or in public health.

Testimony may also pose a significant cost for commissions, in-cluding witness transportation, food, discreet arrival and departure, as well as technical measures to maintain anonymity.[80]

Formal protection is the costliest available method.[81] Post-testimony protection costs at truth commissions may be higher where tes-timony is required in a subsequent prosecution. This is because that case may take a long time to begin and conclude – extending the most costly period of protection (pre-testimony).[82] If a formal protection programme is created, costs will instruct the number of witnesses the programme is able to admit and the consequent admission criteria it employs – a low-budget programme would likely focus on high-value insider witnesses. The number of incidents commissions have jurisdiction to investigate primarily drives cost. The cost of living in Nepal, and its neighbours, is relatively inexpensive. Providing safe accommodation and establishment costs for witness protection could further be mitigated through working

---

[80] These measures include video link with voice distortion – video link from isolated loca-tions to avoid transport costs. Section 17(5) of the Ordinance provides for reimbursement of reasonable testimony related travel, lodging and food expenses.

[81] Costs include set-up costs, temporary protection or relocation, relocation, personnel, travel, witness allowances, psychological assessments, additional prison costs, and social sustenance allowances. Allowances need to be suitable to sustain the person and compara-ble to previous legitimate income until a new life and job can be established. United Na-tions Office on Drugs and Crime, 2008, p. 50, *supra* note 67.

[82] Subsequent meetings with investigators require transportation to neutral locations and testimony before the courts require repatriation to Nepal. A less efficient criminal process may be protracted and require multiple meetings with investigators.

with foreign partners able to assist with post-relocation employment.[83] Where investigation of command structures discloses not only abuses, but also economic crimes, the seizure, freezing and confiscation of criminal proceeds can justify witness protection expenditure.[84]

While seizure of assets may mitigate costs, sourcing financing to cover protection operations often prohibits the creation of protection capacity. The extent to which Nepal's Commission is viewed as independent may determine who provides its funding. Donors appear unwilling to support a programme perceived to be vulnerable to political manipulation, despite expressions of support for the importance of witness protection for long-term justice sector reform.[85] A recent review suggested that donors might be willing to support witness assistance measures (including training on witness sensitive investigations), but not formal witness protec-

---

[83] Getting witnesses into employment as soon as possible divests responsibility for post-relocation witness maintenance. Interview with former prosecution member, 2008, *supra* note 78.

[84] This practice is already enshrined in law relating to criminal cases of human trafficking that provides 10 per cent of the fine levied against a convicted accused to the person or persons who reported the offence. See Section 19, Human Trafficking and Transportation (Control) Act, 2064, 24 July 2007, *supra* note 61. The TRC's mandate: to investigate "the truth of incidents" and "persons involved" in the conflict abuses, empowers investigation. Section 3(1), TRC Ordinance, *supra* note 6; Interview with former prosecution member, 2008, *supra* note 78; "Fake Gold, Diamond Dealers Threaten to Kill American Citizen", *Standard Times Newspaper*, 9 June 2008, p. 1.

[85] Donors view justice sector reform as requiring planning that looks at the entire justice system in all its inter-relatedness over at least a five-year period. Donors have cited the continuing shift in the political economy of justice sector reform, in tandem with continued changes in the political configuration and justice sector leadership (police chief and Attorney-General). This causes donor apprehension as to assistance for reforms that may carry no effect or for commissions that may cause further instability. While most UN agencies appear apprehensive about Nepal's proposals, the UN Office of the High Commissioner for Human Rights has invested a lot of time in creating commissions and may be more willing to assist. One donor cited potential and perceived dilemmas: "If 450 people get amnesty overnight and the Minister has been accused of murder, should we continue to provide justice sector funding?". At the same time, witness protection is constantly cited as an integral requirement of a reformed justice system capable of addressing impunity. Interview with justice sector donors, 23 November 2011, Kathmandu; Interview with justice sector donors, 22 November 2011, Kathmandu, *supra* note 19; Security, Justice and Rule of Law Donor Coordination Group, "Preliminary Mapping, Rule of Law/Security and Access to Justice in Nepal", October 2010, p. 9; United Nations Office of the High Commissioner for Human Rights, 2007, *supra* note 8; Security, Justice and Rule of Law Donor Coordination Group, "Review of International Community Support to Access to Security and Justice and Rule of Law", 31 August 2011.

tion.[86] They appear unwilling to finance legislative, procedural and institutional reform.[87] If the Nepali State is solely responsible for financing the Commission and protection, fiscal intimidation may be a concern.[88] For formal protection, commissions require fiscal sovereignty and a guaranteed budget tied to inflation and energy price fluctuations that accounts for post-commission protection.[89] Fiscal failure or the threat thereof may leave witnesses unprotected or unwilling to co-operate. The justice system's underfunding does not suggest that the commissions will be a financial priority.[90] The Maoists have already suggested that individual perpetrators pay reparations.[91]

Auditing of the commissions must weigh competing values of financial accountability and witness security.[92] High-level personnel vetted by intelligence sources and the commission should conduct audits.[93]

### 10.3.3. Programme's Institutional Location

A protection programme that determines protection provision independent of investigators and politicians best protects report integrity and witness security from:

---

[86]   Security, Justice and Rule of Law Donor Coordination Group, 2011, p. 36, *ibid.*

[87]   *Ibid.*, p. 46.

[88]   Fiscal intimidation of investigative bodies is a concern in Nepal as it is elsewhere. Interview with former member, Ministry of Justice and Constitutional Affairs. Kampala, Uganda. 8 April 2008; Interview with former National Prosecuting Authority member, Pretoria, South Africa, 29 March 2008; Interview with member, Office of the Attorney General, Nairobi, Kenya, 4 April 2008.

[89]   The budget must account for contingency funds. The transport-intensive nature of protecting and assisting witnesses' demands that budgets account for fluctuations in the cost of this critical area of protective function.

[90]   Interview with members, Nepal Police, 22 November 2011, Kathmandu; Interview with member, Attorney-General's office, 22 November 2011, Kathmandu; Interview with justice sector donors, 23 November 2011, Kathmandu.

[91]   Interview with justice sector donors, 23 November 2011, Kathmandu, *supra* note 19.

[92]   The proposed auditing under the witness protection bill fails to account for witness security.

[93]   Their identity should remain top secret, key expenses aggregated, and reports classified and provided to the Minister of Peace and Reconstruction with witness names excluded. Cash should be used to pre-empt hacking of banks or other records. Interview with former prosecution member, 2008, *supra* note 78; Interview with former National Prosecuting Authority member, 2008, *supra* note 88; United Nations Office on Drugs and Crime, 2008, p. 58, *supra* note 67.

1. The provision of protection benefits in exchange for inauthentic and politically informed testimony and;

2. Political interference to intimidate witnesses providing politically sensitive testimony.

At the Special Court for Sierra Leone, for example, prosecution personnel provided key insider witnesses with non-protection, material inducement (including trips to seaside resorts). Concerns about Kenyan political interference, on the other hand, caused programme design at the cutting edge of structural independence. Perception is also important. South Africa's criminal justice programme functions independently, but is located at the National Prosecuting Authority, undermining perceived independence. The ICC has found that investigative conflict of interest in providing protective measures, rather than an independent protection programme, may 'unnecessarily create an increased risk' of investigators inducing inauthentic testimony.

The Nepali Commission's enacting Ordinance is ambiguous as to the structure of potential commission protection. The Ordinance provides discretion to the commissioners to establish, and therefore design a protection programme, by using its power to form 'Sub-committees' or 'Task Forces'.[94]

In order to ensure consistent application of admission criteria and mitigate vulnerability to malicious interference, admission decisions should be centralised in the hands of the programme's chief witness protection officer.[95] Decisions to temporarily relocate or protect witnesses may be made by case officers. Temporary protection should not exceed two weeks.[96]

## 10.3.4. The Residual Question (When a Commission Concludes)

Preserving witness security and having a plan to preserve security at a commission's conclusion is critical to convincing witnesses that their information and security will not fall into the hands of personnel or institutions they do not trust. Dissolution provisions provide the proposed Ne-

---

[94] Sections 17(1), 31, TRC Ordinance, *supra* note 6.

[95] In the event the Chief Witness Protection Officer is absent, the Deputy Chief Witness Protection Officer should assume the Chief Protection Officer's responsibilities.

[96] Within that period the Chief Witness Protection Officer should conclude a decision on admission.

pali Commission's archives to the Ministry of Peace and Reconstruction.[97] The Chief Protection Officer should be provided a continuing role within the Ministry to retain exclusive residual archive access so witnesses that distrust the Government will not fear disclosure of their information. Pseudonyms should be provided in other archives. The Special Court for Sierra Leone has taken provisional steps to provide residual protection responsibility for its witnesses to Sierra Leone's justice system, an entity distrusted by many Sierra Leoneans. A conclusive decision has not yet been made in Sierra Leone.[98]

### 10.3.5. Personnel

The personnel that staff a protection programme are critical to its success. Where personnel will be sourced, how personnel integrity will be ensured, the diverse skills a protection programme requires and the sensitivity of other commission personnel to witnesses' physical and psychological security are all important considerations for a protection programme.

The Ordinance requires the Government to provide personnel, in consultation with the Commission, which may also contract personnel from elsewhere.[99] The Bill also limits remuneration and benefits of personnel to that reflecting their Government equivalents.[100] While these conditions present little incentive for Government personnel to leave permanent positions, the absence of State witness protection may provide scope for flexible interpretation of what equivalent Government conditions constitute. Attractive conditions of service are required to attract foreign or local high-calibre personnel for this historically significant task. The absence of State witness protection in Nepal means some foreign expertise may be required for a formal protection programme.

Because of the need for a sub-committee to be appointed, constituting a protection programme, Commissioners will likely drive personnel procurement. At the TRC, a maximum of seven Commissioners are to be selected from among human rights practitioners that are not political party members. The commissioner appointment process places great power in the hands of the Constituent Assembly Chairperson and the Govern-

---

97 Section 36(3), TRC Ordinance, *supra* note 6.
98 Mahony, 2010, p. 93, *supra* note 40.
99 Section 11, TRC Ordinance, *supra* note 6.
100 *Ibid.*, Section 11(3).

ment.[101] As a consequence, some observers believe that major parties will make appointments that ensure their interests are pursued.[102] The absence of civil society appointed posts has prompted criticism.[103] A key indicator of the Commissioners' independence will be the authority, impartiality and integrity of the appointed Chief Witness Protection Officer, as at the SATRC. South Africa's TRC protection programme head was commonly viewed as the leading witness protection professional in the country. Macadam had previously directed the *ad hoc* programme in the KwaZulu Natal province. He focused the TRC programme on high-profile cases where a threat was originally anticipated, securing 100 percent success in protecting witnesses' physical security. The SATRC's success in avoiding previous experiences of programme infiltration by criminal elements was in no small part due to attractive employment conditions and effective vetting practices. Compromised protection officers at *ad hoc* State programmes assisted criminals seeking to avoid prosecution by placing them in protection programmes. Other criminals provided false testimony to infiltrate a South African programme and pursue protected witnesses.[104]

A witness protection programme requires a diversity of skills. They include intelligence, criminal investigation, law, psychology, gender-specific and youth counselling, cultural and linguistic fluency, as well as security expertise.[105] These personnel should also constantly monitor

---

[101] A selection committee will comprise the Constituent Assembly ('CA') Chairperson, a CA Chairperson appointed human rights commissioner and a government appointed civil society member. The poorly supported National Human Rights Commission also exposes its personnel to political manipulation. The NHRC was scaled back after foreign donor support declined and Government of Nepal responsibility for funding increased. See Sushil Pyakurel, "National Human Rights Commission", in Sapkota (ed.), 2009, p. 302, *supra* note 25; Section 4, TRC Bill 2011.

[102] As a consequence, Madhesi, Maoist, UML, and NC commissioners are likely to be appointed. Interview with member, National Human Rights Commission, Kathmandu, 20 November 2011; Interview with Civil Society actor, 20 November 2011, Kathmandu.

[103] The International Center for Transitional Justice cites civil society nomination and consultation, as well as transparent vetting as best practice for appointment of Commissioners elsewhere. See, for example, ICTJ, 2011, pp. 2–4, *supra* note 8.

[104] "Deputy A–G Appointed Truth Commission's Witness Protector", *South Africa Press Association*, 4 April 1996; Mahony, 2010, p. 102, *supra* note 40; Interview with former National Prosecuting Authority member, 2008, *supra* note 88; Interview with former prosecution member, 2008, *supra* note 78.

[105] Independent intelligence and investigatory capacity are required to design protective strategy based on analysis of the capacity and willingness of hostile actors to carry out threats. Legal personnel are also required to ensure witnesses fully understand the implications of

---

commission-wide witness-oriented practices. They should train personnel and provide best practice where necessary. Personnel not directly involved in witness protection, particularly investigative personnel, are also important to witnesses' physical and psychological security. Given the historical tendency of the Government of Nepal to manipulate investigations of combatant abuse,[106] investigator and statement-taker training and vetting is essential to impede the planting of biased investigative personnel or the misinterpretation of witnesses. The SATRC had problems with inadequate writing skills of statement takers causing commissioner confusion as to what witnesses were trying to say. Statement takers were scarce and predominantly comprised volunteer human rights and social science personnel. Miscommunication may inaccurately inform investigations and threat assessments, with serious consequences for witness risk and the integrity of a commission's final report. Empathy is a critical statement-taker attribute that facilitates uninhibited witness dialogue. Another cited inadequacy relating to SATRC statement-taker training concerned knowledge of available State services to which witnesses may be referred.[107]

Personnel throughout the Commissions, particularly witness protection personnel, require thorough vetting. Thorough vetting and sporadic re-vetting for potential conflicts of interest, breach of conditions of service, psychological vulnerabilities or prior abuses is essential to maintaining programme confidentiality.[108] Working with and protecting psycholog-

---

testifying and signing an admission memorandum of understanding. The programme will require psychologists, particularly gender and child specialists, to evaluate, and explain commission practices and procedures. United Nations Office on Drugs and Crime, 2008, pp. 47–49, *supra* note 67; Interview with former National Prosecuting Authority member, 2008, *supra* note 88; Interview with former prosecution member, 2008, *supra* note 78.

[106] Human Rights Watch, 2010, pp. 3–4, 6, *supra* note 12.

[107] Quinn and Freeman, 2003, p. 1135, *supra* note 44.

[108] Witness protection personnel will require intimate knowledge of Nepalese security dynamics. Former security sector personnel will require particularly rigorous vetting given their historical vulnerability to political coercion. Coercive methods include leverage over individual officers' careers. Conditions of service should require complete transparency of personnel (and family's) financial affairs. The NHRC has not established proposed guidelines for personnel appointment. Crozier and Candan, 2010, pp. 19–20, *supra* note 15; Interview with former National Prosecuting Authority member, 2008, *supra* note 88; The NHRC has not established proposed guidelines for personnel appointment.

ically vulnerable or former criminal witnesses causes psychological repercussions for personnel, who need to have counselling available.[109]

The police and the Army are not currently trained specifically in
witness sensitive practices.[110] International personnel provide a useful
source if commissioners determine local personnel to be too vulnerable to
compromise.[111] However, localised knowledge of Nepali political and security elements critical to threat and protective evaluation will also be required to inform a Chief Protection Officer's threat assessment. Similarly,
culture, language and gender-specific psychosocial personnel may best be
sourced from local civil society.[112]

## 10.4. State Co-operation

### 10.4.1. A Culture of State Non-Cooperation

One donor I spoke with in Nepal told me:

> In Achham I had meetings with the district court judge and
> lawyer. I asked if to get away with rape and murder, the go-
> ing rate is $10,000 (as I had heard). Rather than deny this
> possibility, they discussed whether the rate in Achham dis-
> trict is higher or lower than elsewhere.[113]

States have proven adept at co-operating with truth commission and
criminal processes so as to shape historical narratives and prosecution
case selection.[114] Diminishing the Nepali Commission's need for State co-

---

[109] Counselling provides an outlet for discussing traumatic issues that they are prohibited from
discussing with loved ones.

[110] Govinda Thapa, "The Nepal Police and the Armed Police Force", in Sapkota (ed.), 2009, p.
166, *supra* note 25.

[111] Some civil society actors are concerned that personnel seconded from the security or intelligence apparatus will not be independent. Interview with Civil Society actor, 16 November 2011, Kathmandu.

[112] Even if all protection personnel and investigators were to be sourced from foreign States,
those personnel would still require local translators and an intimate understanding of local
security dynamics. Interview with former prosecution member, 2008, *supra* note 78.

[113] Even the Attorney-General's office note unorthodox pressures on their under-capacitated
staff. Interview with member, Attorney-General's office, 22 November 2011, Kathmandu;
Interview with justice sector donors, 23 November 2011, Kathmandu.

[114] For example, the Rwandan government refused to provide to the International Criminal
Tribunal for Rwanda, documentation and witness access incriminating ruling party personnel, bringing court proceedings to a standstill and forcing the court's prosecutor to be
replaced. While non-punitive commission investigations might not solicit such a belligerent response, interested parties may still employ cooperative methods, including witness

operation will lend them greater independence and legitimacy. Maoist, Nepal Army and political refusal to co-operate with investigation of abuses, in some cases directing investigations to be discontinued, provides impunity and tacit approval to personnel carrying out or ordering witness intimidation or elimination.[115] Like commissions elsewhere, the Nepali Commission would likely disproportionately rely on witness statements and testimony because the State withholds documentary or other corroborating evidence.[116]

State non-cooperation with politically sensitive inquiries and criminal inquiries is founded in Nepali law.[117] The Commission's power to demand documentation and co-operation may have to be contested before the courts, as the Ordinance implies that the Commission may only have power to write and request the removal of non-compliant Government

---

tampering, to skew the content of a commission's report. At the SLTRC many government witnesses did not testify or did so in a particularly sparse fashion. A report perceived as applying disproportionate focus on one party to the advantage of another elevates discontent amongst persecuted groups, elevating the threat to witnesses. United Nations Security Council, Letter Dated 28 July 2003 from the Secretary-General Addressed to the President of the Security Council, UN Doc. S/2003/766, 29 July 2003; Carla Del Ponte, 2009, *Madame Prosecutor: Confrontations with Humanity's Worst Criminals and the Culture of Impunity: A Memoir*, Other Press, New York; Lars Waldorf, "A Mere Pretence of Justice: Complementarity, Sham Trials, and Victor's Justice at the Rwanda Tribunal", in *Fordham International Law Journal*, 2010, vol. 33, no. 4, p. 1221.

[115] Where public pressure for investigation of abuses has required placation, investigative committees and military proceedings producing flawed outcomes that are not acted upon are employed. Implicated personnel, in some instances, are promoted, in a recent case to a ministerial position. The Nepal Army's has previously refused to follow orders of the Nepalese judiciary, the Prime Minister or UN and Human Rights Commission to surrender accused Army personnel and the government has recently ordered an amnesty and a pardon for a conflict related murder. Human Rights Watch, 2010, pp. 2–4, 8–9, *supra* note 12; Crozier and Candan, 2010, p. 19, *supra* note 15; "Monday Interview", *The Kathmandu Post*, 13 November 2011.

[116] The Commission of Historical Clarification in Guatemala was able to employ vast databases compiled by local NGOs as well as US documentation secured *via* a freedom of information request, to compliment 7,338 non-public testimonies. Ordinary police investigations are already disproportionately dependent upon witness testimony due to technological, training and equipment incapacity. See Hayner, 2011, p. 33, *supra* note 48; Quinn and Freeman, 2003, p. 1122, *supra* note 44; Mandira Sharma, 2009, p. 281, *supra* note 57.

[117] The Evidence Act prohibits disclosure of unpublished confidential government documents and prevents compulsion of testimony from public officials when contrary to the public interest. Section 43–44, Evidence Act, 2031, Act no. 24 of Year 2031, 21 October 1974 (https://www.legal-tools.org/doc/97473d/).

---

personnel.[118] Where elements of the State threaten witnesses, the State may refrain from providing protection despite the law. Were Nepal's Commission not to be provided with adequate finance for a Commission-located independent protection programme, they would be left dependent upon co-operation they appear unable to compel.

The Government and the armed forces' reluctance to co-operate with investigations instructs the difficulty Commission investigators are likely to encounter in procuring witness co-operation from security sector personnel. Government co-operative obligations should be incorporated, through focal point personnel, into Security Sector reform that assists attitudinal change towards co-operation.[119]

### 10.4.2. Foreign Co-operation

There is also a global power dynamic to internal Nepali politics that may inform variance in protection assistance from Nepal's neighbours and other States – depending on a witness' perceived affiliation. The Maoists, allegedly viewed by the US and India as agents of Chinese influence, have been included on US Terror and Blocked Persons lists.[120] China reportedly holds a primary interest in procuring Nepali co-operation in securing the Tibet/Nepal border.[121] India (a United States regional ally) was

---

[118] Section 11(3), TRC Ordinance, *supra* note 6.

[119] Thoroughly vetted focal point personnel, of sufficient seniority to command immediate and unquestioned cooperation from their colleagues, should be established within State para-statals. Focal points need not be provided witness' original identity and may instead use pseudonyms.

[120] The US has also blocked visa applications by implicated Maoist personnel. The US and its regional ally, India, have expressed their enthusiasm in supporting the transit of Tibetan refugees through Nepal to India, an issue to which the former Monarchical government was also non-committal. Upon receiving persistent requests from the US Ambassador that Nepal assist in providing safe passage for Tibetan refugees, the then Foreign Minister under the King remained ambiguous. The US intimated a "special, close relationship" with Nepal contingent upon the Royal Government's action on Tibetan refugees. See Human Rights Watch, 2010, p. 3, *supra* note 12; Ambassador James F. Moriarty, "Crunch Time in Nepal?", United States Department of State Cable 002587, Kathmandu, 22 September 2006, (available on the WikiLeaks' web site); Ambassador James F. Moriarty, "FM Pandey Seeks Special, Long-Term Relationship with US", United States Department of State Cable, Ref. A. Kathmandu 2565 B. Kathmandu 2209 C. State 223674 D. Kathmandu 2568,14 December 2005 (available on *The Guardian*'s web site).

[121] China has engaged King Gyanendra as well as the Maoists in strengthening border control and preventing safe passage for Tibetan refugees to India. Maoist favouring of China as its principal external patron is instructed as much by previous US/Indian military support to the Royal Nepalese Army, as by Chinese patronage. The United States cited its military

a long supporter of Nepal's former monarchy, the Nepali Congress and most Madhesi parties, but has recently sought Maoist rapprochement.[122] These external interests instruct the threat posed to witnesses, vicarious support for elements that may threaten witnesses, methods of protection and in particular, territories for relocation given witness affiliation.[123] Nepal's Commission will require MOUs with its neighbours. However, this does not surmount the problem of convincing States to accept witnesses viewed as unsavoury.[124]

---

support to the Royal Government as having a "disproportionately influential role in persuading Maoist leaders to agree to a cease-fire and negotiations with the Government of Nepal", see International Crisis Group, 2011, p. 15, *supra* note 15; Laxmanlal Karna, "Border Security and Management" in Sapkota (ed.), 2009, p. 178, *supra* note 25; Jayshree Bajoria, "Engaging Nepal's Maoists", Analysis Brief, Council on Foreign Relations, 9 July 2008; Deputy Chief of Mission, Robert K. Boggs, "US-Indian Cooperation and Military Assistance to Nepal", United States Department of State Cable, EO 12958, Kathmandu 000280 Ref A.A.02 New Delhi 6938 B.B. New Delhi 267 C.C. New Delhi 641 (available on *The Hindu*'s web site).

[122] The UCPN-M and the UML distrust the Indian government as a result. India has long feared a Maoist government in Nepal would support the Naxalites, a Maoist insurgency in India. India lobbied the Security Council to remove the UN Mission in Nepal based upon the dubious notion that it was impeding the peace process. New Delhi concerns surrounding border disputes, renegotiation of the 1950 Indo-Nepal Peace and Friendship Treaty and China's growing clout in Kathmandu means that Nepal re-engages India from a position of strength. China recently unveiled a planned USD 3 billion tourism, pilgrimage and education centre at the Buddha's acknowledged Nepali birthplace. China also increased, though not to the levels of Indian assistance, its military aid to Tibet. See Miklian, 2008, *supra* note 15; Verma, 2011, *supra* note 15; Council on Foreign Relations, "Engaging Nepal's Maoists", 9 July 2008; International Crisis Group, 2011, pp. 2, 15, *supra* note 15; Ambassador Michael E. Malinowski, "Ambassador Relays Concerns about Activities of Indian Intelligence Agents, United States Department of State Cable, Ref Kathmandu 2282 B. Kathmandu 2298 (available on the WikiLeaks' web site); "Prachanda Seeks to 'Turn over a New Leaf' in Ties with India", *Indian Express*, 10 November 2010; Bajoria, 2008, *ibid.*; Ananth Krishnan and Prashant Jha, "Chinese Foundation Plans $3 Billion Project in Nepal", *The Hindu*, 17 July 2011.

[123] The inherent danger in making judgments as to States' interests is their potential fluidity, particularly during periods of instability or transition. These obstacles elevate the importance of ensuring robust and detailed relocation agreements between States.

[124] Witnesses may have committed or been party to serious international crimes. States, which may have to amend legislation requiring prosecution of a witness, are often apprehensive about accepting witnesses that may threaten their citizens. Amending international crimes legislation attracts domestic attention that may alert hostile elements to a witness's potential destination country. Interview with member, ICC Office of the Prosecutor, 8 June 2009, The Hague, The Netherlands.

Ideally, a TRC programme should be sufficiently capacitated so as not to require State co-operation. Where sufficient capacity is not forthcoming, Commissions need to wield discretion as to what constitutes 'necessitating' Government assistance. Security sector reform, if possible, should precede investigations and focal points of clout and integrity should be established within State institutions.

## 10.5. Commission and Justice System Efficacy, Efficiency and Interdependence

Justice sub-sectors "are inexorably linked one to the other and are best understood in the context of the interactive complexities of the entire Sector".[125] An assessment of an entire criminal justice system is required to ascertain whether independent criminal proceedings can successfully occur as a consequence of a Commission's investigations. If not, the consequences of pursuing sensitive investigations and reporting sensitive findings must be weighed. The Security, Justice and Rule of Law Donor Coordination Group adopted this premise in its analysis of the political economy, institutional capacity, cross-sub-sector relations, social, economic and gender issues that contextualise Nepal's greater criminal justice system. It concluded that criminality and impunity, fuelled by political parties' leverage over law enforcement and justice institutions, undermines the legitimacy of the law and the State.[126]

## 10.5.1. Statement Taking and Other Investigatory Practices

When commissions decide not to name names, not to investigate the chain of command, and not to attribute individual responsibility, investigators may be limited to discreet methods of contacting witnesses and taking statements (see the following section on anonymity). In conducting those investigations, witness co-operation may be assisted with assurances (if the Government grants the commissions permission to do so) that witnesses will not be required to provide that testimony in a criminal trial.

---

[125] Security, Justice and Rule of Law Donor Coordination Group, 2011, *supra* note 85.

[126] This problem is exacerbated by patronage power structures, poverty, unemployment, rising inflation and discrimination that deepen divisions amongst the citizenry and the political parties (including within those parties). They are mitigated by some progressive elements within the police and the Supreme Court is cited as being at the forefront of driving change, see *ibid.*

The Nepali Commission Ordinance places the burden of proof upon the person who "arrested or took control of" the disappeared person in question.[127] Placing the burden of proof on these actors places them in a dilemma between co-operating and implicating their superiors, or attempting to undermine investigations, including by targeting witnesses. Security sector personnel are unlikely to co-operate unless they perceive protection to be available and prosecution to be likely.[128]

As a consequence of the high threat level to insider witnesses in particular, Commission investigators have an obligation to inform witnesses of the ambiguity surrounding criminal consequences of their co-operation. Those consequences include the Government's legal and bureaucratic power not to make the submitted TRC report public; to refuse to prosecute cases referred by either Commission; to prosecute a cooperating witness for admitted criminal acts or for providing a fake fact; and to demand that witnesses are interviewed by police investigators in the presence of the accused.[129] The Ordinance obligates the Commission to provide details of investigated complaints to the Government.[130] Investigators should inform witnesses as to what those details would include, what identity protections will be used and what protections are and are not available in subsequent investigations. Repealing legislation is required to remove these obstacles to witness participation. The Commission's regulations should include these and other witness sensitive practices.

Given the unpredictability of the political process and the inefficient nature of the criminal justice system in Nepal, it is difficult to foresee expeditious criminal processes taking place as a consequence of investigations conducted by the Commission. Investigators should also bring to the attention of witnesses the fact that, were their testimony required in a

---

[127] Section 2(k), TRC Ordinance, *supra* note 6.

[128] For ICC investigators, their capacity to assure witnesses of protection (both security protection and protection from prosecution) greatly assisted procurement of witness cooperation. Interview with Civil Society actor, Kathmandu, 16 November 2011; Mahony, 2010, p. 33, *supra* note 40.

[129] Under the Evidence Act, Nepalese witnesses may not be excused from answering any question in a criminal case, even if they may incriminate themselves in doing so. That testimony may not be used in another case but may prompt an investigation. Section 28(2), Government Cases (Second Amendment) Act, 2049, 23 December 1992; Section 47, Evidence Act, 1974, *supra* note 117 ; Rule 143 and 156 of the Civil Code, 2020, as cited in INSEC, 2011, p. 35, *supra* note 62.

[130] Section 27, TRC Ordinance, *supra* note 6.

criminal case, the period of greatest threat is the period prior to testifying in court. The Commission's investigations prolong that period because subsequent criminal investigations would have to occur after those of the Commission. Expediting statements or testimony of threatened witnesses limits the period of greatest danger to witnesses.

## 10.5.2. Investigating on the Basis of Naming Names

Were names to be named, the Commission should assert its right to refer cases to the Attorney-General prior to submitting its report.[131] The report could then include criticism of cases not pursued. Citing constitutional equality before the law,[132] the National Human Rights Commission ('NHRC') could, under its implementation-monitoring role,[133] advocate on behalf of witnesses. Were the NHRC to fulfil this function, it may mitigate the potential for selective prosecution, the perception of which often exaggerates the threat to witnesses. However, the police have previously ignored many NHRC disappearance case referrals, despite being compelled under law "as soon as possible, [to] investigate and collect evidence".[134]

Commissions also have other bargaining chips at their disposal. Plea-bargaining methods of engaging with witnesses are critical to procuring witness co-operation. Nepal's Commission may, for example, discreetly contact, as quickly as possible, those that carried out crimes, in order to negotiate their co-operation against senior personnel in return for amnesty.[135] Commissioners may agree to criteria with the Attorney-General, which can be employed to waive or reduce sentence in return for witness co-operation, particularly since Commission discretion to provide amnesty is very wide.[136] Clear criteria allow Commission investigators and protection programmes to provide witnesses an indication of the like-

---

[131] *Ibid.*, Section 25(3), 27 (1).

[132] Section 13(1), Interim Constitution of Nepal, 2007, *supra* note 25.

[133] Section 30, TRC Ordinance, *supra* note 6.

[134] Interview with member, National Human Rights Commission, Kathmandu, 20 November 2011; Section 7, Government Cases (Second Amendment) Act, 2049, 23 December 1992.

[135] Courts may also mitigate sentence by 25 per cent for first-time, non-principal trafficking offenders who co-operate with the police, prosecution and the Court. Section 21, Human Trafficking and Transportation (Control) Act, 2064, 2007, *supra* note 61; Section 4(3), Disappearances Bill, *supra* note 2.

[136] Section 23 (1), TRC Ordinance, *supra* note 6.

---

ly reduction in punitive consequence for full witness co-operation.[137] Outreach and other forms of information dissemination of criminal case selection criteria would be of particular assistance in soliciting insider witness co-operation and lending legitimacy to pursued cases.

Implementation of security sector reform processes present opportunities to identify potential insider witnesses who may have diminished allegiance to former superiors. Methods of engaging insider witnesses during security sector reform must ensure their rehabilitation or reintegration experience does not arouse suspicion.[138] Donors can assist Commissions by making rehabilitative provision conditional on full co-operation with the Commission investigations.

### 10.5.3. Psychosocial Protection and Assistance

Trauma associated with witness co-operation is an issue common to Truth Commission investigations elsewhere. At the SATRC, 'briefers' were employed to provide psychological support before, during and post-testimony; as well as to ensure witnesses understood the testimony's procedures and implications.[139] However, the number and training of briefers was inadequate, requiring professionals to volunteer in some communities.[140] The SLTRC's enabling Act required it to:

> [...] implement special procedures to address the needs of
> such particular victims as children or those who have suf-

---

[137] Criteria should also articulate interpretation of persons giving orders or directions (command responsibility).

[138] A security sector reform strategy into which protection of co-operating witnesses is integrated, poses threats to witness security. Insider combatant or officer witnesses benefitting from cooperation with investigators may be identified based on the rehabilitation packages they receive. The difficulty of maintaining anonymity in these circumstances may require temporary or permanent relocation and identity change. However, recommended security sector reform practices, such as engagement of informal security mechanisms including community-, youth- and gender-oriented policing, may also present an opportunity for investigators to discreetly identify potential witnesses. PLA and NA personnel marginalised by security sector reform and subsequently, their former political patrons, might also provide fertile sources of witness cooperation, rather than fertile sources of future instability. Crozier and Candan, 2010, pp. 8, 15, *supra* note 15.

[139] Glenda Wildschut and Paul Haupt, "I'll Walk Beside You: Providing Emotional Support for Testifiers at the South African Truth and Reconciliation Commission", *New Tactics in Human Rights*, 2004; Interview with former National Prosecuting Authority member, 2008, *supra* note 88; Interview with former prosecution member, 2008, *supra* note 78.

[140] Only 14 Briefers were on staff. Quinn and Freeman, 2003, p. 1133, *supra* note 44.

fered sexual abuses, as well as in working with child perpetrators of abuses or violations.[141]

Special hearings, closed sessions, safe interview environments, witness anonymity, and trained psychosocial personnel were employed in
collaboration with reintegration programmes and organisations already
working with victims (including perpetrators).[142] These methods placed
witness interests ahead of testimony volume. These methods were helpful,
but were also impeded by a number of Commission and non-Commission
elements. They included confusion surrounding prosecution, absence in
some districts of child protection agencies ('CPAs'), fear of stigmatisation
and re-traumatisation, and expectation of material support.[143] The SLTRC
experience highlights the need for earlier organisation of key elements
before investigations begin. These elements include:

1. public sensitisation to jurisdiction, goals and processes;

2. multi-lingual, gender sensitive, and human rights trained statement
   takers;

3. psychosocial support structures able to assist throughout the Commission process;

4. assessment and identification of ceremonies and rituals to be made
   available;

5. child- and gender-oriented advocacy of recommendation implementation; and

---

[141] Section 7(4), Truth and Reconciliation Commission Act, 2000, *supra* note 47.

[142] The UN mission to Sierra Leone and UNICEF, which identified child participants through
its child protection and reintegration program, developed these methods. The SLTRC developed a framework for Child Protection Agency ('CPA') identification and support of
child statement givers, using a designated district CPA social worker that prioritised statement quality and child well-being over pursuit of voluminous child accounts. While some
NGOs prevented children from participating because of child absence in designing partici-
patory processes, the framework included progressive child participation principles. They
included the child's best interests, voluntary participation, safety and security, physical,
spiritual and psychological well-being, anonymity, gender sensitive and one-on-one statement taking by trained personnel, and availability of psychosocial support. The principles
were supported by a vulnerability and safety checklist that ensured the psychological capacity and willingness of child witnesses to co-operate before they were allowed to do so.
Saudamini Siegrist, "Children's participation: Truth and Reconciliation Commission for
Sierra Leone", paper presented at Expert Discussion on Transitional Justice and Children,
10–12 November 2005, UNICEF Innocenti Research Centre, Florence, pp. 51, 53–54, 59.

[143] *Ibid.*, p. 54.

---

6.   capacity to provide anonymity.

The Commission Ordinance provides for "special arrangements" to ensure children's dignity and security.[144] Psychosocial assistance should be made available to all psychologically vulnerable witnesses. The Commission Ordinance provides for psychosocial assistance for women and children.[145] Counsellors should accompany investigators when contacting or interviewing potentially vulnerable witnesses. The gender and institutional background of the investigator and counsellor should also be considered on a case-by-case basis in the context of each witness' particularities. Witness sensitive reporting stations and economic provision to facilitate witness travel should be provided.[146] Prior to witnesses testifying before the Commission, programme regulations should be created that require full briefing of witnesses on the anticipated nature of testimony and questioning, practices and procedures, as well as employed and alternative protective and support measures (psychosocial and economic). Regulations should also provide for protection and assistance post-Commission, were testimony to be required in subsequent court cases.[147]

---

[144]  Section 17(7) TRC Ordinance, *supra* note 6.

[145]  *Ibid.*, Section 17(7).

[146]  An absence of financial means to attend court is commonly found by district attorneys to prove prohibitive for many witnesses' ambitions to participate. Some donors including DFID, UNICEF and the Supreme Court, which has a large action plan and is seeking donor support, have advocated special buildings or rooms with psychosocially trained police officers. In addition, there is a joint programme between UNICEF Para-Legal Committees ('PLCs'), UNFPA (health workers) and UNIFEM (law enforcement) to make interventions on GBV. UNFPA has recently commissioned a study to track GBV in national response systems. Interview with justice sector donors, 23 November 2011, Kathmandu; Security, Justice and Rule of Law Donor Coordination Group, 2010, p. 5, *supra* note 85; Interview with member, Attorney-General's office, 22 November 2011, Kathmandu.

[147]  Evidence Act provisions requiring the presence of all parties, do not necessarily prohibit the use of screens, voice distortion and pseudonyms to protect witness identity. A proposed criminal procedure bill, allowing admission of written or video witness testimony without cross-examination, appears to contradict the accused right to cross-examine a witness. Nepali law also provides *ad hoc* anonymity in some circumstances. The Human Trafficking Act for example, criminalises disclosure of a victim's identity and provides for in camera court proceedings. The Supreme Court of Nepal has held that confidentiality may be provided to protect highly personal information which may attach stigma or prevent a person from doing their job, and which is not essential for a specific legal purpose. The court found that the right to privacy has its own significance for women and children when read in the constitutional context of their physical and mental safety. The court found that protection of a witness or party to the conflict's privacy should be assessed on its necessity and appropriateness without prohibiting defence questioning, in an in-camera session, of

Unfamiliar and formal environments can be intimidating for those witnesses that testify rather than provide witnesses statements. Local and international CPAs or gender-oriented NGOs [148] should be consulted whenever a witness or their guardian is considering co-operating in a way that may disclose their co-operation or cause trauma. [149] Investigators should err on the side of anonymity when interpreting witness vulnerability to stigmatisation, age and the capacity to adequately consider the medium to long-term repercussions of co-operating. Distinguishing between the absence of witness apprehension to testify and vulnerability to psychological or other post-testimony harms requires careful consideration of the witness's testimony and psychological condition. Psychosocial officers or, where appropriate, family members should sit with vulnerable witnesses. [150] Accompanying persons should be provided discretion to alert commissioners to particular sensitivities prior to as well as during testimony. Accompanying persons should ensure that witnesses understand their

---

the witness. The Supreme Court's decision, given the clear legislative preference for the right of counsel to cross examination in the Evidence Act, indicates that physical and psychological wellbeing should be given weight by Commissioners when determining the rights of the implicated. While the provision of financial compensation for testimony-related expenses (travel, food, etc.) is provided for in the Commissions' bills, it should also be brought to witnesses' attention that the travel expenses for testimony in subsequent criminal proceedings is also provided for by the States Cases Regulation. However, under the proposed national protection programme the police anticipate only a small stipend being provided. See Section 38–35, 49, Evidence Act, 1974, *supra* note 117; A Bill Made to Amend and Consolidate Prevailing Laws in relation to Criminal Cases, 2067 (2010); Section 25, 27, Human Trafficking and Transportation (Control) Act, 2064, 2007, *supra* note 61; Supreme Court Division Bench of Nepal, *Forum for Women, Law and Development and Advocate Sapana Pradhan Malla v. Office of the Prime Minister and others*, Writ 3561 of 2063 (2006), 25 December 2007, citing Article 20(3) of the Constitution; Rule 15(3) State Cases Regulation 2055 (1999) cited in INSEC, 2011, p. 35, *supra* note 62; Interview with member, Nepal Police, 22 November 2011, Kathmandu.

[148] Often there are many NGOs working on the same issue that may require coordination with all programs – co-ordination that may assist subsequent justice sector reform initiatives. In some instances, there are 25 or so international or national NGOs working on the same issue, stated one donor. Interview with justice sector donor, 23 November 2011, Kathmandu; Security, Justice and Rule of Law Donor Coordination Group, 2010, *supra* note 85.

[149] Para-legal committees of 15–20 women already set up and trained to advise vulnerable complainants may also be consulted. These committees have faced the obstacle of the absence of a formal justice system perceived as safe because many female victims fear that upon reporting rape, police officers may also rape them and refrain from taking the case seriously. Interview with justice sector donor, 23 November 2011, Kathmandu.

[150] Protection personnel should assess the suitability of witness appointed family members where witnesses prefer that form of support.

---

rights, clarify questions, and ensure witnesses are granted time to gather their emotions and thoughts. Fears of stigmatisation on the part of perpetrator or victim witnesses also instruct their participation, which may be inflammatory, particularly if the process is poorly managed. Tim Kelsall provides the most prominent empirical evidence of the antagonising and inflammatory role community 'truth-telling' can play. At SLTRC hearings in Tonkolili district, contested truths provided by former combatants prompted such disharmony that physical altercations almost broke out.[151] Local cultural and religious leaders may also be used to calm audiences and witnesses and, where appropriate, give local hearings legitimacy. Antagonisms, argues Kelsall, were only overcome when the Commissioners stepped aside and allowed local elders to conduct rituals where combatants asked for forgiveness without admitting specific crimes. The TRC Act allowed the Commission to call upon local chiefs and elders to step in and facilitate healing and reconciliation. These ceremonies inevitably compromised witness anonymity and were commonly reserved for perpetrators, but may have been considered for known former child combatants or victims where indigenous processes were available.[152] Travel to and appearance at commissions should ensure anonymity, discretion and psychological well-being.[153]

### 10.5.4. Anonymity

The Commission provides for, at witnesses' discretion, the most effective method of witness protection: anonymity (confidentiality of information that might identify a witness).[154] Vetting and corroboration of testimony instructing the Commission's report or case referral to the Attorney-General becomes more important where anonymity is at the witness' discretion. Maintaining witness anonymity will be challenging in an envi-

---

[151] Tim Kelsall, "Truth, Lies, Ritual: Preliminary Reflections on the Truth and Reconciliation Commission in Sierra Leone", in *Human Rights Quarterly*, 2005, vol. 27, no. 2, pp. 361–391.

[152] See *ibid.*; Section 7(2), Truth and Reconciliation Commission Act, 2000, *supra* note 47.

[153] Immediately prior to testimony, witnesses should be kept with psychosocial personnel in a room. They should be taken to testify *via* a discreet route so as to avoid encountering persons other than the accompanying protection personnel.

[154] Anonymity is also provided for under the Human Trafficking Act. Section 17(6), TRC Ordinance, *supra* note 6. Section 20, Human Trafficking and Transportation (Control) Act, 2064, 2007, *supra* note 61.

ronment where persons are often rightly or wrongly perceived by their communities to be co-operating witnesses.[155]

Truth commissions distinguish themselves from ordinary criminal investigations by their ability to collect and aggregate information corroborated from a wide variety of sources. When investigations focus on a large number of incidents of abuse, human rights and other civil society reports and sources can be used to direct investigations and to corroborate witness testimony. Building public confidence in the professionalism and independence of both Commissions' investigatory apparatus is critical to soliciting witness co-operation. It is particularly important for those familiar with the experience of making first information reports to police.[156]

The availability of anonymity, investigative intent to maintain anonymity, and discreet methods witnesses should employ in contacting the Commissions must be clearly communicated to the public through easily accessible mediums. Like Sierra Leone, South Africa sought to develop institutional legitimacy and witness confidence by sensitising the population to the availability of witness protection and anonymous testimony. At the SLTRC, anonymity was important in ensuring witnesses' physical security. However, in instances where anonymity was compromised, witnesses commonly attracted community stigmatisation. Demonstrating that witnesses could provide anonymous testimony and avoid the stigma of perceived community betrayal may have been as attractive as maintaining one's security, and is often a significant source of encouragement for persons considering providing a statement or testimony. The SLTRC, like the SATRC, used public dissemination of selected witness testimony and availability of anonymity to encourage participation. Radio constituted the primary medium for disseminating information about the TRC (including testimony) that Hayner cites as explaining a 10 percent increase in perpetrator testimony. A poll conducted by a local non-governmental organisation, the Campaign for Good Governance ('CGG'), found that 60 percent thought it was beneficial, 58 percent were willing to testify, and 49 percent thought it should be mandatory for people to testify. However, 83 percent understood the SLTRC partially or not at all, 60 percent believed it would not, or were unsure if it could, provide security and confidentiali-

---

[155] Interview with Civil Society actor, 20 November 2011, Kathmandu.

[156] Victim representative speaking at a meeting with victims and victim representatives, 22 November 2011, Kathmandu.

ty to witnesses and only 43 percent thought the commission would be independent.[157] Similarly, a Nepali Commission should also communicate the level of anonymity achieved and maintained by investigating institutions such as the NHRC that refer cases to it. Commissions should also ensure that witnesses understand the possibility that the State will have to disclose their identity to an accused, if the witness is required to repeat testimony in a criminal trial.[158]

The capacity of a commission to maintain witness anonymity during the commission process is largely dependent upon the quality control of adopted fact-finding practices. These practices are more important in the context of Nepal's socio-political networks.[159] Use of private, one-on-one interviews or statement taking, as well as anonymity of investigative personnel and intermediaries facilitates greater discretion in witness contact. At the ICC, psychosocial assessment and approval by protection programme personnel is required before investigators may approach vulnerable witnesses. In the court's infancy, when investigators elevated the need to quickly contact witnesses above witness security, local populations were alerted to investigators' identities. Revised ICC practices employ local intermediaries to discreetly contact witnesses and set up meetings in secure locations during routine witness departure from communities or work places. At these meetings, protection personnel evaluate witness capacity to testify and endure protective measures, as well as the security implications of witness co-operation. ICC investigators conduct an assessment of the evidential value the witness' testimony will likely provide. Investigation of witnesses' place and nature of residence as well as the number of witnesses' dependents is then carried out. The SLTRC primarily used third party or local investigator methods of contacting and main-

---

[157] See *South Africa Press Association*, 4 April 1996; Campaign for Good Governance, "Opinion Poll Report on the TRC and Special Court", 2002; Hayner, 2011, p. 59, *supra* note 48.

[158] In Nepal, State attorneys are bound to make full disclosure to the accused within 25 days of indictment. These institutions may include both the police and the National Human Rights Commission, in which civil society actors hold little faith as to the extent to which such institutions are able to conduct investigations that preserve anonymity. The NHRC investigators are not trained in witness sensitive practices and would hand over around 1,000 already investigated cases to the commissions, were they created. Interview with Civil Society actors, Kathmandu, 2 December 2011; Interview with member, Attorney-General's office, 22 November 2011, Kathmandu; Interview with member, National Human Rights Commission, Kathmandu, 20 November 2011

[159] Interview with Civil Society actor, Kathmandu, 2 December 2011.

taining contact with witnesses. Private one-on-one interviews were the most common form of testimony. As anonymity was established and maintained, witnesses became more confident about providing sensitive information and less fearful that incriminating evidence would be provided to and acted upon by the Special Court. Nonetheless, combatants were prevented from co-operating due to the Court's close geographic proximity to the TRC, as well as a prosecution statement being the only guarantee of Court/TRC's non-cooperation.[160] Ensuring all precautions are taken should not be subordinated to the interests of speedy access to information, which can have disastrous consequences. Kenya's failure to put appropriate protective measures in place prioritised investigations above its witnesses' physical and psychological well-being. The subsequent killing of co-operating human rights activists and whistle-blowers prompted other witnesses to publicly disassociate themselves from their evidence. The possibility that targeted killings in Guatemala are linked to the infiltration of the CEH or co-operating NGOs' databases, like Kenya, exemplifies the importance of anonymity and the danger of utilising witnesses previously employed by NGOs, or by other investigations.[161]

*Anonymity during testimony* requires a discussion of international legal obligations. A contestation of public goods occurs when the rights of an accused, or in the case of a commission, the right to personality and reputation, confronts witnesses' rights to protection. In contesting implicated persons' rights to avoid defamation or unsubstantiated accusation (particularly relating to international crimes), conflicting bodies of jurisprudence have emerged. In law, the right to examine, or have examined, a witness testifying against you was held as subordinate to a witness's right to anonymity before the International Criminal Tribunal for the former Yugoslavia and the European Court of Human Rights.[162] However, the

---

[160] The author formerly worked at the TRC in 2003. See Mahony, 2010, pp. 32–34, *supra* note 40; Human Rights Watch, "Courting History: The Landmark International Criminal Court's First Years", 2008, p. 56.

[161] Nzau Musau, "Witnesses Targeted over Waki Envelope", *Nairobi Star*, 13 July 2009.

[162] The ECHR held that the accused's right to interrogate the authenticity of testimony including witness credibility outweighed the need to mitigate an organised criminal threat. The European Convention on Human Rights covers both adversarial and inquisitorial systems. International Criminal Tribunal for the Former Yugoslavia, *Prosecutor v. Duško Tadić*, Decision on the prosecutor's motion requesting protective measures for victims and witnesses, Trial Chamber, IT-94-1-T, 10 August 1995 (http://www.legal-tools.org/doc/ff53bf/); European Court of Human Rights. *Kostovski v. The Netherlands*, 10/1988/154/208, 11454/85, 166 Series A, 20 November 1989, p. 43 (http://www.legal-tools.org/doc/14aca1/).

ICC allows judges to weigh the threat with the right to a fair trial.[163] In Nepali law, legal provisions protect witness identity and security, particularly for women and children.[164] A proposed Criminal Code would allow testimony *via* video link for security reasons.[165]

The consequences of witness anonymity are less severe for persons implicated by testimony before a commission of inquiry than a criminal proceeding. A scarcity of jurisprudence exists that considers how the absence of criminal implications instructs re-evaluation of the balance between witness rights to security and the rights of implicated persons. If the commissions decide not to name names or hold public hearings that implicate individuals, this issue will not require consideration. The SATRC's Act barred Commission testimony from admission in criminal proceedings.[166] The High Court held that the witnesses' right to privacy and security[167] outweighed an implicated person's right to disclosure of the witness's identity. However, it did require that implicated persons have rea-

---

[163] The place, time and date of prosecution meetings with witnesses may be redacted from witness statements provided to defence counsel if the threat outweighs the right to a fair trial. International Criminal Court, Situation in the Democratic Republic of the Congo, *The Prosecutor v. Germain Katanga*, Judgment on the appeal of the Prosecutor against the decision of Pre-trial Chamber I entitled "First decision on the prosecution request for authorization to redact witness statements", Appeals Chamber, Case No. 01/04-01/07, 13 May 2008, p. 36 (http://www.legal-tools.org/doc/a76f99/).

[164] Under the Human Trafficking Act, victim's certified statements are admissible "even if the victim does not appear" and the statement assert facts the defence cannot cross-examine. As discussed below under 'psychosocial support', the Supreme Court of Nepal favours anonymity where women and children appear as witnesses. The *in camera* hearing guidelines prepared by the National Judicial Academy with support from UNIFEM have been adopted. They are being disseminated widely at central and district level among judges and law practitioners. Compromising accused rights in adjudicating serious criminal cases suggests Nepali law leans toward the witnesses' security rather than the accused's rights. For example, Section 51, Evidence Act, 1974, *supra* note 117, provides that counsel should not ask questions that unnecessarily insult or annoy the witness. Section 6(3), Human Trafficking and Transportation (Control) Act, 2064, 2007, *supra* note 61; Article 4, Supreme Court of Nepal, The Procedural Directives on Maintaining Secrecy of the Parties in the Cases of Special Nature, 2064; Security, Justice and Rule of Law Donor Coordination Group, 2010, p. 5, *supra* note 85.

[165] Section 109 of Draft Criminal Procedure Code and Criminal Offences (Offence and Implementation) Act 2067 as cited in INSEC, 2011, p. 36, *supra* note 62.

[166] Unless testimony is false, misleading, or prompts a question of law. Section 31(3), Promotion of National Unity and Reconciliation Act 34 of 1995, citing Section 39(d)(ii) of the said Act and Section 319(3) of the Criminal Procedure Act 51 of 1977.

[167] See *ibid.*, Section 11 on the Commission's victim related governing principles.

sonable time to make representation and give information about the implicating incident. The Court held that where witness identity or security would be compromised, disclosure of "witness statements or other relevant documentation" went too far. It also held that "reasonable and timeous" notification allows implicated parties to be present or provide legal representation at the hearing and if able and willing, to contest the evidence and, if permitted, to cross-examine the witness. What constituted "sufficient evidence" would "depend upon the facts of each individual case".[168] Witness anonymity and closed hearings have been the norm in South and Central American Commissions. However, the absence of public cross-examination of witnesses is problematic for a commission seeking to make factual claims in its report about a chain of command or command responsibility. Naming names under circumstances of broad use of anonymity would best be avoided where witnesses are not cross-examined.

### 10.5.5. Post-Testimony Protection (Formal or Advised)

If a Nepali Commission were to provide formal protection and investigate individual criminal responsibility, uncertainty surrounding subsequent punitive processes may complicate the admission of insider witnesses. Because of the identifiable nature of insider witness testimony, formal protective measures (relocation and identity change) are more often required. Focusing protection on insider witnesses also mitigates cost by keeping admission numbers low. The SATRC adopted this model, admitting approximately 150 of 23,000 witnesses.[169] Crime scene witnesses are often either not known to the implicated person or are so numerous that testimony rarely identifies them. In establishing individual command responsibility, few episodes of abuses, where orders or knowledge can be proven, might be focused on to limit the number of formally protected witnesses. A small number of most responsible persons could still be targeted under such circumstances.

How wide a net a prosecutorial phase casts, poses other protective dilemmas for fact-finding commissions. The amnesty in the Nepali Ordi-

---

[168] Supreme Court of South Africa, *Jan Abraham Du Preez and Nicolaas Jacobus Janse Van Rensburg v. The Truth and Reconciliation Commission*, Judgment, Case no 426/96, 18 February 1997, pp. 39, 42–46.

[169] Paul van Zyl, 1999, p. 656, *supra* note 78; Quinn and Freeman, 2003, p. 1121, *supra* note 44.

nance does not appear to have a particular threshold in terms of culpability. Were those of command responsibility to be pursued for prosecution, the immediate subordinates of those persons could be targeted as potential witnesses. However, if the scope and exercise of discretion is greater, those insider witnesses may also be required to serve protected prison time. Prison time requires temporary relocation for the witness' family before release and, if required, permanent relocation. Witnesses likely to encounter this predicament should be avoided, where alternative evidence is available.

Temporary relocation may need to be immediately arranged upon initial contact with a witness, when a threat is reported or perceived.[170] During temporary protection,[171] the programme can collate information and decide on admission to the formal programme or adoption of alternative methods.[172] Alternative methods include temporary relocation for three to four weeks before and after testifying, ensuring witnesses are able to contact protection personnel, regular investigator-witness contact, protection personnel follow up and periodic evaluation of the threat and protective measures.[173] Where a Nepali Commission refers cases to the Attorney-General, the arrest of the accused may also allow for bail conditions that mitigate the threat. Under such circumstances, the Commission programme, in co-operation with police, should closely monitor the enforcement of bail conditions.

The criterion to admit witnesses to formal protection is also ambiguous under the Commission Ordinance.[174] The Ordinance lends arbitrary

---

[170] A period of two weeks was used by the SATRC. Interview with former prosecution member, 2008, *supra* note 78.

[171] As was employed at the South African TRC.

[172] This period of protection should also be employed to build trust by taking victim impact statements, and sensitise witnesses as to the modalities and consequences of various forms of protection.

[173] Continued temporary relocation should cease when the threat has diminished, allowing repatriation and use of other alternative police and programme monitoring measures. These measures are similar to those available under the Human Trafficking Act. The Act provides for any or all protection measures, including: security during travel to and from a case, temporary police protection and access to a rehabilitation centre. Interview with former prosecution member, 2008, *supra* note 78; Section 26, Human Trafficking and Transportation (Control) Act, 2064, 2007, *supra* note 61.

[174] Section 17 provides that the Commission "shall make appropriate arrangements", TRC Ordinance, *supra* note 6.

admission power to the Commission that may lead to unprotected witnesses that merit protection, and inefficient allocation of resources protecting witnesses that do not require it. In creating a witness protection programme, Commissioners should construct admission criteria to be employed by the Chief Protection Officer, including:

1.  Availability and effectiveness of alternative protective methods, including anonymity.

2.  The threat to the witness as a consequence of co-operation:

    - Capacity of the implicated person(s) and affiliates to execute the threat.[175]

    - Willingness of the implicated person(s) and affiliates to execute the threat.[176]

3.  The importance of the witness' testimony (substance, credibility and possibility of alternatives):

    - Psychological capacity to provide credible testimony.

4.  The ability of the witness and family/dependents to temporarily or permanently relocate:

    - The families' cultural and economic adaptability.

    - The threat the witness or accompanying persons may pose to their new community.

    - Psychological capacity to adjust to protective measures.[177]

The Ordinance asserts protection 'as prescribed'.[178] However, best testimony outcomes are achieved through equitable and clearly understood obligations under a memorandum of understanding ('MOU').[179]

---

[175] Including the clout of the implicated person/s as assessed by programme intelligence personnel.

[176] Including the likelihood of effective criminal proceedings against implicated person(s), independence of the criminal justice system, and other implications (including the political, social, economic) of testimony.

[177] Based on counsellor and psychologist reports as well as witness and victim impact statements.

[178] Section 17(8), TRC Ordinance, *supra* note 6.

[179] A detailed negotiation of the admission MOU reduces the likelihood of subsequent disagreement. The MOU should include protective measures, conditions of material, moral support, the identity of accompanying persons, the witness' testimony and other obligations, the witness' voluntary participation, and termination conditions. Where neighbouring or co-operating States have protection programs, MOUs should seek to replicate, as far as

Where the number of accompanying persons asserted by the witness is high, the protection officer must assess relations before deciding to negotiate an MOU.[180] Commissions should also provide a mechanism for appeal of admission or termination decisions that protects anonymity during that process.[181]

In Nepal, the issue of relocation is complicated by its diversity, distinctiveness and community-oriented society.[182] External relocation is

---

is equitable, those States' MOUs. The MOU should also make clear the conditions instructing sanction or termination as a consequence of witness failure to fulfil obligations. This should include conditions under which the witness' identity would be disclosed (for re-engagement in serious criminality for example). Most conditions revolve around the threat subsiding.

[180] Determining accompanying persons' admissibility requires weighing of social, cultural, economic and political elements instructing relations with the witness. In Nepal, where cousins are often referred to as brothers and sisters, the conception of family is wider than in Western culture. Negotiations with witnesses must make clear that, unless exceptional circumstances dictate otherwise, only immediate, and not extended family or loved ones may relocate. While some States legislate to specifically allow witness' 'family', 'associate', 'household', or person 'in a close relationship' to accompany witnesses, it only allows, rather than obligates programs to include those persons. Section 1(1)(xx), Republic of South Africa, Witness Protection Act 112 of 1998, Government Gazette, 19523, 19 November 1998; Interview with Civil Society actors, 5 July 2011.

[181] Kenyan legislation includes a witness protection appeals tribunal on which a high court judge and two other presidential and ministerial appointees sit. In Nepal, three commissioners could sit on an *ad hoc* appeals tribunal. This may be done under the Provision allowing for sub-committees to be established. Commissioners should be appointed, based on their capacity to evaluate threat, testimony value, and witness (and their family's) ability to relocate. Section 3(U), Witness Protection Act, 2006, no. 16 of 2006, Kenya Gazette 3513, 30 December 2006; Sections 31, 34, TRC Ordinance, *supra* note 6.

[182] Whilst Nepal's relatively high population-density indicates internal relocation may be appropriate, the diversity of over 100 ethnicities and over 90 languages and dialects assists identification of relocated persons in a particular area or community. In the early 1990s various groups organised to defend cultures and practices that distinguished some groups from others. Nepali society also instructs a level of neighbourly inquisition unfamiliar to persons from Western metropolitan centres. External co-operation in relocation has been a source of frustration for many witness-protection programmes. In the United States, for example, numerous metropolitan areas with diverse ethnic and cultural populations make internal relocation a particularly viable option. In Sierra Leone, internal relocation is more difficult where only two major metropolitan centres exist and commerce and social interaction is commonly based on ethno-regional relations. External relocation, for many States, is the only viable option in cases where a high level of post-testimony threat persists. In Nepal, large metropolitan centres are sparse and an inquisitorial culture readily identifies persons according to their ethno-regional background, through language and accent. See Jason Miklian, 2008, p. 4, *supra* note 15; Interview with Civil Society actors, ICTJ, 5 July 2011.

therefore preferable to the risk of neighbourly or community suspicion or detection. However, external relocation relies on consistent external co-operation and is expensive, particularly if witnesses are required to testify in subsequent criminal proceedings.[183] Advised relocation (where witnesses bear relocation costs and the protection programme has no official role) may provide a cost-effective alternative.[184]

## 10.6. Conclusion

Fact-finding commissions investigating core international crimes instruct us that quality control must be shaped by the security dynamics of the circumstances in which fact-finding occurs. Relocation may be prohibitively expensive for many crime-scene witnesses. However, using relocation to protect a small number of high-level insider witnesses from each party to the conflict, can obtain information beyond the reach of orthodox investigative practice. Many of the variables instructing the safety of witness co-operation with Nepal's proposed Commission remain unclear or in a constant state of flux. Witness safety requires careful consideration of the merits of sensitive investigations.

The security dynamics instructing quality control is instructed by the sequence of critical elements of post-conflict peacebuilding. Engaging in fact-finding before stabilising processes, such as disarmament, demobilisation and other security sector reform initiatives, increases the threat to

---

[183] Investigator interviews and court testimony may require trips travel back to Nepal. The gap between Commission testimony and criminal proceedings may be exaggerated by an incapacitated investigative, prosecutorial or judicial system, or political interference in criminal processes. Longer processes bear both financial programme cost and psychological burdens for witness. Co-operation with external authorities, or permission to relocate witnesses into other sovereign territories, will be of critical importance. Establishing focal point personnel within the co-operating State's intelligence and security apparatus is essential to responsive and confidential co-operation. Like Nepali government focal points, their authority to make decisions without impediment is critical. Crozier and Candan, 2010, p. 19, *supra* note 15.

[184] The availability of multiple forms of assisted relocation, including assisted application for asylum or other migrant status, may significantly reduce relocation costs comparative to formal programme protection. Witnesses and accompanying persons should be thoroughly briefed on self-deployable methods that obstruct detection by hostile elements. In the context of only 30 of the previously 250 industries operating in the Morang-Sunsari industrial corridor driving Nepali migration to India, economic migration is unlikely to arouse suspicion. The laxity of Nepal's security on both the Chinese and Indian borders facilitates voluntary relocation without ordinarily prerequisite State co-operation. Crozier and Candan, 2010, p. 8, *supra* note 15.

witnesses and the wider community, elevating the required level of fact-finding quality control. In Nepal, the interests of witness security would be enhanced by the sequencing of post-conflict peace-building that placed constitutional reform and security sector reform before the sensitive investigation of abuses. This position must be balanced with the harms of delayed (and potentially denied) justice.[185] The Commission and the Government shall have to weigh the integrity and extent of their historical narratives with the security of the witnesses the Commission hopes to engage. The Ordinance, in its current form, does not provide adequate certainty as to subsequent prosecutorial action (or inaction) or ensure adequate protection for witnesses, given the current security dynamics. The threat to witnesses, therefore, may outweigh the benefit of investigating individual command responsibility. The cause of safely addressing impunity is dependent upon security sector reform, justice sector reform, constitutional reform (establishing a department of public prosecution independent from the executive) and revisions to the Ordinance establishing the Commission that provides independence, capacity and power to compel cooperation.

Five key elements determine the effective function of witness protection programmes and adequate witness-sensitive quality control in fact-finding. The first is the financial, security and political parameters within which protection functions. In Nepal, the recent provision of an ambiguous amnesty lends political, financial and security uncertainty for the Commission's investigative mandate and for witness security. Donors may be willing to fill the financial gap for protection left by a potentially unwilling or unable State. However, a process perceived as established to selectively prosecute or to placate justice pressures could turn donors away.

Political dynamics and donor clout are also instructive as to the second element: programme independence. Donor leverage may be employed to dissuade political pressure on Commissions to use national protection programmes, run by low-level personnel and prone to political manipulation. Commissioners' willingness to establish an independent programme will be critical to the Commission's capacity to protect wit-

---

[185] A report of victims' remains being moved appears to diminish the availability of forms of evidence other than witnesses. Interview with member, National Human Rights Commission, Kathmandu, 20 November 2011.

nesses, procure authentic testimony, and construct a legitimate and objective historical record. A programme structure with clear admission criteria, exclusive admission discretion located in the Chief Protection Officer's hands (an appointee of impeccable integrity), would significantly advance witnesses' physical and psychological security.

The third element: capacity to procure State and non-State co-operation is instructed, in theory, by the Commission's proposed founding documents. The Ordinance compels State co-operation, with caveats of personnel working within their obligations. Security sector elements have proven intransigent in complying with investigations into abuses, a trend potentially exaggerated under the provided amnesty. The effectiveness of security sector reform is a critical prerequisite to the sector's co-operation with investigations, as well as the State's capacity and willingness to apprehend accused in subsequent criminal processes. Commissions perceived as independent and legitimate would instruct non-State, particularly civil society groups', willingness to co-operate. Early engagement of these stakeholders increases the chances of their co-operation.

The Nepal Commission's protection programme will be dependent upon the efficacy and efficiency of the justice system as a whole. This critical fourth element instructs the amount of time witnesses will likely spend under protection before testifying in subsequent criminal cases. This factor also dictates the likely success of attempted prosecution, the cases that are pursued, and the witnesses that are protected.

The final element instructing a protection programme's effective function is the nature and scale of the threat to witnesses. The Commission's diminished punitive consequences and the criminal justice system's uncertain capacity to independently prosecute politically sensitive cases mitigate a historically severe threat from the security sector, the political class and affiliated criminal groups. It is very concerning that elements within the political elite have called for a national programme controlled by the security sector, elements of which pose the greatest threat to potential Commission witnesses.[186] These concerns require the immediate attention of donors, local and international civil society groups and all stakeholders hoping to safely learn the truth about abuses during Nepal's civil conflict.

---

[186] Moves towards this programme have slowed recently. Interview with member, Ministry of Peace and Reconstruction, 20 November 2011, Kathmandu.

Nepal appears to have two broad options before it. One option is to refrain from naming names. If the security and political situation remains precarious, it is unlikely that naming names or investigating and reporting on the chain of command is in the interests of witness security. The best investigative and psychosocial practices should ensure anonymity, and prioritise the interests of vulnerable witnesses Those practices should be made known to the public through a sensitisation campaign that allows potential witnesses to make the best-informed decision as to their own participation. A commission providing amnesty should attempt as best as is possible to facilitate community and indigenous reconciliatory processes that mitigate antagonisms and localised potential for future instability.

The second option is to investigate the chain of command and to name names. Were this approach to be taken, ambiguity relating to amnesty must be clarified. If the Government intends to go forward with prosecutions, Nepal's criminal justice system will require witness sensitive reform as well as reforms enabling capacity to prosecute international crimes cases. The Commission will also require formal protective capacity. The Commission would have to sensitise the broader public, as well as individual witnesses, as to the likelihood of their testimony being used in a subsequent prosecution, the potential consequences for their security, and the available capacity to provide protection should related prosecutions occur. This approach may require significant external support.

Current Nepali capacity and political will does not provide for a level of fact-finding quality control sufficient for safe investigation and prosecution of persons most responsible for crimes during the conflict. Nepali civil society actors must be more transparent about the associated risks of pursuing, in the near term, criminal accountability or even the naming of names for those most responsible for crimes. An over-zealous approach, reproducing witness security outcomes similar to those in Kenya, risks further undermining Nepali faith in government fact-finding and alienating would-be witnesses from future investigations. That scenario would undermine, not advance, the fight against impunity.

# 11

---

# Fact-Finding in the Former Yugoslavia:
# What the Courts Did

## David Re[*]

## 11.1. Introduction

The United Nations sent many fact-finding missions into the former Yugoslavia during the armed conflicts that occurred between 1991 and 1999. The reports of several were influential in persuading the Security Council to establish the first UN war crimes tribunal, the International Criminal Tribunal for the former Yugoslavia, in 1993. The main fact-finding missions – those of the United Nations Commission on Human Rights ('UNCHR') and the Security Council itself – submitted over 20 reports, while fact-finding missions of other intergovernmental and non-governmental organisations undertook their own investigations and published their own reports. The fact-finding missions were area and conflict specific. They employed differing methodologies but generally revealed how crimes had been committed, sometimes specifying alleged or assumed individual perpetrator, by name, unit or organisation. The UN reports were widely publicised, sent directly to the parties to the conflicts, and discussed in the Security Council. Some of these reports became evidence in trials at the International Tribunal for the former Yugoslavia ('ICTY'), mostly tendered as prosecution exhibits. The Tribunal also heard testimony from the authors of the reports and members of their teams who were responsible for investigating the crimes alleged.

By the end of the 1990s, in the conflicts in Kosovo and Macedonia, the reports of NGOs (particularly those of Human Rights Watch), evolved to perform a sophisticated dual role of informing the world at large of suspected breaches of international humanitarian law and of human rights

---

[*]  **David Re**, Presiding Judge, Trial Chamber, Special Tribunal for Lebanon, The Hague. Formerly international judge, Court of Bosnia and Herzegovina; trial attorney and senior prosecuting trial attorney, International Criminal Tribunal for the former Yugoslavia; and barrister and solicitor, Sydney, Australia.

abuses; and of providing a form of legal notice to civilian, paramilitary and military leaders of these crimes and the possible consequences of prosecution for failing to prevent or punish the perpetrators. Their publication and dissemination were tactical, deliberate and strategic.

But what did the ICTY Trial and Appeals Chambers, and the successor mechanism, the International Residual Mechanism for Criminal Tribunals ('IRMCT'), actually do with these reports in their decisions and judgements? How were their findings and conclusions used? Did the courts consider them to be probative, relevant and reliable, and hence admissible as evidence?

The answer is quite mixed. This brief study shows a relatively minimal use of the reports by the ICTY Chambers between 1994 and 2017, and the IRMCT until 2020.[1] The Chambers (i) sometimes used their factual descriptions or conclusions to corroborate other more direct evidence presented at trial; (ii) in some rare cases, accepted factual descriptions or conclusions without corroboration; (iii) several times used the dissemination of the information in the reports to prove notice of the crimes to high-level accused persons; (iv) in a few cases used information in the reports to find the existence of an armed conflict, and hence jurisdiction; and (v) accepted certain legal opinions of one major report (the Security Council's Commission of Experts) while rejecting other recommendations. Some Chambers also explicitly declined to rely upon factual descriptions or conclusions from fact-finding reports, without other supporting or corroborating evidence. The Prosecutor, on the other hand, primarily used the reports as investigative leads.

From this, it can be concluded that the reports of the major UN fact-finding missions to the former Yugoslavia during the 1991 to 1995 conflicts, although used to instigate criminal investigations, ultimately were probably more politically and historically important than judicially influential. The trial judgements reveal that, in the context of the vast amount of material received into evidence in the trials, these reports had compara-

---

[1]  This chapter was originally finalized in October 2013 and then updated in June 2020 to reflect developments between the two dates. The establishment of the IRMCT was one such development. Another was the finalization of six ICC cases, *Lubanga*, *Ngudjolo*, *Katanga*, *Bemba*, *Bemba and others* (Article 70 contempt), and *Al-Mahdi*, and trial judgments in another two, *Gbagbo and Blé Goudé* and *Ntaganda*. For the purposes of comparison, the revision has examined how the International Criminal Court has used fact-finding reports.

tively little effect on either the evidence presented at trial or on the conclusions of these judgements.

In settling their methodology, fact-finding missions should draw from the reasoning of the several ICTY Trial Chambers that have cautioned against relying upon the conclusions of certain reports, absent other corroborating evidence. Although, admittedly, many of these reports were prepared in the 1990s and the standard of investigation and reporting has since improved – and, indeed, the very existence of international criminal courts and tribunals now influences their methodologies – the reasoning of those trial judgements written in 2008 and 2011 stands. These judgements should thus be carefully scrutinised. Lessons can be learned from these, especially if institutions such as the International Criminal Court ('ICC') or hybrid or national courts follow the ICTY's precedent in dealing cautiously with fact-finding reports.

The ICC's approach – properly that of a court applying the appropriate evidentiary standards for receiving and assessing evidence in criminal trials – has had some similarities to the ICTY's. The court, in confirmation decisions and some judgments, has stated its reluctance to rely upon the anonymous hearsay so typically used in fact-finding reports. Chambers and individual judges have expressed the same reluctance to rely on fact-finding reports. Despite this, the ICC prosecution has relied more on fact-finding reports for primary proof than the ICTY prosecution ever did. Fact-finding, even with a distinct and immediate mandate that differs from that of criminal justice institutions, must nonetheless embrace the importance of accuracy in sourcing findings and conclusions.

## 11.2. The Conflicts

The military conflict in the former Yugoslavia (Socialist Federal Republic of Yugoslavia) commenced in June 1991 with a short conflict between the Slovenian Territorial Defence Forces and the Yugoslav People's Army ('JNA'). Another conflict in Croatia between the Croatian military ('HV') and the JNA and its successor in the Federal Republic of Yugoslavia (the FRY, comprised of Serbia and Montenegro from April 1992), the VJ, and the military of a breakaway Serb republic (Army of the Serb Republic of the Krajina, or SVK) occurred from around July 1991 until the end of 1995. In Bosnia and Herzegovina, there were armed conflicts from March 1992 until the signing of the Dayton Peace Agreement on 14 December

1995.[2] The Bosnian conflict was primarily between the Army of Bosnia and Herzegovina ('ABiH') and the military of the breakaway Croatian Republic of Herceg-Bosna, the Croatian Defence Council ('HVO'), and the ABiH and HVO on one side against the Bosnian Serb Army ('VRS'), and paramilitary forces of the FRY's intelligence services on the other. From 1998–1999, an armed conflict occurred in Kosovo between the Kosovo Liberation Army and the VJ and other FRY Government forces. In 2001 in Macedonia, an armed conflict developed between the ethnic Albanian National Liberation Army ('NLA') and Government security forces.

## 11.3. The Fact-Finding Missions

In February 1992, the Security Council established an interim peacekeeping force, the United Nations Protection Force ('UNPROFOR') in the former Yugoslavia.[3] Many months later, and well into an intensifying and increasingly vicious conflict in Bosnia and Herzegovina, two organs of the United Nations, the Security Council and the UNCHR, resolved to send fact-finding missions into the country to inquire into breaches of humanitarian law and human rights abuses.

In August 1992, the UNCHR appointed a Special Rapporteur to investigate first-hand the human rights situation in the former Yugoslavia, in particular within Bosnia and Herzegovina, and to receive relevant, credible information from Governments, individuals and intergovernmental and non-governmental organisations.[4] The Special Rapporteur, former Polish Prime Minister Tadeusz Mazowiecki, immediately visited the country and filed his first report on 28 August 1992. His initial observations commented:[5]

---

[2]  General Framework Agreement for Peace in Bosnia and Herzegovina, A/50/790, S/1995/999, 21 November 1995, signed on 14 December 1995 (https://www.legal-tools. org/doc/de1053/).

[3]  Resolution 743 (1992), 21 February 1992 (http://www.legal-tools.org/doc/e91743/), established a peacekeeping operation as an "interim arrangement to create the conditions of peace and security required for the negotiation of an overall settlement of the Yugoslav crisis".

[4]  Resolution 1992/S-1/1, 14 August 1992.

[5]  UN Doc. E/CN.4/1992/S-1/9, Report on the situation of human rights in the territory of the former Yugoslavia submitted by Mr. Tadeusz Mazowiecki, Special Rapporteur of the Commission on Human Rights, pursuant to Paragraph 15 of Commission Resolution 1992/S-1/1 of 14 August 1992, para. 6.

> Most of the territory of the former Yugoslavia, in particular Bosnia and Herzegovina, is at present the scene of massive and systematic violations of human rights, as well as serious grave violations of humanitarian law. Ethnic cleansing is the cause of most such violations.

Several months later, in October 1992, the Security Council requested the Secretary-General to establish, as a matter of urgency, an impartial Commission of Experts to examine and analyse evidence of grave breaches of the Geneva Conventions and other violations of international humanitarian law committed in the former Yugoslavia.[6] A five-member commission was established later that month. The Commission commenced its work in November 1992, and, between then and April 1994 completed two interim reports.[7] In its first interim report the experts noted,[8]

> [t]he Commission was led to discuss the idea of the establishment of an *ad hoc* International Tribunal. In its opinion, it would be for the Security Council or another competent organ of the United Nations to establish such a tribunal in relation to events in the territory of the former Yugoslavia. The Commission observes that such a decision would be consistent with the direction of its work.

Its final report of 24 May 1994 concluded that grave breaches of the Geneva Conventions and other violations of international humanitarian law had been committed in the former Yugoslavia on a large scale, and were particularly brutal and ferocious in their execution.[9] In December 1994, the Commission submitted to the Security Council all of the annexes to its report, totalling over 3,300 pages. Between August 1992 and August 1995, Special Rapporteur Mazowiecki prepared 18 reports.[10] He re-

---

[6]    Resolution 780 (1992), 6 October 1992.

[7]    Interim Report of the Commission of Experts Established Pursuant to Security Council Resolution 780 (1992), 9 February 1993, S/25274, and Second Interim Report of the Commission of Experts Established Pursuant to Security Council Resolution 780 (1992), 3 October 1993, S/26545.

[8]    Interim Report 9 February 1993, Annex 1, para. 74.

[9]    Letter dated 24 May 1994 from the Secretary-General to the President of the Security Council annexing Final Report of the Commission of Experts Established Pursuant to Security Council Resolution 780 (1992), Add. 1 and Add. 2 (Vol. I–V), S/1994/674 (hereafter 'Final Report') (https://www.legal-tools.org/doc/3a3ae2/).

[10]   The reports are dated 28 August 1992, 27 October 1992, 17 November 1992, 10 February 1993, 5 May 1993 (First Periodic Report), 13 May 1993 (Second Periodic Report), 26 Au-

signed in July 1995 just after the Srebrenica mass atrocities of genocide and crimes against humanity.[11]

Special Rapporteur Mazowiecki's successor, Elisabeth Rehn, visited the former Yugoslavia 19 times between September 1995 and January 1998 and published reports, including six on the situation in the Republic of Croatia.[12]

The Conference on Security and Co-operation in Europe ('CSCE', and from 1 January 1995, the Organization for Security and Co-operation in Europe, or 'OSCE') an intergovernmental organisation, also sent fact-finding teams into the former Yugoslavia to gather evidence of crimes and human rights violations. The European Community had its own monitoring mission, the ECMM,[13] charged with gathering and analysing information. It too investigated and reported on war crimes. UNPROFOR prepared numerous reports, including those of UNCIVPOL ('UNPROFOR Civilian Police'). NGOs including Amnesty International were likewise active in fact-finding. Human Rights Watch was particularly active in Kosovo in 1998 and 1999.

On 25 May 1993, almost two years into the conflict and some seven fact-finding reports later, the UN Security Council passed Resolution 832, formally establishing the ICTY. The two main fact-finding bodies meanwhile continued to visit the former Yugoslavia and to report back to the UN on the recurring mass crimes and human rights abuses.

---

gust 1993 (Third Periodic Report), 6 September 1993 (Fourth Periodic Report), 17 September 1993 (Fifth Periodic Report), 21 February 1994 (Sixth Periodic Report), 10 June 1994 (Seventh Periodic Report), 4 August 1994 (Eighth Periodic Report), 4 November 1994 (Ninth Periodic Report), 13 December 1994 (Special Report on the Media), 9 January 1995 (Tenth Periodic Report), 21 April 1995 (Eleventh Periodic Report), 5 July 1995 (Twelfth Periodic Report), and 22 August 1995 (Thirteenth Periodic Report) with Letter of Resignation.

[11] Final periodic report on the situation of human rights in the territory of the former Yugoslavia submitted by Mr. Tadeusz Mazowiecki, Special Rapporteur of the Commission on Human Rights, pursuant to Paragraph 42 of Commission Resolution 1995/89, 22 August 1995, E/CN.4/1996/9, and 18 September 1995, A/50/441, S/1995/801.

[12] Final report of Ms. Elisabeth Rehn, Special Rapporteur of the Commission on Human Rights on the situation of human rights in Bosnia and Herzegovina, the Republic of Croatia and the Federal Republic of Yugoslavia, 14 January 1998, E/CN.4/1998/63. The reports on Croatia were relevant to the *Gotovina* case at the ICTY.

[13] Established as a consequence of the Brioni Declaration of 8 July 1991.

---

As of 1993, the International Law Commission was continuing its work on drafting a statute for an international criminal court. As no international trials of international crimes had occurred since the aftermath of World War II, the elements of the international crimes of war crimes, breaches of the Geneva Conventions of 1949 and the Additional Protocols, genocide, and crimes against humanity were judicially undefined.

The Final Report of the Commission of Experts, published in May 1994, a year after the ICTY Statute's enactment, contained a fairly lengthy section entitled "Applicable Law" which delved into the international/non-international character of the armed conflict, grave breaches of the Geneva Conventions, the customary international law of armed conflict, command responsibility, superior orders, reprisals, interference with humanitarian aid convoys, crimes against humanity, genocide, and rape and sexual assaults.[14] In explaining its rationale for including this legal analysis the Commission wrote:[15]

> The Commission has chosen to comment on selected legal issues because of their particular significance for understanding the legal context related to violations of international humanitarian law committed in the territory of the former Yugoslavia. The Commission's mandate is to provide the Secretary-General with its conclusions on the evidence of such violations and not to provide an analysis of the legal issues. It will be for the International Tribunal to make legal findings in connection with particular cases.

The report was fully endorsed by the Secretary-General,[16] and elements of the Commission continued until the end of that year to work on compiling the comprehensive annexes that the report had foreshadowed.

The 18 reports of Special Rapporteur Mazowiecki, the reports of Special Rapporteur Rehn on Croatia, and the three reports of the Commission of Experts contained a large quantity of material on the commission of mass crimes in the former Yugoslavia. From December 1992, the Commission of Experts established a database of information gathered, and it was specifically charged with providing that material to the Office

---

[14] Commission of Experts Final Report, paras. 41–109.

[15] Commission of Experts Final Report, para. 41.

[16] Letter dated 24 May 1994 from the Secretary-General to the President of the Security Council, S/1994/674 (submitting the Final Report).

of the Prosecutor of the ICTY.[17] In May 1993, the Security Council resolved that, pending the appointment of the first ICTY Prosecutor, the Commission of Experts should continue to collect evidence of violations of international humanitarian law.[18] The Commission transferred its database to the ICTY Prosecutor in April 1994.[19]

The material provided to the Prosecutor gave him the basis to commence investigations into alleged criminality, resulting in indictments, trials, convictions, sentences and international jurisprudence. As the ICTY's 1994 annual report noted:[20]

> The Office of the Prosecutor has had to invent itself. Starting from nothing in early 1994, a staffing plan was first formulated and qualified and experienced staff were recruited. Then an information management and litigation support system was developed. A great array of information relevant to the Tribunal's jurisdiction, in large part provided by the Commission of Experts [...] was then assembled and registered and is being analysed.

## 11.4. Legal Opinions of the Commission of Experts

The UN fact-finding reports were undoubtedly catalysts in developing international criminal law, at least in facilitating investigations that resulted in court cases and case law. Legally, however, the ICTY Chambers made relatively little use of the Final Report's extensive opinions on humanitarian law as the Commission expressed them in 1994. In this strict literal sense, they appear not to have been overly influential.

The first legal use of the Final Report was in the *Tadić* case, the Tribunal's first, where the Prosecutor – in an application to have Germany defer its jurisdiction to prosecute an ICTY indictee Duško Tadić who had been recently apprehended in Germany and charged domestically with genocide – informed the Tribunal that he was using the Final Report as a source for investigating crimes committed in Prijedor in Bosnia and Her-

---

[17] Commission of Experts Final Report, paras. 21–22.

[18] Resolution 827 (1993) 25 May 1993.

[19] Report of the International Tribunal for the Prosecution of Persons Responsible for Serious Violations of International Humanitarian Law Committed in the Territory of the Former Yugoslavia since 1991, 29 August 1994, A/49/342, S/1994/1007, paras. 157–158 (ICTY Annual Report 1994) (https://www.legal-tools.org/doc/cacdb7/).

[20] ICTY Annual Report 1994, p. 7.

zegovina.[21] The Chamber granted the application and Germany accepted the competence of the Tribunal and transferred Tadić to the ICTY for trial.

However, in the Tribunal's first major legal decision, the *Tadić* Jurisdiction Decision, the Trial Chamber only briefly referred to the Final Report and then only in the context of how its conclusions were used by the Security Council to establish the ICTY, leading to the Trial Chamber's opinion that the Security Council had not acted arbitrarily.[22] On appeal, the majority decision made no mention of the Commission or its reports, despite making legal findings at odds with the Commission's.[23] Judge LI, however, in his dissent, used the report's legal opinion to support his view that customary international law had not developed to allow the prosecution of all violations of the law or customs of law committed in an *internal* armed conflict.[24] He also referenced the Final Report and the reports of Special Rapporteur Mazowiecki to support his view that the armed conflict in Bosnia and Herzegovina was international in character.[25] Judge Sidwa, in a separate opinion, referenced both the Special Rapporteur and the Commission of Experts and their roles in the lead-up to the ICTY's establishment, but did not use the Commission's legal analysis.[26] Major legal findings were made in the Tribunal's first main appellate decision

---

[21]  *Prosecutor v. Duško Tadić*, IT-94-1-D, Decision of the Trial Chamber on the Application by the Prosecutor for a Formal Request for Deferral to the Competence of the International Tribunal for the Former Yugoslavia in the Matter of Duško Tadić (pursuant to Rules 9 and 10 of the Rules of Procedure and Evidence), 8 November 1994, para. 12. The Commission had made a special report on crimes committed in Prijedor in 1992 and 1993.

[22]  *Prosecutor v. Duško Tadić a.k.a. 'Dule'*, IT-94-1-T, Decision on the Defence Motion on Jurisdiction, 10 August 1995, para. 16 (http://www.legal-tools.org/doc/ddd6b0/).

[23]  *Prosecutor v. Duško Tadić a.k.a. 'Dule'*, IT-94-1-AR-72, Decision on the Defence Motion for Interlocutory Appeal on Jurisdiction, 2 October 1995 (http://www.legal-tools.org/doc/866e17/).

[24]  Separate Opinion of Judge LI on the Defence Motion for Interlocutory Appeal on Jurisdiction, para. 8, dissenting on the conclusion of para. 91 of the majority Decision (http://www.legal-tools.org/doc/eb6f75/).

[25]  Separate Opinion of Judge Li, para. 18. The Final Report had stated at para. 42, "The treaty law designed for internal armed conflicts […]. These legal sources do not use the terms of 'grave breaches' or 'war crimes'. Further, the content of customary law applicable to internal armed conflict is debatable. As a result, in general, unless the parties to an internal armed conflict agree otherwise, the only offences committed in internal armed conflict for which universal jurisdiction exists are crimes against humanity and genocide, which apply irrespective of the conflicts classification".

[26]  Separate Opinion of Judge Sidwa on the Defence Motion for Interlocutory Appeal on Jurisdiction, paras. 46, 52, and 99 (http://www.legal-tools.org/doc/03a643/).

against a trial judgement (again *Tadić*) about crimes against humanity, the test for the internationality of an armed conflict and joint criminal enterprise, but without referring to the Final Report.[27]

The Commission's legal opinions were adopted by the ICTY in several specific instances: command responsibility, the definition of 'group' for genocide, the effect of rape and sexual violence on its victims, the definition of 'protected persons for crimes against humanity', and the definition of 'military objectives'. Its most widely accepted opinion is that of the indicia necessary to inform a commander of the criminal acts of subordinates. On the other hand, the Appeals Chamber disagreed with the Commission's opinion that a discriminatory intent was required to commit a crime against humanity, and that certain violations of humanitarian law could only be prosecuted if committed in an international armed conflict. Although far-reaching, this difference of legal opinion between a court and such a commission is quite explicable as these issues were judicially undefined when the Commission expressed its opinion. Moreover, courts hear extensive legal submissions from parties, and appeal courts have the additional benefit of considering the reasoned decisions of lower courts, whereas the Commission relied upon its own internal expertise.

## 11.5. Command Responsibility

The Final Report was most legally influential on the issue of command responsibility. *Delalić*, the first adjudicated case involving Article 7(3) of the ICTY Statute, of superior or command responsibility of commanders for the actions of their subordinates, cited the Final Report's conclusions on command responsibility.[28] *Blagojević* accepted the Commission's policy rationale for Article 7(3), "to ensure that a commander fulfills his obligation to promote compliance with the laws of war by his subordinates

---

[27] *Prosecutor v. Duško Tadić*, IT-94-1-A, Judgement, 15 July 1999 (http://www.legal-tools.org/doc/8efc3a/).

[28] *Prosecutor v. Zejnil Delalić, Zdravko Mucić, a.k.a. 'Pavo', Hazim Delić and Esad Landžo, a.k.a. 'Zenga'*, IT-96-21-T, Judgement, 16 November 1998, para. 90 (http://www.legal-tools.org/doc/6b4a33/). The Final Report was a prosecution exhibit. The *Delalić* and *Aleksovski* Trial Chambers noted the Final Report's observation that political leaders and public officials have been held responsible under the doctrine of command responsibility *Delalić*, para. 90; *Prosecutor v. Zlatko Aleksovski*, IT-95 14/1, Judgement, 26 June 1999, para. 75 (http://www.legal-tools.org/doc/52d982/), holding "this interpretation" was that "chosen by the Commission of Experts". The Final Report, however, only noted that non-military leaders had been held liable under the doctrine, rather than opting for an "interpretation" as such.

---

[…]".[29] And, in finding that command responsibility is responsibility for an omission, *Halilović* noted that "the Commission may have considered that Article 7(3) attached responsibility to commanders for the crimes of their subordinates", but then held that this does not mean "that the commander shares the same responsibility as the subordinates who committed the crimes, but rather that because of the crimes committed by his subordinates, the commander should bear responsibility for his failure to act".[30] This has not been the subject of an appeal decision.

In *Hadžihasanović*, in deciding a defence challenge to the Tribunal's jurisdiction based on the argument that the doctrine of command responsibility was inapplicable in internal armed conflicts, the Trial Chamber, in surveying sources and statements of customary law, relied upon the Commission's view that command responsibility should apply to any war crime or crime against humanity committed in the former Yugoslavia.[31] The Appeals Chamber upheld the decision without referring to the report but while approving the Trial Chamber's survey and analysis.[32]

The ICTY definitively endorsed the Final Report's list of indicia of what factors may constitute a superior's knowledge of subordinates' criminality in determining the superior's mental state or *mens rea*.[33] *Delalić*,

---

[29] *Prosecutor v. Vidoje Blagojević and Dragan Jokić*, IT-02-60-T, Judgement, 17 January 2005 para. 823, referring to para. 57, Final Report (http://www.legal-tools.org/doc/ba75a9/).

[30] *Prosecutor v. Sefer Halilović*, IT-01-48-T, Judgement, 16 November 2005, paras. 51 and 54 (http://www.legal-tools.org/doc/abda04/). Trial Chambers in *Prosecutor v. Naser Orić*, IT-03-68-T, Judgement, 30 June 2006, para. 293 (http://www.legal-tools.org/doc/1c3788/); and *Prosecutor v. Enver Hadžihasanović and Amir Kubara*, IT-01-47-T, Judgement, 15 March 2006, para. 75 (http://www.legal-tools.org/doc/8f515a/), reached the same legal conclusion.

[31] *Prosecutor v. Enver Hadžihasanović, Mehmed Alagić and Amir Kubara*, IT-01-47-PT, Decision on Joint Challenge to Jurisdiction, 12 November 2002 (http://www.legal-tools.org/doc/c46fc0/), findings paras. 141 and 104 referring to paras. 52–53 of the Commision's interim report 9 February 1993 and para. 57, Final Report.

[32] Thus implicitly endorsing the Final Report's conclusions, *Prosecutor v. Enver Hadžihasanović, Mehmed Alagić and Amir Kubara*, IT-01-47-AR72, Decision on Interlocutory Appeal Challenging Jurisdiction in Relation to Command Responsibility, 16 July 2003, para. 27 (http://www.legal-tools.org/doc/608f09/).

[33] Commission of Experts Final Report, para. 58. The list reads in full: To determine whether or not a commander must have known about the acts of his subordinates, one might consider a number of indices, including: (a) the number of illegal acts; (b) the type of illegal acts; (c) the scope of illegal acts; (d) the time during which the illegal acts occurred; (e) the number and type of troops involved; (f) the logistics involved, if any; (g) the geographical

the first command responsibility case, adopted the list.[34] *Blaškić* specifically approved it,[35] and accepted the Commission's test for determining the extent of a commander's responsibility.[36] *Galić* ruled that it could consider this list,[37] *Stakic* followed it,[38] and *Orić* held that it was part of the Tribunal's case law.[39] *Strugar*, too, accepted it,[40] *Brđanin* implicitly endorsed it,[41] and the Appeals Chamber even described it as a "helpful

---

location of the acts; (h) the widespread occurrence of the acts; (i) The tactical tempo of operations; (j) the *modus operandi* of similar illegal acts; (k) the officers and staff involved; and (l) the location of the commander at the time.

[34] *Delalić*, Trial Judgement, para. 386, *supra* note 28.

[35] *Prosecutor v. Tihomir Blaškić*, IT-95-14, Judgement, 3 March 2000, para. 307 (http://www.legal-tools.org/doc/e1ae55/) concerning para. 58, Final Report.

[36] *Ibid.*, paras. 330–332, re paras. 59–60, Final Report. The Trial Chamber also considered the Final Report of the Commission of Inquiry into the Events at the Refugee Camps in Beirut, 7 February 1983 (the massacres at the Shatilla and Sabra refugee camps 1982), the 'Kahan report', in determining the state of customary international law, para. 331, re pp. 35 and 37, Kahan report.

[37] *Prosecutor v. Stanislav Galić*, IT-98-29-T, Judgement, 5 December 2003, para. 174 (http://www.legal-tools.org/doc/eb6006/). It did this deciding a commander's *mens rea* but then somewhat strangely adopted the list under "Individual Responsibility under Article 7 (1) of the Statute" and specifically for "ordering", holding that proof "may be inferred from a variety of factors such as the number of illegal acts, the number, identity and type of troops involved, the effective command and control exerted over these troops [...]". On appeal, the defence unsuccessfully argued that the Trial Chamber was not entitled to take the list into consideration because the Final Report was based on "assumptions and superficial information", *Prosecutor v. Stanislav Galić*, IT-98-29-A, Judgement, 30 November 2006, paras. 180–183 (http://www.legal-tools.org/doc/c81a32/).

[38] *Prosecutor v. Milomir Stakić*, IT-97-24-T, Judgement, 31 July 2003, para. 460 (http://www.legal-tools.org/doc/32ecfb/).

[39] *Prosecutor v. Naser Orić*, IT-03-68-T, Judgement, 30 June 2006, para. 319 (http://www.legal-tools.org/doc/37564c/).

[40] *Prosecutor v. Pavle Strugar*, IT-01-42-T, Decision on Defence Motion Requesting Judgement of Acquittal pursuant to Rule 98 *bis*, 12 June 2004, para. 193 (http://www.legal-tools.org/doc/927ba5/).

[41] *Prosecutor v. Radoslav Brđanin*, IT-99-36-T, Judgement, 1 September 2004, para. 276 (http://www.legal-tools.org/doc/4c3228/).

---

list".[42] And, some 19 years after it was formulated, *Prlić* approved of it.[43] The ICC, in *Bemba* in 2016, also approved it.[44]

## 11.6. Rape and Sexual Violence

The Final Report also analysed the effect of rape and sexual violence on victims. *Delalić*, in finding that rape and other forms of sexual violence could amount to torture for Articles 2 and 3 of the Statute (grave breaches and war crimes) endorsed the Commission's finding on the "profound effects of rape and other forms of sexual assault".[45] *Blaškić* agreed in relation to torture as either a grave breach or contravention of common Article 3 of the Geneva Conventions.[46]

## 11.7. Protected Persons for Crimes Against Humanity

The Final Report examined who could constitute a protected person under Article 5 of the ICTY Statute (crimes against humanity) and concluded that "it applies first and foremost to civilians, meaning people who are not combatants", but that this "should not lead to any quick conclusions concerning people who [...] did bear arms".[47] *Tadić* decided that "the presence of certain non-civilians in their midst does not change the character of the population".[48] And in defining 'protected person', *Jelisić* broadly interpreted 'civilian population' noting the Commission's view that it includes "all those persons bearing or having borne arms who had not,

---

[42]  *Prosecutor v. Stanislav Galić*, IT-98-29-A73.2, Decision on Interlocutory Appeal Concerning Rule 92 bis(C), 7 June 2002, para. 14 (https://www.legal-tools.org/doc/0f588c/).

[43]  *Prosecutor v. Jadranko Prlić, Bruno Stojić, Slobodan Praljak, Milivoj Petković, Valentin Ćorić, Berislav Pušić*, Jugement, IT-04-74-T, 29 May 2013, para. 248 (French original) (https://www.legal-tools.org/doc/ff73ab/).

[44]  *Situation in The Central African Republic in The Case of The Prosecutor v. Jean-Pierre Bemba Gombo*, Judgment pursuant to Article 74 of the Statute, 21 March 2016, ICC-01/05-01/08, para. 193, fn. 443 (https://www.legal-tools.org/doc/edb0cf/).

[45]  *Delalić*, para. 496 and 492, *supra* note 28, citing Commission of Experts Final Report, Annexes IX to XII, Add. 2 (Vol. V), para. 25; Article 2 proscribes grave breaches of the Geneva Conventions, Article 3, violations of the laws or customs of war.

[46]  *Blaškić*, para. 492, *supra* note 35, and noted the Commission's conclusions in the context of international and regional judicial bodies regarding the harm to victims of rape and other forms of sexual violence it could fall within the definition. Article 3 of the ICTY Statute embraces a wider category of crimes than common Article 3 of the Geneva Conventions.

[47]  Commission of Experts Final Report, para. 77.

[48]  *Prosecutor v. Duško Tadić a.k.a. 'Dule'*, IT-94-1-T, Opinion and Judgement, 7 May 1997, para. 638 (http://www.legal-tools.org/doc/0a90ae/), relying upon paras. 77–78, Final Report.

strictly speaking, been involved in military activities" and decided that this includes those *hors de combat* when the crime is committed.[49] *Blaškić* likewise adopted this, holding that crimes against humanity can be committed against members of a resistance movement or former combatants *hors de combat* due to their wounds or detention.[50] In *Martić*, some eight years later, the Appeals Chamber eventually agreed, and by using the 1994 Final Report as an interpretative source, found that persons *hors de combat* are not excluded from Article 5 protection.[51]

## 11.8. Discriminatory Intent for Underlying Crimes of Crimes against Humanity

The Final Report stated that a discriminatory intention was required to commit a crime against humanity. The *Tadić* trial judgement followed this opinion, deciding that a discriminatory intention was required to commit any crime against humanity, including inhumane acts.[52] A Prosecution appeal, however, had this decision reversed – the majority of the Appeals

---

[49] *Prosecutor v. Goran Jelisić*, IT-95-10, Judgement, 14 December 1999, para. 55 (https://www.legal-tools.org/doc/b3ece5/), quoting para. 78 of the Final Report:

It seems obvious that Article 5 applies first and foremost to civilians, meaning people who are not combatants. This, however, should not lead to any quick conclusions concerning people who at one particular point in time did bear arms. One practical example: in the former Yugoslavia, large-scale arbitrary killings were one of the hallmarks of attacks by a given group. Information about such arbitrary killings was then used by the same group to instill fear and demand total subjugation of the other group in other areas as well. Many of the most barbarous onslaughts on villages started with heavy artillery bombardments followed by the villages being stormed by infantry in tandem, while paramilitary groups sought the inhabitants in each and every house. A head of family who under such circumstances tries to protect his family gun-in-hand does not thereby lose his status as a civilian.

[50] *Blaškić*, Trial Judgement, paras. 213–214, *supra* note 35, re para. 78, Final Report.

[51] *Prosecutor v. Milan Martić*, IT-95-11-A, Appeal Judgement, 8 October 2008, para. 306 (http://www.legal-tools.org/doc/ca5eff/), referring to paras. 77–80, Final Report and holding that "under Article 5 of the Statute, a person *hors de combat* may thus be the victim of an act amounting to a crime against humanity, provided that all other necessary conditions are met, in particular that the act in question is part of a widespread or systematic attack against any civilian population", paras. 292–295.

[52] *Prosecutor v. Duško Tadić a.k.a. 'Dule'*, IT-94-1-T, Opinion and Judgement, 7 May 1997, para. 652, relying on para. 84, Final Report: "Isolated acts constituting offences, such as extra-judicial executions or other common crimes punishable under municipal law, do not qualify as crimes against humanity by themselves. The acts must be part of a policy of persecution or discrimination. In addition, the acts must be carried out in a systematic way or by means of a mass action".

---

Chamber, while extensively referencing international sources of law, did not cite the Report.[53]

## 11.9. Definition of a Group for Genocide

The Final Report also examined what could constitute a protected group under the Genocide Convention. *Jelisić* relied upon the Final Report to find that a "stigmatised" group could be categorised either positively or negatively. Negatively, by "identifying individuals as not being part of the group to which the perpetrators of the crime consider that they themselves belong and which to them displays specific national, ethnical, racial or religious characteristics". All rejected individuals would, by their rejection, thus form a 'group'.[54] That finding, while certainly a reasonable interpretation of what the Final Report concluded,[55] was later rejected by the Appeals Chamber. In *Stakić*, the Prosecution unsuccessfully appealed the Trial Chamber's declining to follow *Jelisić* and defining the targeted group separately as Croats and Bosnian Muslims rather than as 'non-Serbs'. The Prosecution argued, relying exclusively on the same passage in the Final Report, that a group could be defined negatively – as not a member of the group doing the attacking. The Appeals Chamber held otherwise, deciding that the citation was unpersuasive and that a 'group' could not be negatively defined.[56]

The Final Report also concluded that targeting the "total leadership" of a group "when accompanied by other acts of elimination of a segment of society" could be genocide.[57] *Jelisić* endorsed this, finding that genocide "may also consist of the desired destruction of a more limited number of persons selected for the impact that their disappearance would have

---

[53] *Prosecutor v. Duško Tadić*, IT-94-1-A, Judgement, 15 July 1999, para. 305.

[54] *Jelisić*, para. 71, *supra* note 49.

[55] The Final Report, para. 96, stated: "for example, that there is evidence group A wants to destroy in whole or in part groups B, C and D, or rather everyone who does not belong to the national, ethnic, racial or religious group A. In a sense, group A has defined a pluralistic non-A group using national, ethnic, racial and religious criteria for the definition. It seems relevant to analyse the fate of the non-A group along similar lines as if the non-A group had been homogenous".

[56] *Prosecutor v. Milomir Stakić*, IT-97-24-A, Judgement, 22 March 2006, paras. 14–28 (http://www.legal-tools.org/doc/09f75f/); Judge Shahabuddeen disagreed, Partly Dissenting Opinion of Judge Shahabuddeen, paras. 8–18.

[57] Commission of Experts Final Report, para. 94.

upon the survival of the group as such".[58] *Tolimir* relied on *Jelisić*'s conclusion and the Final Report's finding that the forcible transfer of the civilian population immediately before killing three civilian leaders supported a finding of genocidal intent.[59]

On appeal, the Appeals Chamber confirmed the legal principle as set out in the Final Report, quoting and italicizing the passage. However, it reversed *Tolimir*'s conviction for genocide in respect of the three leaders as the Trial Chamber had cited no evidence of the impact of the disappearance of the three leaders on the protected group.[60]

In concluding that genocide had occurred in Srebrenica, *Krstić* held that the attack on the leadership of a group "must be viewed in the context of the fate of what happened to the rest of the group".[61]

## 11.10. Military Objectives and Cumulative Convictions

*Strugar*, in trying the JNA's shelling of the Old Town of Dubrovnik in 1991, adopted the Commission's definition of military objectives in defining what was "not justified by military necessity" for the purpose of Article 52 of Additional Protocol I.[62]

---

[58] *Jelisić*, para. 82, *supra* note 49, re para. 94, Final Report. *Blagojević* referred to this in finding that "the forcible transfer of individuals could lead to the material destruction of the group, since the group ceases to exist as a group, or at least as the group it was", *Blagojević*, paras. 663 and 666, *supra* note 29.

[59] *Prosecutor v. Zdravko Tolimir*, IT-05-88/2-T, Judgement, 12 December 2012, paras. 779 and 781 (http://www.legal-tools.org/doc/445e4e/). At paras. 749 and 777 it adopted the *Jelisić* definition, quoting from the Final Report, and finding, by majority, that those responsible for killing the mayor, army commander and head of the civil protection unit of a UN enclave targeted them because of their leadership roles, and that these killings should not be seen in isolation.

[60] *Prosecutor v. Zdravko Tolimir*, IT-05-88/2-A, Judgement, 8 April 2015, paras, 261–270 (https://www.legal-tools.org/doc/010ecb/), holding at para. 263, "The Appeals Chamber finds no legal error in the Trial Chamber's statement that the selective targeting of leading figures of a community may amount to genocide and may be indicative of genocidal intent".

[61] *Prosecutor v. Radislav Krstić*, IT-98-33-T, Judgement, 2 August 2001, para. 587 (https://www.legal-tools.org/doc/440d3a/) regarding Final Report, para. 94. *Sikirica* merely noted defence and prosecution arguments regarding the Final Report, *Prosecutor v. Duško Sikirica, Damir Došen, and Dragan Kolundžija*, IT-95-8-T, Judgement on Defence Motions to Acquit, 3 September 2001 (https://www.legal-tools.org/doc/682ea1/).

[62] *Prosecutor v. Pavle Strugar*, IT-01-42-T, Trial Judgement, 31 January 2005, para. 295 (http://www.legal-tools.org/doc/927ba5/). On cumulative convictions, the *Delalić* Appeals Chamber referred to the Commission's Second Interim Report in discussing whether it was

---

## 11.11. How the ICTY Used the Factual Conclusions of the Fact-Finding Reports

Staff of the Commission of Experts and the Special Rapporteur visited many crime scenes in the former Yugoslavia and collected documents and information from witnesses and many other sources. Sometimes the information collected by fact-finding missions was the first evidence of crimes presented to the international community. Some of this was direct eyewitness testimony, while some was hearsay. Much was anonymous. But what was to be done with this information? In November 1992, Special Rapporteur Mazowiecki wrote, presciently (italics added):[63]

> There is growing evidence that war crimes have been committed. Further investigation is needed to determine the extent of such acts and the identity of those responsible, *with a view to their prosecution by an international tribunal*, if appropriate. In this regard, the Special Rapporteur intends to provide all pertinent information in his possession to the Commission of Experts [...].

He did, and two years later, in December 1994, the Commission of Experts' third Chairman, Professor Cherif Bassiouni, duly submitted 22 annexes of analytical material to the Security Council. They were also given to the ICTY Prosecutor. The annexes included legal studies of rape and investigations into sexual assault, reports on Medak, Prijedor, Sarajevo, Dubrovnik, the policy of ethnic cleansing, prison camps, mass graves, and the destruction of cultural property.[64]

---

possible to cumulatively convict for committing crimes against humanity and war crimes for the same conduct, *Prosecutor v. Zejnil Delalić, Zdravko Mucić, (a.k.a. 'Pavo'), Hazim Delić and Esad Landžo, (a.k.a. 'Zenga')*, IT-96-21-A, Judgement, 20 February 2001, para. 411, fn. 643 (http://www.legal-tools.org/doc/051554/):

> The Commission notes that fundamental rules of human rights law often are materially identical to rules of the law of armed conflict. It is therefore possible for the same act to be a war crime and a crime against humanity'. However, the Report does not indicate whether *convictions* based on the same acts are possible under provisions for war crimes and crimes against humanity.

63 Report of 17 November 1992, para. 140, A/47/666.
64 S/1994/674/Add.2 (Vol. I to V), Transmittal letter dated 28 December 1994 from the Secretary-General to the President of the Security Council, S/1994/674/Add.1, 31 May 1995 (https://www.legal-tools.org/doc/81ffa6/):

> The annexes to the final report contain studies of the historical, political and military aspects of the conflict, analytical studies of the applicable laws of armed conflict and

In 2001, Professor Bassiouni described his own work in these terms:[65]

> Probably the most significant fact-finding operation in UN history was the work of the Commission established by the Security Council pursuant to Resolution 780 in 1992 to investigate war crimes in the Former Yugoslavia. The Commission worked for two years, during which it conducted thirty-five field investigations, established the most extensive database for gathering evidence and information about violations of international humanitarian law, identified over 800 places of detention, estimated 50,000 cases of torture and 200,000 deaths, estimated two million displaced persons as a result of ethnic cleansing that was documented in connection with some 2,000 towns and villages where the practices took place, and conducted the world's first and most extensive investigation into systematic rape. The latter produced over 500 affidavits of victims who identified their perpetrators. Interviews were conducted with 223 victims and witnesses; gathered information led to the identification of close to 1,500 cases; and other information revealed the possibility of an additional 4,500 or so victims.
>
> Over a period of two years, over 140 lawyers and law students worked at the database that produced close to 80,000 documents and 300 hours of videotapes. It was on that basis that the Commission was able to produce some of its Annexes. The report exceeded 3,300 pages and was the longest report made by the Security Council.

At the UN's direction,[66] the Commission transferred this database – which had been prepared under Professor Bassiouni's supervision – to the ICTY Prosecutor's Office, thereby providing the reports, annexes and the materials referenced in the annexes. But most of it was analytical rather than investigatory and, as Professor Bassiouni himself said, the 140 lawyers and law students had worked on compiling the database, and not on gathering the incriminating material. The Final Report and its annexes in fact extensively sourced the reports of other UN bodies such as UN-

---

detailed reports on violations of international humanitarian law committed in the territory of the former Yugoslavia between 1991 and 1993.

[65] M. Cherif Bassiouni, "Appraising UN Justice-Related Fact-Finding Missions", in *Journal of Law and Policy*, 2001, vol. 5, p. 46.

[66] Commission of Experts Final Report, para. 33.

---

PROFOR and the UNHCR, the UNCHR's Special Rapporteur, Governments, the International Committee of the Red Cross ('ICRC') and NGOs such as Amnesty International for its own conclusions.

But could the report and its annexes be used as evidence in a court – as opposed to the obvious uses as historical analysis or as evidentiary leads? The answer by and large is no. The introduction to the annex on prison camps actually carried this disclaimer:[67]

> This report on detention facilities, attempts to identify and provide relevant information concerning all alleged detention facilities (camps) within the territory of the former Yugoslavia. This study is not designed to classify detention sites based on their prosecutorial potential, but is intended to provide a description and analysis of the detention facilities reported to have existed.

The reality is that the ICTY Prosecutor primarily used Professor Bassiouni's database and the materials referenced in the annexes to the Commission of Experts' Final Report in deciding whether to investigate, rather than to indict. Indictments could not have been based on the summary information in the reports. In some cases, the Prosecution tendered or tried to tender some fact-finding reports or portions of them into evidence, but then mainly as background or corroborative evidence. Some internal ICTY criticism was even directed at the utility of the material provided by the Commission of Experts, for example, "Whatever its other virtues it was described [...] by an investigator as 'basically useless' for evidential purposes, since it simply rehashed secondary sources".[68] While the language may seem harsh, the sentiment is probably accurate, as is evidenced by how the ICTY actually used the report in its judgements, regardless of the intentions of the report's authors.

A senior Prosecution official confirms that the database was initially useful to the office in providing investigation leads. Within a very short period, however, the office had obtained its own primary evidence of witness statements and documents, particularly regarding crimes committed in Prijedor, Dubrovnik and Sarajevo. Furthermore, the prosecutors interviewed and took statements from any witnesses whose evidence they

---

[67] S/1994/674/Add.2 (Vol. IV), 27 May 1994, Annex VIII, part 1/10, Prison camps (https://www.legal-tools.org/doc/46fe5d/).

[68] David Chuter, *War Crimes: Confronting Atrocity in the Modern World*, Lynne Rienner, 2003, p. 151.

wished to use in court, including those who had already given a statement or affidavit in the Commission of Expert's project. The prosecutors never considered using these documents as primary evidence in court. Every witness had to be re-interviewed. And, where appropriate, the Commission's statements and affidavits were provided to the defence.[69]

The real and obvious difference between what fact-finding missions and courts can do with this type of information lies in its admissibility under a court's rules of procedure and evidence. Generally, all relevant and probative evidence is admissible, but the ICTY's Rules of Procedure and Evidence, like those of the other international courts and tribunals, restrict when witness statements may be accepted into evidence without the witness testifying. At the very least, absent exceptional circumstances such as death or unavailability, the witness must verify the veracity of the information, either in court or in a declaration attached to the statement.[70] Moreover, any witness statement accepted into evidence must relate to the crimes charged in the indictment, whether or not it connects an accused person to the crimes charged. Additionally, the witness statements and affidavits used by the Commission of Experts were not gathered for case-specific (in the sense of evidence to be used in an indictment against a named person) as opposed to crime incident specific purposes. Logically, they could never have been used as the primary evidence in court in international criminal proceedings.

Filtering irrelevant and inadmissible material from the relevant and admissible can be a complicated task and Prosecution investigators, lawyers and analysts normally re-interview relevant witnesses to take statements relevant to the specific case under investigation or indictment. Only in exceptional circumstances will a statement provided to a fact-finding mission make it onto the court record, for example, to impeach a witness by demonstrating inconsistent accounts. ICTY investigators also took statements from many more witnesses than those who testified or whose

---

[69] Information given to the author by Robert Reid, the ICTY Prosecution's Chief of Operations, in September 2013. According to Morten Bergsmo, who worked in the Office of the Prosecutor at the same time, however, the Commission's Prijedor Study, led by Judge Hanne Greve, as opposed to Professor Bassiouni, "guided the early development of all the Prijedor, Bosanska Krajina and *Republika Srpska* cases" at the ICTY; information given to the author in May 2020.

[70] See Rules 92 *bis*, *ter*, *quinquies*, ICTY Rules of Procedure and Evidence (http://www.legal-tools.org/doc/30df50/), Rule 110 (B), IRMCT Rules of Procedure and Evidence (https://www.legal-tools.org/doc/n7lau1/).

statements were used in court. Professor Bassiouni's statistics are impressive but ascertaining whether those witness statements, affidavits or other documents ever made it to court, and if so, how they were used, would be an extremely time-consuming and potentially fruitless task.[71] The ICTY web site reveals that there had been 4,650 witnesses and 10,800 trial days,[72] but does not make known how many of these had provided statements or affidavits to the Commission.

Other documents used or collected by the Commission fall into a different category. To establish their admissibility as evidence, courts assess other documents individually; the concern is the document's provenance, authenticity and reliability (in addition to its probative value and relevance). Some documents used or sourced in the reports or collected by the Commission may meet these criteria, but each has to be assessed. Automatic admission into evidence cannot be assumed.

In submitting the annexes to the Secretary-General in December 1994, the Chairman of the Commission wrote:[73]

> No other body has been established to pursue the tasks mandated to the Commission by the Security Council in its Resolution 780 (1992). Thus, the Final Report and these Annexes may well be the only relatively comprehensive, historic record likely to be compiled of the policies and practices as well as specific cases, evidencing grave breaches of the Geneva Conventions and other violations of international humanitarian law. The work of the ICTFY will, however, complement this historic record.

---

[71] No records as such are kept of whether the parties before the ICTY, and most particularly the Prosecutor, attempted to tender these documents into evidence (by category) and the judgements do not usually specify the provenance of a witness statement accepted into evidence and referenced in the judgement. Moreover, the parties could have obtained from different sources the same public documents used by the Commission. The Tribunal's publicly available statistical information does not reveal how many of these witnesses had given statements or affidavits to the Commission of Experts, nor whether any of these were ever used in court.

[72] As at the ICTY's closure in November 2017. Its web site, in 2013, had stated that "as of early 2011, more than 4,000 witnesses had told their stories in court".

[73] Letter dated 24 May 1994 from the Secretary-General to the President of the Security Council. Addendum, Annexes to the Final Report of the Commission of Experts Established Pursuant to Security Council Resolution 780 (1992) Volume I – Annexes I to V, 31 May 1995, S/1994/674 Add. 2 (Vol. I), para. 10 (https://www.legal-tools.org/doc/8aab28/).

History has of course overtaken this somewhat pessimistic or, depending on one's viewpoint, perhaps grandiose, contemporary self-assessment as is shown by the 2.5 million (and counting) pages of court transcripts at the ICTY, and IRMCT, the 161 indictments, and 109 final verdicts. The ICTY's Office of the Prosecutor at one stage had 17,297 witness statements and around 9.4 million pages of documents in its own database.[74] The overwhelming majority of these documents, which include military and government archives of the parties to the conflicts, were not available to the Commission of Experts in 1994. Moreover, the Commission's view is unsustainable and indeed contradictory when considering the sources used in compiling the reports; for in the same document the Commission described its own methodology:[75]

> With some exceptions, the information and allegations contained therein have not been verified. However, the cumulative nature of the information, as well as its corroboration from multiple sources evidences a degree of reliability, in the aggregate and in many individual cases. The recurrence of certain factual information from multiple or unrelated sources provides a basis for an inference of reliability and credibility. Viewed in its entirety, the combination of this information warrants the Commission's findings as to the general patterns and policies described in the Final Report and in the Annexes.

This is actually the antithesis of how an international criminal court or tribunal receives its evidence. So, it is hardly surprising that a criminal court such as the ICTY would carefully scrutinise the conclusions of such a report before accepting into evidence as proof of the matters, the conclusions or assertions of fact contained in it. Reliability is a basic requirement for accepting something into evidence, as is illustrated by the *Gotovina* Trial Chamber's methodology in reviewing fact-finding reports:[76]

---

[74]   These figures are as of September 2013. The figure for witness statements is for statements not witnesses as many witnesses have provided more than one statement. In relation to the number of accused, 36 indictments were withdrawn in circumstances that included the death of an accused.

[75]   S/1994/674 Add. 2 (Vol. I), 31 May 1995, para. 5.

[76]   *Prosecutor v. Ante Gotovina, Ivan Čermak, and Mladen Markač*, IT-06-90-T, Judgement, 15 April 2011, para. 39 (http://www.legal-tools.org/doc/7c85bd/).

The Trial Chamber received much evidence on the practice of compiling and processing various reports from international organisations and agencies present on the ground during the Indictment period. It considered all of this evidence in assessing whether and to what extent to rely on such documentary evidence. In general, the Trial Chamber relied on reports from international organizations and agencies, and considered specifically on a case-by-case basis whether the information contained therein was sufficiently sourced and whether it reflected direct observations or (single or multiple) hearsay.

This partly explains why the ICTY Chambers frequently used the findings of these reports only for background material and to corroborate other testimony before the court. In accepting into evidence a 1992 Special Rapporteur's report describing the situation of Kosovar Albanians but in a case relating to events in 1998 and 1999, the *Đorđević* Trial Chamber explained its reasoning and flexibility in the particular circumstances:[77]

> The Chamber accepts that this report contains information that is of some relevance to the background and context of the allegations in the Indictment. The report was prepared by the UN Special Rapporteur of the Commission on Human Rights and transmitted by the UN Secretary General to the UN General Assembly and UN Security Council. In addition, the report details the sources from which information was drawn, including governmental sources, NGOs, witnesses, victims, intergovernmental sources, and human rights organisations such as Amnesty International, Helsinki Watch, and others. It is desirable that documents be tendered for admission through witnesses who would be in a position to comment on them, however, this cannot be viewed as some inflexible rule, and having carefully reviewed the document, the Chamber is of the view that the document itself speaks of its relevance and probative value. The relevant subject matter of the report has also been the subject of other evidence. The Chamber is also convinced that the absence of explanatory

---

[77] Re the report of 17 November 1992, *Prosecutor v. Vlastimir Đorđević*, IT-05-87/1-T, Decision on Prosecution's Motion to Re-Open the Case and Exceed the Word Limit and Second Motion to Admit Exhibits From the Bar Table, 7 December 2009, para. 12 (http://www.legal-tools.org/doc/d7a6a1/).

evidence of the period between 1992 and 1998 in no way vitiates that relevance and probative value.

A typical finding in these judgements using a report as corroborating evidence also highlights and illustrates this point. Here (with italics
added), a Trial Chamber has used a combination of direct eyewitness testimony and fact-finding reports to make a finding about the conditions of
detention:[78]

> As regards shelter and sanitation facilities of the camp, the
> Chamber finds, on the basis of the evidence of Osmanović,
> *as corroborated by the reports of the CSCE and United Na-*
> *tions Commission on Human Rights*, that detainees slept on
> straw bedding and shared insufficient sanitation facilities.
> The shelter and sanitation facilities provided were entirely
> inadequate, given the number of detainees held at the camp.

On the other hand, fact-finding reports seem to have been used as
direct evidence of the 'acts or conduct' of an accused only in command
responsibility cases, and to prove notice to a commander of the potential
criminality of a subordinate. There, it can be used as direct evidence of
the *mens rea* or mental state of an accused. This occurred most notably in
the Kosovo case of *Đorđević* and the Macedonian case of *Boškoski*, and in
the majority judgement of *Perišić* where each used Human Rights Watch
reports to prove inquiry notice. *Perišić* also used the Special Rapporteur's
and Commission of Experts' reports.

Using reports in this manner is understandable and legally permis-
sible as the dissemination of reports of criminality may provide sufficient
evidence to invoke the need for a commander to make the necessary inquiries. In this context, the authorship of the report is less important than
the information contained in it and its dissemination. Moreover, the information about the potential criminality of subordinates need not be
completely reliable to give a commander the inquiry notice necessary to
take reasonable measures to prevent or punish potential crimes.

Several Trial Chambers, however, have explicitly refused to rely on
the findings of NGO reports without corroboration from other sources, as
occurred for example in *Gotovina* and *Boškoski*. How ICTY judgements

---

[78] *Prosecutor v. Mićo Stanišić and Stojan Župljanin*, IT-08-91-T, Judgement, 27 March 2013,
vol. 1, para. 904 (http://www.legal-tools.org/doc/2ed57f/).

have used fact-finding reports can be examined thematically by subject and by geographical area or crime.

## 11.12. Crimes of 'Ethnic Cleansing' or Persecution by Bosnian Serb Authorities in Bosnia and Herzegovina

Both the Commission of Experts and the Special Rapporteur reported on the existence of and conditions in detention centres, primarily those run by the Bosnian Serb authorities in Bosnia and Herzegovina. After his first visit to Bosnia and Herzegovina in August 1992, Special Rapporteur Mazowiecki reported that torture was committed on a systematic scale in the Bosnian Serb camps.[79] In one week between August and September 1992, CSCE teams also visited 19 detention camps and prisons in 13 towns and villages and suspected locations in Bosnia and Herzegovina and Serbia.[80] Some of the information in the reports was sourced to the ICRC. Additionally, a section of the Commission of Experts Final Report was devoted to concentration camps and deportation, in particular the crimes committed in the notorious Keraterm, Omarska, Trnopolje and Manjača camps and some other "improvised detention facilities" in Prijedor.[81] It also contained an annex on prisons[82] that appears not to have been used in ICTY judgements. Another annex was devoted to the role of "special forces", meaning paramilitary units, in committing violations of humanitarian law in Bosnia and Herzegovina, but sourcing some of its findings to the Special Rapporteur's reports.[83]

The ICTY Trial Chambers mainly used the reports for corroborative evidence of the conditions in the camps. Sometimes a report was the only source for a factual finding – such as to establish the washing and sanita-

---

[79] Special Rapporteur to the Commission on Human Rights, Report on the Mission to the former Yugoslavia, 3 September 1992, paras. 23, 29, 33–39, 43 and 54, A/47/418; and Report on the Mission to the former Yugoslavia, 6 November 1992, paras. 10–12 and 15, A/47/635. The UNCHR's Special Rapporteur on Torture also joined Special Rapporteur Mazowiecki's visit to Bosnia and Herzegovina in October 1992 and briefly reported on his observations, Special Rapporteur to the Commission on Human Rights, Report on the Mission to former Yugoslavia, 17 November 1992, A/47/666.

[80] Most relevantly, "Report of CSCE Mission on Places of Detention in BiH, 29 August to 4 September 1992".

[81] Commission of Experts Final Report, Section IV.5.

[82] Commission of Experts Final Report, Annex VIII – part 1/10 Prison camps, S/1994/674/Add.2 (Vol. IV), 27 May 1994.

[83] Commission of Experts Final Report, Annex III.A Special forces, S/1994/674/Add.2 (Vol. I), 28 December 1994.

---

tion facilities available to the prisoners – but where this occurred, it appeared to be in the context of an overwhelming abundance of direct testimony from other sources about the appalling conditions of confinement. Some judgements also noted the conclusions of reports about the existence of systematic persecution, but again, these conclusions were noted within an overall context of a profusion of direct evidence leading to the same result.

*Krajišnik* concerned the persecution of non-Serbs by the Bosnian Serb leadership. The Special Rapporteur had reported extensively on crimes committed in Prijedor in 1992 and *Krajišnik* used the reports to establish some crimes, such as the destruction of the mosque and the Catholic Church.[84] It also used the report to corroborate the murder by machine gun fire of 150 to 200 prisoners in Keraterm, and that some detainees in Omarska were beaten to death.[85] It contrasted the Special Rapporteur's reports with the inaccurate descriptions given by the Bosnian Serb Government of the conditions of detention at Omarska and Keraterm.[86] It used a CSCE report to establish the number of prisoners in Manjača, an UNPROFOR report for the "atrocious" conditions, and a CSCE report on the number of prisoners in Bileća and their condition.[87]

In *Brđanin*, concerning crimes against humanity committed by Bosnian Serb forces against non-Serbs in the Krajina region of north western Bosnia and Herzegovina, the Trial Chamber used a CSCE report to determine the establishment date of Manjača, who ran it, its commander, the number of detainees, and that guards forced detainees to perform heavy physical work.[88]

In *Martić*, the trial of the President of the self-proclaimed Republic of the Serbian Krajina, the Trial Chamber used a Helsinki Watch report of

---

[84] The only source quoted to support the finding, *Prosecutor v. Momčilo Krajišnik*, IT-00-39-T, Judgement, 27 September 2006, para. 473 (http://www.legal-tools.org/doc/62a710/), Special Rapporteur's Report of 17 November 1992, A/47/666, S/24809.

[85] *Krajišnik*, paras. 488 and 490, *supra* note 85.

[86] *Krajišnik*, para. 1070, *ibid.*

[87] Between several hundreds and over 3,000 prisoners at any one time were in Manjača, *Krajišnik*, paras. 383 and 611, *ibid.*; CSCE Report 29 September 1992. 74 detainees were held at the Đački Dom in Bileća in poor conditions and severely mistreated.

[88] *Brđanin*, paras. 748, 749, 436, and 914, *supra* note 41; CSCE note of 3 September 1992; CSCE REPORT of CSCE Mission to inspect places of detention in Bosnia-Herzegovina, 29 August – 4 September 1992.

the killings of civilians in a village, a UNCIVPOL report of house-burning, and a report of the Special Rapporteur showing how 'ethnic cleansing' was being carried out against the non-Serb population.[89]

*Stanišić and Župljanin* concerned crimes against humanity, including persecution, committed across 20 municipalities in Bosnia and Herzegovina in 1992 and 1993 by Bosnian Serb military, police and paramilitary and the FRY's military and paramilitary units. To describe the rationale for the existence of the detention camps, namely that people were detained with the objective of "getting rid" of them for ethnic cleansing and extermination, it used a Special Rapporteur's report and CSCE reports and testimony.[90] It approved the Special Rapporteur's finding that "the military conflict in BiH was aimed at achieving ethnic cleansing and that the Muslims were the principal victims who were "virtually threatened with extermination".[91]

Regarding Manjača camp, the Trial Judgement referred to the Special Rapporteur's attempted visit,[92] and used his reports to corroborate the lack of medical care, its establishment, closure and reopening, its commanders, and the number of prisoners.[93] The CSCE report established the reasons given by the authorities for the detentions.[94] Concerning Trnopolje, the Special Rapporteur's report corroborated the turnover of detainees, that they were not free to leave and the bad conditions of confinement; a CSCE report corroborated the severe mistreatment of detainees, including beatings by guards and the disappearances of prisoners.[95]

---

[89] *Prosecutor v. Milan Martić*, IT-95-11-T, Judgement, 12 June 2007, paras. 324 and 327 (http://www.legal-tools.org/doc/06634c/), Special Rapporteur's Report of 17 November 1992.

[90] *Prosecutor v. Mićo Stanišić and Stojan Župljanin*, IT-08-91-T, Judgement, 27 March 2013, vol. 2, paras. 306 and 659 (CSCE Report 29 September 1992), para. 307 (Special Rapporteur's reports of 28 August and 17 October 1992) (http://www.legal-tools.org/doc/cbc02a/).

[91] The accused were the Republika Srpska's Minister of the Interior and the Banja Luka Regional chief of police, *Stanišić and Župljanin*, vol. 2, para. 306, *ibid.*, quoting the Special Rapporteur's Report, 17 October 1992, paras. 1, 5–6.

[92] *Stanišić and Župljanin*, vol. 1 (http://www.legal-tools.org/doc/2ed57f/), para. 194; Report of 27 October 1992 para. 628 re CSCE Report of 29 September 1992.

[93] *Stanišić and Župljanin*, vol. 1, paras. 182, 170, 171 and 176, *ibid.*

[94] *Stanišić and Župljanin*, vol. 1, paras. 182, 170, 171 and 176, *ibid.*; CSCE Rapporteur's Report on his Visit to Banja Luka, 3 September 1992.

[95] *Stanišić and Župljanin*, vol. 1, paras. 622 and 626, *supra* note 92; Special Rapporteur's Report of 27 October 1992, para. 628; CSCE report, p. 48.

With regard to Batković, the reports helped prove the conditions of detention, including appalling sleeping conditions and malnourishment.[96] The CSCE report was used to determine its establishment, its organisation along military lines, that it had prisoner representatives, the number of detainees, and the conditions of detention.[97] Concerning a camp in Sušica, the CSCE's report sourced the conditions and corroborated and established that the prisoners were not there voluntarily.[98]

The *Vasiljević* Trial Judgement used the Commission's annex on special forces to make findings regarding the arrival of Serb paramilitaries in Višegrad, describing that a "particularly violent and feared group of paramilitaries was led by the co-accused Milan Lukić". It stated that, "[a]s early as June 1992, non-Serb civilians were arbitrarily killed", and described the systematic expulsion of non-Serb civilians who had not already fled.[99] Lukić had been indicted but was not arrested and transferred to the ICTY until 2006, over three years after the end of the *Vasiljević* trial. The *Lukić* Trial Chamber did not use these reports – which do not appear to have been part of the trial record – but nor could it have as these findings went directly to issues in dispute and the criminality attributable to Milan Lukić.[100]

Slightly tangentially, in deciding to appoint counsel over the will of a self-represented accused, Vojislav Šešelj, the Trial Chamber there used

---

[96] *Stanišić and Župljanin*, vol. 1, para. 906, *supra* note 92; Special Rapporteur's Report of 17 October 1992, para. 907; CSCE Report, 29 September 1992.

[97] *Stanišić and Župljanin*, vol. 1, paras. 899, 901, 904, 906, 907 and 910, *supra* note 92 – the CSCE report was the sole source quoted for the shower and medical facilities. The Special Rapporteur's report corroborated that prisoners were sleeping on the floor on straw and hay, para. 906. The findings regarding the conditions included that there were two makeshift showers, and a makeshift latrine for day use, that the detainees seen were thin but not necessarily malnourished, and medical facilities were lacking.

[98] That they appeared hungry, thin and haggard, and water was available only from a single faucet, *Stanišić and Župljanin*, vol. 1, paras. 1456–1467, *supra* note 92. Regarding the deportation of non-Serbs it quoted the Special Rapporteur's reporting that 14,000 displaced Muslims were in Travnik and that Bosnian Muslims were deported from Sanski Most. *Stanišić and Župljanin*, vol. 1, para. 653; re. October 1992 Report, para. 779, re. August 1992 Report.

[99] *Prosecutor v. Mitar Vasiljević* IT-98-32-T, Judgement, 29 November 2002, paras. 45, 46, 72, 49 and 55 (http://www.legal-tools.org/doc/8035f9/) (referring to "Annex III.3.A Special Forces", Final Report); Special Rapporteur Mazowiecki's report of 10 February 1993 was a prosecution exhibit but was not referenced in the judgement.

[100] *Prosecutor v. Milan Lukić and Sredoje Lukić*, IT-98-32/1-T, Judgement, 20 July 2009 (http://www.legal-tools.org/doc/af5ad0/).

some information contained in the Final Report's annex regarding the special forces operating in Bosnia and Herzegovina to conclude that it believed that the accused, who claimed that he only spoke Serbian, actually understood English.[101]

*Šešelj* received the Special Rapporteur's second report into evidence but it is not referred to in the judgement. However, a lengthy "Concurring Opinion of Presiding Judge Jean-Claude Antonetti Attached to the Judgement", has a section entitled "Summary of the Probative Value of Exhibits in the Vojislav Šešelj Case", which ranks 127 principal documents "in seven categories, running from absolute probative value to zero probative value". In an annexed table, the report gets the top ranking of "absolute probative value". However, why or if the judge used it in assessing the evidence is never explained.[102]

*Mladić* also referred to the Special Rapporteur's unsuccessful attempts to visit the Manjača camp in August 1992 and his reports of a "vivid impression of the state of terror under which the detainees were presumably living". It also noted his successful visit to Batković camp in October 1992 and his noting that the approximately 1,000 Muslim prisoners appeared to be in good health and did not complain of ill-treatment.[103]

---

[101] *Prosecutor v. Vojislav Šešelj*, IT-03-67-PT, Decision on Prosecution's Motion for Order Appointing Counsel to Assist Vojislav Seselj with his Defence, 9 May 2003, para. 25 (https://www.legal-tools.org/doc/754b0e/). The report stated that Šešelj had spent a year teaching at a university in the United States of America.

[102] *Prosecutor v. Vojislav Šešelj*, IT-03-67-T, Judgement, 31 March 2016 (http://www.legal-tools.org/doc/9a8e36/), and Concurring Opinion of Presiding Judge Jean-Claude Antonetti Attached to the Judgement (http://www.legal-tools.org/doc/711bb3/), referring to exhibit P00982, in Section 9, "The Probative Value of Documents", and Annex 6, pp. 54, 482 (in English). Judge Antonetti's eccentric concurring opinion of 496 pages (in the English translation) is significantly longer than the 143-page majority judgement, of which only 109 pages comprised the judgement. It also has no paragraph numbers. In a dissenting opinion, Judge Lattanzi complained, and quite correctly, that the majority judgement was unreasoned, Partially Dissenting Opinion of Judge Flavia Lattanzi – Amended Version, paras. 8–13 (http://www.legal-tools.org/doc/9eda6a/). The Prosecution appealed Šešelj's majority acquittal on all counts, and the IRMCT Appeals Chamber reversed the acquittal on one and sentenced him to ten years of imprisonment, *Prosecutor v. Vojislav Šešelj*, MICT-16-99-A, Judgement, 11 April 2018 (http://www.legal-tools.org/doc/96ea58/).

[103] *Prosecutor v. Ratko Mladić*, IT-09-92-T, Judgement – Volume IV of V, 22 November 2017, paras. 4005, 4020-4021 (https://www.legal-tools.org/doc/e8792f/). The reports were in evidence.

## 11.13.  Siege of Sarajevo: 1992–1995

Sarajevo was besieged by the FRY's JNA and then the Bosnian Serb's VRS from April 1992 until the signing of the Dayton Accords at the end of 1995. Near daily sniping and shelling of civilians and civilian and cultural property occurred. Generals Stanislav Galić and Dragomir Milošević, the successive commanders of the responsible VRS unit were separately tried and convicted for inflicting terror on a civilian population as a war crime, and murder and inhumane acts as crimes against humanity. General Momčilo Perišić, the VJ's Chief of Staff based in Belgrade, was also convicted at trial, but acquitted on appeal, not for command responsibility, but for aiding and abetting the crimes committed during the siege. The Prosecutor tendered into evidence in each case the UN fact-finding reports, but they were only substantively used in *Perišić*.

The Special Rapporteur visited Sarajevo between 1992 and 1995 and reported on the siege.[104] The Commission of Experts also published an annex that included a 23-month daily chronology of reports of shelling, sniping and military activity,[105] with additional annexes on the law of armed conflict, and an incident study of a day of shelling in the city.[106] In 1997, the ICTY Prosecutor queried Professor Bassiouni about the source of his information. He responded:

> The source of data is UNPROFOR Reports both published and unpublished, including classified published reports by the BH government and by the city of Sarajevo: media reports, and NGO reports. We did not contact the sources of the reports but compared them internally to assess consistency. No judgement was made as the reliability or veracity of the sources of information. Internal comparison was the basis of our judgement to include the information. Every fact

---

[104]  Second Periodic Report, 26 August 1993, A/47/635.

[105]  Annex VI, Part I, Study of the Battle and Siege of Sarajevo, S/1994/674/Add.2 (Vol. II), 27 May 1994 – from 5 April 1992 to 28 February 1993 (https://www.legal-tools.org/doc/17f8df/).

[106]  The battle of Sarajevo and the law of armed conflict Annex VI.B S/1994/674/Add.2 (Vol. I), 28 December 1994, and Annex VI.A, Incident Study Report Regarding Mortar Shelling Dobrinja, Sarajevo on 1 June 1993: Investigation, S/1994/674/Add.2 (Vol. III), 28 December 1994 (https://www.legal-tools.org/doc/002ea8/).

alleged has been footnoted to one or more sources of information bearing our document number [...].[107]

This may explain why neither the *Galić* nor *Dragomir Milošević* judgements referred to the report. *Galić* sourced neither the Special Rapporteur's nor the Commission of Experts' reports or annexes, but did use the results of an on-site UN investigation team that had investigated the shelling of a market place in Sarajevo.[108] That evidence, however, was more a mixture of expert testimony and fact-finding than of pure fact-finding. The *Dragomir Milošević* judgement's sole reference to these reports was quoting the Special Rapporteur's conclusion that Sarajevo "is shelled on a regular basis, in what appears to be a deliberate attempt to spread terror among the population" and that Serb forces "had attacked cultural centres, including mosques, churches and museums".[109]

In *Perišić*, it was not alleged that the accused, as the Chief of Staff of the military (the 'VJ') of a neighbouring country (the 'FRY'), had personally participated in the attack on Sarajevo. Before determining whether he bore command responsibility for the crimes of Generals Galić and Milošević, who were simultaneously members of the VJ and VRS, the Trial Chamber had to find that the crimes occurred and whether Perišic's providing the VRS with materiel and personnel aided and abetted their crimes in Sarajevo. The Trial Chamber thus used the Commission of Experts' Final Report, which itself had used UNPROFOR estimates, to establish that the crimes had occurred, by concluding that shelling and sniping by the VRS against the whole city were daily events.[110]

---

[107] The quote was available on Case Western Reserve University's web site on 5 October 2013, but can no longer be accessed.

[108] *Prosecutor v. Stanislav Galić*, IT-98-29-A, Judgement, 30 November 2006, paras. 438, 440, 442, 443 and 449. On appeal, the defence unsuccessfully argued that parts of the judgement discussing "control over shelling cannot be relied upon as they contradict the testimony of other witnesses and are challenged in the UN Commission of Experts Report", *Galić*, paras. 369–370.

[109] Under the heading "SRK sniping and shelling of areas within the confrontation lines", *Prosecutor v. Dragomir Milošević*, IT-98-29/1-T, Judgement, 12 December 2007, paras. 148,153 (http://www.legal-tools.org/doc/e706e2/).

[110] And that daily shelling ranged from 200-300 to 800-1,000 impacts per day, *Prosecutor v. Momčilo Perišić*, IT-04-81-T, Judgement, 6 September 2011, para. 1499 (http://www.legal-tools.org/doc/f3b23d/). These figures were also adjudicated facts from the two preceding trials.

The Trial Chamber noted the wide dissemination of the Commission of Experts and the Special Rapporteur's report to show that the FRY leadership (collectively) was aware of and monitored them.[111] However, individual criminal liability is a separate matter, and only the majority used the reports to prove Perišić's own knowledge of the crimes being committed in Sarajevo by the VRS units, concluding that the only reasonable inference was that he generally knew of the allegations of criminality *before* his appointment as VJ's Chief of Staff.[112] They decided that FRY officials were aware of the Special Rapporteur's and Commission of Experts' reports. From the FRY's responses to the Special Rapporteur's reports,[113] and their discussion at the Security Council,[114] "collectively the only conclusion was that the Special Rapporteur's reports were of such interest to Yugoslav authorities and were publicized to such an extent that the information in them was known to Perišić and thus of the VRS' discriminatory intent and criminal conduct in Bosnia and Herzegovina".[115] Perišić was hence well-informed about the marketplace shelling and other attacks on civilians by virtue of these reports, and the publication of several in the Belgrade press. The combination of Bosnian documents provided to the FRY, including these reports and filings and orders in the case between Bosnia and Herzegovina and Serbia and Montenegro in the International Court of Justice thus informed him of the VRS's crimes in Sarajevo.[116]

Judge Moloto dissented – in his view, this established neither that Perišić himself was aware of the reports, nor that he had read them. Moreover, had he read them, they would not have given him actual knowledge of the VRS' discriminatory intent and criminal conduct. The Commission of Experts report generally attributed the crimes to "Bosnian Serb paramilitary forces" but not specifically to the VRS, and there was insufficient evidence that Perišić was aware of the reports. Their mere existence was not enough and the Special Rapporteur's reports "did not contain sufficient detail from which to conclude which group was responsible for the alleged crimes in Sarajevo", only referring to Serb soldiers and

---

[111] *Perišić*, paras. 1451–1454, *ibid.*

[112] Judges David and Picard, *Perišić*, paras. 1451–1454, *ibid.*

[113] *Perišić*, paras. 1465–1473, *ibid.*

[114] *Perišić*, para. 1480, *ibid.*

[115] *Perišić*, paras.1487, *ibid.*

[116] *Perišić*, paras. 1496, 1501, 1499, 1500, 1514, 1518, 1519, 1634–1636, *ibid.*

Serb mercenaries without identifying their organisational affiliation.[117] He would have acquitted Perišić.[118]

The interesting juxtaposition of judicial views – two judges finding that the reports provided both inquiry and actual knowledge of criminality and the other finding the reports were too vague to do so – thus implying that they would not even provide inquiry notice – ironically illustrates both the need for precision in fact-finding reports and the importance of their distribution. Judge Moloto correctly noted that the units responsible for the shelling and sniping were not identified by name, but whether this omission would not provide inquiry notice to a commander is highly debatable.

*Karadžić* also referred to the Special Rapporteur's report back to the UN in August 1992 of the regular shelling and sniping in Sarajevo.[119]

## 11.14. Srebrenica Atrocity Crimes and Genocide of July 1995

The UN Special Rapporteur reported on Srebrenica in September 1995 and the UN Secretary-General published a detailed report, The Fall of Srebrenica, in 1999. The ICTY Trial Chambers, however, made little substantive use of these reports. *Krstić* – the first judgement to find that genocide had occurred – used the Secretary-General's report only to establish the widespread knowledge of the crimes at the time.[120] *Blagojević* extensively referenced the Secretary-General's report but only for background and non-contentious issues.[121]

---

[117] *Perišić*, Dissenting Opinion of Judge Moloto on Counts 1 to 4 and 9 to 12, paras. 43–44, 46, 52, 54, 66 and 68, *supra* note 111.

[118] The Appeals Chamber did, but by majority and without reference to the reasoning relating to notice, confining its brief legal analysis to the test for aiding and abetting a crime, finding that it required an accused person to specifically direct his assistance to the crimes committed, *Prosecutor v. Momčilo Perišić*, IT-04-81-A, Judgement, 28 February 2013 (http://www.legal-tools.org/doc/f006ba/). Judge LIU dissented and Judge Ramaroson separately disagreed with this requirement.

[119] *Prosecutor v. Radovan Karadžić*, IT-95-5/18-T, Judgement, 24 March 2016, paras. 4579, 5788 (https://www.legal-tools.org/doc/173e23/). The report was in evidence.

[120] *Prosecutor v. Radislav Krstić*, IT-98-33-T, Judgement, 2 August 2001, para. 88.

[121] For example, the date when the attack on the Srebrenica enclave commenced and that rockets exploded near the UN peace-keepers headquarters, *Blagojević*, paras. 94, 110, 111, 112, 115, 125, 141, 165, 183, 380 and 469; *supra* note 29, Report of the Secretary-General pursuant to General Assembly Resolution 53/35, The Fall of Srebrenica, A/54/549, 15 November 1999. *Popović*, by contrast, referenced only the Special Rapporteur's report of 5

## 11.15. Crimes Committed by Croat and Croatian Forces

*Prlić* concerned persecution, grave breaches of the Geneva Convention and war crimes committed by HVO Croat forces against Muslims and Serbs in Herzegovina, including Mostar. The Prosecution unsuccessfully moved the Trial Chamber (pre-trial) to take judicial notice of, and admit into evidence Special Rapporteur Mazowiecki's reports and the Final Report and evidentiary annexes of the Commission of Experts. The Trial Chamber refused, holding that it required "a critical examination of the content of the evidence and manner in which it is to be presented at trial" that was not possible to perform at that point in the proceedings.[122]

At trial, the reports of the Commission of Experts and Special Rapporteur Mazowiecki and numerous ECMM reports became evidence. As an example of how these reports were used, the Prlić indictment alleged that Bosnian Muslims were sexually abused during their deportation from East Mostar, but the Trial Chamber decided that the combination of the evidence of one witness and the general allegations in one Special Rapporteur's report were insufficient to prove the allegation.[123] Naletilić, another case of persecution by Croats also used some reports.[124]

---

May 1993 and then only to dismiss as irrelevant to the case some allegations regarding the alleged shelling of civilians in 1993 by subordinates of one accused (Pandurević), *Prosecutor v. Vujadin Popović, Ljubiša Beara, Drago Nikolić, Ljubomir Borovčanin, Radivoje Miletić, Milan Gvero, and Vinko Pandurević*, IT-05-88-T, Judgement, 10 June 2010, para. 2004 (https://www.legal-tools.org/doc/ee2cda/).

[122] *Prosecutor v. Prlić*, IT-04-74-PT, Decision on "Prosecution Motion for Judicial Notice of Facts of Common Knowledge and Admission of Documentary Evidence Pursuant to Rules 94(A) and 89(C)", 3 February 2006 (https://www.legal-tools.org/doc/).

[123] *Prlić* Trial Judgement, paras. 825–828, *ibid.*, referring to, Seventh Periodic Report on the human rights situation in the territory of the former Yugoslavia, submitted by Tadeusz Mazowiecki on 17 November 1993, E/CN.4/1994/47. In another example, it was satisfied that two young Muslim women had been raped by HVO military police (referred to in a Special Rapporteur's Report of 17 November 1993, at para. 23), but was not satisfied that this had occurred in the course of the military operation, *Prlić*, paras. 924–938.

[124] To establish data such as population, for example, to prove the ethnic composition of an area before an incident of criminality, for example, between 1,500 and 2,500 Muslim civilians were rounded up and detained at the Heliodrom detention centre on one day in Mostar in 1994, *Prosecutor v. Mladen Naletilić 'Tuta' and Vinko Martinović 'Stela'*, IT-98-34-T, Judgement, 31 March 2003, para. 45 (http://www.legal-tools.org/doc/f2cfeb/), re Second Periodic Report, 13 May 1993.

---

## 11.15.1. Croatia: Operation Storm August 1995

Operation Storm was a Croatian military operation in August 1995 to re-claim Croatian territory occupied by ethnic Serb and FRY military and paramilitary forces, during which hundreds of ethnic Serb civilians died and several hundred thousand fled. Two Croatian military commanders and one civilian leader were tried for war crimes and crimes against humanity.[125]

The reports of fact-finding missions of the UNCHR Special Rapporteur, HRW, the International Helsinki Federation ('IHF') and the OSCE were used in the *Gotovina* trial. The Trial Chamber, however, refused to use three reports unless they were corroborated by other evidence. These were a Croatian Helsinki Committee report containing "unsourced statements, double entries" and other errors, a HRW report in which the majority of its evidence came from indirect sources, and an IHF report of its fact-finding mission to Knin in August 1995, which was found to be inaccurate and requiring further information.[126]

Four reports of the UNCHR's Special Rapporteur, Elisabeth Rehn, who herself testified, became trial exhibits.[127] These helped establish the number of civilian deaths, the population of the Krajina area, and its ethnic make-up.[128] They were also used to establish the rationale for the Croatian laws on the rights of return and property recovery and their application and effect on those who had fled.[129] The Trial Chamber likewise used a HRW report describing Croatian laws of the rules and mechanisms relating to return of property for Serbs who had left in August 1995.[130]

---

[125] *Prosecutor v. Ante Gotovina, Ivan Čermak, and Mladen Markač*, IT-06-90-T, 15 April 2011.

[126] *Gotovina*, para. 50, *ibid.*; Helsinki Watch Report "Military Operation Storm and its Aftermath", para. 55; HRW Report Impunity for abuses committed during 'Operation Storm' and the denial of the right of refugees to return to the Krajina, para. 57; International Helsinki Federation for Human Rights Report of 25 August 1995.

[127] Special Rapporteur Elisabeth Rehn's reports of 7 November 1995, A/50/727 S/1995/933, "Situation of human rights in the former Yugoslavia", 14 March 1996, E/CN.4/1996/63, 12 November 1996 and 31 October 1997 E/CN.4/1998/14.

[128] *Gotovina*, paras. 1711–1712, *supra* note 125.

[129] *Gotovina*, paras. 2012, 2080, 2188 and 2197, *ibid.*

[130] *Gotovina*, paras. 2085, 2087, *ibid.*; and the "Law on the Lease of Flats in the Liberated Territory". The Rehn report was also used to establish the lack of interest by the Croatian Government and its military leadership in investigating any crimes committed during the operation, and on progress in criminal proceedings, including investigating crimes,

## 11.16. Central Bosnia and Herzegovina Cases

The Special Rapporteur reported on numerous breaches of international humanitarian law in the 1992 to 1994 conflict between the ABiH and the HVO in Central Bosnia and Herzegovina. Trial Chambers used the fact-finding reports in seven relevant cases, but differently in relation to the same crimes.

### 11.16.1. Ahmići Massacre

In April 1993, HVO units launched a co-ordinated attack in Central Bosnia and Herzegovina, including on the small Muslim village of Ahmići. There, about 120 Bosnian Muslim civilians were murdered, and mosques and around 180 homes were destroyed. The Special Rapporteur's field staff visited the village two weeks afterwards and their observations and conclusions were recorded in his second periodic report.[131] The crimes in Ahmići were the subject of four ICTY trials, *Blaškić, Kupreškić, Kordić* and *Furundžija*, one sentence, *Bralo*, and one case that was transferred to the Court of Bosnia and Herzegovina. ICTY Trial Chambers used this report in four of these cases, but differently.

Tihomir Blaškić, the HVO commander in Central Bosnia was not present in the village during the attack. *Blaškić* used the Special Rapporteur's report to establish Ahmići's population and the number of deaths (101),[132] and to provide background information relevant to establishing the hatred towards the Muslim community being propagated by the Croat media before the attack.[133] The report also helped establish that 150 Bosnian Muslims were rounded up and detained in a school, and that 20 civil-

---

*Gotovina*, paras. 2102, 2188 and 2197, *ibid*. And, factually, it established that the police were located on main roads far away from where most of the murders in the Knin area occurred, *Gotovina*, para. 2129.

[131] Second Periodic Report on the situation of human rights in the territory of the former Yugoslavia submitted by Mr. Tadeusz Mazowiecki, Special Rapporteur of the Commission on Human Rights, pursuant to Paragraph 32 of Commission Resolution 1993/7 of 23 February 1993, 19 May 1993, E/CN.4/1994/419, paras. 13–25.

[132] *Blaškić*, paras. 384, 507, *supra* note 35; Second Periodic Report. The Trial Chamber in *Blaškić*, at para. 482 noted that the Special Rapporteur's team had come under sniper fire when visiting Ahmići to obtain testimony from survivors.

[133] *Blaškić*, para. 496, quoting the Special Rapporteur reporting that, for example, "relatively minor incidents involving Croats are exaggerated and sensationalised".

---

ians were killed by very precise shots,[134] and to corroborate that Croat soldiers had shot fleeing civilians.[135] An ECMM report also sourced the number of deaths (103), the destruction of a mosque, that all Muslims had fled, and a concession by Blaškić to the ECMM that crimes had been committed (one he also made in testimony at the ICTY).[136] In reaching its own legal conclusion that "no military objective justified these attacks", the Trial Chamber quoted the Special Rapporteur's conclusion that "by all accounts, including those of the local Croat HVO commander and international observers, this village contained no legitimate military targets and there was no organized resistance to the attack".[137]

*Kordić*, while describing it as a "contemporary report", confined its use of the same report to corroborate eyewitness accounts of the massacre and of property destruction.[138] In sentencing Miroslav Bralo, an HVO military police officer, after he pleaded guilty to committing crimes against humanity in Ahmići, the Trial Chamber used the report to find that all 180 Muslim homes were destroyed and that the surviving Bosnian Muslim residents fled or were forced to leave, noting that "[a] clearer example of 'ethnic cleansing' would be difficult to find".[139]

---

[134] *Blaškić*, paras. 413 and 415. The rounding up was corroborated by witness testimony, while the conclusion regarding the "precise shots" was also sourced to testimony from a Special Rapporteur's team investigator who had visited the village.

[135] *Blaškić*, para. 390, sourcing two international witnesses and the Second Periodic Report of 19 May 1993, para. 15:

> It appears that a large number of residents chose the latter option and ran southwards to an open field where Croat HVO forces were waiting. At least 20 fleeing civilians were ambushed at the field and shot at close range, mainly in the head and neck.

[136] *Blaškić*, paras. 417, 423, 425 and 427; Report on inter-ethnic violence in Vitez, Busovača and Zenica in April 1993, appendix N to ECMM H/S 720, 15 May 1993.

[137] *Blaškić*, paras. 409 and 410; Second Periodic Report, para. 14.

[138] *Prosecutor v. Dario Kordić and Mario Čerkez*, IT-95-14/2-T, Judgement, 26 February 2001, para. 637 (http://www.legal-tools.org/doc/d4fedd/); Second Periodic Report, paras. 14–19.

[139] *Prosecutor v. Miroslav Bralo*, IT-95-17-S, Sentencing Judgement, 7 December 2005, para. 30 (https://www.legal-tools.org/doc/e10281/), quoting Second Periodic Report. *Kupreškić*, conversely, used the Special Rapporteur's report only as general background information to the conflict to corroborate reports of harassment and the arbitrary execution of Croats in Zenica and of the torture and deaths of Croat civilians who were also victims of attacks by the ABiH, *Prosecutor v. Zoran Kupreškić, Mirjan Kupreškić, Vlatko Kupreškić, Drago Josipović, Dragan Papić, and Vladimir Santić, also known as 'VLADO'*, IT-95-16-T, Judgement, 14 January 2000, paras. 66 and 120 (http://www.legal-tools.org/doc/5c6a53/) – Spe-

## 11.16.2. ABiH Crimes

*Delalić*, involving crimes committed by the ABiH against non-Muslim prisoners in a detention centre in Čelebići in Central Bosnia and Herzegovina, used information from the Commission of Experts Final Report only for historical background, and for information regarding the campaign by Serbs to drive non-Serbs out of desired territory or 'ethnic cleansing'.[140] It did not use any information from the report to prove the crimes indicted.

Rasim Delić, the Commander of the ABiH Main Staff, was tried for command responsibility for failing to prevent and punish crimes committed by subordinates. Enver Hadžihasanović, a Corps Commander, and Amir Kubura, a brigade commander, were also tried for command responsibility, in respect of these and other crimes committed in the same area. Letters from the Special Rapporteur to the Bosnian Government were used in both cases to prove notice of crimes – in *Delić*, requesting information on the killing of at least 25 Bosnian Croat civilians, allegedly by soldiers subordinated to the ABiH.[141] In *Hadžihasanović*, for the same crimes, the Trial Chamber used the letter and the Special Rapporteur's reaction to the response to his letter.[142]

The Special Rapporteur's reports were also used for evidence of detention conditions and of the killing of civilians.[143] A report of the UN Centre for Human Rights Field Operations in Zagreb proved housing destruction in villages, but the Trial Chamber decided that it could make no

---

cial Rapporteur's Second Periodic Report, specifically regarding the team's visit to Miletići and report on the torture and death of five Croats there.

[140] Such as the size of the JNA, its withdrawal from Bosnia and Herzegovina, the names and roles of Serb paramilitary units operating in Bosnia, *Delalić*, paras. 94, 116, 119 and 213, *supra* note 28.

[141] In the village of Maljine in June 1993, *Prosecutor v. Rasim Delić*, IT-04-83-T, Judgement, 15 September 2008, para. 233 (http://www.legal-tools.org/doc/a34f45/); and Delić's eventual response, para. 236. Delić was acquitted in relation to this incident because the Trial Chamber was not satisfied that he was the commander when the killings occurred, para. 335.

[142] *Prosecutor v. Enver Hadžihasanović and Amir Kubura*, IT-01-47-T, Judgement, 15 March 2006, paras. 1137, 1138 and 1143 (https://www.legal-tools.org/doc/1941c3/); Sixth Periodic Report, of 21 February 1994, E/CN.4/1994/110 (misquoted as 1993 in footnote 2512).

[143] Killings in the village of Miletići, the number of prisoners detained by the ABiH in the Zenica Music School, the conditions of their detention and the limited access allowed to the school, *Hadžihasanović*, paras. 1099, 1176, 1191 and 1229, *ibid.*; Special Rapporteur's Fifth Periodic Report.

---

findings about whether it was of a large scale not justified by military necessity.[144]

## 11.17. Kosovo

The ICTY heard four cases related to the 1998–1999 conflict in Kosovo and some findings of the Special Rapporteur were used to provide context to the origins of the conflict. The reports of intergovernmental (OSCE) and non-governmental organisations (in particular, Human Rights Watch) provided background, some facts, and served to prove notice to commanders of crimes being committed by their subordinates. The NGOs took a particularly sophisticated approach to distributing their reports during the conflict – HRW published a number of reports documenting war crimes and the responses to their reporting, and issued many media releases.[145]

*Haradinaj* and *Limaj* concerned crimes committed by the Kosovo Liberation Army, while *Milutinović* and *Đorđević* related to crimes committed by FRY forces against Kosovar Albanians. *Limaj* involved two KLA commanders and a camp guard charged with crimes against prisoners at a KLA detention camp. The Trial Chamber used a HRW report for its estimation that 300,000 people were displaced in Kosovo and to estimate the number of Albanians, Serbs and Roma abducted by the KLA. On the issue of jurisdiction – the existence of an armed conflict – the report was used to describe the KLA as an organised military force, and for its conclusion that it was an organised armed group and engaged in an internal armed conflict.[146] *Haradinaj* used NGO reports very sparingly, refer-

---

[144] The villages had been visited by its team, *Hadžihasanović*, paras. 1817–1818, 1828 and 1830, *supra* note 143.

[145] For example, "Humanitarian Law Violations in Kosovo", 1 October 1998; "A Week of Terror in Drenica", 1 February 1999; "A Village Destroyed: War Crimes in Kosovo", 27 October 1999; "Under Orders: War Crimes in Kosovo", 26 October 2001. Media releases included headings such as "Yugoslav Military and Serbian Police Commit War Crimes in Kosovo. Some Abuses by KLA also documented". 1 July 1998, stating, for example, "Powerful evidence that Serbian police forces summarily executed ethnic Albanians in the villages of Likosane and Cirez (28 February–1 March), Prekaz (5–6 March), Poklek (31 May), and Ljubenic (30 May). Eyewitnesses report the rape of three women in Ljubenic".

[146] *Prosecutor v. Fatmir Limaj, Haradin Bala, and Isak Musliu*, IT-03-66-T, Trial Judgement, 30 November 2005, paras. 62, 133, 134, 202, 203, 208 and 209 (http://www.legal-tools. org/doc/4e469a/); HRW Report of October 1998 and with testimony from one of the authors. The KLA was found to have been an organised military force between February and

ring only to witness accounts given to the Humanitarian Law Center in Belgrade.[147]

In *Milutinović*, six FRY political, military and police leaders were tried for crimes against humanity and other crimes committed against the Kosovar Albanian population. The Trial Chamber made very little use of fact-finding reports. To provide historical context to the conflict, it used a report of Special Rapporteur Mazowiecki describing discrimination against the Albanian population in 1992.[148] It did not use the NGO reports in any material sense.

In *Đorđević*, in contrast to *Milutinović*, the Trial Chamber relied extensively on fact-finding reports.[149] The OSCE's Kosovo Verification Mission ('KVM'), staffed by military, political and legal experts seconded by member countries, was charged with monitoring and reporting on the situation, and consequently visited crime scenes and issued reports; its reports were used for proof of tank positions, military clashes and shelling by the VJ.[150] Human Rights Watch also actively monitored events in Kosovo, and between March and July 1999 issued 51 brief statements and reports called 'Flash reports' detailing allegations of criminality, all of which were sent to the Serbian Ministry of the Interior.[151] To prove crimes committed in one town, HRW reports were used as background infor-

---

May 1998 and engaged in an internal armed conflict from May 1998 – relevant to the indictment period. It also used an OSCE Missing Persons Report, *Limaj*, para. 480.

[147] And also to the HLC's Incident Reports, *Prosecutor v. Ramush Haradinaj, Idriz Balaj and Lahi Brahimaj*, IT-04-84-T, Judgement, 3 April 2008, paras. 175 and 183 (http://www.legal-tools.org/doc/025913/).

[148] Including allegations of torture and mistreatment, the dismissal of thousands of Kosovar Albanians, Serbian authorities encouraging Serbian immigration or return, and Albanians leaving in large numbers, *Prosecutor v. Milan Milutinović, Nikola Šainović, Dragoljub Ojdanić, Nebojša Pavković, Vladimir Lazarević, and Sreten Lukić*, IT-05-87- T, Judgement, 26 February 2009, paras. 224, 227 and 230 (https://www.legal-tools.org/doc/9eb7c3/); Report of 17 November 1992.

[149] Đorđević, who was responsible for all police units in Kosovo in 1999, had been indicted in *Milutinović* but was tried separately due to his arrest a year after that trial's commencement, *Prosecutor v. Vlastimir Đorđević*, IT-05-87/1-T, Public Judgement with Confidential Annex, 25 February 2011 (Vol. 1, http://www.legal-tools.org/doc/653651/; Vol. 2, http://www.legal-tools.org/doc/8d4786/).

[150] *Đorđević*, paras. 256, 390, 438 and 1224, *ibid.* The KVM's mandate included, "to report and make recommendations to the OSCE Permanent Council, the UN Security Council and other organizations on areas covered by UN Security Council Resolution 1199 (1998)", Decision No. 263 of 25 October 1998, the Permanent Council, OSCE.

[151] *Đorđević*, para. 1997, *supra* note 149.

---

mation for population and ethnic composition and that the border region was used to smuggle arms and supplies.[152] HRW was also sourced to establish that prominent Albanians were targeted and killed or imprisoned, and for information relating to specific deaths.[153] An OSCE report sourced facts such as the police telling citizens to leave Kosovo, that one refugee buried 10 men – executed by Serbian police as suspected KLA sympathisers – and for the absence of any KLA military presence in an attacked village.[154]

Most substantially, the Trial Chamber used the publication and dissemination of HRW reports to prove that Đorđević, as the effective chief of police, had notice of the crimes allegedly committed by subordinates. For example, in March 1998, in an early incident in the conflict, a police attack on a compound killed at least 54 people, mostly family members. A HRW report described the police action as excessive and causing many deaths, including those of women and children.[155] The Trial Chamber used this and the fact that Đorđević was personally present during the operation, to prove his personal involvement in anti-terrorist activities in Kosovo in which civilians were killed.[156]

Another HRW report was used to prove that he knew of a specific incident that had caused an international outcry. The Trial Chamber found "it is inconceivable on the evidence that Đorđević would not have been aware of the allegations of crimes committed [...] yet he took no measures to follow-up on calls for an investigation".[157]

---

[152] In Đakovica/Gjakove, HRW reports included "Under Orders: War Crimes in Kosovo" documenting war crimes allegedly committed by Serbian and Yugoslav government forces in Kosovo between 24 March and 12 June 1999, *Đorđević*, paras. 852 and 854, *ibid.*

[153] For example, that members of a family in Ćerim/Qerim were killed, burned bodies were in a house, fighting was intense in Đakovica/Gjakove and that 300 bodies were found next to a roadside, *Đorđević*, paras. 861, 891, 898, 1418, 916 and 979, *ibid.*

[154] And that another refugee had seen 30 to 40 bodies on the street of Đakovica/Gjakove, including men, women and children, *Đorđević*, paras. 912 and 744, *ibid.*, referring to OSCE publication "Human Rights Bi-Weekly".

[155] *Đorđević*, para. 1900, *ibid.*, referring to a Human Rights Watch report, "Humanitarian Law Violations in Kosovo", published in October of 1998 regarding the attack on the Jashari family compound in Drenica.

[156] *Đorđević*, para. 1900, *ibid.*

[157] In September 1998 in Gornje Obrinje/Abri-e-Epërme where 21 family members died, *Đorđević*, paras. 339 (1998), referring to the HRW report, "A week of terror in Drenica, Humanitarian law violations in Kosovo", February 1999; *Đorđević*, paras. 1998 and 2083, *ibid.*

A Human Rights Watch report "A Village Destroyed" was sent to the FRY Ministry of the Interior, which was responsible for police units in Kosovo that Đorđević headed.[158] The Trial Chamber used this to prove his knowledge, finding:[159]

> Despite his awareness of crimes committed in Kosovo, the Accused at no point in time set up a commission or body specifically charged with the responsibility to investigate allegations of crimes committed by the police in Kosovo and he took no action to ensure that other appropriate investigative authorities gave due attention to these allegations.

The Trial Chamber also specifically rejected as untrue Đorđević's assertions that he knew nothing of HRW's allegations against the Ministry of the Interior forces when he headed the police. The international media's reporting on the alleged crimes and the local media's response to these and to HRW reports – and his admission that he read newspapers – informed Đorđević of crimes committed or allegedly committed by police, thus making him legally aware that his subordinates had committed or were about to commit crimes. [160]

## 11.18. Macedonia

One ICTY case concerned the 2001 armed conflict in Macedonia between the Albanian National Liberation Army and Macedonian Government forces. *Boškoski and Tarčulovski* related to a Macedonian police attack on an ethnic Albanian village.[161] The Trial Chamber received testimony and reports from intergovernmental organisations – the OSCE and the International Management Group ('IMG') – and NGOs, the International Crisis Group ('ICG') and HRW. It used this evidence as background information, to find jurisdiction and for proof of notice to the accused.

An ICG report provided background information on the NLA's formation.[162] On the jurisdictional existence of an armed conflict, the Trial

---

[158] Relating to a massacre in the village of Cuška/Qyshk in May 1999, *Đorđević*, paras. 1997, 1998, *ibid.*

[159] *Đorđević*, para. 1999, *ibid.*

[160] *Đorđević*, paras. 1996, 1997, 2083, *ibid.*

[161] The village of Ljuboten, near Skopje. Seven civilians were killed, houses were burned and numerous men were detained and maltreated during the attack.

[162] *Prosecutor v. Ljube Boškoski and Johan Tarčulovski*, IT-04-82-T, Judgement, 10 July 2008, para. 28 (http://www.legal-tools.org/doc/939486/), ICG Balkans Report 109 of 5 April 2001.

Chamber considered the ICG, NATO and OSCE reports as generally reliable.[163] OSCE reports were used for some military matters, including the presence of KLA, where a mortar fell, and its observations on ammunition and materiel.[164] OSCE estimates helped establish that some villages were under NLA control; IMG and OSCE reports provided evidence of housing and other property damage.[165]

A report of Human Rights Watch, which actively monitored the escalating tension and conflict, was used to find that Boškoski, as Minister of the Interior, had inquiry notice of the allegations against his subordinates,[166] with the Chamber finding,[167]

> that by virtue of the HRW report, if he had not been fully aware earlier, Ljube Boškoski knew of the serious allegations about the conduct of police in Ljuboten on 12 August and following. While the report in some aspects contradicts the detailed evidence presented in this trial, which is discussed in this Judgement, the nature and seriousness of the allegations, and the existence of an apparent factual basis for them, were sufficient on their own to put Ljube Boškoski on notice of the likelihood of illegal acts by his subordinates.

Boškoski was acquitted, but only after the Trial Chamber had established that the crimes had been committed, that he was in a superior subordinate relationship, and had had notice of the crimes. The Trial Chamber found that he had not failed to take all reasonable steps to punish his subordinates.

Two extracts from the judgement demonstrate the need for care and precision in the conclusions to fact-finding reports and how important proper information sourcing is – and, most particularly, whether it is hearsay or direct evidence. Here, the Trial Chamber was using seven-year-old

---

[163] *Boškoski*, para. 210, *ibid.*

[164] *Boškoski*, paras. 138, 148, 165, *ibid.*; OSCE Special Report on events in Ljuboten 14 August 2001; OSCE Spot Report 15 August 2001.

[165] *Boškoski*, para. 242 (OSCE report re NLA control), paras. 241, 360, 365–368, 371, 372 (IMG reports), paras. 242, 362, 372, 376, 379 (OSCE reports), *supra* note 162.

[166] *Boškoski*, paras. 241, 360, 365–368, 371, 372 (OSCE reports), paras. 448–451 (OSCE reports), *ibid.*

[167] *Boškoski*, para. 451, *ibid.*

contemporary fact-finding reports and testimony from their authors. In relation to one HRW witness and the relevant report it held:[168]

> His observations were made 11 days after the events. Further, the HRW report on the relevant events in Ljuboten, to which he was the main contributor, and which is a cornerstone of his evidence, is sourced primarily by unchallenged accounts of ethnic Albanian residents from Ljuboten which have not been tested against the other differing accounts which the Chamber has heard.

Additionally, it was footnoted "[t]he Chamber notes that aspects of his observations may have been influenced by media reports". And concerning an OSCE report, it held,[169]

> The Chamber notes that there is no specific evidence as to the circumstances in which Muharem Ramadani was killed. There is no support, however, in the evidence for the suggestion in the OSCE report that the death of Muharem Ramadani could have occurred during the operation by the Macedonian forces to 'clear' the area of hostile forces on their way to the houses in the 'north edge of town'. The same suggestion is made in the report with respect to the body of Sulejman Bajrami. The source of that suggestion is not disclosed.

## 11.19. The International Criminal Court

The ICC appears to have adopted a less cautious approach than the ICTY and the IRMCT in assessing fact-finding reports. Just like the ICTY, it has used fact-finding reports for investigative purposes.[170] It also used fact-

---

[168] *Boškoski*, para. 134, *ibid.*

[169] *Boškoski*, para. 324, *ibid.*

[170] For example, the ICC Prosecutor issued a press release in relation opening an investigation into the Situation in Darfur, Sudan, stating that:

> [f]ollowing the referral from the United Nations Security Council on 31 March 2005, the Prosecutor received the document archive of the International Commission of Inquiry on Darfur. In addition, the Office of the Prosecutor requested information from a variety of sources, leading to the collection of thousands of documents. The Office also interviewed over 50 independent experts. After thorough analysis the Prosecutor concluded that the statutory requirements for initiating an investigation were satisfied. [...] [And multiple] sources of information have been used for the OTP analysis, including reports from the Government of Sudan, the African Union, the United Nations, and other organizations, local and international media, academic experts and others.

finding reports including the Report of the International Commission of Inquiry on Darfur,[171] in deciding to issue an arrest warrant in the Situation in Darfur, Sudan.[172]

In confirmation proceedings, in a manner similar to some judgements at the ICTY, the court has termed the heavy reliance on anonymous hearsay evidence typically found in NGO reports as "problematic" for the defence. Moreover, it is,[173]

> [...] highly problematic when the Chamber itself does not know the source of the information and is deprived of vital information about the source of the evidence. In such cases, the Chamber is unable to assess the trustworthiness of the source, making it all but impossible to determine what probative value to attribute to the information.

The ICC has received fact-finding reports into evidence at trial and has used them both as background material and as primary evidence of crimes.

The *Lubanga* judgement extensively referred to MONUC reports, although it noted in describing the investigation phase that the Prosecution's lead investigator "was surprised by the differences between the reports from the NGOs and the situation that confronted the investigation team during its work". The judgement also quoted an article referring to an NGO leader, William R. Pace, the former Convenor of Coalition for

---

ICC, The Prosecutor of the ICC opens investigation in Darfur, Press Release, ICC-OTP-0606-104, 6 June 2005.

[171] Report of the International Commission for Inquiry on Darfur to the United Nations Secretary-General, Pursuant to Security Council Resolution 1564 of 18 September 2004, S/2005/60, 25 January 2005.

[172] The reports included those of HRW, ICG, the UN High Commissioner for Human Rights, Amnesty International, *Situation in Darfur, Sudan in the Case of The Prosecutor v. Omar Hassan Ahmad Al Bashir ('Omar Al Bashir')*, Decision on the Prosecution's Application for a Warrant of Arrest against Omar Hassan Ahmad Al Bashir, 4 March 2009, ICC-02/05-01/09 (http://www.legal-tools.org/doc/e26cf4/).

[173] *Situation in the Republic of Cote d'Ivoire in the case of The Prosecutor v. Laurent Gbagbo*, Decision adjourning the hearing on the confirmation of charges pursuant to Article 61(7)(c)(i) of the Rome Statute, 3 June 2013, ICC-02/11-01/11-432, para. 29 (http://www.legal-tools.org/doc/2682d8/). See also, *Situation in the Central African Republic in the case of The Prosecutor v. Jean-Pierre Bemba Gombo*, Pre-Trial Chamber II, Decision Pursuant to Article 61(7)(a) and (b) of the Rome Statute on the Charges of the Prosecutor Against Jean-Pierre Bemba Gombo, 15 June 2009, ICC-01/05-01/09-424, paras. 49–51 (http://www.legal-tools.org/doc/07965c/).

the ICC, stating that "human rights and humanitarian organizations are lousy criminal investigators. They are not producing forensic evidence that can be used by a prosecutor".[174]

Lubanga was convicted of conscripting and enlisting children under fifteen and using them to participate actively in hostilities. His conviction was upheld by majority on appeal. In a strong dissent, Judge Ušacka attacked the use of the MONUC evidence in establishing the age of children who were alleged to have been child soldiers:

> First, although the witness described the steps that she and other members of her organisation took to verify the stories of the children that she encountered, these methods of verification were not to the standard applied during a criminal investigation, the purpose of which is to establish certain facts beyond reasonable doubt. In this regard I reiterate my concerns about reliance on anonymous hearsay evidence, especially when such evidence emanates from the work of states, international organisations or non-governmental organisations. This is because the mandates and objectives of such organisations do not require their working methods to reach the level required by the "more exacting process of establishing a legally sufficient case for prosecution". Second, it is notable that the witness did not reveal the identities of any of the children about whom she testified.[175]

In *Ngudjolo*, the Trial Chamber cautiously approached NGO and UN reports, principally using two MONUC reports for background information. It held that in the absence of direct eyewitness evidence, "it

---

[174] *Situation in the Democratic Republic of the Congo in the Case of The Prosecutor v. Thomas Lubanga Dyilo*, Judgment pursuant to Article 74 of the Statute, 14 March 2012, ICC-01/04-01/06-2842, para. 129 (http://www.legal-tools.org/doc/677866/). It used several reports of the Mission des Nations Unies en République démocratique du Congo (United Nations Organization Mission in the Democratic Republic of the Congo). The investigator, Bernard Lavigne, a non-protected witness referred to as 'P-0582' in the judgement, testified that "nonetheless investigations carried out by humanitarian groups, in his opinion, are more akin to general journalism than a legal investigation", para. 131.

[175] *Situation in the Democratic Republic of the Congo in the Case of The Prosecutor v. Thomas Lubanga Dyilo*, Judgment on the Appeal of Mr Thomas Lubanga Dyilo against His Conviction, 1 December 2014, ICC-01/04-01/06-3121-Red (http://www.legal-tools.org/doc/585c75/); Dissenting Opinion of Judge Anita Ušacka, para. 75 (footnotes omitted) (http://www.legal-tools.org/doc/df4480/). In footnote 126 she noted, that "[n]otably, NGOs' reports generally refer to "child soldiers", without indicating any age, or refer to children under eighteen when an age is mentioned".

was necessary to rely primarily on witness statements and reports by MONUC investigators or representatives of various NGOs", but specified that as a general principle "excerpts from the report on human rights violations" were only "included on the proviso that the information relating directly to the events […] has been corroborated beforehand".[176]

Referring to a MONUC report drafted by its Human Rights and Child Protection Section on mass atrocities committed in the Ituri district of the DRC, and after hearing evidence from its author, it stated that it "provides useful information on the events that took place in Ituri". The Chamber then elaborated on the essential differences between criminal investigations and those of most fact-finding missions stating that:

> […] conducting an investigation into human rights violations is not subject to the same rules as those for a criminal investigation. Reports are prepared in a non-adversarial manner; they are essentially based on oral testimony, sometimes derived from hearsay, and the identity of sources is always redacted.

> The Chamber specifies that excerpts from the report on human rights violations which might be mentioned in the judgment will be included on the proviso that the information relating directly to the events of Bogoro has been corroborated beforehand.[177]

The accused was acquitted of all counts charged, of war crimes and crimes against humanity in respect of an attack on the village of Bogoro in February 2003. The same Trial Chamber in *Katanga*, in the continued trial of the co-accused after its mid-trial severance, repeated the passages directly above from *Ngudjolo*, replacing "same rules" with "same criteria".[178]

---

[176] *Situation in the Democratic Republic of the Congo in the Case of The Prosecutor v. Mathieu Ngudjolo*, Judgment pursuant to Article 74 of the Statute, 18 December 2012, ICC-01/04-02/12-3-tENG, paras. 117 and 296 (http://www.legal-tools.org/doc/2c2cde/). Special report on the events in Ituri, January 2002-December, 2003, S/2004/573, 16 July 2004.

[177] *Ngudjolo*, paras. 294, 296, *ibid.*

[178] *Situation in the Democratic Republic of the Congo in the Case of The Prosecutor v. Germain Katanga*, Judgment pursuant to Article 74 of the Statute, 7 March 2014, ICC-01/04-01/07, paras.324-327 (https://www.legal-tools.org/doc/f74b4f/). The case did not proceed to an appeal.

Katanga was convicted by majority as an accessory to crimes against humanity and war crimes committed by his Ngiti fighters. In September 2002, some months before the Bogoro attack, the village of Nyankunde was attacked and civilians were killed. Judge Van den Wyngaert dissented and was strongly critical of the majority's use of the MONUC report to find that killings in Nyankunde were committed by Ngiti fighters under Katanga's control and that this incident was evidence of Katanga's criminality for the attack by same fighters in Bogoro. She stated of the MONUC report:

> I cannot fail but notice that it seems rather unconvincing to base a finding beyond reasonable doubt on a report that (a) has been proved rather inaccurate in other parts and (b) which, in relation to the most important point – i.e. the responsibility for the civilian killings – states that "From 80 survivors' statements gathered by MONUC, *it appears* that mainly Ngiti forces were responsible for the killings." Clearly this is insufficient evidence for even the most basic findings, which once again demonstrates how important it was to have additional investigations into what occurred in Nyankunde.[179]

In *Bemba*, the Trial Chamber, referring to an earlier decision admitting NGO reports into evidence,[180] held:[181]

---

[179] *Situation in the Democratic Republic of the Congo in the Case of The Prosecutor v. Germain Katanga*, Minority Opinion of Judge Christine Van den Wyngaert, 7 March 2014, ICC-01/04-01/07-3436-AnxI, 7 March 2014, at para. 241 (with footnotes omitted) (https://www.legal-tools.org/doc/9b0c61/). And, at para. 244: "Accordingly, it is not at all clear who did most of the killing at Nyankunde. I note in passing that there is simply no reliable evidence about the scale of the massacre at Nyankunde. The Majority does not venture to suggest a minimum number of casualties, but simply informs us about what the UN Special Report has to say in this regard. As the Chamber is not entitled to take judicial notice of findings by the UN, one wonders what the value of such a reference is. More importantly, one may ask whether the Majority has carried out its responsibility to enter its own findings on the basis of the applicable standard of proof".

[180] *Situation in The Central African Republic in The Case of The Prosecutor v. Jean-Pierre Bemba Gombo*, Decision on the Prosecution's Application for Admission of Materials into Evidence Pursuant to Article 64(9) of the Rome Statute of 6 September 2012, 8 October 2012, ICC-01/05-01/08-2299-Red, paras. 35-36 (https://www.legal-tools.org/doc/13ca4b/). Judge Ozaki dissented on this point, Partly Dissenting Opinion of Judge Ozaki on the Prosecution's Application for Admission of Materials into Evidence Pursuant to Article 69(4) of the Rome Statute (https://www.legal-tools.org/doc/46fdb1/), holding, at para. 12: "Due to the lack of guarantees concerning the reliability of these reports' sources and without hearing the testimony of the authors of these reports, in my judgment their probative

Concerning official NGO reports, the Majority found that they can be considered (i) "prima facie reliable, provided that they offer sufficient guarantees of impartiality"; and (ii) admissible "for the limited purpose that the information contained therein may serve to corroborate other pieces of evidence". Noting the Defence submissions on the limited use and weight that should be accorded to press and NGO reports, the Chamber has cautiously considered the information contained in press and NGO reports in light of the principles articulated in its decisions admitting these items, as set out above.

The Trial Chamber apparently used an NGO report on attacks in Bangui committed by Bemba's soldiers to prove his knowledge of these crimes. The NGO report had also analysed Bemba's possible criminal liability. Bemba, after first dismissing the report as "of a political character" then offered to work with it to establish the truth about what happened.[182]

Bemba was acquitted on appeal in a three to two majority decision.[183] In their joint separate opinion Judges Morrison and Van den Wyngaert stated generally of fact-finding reports that:

Indeed, what distinguishes judgments from reports of special investigation commissions, NGOs and the media is precisely the strength and quality of the evidential foundations of judicial findings of fact.[184]

---

value is low. Considering in turn the high potential for prejudice to the defence if the reports are admitted, it is my view that these reports do not satisfy the test for admission".

[181] *Situation in The Central African Republic in The Case of The Prosecutor v. Jean-Pierre Bemba Gombo*, Judgment pursuant to Article 74 of the Statute, 21 March 2016, ICC-01/05-01/08-3343, para. 270 (https://www.legal-tools.org/doc/edb0cf/). The reports were from the *Fédération Internationale des ligues des Droits de l'Homme* ('FIDH').

[182] *Bemba*, paras. 607-611, "On 13 February 2003, the FIDH issued a report on its investigative mission in Bangui between 25 November and 1 December 2002 entitled Crimes de guerre en République Centrafricaine "Quand les éléphants se battent, c'est l'herbe qui souffre"", para. 607, referring to crimes against civilians, MLC victims, rape, pillaging and murder.

[183] *Situation in The Central African Republic in The Case of The Prosecutor v. Jean-Pierre Bemba Gombo*, Judgment on the appeal of Mr Jean-Pierre Bemba Gombo against Trial Chamber III's "Judgment pursuant to Article 74 of the Statute", 8 June 2018, ICC-01/05-01/08 A (https://www.legal-tools.org/doc/40d35b/).

[184] *Situation in The Central African Republic in The Case of The Prosecutor v. Jean-Pierre Bemba Gombo*, Separate opinion, Judge Christine Van den Wyngaert and Judge Howard

In *AlMahdi*, where the accused pleaded guilty to the war crime of attacking protected objects (UNESCO protected tombs in Timbuktu in Mali), the Trial Chamber, according to an agreement between the Prosecution and Defence, relied on UN and other reports for background information about the conflict.[185] The facts were uncontested.

In *Gbagbo and Blé Goudé* the two Accused were acquitted, by majority and at the close of Prosecution's case, of committing crimes against humanity in Côte d'Ivoire. They had been charged with five incidents.

To prove that the attacks were part of a widespread and systematic attack on a civilian population pursuant to a State policy, the Prosecution had led evidence of "20 other incidents" involving at least 259 victims. To prove these the Prosecution relied in part upon UN reports, including of those of the mission in Côte d'Ivoire ('UNOCI'), the UNHCR and OHCHR. It also relied on NGO reports from Human Rights Watch and Amnesty International. These reported incidents involving the *Forces de Défense et de Sécurité* ('FDS'), the military of which Gbagbo was the supreme commander, and other pro-Gbagbo forces.

Judge Henderson critically analysed the reports.[186] The Prosecution, to prove an incident near the Great Mosque of Koumassi, relied on the HRW report which states that a young boy was "killed by a fragmentation grenade". However, the police report stated that he was struck six times in the leg by bullets. Judge Hendeson concluded that it was possible that they were not referring to the same person.[187]

---

Morrison, 8 June 2018, ICC-01/05-01/08-3636-Anx2, para. 5 (https://www.legal-tools.org/doc/c13ef4/).

[185] *Situation in the Republic of Mali in The Case of The Prosecutor v. Ahmad Al Faqi Al Mahdi*, Judgment and Sentence, 27 September 2016, ICC-01/12-01/15-171, para. 31 (http://www.legal-tools.org/doc/042397/).

[186] *Situation in the Republic of Côte d'Ivoire in The Case of The Prosecutor v. Laurent Gbagbo and Charles Blé Goudé*, Reasons for oral decision of 15 January 2019 on the Requête de la Défense de Laurent Gbagbo afin qu'un jugement d'acquittement portant sur toutes les charges soit prononcé en faveur de Laurent Gbagbo et que sa mise en liberté immédiate soit ordonnée, and on the Blé Goudé Defence no case to answer motion, 16 July 2019, ICC-02/11-01/15-1263 (https://www.legal-tools.org/doc/440017/). Reasons of Judge Geoffrey Henderson, 16 July 2019, ICC-02/11-01/15-1263-AnxB-Red (https://www.legal-tools.org/doc/j0v5qx/). Judge Tarfusser stated that he subscribed to Judge Henderson's factual and legal findings, Opinion of Judge Cuno Tarfusser, para. 1 (https://www.legal-tools.org/doc/f6c6f3/).

[187] Reasons of Judge Geoffrey Henderson, para. 1414.

---

The Prosecutor also alleged the deaths of two civilians in Port-Bouët, one from Burkina Faso. An Amnesty International report containing an eye-witness account of one death stated that the victim was killed when he went to buy cigarettes after the end of a curfew. The police report, however, only stated that two bodies were found with bullet wounds but with unknown circumstances of death. Judge Henderson concluded that:

> it is not possible to ascertain whether or not these two individuals were killed by the FDS as alleged. Even if the bullet injuries were caused by the FDS as indicated by the Amnesty International report, it is not known why these individuals were targeted, if at all. The Prosecutor's implied suggestion that they were killed because of their nationality is entirely speculative.[188]

A UNOCI Daily Situation Report refers to FDS elements raiding a neighbourhood and killing at least 18 people. However, a UNHCR report to the Human Rights Council reported that FDS members had stormed four mosques on the same dates, killing one and injuring at least 27. Judge Henderson noted that it was not known to what extent the information in the UNHCHR report was based on the UNOCI report and hence to what extent they corroborated each other. Further:

> Given that these documents are the main available source of evidence about what allegedly happened, and are largely composed of (anonymous) hearsay, no reasonable trial chamber could consider this as a sufficient basis to make findings against the accused.[189]

An OHCHR report, relied on by the Prosecution, provided information regarding the wounding of 11 people in Cocody that contradicted police reports.[190]

In relation to crimes allegedly committed at roadblocks, the Prosecution relied on a UN Report on Human Rights Violations in Abijan. Judge Henderson rejected it finding:

> The UN Report succinctly addresses incidents that purportedly occurred in Yopougon on 25 February 2011 and lists the names of 11 victims. The information in the report is based

---

[188] *Ibid.*, paras. 1415-1416.

[189] *Ibid.*, para. 1607, footnote omitted.

[190] *Ibid.*, para. 1614.

on anonymous hearsay and has been contradicted by direct testimonial evidence. When it comes to the CVQDY list, the difficulty to assess the reliability of the information therein stated and its sources is noted.[191]

The Prosecutor also alleged that elements of the *Garde Républicaine* shelled a bakery killing at least four. It was referenced in the UNOCI report, but Judge Henderson noted:

> It is not known who ordered this shelling. It is also not known how many shells were fired or what they were aimed at. No information is available as to how it was known that it was the *Garde Républicaine* that fired the mortar(s).[192]

It is difficult to understand why the Prosecution chose to rely on fact-finding reports containing anonymous hearsay to establish these 20 additional incidents. It appeared to be inviting trouble in court.

In her dissent, however, Judge Herrera Carbuccia took a more liberal approach to using UN and NGO reports in relation to the uncharged incidents, and adopted the *Bemba* Trial Chamber view, stating:[193]

> As regards United Nations and NGO reports, they are considered *prima facie* reliable provided that they offer sufficient guarantees of impartiality. They were relied upon only to corroborate other evidence concerning a particular incident or to give further detail about the circumstances in which the alleged crimes were committed. They did not serve as the sole source of evidence to prove any allegations related to the acts and conduct of the accused or other matters material to the charges.

As an example of her approach, which differed from the majority's, regarding an uncharged incident in Port-Bouët in which the Iman of a mosque and 35 others were killed, Judge Herrera Carbuccia stated:[194]

> Two UNOCI reports refer in more detail to the incident. Although, in general, UNOCI or NGO reports are deemed in-

---

[191] *Ibid.*, para. 1743.

[192] *Ibid.*, para. 1847.

[193] *Situation in the Republic of Côte d'Ivoire in The Case of The Prosecutor v. Laurent Gbagbo and Charles Blé Goudé*, Dissenting Opinion, Judge Herrera Carbuccia (footnotes omitted), 16 July 2019, ICC-02/11-01/15-1263-AnxC-Red, para. 31 (https://www.legal-tools.org/doc/6ak9rf/).

[194] *Ibid.*, para. 199, fn. 426.

admissible for the accuracy of their content, the following reports are admissible but solely in relation to the said incident, which was confirmed as reported by P-0046. The reports are admissible, as they give greater detail about the context in which the alleged incident took place, the alleged perpetrators and victims.

Judge Henderson, on the other hand, was of the view that "the details of the so-called operation are derived from the undated UN report which constitutes anonymous hearsay", and did not find the incident established.[195]

In analysing the charges, however, Judge Herrera Carbuccia clearly stated that "Documentary evidence containing anonymous hearsay has been excluded for the purpose of the analysis of the counts", including some UN reports, footnoting to five UNOCI documents. She was firmly against using information of this kind to establish criminal liability, stating:[196]

These documents are *prima facie* unreliable as the sources of information contained therein are unknown. As the information in these documents relates to matters central to the charges, it would be inappropriate to admit them for the truth of their contents.

In *Ntaganda*, in its factual findings, the Trial Chamber referred to some unidentified MONUC reports. In relation to a specific incident of fighting (in Komanda and Mambasa), the Chamber noted the evidence of two witnesses came from what they learned in a MONUC investigation in which hundreds were interviewed, including victims and community leaders. Consequently:

The Chamber considers that the information contained in these reports shall only be used in corroboration and, considering the fact that the evidence of P-0046 and P-0317 is based on the same investigation as the reports, it makes no

---

[195] Reasons of Judge Geoffrey Henderson, para. 1801.

[196] Dissenting Opinion, Judge Herrera Carbuccia, para. 373 (footnotes omitted). Judge Henderson's Reasons describe these documents as "UNOCI Call Centre daily reports" and a UNOCI report dated 10 May 2011, *Rapport sur les violations des droits de l'homme et du droit international humanitaire commises à l'Ouest de la Côte d'Ivoire*, UNOCI/HRD/2011/02. Only the latter is a fact-finding report.

finding concerning the involvement of the MLC and RCD-N and/or concerning an alleged assault on Mambasa.[197]

Further, in relation to an attack on Sayo, in which Ntaganda communicated orders to soldiers involved in the attack, the Trial Chamber footnoted an example of circular corroboration:

> The Human Rights Watch report 'Ituri: Covered in Blood' states that some 'civilians' tried to hide in Sayo, including inside a church called 'Mungu Samaki'; when the UPC/FPLC soldiers found them, they 'slaughtered' them (DRC-OTP-0074-0797, at 0829). SIT report DRCOTP-0074-0422 also refers to the killing of 'civilians' inside the 'Mungu Samaki' church in Sayo, but states that its source is the aforementioned Human Rights Watch report (DRC-OTP-0074-0422, para. 102 and footnote 39). The Chamber notes that the evidence of P-0017 in relation to this alleged killing is hearsay. A far as the Human Rights Watch report is concerned, the Chamber notes that it has relied on the information contained therein only in corroboration. It further notes that the report refers to people hiding inside the church as having been killed by 'UPC combatants', while according to P-0017 they were killed by persons who did not form part of the UPC/FPLC, that the witness referred to as Hema Gegere 'combatants'. As the MONUC report cites the Human Rights Watch report in relation to information concerning people having allegedly been killed inside the church in Sayo, it cannot be considered as an additional source of information. The Chamber thus considers that all the evidence received in relation to the fate of people who had sought refuge inside the church is weak. Under these circumstances, the Chamber is unable to make a finding on the matter.[198]

On a more general note, the ICC judgments are, in some respects, difficult to follow. Witnesses are referred to by à P number, for example, P-317, rather than by their name even when there are no protective measures. Exhibits are frequently not adequately described, but are referenced by their exhibit number, and the exhibits are (still) not available on

---

[197] *Situation in the Democratic Republic of the Congo in The Case Of The Prosecutor v. Bosco Ntaganda*, Judgment, 8 July 2019, ICC-01/04-02/06-2359, para. 460, fn. 1312 (https://www.legal-tools.org/doc/80578a/).

[198] *Ibid.*, para. 504, fn. 1473. This finding is repeated in para. 508, fn. 1492. This judgment is noted for its lengthy and complex footnotes.

the ICC website.[199] Decisions cited are footnoted by filing numbers rather than decision titles. Summaries of the judgment read in court are light on the facts and full of arcane procedural details of little interest, one would think, to the audience. Unfortunately, clear detail is sometimes lacking explaining what the accused is alleged to have done and what the court found that they did.

## 11.20. Special Tribunal for Lebanon

In *Ayyash*, the STL Trial Chamber, on a Defence application, took judicial notice of nine facts contained in three reports of UN fact-finding missions to Lebanon ('UNIIIC').

The Defence had asked the Trial Chamber to take judicial notice of the entire contents of twelve such reports, or alternatively, of "facts of common knowledge" in 155 selected paragraphs and eleven excerpts of summaries from the reports. The Trial Chamber declined to do so on the basis that many facts related "to matters highly contested between the Parties" that were central to the case, and to take judicial notice of these facts "would be absurd".

It took judicial notice of nine facts of common knowledge, such as relating to the UNIIIC's mandate and existence, the historical relationship between Lebanon and Syria, the fact of Rafik Hariri's death, and some well-known contemporaneous political events. It also invited the Prosecution and Defence to explore entering into agreements as to evidence in relation to other aspects of the reports, and ordered them to meet to consider a table of selected facts from ten of the reports.[200] Some agreements as to evidence resulted.

---

[199] The *Ntaganda* trial judgment, for example, issued in 2019, refers eleven times to MONUC reports by exhibit numbers, but without describing the reports by title or date. It also twice refers to a "SIT report" followed by an exhibit number. Annex B "List of short forms and acronyms" defines "SIT" as "Special investigation team", but does not explain what that is. The judgment does not tell us.

[200] *The Prosecutor v. Salim Jamil Ayyash, Hassan Habib Merhi, Hussein Hassan Oneissi, Assad Hassan Sabra*, STL-01-11/T/TC, Decision on Sabra Defence Motion Seeking Judicial Notice of United Nations Fact-Finding Mission and UNIIIC Reports, F2665, 26 July 2016, paras. 1, 2, 23, 24 (https://www.legal-tools.org/doc/c77014/). These were: Report of the Fact-finding Mission to Lebanon inquiring into the causes, circumstances and consequences of the assassination of former Prime Minister Rafzk Hariri, S/2005/203, 24 March 2005, prepared pursuant to the statement by the President of the United Nations Security Council (S/PRST/2005/4) of 15 February 2005 (http://www.legal-tools.org/doc/e87566/),

## 11.21. Conclusion

The ICC's experience to date appears to differ somewhat from that of the ICTY and IRMCT from 1994 onwards. The ICTY Chambers treated with great caution the information in fact-finding reports and carefully assessed their reliability before admitting them into evidence. They were infrequently used to corroborate facts, and were only used as direct evidence to prove notice to a commander of the criminality of subordinates.

ICC Chambers have generally made statements to the same effect about exercising caution, but in some instances have used the reports to prove the primary crimes. In *Bemba*, the Trial Chamber appears to have used an NGO report to demonstrate Bemba's inquiry notice of crimes committed by subordinates, as the ICTY Chambers did. This is of course perfectly legitimate.

The fundamental difference between the two institutions appears to be that the ICC Prosecution has more readily relied upon intergovernmental and NGO fact-finding reports than the ICTY Prosecution did. *Gbagbo and Blé Goudé* provides the most extreme example in using UN and NGO reports to prove uncharged incidents in an attempt to prove that the five incidents charged were part of a widespread or systematic attack against a civilian population according to a State policy. In hindsight, this appears not to have been a wise move.

Using anonymous hearsay at any time, even to prove uncharged incidents, is problematic. It is intrinsically unfair to the Defence. In saying this though, it is accepted that in some circumstances, NGO and UN reports, albeit based on anonymous hearsay, might reach a threshold of having some limited probative value. It could provide background contextual information. But even this would require careful scrutiny, and analysing other evidence to ensure that reports are not simply cross-corroborating each other or other facts, meaning that they are not corroborative of anything. Multiple reports relating to attacks by the same unit, for example, could fall within this category.

However, it is stressed that without knowledge of the source of the information, an element of unfairness is almost inevitable. In this respect, though, the court must carefully assess the purpose of the report: namely,

---

and Report of the International Independent Investigation Commission established pursuant to Security Council resolution 1595 (2005), S/2005/662, 19 October 2005 (http://www.legal-tools.org/doc/8e45b0/), and ten subsequent UNIIIC reports.

is it being tendered for the truth of its contents, that what is reported is accurate, as opposed to the fact that it was said. A report based on anonymous hearsay of alleged attacks by a unit subordinated to an accused person can quite legitimately be used to prove that the commander had inquiry notice of possible subordinate criminality.

As the ICC judges have pointed out, the aims and objectives of fact-finding missions differ from those of prosecutors, defence counsel, victims' advocates and courts. But they also overlap in that both seek some sort of justice. For their conclusions, both fact-finders and courts need reliable and credible information – for the fact-finder, it is the report or recommendation; for the court, the judgement or decision.

Some of the overlap lies in gathering material – or 'evidence' if it gets to court. For the credibility of both types of institutions, it must be accurate and reliable. Even recognising the obvious differences in institutional mandates, accuracy is paramount for both.

Fact-finding organisations, although not applying criminal rules of admissibility, much less the standard of beyond reasonable doubt for asserting a fact or conclusion, can and should learn from how criminal courts scrutinise the conclusions and information in their reports. This is especially critical where a mandate requires a fact-finder to investigate, gather evidence and make findings of something as comprehensive as, for example, 'all violations of international humanitarian law' or 'human rights abuses'.

ICC judges have made some powerful statements against using these reports in criminal proceedings as primary evidence of criminality. Experience has shown that the information in these reports is mostly better used for investigatory leads than as evidence in court. A common exception is for historical or background information that may provide context to the charges. They could also be used in establishing the legal classification of an armed conflict.

The fundamental principle though is that fact-finding reports must state as accurately as possible the primary sources of the information relied upon. This principle is more important to a criminal investigation, and a court, than the report's ultimate assessment of what happened.

Why? Because the findings, or their bases, could one day end up in a court somewhere. For this reason it is essential that fact-finding organisations adhere to rigid best international practice in their important work.

# 12

---

# International Criminal Law Outside the Courtroom: The Impact of Focusing on International Crimes for the Quality of Fact-Finding

## Dov Jacobs and Catherine Harwood[*]

### 12.1. Introduction: Taking International Criminal Law Out of the Courtroom

The 1990s marked the coming of age of international criminal law ('ICL'), which had not developed in any significant way since the end of World War II, with an attendant proliferation of international criminal tribunals. This revitalisation was connected to a shift in international discourse towards the 'fight against impunity' and 'accountability'. Echoing Robert H. Jackson's words at the opening of the Nuremberg Trial,[1] prosecutions were seen as the 'civilized' way through which the international community expressed its disapproval of conduct "shocking to the conscience of mankind".[2] This narrative shift has led to ICL providing key tools of se-

---

[*] At the time of writing, Dr. **Dov Jacobs** was Assistant Professor in International Law, Grotius Centre for International Legal Studies, Leiden University; and **Catherine Harwood** was a Ph.D. Researcher at the Grotius Centre.

[1] *Trial Of The Major War Criminals Before The International Military Tribunal*, vol. 2, p. 99 (https://www.legal-tools.org/doc/3c08b1/):

> That four great nations, flushed with victory and stung with injury stay the hand of vengeance and voluntarily submit their captive enemies to the judgment of the law is one of the most significant tributes that Power has ever paid to Reason.

[2] Rome Statute of the International Criminal Court 1998, Preamble (https://www.legal-tools.org/doc/9c9fd2/). See also *Prosecutor v. Tadić*, Case No. IT-94-1, Trial Chamber, Decision on the Defense Motion on Jurisdiction, 10 August 1995, para. 42 (https://www.legal-tools.org/doc/ddd6b0/), cited with approval in *Prosecutor v. Tadić*, Case No. IT-94-1, Appeals Chamber, Decision on the Defence Motion for Interlocutory Appeal on Jurisdiction, para. 59 (http://www.legal-tools.org/doc/866e17/):

> Before leaving this question relating to the violation of the sovereignty of States, it should be noted that the crimes which the International Tribunal has been called upon to try are not crimes of a purely domestic nature. They are really crimes which are uni-

---

mantic legitimacy in international discourse, with allegations of international crimes at the heart of most discussions on particular conflicts[3] and calls for international prosecutions being (at least publicly) a preferred way to place pressure on governments to abide by international legal obligations.[4]

As a result, normative and institutional developments in the field of ICL resonated in contexts beyond the courtroom, including in the fact-finding work of international commissions of inquiry ('commissions'), which are the focus of this chapter. Many commissions established under the auspices of the UN Security Council, Secretary-General and the Human Rights Council[5] have engaged with ICL concepts substantively and

---

versal in nature, well recognised in international law as serious breaches of international humanitarian law, and transcending the interest of any one State. The Trial Chamber agrees that in such circumstances, the sovereign rights of States cannot and should not take precedence over the right of the international community to act appropriately as they affect the whole of mankind and shock the conscience of all nations of the world. There can therefore be no objection to an international tribunal properly constituted trying these crimes on behalf of the international community.

[3] See, for example, the Darfur 'genocide' debate, where the Commission of Inquiry for Darfur (hereinafter 'Darfur Commission') found serious violations of IHL and international human rights law that could amount to international crimes, but that the Government of the Sudan had not pursued a policy of genocide. Schabas observes that critics of the Commission "are preoccupied with its determination that genocide is an inappropriate term to describe the atrocities": William Schabas, "Genocide, Crimes Against Humanity, and Darfur: the Commission of Inquiry's Findings on Genocide", in *Cardozo Law Review*, 2006, vol. 27, no. 4, p. 1719; and Michael Kelly, "The Debate over Genocide in Darfur, Sudan", in *University of California Davis Journal of International Law and Policy*, 2011, vol. 18, no. 1, pp. 205–224.

[4] For instance, on 14 January 2013, Switzerland on behalf of 56 states wrote to the Security Council, requesting it to send "an unequivocal message urging [Syria] and all other parties to fully respect international human rights and humanitarian law in the ongoing conflict and announcing that it intends to refer the situation to the ICC unless a credible, fair and independent accountability process is being established in a timely manner": Letter dated 14 January 2013 from the *Chargé d'affaires* a.i. of the Permanent Mission of Switzerland to the United Nations addressed to the Secretary-General, UN Doc. A/67/694–S/2013/19, 16 January 2013, Annex; see also Alvarez, who observes that "international trials are seen as superior methods of meeting the symbolic and practical needs of the international community", José Alvarez, "Crimes of States/Crimes of Hate: Lessons from Rwanda", in *Yale Journal of International Law*, 1999, vol. 24, no. 365, p. 375.

[5] Charter of the United Nations 1945, Article 34 (https://www.legal-tools.org/doc/6b3cd5/) empowers the Security Council to investigate "any situation which might lead to international friction or give rise to a dispute [...] to determine whether the situation might endanger international peace and security". The Declaration on Fact-finding by the United Nations in the Field of the Maintenance of International Peace and Security 1991 provides,

---

through fact-finding methodologies. While the mandates and activities of commissions have moved normatively and procedurally closer to the field of ICL, there is a growing realisation that prosecutions are no panacea to global conflict, and disenchantment with the ICL project is on the rise.[6] It is therefore timely to reflect on the impact that an ICL-focus may have on the quality of fact-finding by international commissions of inquiry, which are claimed to cater to a variety of transitional justice goals.

This evaluation depends on the way the notion of 'quality' is approached. If approached from a technical angle, an ICL-focus may contribute to a more rigorous fact-finding methodology, which may increase the certainty of findings, enhance the credibility of reports and possibly make information gathered by commissions more usable in international prosecutions. However, if 'quality' is considered more as a holistic notion linked to normative and narrative agendas, an ICL-focus might in fact reduce quality by unnecessarily narrowing the focus and outcomes of fact-finding, both in terms of the scope of facts considered and the persons or entities investigated.

In light of this ambition, this chapter first traces the evolution of the functions of international commissions of inquiry and tracks the migration of ICL concepts from the courtroom and into commissions' investigations (section 12.2.). It then identifies the impact of this migration in terms of the quality of procedural aspects of commissions' work, including through the adoption of evidentiary standards (section 12.3.) and substantive aspects of fact-finding (section 12.4.). Finally, in a concluding section, this chapter interrogates the use of ICL as a point of reference, both because the international justice system that is taken as a standard does not in fact exist and because, more technically, ICL outside the courtroom might not actually *be* ICL.

---

"[f]act-finding missions may be undertaken by the Security Council, the General Assembly and the Secretary-General, in the context of their respective responsibilities for the maintenance of international peace and security in accordance with the Charter", GA Res. 46/59, UN Doc. A/RES/46/59, 9 December 1991, Article 7.

6   See, *e.g.*, William Schabas, "The Banality of International Justice", in *Journal of International Criminal Justice*, 2013, vol. 11, no. 3, p. 545.

## 12.2. Migration of ICL Concepts into International Commissions of Inquiry

Though it is now common for international commissions of inquiry to make findings of violations of international law, this has not always been the case. The function of commissions significantly evolved during the twentieth century. In the early 1900s, commissions made factual determinations and acted as conciliators to encourage the peaceful resolution of international disputes. The 1907 Hague Convention for the Pacific Settlement of International Disputes provided that in respect of an international dispute "arising from a difference of opinion on points of fact", states could establish an international commission of inquiry to "facilitate a solution of these differences by elucidating the facts by means of an impartial and conscientious investigation".[7] A commission's report was limited to a "statement of facts",[8] while legal questions could be determined by arbitration.[9] While in practice a few commissions were instructed to make legal evaluations,[10] the traditional role of commissions endured through to 1991, evidenced by a General Assembly declaration on fact-finding in matters of international peace and security which provided that a commission's report "should be limited to a presentation of findings of a factual nature".[11]

The establishment of a Commission of Experts for the former Yugoslavia (hereinafter 'Yugoslavia Commission') by the Security Council in 1992[12] heralded a new era of international commissions of inquiry and triggered the renaissance of ICL.[13] The Yugoslavia Commission was in-

---

[7] Hague Convention for the Pacific Settlement of International Disputes 1907, Article 9.

[8] *Ibid.*, Article 14.

[9] *Ibid.*, Article 16.

[10] For instance, the former Commission on Human Rights established an Ad Hoc Working Group of Experts, which was asked to investigate various situations. The Special Working Group of Experts for Israel was instructed to investigate allegations of IHL violations in territories occupied by Israel: Commission Res. 6 (XXV), UN Doc. E/CN.4/RES/6 (XXV), 4 March 1969, para. 4.

[11] Declaration on Fact-finding by the United Nations in the Field of the Maintenance of International Peace and Security 1991, GA Res. 46/59, UN Doc. A/RES/46/59, 9 December 1991, Article 17.

[12] SC Res. 780 (1992), 6 October 1992 (https://www.legal-tools.org/doc/5887b3/).

[13] Bassiouni considers that the Commission of Experts concerning the former Yugoslavia "tore down [the] psychological iron curtain" which allowed ICL to develop: M. Cherif Bassiouni, "Appraising UN Justice-Related Fact-Finding Missions", in *Washington Uni-*

---

structed to inquire into violations of international humanitarian law ('IHL'), which departed from the traditional model for commissions of inquiry. In an early report to the Security Council, the Commission determined that ICL was part of its legal framework of analysis[14] and intimated that "the establishment of an ad hoc international criminal tribunal [...] would be consistent with the direction of its work".[15] The Security Council subsequently resolved to establish the International Criminal Tribunal for the former Yugoslavia ('ICTY'),[16] which marked the revitalisation of ICL that had laid largely dormant post-Nuremburg. A multiplicity of international and internationalised criminal tribunals arose in the following years, most notably the first permanent international criminal tribunal in 1998, the International Criminal Court ('ICC'). Since the Yugoslavia Commission, UN organs have established over 30 international commissions of inquiry (see the table in section 1.6. above).[17] Although a few commissions held factual mandates,[18] many others followed in the footsteps of the Yugoslavia Commission by investigating violations of international law and recommending measures to ensure accountability for those violations.

An examination of the mandates and reports of these commissions reveals that ICL has been included in their investigations in several ways. Commissions have sometimes been instructed through their mandates to investigate international or general crimes. Other commissions lacking express mandatory permission have also determined that ICL is part of the legal framework relevant to their investigations (for ease of reference

---

*versity Journal of Law and Policy*, 2001, vol. 5, p. 47. See also Bassiouni, "The Commission of Experts Established Pursuant to Security Council Resolution 780: Investigating Violations of International Humanitarian Law in the Former Yugoslavia", in *Criminal Law Forum*, 1994, vol. 5, no. 2, p. 279.

[14] Interim Report of the Commission of Experts Established Pursuant to Security Council Resolutions 780 (1992), UN Doc. S/25274, 10 February 1993.

[15] *Ibid.*, para. 74.

[16] SC Res. 827 (1993), 25 May 1993 (http://www.legal-tools.org/doc/dc079b/).

[17] A list of UN commissions of inquiry established since 1992 is on file with the authors.

[18] *E.g.*, Commission of Inquiry established pursuant to Resolution 885 (1993) concerning Somalia, SC Res. 885, 16 November 1993 (http://www.legal-tools.org/doc/6e9cc7/); Fact-finding Mission to Lebanon inquiring into the causes, circumstances and consequences of the assassination of former Prime Minister Rafik Hariri, UN Doc. S/PRST/2005/4, 15 February 2005; UN Commission of Inquiry into the Benazir Bhutto assassination, UN Doc. S/2009/68, 3 February 2009; Panel of Inquiry on the 31 May 2010 Flotilla Incident, UN Doc. S/2010/414, 2 August 2010.

termed the 'applicable law'). These determinations have been made by reference to the interrelationship of different fields of international law and on the basis of teleological reasoning. Each basis for the inclusion of ICL is discussed below.

## 12.2.1. Inclusion through the Commission's Mandate

International criminal law concepts have been incorporated into the work of some international commissions of inquiry directly through their mandates. The Human Rights Council has established two commissions whose mandates refer to the investigation of "crimes against humanity".[19] These commissions are among the most recent established by the Council, which perhaps signals the future direction of commissions created by this body. Several other commissions' mandates refer to the investigation of "crimes".[20] This broad wording may be interpreted to include both international and domestic criminal law. In almost every case where a com-

---

[19] HRC Res. 22/13, UN Doc. A/HRC/RES/22/13, 21 March 2013, para. 5 (North Korea Commission) (https://www.legal-tools.org/doc/44666d/):

> The International Commission of Inquiry on North Korea was instructed to investigate violations of human rights "with a view to ensuring full accountability, in particular where these violations may amount to crimes against humanity".

HRC Res. S-17/1, UN Doc. A/HRC/RES/S-17/1, 23 August 2011, para. 13 (Syria Commission):

> The Independent International Commission of Inquiry on the Syrian Arab Republic was mandated to "establish the facts and circumstances that may amount to such violations and of the crimes perpetrated and, where possible, to identify those responsible with a view to ensuring that perpetrators of violations, including those that may constitute crimes against humanity, are held accountable".

[20] International Commission of Inquiry for Libya, HRC Res. S-15/1, UN Doc. A/HRC/RES/S-15/1, 25 February 2011, para. 11 (hereinafter 'Libya Commission') (https://www.legal-tools.org/doc/233009/); Mission to the Syrian Arab Republic to Investigate Alleged Violations of International Human Rights Law, HRC Res. S-16/1, para. 7 (hereinafter 'OHCHR Mission to Syria') ((https://www.legal-tools.org/doc/37fa81/); Special Inquiry on Events in Al-Houla, HRC Res. S-19/1, UN Doc. A/HRC/RES/S-19/1, 1 June 2012, para. 8 (hereinafter 'Al-Houla Inquiry') (https://www.legal-tools.org/doc/d3a043/); International Commission of Inquiry Mandated to Establish the Facts and Circumstances of the Events of 28 September 2009 in Guinea, Letter dated 28 October 2009 from the Secretary-General addressed to the President of the Security Council, UN Doc. S/2009/556, Annex, para. 2 (hereinafter 'Guinea Commission') (https://www.legal-tools.org/doc/df9140/); Group of Experts for Cambodia established pursuant to GA Res 52/135, UN Doc. A/RES/52/135, 12 December 1997, p. 1 (hereinafter 'Cambodia Commission') (https://www.legal-tools.org/doc/6e9a5f/).

mission was mandated to establish the reality of 'crimes' perpetrated, findings of international crimes were made.[21]

Some commissions have been instructed to identify perpetrators and bring them to justice. Commissions have interpreted this instruction as invoking ICL. The Darfur Commission, for instance, explained that "[i]n order to name particular persons as suspected perpetrators, it is necessary to define the international crimes for which they might be held responsible".[22] Another example is the International Commission of Inquiry for Côte d'Ivoire, which was instructed to investigate allegations of serious violations of human rights committed following the 2010 presidential election "in order to identify those responsible for such acts and to bring them to justice".[23] The Commission reported that violations of human rights and IHL might amount to crimes against humanity and war crimes, and noted that although a final determination of individual criminal responsibility must be made by a court, it was required to identify those responsible.[24]

---

[21]    The Libya Commission made findings of war crimes and crimes against humanity: Report of the Libya Commission, UN Doc. A/HRC/17/44, 12 January 2012, para. 246 (hereinafter 'First Report of the Libya Commission'). The OHCHR Mission to Syria made findings of crimes against humanity: Report of the OHCHR Mission to Syria, UN Doc. A/HRC/18/53, 15 September 2011, para. 69 (https://www.legal-tools.org/doc/5bf068/). The Guinea Commission made findings of crimes against humanity: Report of the Guinea Commission, UN Doc. S/2009/693, 18 December 2009, p. 3. The Cambodia Commission recommended that prosecutions for genocide, crimes against humanity and war crimes be pursued: Report of the Cambodia Commission, UN Doc. A/83/850, 16 March 1999, para. 91. An exception is the UN Independent Special Commission of Inquiry for Timor-Leste, which focused on domestic criminal law: Report of the UN Independent Special Commission of Inquiry for Timor-Leste, 2 October 2006, para. 109 (hereinafter 'Report of the Timor-Leste Commission') (https://www.legal-tools.org/doc/386b70/).

[22]    Report of the International Commission of Inquiry on Darfur to the UN Secretary-General, 25 January 2005, para. 4 (hereinafter 'Report of the Darfur Commission') (https://www. legal-tools.org/doc/e684bb/).

[23]    HRC Res. 16/25, UN Doc. A/HRC/RES/16/25, 25 March 2011 (https://www.legal-tools. org/doc/7b9efc/).

[24]    Report of the independent, international commission of inquiry on Côte d'Ivoire, A/HRC/17/48, 1 July 2011, para. 116 (https://www.legal-tools.org/doc/9d910a/):

    La Commission est bien consciente du fait que la détermination finale de la responsabilité pénale d'un individu doit être effectuée par un tribunal pour assurer la garantie des droits des personnes concernées; néanmoins, le mandat du Conseil des droits de l'homme lui prescrit d'identifier les responsables.

### 12.2.2. Inclusion by Reason of the Interrelationship of Fields of International Law

Some commissions have included ICL as part of the applicable law by citing the links between ICL and other fields of international law. Commissions have characterised ICL as the 'enforcement arm' of human rights law and IHL. For instance, the International Commission of Inquiry for Libya stated that ICL is the "means of enforcement at the international level of penalties for grave violations of customary law, [human rights] and serious violations of IHL which are recognized as attracting individual liability".[25] The UN Fact-Finding Mission on the Gaza Conflict, also known as the Goldstone Commission (discussed in Chapter 2 above), was instructed to investigate violations of IHL and human rights. It reported that ICL was "a necessary instrument for the enforcement"[26] of IHL and international human rights law, and that:[27]

> The international community increasingly looks to criminal justice as an effective mechanism of accountability and justice in the face of abuse and impunity. The Mission regards the rules and definitions of international criminal law as crucial to the fulfilment of its mandate to look at all violations of IHL and IHRL by all parties to the conflict.

A similar statement was made by the Darfur Commission, which reported that individual criminal responsibility was a "critical aspect of the enforceability of rights and of protection against their violation".[28]

### 12.2.3. Inclusion on the Basis of the Goal of Ensuring Accountability

The migration of ICL concepts into the work of commissions has also occurred as a result of normative discourse relating to accountability and the right of victims to justice.[29] In respect of violations constituting interna-

---

[25] Report of the Libya Commission, UN Doc. A/HRC/19/68, 2 March 2012, para. 23 (hereinafter 'Second Report of the Libya Commission') (https://www.legal-tools.org/doc/a7b7ee/pdf/).

[26] Report of the UN Fact-Finding Mission on the Gaza Conflict, UN Doc. A/HRC/12/48, 25 September 2009, para. 286 (hereinafter 'Report of the Goldstone Commission') (https://www.legal-tools.org/doc/ca9992/).

[27] *Ibid.*

[28] Report of the Darfur Commission, para. 407.

[29] See, *e.g.*, General Assembly, "Basic Principles and Guidelines on the Right to a Remedy and Reparation for Victims of Gross Violations of International Human Rights Law and

tional crimes, there is a strong emphasis on judicial accountability[30] as a result of the norm that states have a duty to prosecute international crimes.[31] The perception that international crimes threaten international peace and security[32] depicts ICL as a vital enforcement mechanism of international law and a tool to achieve lasting peace. Bassiouni writes that "accountability must be recognized as an indispensable component of peace"[33] and that "[f]act-finding and investigation are a means to an end. With respect to the values of truth and justice, the end is accountability of the perpetrators".[34]

Many commissions claim to share the same broad goals as international criminal tribunals of ending impunity and ensuring accountability for perpetrators. References to accountability are found in many commissions' mandates. For instance, the International Commission of Inquiry concerning Burundi ('Burundi Commission') was asked to recommend measures "with regard to the bringing to justice of persons responsible for

---

Serious Violations of International Humanitarian Law", GA Res. 60/147, UN Doc. A/RES/60/147, 21 March 2006; UN Commission on Human Rights, "Updated Set of Principles for the Protection and Promotion of Human Rights Through Action to Combat Impunity", UN Doc. E/CN.4/2005/102/Add.1, 8 February 2005; Office of the United Nations High Commissioner for Human Rights, "Study on the Right to the Truth", UN Doc. E/CN.4/2006/91, 8 February 2006; HRC Res. 21/7 (hereinafter 'Right to Truth'), UN Doc. A/HRC/RES/21/7, 10 October 2012 (https://www.legal-tools.org/doc/dcac1a/).

[30] But note the view of Ambos, who considers that although a duty to prosecute specific violations is found in treaty law, it is not yet settled that the duty exists in customary international law; and that the duty cannot arise purely from victims' right to a remedy, as this does not necessarily equate to an obligation of criminal prosecution: Kai Ambos, "The Legal Framework of Transitional Justice: A Systematic Study with a Special Focus on the Role of the ICC", in Kai Ambos *et al.* (eds.), *Building a Future on Peace and Justice: Studies on Transitional Justice, Peace and Development*, Springer-Verlag Berlin, 2009, p. 30.

[31] See, *e.g.*, Rome Statute, Preamble; SC Res. 1674 (2006), 28 April 2006 (https://www.legal-tools.org/doc/4bf3cc/), where the Security Council resolved that states have a responsibility to "comply with their relevant obligations to end impunity and to prosecute those responsible for war crimes, genocide, crimes against humanity and serious violations of international humanitarian law".

[32] See, *e.g.*, Rome Statute of the International Criminal Court 1998, Preamble, where States Parties recognised that "such grave crimes threaten the peace, security and well-being of the world".

[33] M. Cherif Bassiouni, "Searching for Peace and Achieving Justice: The Need for Accountability", in *Law and Contemporary Problems*, 1996, vol. 59, no. 4, p. 19.

[34] *Ibid.*

those acts" and to "eradicate impunity".[35] The Commission of Inquiry for Darfur undertook investigations "with a view to ensuring that those responsible are held accountable",[36] and the Libya Commission was asked to recommend measures "with a view to ensuring that those individuals responsible are held accountable".[37] A commission established in 2013 to examine human rights abuses in the Democratic People's Republic of Korea ('North Korea Commission') was asked to investigate "with a view to ensuring full accountability".[38]

International criminal law thus finds its way into commissions' work through mandates; as a result of commissions' views regarding the interrelationship of ICL, international human rights law and IHL; and by reference to the goal of ensuring accountability for violations of international law. The next sections explore the consequences of the inclusion of ICL concepts *vis-à-vis* the quality of fact-finding work undertaken by commissions.

## 12.3. Impact of ICL-focus on the Technical Quality of Fact-Finding

As a result of the emigration of ICL beyond the courtroom, commissions have shown a desire to adopt procedures that mirror those found in judicial contexts in the claimed interests of improving the quality of investigations, strengthening findings and assisting future prosecutions. The impact of ICL can be witnessed on a number of levels: in the desire to produce credible reports and collect information which may assist subsequent prosecutions (section 12.3.1.), in a preference for a judicialized assessment of the veracity of evidence (section 12.3.2.), in the adoption of evidential thresholds (section 12.3.3.) and in the attachment to principles of due process (section 12.3.4.).

### 12.3.1. Facilitation of International Criminal Investigations

While commissions might adopt procedures to facilitate the use of evidence gathered by international tribunals (section 12.3.1.1.), this practice is not without its limits (section 12.3.1.2.).

---

[35] SC Res. 1012 (1995), 28 August 1995, para. 1(b) (http://www.legal-tools.org/doc/80c1a0/).
[36] SC Res. 1564 (2004), 18 September 2004, para. 12 (http://www.legal-tools.org/doc/1ba770/).
[37] Libya Commission, para. 11, *supra* note 21.
[38] HRC Res. 22/13, para. 5.

---

## 12.3.1.1. Paving the Way for Future Prosecutions

Some commissions have determined that information gathered during their investigations may be useful in subsequent prosecutions, and have shaped their methodologies so as to facilitate criminal investigations. Indeed, the mandate of the Special Inquiry into Al-Houla, undertaken by the International Commission of Inquiry on Syria ('Syria Commission'), instructed it to "preserve the evidence of crimes for possible future criminal prosecutions or a future justice process".[39] The Burundi Commission, established over a decade earlier, decided to conform as much as possible to "judicial standards" in order to "amass evidence that could be of use for any later judicial action".[40] These 'judicial standards' included taking witness testimony under oath[41] and seeking to hear witnesses from different parties to the conflict.[42] When explaining its working methods, the International Commission of Inquiry on Darfur (Darfur Commission) reported that "in classifying the facts according to international criminal law, [it] adopted an approach proper to a judicial body. It therefore collected all material necessary for such a legal analysis",[43] and reported that it would "make an assessment of possible suspects that would pave the way for future investigations, and possible indictments, by a prosecutor".[44]

One can also note that a number of commissions have collected and stored information in such a way as to enable it to be transferred to criminal investigators. The last chairman of the Yugoslavia Commission, Professor Bassiouni, created an extensive database of evidence and transferred this to the ICTY Prosecutor,[45] which helped to "establish the location, character and scale of violations".[46] Likewise, the former ICC Prose-

---

[39] HRC Res S-19/1, UN Doc. A/HRC/RES/S-19/1, 1 June 2012 (http://www.legal-tools.org/doc/d3a043/).

[40] Report of the Burundi Commission, para. 6.

[41] *Ibid.*, para. 8. Note however that not all interviews had been transcribed by the time the report was published: para. 58.

[42] *Ibid.*, para. 11.

[43] Report of the Darfur Commission, para. 14.

[44] Report of the Darfur Commission, para. 15 (footnotes omitted).

[45] Bassiouni, 1994, *supra* note 13. See also Final Report of the Commission of Experts Established Pursuant to Security Council Resolution 780 (1992), UN Doc. S/1994/674, 27 May 1994, para. 22 (hereinafter 'Final Report of the Commission of Experts for the Former Yugoslavia') (https://www.legal-tools.org/doc/3a3ae2/).

[46] Lyal Sunga, "How Can UN Human Rights Special Procedures Sharpen ICC Fact-Finding?", in *The International Journal of Human Rights*, 2011, vol. 15, no. 2, p. 193.

cutor has written that information collected by the Darfur Commission[47] helped his Office to plan its investigation into the situation in the Sudan.[48] In addition to generating information about the nature of violations, several commissions have identified suspected perpetrators and either given a confidential list of names to the High Commissioner for Human Rights, or more rarely, published those names in their reports.

These efforts to facilitate prosecutions have therefore been partially fruitful. The report of the Darfur Commission[49] prompted the Security Council to refer the situation in the Sudan to the ICC. A similar relationship existed between the Yugoslavia Commission and the ICTY. However, there is not always a causal relationship between a commission of inquiry and an international judicial investigation. For instance, the Security Council referred the situation in Libya to the ICC Prosecutor one day after the Human Rights Council established the Libya Commission.[50] Conventional wisdom regarding the causal relationship between the Commission of Experts on Rwanda and the ICTR has been challenged by Bassiouni, who considers that the Commission was, in essence, window-dressing for the Security Council's intention to create another *ad hoc* international criminal tribunal.[51]

### 12.3.1.2. The Limits of the Practice

First of all, it should be pointed out that commissions are also aware that their findings are not identical to, nor a substitute for, prosecutions. For instance, an OHCHR fact-finding mission in the Democratic Republic of the Congo ('DRC Mapping Exercise') stated that the question of whether serious acts of violence committed against the Hutus constituted genocide remained unresolved and that "this question can only be decided by a court decision on the basis of evidence beyond all reasonable doubt".[52]

---

[47] Report of the Darfur Commission, paras. 25 and 645.

[48] Luis Moreno-Ocampo, "The International Criminal Court in Motion", in Carsten Stahn and Göran Sluiter (eds.), *The Emerging Practice of the International Criminal Court*, Brill/Martinus Nijhoff, 2009, p. 15.

[49] Report of the Darfur Commission, para. 584.

[50] Libya Commission, *supra* note 21; SC Res. 1970 (2011), 26 February 2011.

[51] Bassiouni, 2001, p. 43, *supra* note 13.

[52] Report of the Mapping Exercise documenting the most serious violations of human rights and international humanitarian law committed within the territory of the Democratic Republic of the Congo between March 1993 and June 2003, August 2010, paras. 28 and 510

Likewise, the Darfur Commission noted that its role was to "collect a reliable body of material that indicate which individuals may be responsible for violations committed in Darfur and who should therefore be brought to trial with a view to determining their liability".[53] Moreover, prosecutions are not a necessary corollary of all commissions which make findings of international crimes. Despite commissions' findings that genocide occurred in Burundi in 1972[54] and 1993,[55] no prosecutions of genocide have occurred. While institutional links between commissions and judicial mechanisms should not be overstated, the possibility of prosecution represents an important motivation on the part of commissions to have regard to ICL when conducting non-judicial fact-finding.

Finally, the adoption of methodologies mimicking law-enforcement procedures for the search and collection of evidence could be, in some cases, legally irrelevant from the perspective of a judicial body, at least from the point of view of admissibility of evidence. Rules that have been adopted in relation to the 'public' exercise of the investigative function (*id est*, by an authority formally granted this function), cannot just be transposed to 'private' exercises of this investigative function. To illustrate, should a private citizen cordon off a crime scene, gather evidence with gloves and put it in a labelled plastic bag, this would not be considered as an acceptable investigative method from a court's perspective, but rather as a contamination of a crime scene, albeit with good intentions. In the case of commissions, this means that, for example, a statement taken under oath does not have additional value before a court of law as compared with a statement taken in the absence of an oath. Only an oath taken before the institution itself has such legal relevance. Perhaps asking witnesses to give statements under oath may dissuade some individuals from giving false information, but it does not improve the legal quality of the information. Moreover, adopting such procedures does not remove the fact that the involvement of a commission in a given case might actually taint evidence, either by removing it from the scene, thus not allowing for prosecutorial investigators (or for that matter the defense) to make their

---

(hereinafter 'Report of the DRC Mapping Exercise') (http://www.legal-tools.org/doc/ae3026/).

53  Report of the Darfur Commission, para. 6.

54  Report of the Preparatory Fact-Finding Mission to Burundi, UN Doc. S/1995/157, 24 February 1995, para. 36.

55  Report of the Burundi Commission, para. 483.

---

own findings, or, in the case of witnesses, by inadvertently influencing them, creating the risk that they might adapt their stories from one interview to another.

### 12.3.2. Judicialised Assessment of Veracity of Evidence

Like courts, commissions prefer to reach findings on the basis of eye-witness accounts and first-hand information.[56] The International Fact-Finding Mission to Investigate Violations of International Law Resulting from the Israeli Attacks on the Flotilla of Ships Carrying Humanitarian Assistance ('Gaza Flotilla Commission') treated with "extreme caution" information from Israeli authorities which did not coincide with evidence of eyewitnesses.[57] The Gaza Flotilla Commission accepted hearsay evidence, noting that it gave such information "such weight as the circumstances merited".[58] Some commissions also required evidence to be corroborated in order to make findings.[59]

Many commissions evaluated the veracity of witness testimony in manner similar to judicial appraisal. The Gaza Flotilla Commission examined the "content of the evidence and demeanour of the persons appearing before it in deciding whether, and if so, what part of the information provided should be accepted".[60] The DRC Mapping Exercise reported that it assessed the veracity of information by evaluating the reliability and credibility of the source as well as the veracity of the information itself.[61] Commissions also show a similar reluctance as judicial bodies in reaching findings on the basis of hearsay evidence in documentary materials.[62]

---

[56] See, for example, Commission of Inquiry on the Events Connected with the March Planned for 25 March 2004 in Abidjan, UN Doc. S/2004/384, para. 8 (https://www.legal-tools.org/doc/1d941c/pdf/).

[57] Report of the International Fact-Finding Mission to Investigate Violations of International Law Resulting from the Israeli Attacks on the Flotilla of Ships Carrying Humanitarian Assistance, UN Doc. A/HRC/15/21, para. 20 (hereinafter 'Gaza Flotilla Commission') (https://www.legal-tools.org/doc/32f94d/).

[58] *Ibid.*

[59] See, *e.g.*, Report of the Guinea Commission, para. 22; Second Report of the Libya Commission, para. 806; Report of the DRC Mapping Exercise, para. 10.

[60] Report of the Gaza Flotilla Commission, para. 24.

[61] Report of the DRC Mapping Exercise, para. 10.

[62] See, for instance, *Prosecutor v. Laurent Gbagbo*, Decision adjourning the hearing on the confirmation of charges pursuant to Article 61(7)(c)(i) of the Rome Statute, ICC No. ICC-02/11-01/11-432, Pre-Trial Chamber I, 3 June 2013, para. 28 (https://www.legal-tools.org/doc/2682d8/):

Some commissions stated that reports of other commissions or non-governmental organisations were consulted but not used directly as evidence.[63] The Goldstone Commission verified sources and methodology in reports and cross-referenced material to analyse whether there was sufficient credible and reliable information to make a finding in fact.[64]

### 12.3.3. Use of Evidentiary Thresholds

While the adoption of particular evidentiary thresholds by commissions mirrors the practice of judicial institutions (section 12.3.3.1.), it requires a difficult balancing exercise (section 12.3.3.2.) and may ultimately not be particularly suited for the non-judicial fact-finding context (section 12.3.3.3.).

### 12.3.3.1. From Courts to Commissions: The Emigration of 'Standards of Proof'

Satisfaction of a particular standard of proof is a key feature of judicial decision-making, and is combined with the notion of the *burden* of proof – responsibility for satisfying the standard of proof generally rests on one party to proceedings. In international and domestic criminal law, the standard of proof that the prosecution must meet in order for an accused to be convicted is very high, typically exemplified by the common law standard of 'proof beyond a reasonable doubt'.[65]

Other evidential thresholds are relevant at different stages of the criminal process. At the ICC, a warrant of arrest may be issued if the Pre-Trial Chamber is satisfied that there are "reasonable grounds to believe" that the person committed a crime within the Court's jurisdiction[66] and

---

Although there is no general rule against hearsay evidence before this Court, it goes without saying that hearsay statements in the Prosecutor's documentary evidence will usually have less probative value. Reliance upon such evidence should thus be avoided wherever possible.

[63] See Report of the Burundi Commission, paras. 107–108; Report of the International Commission of Inquiry established under Resolution 1013 (1995) concerning Rwanda, UN Doc. S/1996/195, para. 53; Report of the DRC Mapping Exercise, para. 10.

[64] Report of the Goldstone Commission, para. 24.

[65] Rome Statute, Article 66. For an analysis of the adoption of this standard in international criminal tribunals, see Dov Jacobs, "The Burden and Standard of Proof", in Goran Sluiter *et al.* (eds.), *International Criminal Procedure, Principles and Rules*, Oxford University Press, Oxford, 2013, pp. 1128–1150.

[66] Rome Statute, Article 58(1)(a).

---

may confirm charges against an accused if it determines that there is "sufficient evidence to establish substantial grounds to believe" that the person committed the crimes charged.[67] At the *ad hoc* tribunals, indictments are confirmed by a Judge of the Trial Chamber if satisfied that a "prima facie case"[68] is established. Other evidential thresholds, such as the 'balance of probabilities', are found in civil proceedings.[69]

As commissions increasingly make findings not only on the existence of facts, but also in relation to the legal characterisation of those facts, the evidential strength of findings has come under scrutiny. Scholars argue that formulating clear evidentiary standards is important to indicate the level of confidence in findings, ensure that findings are accurate[70] and demonstrate procedural integrity.[71] As commissions are non-judicial and non-adversarial in nature, there is no 'party' on which the burden of proof rests. Moreover, the application of a standard of proof is not an essential aspect of a non-judicial fact-finding process. Nevertheless, many commissions have applied minimum 'evidentiary thresholds' when making findings.

While some commissions' reports do not expressly adopt a particular evidentiary threshold, a close reading of their reports shows that most do in fact apply thresholds when making findings. Many different evidentiary indicators have been used, some of which recall judicial concepts. Several commissions have adopted the threshold of 'reasonable suspicion', defined by the Syria Commission as "a reliable body of evidence, consistent with other information, indicating the occurrence of a particular

---

[67] *Ibid.*, Article 61(7).

[68] Statute of the International Criminal Tribunal for the former Yugoslavia, Article 19(1) (http://www.legal-tools.org/doc/b4f63b/); Statute of the International Criminal Tribunal for Rwanda, Article 18(1) (http://www.legal-tools.org/doc/8732d6/).

[69] See, *e.g.*, the House of Lords judgment *R. (McCann) v. Crown Court at Manchester* (2003) 1 AC 787, para. 37, where Lord Steyn wrote that the standard of proof applicable in civil proceedings is the balance of probabilities. See also Peter Murphy, *Murphy on Evidence*, Oxford University Press, Oxford, 2008.

[70] Stephen Wilkinson, "Standards of Proof in International Humanitarian and Human Rights Fact-Finding and Inquiry Missions", 2012 (available on the Geneva Academy's web site).

[71] Thomas Franck and H. Scott Fairley, "Procedural Due Process in Human Rights Fact-Finding by International Agencies", in *American Journal of International Law*, 1980, vol. 74, p. 310.

incident or event".[72] The 'reasonable suspicion' threshold closely corresponds to the standard of proof applied at the arrest warrant stage of ICC proceedings. The Yugoslavia Commission made some findings by reference to a *prima facie* standard.[73] The Libya Commission made assessments "based on a 'balance of probabilities' as to whether the information gathered supported a finding that a violation had in fact occurred".[74] Other commissions indicated the strength of findings by using a wide variety of terms, some of which do not clearly correspond to judicial standards of proof. High evidential certainty has been communicated by terms such as 'no doubt',[75] 'unquestionable',[76] 'undeniable',[77] or 'overwhelmingly established'.[78] Lower evidential certainty has been communicated by phrases such as "reasonable to presume",[79] a "reasonable degree of certainty",[80] "ample grounds to conclude",[81] or simply "credible evidence".[82] While commissions' practices in respect of evidentiary thresholds are widely divergent, there is some congruence with judicial standards of proof.

### 12.3.3.2. Balancing Interests in the Choice of Evidentiary Standards

The adoption of a particular evidentiary standard will depend on a balance that needs to be struck between two particular interests: efficiency and credibility. Indeed, while high evidentiary thresholds communicate a

---

[72] Report of the Syria Commission, UN Doc. A/HRC/S-17/2/Add.1, 23 November 2011, para. 5 (https://www.legal-tools.org/doc/925e44/). Commissions which have adopted a reasonable suspicion threshold include the Darfur Commission, UN Independent Special Commission of Inquiry for Timor-Leste and the DRC Mapping Exercise.

[73] Final Report of the Commission of Experts for the Former Yugoslavia, paras. 201 and 209.

[74] Second Report of the Libya Commission, para. 7.

[75] *Ibid.*, para. 290; Report of the Commission of Experts established pursuant to Resolution 935 (1994) concerning Rwanda, UN Doc. S/1994/1405, 9 December 1994, para. 106 (hereinafter 'Report of the Rwanda Commission') (https://www.legal-tools.org/doc/361096/).

[76] Final Report of the Commission of Experts for the Former Yugoslavia, para. 182.

[77] Report of the Darfur Commission, paras. 293 and 633.

[78] Report of the Burundi Commission, para. 473.

[79] Final Report of the Commission of Experts for the Former Yugoslavia, para. 205.

[80] *Ibid.*, para. 209.

[81] Report of the Rwanda Commission, para. 146.

[82] Report of the Darfur Commission, para. 639.

strong level of confidence in findings, commissions have generally declined to adopt such thresholds, both because it is inappropriate for the
type of investigation being undertaken and because they lack the coercive
powers required to amass all information required to make such determinations. For instance, the UN Independent Special Commission of Inquiry
for Timor-Leste observed that because it did not have powers of subpoena,
it was not appropriate to apply the criminal standard of proof beyond reasonable doubt.[83] The Goldstone Commission reported that although it
found that acts had been committed which triggered individual criminal
responsibility, its findings did not "pretend to reach the standard of proof
applicable in criminal trials".[84] The Darfur Commission likewise noted
that in respect of identifying individual suspects, in light of limitations in
its powers, it could not adopt the threshold of beyond a reasonable doubt
or the *prima facie* standard used to confirm indictments. Rather, it considered the most appropriate standard to be that of a reasonable suspicion.[85]
Indeed, adoption of the 'beyond reasonable doubt' threshold by a fact-
finding mission outside of the UN context prevented it from reaching
findings in respect of key aspects of its investigation.[86]

However, an evidential threshold which is too low may invite criticism that findings cannot be relied upon. For instance, the DRC Mapping
Exercise reasoned that a 'reasonable suspicion' threshold was appropriate
that since its objective was to gather basic information on incidents.[87] Its
report included allegations of genocide against Hutus. In response, the
Rwandan Government issued a press release dismissing the report on several grounds, including on the basis of the "application of the lowest im-
aginable evidentiary standard".[88] While the threshold of 'reasonable suspicion' is in fact commonly adopted by commissions, the Rwandan response demonstrates how a lower evidentiary threshold may be vulnerable
to criticism.

---

[83] Report of the Timor-Leste Commission, paras. 12 and 110.

[84] Report of the Goldstone Commission, para. 25.

[85] Report of the Darfur Commission, para. 15.

[86] Geneva Call, "Report of the 2009 Verification Mission to the Philippines to Investigate
Allegations of Anti-Personnel Landmine Use by Moro Islamic Liberation Front", June
2010, paras. 9 and 39 (available on its web site).

[87] Report of the DRC Mapping Exercise, para. 7.

[88] Republic of Rwanda (Ministry of Foreign Affairs and Cooperation), "Flawed and Dager-
ous Report Threatens Regional Stability", Press Statement, 30 September 2010, para. 4.

---

### 12.3.3.3.  The Limits of the Use of Evidentiary Thresholds

In reaction to the diversity of the practice of commissions, some commentators argue that there should be some standardisation of evidentiary thresholds, ranging from a lower balance of probabilities,[89] to a higher 'clear and convincing' threshold if commissions publicly name individual suspects.[90] However, in light of the fact that evidence cannot be tested before commissions to the same degree as in the judicial context, it is questionable whether it makes sense to apply evidential thresholds. Where a key actor refuses to co-operate with a commission, the commission may not have access to vital information. One now infamous example of the effect that non-co-operation may have on the strength of findings is found in the report of the Goldstone Commission, where Israel was found responsible for serious IHL violations. Israel had refused to co-operate with the investigation, and only after the report was issued did it provide further information to one of the Commissioners. That information led the Commissioner to unilaterally and publicly retract some of the findings of the report, as described in Chapter 2 above.[91] The lack of co-operation meant that key information was not conveyed to the Commission, which might have influenced its findings.

### 12.3.4.  Concerns Regarding Due Process

International commissions of inquiry have also been keen to comply with principles of due process. Requirements flowing from this principle include the independence and impartiality of decision-makers and the right to reply in respect of actors implicated or suspected of committing violations. The Updated Principles on Impunity 2005, a set of principles produced under the auspices of the former Commission on Human Rights, provides:[92]

> Before a commission identifies perpetrators in its report, the individuals concerned shall be entitled to the following guar-

---

[89]  Wilkinson, 2012, p. 51, *supra* note 70.

[90]  *Ibid.*, p. 54.

[91]  Richard J. Goldstone, "Reconsidering the Goldstone Report on Israel and War Crimes", Washington Post, 1 April 2011.

[92]  Report of Diane Orentlicher, Independent Expert to update the Set of Principles to Combat Impunity – Updated Set of Principles for the Protection and Promotion of Human Rights through Action to Combat Impunity, E/CN.4/2005/102/Add.1, 8 February 2005, Principle 9.

antees: (a) The commission must try to corroborate information implicating individuals before they are named publicly; (b) The individuals implicated shall be afforded an opportunity to provide a statement setting forth their version of the
facts either at a hearing convened by the commission while
conducting its investigation or through submission of a document equivalent to a right of reply for inclusion in the
commission's file.

The Chair of the North Korea Commission, Michael Kirby, was
quoted in an interview as stating:

I have no preconceptions about the government of North Korea and I'll proceed as one should: with impartiality and just
giving them the opportunity to have their say and to respond
to testimony. That's due process.[93]

In respect of identifying individual suspects, commissions have
been concerned of the risk of prejudicing trial fairness, should a prosecution be initiated following its report. Juan Méndez, writing as Special
Rapporteur, stated that:[94]

Certain steps must be taken to ensure that the activities of a
commission of inquiry do not jeopardize criminal due process standards, including, importantly, the rights of potential
criminal defendants. Commissions of inquiry should not
identify individuals as being criminally responsible for acts
described in the final report if doing so violates the rights of
the identified individuals, who should be presumed to be innocent, and may inject additional bias into any subsequent
official criminal investigation or prosecution.

While two commissions have publicly identified individual suspects,[95] others have kept lists of suspects confidential.[96] For example, the
Libya Commission identified individuals suspected of committing international crimes[97] but decided not to include those names in its report ex-

---

[93] Tony Eastley, "Former High Court judge to lead North Korea human rights commission",
ABC News, 8 May 2013.

[94] Juan Méndez, "Report of the Special Rapporteur on torture and other cruel, inhuman or
degrading treatment or punishment", UN Doc. A/HRC/19/61, 18 January 2012, para. 72
(footnote omitted).

[95] Guinea Commission and Timor-Leste Commission.

[96] Commissions on Cote d'Ivoire, Syria and Libya, as well as the OHCHR Mission to Syria.

[97] Second Report of the Libya Commission, paras. 758–759.

cept for senior figures who were already publicly known, to reduce the risk of harm to those in custody and avoid jeopardizing fair trial rights of those who may be brought to trial.[98] Likewise, the Darfur Commission chose to keep its list of suspects confidential in recognition of "the importance of the principles of due process and respect for the rights of the suspects".[99]

Commissions have therefore adopted various procedures and standards to enhance the precision of findings and strengthen the credibility of reports, in the hope that their work will motivate the political will to initiate enforcement mechanisms and provide assistance to criminal investigations. In fact, whether findings are considered to be credible may not depend so much on the standards adopted by a commission as the competence of the individuals undertaking the investigation and acknowledgement in the report of the strength of evidence, including limitations to the investigation. If procedures and reporting are not sound, the adoption of a particular methodological device is unlikely to improve the credibility or reliability of findings.

## 12.4. Impact of ICL-Focus on the Substantive Quality of Fact-Finding

As "the relevance of a fact is linked to the choice of the applicable law",[100] the particular legal lenses adopted by a fact-finder shape the investigative focuses of an inquiry. The investigative focus necessarily shapes the range of findings, the actors considered responsible, and the character of recommendations generated by a commission. Inclusion of ICL in a commission's applicable law and an emphasis on ensuring individual accountability have the potential to influence a commission's investigative focus and, as a corollary, the nature of its findings and recommendations.

---

[98] *Ibid.*, para. 760.

[99] Report of the Darfur Commission, para. 645.

[100] Théo Boutruche, "Credible Fact-Finding and Allegations of International Humanitarian Law Violations: Challenges in Theory and Practice", in *Journal of Conflict and Security Law*, 2011, vol. 16, no. 1, p. 111, citing J. Salmon, "Le fait dans l'application du droit international", in *The Collected Courses of the Hague Academy of International Law*, 1982, vol. 75, p. 296.

### 12.4.1. Focus on International Crimes

When a commission analyses whether international crimes have been committed, the substantive fact-finding exercise will narrow its enquiry to concentrate on those incidents which could be legally characterised as international crimes. This tendency is particularly marked when commissions perceive ICL as the 'enforcement arm' of IHL and international human rights law, and when these bodies of law are also referred to as applicable law of the commissions. As a result, the investigative focus is narrowed, as only some incidents that may be characterised as violations of human rights law and IHL form the constitutive elements of crimes against humanity and war crimes.

Violations of international law that do not appear on ICL's 'radar' may nonetheless significantly impact the wellbeing of populations, but may not receive as much attention. Much of IHL is outside the scope of ICL. For example, Additional Protocol I to the Geneva Conventions lists as a grave breach the unjustifiable delay in repatriation of prisoners of war or civilians,[101] but this has no equivalent in the Rome Statute. IHL also regulates the mundane everyday of armed conflict, such as the rule that in prisoner of war camps, canteens must be installed where prisoners of war may procure food, tobacco and everyday items, for which prices must not exceed those of the local market.[102] Those rules do not attract criminal sanction, but still affect the quality of life of individuals in armed conflicts. In a similar vein, a commission which has embraced ICL within its applicable law may focus on human rights violations which could form the basis of crimes against humanity. This could diminish the degree of scrutiny into violations of other human rights outside the ICL framework, particularly social and economic rights such as the right to education and the right to work.

More generally, an ICL-focus may limit broader inquiries and the construction of narratives beyond the realm of ICL. In fact, commissions' inquiries are broader than criminal trials, and often include in their reports historical and political narratives, and findings of patterns of violations.

---

[101] Protocol Additional to the Geneva Conventions of 12 August 1949, and relating to the Protection of Victims of International Armed Conflicts, 8 June 1977, Article 85(4)(b) (http://www.legal-tools.org/doc/d9328a/).

[102] Convention (III) Relative to the Treatment of Prisoners of War, 12 August 1949, Article 28 (https://www.legal-tools.org/doc/365095/).

The DRC Mapping Exercise, for instance, stated that as its goal was to identify broad patterns of violations, it did not focus on ICL:[103]

> Unlike some commissions of inquiry with a specific mandate to identify the perpetrators of violations and make them accountable for their actions, the objective of the Mapping Exercise was not to establish or to try to establish individual criminal responsibility of given actors, but rather to expose in a transparent way the seriousness of the violations committed, with the aim of encouraging an approach aimed at breaking the cycle of impunity and contributing to this.

This being said, it should be noted that the definitions of international crimes most certainly take into account the collective nature of their commission, through the contextual elements that need to be proven for the crime to be established. For example, crimes against humanity require the existence of a widespread or systematic attack against a civilian population in furtherance of a state or organisational policy.[104] Equally, war crimes require the existence of an armed conflict[105] and the crime of aggression, the existence of an act of aggression by a state.[106] In relation to genocide, while there is some debate as to the requirement of a plan or policy[107] to commit such a crime, the Rome Statute generally requires "a pattern of similar conduct"[108] and Lemkin, when first describing the crime, truly had the collective dimension in mind of one group attempting to destroy another.[109] However, a strong ICL-focus still has the potential to move wider narratives into the background. Rather than in the interests of creating a broad historical narrative, the detection of patterns of violations is undertaken in order to satisfy the contextual elements of international crimes.

---

[103] Report of the DRC Mapping Exercise, para. 8.

[104] Rome Statute, Articles 7(1) and 7(2)(a).

[105] *Ibid.*, Article 8.

[106] *Ibid.*, Article 8*bis*(2).

[107] See, *e.g.*, Schabas, 2006, p. 1711, *supra* note 3; and Paola Gaeta, "On What Conditions Can a State Be Held Responsible for Genocide?", in *European Journal of International Law*, 2007, vol. 18, no. 4, p. 631.

[108] International Criminal Court, *Elements of Crimes*, 2011, Article 6.

[109] Lemkin wrote that "by its very nature [genocide] is committed by the state or by powerful groups which have the backing of the state": Raphael Lemkin, "Genocide", in *American Scholar*, 1946, vol. 15, no. 2, p. 228.

## 12.4.2. Focus on Individual Accountability

An ICL-focus may also narrow investigations in terms of the actors under examination. Indeed, while there is much discussion today on the possible criminal responsibility of non-state actors such as corporations,[110] the fact remains that only individuals may be found guilty of committing international crimes before international criminal tribunals.[111] As such, an inquiry into the commission of international crimes focusses on the actions of individuals, rather than the responsibility of collective entities. Findings that states or non-state armed groups have violated human rights law or IHL appear to be made in order to substantiate criminal liability through command responsibility, rather than to stimulate international sanction for state responsibility.

An emphasis on violations committed by individual actors could diminish the degree of scrutiny into the wrongful behaviour of other subjects of international law, and on the existing systemic forces and conditions which permit mass atrocities to occur. Nollkaemper writes:[112]

> Criminal law is not capable of capturing the complex mechanisms and relations of organizations which engage in mass crimes. It provides a distorted and fragmentized picture of reality in which the blame rests on a few individuals who, understandably, resent their being sacrificed as scapegoats. State responsibility epitomizes a more holistic approach which recognizes the responsibility of the wider periphery of bystanders who, though not directly involved, create the breeding ground for mass atrocity.

Nielsen similarly writes that ICL:[113]

> [...] fails to account for the structural causes of violence or to look at the role of international institutions or powerful

---

[110] See, *e.g.*, Norman Farrell, "Attributing Criminal Liability to Corporate Actors: Some Lessons from the International Tribunals", in *Journal of International Criminal Justice*, 2010, vol. 8, no. 3, p. 725; Volker Nerlich, "Core Crimes and Transnational Business Corporations", in *Journal of International Criminal Justice*, 2010, vol. 8, no. 3, p. 895; and Michael Kelly, "Prosecuting Corporations for Genocide under International Law", in *Harvard Law and Policy Review*, 2012, vol. 6, no. 2, p. 339.

[111] Rome Statute, Article 25(1); ICTY Statute, Article 6; ICTR Statute, Article 5.

[112] André Nollkaemper, "Systemic Effects of International Responsibility for International Crimes", in *Santa Clara Journal of International Law*, 2010, vol. 8, no. 1, p. 352.

[113] Claire Nielsen, "From Nuremburg to The Hague: The Civilizing Mission of International Criminal Law", in *Auckland University Law Review*, 2008, vol. 14, p. 99.

states in creating the conditions under which mass atrocity
takes place. For example, there is no scope within the system
of international criminal law for the ICTR to examine the colonial roots of the violence and conflict, nor for it to address
the failure of the United Nations and Western states to intervene and prevent the genocide from occurring. Further, its
limited scope does not allow international criminal law to
address the complicity of Western powers, such as France, in
aiding those committing the atrocities. […] The system privileges crimes that are able to be linked back to direct individual action or inaction, conveniently obscuring and avoiding
discussion of the global inequality in which powerful states
are profoundly implicated.

An illustration may be drawn from Kent's evaluation of the Serious
Crimes Process in Timor-Leste as a post-conflict justice mechanism. She
writes that war crimes trials were "restricted in their capacity to delve into
the complex politics and histories that underlie conflicts, including the
role of international actors, institutions, and bystanders" and that "by lo-
cating the origins of atrocity in the acts of the individual accused, trials
were unable to consider broader questions of responsibility"[114] which implicated Indonesia and several Western states. Summarising these arguments, Tallgren remarks:[115]

By focusing on individual responsibility, criminal law reduces the perspective of the phenomenon to make it easier for
the eye. Thereby it reduces the complexity and scale of multiple responsibilities to a mere background. We are not discussing state responsibility, we are discussing criminal law.
We are not really discussing a crime of aggression, we are
busy discussing rape or murder. We are not really discussing
nuclear weapons, we are discussing machete knives used in
Rwanda. We are not much discussing the immense environ-
mental catastrophes caused by wars and the responsibility for
them, we are discussing the compensation to be paid by individual criminal to an individual victims. Thereby the exercise which international criminal law induces is that of mo-
nopolizing violence as a legitimate tool of politics, and pri-

---

[114] Lia Kent, "Interrogating the 'Gap' Between Law and Justice: East Timor's Serious Crimes Process", in *Human Rights Quarterly*, 2012, vol. 34, no. 4, pp. 1033–1034.

[115] Immi Tallgren, "The Sense and Sensibility of International Criminal Law", in *European Journal of International Law*, 2002, vol. 13, p. 594.

vatizing the responsibility and duty to compensate for the damages caused.

While these assessments of the limits of ICL are accurate on principle, it should be pointed out that ICL has developed conceptual tools to cater, to some extent, to the collective nature of international crimes. For example, the Nuremberg Charter provided for the possibility of the Military Tribunal to recognise the criminality of organisations.[116] As a result, the International Military Tribunal ('IMT') declared that a number of state organisations were criminal, such as the SS and the Gestapo.[117] While this possibility was not carried over into future experiences of international criminal justice, it remains an option to be explored in the future, in order to align ICL more closely with the collective nature of international crimes.[118]

Moreover, this collective nature is reflected in the modes of liability of ICL. The ICTY famously championed the concept of 'joint criminal enterprise'[119] and the ICC has adopted a somewhat similar concept of indirect co-perpetration.[120] These forms of liability require that particular collective elements, in terms of organisation or decision-making processes, be established. To a certain extent, the doctrine of superior responsibility[121] has the same effect, by escalating responsibility along the organisational chain, thus going beyond strict individual responsibility, at least in

---

[116] Article 9, London Charter.

[117] *Trial Of The Major War Criminals Before The International Military Tribunal*, vol. XXII, p. 493 (http://www.legal-tools.org/doc/8eba20/).

[118] For such a proposal in relation to aggression, see Dov Jacobs, "The Sheep in the Box: The Definition of the Crime of Aggression at the International Criminal Court", in Christoph Burchard, Otto Triffterer, and Joachim Vogel (eds.), *The Review Conference & The Future Of The ICC: Proceedings Of The First AIDP Symposium For Young Penalists*, Kluwer Law International, 2010, pp. 131–151.

[119] *Prosecutor v. Tadić*, Case No. IT-94-1, Judgment, Appeals Chamber, 15 July 1999, paras. 185–229; Kai Ambos, *Treatise on International Criminal Law*, Volume I, Oxford University Press, Oxford, 2013, pp. 123–127; and Jens Ohlin, "Three Conceptual Problems with the Doctrine of Joint Criminal Enterprise", in *Journal of International Criminal Justice*, 2007, vol. 5 pp. 69–90.

[120] Rome Statute, Article 25(3)(a); *Prosecutor v. Katanga and Chui*, Case No. ICC-01/04-01/07, Decision on the Confirmation of Charges, Pre-Trial Chamber I, 30 September 2008, para. 489 *et seq.* (http://www.legal-tools.org/doc/67a9ec/); Thomas Weigend, "Perpetration through an Organization: The Unexpected Career of a German Legal Concept", in *Journal of International Criminal Justice*, 2011, vol. 9, pp. 91–111.

[121] Rome Statute, Article 28; ICTY Statute, Article 7(3).

---

spirit.[122] However, recognition of the collective nature of international crimes is bounded by the fundamental principle of individual culpability, where individual criminal responsibility is only established – in other words, a crime is committed – where an individual commits a relevant act (*actus reus*) while holding the requisite intention (*mens rea*).[123]

### 12.4.3. Focus on Prosecutorial Responses

As international judicial institutions have evolved, so too have the recommendations generated by commissions. Commissions have recommended an array of measures to prevent future violations, including institutional reform, reparations schemes and capacity building initiatives. Notably, developments in international criminal institutions are mirrored in the recommendations put forward by commissions. Following the establishment of the *ad hoc* tribunals and prior to the entry into force of the Rome Statute, commissions recommended that the UN create further *ad hoc* tribunals to respond to violations.[124] By contrast, commissions established after the entry into force of the Rome Statute, in the knowledge that the establishment of further *ad hoc* tribunals was unlikely, have recommended that the Security Council refer situations to the ICC Prosecutor.[125]

It might be argued that recommendations with an ICL-focus encourage limited resources to be channelled towards ensuring the account-

---

[122] For an extensive discussion of the collective dimensions of ICL, see Darryl Robinson, "A Cosmopolitan Liberal Account of International Criminal Law", in *Journal of International Criminal Justice*, 2013, vol. 26, p. 127.

[123] Limitations in the work of commissions in respect of modes of liability are explored below in section 12.5.

[124] For instance, the Cambodia Commission concluded in 1998 that Khmer Rouge leaders should be prosecuted for international crimes and considered different options for trials. It strongly recommended the establishment of an *ad hoc* international tribunal: Report of the Cambodia Commission, para. 139. In 2000, the Commission of Inquiry for Timor-Leste recommended that the UN establish an international prosecution body to investigate violations, prosecute those responsible and order reparations: Report of the International Commission of Inquiry on East Timor to the Secretary-General, UN Doc. S/2000/59, 31 January 2000, para. 152 (http://www.legal-tools.org/doc/65a1e5/).

[125] Report of the Darfur Commission, para. 647; Report of the Goldstone Commission, para. 1969(c); Report of the Guinea Commission, para. 266. The Syria Commission has refrained from formally recommending referral to the ICC but stated that "the ICC is the appropriate institution for the fight against impunity in Syria": Report of the Syria Commission, UN Doc. A/HRC/22/59, 5 February 2013, p. 127 (https://www.legal-tools.org/doc/802b1c/).

ability of those who committed the most egregious violations.[126] However, international crimes and violations of human rights and IHL do not represent a hierarchy of violations. While the term 'crimes against humanity' requires that human rights violations occur in a widespread or systematic way, this does not mean that human rights violations *per se* are less serious than crimes against humanity. Individuals cannot be held legally responsible for breaching international human rights law, and the same is true in respect of states *vis-à-vis* ICL. These fields therefore give rise to responsibility regimes for different types of actors, and findings of one species of violation or another do not necessarily indicate the seriousness of violations. Insisting on qualifying human rights violations as crimes against humanity may in fact perpetuate the false notion of a hierarchy of violations, as it may be perceived that human rights violations in the absence of findings of crimes against humanity are less serious, when in fact that omission may be due to a methodological decision to focus on state responsibility, rather than that of individuals. To ensure fuller accountability, recommendations should recognise responsibility arising from regimes beyond ICL and propose measures to hold all involved actors to account. This also requires the international community to demand that accountability recommendations directed at other responsible actors are fulfilled, such as through the establishment of reparations schemes.[127]

## 12.5. Conclusion: Sending ICL Back to the Courtroom?

In light of the above, it is difficult to draw an overly optimistic picture of the effects of the import of ICL standards and norms within the work of commissions. While there might be some benefits on the margins in terms

---

[126] See, *e.g.*, Tomuschat who writes that in respect of the Darfur conflict, in addition to victims' rights to the truth and to compensation, "those bearing the greatest responsibility for the tragic course of events must be made accountable" through prosecutions: Christian Tomuschat, "Darfur – Compensation for the Victims", in *Journal of International Criminal Justice*, 2005, vol. 3, p. 581.

[127] For instance, the Commission of Inquiry established pursuant to resolution 885 (1993) concerning Somalia concluded that compensation should be considered for civilians who suffered harm from the actions of UN peacekeepers and suggested that the UN establish a compensation mechanism: UN Doc. S/1994/653, 24 February 1994, paras. 264–265. However, this recommendation was not implemented. A key recommendation of the Darfur Commission was that that a compensation commission should be set up to provide reparations to victims: Report of the Darfur Commission, paras. 590-603. While the Darfur Compensation Commission was established in 2011, little practical progress appears to have been made in processing claims.

of the quality or credibility of commission reports, it appears that adoption of ICL concepts does not necessarily solve problems related to the technical quality of reports, and possibly creates new problems related to the substantial scope of investigations. Ultimately, one can wonder if these findings are not in fact predictable, when one questions two implicit assumptions that underlie the import of ICL in the work of commissions: that ICL actually has an answer to the questions asked, and, more fundamentally, that ICL can be taken out of the courtroom at all.

In relation to the first assumption, it quickly becomes apparent that ICL is seen as a solution because it is draped with virtues that it in fact does not possess, more particularly in relation to technical quality. Indeed, while the procedures adopted in international criminal institutions are arguably more rigorous than those adopted by many human rights fact-finding bodies, they generally do not reach basic domestic criminal law standards. For example, international criminal tribunals have adopted very flexible principles in relation to the admissibility[128] and evaluation of evidence.[129] Moreover, international criminal judgments have not set the bar very high in terms of length and accessibility, nor in terms of quality of argumentation. It is therefore doubtful whether ICL, as it is practiced today, should really be a model for commissions.

In relation to the second assumption, there is a surprising dearth of theoretical discussion on whether ICL can in fact be so easily imported into the context of commissions. However, a certain number of the difficulties raised in this chapter might be linked to the fact that ICL outside the courtroom does not actually make sense. For example, as recalled above, standards of proof in the judicial context have a specific function in the achievement of a particular procedural goal, most notably the determination of the innocence or guilt of a particular individual, with the very concrete effect of incarceration. In other words, in criminal law, standards of proof are intrinsically linked to the protection of the rights of

---

[128] Gideon Boas, "Creating Laws of Evidence for International Criminal Law: The ICTY and the Principle of Flexibility", in *Criminal Law Forum*, 2001, vol. 12, pp. 41–90; Guido Acquaviva, "Written and Oral Evidence", in Linda Carter and Fausto Pocar (eds.), *International Criminal Procedure: The Interface of Civil Law and Common Law Legal Systems*, E. Elgar, 2013, pp. 99–123. Generally, on international rules of evidence, see Sluiter *et al.*, 2013, Chapter 7, *supra* note 65.

[129] Nancy Combs, *Fact-Finding without Facts: The Uncertain Evidentiary Foundations of International Criminal Convictions*, Cambridge University Press, Cambridge, 2010.

the accused, more particularly in respect of the presumption of innocence. The two cannot be separated and, given the nature of commissions, which do not have a judicial function, nor specific legal powers over individuals, the adoption of evidentiary thresholds might not be conceptually sound.

The same holds true of discussions on due process rights. These rights are linked to a judicial process leading to the incarceration of a specific individual and are integrated into a comprehensive procedural framework. This is not the case for commissions, which in essence express more or less persuasive opinions, not binding legal decisions. Individuals cannot therefore be said to have due process rights before commissions. Complaints at being named as a perpetrator of an international crime would not technically be based on a violation of due process rights, but would rather fall within the realm of libel or defamation, just as it would if a newspaper made accusations against someone. Perhaps a more pertinent issue is that due to the privileges and immunities routinely granted to commissioners,[130] named individuals are in practice unable to seek legal recourse.

In relation to the substance of the reports, there are a number of problems with commissions attempting to legally characterise facts as international crimes that arise from taking ICL outside its natural environment. The most obvious one is that technically, only a court can determine that a fact pattern constitutes a crime. It is not because commissions use the language of ICL in terms of standards of evidence that they are imbued with legal authority. Another problem is the more or less systematic ignorance of the *mens rea* dimension of crimes in commissions' reports, especially those which do not focus on particular individuals. This is a misunderstanding of the nature of criminal law, which requires both *actus reus* and *mens rea* for a crime to be constituted. In light of this, it is inaccurate to determine the existence of a crime without entering into an evaluation of the intention of particular individuals. The same fact pattern can constitute, for example, both a crime against humanity and genocide, depending on the intention of the perpetrators. Commissions' reports which

---

[130] Convention on the Privileges and Immunities of the United Nations 1946, Article VI, s. 22 (http://www.legal-tools.org/doc/f68109/).

ignore that dimension[131] are misrepresenting ICL, while pretending to apply it.

Ultimately, however, all these considerations might not in fact be relevant at all. As already mentioned in the introduction, ICL is not so much imported as a body of law to be applied, but rather as a legitimisation tool, to increase credibility of reports, and as a meta-narrative of conflict situations. In this sense, one can wonder if legal critiques of the practice of commissions are not ancillary to the questions of whether ICL in fact enhances the credibility of commissions' reports and whether ICL works adequately as a narrative framework. While it is beyond the scope of this contribution to address these questions in detail, two final thoughts can be submitted.

In relation to credibility, while the use of ICL vocabulary might have a superficial impact on whether commissions are taken seriously, it will not have any lasting impact on the quality of reports if more care is not taken in addressing the core problem, common to many international institutions: the competence of those conducting the investigations and drafting reports. The credibility of reports does not depend on the adoption of such and such standard of evidence, or characterising a fact pattern as a crime against humanity rather than a mass atrocity. It depends on the credentials and competence of the staff of those commissions.[132]

In relation to the narrative quality of ICL, we have shown previously that the narratives proposed in that context are possibly too narrow as an explanatory tool of complex situations. While the narrow focus of ICL makes sense inside the courtroom, where the key inquiry is into the criminal responsibility of a particular individual, commissions do not have the same end goal. Importing an ICL narrative into commissions' reports leads to the result that rather than being a useful complementary tool to prosecutions by providing other narratives of conflicts, commissions are duplicating, less rigorously, the work of international tribunals, thus raising the question of their usefulness. Ironically, while commissions may seek to gain credibility by using an ICL framework, international criminal tribunals attempt to gain more legitimacy by trying to expand their func-

---

[131] See, for example, the definition of crimes against humanity in the Goldstone Report, which refers to the *actus reus* only (Report of the Goldstone Commission, para. 293) and its finding that crimes against humanity may have been committed without any reference to the *mens rea* of particular individuals (Report of the Goldstone Commission, para. 1335).

[132] On this, see also Chapter 8 above.

tions above and beyond the core application of criminal law norms. Indeed, over the years, ICL has been assigned many lofty goals such as recognition of harms committed against victims, promotion of human rights and respect for the rule of law, and fostering reconciliation.[133] Ultimately, however, its key task is to determine whether an accused is individually criminally responsible,[134] and some commentators consider that it is unrealistic to expect ICL to fulfil multiple conflicting goals.[135] A commission which seeks to ensure accountability by relying on an ICL framework may be faced with similar limitations.

This therefore seems to be a case of the grass always being greener on the other side of the fence: commissions searching for greater recognition through the adoption of an ICL narrative and international criminal tribunals seeking to position themselves within a human rights narrative. Ultimately, one can wonder if, rather than being Trojan horses of difficulties for each other, commissions should not refocus on their core function of determining facts, while ICL should be put back where it belongs, in the courtroom.

---

[133] Kent, 2012, p. 1022, *supra* note 114. The Rome Statute Preamble provides that States Parties are "determined to put an end to impunity for the perpetrators of these crimes and thus to contribute to the prevention of such crimes". The Human Rights Council Resolution 'Human rights and transitional justice' recognised the role of the ICC in a "multilateral system that aims to end impunity, establish the rule of law, promote and encourage respect for human rights and [IHL] and achieve sustainable peace": HRC Res 21/15, UN Doc. A/HRC/RES/21/15, 11 October 2012 (http://www.legal-tools.org/doc/f2c7f0/).

[134] International criminal law is "a body of international rules designed both to proscribe certain categories of conduct [...] and to make those persons who engage in such conduct criminally liable": Antonio Cassese, *International Criminal Law*, Oxford University Press, 2013, p. 3.

[135] See, *e.g.*, Damaška who writes that international criminal law has set itself too many goals which are in tension with one another and could damage perceptions of its legitimacy: "no single goal can be found around which other objectives can be rigorously organized. There is no trellis, so to speak, to support the ivy of the courts' aspirations" and that "when pruned of presently unrealistic aspirations, these institutions are likely to grow more vigorously in the future": Mirjan Damaska, "What is the Point of International Criminal Justice?", in *Chicago-Kent Law Review*, 2008, vol. 83, no. 1, pp. 330 and 365.

# 13

---

# Can International Criminal Investigators and Prosecutors Afford to Ignore Information from United Nations Human Rights Sources?

## Lyal S. Sunga[*]

## 13.1. Introduction

If and when criminal investigators show up in the aftermath of violent conflict to investigate genocide, war crimes or crimes against humanity, they can suffer sensory overload and emotional shock from the horrific scenes that confront them, an experience for which they might be quite unprepared. At the same time, from chaotic scenes of blood, broken bodies, busted buildings and shredded lives, they have to figure out the big picture quickly. Unless they acquire balanced and broad perspective on what transpired, international criminal investigators will be unable to identify planners, organisers and direct perpetrators of crimes that far exceed the ordinary in terms of intensity, scale and gravity. Nor will they be able to situate individual suspects in the relevant command structure and to connect that relationship to the crime. As the clock starts ticking and the international community, including victims, clamour for justice, prosecutors have to piece together the historical, political, social and military

[*] **Lyal S. Sunga** is Visiting Professor at the Raoul Wallenberg Institute of Human Rights and Humanitarian Law, Lund University, Sweden. He was Human Rights Officer at the UN High Commissioner for Human Rights ('OHCHR') from 1994 to 2001. In 1994, he was responsible for assisting the UN Security Council's Commission of Experts on Rwanda to investigate facts and responsibilities relating to the genocide and associated violations perpetrated during Rwanda's Civil War and for drafting the Preliminary and Final Reports for the Commission recommending the establishment of the ICTR. He then became backstopping officer in Geneva to establish and maintain the UN Human Rights Field Operation in Rwanda for several years, before becoming Coordinator *ad interim* for the Asia-Pacific team in the Special Procedures Branch and, *inter alia*, OHCHR's Observer to the Preparatory Commission meetings in New York and the 1998 Rome Diplomatic Conference of Plenipotentiaries for the Establishment of a Permanent International Criminal Court. From September to December 2007, Dr. Sunga rejoined OHCHR's Special Procedures Branch as Coordinator of the UN Human Rights Council's Group of Experts on Darfur, and has acted as served OHCHR as expert consultant on national human rights institutions.

context in which the alleged crimes were perpetrated: by whom, against whom, when, where, why and how. Since facts in themselves mean little without context, prosecutors have to make their case as coherently and compellingly as possible, particularly since international criminal court and tribunal judges are not interested in vague charges, poorly substantiated allegations or weak evidence.

Yet even the Prosecutor of the International Criminal Court ('ICC') – the world's pre-eminent symbol of international criminal justice – has nowhere near enough resources to become expert in situations from Colombia to Côte d'Ivoire, Syria to Sudan, Mali to Kenya to Uganda to whichever other Rome Statute crime scenario crops up. International crimes are highly complex, often involving nuanced or normatively convoluted violations of human rights or humanitarian law in terms of the way they are defined and the circumstances surrounding their perpetration. Practically speaking, criminal investigators and prosecutors, whether from the ICC, international criminal tribunals, and even at domestic levels, have little choice but to draw upon the great wealth of information on human rights violations routinely collected by international, regional and sub-regional organisations, the strictly neutral ICRC, Governments, and human rights NGOs. Not only do these bodies carry out competent, regular and balanced human rights monitoring the world over and have been doing so for decades, but they often have extensive knowledge of the local situation, and have the capacity to identify and locate witnesses, victims and survivors, and in some instances, suspected perpetrators, even before the ICC could start planning its initial field mission to the crime scene.

At the same time, information on human rights situations may be as biased, politically slanted, vague, partial and prejudicial as its source. Controls on the collection, authentication, storage and analysis of information designed to ensure criminal prosecutions are accurate, fair and effective, do not apply in the realm of human rights investigation, monitoring and reporting. Investigative procedures for human rights violations differ from those for international criminal prosecutions and the dissimilarities between their respective purposes, formats and probative value, seem wide and even unbridgeable in particular instances. Further complicating the challenge for international criminal investigators and prosecutors is that many different kinds of actors collect, analyse and report on human rights matters including intergovernmental organisations, Governments, the ICRC, NGOs, journalists, academics, and research institutes. This bewildering array of sources feeds information into UN human rights reports.

For the international criminal investigator and prosecutor, many of whom may have had little or no international experience and have been drawn from domestic criminal practice to serve the ICTY, ICTR, ICC, Special Court for Sierra Leone, Special Court for Lebanon, Extraordinary Chamber in the Courts of Cambodia or other international, hybrid or mixed venue, UN human rights information might be somewhat mystifying because of the following paradoxes. On the one hand, UN human rights reports do not resemble evidence gathered in the course of ordinary criminal investigations, but on the other hand, such reports could contain information on mass violations or the events leading up to such violations that might assist the Prosecutor to prepare his or her case, not least because the crimes themselves are defined also as violations of international human rights law or grave breaches of humanitarian law. On the one hand, the UN is a political organisation that was set up by Governments, each of which has its own political agenda, yet on the other hand, UN reports are often cited as relatively independent and objective. On the one hand, UN human rights fact-finding bodies do not have a mandate to indict individuals or produce evidence for an eventual criminal trial, yet on the other hand, several UN human rights fact-finding bodies have been requested to identify violations including crimes under international law and to compile lists of the names of possible perpetrators for submission to the UN Secretary-General and the High Commissioner for Human Rights, as discussed below. On the one hand, UN human rights fact-finding exercises have frequently led the way for the establishment of international criminal tribunals themselves, such as the ICTY and ICTR, but those same tribunals then have often treated information from UN human rights sources with great scepticism, or dismissed it altogether as discussed in Chapter 11 above, perhaps because its value and potential role is not fully appreciated.

It is therefore worth considering first the information needs relating to international criminal prosecutions; second, whether UN human rights information in general can be trusted; third, the relationship between the UN and intelligence gathering; fourth, the pre-eminence of Government information gathering capacity; fifth, the value of information from UN human rights sources including the treaty bodies, special procedures and the Universal Periodic Review ('UPR'); sixth, whether information from UN human rights sources could be admitted as direct evidence in international criminal proceedings and whether rules against hearsay exclude UN human rights reports; and finally, whether international criminal investigators and prosecutors can afford to ignore information from UN human rights sources.

## 13.2. What Kinds of Information Do International Criminal Prosecutions Need?

Very few, if any, situations that deteriorate to the point of genocide, war crimes or crimes against humanity, blow up overnight. Serious human rights and humanitarian law violations amounting to crimes under international law are almost always preceded by an accelerando of violations of lesser intensity, gravity and scale. It follows that understanding patterns and developments of precursor violations can shed light on the context in which genocide, war crimes or crimes against humanity have been perpetrated, or are about to be perpetrated. Consider Hitler's Final Solution to the Jewish Question – the Nazis' euphemism for the attempted annihilation of all Jews in Europe. Before it was fully implemented in 1942,[1] hundreds of thousands of Jews, Roma, Sinti and others, had already been massacred, and these massacres were themselves preceded by years of persecution and violations of lesser gravity that were launched by the Nazi regime once Hitler was appointed Chancellor of Germany on 30 January 1933 and they had been ramped up over many years.[2] Mass violations, such as those committed from 1966 to 1996 in Guatemala, during the 1971 Bangladesh War of Liberation, Burundi in 1972 and 1993, Equatorial Guinea (1968–1979), Argentina's Dirty War (1976–1983) , the Cambodian Civil War (1976–1979) , the 1994 Rwandan Civil War, the Yugoslav Wars (1991–1999), the Darfur Conflict (2003–present), the various armed conflicts in the Democratic Republic of the Congo (including the first and second Congo wars, the Ituri and Kivu conflicts and the still ongoing M23 Rebellion), and the Sri Lanka Civil War (1983–1999), to mention only a

---

[1] See the Minutes of the Wannsee Conference, held in Berlin, am Grossen Wannsee, No. 56/58 on 20 January 1942 concerning the Final Solution of the Jewish Question, translation in English in John Mendelsohn, 11 The Holocaust: selected documents in eighteen volumes (1982) at 18–32.

[2] See, for example, Robert A. Michael, *The Holocaust: A Chronology and Documentary*, 1998.

few, seem all to have been perpetrated in the context of protracted armed
conflict and severe political instability that sometimes took many years to
get to the point of open, large-scale violence. Many of them were exacerbated by deep ethnic or religious hatred that lasted for many generations.
By the time violations reach the gravity of genocide, war crimes or crimes
against humanity, patterns of human rights violations, at least viewed in
retrospect, indicate the pathways that led to such intense violence. Situat-
ing individual criminal suspects in these pathways and relating them to
the *actus reus* and *mens rea* in crimes of genocide, war crimes and crimes
against humanity could therefore be essential for international criminal
investigators and prosecutors to develop their case.

## 13.3. Understanding the Constitutional, Legal and Political System

International criminal prosecutors also have to understand thoroughly the
structure, function and operation of the legal system of countries where
genocide, war crimes or crimes against humanity are alleged. In the situations of Nazi Germany, the period leading up to the 1994 Rwandan Civil
War, and in Darfur, Sudan, the legal system itself, in one way or another,
functioned as an instrument of discrimination, oppression and persecution.
Examination of the constitutional framework could itself provide clear
evidence of the differences in power among national, ethnic, racial or religious groups. Charting how constitutional arrangements came into being
and the configuration of the role of the courts, legislative system, Executive, and the presence or absence of checks and balances, offers a blue-
print of the distribution of legal and political power in a given country.
Lack of civilian control over the military, non-functioning alternatives to
Executive power, and frequent changes in constitutional arrangements
could flag political under-representation, disenfranchisement of certain
groups, and root causes of deep dissatisfaction, persistent unrest, and politically motivated violence. Equally, a lack of accessible legal avenues to
redress human rights grievances, such as through national human rights
commissions, ombudsmen, anti-corruption commissions, commissions on
the human rights of women, and weak minority rights protection, could
help show the details of a governmental structure that operated on a more
authoritarian than democratic basis, which in turn could help explain cata-
lytic factors leading to genocide, war crimes or crimes against humanity.

Laws stigmatising certain groups or enforcing systematic discrimination against them could lend weight to a prosecutor's assertion that one or other group had long been targeted by the country's government or singled out for marginalisation or relegation to inferior status within society. Genocide, war crimes or crimes against humanity can be perpetrated as an extension of long practiced discriminatory government policy, as exemplified in Nazi Germany, Rwanda and Darfur, and arguably in Sri Lanka and East Timor.

Examining the administration of criminal justice in a country implicated in genocide, war crimes or crimes against humanity is important also because according to the Rome Statute, the ICC should only assert jurisdiction over a situation where the concerned country authorities themselves will not or cannot prosecute Rome Statute crimes. Documenting established patterns of governmental discrimination of certain groups and the politicisation of the justice system therefore becomes a crucial point because of the complementary nature of ICC jurisdiction. A related area for fruitful investigation could be electoral laws which might exclude members of certain national, ethnic, racial or religious groups from voting in or standing for election. Laws relating to elections and political representation might diminish or exclude certain constituencies altogether, which could form part of the historical, political and legal puzzle leading up to serious crimes. Laws, policies and practices relating to the treatment of women, children and sexual minorities could also shed light on existing patterns of persecution and discrimination, which might help explain why and how certain crimes were actually committed.

## 13.4. Meeting Evidentiary Requirements

In terms of evidentiary requirements, the Prosecutor must prove the guilt of the accused beyond a reasonable doubt. At the same time, the basic fair trial principle of the presumption of innocence prevents the Prosecutor's burden of proof from ever being shifted to the accused instead to prove his or her innocence. This principle, perhaps clear enough in the abstract, can be fraught with difficulty in its application. In the *Zigiranyirazo Case* for example, the ICTR Appeal Chamber strongly criticised the Trial Chamber for the way it treated alibi evidence which had been adduced to show that the accused could not possibly have committed the crime because he was not physically present at the crime scene at the material time[3]; as well as the Prosecutor for adding charges as the trial proceeded, including one that had no foundation in the applicable law.

The evidentiary requirements for establishing criminal guilt depend on several factors, first and foremost on the definition and elements of the particular alleged crime. To prove the crime of genocide for example, as set out in Article 6 of the Rome Statute[4] (found also in Articles 4 and 2 of the Statutes for the International Criminal Tribunals for the former Yugoslavia and Rwanda, respectively), the prosecution has to prove that the *actus reus* was perpetrated with the specific intent "to destroy, in whole or in part, a national, ethnical, racial, or religious group" – a quite high evidentiary burden. To take another example, establishing that a crime against humanity was committed[5] requires the prosecution to prove that it was "committed as part of a widespread or systematic attack directed against any civilian population, with knowledge of the attack". Article 7(2)(a) of the Rome Statute provides that: "Attack against any civilian population" means a course of conduct involving the multiple commission of acts referred to or against any civilian population, pursuant to or in furtherance of a State or organizational policy to commit such attack", which the Prosecutor has to prove. For war crimes, the Prosecutor first has to prove that there was a situation of armed conflict within the sense of the

---

3   The ICTR Appeal Chamber in the *Zigiranyirazo Case* faulted the Trial Chamber for requiring the defense to prove its alibi to a high level of certainty rather than merely to have to raise a reasonable doubt, which in effect shifted the burden of proof to the accused to prove his innocence. The ICTR Appeal Chamber ruled that: "An accused does not bear the burden of proving his alibi beyond reasonable doubt". Rather, "[h]e must simply produce the evidence tending to show that he was not present at the time of the alleged crime" or, otherwise stated, he must present evidence "likely to raise a reasonable doubt in the Prosecution case". If the alibi is reasonably possibly true, it must be accepted". See Judgement, *Zigiranyirazo v. Prosecutor*, Case No. ICTR-01-73-A, Appeal Chamber, 16 November 2009, para. 17 (http://www.legal-tools.org/doc/8c455f/). See further Lyal S. Sunga, "Commentary on Judgement of the ICTR Case of *The Prosecutor v. Zigiranyirazo*", in *Annotated Leading Cases of International Criminal Tribunals*, 2011, vol. 32, pp. 240–258.

4   Statute of the International Criminal Court, adopted on 17 July 1998, entered into force on 1 July 2002 (A/CONF. 183/9) (https://www.legal-tools.org/doc/9c9fd2/).

5   Article 7(1) of the Rome Statute defines a 'crime against humanity' to encompass one or more of the following: "murder, extermination, enslavement, deportation or forcible transfer of population, imprisonment or other severe deprivation of physical liberty in violation of fundamental rules of international law, torture, rape, sexual slavery, enforced prostitution, forced pregnancy, enforced sterilization, or any other form of sexual violence of comparable gravity, persecution, enforced disappearances, apartheid, and other inhumane acts of a similar character intentionally causing great suffering, or serious injury to body or to mental or physical health".

four Geneva Conventions of 12 August 1949.[6] Moreover, Article 8(1) of the Rome Statute establishes threshold criteria limiting the ICC's exercise of jurisdiction to war crimes only where they were "committed as part of a plan or policy or as part of a large-scale commission of such crimes".

Not only does the evidence have to satisfy the definition and threshold requirements of the crimes alleged, but those of basic admissibility rules as well, including that it must tend to prove or disprove a fact material to the allegation, be authentic rather than false, and brought from a reliable and credible source to court along an unbroken chain of custody to avoid contamination, tampering or fabrication. Moreover, even testimony that originates from a reliable and credible source, and is true, relevant and probative, could still be excluded on grounds that its introduction into evidence would be so overwhelmingly prejudicial to the accused's right to be presumed innocent, that its admission would preclude a fair trial.

The Rome Statute expresses these conditions in a broad way. Article 69 on evidence requires each witness to give an undertaking as to the truthfulness of the evidence, provide testimony in person except where special measures are necessary to protect victims and witnesses pursuant to Article 68 or in relation to the Rules of Procedure and Evidence, or by recorded oral, video or audio means, and through documents or written transcripts as long as such evidence conforms to the Statute and its Rules of Procedure and Evidence and do not prejudice or infringe the rights of the accused. Significantly, Article 69(3) confers upon the ICC "the authority to request the submission of all evidence that it considers necessary for the determination of the truth", favouring a more inclusive approach to the admissibility of evidence. Article 69(4) empowers the Court to exclude evidence on grounds that it would prevent a fair trial or fair evaluation of witness testimony. Articles 69(5) and (6) oblige the Court to respect confidentiality privileges and not to require proof of facts of common knowledge and that the Court should take judicial notice of them instead. Crucially, Article 69(7) states that evidence shall not be admissible wherever it has been obtained in violation of the Rome Statute or "internationally recognized human rights", in particular, where "the violation casts

---

[6]   In *Tadić*, the ICTY Appeal Chamber held that: "an armed conflict exists whenever there is a resort to armed force between States". See *The Prosecutor v. Duško Tadić*, Decision on the Defence Motion for Interlocutory Appeal on Jurisdiction, IT-94-1-A, 2 October 1995, para. 70 (http://www.legal-tools.org/doc/866e17/).

substantial doubt on the reliability of the evidence", or for whatever reason the "admission of the evidence would be antithetical to and would
seriously damage the integrity of the proceedings". Finally, the ICC provides that: "When deciding on the relevance or admissibility of evidence
collected by a State, the Court shall not rule on the application of the
State's national law", thereby preventing the ICC from mixing up and
confusing international with domestic application of law.

In addition to the commonly accepted restrictions on admissibility
of evidence found in Article 69 of the Rome Statute and its Rules of Procedure and Evidence, several practical aspects of information collection
make the Prosecutor's responsibility to prove genocide, war crimes or
crimes against humanity a particularly difficult one. First, Governments
often are sources of information on human rights, but in many instances,
they refuse or limit their own co-operation with international criminal investigators, especially where individuals at higher echelons of power
seem implicated in the crimes, for example, in the ICC's indictment of the
President of the Sudan, Omar al Bashir.[7] In other cases, a rebel movement
succeeds in taking over the Government and has every interest to prosecute individuals from the previous regime. This has been the case in Libya
following the ouster of Colonel Muammar Qadhafi who, after ruling Libya for almost 42 years, was captured and killed on 20 October 2011 by
rebel forces in Sirte.[8] At the time of writing, it seemed doubtful that
Qadhafi's son, Saif Al-Islam who acted as Libyan *de facto* Prime Minister
and whom the ICC indicted on two counts of crimes against humanity,
would be fairly tried by the Libyan courts, but the Libyan Government
had still refused to transfer the suspect from Libyan to ICC jurisdiction,[9]
and at one point, even detained ICC counsel for the defense in Libya.[10]

---

[7] See Second Warrant of Arrest for Omar Hassan Ahmad Al Bashir, Situation in Darfur,
Sudan, in the case of *The Prosecutor v. Omar Hassan Ahmad Al Bashir ('Omar Al Bashir')*,
issued by Pre-Trial Chamber I; ICC-02/05-01/09 of 12 July 2010 (http://www.legal-tools.
org/doc/307664/).

[8] See "Muammar Gaddafi killed as Sirte falls: Former Libyan leader dies as last bastion
falls, but questions remain about the circumstances of his death", *Al Jazeera*, 20 October
2011.

[9] See ICC Appeals Chamber rejects the Libyan authorities' request to suspend the surrender
of Saif Al-Islam Gaddafi to the Court: ICC Press Release; ICC-CPI-20130718-PR934 of
18 July 2013.

[10] See Julian Borger, "ICC lawyer: Saif al-Islam Gaddafi will not get a fair trial in Libya:
Melinda Taylor says her detention in Libya was unjustified and showed her client would
not be tried impartially in the country", *The Guardian*, 6 July 2012.

Second, criminal investigators seconded by Governments to work with international courts and tribunals may be quite adept at collecting evidence at home, but they might be quite inexperienced working in conditions such as those present in affected regions of Uganda, the Democratic Republic of the Congo, Darfur (Sudan), Central African Republic, Kenya, Libya, Côte d'Ivoire or Mali, where the ICC was trying to conduct investigations at the time of writing. Disrupted infrastructure, weak information and transportation links and lack of physical security in some of these countries pose special obstacles in the way of efficient criminal investigation of mass scale crimes. Third, in many instances, the ICC might not be in a position to protect victims and witnesses, which could leave them exposed to retaliation, reprisal and bribery from alleged perpetrators. ICC Prosecutor Fatou Bensouda stated that this kind of scenario was behind her dropping of the indictment against Mr. Francis Muthaura, who was supposed to stand trial in July 2013 alongside Mr. Uhuru Kenyatta:[11]

> I explained to the Judges the reasons for my decision, specifically, the severe challenges my Office has faced in our investigation of Mr. Muthaura;
>
> - the fact that several people who may have provided important evidence regarding Mr Muthaura's actions, have died, while others are too afraid to testify for the Prosecution.
>
> - the disappointing fact that the Government of Kenya failed to provide my Office with important evidence, and failed to facilitate our access to critical witnesses who may have shed light on the Muthaura case.
>
> - the fact that we have decided to drop the key witness against Mr. Muthaura after this witness recanted a crucial part of his evidence, and admitted to us that he had accepted bribes.[12]

Efforts to gather information and evidence *in situ* to prosecute genocide, war crimes or crimes against humanity have to be carried out often in the aftermath of armed conflict or serious social upheaval. These al-

---

[11] See Situation in the Republic of Kenya in the Case of *The Prosecutor v. Francis Kirimi Muthaura, Uhuru Muigai Kenyatta and Mohammed Hussein Ali*; ICC-01/09-02/11-382-Red of 23 January 2012.

[12] See "Statement by ICC Prosecutor on the Notice to withdraw charges against Mr. Muthaura Statement", 11 March 2013.

ready difficult conditions, worsened by the non-cooperation of the territorial Government or authority, or even outright aggressive efforts to hinder
investigations, combined with weak investigative capacity on the part of
international criminal courts and tribunals, forces the Prosecutor to rely
upon other sources, the merits and demerits of which are discussed next.

To be more precise, in many situations, the challenge is not a lack
of information or evidence *per se*. Mass scale violations typically involve
a large number of perpetrators, victims and witnesses, and are therefore
'fact-rich'.[13] The challenge is getting hold of the right information and
evidence that will prove the connections between a specific criminal suspect, a particular victim or victims, and the position of that individual
suspect in a command structure, or a *de facto* hierarchy, as well as his or
her criminal intent and its direct relation to the *actus reus*. International
criminal courts and tribunals must obtain as much first-hand information
and eyewitness testimony as possible. Particularly where criminal investigators cannot get sufficient access to the territory in order to conduct interviews, collect physical and documentary evidence, and examine massacre sites or other *loci delicti*, official UN human rights reports could
prove valuable, perhaps indispensable information to allow the Prosecutor
to figure out the main players, historical, cultural and ethnic context, the
proximate events that led to the commission of the crimes, and the relationship between perpetrator and victim.

The central issue has always been about what information can be
trusted. Sorting out reliable from less reliable information requires background checking, getting as wide a picture as possible, corroboration from
differing and hopefully opposing sources (in terms of political affiliation,
ethnic, cultural, religious, ideological, social or other aspect), as well as
multiple accounts so that what is known is clear and even more important,
what is not known, ambiguous or unclear, is identified and marked as
such.

## 13.5. Can UN Human Rights Information be Trusted?

Before discussing the specifics of UN human rights information, and their
possible uses, it is important not to bypass a more general but critical issue: can UN human rights reports really be *trusted* for the purposes of in-

---

[13] See further Christian Ranheim, "Introducing Modern Technology in the Search for War
Criminals", in *Web Journal of Current Legal Issues*, vol. 1, 2009.

ternational criminal prosecutions of genocide, war crimes and crimes against humanity? After all, as the world's pre-eminent intergovernmental organisation, the UN was set up, and is funded and supported by Governments, each one of which has its own set of political agendas. Key UN organs dealing with human rights issues, including the Security Council, General Assembly, and Human Rights Council, whose memberships are made up of States, are explicitly political in terms of agenda, focus and operation. Is the information these organs gather, receive and analyse irremediably tainted so that it becomes too political, too biased, too subjective and too unreliable to meet the demands of fair and effective international criminal justice?

The UN, and indeed the League of Nations that preceded it, have long track records in producing high quality analytical reports on the full range of human rights issues around the globe. The UN Office of the High Commissioner for Human Rights ('OHCHR'),[14] by December 2012, had 573 professional staff responsible for servicing the UN human rights system.[15] A cursory look at the OHCHR website turns up thousands of detailed UN, intergovernmental, Government and NGO reports on any country according to any one of dozens of themes and topics. Despite its faults, and its explicitly intergovernmental and political character, the UN is widely viewed as more independent and objective in human rights and humanitarian assistance fields because its priorities and actions represent the concerns of the international community as a whole, rather than only of one or few governments, even if some governments exercise considerably more influence than others. Significantly, public opinion in many countries holds that the UN should be strengthened, including its peacekeeping powers and capacity to prevent genocide.[16]

---

[14] OHCHR claimed 2.8% (amounting to USD 142,743,800) of the UN regular biennial budget in 2010–2011, and that amount constituted one-third of OHCHR's funding, which was further supplemented by voluntary and project funding. See OHCHR, "OHCHR's Funding and Budget" (available on its web site).

[15] See Composition of the staff of the Office of the United Nations High Commissioner for Human Rights, Report of the United Nations High Commissioner for Human Rights, A/HRC/22/69 of 25 January 2013.

[16] See "World Publics Favor New Powers for the UN, Most Support Standing UN Peacekeeping Force, UN Regulation of International Arms Trade, Majorities Say UN Should Have Right to Authorize Military Force to Stop Terrorism, Nuclear Proliferation, Genocide", Report of the Chicago Council on Global Affairs, 2007.

The UN's explicitly intergovernmental and political character counts as both strength and weakness in terms of the reliability of the information it collects and analyses, including on genocide, war crimes and crimes against humanity. To understand why and how, it is important to recall the UN's relationship to intelligence gathering and then to explore the relevance of information coming from UN human rights mechanisms for investigation, monitoring and reporting.

## 13.6. The UN and Intelligence

In criminal investigations, secrecy in information gathering for evidentiary purposes is standard operating procedure. Sources, information gathering techniques and investigation targets have to be kept confidential to avoid compromising the effectiveness and integrity, as well as the safety and security, of the Prosecution effort. This contrasts starkly with UN human rights fact-finding, mainly because of the peculiar status of intelligence gathering *vis-à-vis* the UN.

The UN itself does not have *intelligence* gathering capacity in the sense of covert information gathering, nor has it ever been nor will it ever likely function as an intelligence gathering body in future, unless member States so wish. The simple reason is that, until the present, no Government has shown any particular enthusiasm for conferring upon a supranational organisation beyond its own control the authority to collect information that could eventually challenge the State's exercise of its sovereign power in unpredictable ways. A very narrow exception operates to the extent that the UN has been requested by its member States to assist them to improve multilateral co-operation with regard to specific transnational crimes, but even here, the emphasis is squarely on intelligence co-operation between and among States, rather than with the UN itself. With regard to human trafficking for example the UN Office of Drugs and Crime ('UNODC') acknowledges that:

> Intelligence gathering and exchange between relevant authorities of States parties is crucial to the success of measures to attack transnational criminal networks.

The UNODC Toolkit on Intelligence Gathering and Exchange explains the difference between strategic and tactical intelligence and delves into the relationship between the two, but it carefully restricts its focus to open sources of information and mutual State co-operation in criminal matters and police enforcement.[17]

Contrary to the paranoiac gibberish spouted by some conspiracy theorists,[18] the UN has always been easy prey, rather than predator, right from the time of its establishment, in terms of intelligence collection, as Simon Chesterman has pointed out:

> During the 1945 conference in San Francisco that drafted the UN Charter, the US Army's Signal Security Agency, the precursor of the NSA [National Security Agency],[19] was obtaining intercepts on at least 43 of the original 45 nations in attendance.[20]

Spying on the UN is old news, and during the Cold War, many countries seemed to treat the UN offices in New York, Geneva and Vienna as their covert operations playgrounds. Since the Berlin Wall fell, rather than disappearing, the antics have become more high-tech.

In 2004, a UN spokeswoman indicated that the UN Headquarters in Geneva had been bugged, which was reported first by Television Suisse

---

[17] The UNODC Toolkit observes that tactical intelligence forms the basis for concrete criminal investigations that could lead enforcement agencies to intercept smuggling operations and it is therefore essential in the preparation and planning of such operation. It helps to identify specific opportunities to detect, disrupt and prevent further criminal activity. Strategic intelligence, on the other hand, produces accurate assessments of the nature and scale of smuggling at all levels, facilitates legislative amendment, international co-operation linkages, and strategies for education, awareness-raising and prevention, aids policymakers, and shares information with the media and the general public. Thus, the "overall picture of smuggling of migrants is formed by strategic intelligence, which is fed by tactical intelligence". UNODC, Toolkit to Combat: Smuggling of Migrants – Tool 1: Understanding the smuggling of migrants, United Nations Office of Drugs and Crime, 2010 at Chapter 7.15.

[18] See, for example, Michael Benson, *The United Nations Conspiracy to Destroy America*, 2010; and Pedro A. Sanjuan, *The UN Gang: A Memoir of Incompetence, Corruption, Espionage, Anti-Semitism, and Islamic Extremism at the UN Secretariat*, 2005; and Robert W. Lee, *The United Nations Conspiracy*, 1981. These days, there are plenty of bloggers, radio talk show hosts and journalists in many countries who spout incendiary diatribes against the United Nations Organization, as a cursory internet check will confirm.

[19] Author's note.

[20] See Simon Chesterman, "Does the UN Have Intelligence?", in *Survival*, 2006, vol. 48, no. 3, pp. 149–164. See also Ian Davis and David Isenberg, "The long history of UN espionage: Spying at the United Nations helped to shape the UN Charter itself. But if spying is an inevitable part of global diplomacy, it won't necessarily help the Bush administration to win friends and influence people at a time of global crisis", *The Observer*, 9 March 2003.

---

Romande.[21] Embarrassing for the United Kingdom's Prime Minister Tony
Blair, was the revelation by his cabinet minister, Ms. Clare Short, that the
confidential conversations of UN Secretary-General Kofi Annan in the
period leading up to the Iraq War were listened to by British spies and that
she had personally read the transcripts of these conversations.[22] In 2010,
The Guardian reported that the leaked Wikileaks cables included a di-
rective from Secretary of State Hillary Clinton, that was sent to United
States missions at the UN in New York, Vienna and Rome as well as 33
embassies and consulates, "demanding forensic technical details about the
communications systems used by top UN officials, including passwords
and personal encryption keys used in private and commercial networks for
official communications". The cable:

> [...] called for detailed biometric information 'on key UN of-
> ficials, to include undersecretaries, heads of specialised
> agencies and their chief advisers, top SYG [secretary general]
> aides, heads of peace operations and political field missions,
> including force commanders' as well as intelligence on Ban's
> 'management and decision-making style and his influence on
> the secretariat'.[23]

This US intelligence gathering programme involved the co-
ordinated efforts of the "CIA's clandestine service, the US Secret Service
and the FBI".[24]

Leaps in electronic surveillance capabilities enable Governments to
conduct, filter and analyse content and communications patterns of massive volumes of e-mail, Skype and internet traffic of millions of people
very efficiently and with scant judicial oversight. Edward Snowden, former NSA and CIA information specialist turned whistle-blower, stunned
the world by revealing to *The Guardian* and *Washington Post* detailed accounts of the extent of US Government electronic surveillance of the daily
internet use of millions of ordinary Americans, as well as people abroad,

---

21  See "Bugging device found in UN room: The United Nations says it has found a bugging
    device in a room at its European offices in Geneva", *BBC News*, 17 December 2004.

22  See "UK 'spied on UN's Kofi Annan' British spies listened in to UN Secretary General
    Kofi Annan's office in the run up to the Iraq war, former UK cabinet minister Clare Short
    says", *BBC News*, 26 February 2004.

23  See Robert Booth and Julian Borger, "US diplomats spied on UN leadership", *The Guard-
    ian*, 28 November 2010.

24  *Ibid.*

---

including even the political leaders of its closest European allies leading up to, during and following major summits.[25]

In short, the UN has no intelligence gathering capacity of its own in the sense of clandestine operations and this implies at least three things. First, the UN must resort to collecting public information as well as information provided to it freely on an *ad hoc* basis by Governments, intergovernmental organisations, the ICRC, NGOs, individuals and other entities, relating to genocide, war crimes or crimes against humanity. Second, the UN can draw upon information it receives on a regular and systematic basis through UN human rights treaty bodies, UN Human Rights Council special procedures and the Universal Periodic Review, which are discussed below. Third, UN criminal investigative work, which from time-to-time requires information secretly acquired, or more precisely, information the sources and content of which must be kept confidential, takes us back to Government willingness to share the fruits of their prodigious intelligence gathering machines. Not addressed in the present chapter is a fourth consideration which relates to the increasing impact of whistle blowers, non-governmental computer hackers and leakers of official Government secrets, and whether the UN, given its intergovernmental character, is in any position to take even the slightest account of such information.

## 13.7. Back to Governments

Any information that the UN requires for its investigations leads right back to Governments because States continue to be the principal sources of official information on most human rights issues in their own sovereign territory. Many States collect substantial quantities of information on human rights practices in other countries, even if they do not always publish them, in order to keep informed of a vital aspect of inter-state relations. Some Governments, such as that of the United States, systematically collect, review and publish annual reports that include critical comments on

---

[25] See Michael Birnbaum, "Merkel, other European leaders raise concerns on U.S. surveillance", *Washington Post*, 10 June 2013; and Veit Medick, Annett Meiritz and Philipp Wittrock, "'No Longer in the Cold War': Merkel Infuriated by US Spying", *Der Spiegel Online International*, 1 July 2013. See also "Edward Snowden documents show NSA broke privacy rules: The US National Security Agency (NSA) broke privacy rules and overstepped its legal authority thousands of times in the past two years, according to documents leaked by Edward Snowden", *BBC News Online*, 15 August 2013.

the human rights situation of almost every country (except itself).[26] Long feeling itself to have been singled out by the US Government for especially sharp criticism, the Government of the Peoples' Republic of China has begun to respond by publishing an annual report of its own on human rights practices in the United States.[27] That Governments clearly have their own interests and particular historical, cultural, political and geo-strategic lenses through which they view human rights situations inside and outside the country is an obvious red flag for international prosecutors to take account of these kinds of bias when reading government human rights reports, and reports of national human rights institutions, depending on how independent or not they are from the Government.

Governments are also the main entities responsible for implementing international human rights law, including the UN human rights conventions they have ratified. Indeed, the main UN human rights conventions require State parties to collect information and report to UN human rights treaty bodies on the status of their implementation of their treaty obligations. Also, the UN Human Rights Council's Universal Periodic Review, which systematically covers human rights practices in every UN member State, is premised on the willingness of every State under review to collect, analyse and share information with the Human Rights Council to enable this process to work effectively. Furthermore, government statistics on a wide range of issues from crime, to health, education, labour, poverty, and just about any other field of economic, legal, social and political activity, usually relate to the State's human rights performance in some way or other. In short, Governments, being the legally authorised entities with criminal enforcement power to the extent of its sovereign jurisdiction, remain the first and in many cases the most credible sources of information on human rights issues.

While Government remains the most powerful information source, it is at the same time, the 'usual suspect' in terms of serious violations of human rights, humanitarian law and international criminal law, together with rebel movements or militia allied to an aspirant for government. For this reason, guarantees of human rights have been deliberately defined to restrain mainly the State from violations, and to oblige the State to pro-

---

26  See, for example, the annual country reports published by the US Department of State.

27  See Full Text of Human Rights Record of the United States in 2012, published by the State Council Information Office of the People's Republic of China (available on XinHuanet's web site).

mote and protect human rights, because it is the State and its agencies that have pre-eminent power both to protect and abuse the rights of individuals and groups under its jurisdiction. It also means that States have a fundamental conflict of interest: on the one hand, they must collect, analyse and make public information on human rights matters within their jurisdiction in order to meet their international and domestic obligations to promote and protect human rights; but on the other hand, the impulse of Governments to keep embarrassing information on human rights secret, not to share it, to minimise it and in some cases, even to falsify it, can be overwhelming despite freedom of information laws, and political rhetoric about the Government's commitment to democracy, transparency and accountability. Thus, coaxing Governments to disclose information that could implicate it in egregious human rights shortcomings, particularly where allegations concern genocide, war crimes or crimes against humanity, has remained a tough challenge. UN access to Government information depends mainly on co-operation and where this is lacking, the challenge naturally gets more difficult, but fortunately, there are very well-established diplomatic and multilaterally established information channels that are discussed next, which can help clarify factually and politically opaque situations involving serious crimes under international law.

### 13.8. Could UN Human Rights Treaty Body Reports Inform International Criminal Investigations?

It is important to recall the wealth of information that has built up over many years in respect of a country's compliance to its voluntarily assumed human rights treaty obligations. Currently, 10 UN human rights treaty bodies are in operation:

- The Committee on the Elimination of Racial Discrimination ('CERD') which monitors the International Convention on the Elimination of All Forms of Racial Discrimination;[28]

- The Human Rights Committee which monitors the International Covenant on Civil and Political Rights;[29]

---

[28] International Convention on the Elimination of All Forms of Racial Discrimination, adopted by General Assembly Resolution 2106 (XX) of 21 December 1965, entered into force 4 January 1969 (http://www.legal-tools.org/doc/43a925/). By January 2013, it had 175 State Parties, 64 of which had recognized the Committee's competence to receive individual complaints.

- The Committee on Economic, Social and Cultural Rights ('CESCR') which monitors the International Covenant on Economic, Social and Cultural Rights;[30]

- The Committee on the Elimination of All Forms of Discrimination against Women ('CEDAW') which monitors the International Convention on the Elimination of All Forms of Discrimination against Women;[31]

- The Committee against Torture ('CAT') which monitors the Convention against Torture and Other Cruel, Inhuman or Degrading Treatment or Punishment;[32]

- The Subcommittee on the Prevention of Torture;[33]

---

[29] International Covenant on Civil and Political Rights, adopted 16 December 1966; entered into force 23 March 1976; UNTS No. 14668, 1976, vol 999, p. 171 (http://www.legal-tools. org/doc/2838f3/). As of January 2013, there were 167 States Parties to the ICCPR. There were 114 States Parties to the first Optional Protocol to the ICCPR which in Article 1 provides that:

> A State Party to the Covenant that becomes a Party to the present Protocol recognizes the competence of the Committee to receive and consider communications from individuals subject to its jurisdiction who claim to be victims of a violation by that State Party of any of the rights set forth in the Covenant.

[30] International Covenant on Economic, Social and Cultural Rights, adopted 16 December 1966; entered into force 3 January 1976; UNTS No. 14531, 1976, vol. 993, p. 3 (http:// www.legal-tools.org/doc/06b87e/). As of January 2013, there were 160 States Parties to the ICESCR, eight of which had recognised the Committee's competence to receive individual complaints from their jurisdictions.

[31] The Convention on the Elimination of All Forms of Discrimination against Women, adopted by the General Assembly in Resolution 34/180 of 18 December 1979, entered into force 3 September 1981 (http://www.legal-tools.org/doc/6dc4e4/). Article 17(1) of the Convention provides for a Committee of 18 independent experts to monitor compliance. In Resolution A/Res/54/4, the General Assembly adopted Optional Protocol 1 to the Convention on 6 October 1999, opened for signature on 10 December 1999 and entered into force on 22 December 2000, following the tenth instrument of ratification. As of January 2013, there were 174 States Parties to the Convention and 53 States Parties to Optional Protocol 1.

[32] UN Convention against Torture and Other Cruel, Inhuman or Degrading Treatment or Punishment, adopted by consensus by the General Assembly on 10 December 1984, opened for signature on 4 February 1985, entered into force on 26 June 1987 (http://www.legal-tools.org/doc/713f11/). The Convention forms the Annex to General Assembly Resolution 39/46. As per Article 22, the Committee can receive allegations of torture from the individual where the State Party has so declared that it recognises the competence of the Committee to receive individual allegations. As of January 2013, there were 153 States Parties to the Convention, 56 of which had recognised the competence of the Committee to receive complaints from individuals under its jurisdiction.

- The Committee on the Rights of the Child ('CRC') which monitors the Convention on the Rights of the Child;[34]

- The Committee on the Protection of the Rights of All Migrant Workers and Members of Their Families which monitors the International Convention on the Protection of the Rights of All Migrant Workers and Members of Their Families;[35]

- The Committee on the Rights of Persons with Disabilities which monitors the Convention on the Rights of Persons with Disabilities;[36] and

- The Committee on Enforced Disappearances which monitors the Convention on Enforced Disappearances.[37]

These bodies consist of independent experts of recognised competence in human rights who serve in a personal capacity. Each of the conventions listed above obliges the State Party to submit to the UN Secre-

---

[33] The Optional Protocol to the Convention against Torture and Other Cruel, Inhuman or Degrading Treatment or Punishment, adopted by the General Assembly on 18 December 2002, entered into force on 22 June 2006 (http://www.legal-tools.org/doc/59c926/), by January 2013, had 69 States Parties. The Subcommittee on Prevention of Torture and other Cruel, Inhuman or Degrading Treatment or Punishment which has 25 experts and began operation in February 2007 is mandated to prevent torture and ill treatment.

[34] The Convention on the Rights of the Child, adopted by the General Assembly in Resolution 44/25 of 20 November 1989, entered into force 2 September 1990 (http://www.legal-tools.org/doc/f48f9e/). Article 43 of the Convention provides that for "the purpose of examining the progress made by States Parties in achieving the realization of the obligations undertaken" in the Convention, there shall be established a Committee of ten experts. As of January 2013, there were 193 States Parties to the Convention, and an Optional Protocol allowing for individual complaints adopted on 19 December 2011.

[35] International Convention on the Protection of the Rights of All Migrant Workers and Members of Their Families, adopted by General Assembly Resolution 45/158 of 18 December 1990, entered into force on 1 July 2003 (http://www.legal-tools.org/doc/a6a403/). The Committee consists of 14 experts serving in their personal capacity. As of January 2013, there were 46 States Parties to the Convention.

[36] Convention on the Rights of Persons with Disabilities, adopted by General Assembly Resolution 61/106 of 13 December 2006, entered into force on 3 May 2008 (http://www.legal-tools.org/doc/06e036/). The Committee consists of 18 experts serving in their personal capacity. As of January 2013, there were 123 States Parties, 74 of which had recognised the competence of the Committee to receive complaints from individuals under its jurisdiction.

[37] International Convention for the Protection of All Persons from Enforced Disappearance, adopted by General Assembly Resolution 61/177 of 20 December 2006, entered into force on 23 December 2010 (http://www.legal-tools.org/doc/0d0674/). The Committee consists of 18 experts serving in their personal capacity. As of January 2013, there were 36 States Parties and 90 signatories to the Convention.

---

tary-General for consideration by the corresponding Committee a report
on the legislative, judicial, administrative or other measures the State Party has taken to implement the convention. State reports have to be submitted within one year following the Convention's entry into force and peri-
odically thereafter and whenever the Committee requests a report. The
treaty bodies examine the State reports, together with information from
other sources and after a dialogue with the State's delegation, the committee adopts 'concluding observations' or 'comments' expressing positive
and negative aspects of the substance of the State's report and recommends measures the State should take to brings its practice into closer
conformity with its conventional obligations. In addition, the optional individual complaints procedure also sheds light on the kinds of allegations
of violations of concern within the State's jurisdiction.

Information contained in State reports to the UN human rights treaty bodies, 'shadow reports' submitted by NGOs, and the recommendations of the relevant treaty body itself, could help Prosecutors fill in the
gaps in their understanding of the status and operation of a country's judicial system, its law, policies and practices. All of this information is public,
available and easily accessed from OHCHR's website. It is important to
remember that nothing forces a particular country to sign and ratify any of
the multilateral human rights conventions, and a Government cannot be
forced to submit its State report or provide information on the level of its
compliance with its treaty obligations, much less to recognise the competence of the relevant Committee to receive individual complaints from its
jurisdiction. All the same, the fact that every country is a party to at least
one multilateral human rights convention and that most countries have
ratified several human rights treaties means that a considerable quantity of
information relating to human rights violations is easily accessible to international criminal investigators and prosecutors. This was the situation
with regard to Darfur for example. The Government of the Sudan had ratified the International Covenant on Civil and Political Rights, 1966; the
Convention on the Rights of the Child, 1989; the Convention on the Elimination of All Forms of Racial Discrimination, 1965; the Covenant on
Economic, Social and Cultural Rights, 1966; as well as to the four Geneva
Conventions of 12 August 1949. The Government was very late in submitting its periodic reports to the UN Human Rights Committee. Despite
this shortcoming, in 2007, reviewing Sudan's Third Periodic Report, UN
the Human Rights Committee felt that it was in a position to express that:

> Despite the information provided by the State party about prosecutions of a number of perpetrators of human rights violations, the Committee notes with concern, particularly in the context of armed conflict, that widespread and systematic serious human rights violations, including murder, rape, forced displacement and attacks against the civil population, have been and continue to be committed with total impunity throughout Sudan and particularly in Darfur. It is particularly concerned at the immunity provided for in Sudanese law and untransparent procedure for waiving immunity in the event of criminal proceedings against State agents.[38]

A few years earlier, in 2005, the UN Committee on the Elimination of All Forms of Racial Discrimination recalled its obligation, in line with its early warning and urgent action procedure to signal that a situation might further deteriorate, and recommended:

> [...] to the Secretary-General, and through him, the Security Council, the deployment, without further delay, of a sufficiently enlarged African Union force in Darfur with a Security Council mandate to protect the civilian population, including those in camps, displaced persons and refugees returning to their homes in Darfur, against war crimes, crimes against humanity, and the risk of genocide.[39]

Thus, information from Government reports to the UN human rights treaty bodies often provides the most detailed explanation of the constitutional, political and legal system, and can shed light on root causes of conflict which in turn can help place crimes under international law in context and help international prosecutors make their case. The Government report, together with the observations and recommendations of the treaty body itself and NGO shadow reports, could help international investigators and prosecutors to trace pathways leading up to the commission of crimes under international law, as well as the Government's official attitude towards them.

---

[38] Consideration of Reports Submitted by States Parties under Article 40 of the Covenant: Concluding Observations of the Human Rights Committee on Sudan; CCPR/C/SDN/CO/3/CRP.1 of 26 July 2007 at para. 9.

[39] UN Committee on the Elimination of All Forms of Racial Discrimination Decision 2 (66) on the Situation in Darfur; CERD/C/66/DAR/Dec.2, 11 March 2005.

### 13.9. Could UN Human Rights Council Special Procedures and Investigative Missions Inform International Criminal Prosecutions?

In situations of genocide, war crimes or crimes against humanity the implicated government or territorial authority might not have ratified the relevant multilateral convention, for example, on genocide, torture, racial discrimination or the International Covenant on Civil and Political Rights. Even where it has ratified the relevant convention, it might not have offered much information on the state of its human rights observance through the UN human rights treaty body system. In other instances, even with the full co-operation of the State with the UN human rights treaty bodies, the information might be too general to be of much use to an international criminal investigator or prosecutor searching for evidence of a clear pattern of crimes or *modus operandi* of particular armed forces, paramilitary, police or militia units that might corroborate witness testimony in particular criminal instances. To fill these kinds of gaps in a prosecutor's understanding of the law enforcement structure and the operating standards of particular entities that might be implicated in genocide, war crimes or crimes against humanity, UN Human Rights Council special procedures could be especially valuable.

Whereas UN human rights treaty bodies monitor a State Party's observance of the specific human rights set forth in the relevant convention it ratified, 'special procedures' monitor and report on human rights issues regardless of the consent of the particular State or territorial authority concerned. Special procedures operate either through 'country mandates' to examine human rights situations in particular countries or territories, or through 'thematic mandates' which cover the situation in any country with regard to enjoyment of a particular human right or cluster of rights. As mentioned above, genocide, war crimes or crimes against humanity do not normally arise from peaceful or stable situations, but rather from situations where human rights, democracy and the rule of law are weak. These are the same situations, which are likely to have become subject to a Human Rights Council country or one or more thematic mandates.

Reports of special rapporteurs have led or contributed to the establishment of commissions of enquiry to investigate facts and responsibilities concerning criminal violations of human rights and humanitarian law in the former Yugoslavia,[40] Rwanda, East Timor[41] and Darfur,[42] to name just a few examples. Special procedures mechanisms have also co-ordinated visits and received information from UN human rights field presences deployed in particular countries.

In the former Yugoslavia for example, the Commission on Human Rights appointed a special rapporteur to report on the scale and character of violations. Commission Special Rapporteur on the human rights situa-tion in the former Yugoslavia, Mr. Tadeusz Mazowiecki argued that the perpetrators of severe violations should be prosecuted, and in this connec-tion, he underlined the importance of the "the systematic collection of documentation on such crimes and of personal data concerning those re-sponsible".[43] Mazowiecki also recommended that a commission should be established actually to identify specific persons and conduct investigations to prepare the way for eventual criminal prosecution.[44] In subsequent re-ports, the Special Rapporteur further urged the expeditious collection of information to support criminal investigation of war crimes and serious violations of humanitarian law,[45] that there was growing evidence that war crimes had been committed and that further investigation was needed to determine their scale and the individual perpetrators for "prosecution by an international tribunal, if appropriate".[46]

---

[40] See Report on the situation of human rights in the territory of the former Yugoslavia sub-mitted by Mr. Tadeusz Mazowiecki, Special Rapporteur of the Commission on Human Rights, pursuant to Paragraph 14 of Commission Resolution 1992/S-1/1 of 14 August 1992 and E/CN.4/1992/S-1/9 of 28 August 1992.

[41] See the Report of the Special Rapporteur on Torture (E/CN.4/1997/7), the Special Rappor-teur on Extrajudicial, Summary or Arbitrary Executions (E/CN.4/1997/60), the Working Group on Arbitrary Detention (E/CN.4/1997/4 and Add.1) and the Working Group on En-forced or Involuntary Disappearances (E/CN.4/1997/34).

[42] See, for example, the Report of the Special Rapporteur on Extrajudicial, Summary and Arbitrary Executions on Her mission to the Sudan (E/CN.4/2005/7/Add.2), the Special Rapporteur on Violence against Women, Its Causes and Consequences, on her mission to the Darfur region of the Sudan (E/CN.4/2005/72/Add.5), among numerous others.

[43] See Report on the situation of human rights in the territory of the former Yugoslavia sub-mitted by Mr. Tadeusz Mazowiecki, Special Rapporteur of the Commission on Human Rights, pursuant to Paragraph 14 of Commission Resolution 1992/S-1/1 of 14 August 1992, E/CN.4/1992/S-1/9, 28 August 1992 at para. 69.

[44] *Ibid.*, at para. 70.

[45] See for example, E/CN.4/1992/S-1/10 of 27 October 1992 at para. 18 as well as Annex II (Statement by Dr. Clyde Snow).

[46] See Report of the Special Rapporteur (transmitted by the Secretary-General to the Security Council and General Assembly) A/47/666; S/24809 of 17 November 1992 at para. 140.

The accumulation of credible and reliable information coming from
the Commission of Experts, the Special Rapporteur and increasingly from
UN human rights field presences set up in some of the territories of the
former Yugoslavia, together with media and NGO reports and rising public pressure over the plight of civilians and detainees in the former Yugoslavia, pushed the Security Council to adopt resolution 780[47] on 6 October
1992, requesting the Secretary-General to establish urgently a commission
of experts on the former Yugoslavia. Resolution 780 mandated the Commission of Experts to examine and analyse information received from
States, conduct investigations and gather information from other persons
or bodies and to inform the Secretary-General as to whether grave breaches of the Geneva Conventions of 12 August 1949 were committed in the
former Yugoslavia. In fact, the Secretary-General indicated his expectation that the Commission of Experts and the Special Rapporteur on the
former Yugoslavia should coordinate with one another to ensure that human rights information relevant to prosecutions would be channelled to
the Commission of Experts, and that information the Commission of Experts collected that was relevant to the Special Rapporteur's mandate
would reach him.[48] The Commission of Experts carried out investigations
from November 1992 until April 1994 and in its three reports to the Secretary-General, it documented widespread patterns of "wilful killing", "ethnic cleansing", "mass killings, torture, rape, pillage and destruction of civilian property, destruction of cultural and religious property and arbitrary
arrests".[49]

The Security Council's establishment of the International Criminal
Tribunal for the former Yugoslavia ('ICTY') on 25 May 1993 by way of
resolution 827 figures as a landmark advance in international criminal law
implementation, but it is important to recall that the Commission of Experts for the former Yugoslavia continued to operate and gather information until April 1994. The Chair of the Commission of Experts stated

---

[47] See S/RES/780 (1992) adopted by the Security Council at its 3119 meeting, 6 October
1992. Reprinted in 31 International Legal Materials (1992) 1476 (http://www.legal-tools.
org/doc/cdc5ad/).

[48] See Report of the Secretary-General on the Establishment of the Commission of Experts
pursuant to Paragraph 2 of Security Council Resolution 780(1992), S/24657 at paras. 7 and
10.

[49] See UN Doc. S/25274 of 9 February 1993.

that a large amount of materials was sent to the ICTY Prosecutor, including some three hundred videotapes, documents and interview transcripts.[50]

With regard to Rwanda, the August 1993 report[51] of the UN Commission on Human Rights Special Rapporteur on extrajudicial, summary or arbitrary executions, Mr. Bacre Waly Ndiaye, is particularly striking. On the basis of his 10-day mission to Rwanda in April 1993, a full year before the Rwandan genocide, he warned that massacres of civilians, death threats, political assassinations, widespread use of the death penalty and other serious human rights violations, might already qualify as 'genocide'.[52]

On 1 July 1994, the day after the Rwandan Patriotic Front took effective control over the country after halting the genocide, the Security Council established the Commission of Experts on Rwanda[53] to provide the Secretary-General with "its conclusions on the evidence of grave violations of international humanitarian law committed in the territory of Rwanda, including the evidence of possible acts of genocide".[54] The Commission of Experts on Rwanda, which was serviced by OHCHR in Geneva, gathered information from the UN Human Rights Field Operation in Rwanda (which in late 1994 consisted of only a few human rights officers deployed in Rwanda), the UN Special Rapporteur on Rwanda ('UNAMIR'), and "from the two parties to the conflict thousands of pages of documents, letters, written complaints, testimony and other items (sound and audio-visual recordings) instancing serious violations of international humanitarian law", the value of which varied widely. The Commission of Experts noted that "[s]ome of these documents contain non-exhaustive lists of the principal suspects".[55] The interim report recommended prosecution of the perpetrators of genocide and associated viola-

---

[50] See Cherif Bassiouni, "The Commission of Experts established pursuant to Security Council Resolution 780: Investigating Violations of International Humanitarian Law in the Former Yugoslavia", *Criminal Law Forum*, 1994, vol. 5, no. 2–3, pp. 291–293.

[51] The report of Mr. Bacre Waly Ndiaye on his mission to Rwanda from 8–17 April 1993, E/CN.4/1994/7/Add.1 of 11 August 1993.

[52] *Ibid.*, at para. 79.

[53] UN Security Council Resolution 935 adopted unanimously on 1 July 1994; S/RES/1994.

[54] *Ibid.*

[55] Final Report of the Commission of Experts established pursuant to Security Council Resolution 935 (1994) (http://www.legal-tools.org/doc/1594bd/); UN Doc. S/1994/1405 of 9 December 1994 at para. 54 (https://www.legal-tools.org/doc/361096/).

tions by an international criminal tribunal, a recommendation that was acted on by the Security Council on 8 November 1994 by way of resolution 955 establishing the ICTR.[56] As in the former Yugoslavia, information from UN human rights sources provided an early indication of the scale and character of crimes under international law, the parties responsible for the genocide, the relationship between perpetrators and victims in terms of legally designated ethnicity, as well as the names of a certain number of criminal suspects, several months before the ICTR was set up and prosecutors could commence investigations.

It must be recalled that the Security Council investigations differ from investigations deployed under the auspices of the Commission on Human Rights and its successor, the Human Rights Council. One of the important differences is that Security Council investigations mandated under Chapter VII of the Charter of the United Nations require a resolution conferring this authority, which is always dependent on a draft resolution being supported by 9 affirmative votes including the 5 concurring votes of the permanent members. Because one or more Security Council permanent members could oppose strong investigative action, as Russia and China did on Syria,[57] even in relation to situations involving genocide, war crimes and crimes against humanity, commissions of inquiry mandated under Human Rights Council authority have had to make up for this lost ground. No state has a veto in the Human Rights Council and decisions are reached on a majority basis among the 47 member States which means that UN human rights special procedures as a source for international criminal investigations and prosecutions have become commensurately more important, as demonstrated in Darfur, the Israeli Occupied Palestinian territories, Côte d'Ivoire, Libya and Syria.

With regard to the Darfur situation, where the Security Council referred the situation to the ICC in March 2005,[58] sitting President Omar Al Bashir, as well as certain other high-ranking officials, was indicted for

---

[56] See generally Lyal S. Sunga, "The Commission of Experts on Rwanda and the Creation of the International Criminal Tribunal for Rwanda, a Note", in *Human Rights Law Journal*, 1995, vol. 16, no. 1–3, pp. 121–124.

[57] Neil MacFarquhar and Anthony Shadid, "Russia and China Block UN Action on Crisis in Syria", *New York Times*, 4 February 2012.

[58] Security Council 1593 (2005), adopted by a vote of 11 in favour, none against and 4 abstentions (Algeria, Brazil, China, United States) on 31 March 2005 (http://www.legal-tools.org/doc/4b208f/).

war crimes and crimes against humanity. The Security Council set up the International Commission of Inquiry on Darfur on 18 September 2004 to determine whether or not acts of genocide were committed and to identify the responsible individuals. This Commission received and gathered information including from UN human rights sources and human rights and humanitarian NGOs, on serious violations of international human rights and humanitarian law in Darfur and submitted a list of names of persons suspected of having committed crimes under international law in a sealed file to the Secretary-General and UN High Commissioner for Human Rights.[59] The International Commission of Inquiry however was only the first of several important steps in gathering information relevant for eventual international criminal investigations and prosecutions.

A number of UN human rights mechanisms, with varying mandates, followed the Commission of Inquiry. The Human Rights Council's High Level Mission on the Human Rights Situation in Darfur in December 2006 established in its final report of March 2007, that the Sudanese "justice system as a whole was unable or unwilling to pursue justice or prevent attacks" and that impunity prevailed – a critical element given the complementary character of the ICC that called for international criminal prosecutions. Once the High Level Mission was dissolved in March 2007, the Human Rights Council established a Group of Experts on Darfur comprising the Special Rapporteur on the situation of human rights in the Sudan, the Special Rapporteur on extrajudicial, summary or arbitrary executions, the Special Representative of the Secretary-General for children and armed conflict, the Special Rapporteur on violence against women, its causes and consequences, the Special Representative of the Secretary-General on the situation of human rights defenders, the Representative of the Secretary-General on the human rights of internally displaced persons, and the Special Rapporteur on the question of torture and other cruel, inhuman or degrading treatment or punishment.[60] While the Group of Ex-

---

[59] Report of the International Commission of Inquiry on Darfur to the United Nations Secretary-General pursuant to Security Council Resolution 1564 of 18 September 2004 (2005); Report of the High-Level Mission on the Situation of Human Rights in Darfur pursuant to Human Rights Council decision S-4/101; A/HRC/4/80 of 9 March 2007 at para. 46.

[60] Human Rights Council Resolution 4/8, adopted on 30 March 2007 without a vote, is entitled "Follow-up to decision S-4/101 of 13 December 2006 adopted by the Human Rights Council at its fourth special session entitled 'Situation of human rights in Darfur'"; Final Report on the situation of human rights in Darfur prepared by the Group of Experts mandated by the Human Rights Council in its Resolution 4/8; A/HRC/6/19 of 28 November

perts on Darfur was not primarily a fact-finding body, it evaluated the extent to which the Government of Sudan had implemented the outstanding recommendations in its final report of 10 December 2007 by reviewing and updating information from a large number of credible and reliable sources, including the Government of the Sudan, the UN Mission in Sudan, other UN agencies, bodies and programmes operational in Darfur, and from humanitarian and human rights NGOs which had not yet been expelled from Sudan.

Another example where information from UN human rights sources has been an important part of determining whether or not crimes under international law have been committed has arisen with regard to the Israeli Occupied Palestinian territories. Security Council action to investigate the Government of Israel's violations of human rights and humanitarian law, some of which could qualify as crimes under international law, has been rendered impossible because of the Government of the United States' continual casting of a veto on all pertinent draft Security Council resolutions. As in the case of Syria where, as discussed below, Russia and China have been responsible for blocking Security Council action, investigation into Israeli crimes under international law had to be taken up by the UN Human Rights Council because of the veto of the US in the Security Council. For example, the Human Rights Council expressed its concern over Israeli military operations in Beit Hanoun, Gaza, in November 2006,[61] as imposing 'collective punishment' on civilians and exacerbating the humanitarian crisis in the Occupied Palestinian Territory. In the same resolution, the Council established a high-level fact-finding mission to deploy to Beit Hanoun in order to assess violations of human rights and humanitarian law. In April 2009, the President of the Human Rights Council established the Fact-Finding Mission on the Gaza Conflict

> [...] to investigate all violations of international human
> rights law and international humanitarian law that might
> have been committed at any time in the context of the mili-

---

2007. For the long list of Security Council draft resolutions critical of Israel where the US has cast a veto, often the only dissenting vote, see "U.S. Vetoes of UN Resolutions Critical of Israel: (1972–2011)" (available at http://www.jewishvirtuallibrary.org/jsource/UN/usvetoes.html).

61 See UN Human Rights Council Resolution on human rights violations emanating from Israeli military incursions in the Occupied Palestinian Territory, including the recent one in northern Gaza and the assault on Beit Hanoun; A/HRC/S-3/1, 15 November 2006; adopted by a recorded vote of 32 to 8, with 6 abstentions, preamble, paras. 5, 7.

tary operations that were conducted in Gaza during the period from 27 December 2008 and 18 January 2009, whether
before, during or after.[62]

On 31 May 2010, Israel attacked a flotilla of ships headed for Gaza
with humanitarian supplies, resulting in the death of nine activists and the
wounding of 55 others on the *Mavi Marmara*. As usual with respect to the
Israeli Occupied Palestinian territories, the Security Council found itself
unable to agree on establishing a commission of inquiry under its own
auspices and merely called for an impartial investigation, which then fell
to the Human Rights Council.[63] In June 2010, the Human Rights Council
adopted resolution 14/1 establishing a fact-finding mission which determined that the Israeli naval blockade of the Gaza strip, the attack on the
flotilla and certain other actions constituted serious violations of international humanitarian and human rights law.[64] In short, given both the Government of Israel's long history of non-co-operation with the international
community, as well as the inability of the Security Council to agree to investigate Israeli action in the Occupied Territories, international criminal
investigations and prosecutions into Israeli Government practices (itself
admittedly a highly unlikely eventuality) would have to rely heavily on
information coming from the array of UN human rights sources, including
commissions of inquiry, that have been activated by the Human Rights
Council from time-to-time. In this respect, one should not overlook the
work of the General Assembly's Special Committee on Israeli Practices
that has been in operation since 1968.[65]

---

[62] *Ibid.*, para. 1.

[63] See Security Council Presidential Statement S/PRST/2010/9 of 1 June 2010 which says
that:

> The Security Council takes note of the statement of the UN Secretary-General on the
> need to have a full investigation into the matter and it calls for a prompt, impartial,
> credible and transparent investigation conforming to international standards.

[64] See Report of the international fact-finding mission to investigate violations of international law, including international humanitarian and human rights law, resulting from the Israeli attacks on the flotilla of ships carrying humanitarian assistance; A/HRC/15/21 of 27 September 2010 at paras. 260–278 (https://www.legal-tools.org/doc/32f94d/).

[65] The UN Special Committee to Investigate Israeli Practices affecting the Human Rights of
the Palestinian People and Other Arabs of the Occupied Territories was established by
General Assembly Resolution 2443 (XXIII) of 19 December 1968 to monitor: "respect for
and implementation of human rights in occupied territories".

---

The response of the international community through the UN to the 2010 election crisis in Côte d'Ivoire, where President Laurent Gbagbo tried to cling to power after the first elections in ten years, despite the Electoral Commission's declaration on 2 December 2010 that opposition leader Alassane Dramane Ouattara had won, is also instructive in terms of UN information gathering in the context of a situation involving crimes under international law. Following the election, rival political groups engaged in massacres, torture, mass rape, summary executions and other atrocities along ethnic lines which intensified during the first months of 2011.[66] In March 2011, the Human Rights Council decided to dispatch an independent, international commission of inquiry to investigate serious human rights violations committed in Côte d'Ivoire following the election, to identify individuals responsible for such acts with a view to bringing them to justice, and to report back to the Council at its next session.[67] The Council also reaffirmed the "responsibility of Côte d'Ivoire to promote and protect all human rights and fundamental freedoms, to investigate alleged violations of human rights and international law and to bring to justice the perpetrators of such acts, who are answerable for their deeds before the judicial process". In its July 2011 report, the Commission of Inquiry stated that Gbagbo's rejection of the election results made him responsible for the serious violations of human rights and humanitarian law and that some of the violations might constitute war crimes or crimes against humanity.[68] On 3 May 2011, President Ouattara requested the ICC prosecutor to open an investigation,[69] and in October 2011, ICC Pre-Trial Chamber III endorsed the prosecutor's request to commence an investiga-

---

[66] See, for example, "Côte d'Ivoire: Warning of 'human rights catastrophe' as forces reach Abidjan", Amnesty International, 31 March 2011.

[67] Human Rights Council Resolution 16/25 on the situation of human rights in Côte d'Ivoire; A/HRC/16/25 of 25 March 2011 (http://www.legal-tools.org/doc/7b9efc/).

[68] Rapport de la Commission d'enquête internationale indépendante sur la Côte d'Ivoire, A/HRC/17/48 of 1 July 2011 at para. 91 (http://www.legal-tools.org/doc/234c50/).

[69] On 23 June, the prosecutor then requested ICC judges for authorisation to initiate a criminal investigation into war crimes and crimes against humanity committed in Côte d'Ivoire since 28 November 2010. In his request for authorisation, the prosecutor cited reports that more than 3000 individuals had been killed, 72 disappeared, and 520 people subjected to arbitrary arrest and detention in Côte d'Ivoire following the November 2010 election. More than 100 cases of rape were reported, but the prosecutor indicated that the number of unreported incidents of rape were believed to be much higher. See "Situation of Côte d'Ivoire: Request for authorization of an investigation pursuant to Article 15"; ICC-02/11-3 of 23 June 2011 (http://www.legal-tools.org/doc/1b1939/).

---

tion in Côte d'Ivoire with respect to crimes committed since 28 November 2010.[70] In the Côte d'Ivoire situation, the UN Human Rights Council was the preferred forum for investigation rather than the Security Council and therefore any action taken by international criminal investigators and prosecutors had to be guided by the work of the Human Rights Council's Commission of Inquiry as well as by information that might have been collected by UN Special Rapporteurs, working groups or other human rights mechanisms.

Turning to the situation in Libya, both the Security Council and the Human Rights Council entered the fray early on, with the Security Council discharging its UN Charter responsibilities to restore and maintain peace and security, while the Human Rights Council established a mechanism to investigate possible crimes under international law. The crisis began with peaceful protests in February 2011 against Colonel Muammar Qadhafi's rule that had endured for almost 42 years, and escalated into mass Arab Spring demonstrations that were met with severe military crackdowns on protestors and civilians. In February 2011, the Human Rights Council established an international commission of inquiry to investigate the violations and recommend measures to enforce criminal responsibility of the perpetrators.[71] By way of resolution 1970, adopted on 26 February, the Security Council referred the situation to the ICC,[72] enforced an arms embargo upon all UN member States on the direct or indirect supply of arms to Libya,[73] put in place a travel ban on 16 members of the Qadhafi family and persons close to the regime[74] as well as an assets freeze on six Qadhafi family members,[75] established a Sanctions Committee and criteria for identifying individuals involved or complicit in ordering, controlling, or otherwise directing, the commission of serious human rights abuses.[76] The Human Rights Council's Commission of Inquiry's

---

[70] Decision pursuant to Article 15 of the Rome Statute on the Authorization of an Investigation into the Situation in the Republic of Côte d'Ivoire, ICC-02/11 of 3 October 2011 at para. 212 (http://www.legal-tools.org/doc/7a6c19/).

[71] Human Rights Council Resolution on the situation of human rights in the Libyan Arab Jamahiriya; A/HRC/S-15/1 of 3 March 2011, adopted on 25 February 2011, at para. 11.

[72] *Ibid.* at paras. 4–8 (https://www.legal-tools.org/doc/233009/).

[73] *Ibid.* at paras. 9–14.

[74] *Ibid.* at paras. 15 and 16 and see Annex I to the resolution.

[75] *Ibid.* at paras. 17–21 and see Annex II to the resolution.

[76] *Ibid.* at paras. 22–25.

June 2011 report states that it gathered information from the Government,
the National Transitional Council, civil society representatives and other
individuals throughout Libya, as well as doctors, medical staff, patients
and members of their families in 10 hospitals, detainees, internally displaced persons and refugees.[77] As in the international community's response to Côte d'Ivoire, it was the Human Rights Council rather than the
Security Council that established an investigative commission and it was
therefore the UN human rights system to which international criminal investigators had to turn for information to prepare prosecution dossiers.

The Human Rights Council's investigative capacity again proved
essential to possible future international criminal prosecutions with regard
to Syria. In late August 2011, the Human Rights Council established an
international commission of inquiry to investigate, monitor and report on
human rights violations in Syria.[78] As in the Libya scenario, the Human
Rights Council with regard to Syria was more prepared than the Security
Council to field an investigation into the atrocities which meant that any
eventual international criminal prosecutions would have to draw substantially on the information collected under the auspices of the Human
Rights Council.

In short, UN human rights thematic and country special procedures,
and particularly investigations mandated to assess serious violations of
human rights or humanitarian law that could qualify as Rome Statute
crimes, offer a leading source of credible and reliable information for international criminal investigators and prosecutors. As discussed above,
UN human rights special procedures are themselves broad ranging in that
they sweep in information from the Government, national human rights
institutions, intergovernmental organisations, other UN human rights
agencies, bodies or programmes, the ICRC, NGOs, journalists, detainees,
refugees and internally displaced persons, witnesses, victims and survivors and their family members, to analyse and chronicle events which
might help to identify and implicate individual criminal suspects. As discussed above, in some instances, investigative missions deployed under

---

[77] See Report of the International Commission of Inquiry to investigate all alleged violations
of international human rights law in the Libyan Arab Jamahiriya; A/HRC/17/44 of 1 June
2011 at Summary.

[78] See OHCHR Press Statement on "Human Rights Council decides to dispatch a commission of inquiry to investigate human rights violations in the Syrian Arab Republic" of 23
August 2011.

the auspices of the Security Council or Human Rights Council have been mandated to submit lists of individuals suspected of having perpetrated crimes under international law, which surely give international investigators and prosecutors a head start.

### 13.10. Could Information from the Human Rights Council's Universal Periodic Review Help to Broaden Out the Picture?

The Universal Periodic Review provides another source of human rights information that could relate to international criminal investigations and prosecutions. The UPR, as per General Assembly resolution 60/251, is a co-operative process based on objective and reliable information concerning the State's fulfilment of its human rights obligations. It is based on a peer review of every State by three other, randomly-chosen States that takes place every four years. It is universal in coverage, thereby providing equal treatment to all countries. It is based on an interactive dialogue, with the full involvement of the country concerned and there is consideration to a State's capacity-building needs. The UPR complements rather than duplicates the work either of UN human rights treaty bodies or human rights special procedures, but builds on both, and the process also brings in information from intergovernmental organisations, national human rights institutions and NGOs. Although the UPR mechanism began operating only in 2008, it seems to hold promise as a source of reliable information in that it offers the State subject to review full opportunity to present its side of the picture, and after the first round of reviews, the focus has now shifted to implementation of recommendations. Information in the various reports, including the Outcome Document which summarises the results of the peer review process and takes into account the Government's response, could help international investigators and prosecutors to pinpoint historical and current issues, such as those relating to excessive use of force by law enforcement personnel and military, lack of independence of the judiciary, weak access of minorities to justice, patterns of marginalisation, exclusion or persecution relating to the eventual outbreak of genocide, war crimes or crimes against humanity.

### 13.11. Could Information from UN Human Rights Sources Be Admitted as Direct Evidence in an International Criminal Trial? What about Hearsay?

The foregoing argument contends that information from UN human rights sources, which is often drawn from interviews of Government officials, rebel and militia personnel, parliamentarians, officials of intergovernmental organisations and NGOs present in the territory where crimes under international law were alleged to have been committed, journalists, key political party members, detainees, refugees and internally displaced persons, victims, witnesses, survivors or their family members, often prove to be essential in assembling the background picture and antecedent circumstances surrounding genocide, war crimes and crimes against humanity. Taking this point further, it is worth pondering whether such information could be admitted directly as evidence at an international criminal trial or would it have to be excluded on grounds that it constituted second hand information, that is, hearsay?

It is important to bear in mind that because their main aim is to establish facts surrounding human rights related incidents, events and situations in terms of the responsibility of the State or other entities exercising effective control over the territory, rather than to determine individual criminal responsibility, human rights investigators have, until recently, generally not taken systematic measures to:

- record carefully all relevant particulars of events witnessed by the investigator himself or herself, in order to aid accuracy of recollection in case he or she is called to testify at trial;

- record carefully all relevant particulars of events recounted by sources of information on violations which might qualify as acts of genocide, war crimes or crimes against humanity;

- grade and note the credibility and reliability of sources according to standard open source information gathering techniques, such as those outlined in the NATO Open Source Intelligence Handbook[79]

---

[79] See NATO Open Source Intelligence Handbook (2001). See also William S. Brei, "Getting Intelligence Right: The Power of Logical Procedure", *Occasional Paper*, no. 2, Joint Military Intelligence College, Washington, D.C., 1996.

or with regard to interviews, the Admiralty Code (also known as the Admiralty Grading System);[80]

- note clearly and consistently the identity, addresses, e-mail and mobile phone contact information of witnesses to allow for their eventual appearance at trial for cross-examination;

- ensure an unbroken and secure chain of evidence from source to trial; and

- consistently apply up-to-date encryption technology to keep information gleaned from interviews, documents or first hand eye witness accounts secret during storage at local field offices and field headquarters and during transmission to New York and Geneva, and to take adequate measures to guard against physical, fixed wire, wireless, satellite or other forms of hostile electronic surveillance, monitoring or interception.

M. Cherif Bassiouni, the last Chair of the Security Council's Commission of Experts for the former Yugoslavia, has commented that the major part of information collected by the Commission of Experts could be used only to establish the location, character and scale of violations, that is, to construct the case background and context, and not as evidence directly relevant to the Prosecution's case. Sources of information were not properly recorded which precluded corroboration and Defence cross-examination, thereby rendering it inadmissible at trial.[81]

Yet the adduction of information from UN human rights sources into evidence in international criminal proceedings is not *a priori* inadmissible, as demonstrated in at least one striking instance. In the ICC case of the *Prosecutor v. Germain Katanga and Mathieu Ngudjolo Chui* where

---

[80] See American, British, Canadian, Australian, and New Zealand Armies Program, "Coalition Operations Handbook", 4th ed., 14 April 2008 (available on Public Intelligence's web site). See also United Kingdom Ministry of Defense, Understanding and Intelligence Support to Joint Operations, Joint Doctrine Publication 2-00: Third ed., August 2011.

[81] Bassiouni, 1994, *supra* note 50. Bassiouni observed that:

Governments did not provide any intelligence information in their possession – such as satellite and aerial photographs; intercepted telephone, radio, and cable communications; and other materials that could have revealed the disposition and movement of troops and supplies, particularly important where national borders were crossed. Such information would help to establish the role of different governments in these multiple conflicts, the international character of the conflict, the chain of command, and the apex of command and control.

two high-level Congolese militia leaders were prosecuted for war crimes and crimes against humanity,[82] testimony from the Assistant Head of the Human Rights Section of the UN Organization Mission in the Democratic Republic of the Congo ('MONUC')[83] was admitted into evidence, despite Defence objections that the information was unreliable. Presiding Judge Bruno Cotte observed that UN human rights officer information gathering procedures reflected traditional UN practice and were 'tried and tested'. Moreover, the Chamber considered that the reports were relevant to the case, authentic, and that with the aid of the drafter of the relevant UN report testifying also in person orally, the Court could assess their probative value.[84] Furthermore, while the Chamber acknowledged that the UN human rights information was not collected specifically for the purposes of criminal prosecution, it underlined that:

> The Chamber is perfectly aware that the methods utilized were not the same as the methods employed by police investigators or legal investigators, and it is quite precisely because they are not police investigations or legal investigations that the Chamber, when the time comes, shall accord them the appropriate weight of probative value. In other words, they will – the probative value will be given to the appropriate excerpts and paragraphs from these reports. This probative value will be given bearing in mind that these are reports established by UN services in an impartial manner with a concern to understand the events in question. The Chamber recalls yet again that these are neither police reports nor [Office of the Prosecutor] investigations.[85]

The Chamber thus ruled that the information was admissible as evidence, confirming that under certain conditions information from UN human rights sources could be adduced directly in international criminal proceedings, and the Chamber also endorsed their impartiality.

What about the hearsay rule? Is there not a serious risk that UN human rights officers could be misled into recycling unfounded rumours, false accounts deliberately pressed on them by organised agents of Gov-

---

[82] ICC, *The Prosecutor v. Germain Katanga and Mathieu Ngudjolo Chui*, ICC-01/04-01/07.

[83] See Sonia Bakar's testimony of 6 December 2010; ICC-01/04-01/07-T-228-ENG ET WT 06-12-2010 1/86 RM T (http://www.legal-tools.org/doc/be3a03/).

[84] See the Ruling at DRC OTP P 0317 (Resumed) open session on 7 December 2010.

[85] *Ibid.*, at p. 24, at lines 8–18.

ernment or other parties, or factually incorrect and groundless allegations of genocide, war crimes or crimes against humanity? In other words, apart from the instance discussed above where the drafter of the UN report was brought before the ICC to testify in person, should UN human rights reports based on witness statements and interviews be ruled as hearsay and therefore inadmissible in international criminal proceedings?

Hearsay, is an oral, written or nonverbal assertion that was intended as an assertion and was made out of court, which the declarant offers in court as evidence to prove the truth of the matter asserted in the statement, and not merely that the statement was made.[86] A substantial body of lawyerly and judicial opinion considers hearsay to be inherently unreliable because it "may range all the way from very reliable evidence to idle or malicious gossip, and may have been distorted or embroidered in retelling. [...] Our system relies very heavily on cross-examination as a means of exposing falsehood or error, and few other means of discrediting a witness are permitted".[87] In the adversary system, the rule against hearsay ensures that a witness verifies a fact from his or her own observation instead of merely repeating statements heard from others.

Aside from the issue of unreliability, the hearsay rule, used more in common law jurisdictions, seeks to protect a very important principle:

> This is the principle that a person may not offer testimony against a criminal defendant unless it is given under oath, face to face with the accused and subject to cross-examination. It is this principle – and not concerns about the reliability of hearsay evidence or the supposed inability of the jury to deal with the weaknesses of evidence – that should drive the law concerning secondary evidence.[88]

While the hearsay rule honours some key principles of fairness in criminal justice, it has proven to be of much less importance in international criminal proceedings than in domestic common law jurisdictions for two main reasons. First, the hearsay rule has less application in international criminal trials, which mix adversarial and inquisitorial procedure.

---

[86] See for example, United States Federal Rules of Evidence, Rule 801; Pub. L. 93–595, §1, 2 January 1975, 88 Stat. 1926.

[87] 29 New South Wales NSW Law Reform Commission Report (1978) – The Rule against Hearsay, p. 6.

[88] Richard D. Friedman, "Thoughts from across the Water on Hearsay and Confrontation", in *Criminal Law Review*, October 1998, p. 697.

In criminal law jurisdictions with an adversarial procedure and a jury, the judge is expected to act as a more passive and neutral arbiter between Prosecution and Defense and the jury is the main trier of fact, whereas in continental European systems, the judge participates more actively in questioning witnesses, even suggests lines of enquiry, and decides on law and fact.[89] The hearsay rule was developed partly to prevent jurors from being misled by second hand information – a rationale that applies less to judges experienced in assessing probative value and credibility of evidence. As D'Aoust has observed, the ICTY and ICTR have:

> [...] opted for an extensive admission of evidence as long as it was ruled relevant, reliable and had a probative value that was not substantially outweighed by the need to ensure a fair trial, preferring to leave to the Trial Chamber, after the presentation of the whole of the evidence, the assessment and the determination of its proper weights.[90]

D'Aoust cites dicta from the ICTY *Delalic* and *Nikolić* Cases confirming this point.[91] In the *Thomas Lubanga Case,* the ICC cited dicta from the *Bemba Case* that: "The determination of admissibility is to be made in light of "the relevance, probative value and the potential prejudice of each item of evidence".[92] In the *Bemba Case*, Pre-Trial Chamber II indicated that with regard to deciding on the confirmation of charges (albeit a lower threshold proceeding than that of the trial itself), in review-

---

[89] As Christopher B. Mueller argues:

> The conventional reason for excluding hearsay is mistrust of juries – a fear that lay fact finders cannot properly appraise remote statements and are too unsuspecting. [...] And in criminal cases especially, the serious limitations that hearsay doctrine puts on use of statements produced or gathered by government agents reflects multiple concerns: jury credulity and care in fact-finding are implicated. [...] [J]uries are unlikely to appreciate the pressures faced by prosecution witnesses and law enforcement agents, and probably no fact finder can reliably appraise statements by such people. Further, as a matter of intrinsic policy we discourage both police and prosecutors from generating the out-of-court statements to be used against people charged with crime.

Christopher B. Mueller, "Meta-Evidence: Do We Need It?", in *Loyola of Los Angeles Law Review*, 1992, vol. 25, pp. 822–823.

[90] See Josee D'Aoust, "The Conduct of Trials", in Jose Doria *et al.* (eds.), *The Legal Regime of the International Criminal Court*, 2009, pp. 779-80.

[91] *Ibid.*, p. 880.

[92] Situation in the Democratic Republic of the Congo, *The Prosecutor v. Thomas Lubanga Dyilo*; ICC-01/04-01/06 of 14 March 2012 (Trial Chamber 1) at para. 100 (https://www.legal-tools.org/doc/677866/).

---

ing hearsay evidence, UN, NGO and media reports, it generally assigned lower probative value to indirect evidence than to direct evidence,[93] and it adopted a two-stage approach with regard to indirect evidence:

> [...] it assesses the relevance, probative value and admissibility of indirect evidence, as it would undertake with respect to direct evidence. Once this assessment is made, it then turns to the second step, namely whether there exists corroborating evidence, regardless of its type or source. Thus, the Chamber is able to verify whether the piece of evidence in question, considered together with other evidence, acquires high probative value as a whole.[94]

The ICC has therefore adopted a broad, inclusive approach to evidence, including hearsay, but consciously applied a careful and discerning approach to its reliability, fully in line with the relevant provisions of the Rome Statute and its Rules of Procedure and Evidence.

Second, the hearsay rule itself has fallen into serious disrepute in many common law jurisdictions – its home turf. Already in 1979, the New South Wales Law Reform Commission opined that the hearsay rule:

> [...] continues to annoy and bewilder witnesses, who are not allowed to tell the court what they know in a natural way. It continues to frustrate litigants, who cannot use obviously cogent evidence to prove their cases. It continues to add to the expense and delay of litigation. Parties who wish to embarrass their opponents can require strict first-hand proof of matters not really in dispute. In short, it lowers public respect for the courts by making their operation less sure, less just, more expensive, less comprehensible, and at times simply ridiculous.[95]

Law reform efforts in other countries have considered abolishing the hearsay rule entirely[96] and in recent years a body of empirical research

---

93  *The Prosecutor v. Jean-Pierre Bemba Gombo*; ICC-01/05-01/08 of 15 June 2009 at para. 51 (http://www.legal-tools.org/doc/07965c/).

94  *Ibid.*, at para. 52.

95  NSW Law Reform Commission Report (1978), p. 3, *supra* note 87.

96  See Eleanor Swift, "Abolishing the Hearsay Rule", in *California Law Review*, 1987, vol. 75, no. 1, pp. 495–519. See also David Crump, "The Case for Selective Abolition of the Rules of Evidence", in *Hofstra Law Review*, 2006, vol. 35, p. 585. See further Adrian A.S. Zuckerman, "The futility of hearsay: Law Commission Consultation Paper No.138 on hearsay (Part 1)", in *Criminal Law Review*, vol. 4, 1996.

has cast doubt on the presumption that jurors are unable to distinguish hearsay from direct evidence or to assess carefully its reliability.[97]

In short, the rationale behind excluding hearsay from being admitted into evidence has less persuasive force for international criminal proceedings which mix continental and common law approaches, do not use jurors, and are presided over by judges who are presumably experienced in assessing evidentiary relevance, probative value, reliability, weight and risk of prejudice to fair trial. UN human rights reports based on interviews of witnesses and other individuals therefore should not be excluded *holus-bolus* as evidence in international criminal proceedings, even where the report drafter could not be brought into court to testify, but rather assessed individually in terms of relevance, probative value and potential prejudice – an approach the ICC and *ad hoc* tribunals have already endorsed, as discussed above.

## 13.12. Can International Criminal Investigators and Prosecutors Afford to Ignore Information from UN Human Rights Sources?

International criminal investigators and prosecutors are rarely, if ever, among the first persons to arrive at crime scenes of genocide, war crimes or crimes against humanity. Aside from perpetrators and victims, survivors, witnesses, journalists and eventually local NGO staff are usually the most physically proximate and knowledgeable about the various facets of the crimes in question that international criminal investigators and prosecutors have to piece together months or years after the fact. As discussed above, serious violations of human rights and humanitarian law often get picked up by the UN human rights system antennae which include the human rights treaty bodies, human rights special procedures including special investigative missions or commissions of inquiry deployed under Security Council authority, the Universal Periodic Review and a range of

---

[97] See for example, Richard F. Rakos and Stephan Landsman, "Researching the Hearsay Rule: Emerging Findings, General Issues, and Future Directions", in *Minnesota Law Review*, 1992, vol. 76, pp. 655–682; and Angela Paglia and Regina A. Schuller, "Jurors' Use of Hearsay Evidence: The Effects of Type and Timing of Instructions", in *Law and Human Behavior*, 1998, vol. 22, no. 5. On the question of hearsay introduced by way of expert testimony, see Ronald L. Carlson, "Experts, Judges, and Commentators: the Underlying Debate about an Expert's Underlying Data", in *Mercer Law Review*, 1996, vol. 47 (Winter), pp. 481–493. See also Regina A. Schuller and Angela Paglia, "An Empirical Study: Juror Sensitivity to Variations in Hearsay Conveyed via Expert Evidence", in *Law and Psychology Review*, 1999, vol. 23, pp. 131–149.

other UN human rights related agencies, bodies and programmes such as the OHCHR Secretariat, UN human rights field presences including human rights components of peacekeeping mission, the UN High Commissioner for Refugees, the UN Office for the Coordination of Humanitarian Affairs, UNICEF, UNESCO, the World Food Programme and the World Health Organization, the UN Development Program, and UNODC. The sheer vastness and complexity of the UN family of agencies, their mandates, differing *modus operandi* and distinct management and staff cultures pose formidable obstacles for anyone trying to identify, assess and relate information from these sources to proving guilt beyond a reasonable doubt of perpetrators of the worst crimes known to humanity. Yet the urgency of international criminal justice for victims, survivors, affected communities, societies seeking to transit from conflict, and the international community at large, demands that crimes, their victims and perpetrators are placed accurately in a large and detailed tableau. That requires a wide and high-resolution field of perception on the part of international criminal investigators and prosecutors. In order to discharge their solemn responsibility towards fair and effective international criminal justice, international criminal investigators and prosecutors cannot afford to ignore information from UN human rights sources.

# 14

---

# Non-Governmental Organisation Fact-Work: Not Only a Technical Problem

## Wolfgang Kaleck and Carolijn Terwindt[*]

[W]e are trying to get the facts but they're not facts that have to stand up in a court of law.[1]

## 14.1. The Quality of NGO Fact-Work

During the past decades, non-governmental organisations ('NGOs') have become involved in fact-finding regarding human rights abuses. Indeed, the documentation of human rights violations has become the *raison d'être* for more than a few NGOs. It is more of a recent development that their contributions have also come before courts as evidence in criminal trials.

As the standards for evidence to be admissible and credible in court are high, the fact-work methodology from NGOs has not always been sufficient to fulfill such requirements. This has led to calls for and attempts

[*] **Wolfgang Kaleck** is General Secretary of the European Center for Constitutional and Human Rights ('ECCHR'), which he founded in 2007. He is a member of the Centre of European Law and Politics at the University of Bremen, the CILRAP Advisory Board, the lawyers collective CCAJAR in Colombia, the Mexican non-governmental organization ProDESC, FIAN Germany as well as the Paul Grueninger Foundation. Two of his books were recently published in English: *Law versus Power. Our Global Fight for Human Rights*, OR Books, New York-London, 2019; and *Double Standards: International Criminal Law and the West*, Torkel Opsahl Academic EPublisher, Brussels, 2015. He has published several books in German. In recognition of his human rights work, he received the 2019 M.C. Bassiouni Justice Award and the Bayerischer Anwaltverband (Bavarian Lawyer's Association) Max Friedlaender Prize in 2018. **Carolijn Terwindt** wrote her doctoral dissertation "Ethnographies of Contentious Criminalization" at Columbia Law School, NYC, and worked as a lecturer and researcher in Utrecht, Amsterdam and Freiburg. Her work was published in a variety of journals, including *Nationalism and Ethnic Politics*, *Development in Practice*, and *Crime, Law, and Social Change*.

[1] Interview with representative of Amnesty International, in Eric Meldrum, "Time for a Change? The Traditional Human Right NGO Fact Finding Methodology in Relation to National and International Prosecutions of Gross Human Right Violations", Written for M.A., Oxford, 31 August 2009, p. 36.

to create a system for quality control of such fact-finding by NGOs. For example, in order to ensure that the quality of their contributions would be up to courtroom standards, the prosecutor's office of the International Criminal Tribunal for the former Yugoslavia ('ICTY') issued guidelines for NGOs to follow.[2]

Fact-finding by NGOs, including the choices of which 'facts' to find, and how to interpret and report or not report them, is never a neutral process, but always part of a political struggle.[3] The politics of fact-work is visible, for example, in the selection of facts that are worthy of documentation or to be further investigated in a fact-finding mission.[4] Indeed, it is often exactly because of the political biases behind such questions that NGOs get active in the first place, for example, to draw attention to forgotten victim groups. It is also because of the many real, perceived, or alleged political motives behind human rights fact-work that, from its start, credibility has been emphasised as a core condition for such work.[5]

There are no uniform standards regarding NGO fact-finding, even though there are multiple publications addressing methods and best practices.[6] Scholars and practitioners have criticised the lack of a standardised and universal methodology for fact-finding by NGOs.[7] This is not a new debate. In 1980, Franck and Scott Fairley warned against mere propaganda and called for universally applicable minimal standards to avoid anoth-

---

[2]   Meldrum, 2009, p. 31, see *supra* note 1.

[3]   For example, on the role of human rights organisations in the civil war in El Salvador, see Ralph Sprenkels and Chris van der Borgh, "De politiek van civiele diplomatie. Burgeroorlog en mensenrechten in El Salvador", Chapter 5, in Beatrice de Graaf and Duco Hellema (eds.), *Civic Diplomacy. Diplomatie tussen macht en Mensenrechten*, SIM Special, 2010, Utrecht, no. 33.

[4]   Godoy has described how in Guatemala the appropriate focus of human rights work has become an issue. The focus on allegedly political crimes while ignoring common crimes has led to accusations that human rights NGOs would only be protecting criminals. Angelina Godoy, "La Muchacha Respondona: Reflections on the Razor's Edge between Crime and Human Rights", in *Human Rights Quarterly*, 2005, pp. 597–624.

[5]   Diane Orentlicher, "Bearing Witness: The Art and Science of Human Rights Fact Finding", in *Harvard Human Rights Journal*, 1990, vol. 3, p. 95.

[6]   For instance, see *ibid.*

[7]   For example, Gerald M. Steinberg, Anne Herzberg, and Jordan Berman, *Best Practices for Human Rights and Humanitarian NGO Fact-Finding*, Martinus Nijhoff Publishers, 2012.

er "chimera".[8] At around the same time, Weissbrodt and McCarthy asked whether NGOs should adopt formal fact-finding procedures.[9] Also in the early 1980s, the Netherlands Institute of Human Rights ('SIM') organised a conference on human rights fact-finding in which they especially focused on NGOs and the development of procedural rules to improve future fact-finding efforts.[10] Thus, the problems with NGO fact-finding, the lack of uniform standards and the possible need for them have been discussed for a few decades already, even though literature on the topic has been scarce.[11]

The emergence of the international criminal tribunals and extraterritorial cases in domestic courts has introduced a different standard for doing human rights fact-work internationally and added a new layer to this debate.[12] Fact-finders now have to face the questions of whether, how, and to what extent their fact-work could or should be compatible with such criminal justice standards. For example, Talsma has undertaken a study comparing the rules of evidence of the *ad hoc* criminal courts to the rules adopted by UN human rights fact-finding missions. She found that while

---

[8]    Thomas M. Franck and H. Scott Fairley, "Procedural Due Process in Human Rights Fact-Finding by International Agencies", in *The American Journal of Law*, 1980, vol. 74, no. 2, p. 309.

[9]    D. Weissbrodt and J. McCarthy, "Fact-Finding by International Nongovernmental Human Rights Organizations", in *Virginia Journal of International Law*, 1981, vol. 22, no. 1.

[10]   Studie en Informatiecentrum Mensenrechten, SIM Newsletter, 1984, no. 6, p. 1; a more in-depth discussion of the report can be found in Robert Charles Blitt, "Who Will Watch the Watchdogs? Human Rights Nongovernmental Organizations and the Case for Regulation", in *Buffalo Human Rights Law Review*, 2004, vol. 10, pp. 334–339.

[11]   Regarding governmental fact-finding, former UN Rapporteur Philip Alston specifically calls for more engagement with the topic, pointing out that the proliferation of fact-finding missions might be viewed as a development as significant for the human rights field as the establishment of international and mixed criminal courts. Philip Alston, "Commissions of Inquiry into Armed Conflict, Breaches of the Laws of War, and Human Rights Abuses: Process, Standards, and Lessons Learned", in *American Society of International Law Proceedings*, 2011, vol. 105, p. 84.

[12]   We have witnessed the emergence of NGOs with qualifications and knowledge about evidentiary standards, which are proactively using them in their litigation work (for instance, TRIAL International or the ECCHR). These organizations are often directly involved in litigation. When working on transnational cases, which happens frequently when litigating cases of human rights abuses, these specialized organisations often train smaller partner NGOs that are sometimes performing documentation ground work while human rights abuses are still ongoing (examples are trainings by NGOs or organisations such as the International Bar Association, for NGOs working on the ground in Syria or Yemen that are trying to document international crimes).

---

fact-finding missions admit almost all evidence, stricter rules apply in the court.[13] Since starting to co-operate with the prosecutors at international tribunals, NGOs now face this dilemma of managing this difference as well.

Efforts have been made to adapt criminal investigation principles for the purposes of human rights fact-finders.[14] Others have attempted to grapple with the different evidentiary standards generally adopted in fact-finding missions and in a criminal courtroom.[15] From such manuals, NGOs can learn technical advice about how to estimate the credibility of their reports, to develop a witness statement file, how to document a physical injury, or how to maintain a 'chain of custody' for possibly forensic evidence (that is, including dates, places, and signatures from everyone that has been in possession of the material, as well as a label where the evidence is from, with appropriate packaging material). The ICTY, for example, has developed the following concrete advice for NGOs that want to contribute to their criminal investigations:

> [I]nstitutions and agencies should be encouraged to record the details of potential witnesses, including and especially their future contact information, but should be encouraged not to attempt to take comprehensive witness statements. Rather, they should simply record in a general way the statements of potential witnesses based on their own direct experiences, and they should understand that the taking of statements is a professional process that is best left to the criminal justice system and to trained investigators.[16]

While such manuals can give guidance to NGOs when they want their materials to contribute to courtroom procedures, it is recognised that NGOs will have to determine whether such guidelines indeed suit them in

---

[13] Lara Talsma, "UN Human Rights Fact-Finding: Establishing Individual Criminal Responsibility?", in *Florida Journal of International Law*, 2012, vol. 24.

[14] Dermot Groome, *The Handbook of Human Rights Investigation: A Comprehensive Guide to the Investigation and Documentation of Violent Human Rights Abuses*, Northborough, MA, Human Rights Press, 2001.

[15] Stephen Wilkinson, "Standards of Proof in International Humanitarian and Human Rights Fact-Finding and Inquiry Missions", Geneva Academy of International Humanitarian Law and Human Rights, p. 5 (available on its web site).

[16] ICTY, "Manual on Developed Practices", UNICRI Publisher, Turin, Italy, 2009, p. 16 (https://www.legal-tools.org/doc/0cc55d/).

the particular situation that they are in.[17] Clearly, fact-work in preparation for a legal case is different from fact-work done for the traditional purposes of human rights NGOs. Two full days may be required to draft a courtroom testimony with the level of detail and in the particular form needed by a litigation lawyer. On the other hand, for the purpose of an NGO report, one hour might be sufficient.[18] This difference alone would be enough to indicate the tension that inevitably arises when NGOs consider turning their fact-work into evidence.

What makes this more complicated is that it is really difficult to define standards because they might differ considerably depending on where and how a piece of evidence is to be used. When trying to bring a civil claim for damages (for instance, Marie Colvin in the United States), lawyers had to present detailed evidence according to strict admissibility standards, whereas in criminal investigations in many civil or continental legal systems, rather general information is being handed over to prosecutors who then conduct the investigations. If NGOs collect information in a manner that is too detailed, it might even reflect negatively on the case, because it increases the risk of differences between testimonies, which in turn can negatively affect the credibility of a witness. This means that the best evidence is completely tailored to the kind of forum in which it will be used in the future, which demands the legal knowledge of the prerequisites for the admissibility of evidence in that forum. Often, however, that forum is unknown to the NGO when the evidence is being collected.

Further, the development to co-operate with criminal justice officials is a striking change from the distrust that traditionally existed among human rights NGOs (and still continues to exist among many) towards state institutions and, particularly, the prosecution. Still, not all NGOs are willing to hand over documents to the prosecution or appear as witnesses – for good and bad reasons.[19]

Therefore, before it is possible to enter a discussion about quality control and delve into the more detailed and technocratic questions of standardised procedures, it is important to take a step back and reflect on

---

[17] In his introduction, Groome explicitly writes that NGOs will have to decide whether to adopt the advice. Groome, 2001, see *supra* note 14.

[18] Personal conversation Carolijn Terwindt with current litigator and former Amnesty International investigator, 2 March 2013, Delhi, India.

[19] Meldrum, 2009, pp. 42–44, see *supra* note 1.

the problem from a socio-political perspective. Recognising the differences between NGOs, including the different situations within which they conduct their fieldwork and the varied interests and purposes they serve; the question shifts from whether guidelines or standards *should* be implemented, to *which* standards should be adopted, *when* and by *whom*. It is argued, that as a preliminary step to fact-work, it is essential that NGOs clarify their role, goal, and methods, and especially also their approach to, and possibly future role in, legal procedures.

This chapter first reflects briefly on the differences between NGOs and the situations in which they conduct their fact-work. It further discusses the problems that are related to fact-finding and the debate about the development of standards to implement a system of quality control. The chapter then turns to the specific problems that arise when NGO fact-work comes to play a role in criminal investigations and courtroom proceedings. Instead of dealing with these problems head-on in terms of specific suggestions for guidelines or standards, the authors address the underlying role conflicts that are bound to occur when NGOs become intermediaries between criminal justice officials on the one hand and affected communities on the other. The chapter concludes by reiterating the importance of early reflection on the possibility that fact-work turns into evidence and the need for a clear position of the NGO both *vis-à-vis* the people that were the basis for the production of the facts, and in relation to the courtroom rules and procedures.

## 14.2. Differentiating NGOs and Fact-Work Situations

Robertson traces NGO fact-finding to the foundation of Amnesty International in 1961[20] and estimates the current number of human rights NGOs engaged in monitoring or fact-finding at several thousand.[21] Just as the concept 'civil society' has come to be filled with different meanings,[22] so too has the term NGO become a catch-all term.[23] As the NGO sector

---

[20] Robertson mistakenly dates the foundation of Amnesty International in 1959 (Geoffrey Robertson, "Human Rights Fact-Finding: Some Legal and Ethical Dilemmas", in *University College London Human Rights Review*, 2010, vol. 3, p. 21).

[21] *Ibid.*, p. 38.

[22] Michael Edwards, *Civil Society*, Polity, 2009.

[23] For a discussion regarding a definition of NGOs generally and human rights NGOs in particular, see also George E. Edwards, "Assessing The Effectiveness Of Human Rights Non-Governmental Organizations (NGOs) From The Birth Of The United Nations To The 21st

worldwide has boomed over the past decades, the term has increasingly been used to describe a range of diverse organisations with little in common. For example, the fact that some NGOs are actually set up or funded by governments, even led to the pitching of the term GONGO (government-sponsored non-governmental organisations).[24] Moreover, NGOs do not necessarily promote tolerance and civic virtues, hence the emergence of the term 'uncivil' society.[25]

The many possible differences between NGOs have been captured by categorising them in several ways.[26] This chapter will only briefly mention some of the factors that inevitably influence the way an NGO approaches fact-work. The focus here is on the particular subset of NGOs that addresses human rights. This can include professionally run organisations (for example, Human Rights Watch) and grassroots membership organisations (for example, a victim's organisation such as the Khulumani Support Group in South Africa).[27] Some NGOs act globally, such as Amnesty International, whereas others work regionally or locally.

This, however, is not enough to differentiate between the different kinds of fact-work that these NGOs engage in. Access to resources and know-how are key factors as well. Further, some NGOs work on the basis that they are outsiders, whereas others receive their mandate from being in close connection to particular groups. Thus, some NGOs are embedded in

---

Century: Ten Attributes Of Highly Successful Human Rights NGOs", in *Michigan State University College of Law Journal of International Law*, 2009–2010, vol. 18, p. 169.

[24] Moisés Naím, "What is a GONGO?", in *Foreign Policy*, 18 April 2007.

[25] For a critical position regarding this term, see Clifford Bob, "Civil and Uncivil Society", in *The Oxford Handbook of Civil Society*, 2011; see also Geoffrey Robertson, "Human Rights Fact-Finding: Some Legal and Ethical Dilemmas", in *UCL Human Rights Review*, 2010, vol. 3, p. 38.

[26] Edwards developed an NGO 'taxonomy' differentiating NGOs on the basis of the geographical emphasis of their operations, staff or members' nationality, status of personnel (that is, paid or voluntary), geo-political and economic origin (for example, North or South, democratic regime or totalitarian), structure (consultancy basis, project, academic, *et cetera*), size, substantive area of human rights concern, nature of mandates and work, funding levels and funding sources, how they lobby or consult domestic governments or IGOs, how they gather information, how they share information, and their affiliations. Edwards, 2009–2010, see *supra* note 22.

[27] The distinction between professionally run versus grassroots comes from Harry Blair, "Civil society and Building Democracy: Lessons from International Donor Experience", in Amanda Bernard, Henny Helmich and Percy B. Lehning (eds.), *Civil Society and International Development*, OECD, 1998, p. 66.

a domestic social movement or political struggle[28] (for example, human rights organisations Karapatan in the Philippines or Behatokia in the Basque Country) whereas others pride themselves on their independence (for example, International Crisis Group). Each of these actors moves within a different discursive and institutional field, and therefore has different opportunities for engaging with local communities or exerting influence on national governments.[29]

Not only are there major differences between NGOs, the situations in which fact-work occurs may also differ dramatically.[30] Some NGOs conduct incident-based missions, whereas others do fact-collection on an ongoing basis. Some may rely on independent experts for their reports, whereas others may use human rights reports from amateur activists.[31] Human Rights Watch also distinguishes between situations in which they research an emergency incident versus those situations where they deal with long-running (systematic or repeated) violations.[32] Also, in the reporting of fact-finding, NGOs have relied on a variety of formats ranging from quantitative tables listing violations, narrative background reports, case studies, legal assessments, or personal accounts.

NGOs can thus differ in their capacities and conditions for undertaking fact-finding. It is disputed, however, whether different situations

---

[28]　For a discussion on the politicisation of NGOs, and particularly the establishment of human rights organisations by political party activists to benefit from the realm of objectivity, see Robert Charles Blitt, "Who Will Watch the Watchdogs? Human Rights Nongovernmental Organizations and the Case for Regulation", in *Buffalo Human Rights Law Review*, 2004, vol. 10, pp. 359–360.

[29]　For an analysis of the differential power of human rights NGOs in Israel, see Neve Gordon, "Human Rights, Social Space and Power: Why do some NGOs Exert More Influence than Others?", in *The International Journal of Human Rights*, 2008, vol. 12, no. 1, pp. 23–39

[30]　Robertson identifies five types of fact-finding: (i) The Commission of Inquiry with statutory powers; (ii) an official inquiry without legal power; (iii) an inquiry set up by an NGO but executed by an independent person; (iv) a confidential expert mission which later feeds into an NGO report; (v) the previous 'single-visit' missions have to be distinguished from ongoing and systematic in-country monitoring by local actors or country representatives, that is, a 'permanent fact-finding mission', also called human rights reporters (Robertson, 2010, pp. 16–17, *supra* note 20).

[31]　Beutz Land specifically analyses the difficulty that this amateur model poses to ensure the accuracy of facts (Molly Beutz Land, "Peer Producing Human Rights", in *Alberta Law Review*, 2008–2009, vol. 46, p. 1116).

[32]　Human Rights Watch, "Our Research Methodology" (available on its web site).

would require different approaches or standards.[33] It is clear, though, that interviewing witnesses in a rural area in a war zone about ongoing sexualised violence by warring parties poses different challenges to an NGO than fact-finding about war crimes that occurred 40 years ago, or factfinding into corporate responsibility for alleged health damages due to the use of pesticides by migrant workers on plantations.

In the ongoing universal jurisdiction investigations in Western European States many Syrian witnesses have been accompanied by different NGOs. Their accounts included heavily traumatizing incidents in an ongoing conflict, far from the forum State. The sheer number and the content of their testimonies pose challenges of all kinds.

Having disaggregated the term 'NGO', it is equally important to explain what fact-finding means here. In line with this publication, factfinding is understood as 'fact-work', which involves the "work processes to identify, locate, obtain, verify, analyze, corroborate, summarize, synthesize, structure, organize, present and disseminate facts".[34] Fact-work thus expressly also includes analysis. Indeed, fact-work does not necessarily mean collecting new facts; it can also mean digesting fact-finding of others. Such is the core contribution, for example, of the Human Rights Data Analysis Group, whose statistical analyses of existing datasets can yield new insights.[35]

More than ever before, a major part of fact-finding today consists of sifting through the quantity of information available "separating facts

---

[33] Meldrum describes that Human Rights Watch does not have specific interview standards because of the need to adapt to the case at hand (Meldrum, 2009, pp. 15–16, see *supra* note 1) – he explicitly addresses the tension between this assertion and the belief at the Police that there are best practice tools that should apply anywhere (Meldrum, 2009, p. 41, see *supra* note 1).

[34] See the concept note of the 2013 LI Haopei Seminar co-organized by CILRAP, European University Institute, and Peking University International Law Institute (available on http://www.fichl.org/activities/quality-control-in-international-fact-finding-outside-criminal-justice-for-core-international-crimes/).

[35] For example, its statistical analyses of the killings of trade unionists in Colombia, particularly also taking into account the number that would not have been registered, have claimed to be able to offer statistical estimates of unknown, unreported trade unionists killed, which is estimated at about 30%. Daniel Guzmán, Tamy Guberek and Megan Price, "Unobserved Union Violence: Statistical Estimates of the Total Number of Trade Unionists Killed in Colombia, 1999–2008", in *Benetech Human Rights Program*, 13 November 2012, p. 1 (available on the Human Rights Data Analysis Group's web site).

from rumour, propaganda and blogging fantasies".[36] Analysis also includes the legal assessment of facts, which can have great significance,
for example, when facts are concluded to indicate the occurrence of
crimes against humanity or genocide.[37] Equally significant can be the val-
uation of a trial as being in accordance with due process or not.[38] For this
reason, Blitt fears the risks of poor interpretation methods.[39]

Fact-work by NGOs often goes beyond the collection and analysis
of facts. For local NGOs to achieve the goals of their fact-work, such facts
have to get attention and be recognised as important and legitimate facts.[40]
For this, these facts may need to be reproduced by more official institutions, such as UN Special Rapporteurs or governmental *ad hoc* inquiry
commissions. Initial fact-finding by grassroots NGOs can thus be used to
push official public institutions to send fact-finding missions. For example,
in the Philippines, a coalition of NGOs started a "Stop-the-Killings" campaign and advocated explicitly for a fact-finding mission by the UN Special Rapporteur on Extra-Judicial Killings.[41]

While NGOs try to get attention from more formal institutions, international fact-finders (including globally working human rights NGOs
such as Amnesty International and Human Rights Watch) often depend
heavily on fact-work by local and national human rights NGOs in order to
get access to sites, victims, and witnesses during their missions.[42] Local
and national human rights documentation thus often finds its way into the
reports of *ad hoc* inquiry missions. Blitt criticises this reliance by international fact-finders on local NGOs because they tend to be underfunded
and have less stringent fact-finding standards.[43]

---

[36] Robertson, 2010, p. 18, see *supra* note 20.

[37] *Ibid.*, p. 17.

[38] Robertson, 2010, p. 22, see *supra* note 20.

[39] Blitt, 2004, p. 289, see *supra* note 28.

[40] Keck and Sikkink have described NGO activities to achieve such recognition in their book
about advocacy. They describe that NGOs are involved in what they call network politics,
information politics, symbolic politics, leverage politics, and accountability politics (Mar-
garet E. Keck and Kathryn Sikkink, *Activists beyond Borders: Advocacy Networks in International Politics*, Cornell University Press, 1998).

[41] Interviews by Carolijn Terwindt with representatives of human rights organisations
Karapatan and Task Force Detainees of the Philippines, 20–21 March 2012, Manila.

[42] See, for example, Human Rights Watch, "Our Research Methodology", see *supra* note 32.

[43] Blitt, 2004, pp. 342 and 354, see *supra* note 28.

NGOs are thus just one of the actors within a larger field of national and international human rights actors engaged in fact-work. As NGOs engage in fact-finding, they can do so in the absence of any investigation by public institutions (including prosecutors, but also state human rights commissioners, ombudsmen, or UN Special Rapporteurs). NGO fact-finding can, however, also take place in addition to such state or supra-state investigations. Such factors can be relevant for NGOs to decide the purpose of their fact-work.

This leads to the different goals of fact-finding, a last factor influencing fact-work approaches. Fact-finding is often the basis for other work that the NGO pursues. An important goal is public scandalising of human rights abuses that occurred or are going on and calling attention to the actors that are held to be responsible for them. NGOs may also claim an early warning function to attract external observers to otherwise possibly unnoticed violations. If public institutions did engage in fact-work, NGOs might become active to counter existing information, submit shadow reports, contribute to public debate and decision-making, or contribute to the historical record.[44] Fact-work may also be part of ongoing support to victims and their communities as well as social movements and a way to give their voice in the public debate. Fact-finding can further be used to promote law-making[45] or to serve a quasi-judicial function and come to a legal assessment of facts and attribution of (criminal) responsibility. Finally, fact-finding may explicitly be undertaken in order to support adjudication in court.

The goals of NGO fact-work can thus be very different from those of criminal investigation. This is reflected, for example, in the fact that traditional NGO fact-finding mainly consists of taking interview statements. Only sporadically do NGOs collect physical evidence, even though

---

[44] For example, after a massacre in Mesuji, Indonesia, where allegedly police officers were responsible for the deaths of one or more farmers, NGOs in Jakarta distrusted the independent fact-finding mission which was set up by the government (even though a well-respected human rights lawyer was made part of the mission) and a coalition of national NGOs sent its own fact-finding mission in order to publish an alternative report (interview by Carolijn Terwindt with a spokesperson for the Consortium for Agrarian Reform ('KPA'), 28 March 2012, Jakarta).

[45] Tamar Ezer and Susan Deller Ross, "Fact-Finding as a Lawmaking Tool for Advancing Women's Human Rights", in *The Georgetown Journal of Gender and the Law*, 2006, vol. 7.

they may actively take pictures.[46] The data that NGOs collect should be accurate and credible, but, often, it should also provide the emotional element needed to achieve the goal that NGOs have to "create issues". For that purpose, information should not only be credible, but also dramatic in order to persuade audiences.[47]

The way in which fact-work is done and the kinds of facts that are collected thus depend not only on the characteristics and function of an NGO, but also on the context within which such fact-work takes place, and the goals of the fact-finding. Quality control is problematic as the goals of fact-work are often multiple, unstated, and can change over time. Furthermore, many NGOs engage in fact-finding to have a political and public impact as well as to turn information into evidence for court adjudication.

## 14.3. General Problems in NGO Fact-Finding: Early Guidelines

NGOs, as well as their counterparts from legal and institutional bodies, can face a variety of challenges as they embark on fact-work, ranging from a lack of access to information, to security issues and a lack of resources. Access to information is a problem that has particular salience in closed societies (such as North Korea) or dictatorships.[48] But even in established democracies, access to information can be barred due to government secrecy.[49] Accessibility of geographical areas and witnesses can also be an issue. Of course, NGOs rely on publicly available materials and the goodwill from people to provide it. Human Rights Watch, for example, described that their requests for interviews, especially requests to government officials, or any other accused perpetrators of abuses, are often refused.[50] NGOs also lack subpoena power from official institutions. It should be noted, however, that while access to specific information can be

---

[46] Meldrum, 2009, see *supra* note 1.

[47] Keck and Sikkink, 1998, p. 19, see *supra* note 40.

[48] Orentlicher, 1990, p. 94, see *supra* note 5.

[49] For example, in relation to the programme of extraordinary rendition, savvy use of the right to information regarding on flight data and air traffic management yielded some information to identify planes connected with the renditions program. Most countries, however, obstructed the freedom of information requests (Reprieve and Access Info Europe, "Rendition on Record: Using the Right of Access to Information to Unveil the Paths of Illegal Prisoner Transfer Flights", 19 December 2011 (available on the Rendition Project's web site).

[50] Human Rights Watch, "Our Research Methodology", see *supra* note 32.

a problem, an overwhelming quantity of data can also pose a challenge to NGOs in terms of the appropriate analysis of the information.

Security issues are rampant. Apart from the general security threat posed by entering violent environments such as war zones or failed states, those involved in the documentation and publication of human rights abuses frequently become the target of threats and, in some cases, even extra-judicial killings. Such was the case, for example, when human rights advocate Munir, the director of Imparsial in Indonesia was poisoned after calling attention to abuses by the Indonesian military.[51] Increased international attention to 'human rights defenders' is a testimony to the reality of these risks.[52]

Besides security issues, NGOs can face libel claims, as they do not enjoy the immunity guaranteed to some other fact-finders, for example, UN rapporteurs.[53] Also, human rights organisations that are engaged in judicial procedures are vulnerable to such backlashes, for example, in the form of charges for criminal defamation.[54]

A lack of resources and know-how can further hamper NGO fact-work. Beyond hard costs, such as access to computers, adequate software, and travel allowances, many NGOs are small and rely on volunteers to fulfill core tasks. While there is no doubt that such organisations can produce excellent work, the lack of resources also means that there are limits to what can be done.

In the literature, the problems with fact-finding have been discussed not only with regards to NGOs, but also in relation to national human rights commissions, UN Special Rapporteurs, *ad hoc* inquiry fact-finding missions by UN agencies, and fact-finding by regional human rights

---

[51] Rusdi Marpaung, J. Heri Sugianto and Cahyadi Satriya (eds.), *Test of Our History??? A Thick Wall on the Murder Investigation of Munir*, Imparsial, Jakarta, 2006.

[52] For example, in 1999 the UN issued a Declaration on Human Rights Defenders, adopted with United Nations General Assembly, Resolution 53/144, 8 March 1999; and the EU issued guidelines in "Human Rights Defenders – EU support", EUR-Lex (available on the European Union's web site); since 2000, there is a UN Special Rapporteur dedicated to this issue.

[53] Robertson, 2010, pp. 18, 41–43, see *supra* note 20.

[54] Criminal defamation charges are a serious issue for anti-corruption NGOs in Indonesia, see Human Rights Watch, "Turning Critics into Criminals", 4 May 2010 (available on its web site).

courts.[55] Indeed, most literature has centred on fact-finding missions by UN or governmental agencies.[56] Efforts to arrive at guidelines and standards have, therefore, often focused on such specialised *ad hoc* missions. In 1980, for example, attempts by the International Law Association to establish standards to assess the quality of fact-finding reports resulted in the Belgrade Minimal Rules of Procedure for International Human Rights Fact-Finding Missions.[57]

A few authors, however, have given specific recommendations regarding data collection by NGOs.[58] Recommendations by Thoolen and Verstappen (based on their survey of NGO fact-finding reports) included the request to include a description of the methodology as well as suggestions to distinguish clearly between direct evidence and factual inferences from indirect evidence, and to distinguish between findings and conclusions.[59]

Early guidelines for NGO fact-finding were generally made with the objective that facts should create public political pressure, and thus focused mainly on enhancing the credibility of allegations. Part of the public battle about the authenticity of facts involves attacks on credibility of the NGO, for example, by defaming the authors of such reports.[60]

---

[55]  See, for example, Frans Viljoen, "Fact-Finding by UN Human Rights Complaints Bodies – Analysis and Suggested Reforms", in Max Planck Yearbook of United Nations Law, 2004, vol. 8, p. 49; Philip Leach, Costas Paraskeva and Gordana Uzelac, "Human Rights Fact-Finding. The European Court of Human Rights at a Crossroads", in *Netherlands Quarterly of Human Rights,* 2010, vol. 28, pp. 41–77; Franck and Scott Fairley, 1980, see *supra* note 8.

[56]  For example, as early as 1970, Miller wrote about the challenges to UN fact-finding missions given the lack of cooperation by the relevant states. Robert Miller, "United Nations Fact-Finding Missions in the Field of Human Rights", in *Australian Yearbook of International Law,* 1970–1973, p. 40. In a more recent article, former Special Rapporteur Philip Alston analysed the problems that can be observed regarding *ad hoc* government initiated commissions of inquiry after extra-judicial executions. Philip Alston, "Commissions of Inquiry into Armed Conflict, Breaches of the Laws of War, and Human Rights Abuses: Process, Standards, and Lessons Learned", in *American Society of International Law Proceedings,* 2011, vol. 105, p. 83.

[57]  Nigel S. Rodley, "Assessing the Goldstone Report", in *Global Governance,* 2010, vol. 16, p. 191.

[58]  For example, Orentlicher, 1990, pp. 109–130, see *supra* note 5.

[59]  Blitt discusses this study by H. Thoolen and B. Verstappen, "Human Rights Missions: A Study of the Fact-Finding Practice of Non-Governmental Organizations", 1986, in Blitt, 2004, pp. 335–337, see *supra* note 28.

[60]  Beutz Land, 2008–2009, p. 1119, see *supra* note 31.

---

Therefore, NGOs have adopted policies, such as always disclosing sources of funding and, for some NGOs, refusing funders like governments.[61] Besides credibility as a key factor, it has long been recognised that accuracy is the most important asset of a human rights organisation.[62] For this reason, over the past decades, fact-finding by larger NGOs such as Human Rights Watch and Amnesty International has professionalised in the sense that they have an internal review process as well as centralised training and editing procedures.[63] While key factors such as credibility and accuracy are thus recognised and shared, there is no uniform standard on which NGOs have agreed to assess the quality of fact-finding reports. Blitt, a forceful advocate of uniform standards has pointed out what is at stake here:

> [I]t is the lack of standards that threatens to downgrade the authority of the human rights NGO community and further risks undermining the legitimacy of recognized international human rights norms.[64]

The basic guiding principles of fact-finding – neutrality, impartiality, and independence – are not controversial for most NGOs. However, a matter of dispute has been whether NGOs should indeed adopt the same guidelines as those adopted by international governmental organisations, whether NGOs should be allowed to decide flexibly what fits their particular situation, or whether there should be a set of standards that applies specifically to NGOs.[65] Orentlicher explicitly addressed the fact that NGOs have generally been reluctant to accept standardised methodologies.[66] A particular concern she mentions is fact-finding in very repressive countries, where more flexibility would be needed. Another concern is that setting standards too high would make it easy for governments to discredit domestic monitoring NGOs, making them vulnerable to repression.[67]

---

[61] Robertson, 2010, p. 21, see *supra* note 20.

[62] Beutz Land, 2008–2009, p. 1119, see *supra* note 31.

[63] *Ibid.*, p. 1118.

[64] Blitt, 2004, p. 321, see *supra* note 28.

[65] *Ibid.*, pp. 348–349.

[66] Orentlicher, 1990, p. 105, see *supra* note 5.

[67] *Ibid.*

One suggestion to deal with the need for flexibility, while maintaining credibility, has been the device of a "threshold standard of credibility".[68] Suggested in 1990 by Orentlicher, the idea has been taken up by the Geneva academy of international humanitarian law and human rights[69] which identifies four different standards of proof which can be attached to fact-work: 'reasonable suspicion',[70] 'balance of probabilities',[71] 'clear and convincing evidence',[72] and 'overwhelming evidence'.[73] This is also a first step to make NGO fact-work amenable for litigation as these standards can be translated into different standards of suspicion and evidence in different domestic and international law procedures.

## 14.4. NGO Fact-Work and Formal Investigation or Litigation

Human rights fact-finding has come to play an important role in court proceedings, especially since the establishment of international criminal tribunals, the rise of domestic procedures, and the growing number of universal jurisdiction cases concerning the systematic torture of the Assad regime in Syria. In addition to being called the best documented conflict with regards to international crimes,[74] its documentation has been gathered by NGOs in most cases.

This is due to the fact that in 2011, when the protests started, smartphone technology was widely available in Syria and proved to be important in organising the protests in the first place. This has led to an unprecedented level of documentation that was, in many instances, aimed

---

[68]  *Ibid.*, p. 106.

[69]  Wilkinson, p. 5, see *supra* note 15.

[70]  "Grounds for suspicion that the incident in question occurred, but other conclusions are possible. (40%) Classic expression is may be reasonable to conclude", Wilkinson, p. 5, see *supra* note 15.

[71]  "More evidence supports the finding than contradicts it. (51%) Classic expression is reasonable to conclude", *ibid.*

[72]  "Very solid support for the finding; significantly more evidence supports the finding and limited information suggests the contrary. (60%) Classic expression is it is clear that", *ibid.*

[73]  "Conclusive or highly convincing evidence supports the finding. (80%) Classic expression is it is overwhelming, it is undeniable", *ibid.*

[74]  Wolfgang Kaleck and Patrick Kroker, "Syrian Torture Investigations in Germany and Beyond Breathing New Life into Universal Jurisdiction in Europe?", in *Journal of International Criminal Justice*, 2018, vol. 16, no. 1, pp. 165-191; Ingrid Elliott, "A Meaningful Step towards Accountability? A View from the Field on the United Nations International, Impartial and Independent Mechanism for Syria", in *Journal of International Criminal Justice*, 2017, vol. 15, no. 2, p. 240.

---

to document the human rights abuses. Once the calls for accountability were obtaining increased traction, organizations switched to document for these purposes as well. Other organizations specialized in analysing and cataloguing information and documentation that had been uploaded to the internet by activist-journalists or documentarists.[75]

It is still too early to assess how much of this evidence has made or will make its way into the courtroom, and the extent of its value in court. What can be said is that it contributed enormously to raise public attention to the issue of the abuses that were being committed in Syria and made prosecutors aware of this problem. In such a way, it might have contributed to the far-reaching steps that were taken: for instance, the arrest warrants against Jamil Hassan in Germany and France and against Fajr Mahmoud and Ali Mamluk in France.

At the same time, these organisations were not only being trained in how to provide evidence, but also played a major role in driving the steps towards accountability that were taken.[76] These NGOs and Syrian lawyers engaged in documentation, together with international NGOs, were strategically shaping prosecutions that had been started in European countries with the criminal complaints that they filed in several of them. The evidentiary foundations these complaints were based on were collected by Syrian organisations and lawyers, comprising mainly of witness testimonies from survivors of torture prisons.

For example, prosecutorial decisions to initiate proceedings have been taken on the basis of fact-finding reports.[77] This is so for fact-finding reports in general, and it has also been the case with NGO fact-finding.

The general problems related to access to information, security, and resources continue to play a role when NGO fact-work becomes the basis for courtroom evidence. They may even obtain new salience in this context. For example, while establishing credibility has been a major focus since the early days of NGO fact-finding, if NGO-fact-work becomes the basis for a criminal complaint, the lawyer can face counter-charges of "false complaint", if the facts are believed to be tampered with.[78]

---

[75] Such as the Syrian Archive.

[76] Kaleck and Kroker, 2018, see *supra* note 74.

[77] Talsma, 2012, p. 386, see *supra* note 13.

[78] For an analysis of such charges in Spain regarding torture allegations, see Carolijn Terwindt, "Were They Tortured or Did They Make That Up? Ethnographic reflections on tor-

New challenges for NGOs that aim to contribute to criminal proceedings have arisen in relation to material evidence (such as weapons or photographs), witness testimonies, and the possibility that NGO representatives are summoned to appear in court. It is clear that the gathering, analysis, and storage of forensic evidence require both resources and expertise. This means that accurate professional and technical standards are only possible for well-equipped organisations. Dangers are that evidence is contaminated and that mistakes are reproduced. An example of such mismanagement was reported to have occurred when an eyewitness took NGO staff to the local offices of the government. While the NGO seized all records, they did not implement any kind of chain of custody. For this reason, the trial chamber at the International Criminal Tribunal for Rwanda did not admit the records as evidence.[79]

The collection of witness testimonies can be an equally sensitive matter if the testimonies are to be used by a court and if the witness has to be prepared to be cross-examined. Witnesses are generally considered to be the weakest form of evidence in criminal trials. It is well-known that memories can be unreliable. In the context of human rights abuse, however, there are additional challenges. People can be severely traumatised, the time that often passes between the incidents and judicial proceedings can be very long, and in protracted violent conflicts people are even more likely to be biased. Furthermore, politically sensitive trials can increase the pressure on witnesses and victims might have their own interests. Especially in the Syrian torture cases, there is a high risk of re-traumatisation and victims that are potential witnesses might need professional psychological treatment that is not always guaranteed by the interviewing NGOs. Additionally, the security issues mentioned earlier are an issue for potential witnesses. Indeed, there have been incidents of harassment and even killings of witnesses.[80] Further, as NGOs take witness statements, they have to be careful not to hamper subsequent litigation. For example, there have been instances where different NGOs had taken

---

ture allegations in the Basque Country in Spain", in *Oñati Socio-Legal Series*, 2011, vol. 1, no. 2, pp. 5–6.

[79] This example was provided in an interview at the ICTY in 2009, in Eric Meldrum, 2009, p. 33, see *supra* note 1.

[80] Robertson, 2010, p. 37, see *supra* note 20.

statements from the same witnesses. This subsequently served the defense to question the credibility of conflicting accounts.[81]

Finally, NGO representatives can be summoned to appear as a witness in a trial and be subjected to cross-examination. As Robertson points out, the success of a fact-finding mission (in terms of the ability to secure accurate information) often depends on the ability to guarantee confidentiality. With the possibility of upcoming litigation, however, balancing this trade-off has to be done early on. Among NGOs, only Red Cross (former) employees are entirely discharged from the obligation to appear as witnesses. Indeed, they cannot be called to testify, even if they would want to.[82] If, however, human rights monitors are granted the same privilege as, for example, war correspondents to keep their sources confidential to protect them against reprisals, this also means that the Court is allowed – for good reason – to give less weight to those testimonies that are based on anonymous sources and never to base findings of guilt solely on their information.[83] Thus, before embarking on their fact-finding, NGOs would have to reflect on this because this has implications for the evidentiary value of NGO fact-work.

Given these concerns, Meldrum argues that, as the information of human rights NGOs can be important in criminal justice processes, it is important to think of a "method of passing this information across in an acceptable format that will aid rather than hinder investigations".[84] Technically, the question is thus how NGOs can overcome the challenge of bridging the different evidentiary standards[85] for NGO fact-finding and criminal procedures. In criminal courts, the evidence has to prove facts beyond a reasonable doubt, whereas a less strict standard is applied in fact-finding missions as different information is weighed against each other to determine what account is more probable ('balance of probabili-

---

[81]  Meldrum, 2009, p. 40, see *supra* note 1.

[82]  Robertson, 2010, pp. 15 and 19, see *supra* note 20. Journalists and academics obviously face similar questions. Some have decided to refuse to provide information about their sources, which in more than one case has led to contempt of court and their imprisonment, see, for example, Rik Scarce, *Contempt of Court: A Scholar's Struggle for Free Speech from Behind Bars*, Walnut Creek, California, Alta Mira Press, 2005.

[83]  Robertson, 2010, pp. 36–38, see *supra* note 20.

[84]  Meldrum, 2009, p. 40, see *supra* note 1.

[85]  Rob Grace and Claude Bruderlein, "On Monitoring, Reporting, and Fact-finding Mechanisms", in *ESIL Reflections*, 15 July 2012, vol. 1, no. 2, p. 3.

ties').[86] However, before the technicalities (such as to how to obtain and handle information, how to deal with balancing the need for increased accuracy and the lack of time and resources, and the question of how to protect witnesses against possible repercussions), there are preliminary questions. First, NGOs have to decide on their intermediary position and the responsibility that comes with having such power.

## 14.5. Role Conflicts

Managing the potential conflicts of interest when fact-work is aimed to serve as evidence in litigation is perhaps even trickier than ensuring the evidentiary value of NGO fact-work. This issue is seldom openly addressed[87] and probably often underestimated. In order to avoid such role conflicts, NGOs should clarify their aims and position and stick to them. On the one hand, NGOs have to determine their position towards those that are affected by human rights violations (the 'victims'). On the other hand, NGO have to take a position in relation to the relevant judicial system, whether national or supranational.

First, regarding a position in relation to those very people whose facts were collected, NGOs have to take post-colonial critique into account, which counsels against claims to represent or merely engage in the appropriation and production of victims and their stories.[88] Instead, NGOs have to reflect carefully what it means to act responsibly, which, as Madlingozi, a member of the Khulumani Support Group says "should mean more than being nice to victims".[89] Whereas fact-finding is often conducted in a top-down manner, treating victims as objects, critics advocate for a non-hierarchical and co-operative approach, as otherwise the subordinated position of victims may actually be increased.[90]

---

[86]  *Ibid.*, p. 3.

[87]  There are some exceptions. See, for example, a brief discussion in: Groome, 2001, pp. 43–45, see *supra* note 14; see also the initiative of a fact-finding conference in which such issues as imperialism or fact extraction are addressed: "International Human Rights Fact-Finding in the Twenty-First Century: Conference", 1 November 2013, New York University Law School.

[88]  Tsheplo Madlingozi, "On Transitional Justice Entrepreneurs and the Production of Victims", in *Journal of Human Rights Practice*, 2010, vol. 2, no. 2.

[89]  *Ibid.*, p. 208.

[90]  Barbora Bukovská, "Perpetrating Good: unintended consequences of international human rights advocacy", in *SUR – International Journal on human Rights*, 2008, vol. 9, pp. 8–9.

Bukovská addresses three ways in which NGO fact-finding, and especially such work by international human rights organisations, can be harmful for those affected by human rights violations: (i) Perpetuating victimisation, as the human rights narrative reproduces "images of incompetence, dependence, and weakness";[91] (ii) Disrespectful collection of testimonies, as little information is provided as to what will happen with the statement; (iii) Monopolising the struggle, by relegating victims to the margins as sources of material while excluding them as "subjects in the production of their own narratives".[92] Clearly, these critical observers of NGO activity in relation to affected communities call for a higher responsibility and a deeper engagement than the mere "do no harm" principle which is currently widely recognised.[93] Especially when NGOs decide to engage in fact-work for litigation purposes, they have to be aware that the translation of narratives into legal categories and arguments can disempower and exclude those suffering from the human rights violations and even contradict their political demands. While this is not an argument against litigation, it should be a consideration for NGOs as to how to approach it.

NGOs may further be fact-finding in a context where a court is not supported by the entire local population. For example, the International Criminal Court ('ICC') indictments against the Lord Resistance Army in Uganda were criticised by local Acholi leaders for hampering local peace mechanisms. Others voiced concern that the ICC intervention could re-escalate the violence and that the lack of investigations of government soldiers indicated a bias.[94] Before NGOs decide to support such litigation with their fact-work, they should reflect on their role in a potentially polarized environment.

For international NGOs, there is the additional responsibility to be aware of their relation, not only with the affected people, but also with the domestic NGO that has served as an intermediary. Any discontent among the affected people with the results of the human rights fact-finding can

---

[91]   *Ibid.*, p. 10.

[92]   *Ibid.*, p. 11.

[93]   Grace and Bruderlein, 2012, p. 3, see *supra* note 85.

[94]   This was voiced, for example, by a representative of the Refugee Law Project in an interview with Meldrum, 2009, p. 38, see *supra* note 1.

namely also have a negative impact on the ability of the domestic NGO to do its work as they may be blamed for it.[95]

Second, regarding a position in relation to the judicial system, it was already indicated earlier that not all NGOs are comfortable with playing a role alongside a prosecutor. Besides the fear to appear partial when co-operating with prosecutors, NGOs have expressed concerns about the costs of court proceedings and the low number of prosecutions that are completed. Some NGOs therefore prefer to put their scarce resources to a different use.[96] As NGOs position themselves *vis-à-vis* a judicial system, there are several options which can sometimes contradict each other, for example: (i) NGOs can claim neutrality and independence, without co-operating with prosecutors;[97] (ii) NGOs can claim that they are close to victims and their communities and correspondingly advocate for their interests with a high degree of legitimacy; (iii) NGOs can be pleased to play a role in the activities of the judicial institutions and correspondingly adopt the rules of the criminal justice game and comply with these legal standards.

Of course, NGOs do not have to approve wholesale of the judicial proceedings to which they contribute with their fact-work. On the contrary, their active involvement gives them a different basis from which to comment, criticise or provide legal analysis. NGOs can also offer additional political background, point to gaps, or call out double standards. For example, NGOs can denounce the lack of investigation in higher-level officials or point to corporate accountability.

If an NGO decides to play a role in judicial proceedings, it can do so either by initiating or triggering legal cases or by supporting pending cases. In support of pending cases, NGOs will have to respect the evidentiary rules and fair trial principles and be cautious not to hamper official investigations. Thus, if NGOs do not have the resources or the know-how

---

[95] Bukovská, 2008, p. 12, see *supra* note 90.

[96] Meldrum 2009, p. 38, see *supra* note 1.

[97] The research done by Meldrum indicates that a distinction should be made between bigger international NGOs such as Amnesty International and Human Rights Watch on the one hand and local NGOs that are immersed in one particular conflict on the other hand. For the larger international human rights organisations, contribution to and participation in court proceedings is expressly not a part of their goal or the role they see for themselves, whereas local organisations can view this as an integral part of their work and can co-operate closely with the prosecutor's office. Meldrum 2009, see *supra* note 1.

for proper evidence taking, the basic rule is to identify the evidence, especially witnesses, and to refrain from starting to collect it in a rudimentary and potentially harmful manner. Witness statements ideally adhere to the advice that there should be no doubt in the statement whether the witness him or herself saw and experienced an event, or whether it is something he or she has heard from others (hearsay). Preferably, NGOs should only obtain general information regarding the kind of events the witness could testify about and include the contact details of the witness. An actual statement could then be taken later by a professional investigator. This avoids the existence of multiple possibly diverging or even contradictory statements that the defense can later use against the prosecution. Finally, it should be made very clear in advance to the witness what the role of NGO workers is and what the role of the prosecutor is. It should be avoided that a witness confuses a testimony to an NGO worker with a testimony given to a prosecutorial investigator.[98] There are also additional issues concerning witness protection which should be taken into account. If the name or the details of a testimony are being submitted to investigators or courts, and these become part of a case file, there is no way to guarantee the anonymity of that witness.

If NGOs initiate or trigger legal proceedings, NGOs have to be conscious of the fact that this can lead to legal obligations, for example, being a witness, giving evidence or entrusting a witness to be interviewed by the prosecutors. Not all NGOs are ready for this commitment. For example, Meldrum noted that an investigations staff member at the ICTY perceived NGOs "to view some of the female victims as their own personal property".[99]

An early decision to contribute to court proceedings can help NGOs to include physical evidence within their repertoire of fact-finding, especially where this is stronger than witness statements. If they do so, they should take account of the courtroom demands for admitting such evidence. Concretely, this means that a chain of custody should be kept. The few anecdotes mentioned by Meldrum illustrate that it is actually quite likely that NGOs will encounter such physical evidence if they are open to

---

[98] These were the concerns with NGO fact-work for courtroom purpose expressed by prosecutors at the ICTY, the National War Crimes Courts of Serbia, Bosnia and Herzegovina and the International Criminal Court due to their experiences with witness statements provided by NGOs in interviews with Meldrum in Meldrum, 2009, see *supra* note 1.

[99] *Ibid.*, p. 32, see *supra* note 1.

and pro-active about it, given that they are often the closest to the people and events on the ground. For those NGOs that choose to cooperate with criminal investigations, it would be misguided to stick to the "interviews-only" approach, which was informed by a different kind of NGO-politics.

## 14.6. Conclusions

In academia and within the human rights community there is a debate about standards for fact-finding missions in general and a more special-ised debate for NGO fact-finding and ways to implement a system of quality control. In these debates, there is criticism of a lack of such stand-ards. Biased reports and a lack of verifiability of anonymous sources are especially criticised. Defenders of flexible standards for NGOs point to their different realities, the need for an early warning system, and the im-portance of local fact-finding by under-resourced NGO-workers. The question then is whether NGOs should follow the same standards as fact-finding missions by international governmental organisations.

In this chapter, we have not addressed these debates about the pos-sible need for standards for fact-finding missions in general or for NGO fact-finding in particular. Instead, we looked at those instances where NGO fact-work plays a role in courtroom proceedings, either as a basis for the initiation of a prosecution or as evidence in a trial. This means that NGOs may co-operate with prosecutors and it may require NGOs to func-tion as intermediaries between criminal justice officials and affected communities, as victims or witnesses. Because it has become more com-mon that NGOs co-operate with prosecutors in the production of evidence, efforts have been made to produce uniform standards and to instruct NGOs on how they should do their fact-work for criminal justice purposes. These efforts have produced quite technocratic guidelines. We have taken a step back and counselled for a reflection on the role of NGOs and their fact-work in the courtroom and the ways in which they could or should position themselves and their work.

We have argued that NGOs have to be aware of the possibility that their fact-work becomes a basis for or evidence in courtroom litigation. Before the quest for quality control can meaningfully be started in the form of technical guidelines, NGOs have to reflect on their role and pos-sible conflicts of interest. NGOs have to make a clear decision internally and to the outside actors regarding their position in relation to possible or ongoing litigation. This means that they take a clear stance both towards the people with whom they work and whose facts they are collecting, and towards the courtroom procedures. Thus, between an easy consensus on general principles (neutrality, impartiality, and independence) and the jump to a technical approach (such as the details of maintaining a chain of custody), there is a more political and strategic level that should first be addressed head-on. Clear choices have to be made and the consequences of these choices have to be understood and accepted.

A call for and focus on creating a uniform standardised methodology for NGO fact-work to contribute to judicial proceedings may too easily assume that it is a good thing to promote litigation-based NGO fact-finding and the reliance of legal practitioners on such fact-work. NGOs may indeed have plenty to contribute to court proceedings and it is certainly a good thing to provide clear standards for the fact-work if they do so. It is, however, essential to first create clarity about the NGO's position *vis-à-vis* the communities with which they work on the one hand and the legal actors and mechanisms on the other. Jumping to technical details too soon and sidestepping these preliminary questions is bound to backfire.

# 15

---

# Fact-Finding and the International Humanitarian Fact-Finding Commission

### Charles Garraway[*]

## 15.1. Introduction

Fact-finding seems to have become the flavour of the age. Wherever there is a situation of violence or conflict, there is a call to "establish the facts". Whether it was in the former Yugoslavia,[1] Sudan,[2] Libya,[3] Syria[4] or Yemen,[5] commissions have been established to look into the events and report. Such reports have indeed led to changes in the international response to such situations, in particular through the establishment of international criminal justice mechanisms such as the International Criminal Tribunals for the former Yugoslavia[6] and Rwanda,[7] and the activation of the Interna-

---

[*]  **Charles Garraway** is Visiting Fellow at the Human Rights Centre of the University of Essex. At the time of the First Edition, he was Vice-President of the International Humanitarian Fact-Finding Commission and a Member of the Group of Eminent Experts on Yemen. The opinions and views expressed in this chapter are those of the author acting in his personal capacity and do not necessarily reflect the views of the Commission itself or any other organisation.

[1]  United Nations Security Council Commission Established Pursuant to Resolution 780 (1992) to Investigate Violations of International Humanitarian Law in the Former Yugoslavia (https://www.legal-tools.org/doc/cdc5ad/).

[2]  High-Level Mission on the Situation of Human Rights in Darfur, pursuant to Human Rights Council decision S-4/101, 13 December 2006.

[3]  International Commission of Inquiry to Investigate All Alleged Violations of International Human Rights Law in the Libyan Arab Jamahiriya, pursuant to Human Rights Council Resolution S-15/1, 25 February 2011 (https://www.legal-tools.org/doc/233009/).

[4]  Mission to the Syrian Arab Republic to Investigate All Alleged Violations of International Human Rights Law and to Establish the Facts and Circumstances of such Violations and of the Crimes Perpetrated, pursuant to Human Rights Council Resolution S 16/1, 29 April 2011 (https://www.legal-tools.org/doc/233009/).

[5]  Group of Eminent International and Regional Experts on Yemen, see Human Rights, Technical Assistance and Capacity-building in Yemen, A/HRC/RES/36/31, 29 September 2017.

[6]  See United Nations Security Council Resolution 827, 25 May 1993 (https://www.legal-tools.org/doc/dc079b/).

tional Criminal Court through the references by the Security Council in the cases of Sudan[8] and Libya.[9]

This is perhaps not surprising. "In war, truth is the first casualty". This well-known saying is as old as the laws of war themselves, being ascribed first to the Greek dramatist Aeschylus. In every conflict, the air has been thick with claim and counter-claim. In August 2013, the chemical attack in Damascus caused an initial divide in the international community with the United States and the others arguing that this could only have been carried out by the Assad regime whilst the regime itself, supported by Russia, insisted that blame rested with the rebel 'terrorists' fighting against the regime. The controversial votes in the British House of Commons over a military response, in which both Government and Opposition motions were defeated, took place in the middle of this argument.[10]

There can be no doubt therefore that fact-finding is both important and plays an increasing role in international relations in the 21st century. However, what is still unclear is how that fact-finding should be carried out and under what parameters. This is largely caused by the growing confusion over the varying legal regimes governing situations of violence and conflict.

## 15.2. The Legal Frameworks

Until the Second World War, there was a comparatively clear divide between the legal regimes operating in war and peace. Peace was a matter for domestic law, though increasingly, with the growth of global interaction, international law was beginning to impinge in areas such as trade. However, in war, domestic law was to a considerable extent replaced by the international laws of war, a mixture of treaty law, developed since the mid-19th century, and custom. 'War', however, consisted of inter-State conflict. Violence within a State was still a matter for domestic law. Obviously, within domestic law, criminal law played a major role. Rebels in a

---

[7]    See United Nations Security Council Resolution 955, 8 November 1994 (http://www.legal-tools.org/doc/f5ef47/).

[8]    See United Nations Security Council Resolution 1593, 31 March 2005 (http://www.legal-tools.org/doc/4b208f/).

[9]    See United Nations Security Council Resolution 1970, 26 February 2011 (http://www.legal-tools.org/doc/00a45e/).

[10]    Syria crisis: Cameron loses Commons vote on Syria action, BBC News, 30 August 2013.

domestic environment were subject to criminal sanction for treason and other offences. Criminal law played a much lesser role on the international stage where the attempts to try German officials for war crimes at the end of World War I met with limited success.[11]

The end of World War II led to three critical developments, each of which would take decades to come to full fruition. The first was the establishment of the war crimes Tribunals at Nuremberg[12] and Tokyo.[13] Although these were not to be followed up on in any meaningful way for almost 50 years, they set the ball rolling for the subsequent establishment of international criminal justice. The Statutes of both the International Criminal Tribunals for the former Yugoslavia[14] and Rwanda[15] were firmly based on the precedents of Nuremberg.

The second major development was in the attempts by the International Committee of the Red Cross ('ICRC') to extend the laws of war – at least in their protective elements – to non-international armed conflicts, that is, conflicts within a State. The horrors of World War II, and those revealed within some of the conflicts that arose at the end of that war as factions within States fought for control of territories abandoned by their occupiers, had made the ICRC realise that protection needed to be given in situations of violence that fell below the level of inter-State conflict. Domestic law was simply insufficient to protect the victims of such violence. Whilst they were not wholly successful in their endeavours, the ICRC did succeed in having an article covering non-international armed conflicts inserted into each of the four Geneva Conventions of 1949, Common Article 3.[16] This incursion into an area that had previously been

---

[11]  Jackson Maogoto, "Early Efforts to Establish an International Criminal Court", in José Doria, Hans-Peter Gasser and M. Cherif Bassiouni (eds.), *The Legal Regime of the International Criminal Court*, Martinus Nijhoff, Leiden, 2009, pp. 16–18.

[12]  Agreement for the Prosecution and Punishment of the Major War Criminals of the European Axis Powers and Charter of the International Military Tribunal, 8 August 1945, 82 UNTS 15 (https://www.legal-tools.org/doc/844f64/).

[13]  International Military Tribunal for the Far East, Established at Tokyo, 19 January 1946 (General Orders No. 1), as amended (General Orders No. 20), 26 April 1946, TIAS No.1589 (https://www.legal-tools.org/doc/242328/).

[14]  See *supra* note 6.

[15]  See *supra* note 7.

[16]  Common Article 3 to the four Geneva Conventions of 12 August 1949, reprinted in Adam Roberts and Richard Guelff (eds.), Documents on the Laws of War, Oxford University Press, 3rd ed., 2000, pp. 198, 223, 245 and 302 respectively.

left to domestic law was followed in 1977 by Additional Protocol II to the 1949 Conventions, covering "all armed conflicts which are not [international armed conflicts] and which take place in the territory of a High Contracting Party between its armed forces and dissident armed forces or other organized armed groups which, under responsible command, exercise such control over a part of its territory as to enable them to carry out sustained and concerted military operations and to implement this Protocol".[17] The divide between 'peace' and 'war' was becoming eroded.

The third, and perhaps most critical, development took place under the auspices of the United Nations. The United Nations Charter, in its Preamble, determined "to save succeeding generations from the scourge of war, which twice in our lifetime has brought untold sorrow to mankind".[18] In order to do this it sought "to reaffirm faith in fundamental human rights, in the dignity and worth of the human person, in the equal rights of men and women and of nations large and small".[19] The way this was to be done was by the development of what was essentially a new strand of public international law, human rights law. This was designed principally to protect the individual from the overweening power of the State and was seen as part of the 'law of peace'. However, whilst many saw human rights as applying only in times of peace and being superseded in times of war by the laws of war, now more commonly called the laws of armed conflict, the actual scope of application was never so clear cut. The derogation clause in the European Convention for the Protection of Human Rights, adopted on 4 November 1950, specifically stated that

> [i]n time of war or other public emergency threatening the life of the nation any High Contracting Party may take measures derogating from its obligations under this Convention to the extent strictly required by the exigencies of the situation, provided that such measures are not inconsistent with its other obligations under international law.[20]

---

[17] Art. 1(1), Protocol Additional to the Geneva Conventions of 12 August 1949, and Relating to the Protection of Victims of Non-International Armed Conflicts, 8 June 1977 (hereinafter 'AP II') (https://www.legal-tools.org/doc/fd14c4/pdf); *ibid.*, p. 484.

[18] Preamble, Charter of the United Nations, 24 October 1945, 1 UNTS XVI (https://www.legal-tools.org/doc/6b3cd5/).

[19] *Ibid.*

[20] Art. 15, European Convention for the Protection of Human Rights (hereinafter 'ECHR'), 4 November 1950, 213 UNTS 221 (No. 2889) (https://www.legal-tools.org/doc/8267cb/). It entered into force on 3 September 1953.

'War' in 1950 was inter-State war but internal armed conflicts would certainly be covered by the phrase "other public emergency threatening the life of the nation". It followed that, even in those extremes of violence, the Convention applied in principle, subject to such derogations as may have been authorised. However, what was left unclear in all human rights treaties was the relationship between human rights law and the traditional laws of war.

## 15.3. The Developing Relationship

As the character of conflict has changed, so has the legal response. The laws of armed conflict were always much more developed in relation to international armed conflict, due to States' reluctance to allow outside interference in internal armed conflicts, which they saw as falling within their domestic prerogative. However, human rights law, clearly applicable in times of peace, had already breached that particular legal barrier. There was thus indeed international law that applied within the domestic realm and could be applied in times of internal violence, subject to derogation. There was, initially, little controversy about the laws of armed conflict, insofar as they applied to internal armed conflict as, under treaty law at least, this application was restricted principally to the protection of victims, a matter on which the two bodies of law were substantially complementary. The underlying problems arose in high intensity conflicts where the 'law enforcement' model on which the use of force under human rights law was based, was simply unworkable and the laws of war paradigm came into play. This allowed targeting by status rather than threat and accepted the risk of collateral damage to innocent civilians, provided that it was not expected to be excessive in relation to the military advantage anticipated.[21] But, despite the apparent wishes of States, who had inserted a higher threshold for the application of Additional Protocol II[22] than that generally accepted for Common Article 3,[23] there seemed to be no appetite from the ICRC or others to sub-divide internal conflicts into those of high intensity where laws of war principles would apply to the

---

[21] Art. 57(2)(a)(iii), Protocol Additional to the Geneva Conventions of 12 August 1949, and Relating to the Protection of Victims of International Armed Conflicts, 8 June 1977 (hereinafter 'AP I') (https://www.legal-tools.org/doc/d9328a/), Roberts and Guelff, p. 453, see *supra* note 16.

[22] See *supra* note 17.

[23] See *supra* note 16.

---

use of force, and low intensity where law enforcement principles would be the default position. The danger, therefore, grew of an overlap in the applicability of these two bodies of public international law, and of possible incompatibilities occurring.

The matter was complicated by the decisions of the International Criminal Tribunal for the former Yugoslavia, which, in seeking to avoid the difficulties inherent in having to classify individually the various conflicts that had erupted in the former Yugoslavia, sought instead to level the playing field by introducing law relating to the 'conduct of hostilities' into non-international armed conflicts. The Appeals Chamber stated:

> [...] it cannot be denied that customary rules have developed to govern internal strife. These rules... cover such areas as protection of civilians from hostilities, in particular from indiscriminate attacks, protection of civilian objects, in particular cultural property, protection of all those who do not (or no longer) take active part in hostilities, as well as prohibition of means of warfare proscribed in international armed conflicts and ban of certain methods of conducting hostilities.[24]

A further impetus was provided by the Study on Customary International Humanitarian Law published by the ICRC in 2005.[25] This study found 161 'rules' of customary international law relating to armed conflict, of which 159 applied to international armed conflict and two were only applicable to non-international armed conflict. However, of the 159, 147 of these rules were applicable across the board to international and non-international armed conflict alike.[26] Essentially, insofar as the conduct of hostilities was concerned, the rules were the same.

Just as judicial pronouncements were extending the coverage of non-international armed conflict by the laws of armed conflict, so too had the International Court of Justice been looking at the relationship between

---

[24] ICTY Appeals Chamber, *Prosecutor v. Tadić*, Case No. T-94-1-A, Decision on the Defence Motion for Interlocutory Appeal on Jurisdiction of Trial Chamber I, 3 June 1999, 105 International Law Reports 453, 520, para. 127 (https://www.legal-tools.org/doc/602186/).

[25] Jean-Marie Henckaerts and Louise Doswald-Beck (eds.), Customary International Humanitarian Law (two volumes: Vol. I, Rules; Vol. II, Practice (two Parts)), Cambridge University Press, 2005.

[26] Jean-Marie Henckaerts, The ICRC Study on Customary International Humanitarian Law – An Assessment, in Larry Maybee and Benarji Chakka (eds.), *Custom as a Source of International Humanitarian Law*, ICRC, 2006, p. 50.

those laws, referred to now as international humanitarian law, and human rights law. In the Nuclear Weapons Advisory Opinion, the Court stated:

> The Court observes that the protection of the International Covenant of Civil and Political Rights does not cease in times of war, except by operation of Article 4 of the Covenant whereby certain provisions may be derogated from in a time of national emergency. Respect for the right to life is not, however, such a provision. In principle, the right not arbitrarily to be deprived of one's life applies also in hostilities. The test of what is an arbitrary deprivation of life, however, then falls to be determined by the applicable *lex specialis*, namely, the law applicable in armed conflict which is designed to regulate the conduct of hostilities. Thus whether a particular loss of life, through the use of a certain weapon in warfare, is to be considered an arbitrary deprivation of life contrary to Article 6 of the Covenant, can only be decided by reference to the law applicable in armed conflict and not deduced from the terms of the Covenant itself.[27]

In the Barrier Advisory Opinion, the Court went further and said:

> As regards the relationship between international humanitarian law and human rights law, there are thus three possible situations: some rights may be exclusively matters of international humanitarian law; others may be exclusively matters of human rights law; yet others may be matters of both these branches of international law. In order to answer the question put to it, the Court will have to take into consideration both these branches of international law, namely human rights law and, as *lex specialis*, international humanitarian law.[28]

However, what the Court did not say was where the dividing lines were. What was clear, however, was that these two legal frameworks now overlapped. This was further confirmed in the later Case Concerning

---

[27] *Case Concerning Legality of the Threat or Use of Nuclear Weapons*, Advisory Opinion, ICJ Report, 8 July 1996, pp. 226 and 240 (https://www.legal-tools.org/doc/d97bc1/).

[28] *Case Concerning Legal Consequences of the Construction of a Wall in the Occupied Palestinian Territory*, Advisory Opinion, 9 July 2004, 43 ILM 1009, p. 1048 (http://www.legal-tools.org/doc/e5231b/).

Armed Activities on the Territory of the Congo (Democratic Republic of the Congo *versus* Uganda).[29]

Various human rights bodies, not least the European Court of Human Rights, have also sought to pronounce upon the relationship with differing amounts of clarity. This is not the place to enter into a detailed analysis of that relationship, but it suffices to say that it is complex and far from subject to universal agreement.

The effect of international criminal law is also underestimated. Although the various international courts that have grown up over the last 20 years, including the International Criminal Court, base their jurisdiction principally on tenets of international humanitarian law and human rights law – genocide, crimes against humanity and war crimes – this discipline, too, has taken on a life of its own with new interpretations of traditional legal concepts. Methods of participation such as command responsibility and joint criminal enterprise have been refined and, in some cases, expanded and attempts have been made to provide stricter parameters for some of the terms used in the laws of armed conflict, such as indiscriminate attack.[30] Increasingly, international humanitarian law, the law of armed conflict, is being interpreted by judges operating under international criminal law principles.

## 15.4. The Effect on Fact-Finding

How has this affected fact-finding? The need for fact-finding has probably never been greater and yet the nature of fact-finding changes according to its conceived purpose. Each of the legal regimes, namely, the law of armed conflict, human rights law and international criminal law, has a different end-state and thus both the nature of fact-finding and the facts required will be different.

In reverse order, international criminal law seeks to bring individual perpetrators to justice. In the words of the Nuremburg Tribunal, "[c]rimes against international law are committed by men, not by abstract entities, and only by punishing individuals who commit such crimes can the provi-

---

[29] *Armed Activities on the Territory of the Congo (New Application: 2002), (Democratic Republic of the Congo v. Uganda)*, Judgment, ICJ Report, 19 December 2005, p. 168 (http://www.legal-tools.org/doc/e31ae7/).

[30] *Prosecutor v. Ante Gotovina and Mladen Markac*, Case No. IT-06-90-A, 16 November 2012 (http://www.legal-tools.org/doc/03b685/).

sions of international law be enforced".[31] This requires the establishment of a crime under international criminal law, the identification of a suspect and a finding that the suspect is responsible for the crime. The criminal standard of proof is one of beyond reasonable doubt. This is perhaps the most difficult form of fact-finding in the light of its possible outcome, a criminal conviction. It requires painstaking attention to detail and the connection of seemingly unrelated facts. It is thus extremely time-consuming and expensive, as the costs of the various international criminal courts show. Costs indeed may be a contributing factor to the reluctance of domestic courts to become involved in international prosecutions.

Human rights fact-finding, on the other hand, is more broad-brush. The result is much more important. Put simply, if a right has been violated, then the burden shifts to the State to justify that violation. The burden of proof will differ according to the purpose for which the fact-finding is being carried out, but will not normally exceed the civil standard of balance of probabilities. Indeed, as recent studies have revealed, there is no set standard of proof and numerous different formulations have been used.[32] In non-international armed conflict, human rights fact-finding has a particular problem in that it is generally accepted that human rights treaties only bind States. Whilst reports can, and frequently do, make reference to alleged breaches of human rights norms by non-State actors, the legal consequences of such breaches are disputable.

International humanitarian law fact-finding is different. Whilst international humanitarian law binds all parties to armed conflicts, both States and non-State parties, it is essentially civil in nature. Whilst much of the law on the protection of victims of armed conflicts is similar to human rights law, the law on the conduct of hostilities is not, as it is based much more on a balance between military necessity and the interests of humanity. Thus, if a prisoner of war dies in captivity, the burden will be on the detaining power to explain the nature of the death. However, the death of civilians during a military operation may not be so clear-cut. If it can be shown that the attack was directed against the civilians, that would

---

31 Trial of the Major War Criminals before the International Military Tribunal, Nürnberg, 14 November 1945 – 1 October 1946, published at Nürnberg, Germany, 1947, p. 223 (https://www.legal-tools.org/doc/f21343/).

32 See Stephen Wilkinson, "Standards of Proof in International Humanitarian and Human Rights Fact-Finding and Inquiry Missions", Geneva Academy of International Humanitarian Law (available on its web site).

undoubtedly be considered a violation. However, if the attack was directed against a military objective, it would be necessary to assess the proportionality of that attack. This is based on the expected incidental loss of civilian life, injury to civilians, damage to civilian objects, or a combination thereof, as opposed to the anticipated concrete and direct military advantage.[33] This means that the result can only take the decision maker so far.

An example would be an attack on a civilian factory, causing limited civilian casualties. Under human rights law, the civilian deaths would automatically trigger the need for investigation by the State for justification of those deaths, bearing in mind that the right to life is non-derogable. The burden is instantly on the State. On the other hand, under international humanitarian law, the test is different. If the facts found were that the factory was attacked at night when civilian casualties were likely to be at their lowest level; and that a precision guided munition was used to attack a particular area of the factory; these findings might be irrelevant to a human rights body. However, they would indicate to an international humanitarian law body that the attacker had taken precautions to reduce civilian casualties,[34] and, through the use of an expensive precision guided missile, that this was a high value target. On that basis, the indication would be that if the civilian casualties were low, the attack might well have been proportionate though no actual finding could be made without examining the intelligence available to the attacker to identify what the anticipated military advantage was and the expected civilian casualties and damage.

A classic example of this in real life is that of the Al Firdus bunker in Baghdad during the 1991 Gulf War. Here, military planners identified the site as a command and control centre, which in itself was an important military objective. Barbed wire surrounded the complex; it was camouflaged, and armed sentries guarded its entrance and exit points. However, it later transpired that Iraqi civilians used the site at night as an underground shelter. The complex was bombed, resulting in a large number of civilian casualties.[35] The test here under international humanitarian law is

---

[33] See *supra* note 21.

[34] Art. 57, AP I, see *supra* note 21.

[35] See US Department of Defence, "Conduct of the Persian Gulf War", Final Report to Congress, p. 189 and Annex O-14 (available on the Global Security's web site).

---

not the result itself but what the military planners knew and whether that knowledge was reasonable.

It follows from this that fact-finding under international humanitarian law will need to gather a greater degree of information than is strictly required for human rights fact-finding. Whilst it is possible to conduct human rights fact-finding without the co-operation of one or even both parties, it is much more difficult to do that under international humanitarian law.

## 15.5. Fact-Finding Bodies

The initial structure of fact-finding was inevitably *ad hoc*. This was partly because, at that time, nobody was sure of the purpose of the initial missions. Thus, in 1992, the Security Council adopted resolution 780 (1992), by which it requested the Secretary-General to establish a Commission of Experts to examine and analyse, *inter alia*, information submitted pursuant to Security Council resolutions 771 (1992) of 13 August 1992 and 780 (1992) of 6 October 1992, with a view to providing the Secretary-General with its conclusions on the evidence of grave breaches of the Geneva Conventions and other violations of international humanitarian law committed in the territory of the former Yugoslavia.[36] This Commission, led initially by Professor Frits Kalshoven and subsequently by Professor Torkel Opsahl and then Professor Cherif Bassiouni, resulted in the establishment of the International Criminal Tribunal for the former Yugoslavia. It is perhaps worthy of note that the mandate specified "evidence of grave breaches of the Geneva Conventions and other violations of international humanitarian law", that is to say, it was a mandate involving the law of armed conflict rather than human rights law. However, it was established by the Secretary-General of the United Nations, following a Security Council Resolution.

Such inquiries could not, in themselves, satisfy the requirements of criminal proceedings. As the conclusions of the Commission stated:

> The Commission finds significant evidence of and information about the commission of grave breaches of the Geneva Conventions and other violations of international humanitarian law which have been communicated to the Office of the Prosecutor of the International Tribunal.

---

[36] See *supra* note 1.

---

> Some of the conclusions relative to these violations are re-
> flected in the present report, but for obvious reasons infor-
> mation and evidence of a prosecutorial nature are not de-
> scribed herein.[37]

International criminal law quickly established its own fact-finding mechanisms through the workings of the relevant international tribunals and courts. Although the majority of these international tribunals are re-ferred to as *ad hoc*, each had its own Prosecutor's Office with investiga-tive teams. Thus, the investigations carried out by these teams were not *ad hoc* within the meaning of their own mandates, but were carried out by regular staff attached to the responsible body. Each tribunal could estab-lish its own working practices to cover its operations, although, inevitably, there was a considerable degree of experience sharing and, indeed, trans-fer of staff.

Thus, by the time the International Criminal Court was established, there was a wealth of experience in fact-finding by investigative teams operating from the international tribunals and international criminal jus-tice had started to develop a clear set of parameters and standards for such investigations.

However, outside the sphere of international criminal justice, there was no such standardisation. Fact-finding remained an ad hoc phenome-non. Increasingly, the responsibility was taken up by the United Nations. For example, in September 2004, the Security Council adopted resolution 1564 requesting, *inter alia*, that the Secretary-General "rapidly establish an international commission of inquiry in order immediately to investigate reports of violations of international humanitarian law and human rights law in Darfur by all parties, to determine also whether or not acts of geno-cide have occurred, and to identify the perpetrators of such violations with a view to ensuring that those responsible are held accountable".[38]

Here, it is possible to see the widening of the mandate to include in-ternational humanitarian law and human rights law, as well as the inten-tion of seeking accountability for perpetrators. With regard to this latter point, the Commission stated:

---

[37] Final Report of the Commission of Experts Established pursuant to Security Council Reso-lution 780 (1992), Annex to UN Doc. S/1994/674, 27 May 1994, paras. 311–312 (https://www.legal-tools.org/doc/5887b3/).

[38] United Nations Security Council Resolution 1564, 18 September 2004, para. 12 (http://www.legal-tools.org/doc/1ba770/).

> As requested by the Security Council, to 'identify perpetra-
> tors' the Commission decided that the most appropriate
> standard was that requiring that there must be 'a reliable
> body of material consistent with other verified circumstances,
> which tends to show that a person may reasonably be sus-
> pected of being involved in the commission of a crime.' The
> Commission therefore has not made final judgments as to
> criminal guilt; rather, it has made an assessment of possible
> suspects that will pave the way for future investigations, and
> possible indictments, by a prosecutor, and convictions by a
> court of law.[39]

Although the Commission was appointed by the Secretary-General,
it was staffed by a Secretariat, as well as a legal research team and an investigative team composed of investigators, forensic experts, military analysts, and investigators specialising in gender violence, all appointed by
the Office of the United Nations High Commissioner for Human Rights
('UNHCHR'). It should be noted that there is no United Nations or other
body which is mandated to support such missions under international humanitarian law, not even the ICRC. It would not have been appropriate,
nor would the ICRC have agreed, for the Secretary-General to pass the
support function across to them. Thus the UNHCHR operated *faute de
mieux*. However, it should be noted that the mandate given to the Commissioner under General Assembly Resolution 48/141[40] deals only with
human rights and has no mention of international humanitarian law.

Other United Nations human rights bodies such as the Commission
on Human Rights (now the Human Rights Council) also became increasingly involved in fact-finding. Initially, the mandates dealt with "violations of human rights".[41] However, as these inquiries increasingly involved situations of armed conflict, the mandates widened. The Lebanon
Inquiry in 2006 had a mandate:

---

[39] Report of the International Commission of Inquiry on Darfur to the United Nations Secretary-General, Geneva, 25 January 2005, para. 643 (https://www.legal-tools.org/doc/
1480de/).

[40] United Nations General Assembly Resolution 48/141, 20 December 1993.

[41] Human Rights Situation in the Occupied Palestinian Territory, HRC Res. S-1/1, 13 November 2006, para. 6 (https://www.legal-tools.org/doc/e9d538/). There were references to
international humanitarian law in the Resolution but the mandate was limited to human
rights.

1. to investigate the systematic targeting and killings of civilians by Israel in Lebanon;

2. to examine the types of weapons used by Israel and their conformity with international law; and

3. to assess the extent and deadly impact of Israeli attacks on human life, property, critical infrastructure and the environment.[42]

This clearly went beyond pure human rights law and would require an assessment of international humanitarian law issues as well. Indeed, the mandate required "eminent experts on human rights law and international humanitarian law" to be appointed.[43]

Although the mandate of the Darfur Mission in 2006 referred only to human rights,[44] the Goldstone Mission in relation to Gaza in 2009 specifically referred to "all violations of international human rights law and international humanitarian law by the Occupying Power".[45] The Human Rights Council also included specific reference to international humanitarian law in the inquiry into the Gaza Flotilla in 2010.[46] However, the inquiries into Libya[47] and Syria[48] in 2011 did not, referring only to human rights violations. In the case of Libya, this omission was picked up by the NATO Legal Adviser, Peter Olsen, who, when requested to supply information on NATO air strikes in Libya, politely challenged the mandate of the Commission to examine alleged violations of international humanitarian law.[49] In the case of Syria, when the Commission was appointed, there was at least doubt as to whether the situation in Syria amounted to an

---

[42] The Grave Situation of Human Rights in Lebanon Caused by Israeli Military Operations, HRC Res. S-2/1, 11 August 2006, para. 7 (https://www.legal-tools.org/doc/9e7f9b/).

[43] *Ibid.*

[44] Situation of Human Rights in Darfur, HRC Res. S-4/101, 13 December 2006.

[45] The Grave Violations of Human Rights in the Occupied Palestinian Territory, Particularly Due to the Recent Israeli Military Attacks against the Occupied Gaza Strip, HRC Res. S-9/1, 12 January 2009, para. 14 (https://www.legal-tools.org/doc/edc0db/).

[46] The Grave Attacks by Israeli Forces against the Humanitarian Boat Convoy, HRC Res. 14/1, 2 June 2010, para. 8 (https://www.legal-tools.org/doc/1a6296/).

[47] Situation of Human Rights in the Libyan Arab Jamahiriya, HRC Res. S-15/1, 25 February 2011, para. 11 (https://www.legal-tools.org/doc/6012d0/).

[48] The Current Human Rights Situation in the Syrian Arab Republic in the Context of Recent Events, HRC Res. S-16/1, 29 April 2011, para. 7 (https://www.legal-tools.org/doc/37fa81/).

[49] Annex II, Report of the International Commission of Inquiry on Libya, A/HRC/19/68, 8 March 2012, p. 26.

---

armed conflict and, therefore, if human rights alone would have been applicable. However, the mandate was extended in 2012:

> [...] to conduct an international, transparent, independent and prompt investigation into abuses and violations of international law, with a view to hold to account those responsible for violations and abuses, including those that may amount to crimes against humanity and war crimes.[50]

The mandate for the Group of Eminent Experts on Yemen required them:

> [t]o monitor and report on the situation of human rights, to carry out a comprehensive examination of all alleged violations and abuses of international human rights and other appropriate and applicable fields of international law committed by all parties to the conflict since September 2014, including the possible gender dimensions of such violations, and to establish the facts and circumstances surrounding the alleged violations and abuses and, where possible, to identify those responsible.[51]

The key point about the various inquiries instituted by the Human Rights Council is that all are *ad hoc*. Whilst both the Secretariat and support staff are provided by the Council, usually through the auspices of the High Commissioner, the Members are individually selected for each inquiry. It is perhaps inevitable that these selections will be primarily based on relevant expertise in human rights. Apart from Yemen, there appears to have been little concentration on international humanitarian law expertise. This has led to criticisms of the methodology of some inquiries, particularly the Goldstone Report into Operation Cast Lead in Gaza.[52]

When challenged as to why the Human Rights Council is seeking to investigate alleged violations of a branch of public international law that appears to be outside its mandate or expertise, the answer is often made

---

[50] Situation of Human Rights in the Syrian Arab Republic, A/HRC/RES/21/26, 17 October 2012, para. 10 (https://www.legal-tools.org/doc/4e9c2a/).

[51] Human Rights, Technical Assistance and Capacity-building in Yemen, A/HRC/RES/36/31, 29 September 2017, para. 12(a) (https://www.legal-tools.org/doc/1abd18/).

[52] For example, see the European Centre for Law and Justice, "Written Statement Addressing Resolution S-9/1 and the "Goldstone Report"", Submission to the 13th Session of the Human Rights Council.

that there is nobody else doing it.[53] There is a large degree of truth in this. But it is often overlooked that the need for fact-finding in international humanitarian law was foreseen as early as 1949. The four Geneva Conventions of that year provided for enquiries to be instituted "in a manner to be decided between the interested Parties, concerning any violation of the [Conventions]".[54] This mechanism was never used and was supplemented in the 1977 Additional Protocol I to the 1949 Geneva Conventions by a permanent body, the International Humanitarian Fact-Finding Commission ('IHFFC').[55] Sadly, this body has only been used once when the IHFFC was asked by the Organization for Security and Co-operation in Europe (OSCE) to lead an independent forensic investigation in relation to an incident in April 2017 that occurred in the Ukraine involving the death of a paramedic and the injury of two monitors of its Special Monitoring Mission to Ukraine.[56]

### 15.6. What is the International Humanitarian Fact-Finding Commission?

The International Humanitarian Fact-finding Commission) consists of 15 "members of high moral standing and acknowledged impartiality". States that have signed up to the Commission may each nominate one candidate and elections are then carried out. The Commissioners are elected for a five-year period but they are free to stand again for further terms. The last elections were in December 2016.

Although there are 174 State Parties to Additional Protocol I, only 76 of them have made the declaration to accept the competence of the Commission. Although the intention is to have an equitable geographic spread, there are many notable absentees and some areas of the world are

---

[53] Presentation by Dr. Annyssa Bellal, OHCHR, to the 36th Round Table of the International Institute of Humanitarian Law, San Remo, on 6 September 2013.

[54] Convention for the Amelioration of the Condition of the Wounded and Sick in Armed Forces in the Field, 12 August 1949, 6 UST 3114, 75 UNTS 31; Convention for the Amelioration of the Condition of Wounded, Sick and Shipwrecked Members of Armed Forces at Sea, 12 August 1949, 6 UST 3217, 75 UNTS 85; Convention Relative to the Treatment of Prisoners of War, 12 August 1949, 6 UST 3316, 75 UNTS 135; Convention Relative to the Protection of Civilian Persons in Time of War, 12 August 1949, 6 UST 3516, 75 UNTS 287, Arts. 52, 53, 132 and 149 respectively.

[55] Article 90, AP I, Roberts and Guelff, p. 473, *supra* note 16.

[56] See IHFFC, "OSCE Special Monitoring Mission Was Not Targeted, Concludes Independent Forensic Investigation into Tragic Incident of 23 April 2017", 7 September 2017.

---

under-represented – not least Africa and Asia. Despite this, the Commissioners are designed to reflect the geographic diversity of the Parties and come from all parts of the world, reflecting many different disciplines. There are lawyers, doctors, military experts and others. Previous Commissioners have included people of such stature as Professors Frits Kalshoven, Michael Bothe and Ove Bring, as well as Ambassador Erich Kussbach and Judge Sir Kenneth Keith.

What is the Commission mandated to do? The answer lies in Article 90 itself. It can investigate grave breaches and other serious violations of the Conventions and Additional Protocol I, as well as offer its good offices. Between States that have made the Article 90 Declaration, there is a right to inquire, but in any other case, it is only by consent. As a matter of practicality, consent would be required in any event as the Commission, like the International Criminal Court, has no enforcement arm. The Commission has promulgated rules, financial regulations and operational guidelines in order to enable it to achieve its mandate.

It is regrettable that, in the two decades that the Commission has been established, so little use has been made of its services. In the early days, little was known of the Commission, but in recent years, a series of promotional activities have been undertaken to raise consciousness amongst States. In the view of the Commission, it has an important role to play in the modern world and is anxious to fulfil this.

Despite the lack of official activity, members of the Commission have been involved in their private capacity in other enquiries. Members of the Commission have been involved in separate enquiries in Lebanon and, occasionally, Commissioners are approached as to their availability for other such missions. One Commissioner has been involved in a mission for Geneva Call involving the alleged use of mines by non-State actors. However, in such cases, Commissioners are acting within the mandate of the particular organisation concerned and not as Commission members. At the same time, the Commission has offered its services and its good offices in a number of situations, and delicate negotiations have taken place with various parties. However, none of these initiatives have come to fruition.

### 15.7. The Future of the International Humanitarian Fact-Finding Commission

So is the IHFFC a white elephant, or does it have a role in the 21st century? Could it provide added value?

The Commission would seem to offer two particular advantages. The first is legitimacy. It is a treaty body with an international mandate. It is not an NGO with a duty to its funders. It is the States themselves who fund the Commission. As a result, there is a stronger argument for States to co-operate with it. Indeed, in cases where States have made the Article 90 Declaration, the Commission would expect that co-operation, both as a matter of law and also of common sense.

Secondly, the Commission offers a degree of efficiency in that any enquiry carried out must adopt a low-key, confidential approach. A report is submitted to the Parties with recommendations and that report will not be made public "unless all the Parties to the conflict have requested the Commission to do so" (Article 90(5)(c)). However, "if the Chamber is unable to secure sufficient evidence for factual and impartial findings, the Commission shall state the reasons for that inability". The task of the Commission is not to 'blame and shame' but to try to resolve disputes. The intention is to try to take some of the heat out of the propaganda wars that develop at present.

Furthermore, the Commission is the only standing body designed to investigate alleged violations of international humanitarian law and with Commissioners who are elected partly for their expertise in this area of law.

However, the Commission has a number of weaknesses, reflected to a large extent in its treaty mandate. First, by its terms, it is limited to dealing with alleged grave breaches and serious violations of the Geneva Conventions and Additional Protocol I. It therefore has no treaty mandate to investigate violations of other parts of international humanitarian law, although the Commission has expressed its willingness to do so in appropriate circumstances. This would, however, depend on the consent of the parties. Secondly, although the Commission has offered its services in situations of non-international armed conflict, it has been argued again that this also does not fall within its treaty mandate.

A further practical difficulty is the way that the Commission is funded. Although States Parties provide the basic funding for the Commission to exist and operate, Article 90 envisages that any inquiry will be funded by the parties involved. This is clearly a disincentive to use the Commission and effectively rules out involvement in non-international armed conflict unless the State Party is prepared to fund the complete mission (which the non-State Party might see as casting doubt on its impartiality) or some third party is prepared to contribute. This uncertainty over financing inevitably casts doubts on the ability of the Commission to immediately respond to a request, even though it has prudently developed a small reserve fund over the years in order to fund the initial stages of any mission.

Under Article 90(1)(f), Switzerland is required to "make available to the Commission the necessary administrative facilities for the performance of its functions". It fulfils this mandate by providing that the Federal Department of Foreign Affairs acts as the Secretariat to the Commission. Whilst this was appropriate in 1977, it has to be asked whether in the 21st century, it is still appropriate to have a State Party providing the Secretariat. Inevitably, there will be tensions between the policies of an independent organisation and those of a State and it could place Secretariat staff, who are employees of the Federal Department of Foreign Affairs, in an invidious position. No such conflict has yet arisen in practice, but the possibility is there.

## 15.8. The Swiss/ICRC Initiative on Strengthening Compliance with International Humanitarian Law

At the 31st International Conference of the Red Cross and Red Crescent in 2011, a joint initiative was launched by Switzerland and the ICRC on strengthening compliance with international humanitarian law.[57] There were high hopes that this might include a strengthening of support for the International Humanitarian Fact Finding Commission. A series of meetings took place with States, with a view to developing a report which was duly presented at the 32nd conference in 2015. The report proposed options to enhance the effectiveness of mechanisms of compliance with in-

---

[57] Strengthening Legal Protection for Victims of Armed Conflicts, Resolution 1, 31IC/11/R1, 31st International Conference of the Red Cross Red Crescent, 28 November – 1 December 2011, para. 7.

ternational humanitarian law, and to strengthen dialogue between States.[58] Regrettably, no consensus could be reached and the adopted Resolution only recommended initiating a new process.[59] Despite a number of meetings conducted by Switzerland and the ICRC in accordance with the Resolution, no agreement could be reached on further methods of strengthening compliance and the process was ended with a formal Report to the 33rd Conference in 2019.[60]

All of the three main mechanisms of compliance, Protecting Powers, the inquiry mechanisms initiated under the 1949 Geneva Conventions, and the IHFFC, are currently unused, the IHFFC at least in its treaty form. However, whilst all were initially designed for use in situations of international armed conflict, only the IHFFC has the potential to be made relevant in non-international armed conflict. But, as currently established, it could be seen as a 20th century construct seeking to deal with 21st century problems. Clearly, if international humanitarian law is to continue to be relevant, it needs effective compliance mechanisms to sit alongside those already in existence for international criminal justice and human rights. Fact-finding is a key element in those mechanisms and must be at the centre of any similar mechanism for international humanitarian law.

The question is how to move from the 20th century model under Article 90, to the sleeker model required for the 21th century, with an expanded mandate and a more secure logistical and financial base. Any attempt to re-negotiate the terms of Article 90 is likely to be resisted by many who would see this as possibly opening up other areas of Additional Protocol I. A more likely option therefore might be to establish less formally an expanded version of the IHFFC. This would sit alongside the existing mechanism, and either could be used as appropriate. Commissioners could be to a degree interchangeable, though if States not currently signed up to the IHFFC were to be involved in the new mechanism, there might need to be a wider pool of Commissioners involved in the

---

[58] See International Committee of the Red Cross, Swiss Federal Department of Foreign Affairs, "Strengthening Compliance with International Humanitarian Law", Concluding Report, 32IC/15/19.2, Geneva, October 2015.

[59] Strengthening Compliance with International Humanitarian Law, 32IC/15/R2, 32nd International Conference of the Red Cross and the Red Crescent, 8-10 December 2015.

[60] See Factual Report on the Proceedings of the Intergovernmental Process on Strengthening Respect for International Humanitarian Law, 33IC/19/9.2, 33rd International Conference of the Red Cross Red Crescent, 9–12 December 2019.

new body. Trigger mechanisms would remain an issue but as the practice of international humanitarian law fact-finding requires the co-operation of both sides to reach conclusions, this may not be as much of an issue as it appears.

## 15.9. Conclusions

Fact-finding is here to stay and plays an important role in international relations. However, as international criminal law and human rights law have both become more influential in situations of armed conflict, each has developed its own fact-finding mechanisms. International humanitarian law will need to catch up if it is not to be left behind. Otherwise, the danger will be that fact-finding is left to the other two bodies of law with the effect that international humanitarian law will find itself subject to interpretation through the prism of either or both bodies, and ceasing to have an existence of its own. The laws of war have been in existence in custom for millennia, and in treaty form for over 150 years. The need for such laws is not going to dissipate any time soon. It would be unfortunate if their relevance became increasingly challenged because the only compliance mechanisms worth pursuing were in different bodies of law. Solutions to this challenge are possible, but require a degree of political will to achieve them.

# 16

---

# Information Technology and Quality Control in Non-Criminal Justice Fact-Work

## Ilia Utmelidze[*]

## 16.1. Introduction

The use of information technology in fact-finding work is often associated with empirical examples of successfully implemented database projects; but also with the disappointments, frustration and failures frequently caused by a lack of good communication between professionals of different disciplines such as law, information technology, political science, statistics, or sociology.

The difficulties of establishing a comprehensive dialogue between humanitarian and technical scholarships on this topic is probably one of the reasons why there has, so far, been only limited academic discussion around this issue. Instead, the primary focus of discussion has been on the practical developments of different methodological models and technical tools that can be utilised in fact-finding work – or 'fact-work', the term coined for this book and its preceding 2013 LI Haopei Seminar.

There is nothing negative *per se* in such a utilitarian approach to the issue. Potentially, such pragmatic and low-key approaches can play an instrumental role in keeping developments, including discourse around

---

[*] **Ilia Utmelidze** is Director of the Case Matrix Network ('CMN'), a department of the Centre for International Law Research and Policy (CILRAP). He has been involved in the full spectrum of CMN activities, including participating in numerous missions to countries around the world and the development of CMN tools and services. He is a Senior Legal Adviser at the Norwegian National Human Rights Institution. He advises the Norwegian Helsinki Committee on methodologies and tools for the documentation of mass atrocities. In the past, he served as Legal Adviser in the Human Rights Department of the Organization of Security and Cooperation in Europe's Mission to Bosnia and Herzegovina, advising on transitional justice and institution-building in areas such as domestic war crimes prosecution mechanisms (including the development of a national strategy for war crimes prosecution), specialised investigative commissions for Srebrenica and Sarajevo, and the reform of ombudsman institutions.

this topic, result-oriented and driven by the practical needs and requirements of fact-finders.

However, alongside these practical developments, there is also a need for more conceptual discussion around this issue. Discourse that considers all relevant aspects (including those of a practical nature) of information technology and its use in fact-finding work can help to identify some of the major challenges in this area, and positively affect the development of a common theoretical platform.

## 16.2. Possible Definitions for Fact-Finding and Information Technology

### 16.2.1. Fact-Finding

Understanding the relevance of information technology for fact-finding, including how it can facilitate the quality control of its work, has to start with an actual definition of fact-finding work. This will help to identify the elements of fact-finding work where the use of information technology is most relevant; as well as assist to analyse the qualitative effects of information technology on this work.

The 2013 LI Haopei Seminar concept note defines fact-finding as:

> [...] work on facts or alleged facts, including work processes to identify, locate, obtain, verify, analyse, corroborate, summarize, synthesize, structure, organize, present and disseminate facts.[1]

According to Oppenheim the primary purpose of inquiry in international law "is the elucidation of the facts".[2] However, fact-finding work in the areas of international criminal, humanitarian and human rights law is not only a means of producing an authoritative account of a situation that involves issues of major public interest. It is also a specific work process for the analysis and evaluation of such situations, in accordance with the normative framework of the applicable legal disciplines.

It would perhaps be accurate to say that the main objective of fact-finding work is the clarification of the factual circumstances of a situation

---

[1]  The concept note of the Quality Control in International Fact-Finding LI Haopei Lecture and Seminar is available at https://www.fichl.org/activities/quality-control-in-international-fact-finding-outside-criminal-justice-for-core-international-crimes/.

[2]  Lassa Oppenheim, *International Law*, Hersh Lauterpacht (ed.), Longmans, Green and Co., London, 7th Edition, 1952, vol. 2, p. 13.

that usually concerns allegations of human rights violations and breaches of international humanitarian or criminal law.

This means that fact-finding in the fields of international criminal, humanitarian and human rights law is, in principle, a quasi-judicial or "quasi-judicial like" process. It operates with the framework of applicable substantive law and less formally defined procedural rules that regulate its work processes. How strict or detailed such procedural rules are, largely depends on the nature and mandate of the fact-finding missions, although these never appear to be as strict or vigorous as those of judicial proceedings. Nevertheless, it is possible to see some similarities in the work processes of these two mechanisms.

Fact-finding as a quasi-judicial or "quasi-judicial like" work process can, in general, be summarised into three main stages. Each stage should ideally be guided by the applicable international criminal, humanitarian and human rights law, as well as by procedural rules. The three stages might be defined as follows:

a)    The searching and gathering of information – that is, to *identify, locate, obtain and verify* different sources and materials that are reliable and trustworthy, and can serve as a factual account of the matter under inquiry. In comparison to judicial proceedings, especially criminal proceedings, fact-finders are not bound to very strict and vigorous rules of evidence. However, as a quasi-judicial process, fact-finders have to also evaluate the information they are gathering and consider its factual value before it can be used for assessment and conclusion. This would include looking at the sources of information, how the information was collected and directed to the fact-finders, as well as assessing the content of the information with regard to its reliability.

b)    The assessment and analysis of factual information – that is, to analyse, *corroborate, summarise, synthesise, structure and organise* facts that have been gathered with the primary objective of evaluating a given situation and allegations of human rights violations and breaches of international humanitarian or criminal law. This stage of the work process is primarily based on the methodologies of legal analysis. Its main objective is to place a factual map of the situation against the applicable international legal framework. How detailed such legal analysis can be will largely depend on the mandate and nature of the fact-finding mission. Nonetheless, expectations with regard to the quality and accuracy of the related factual analysis are usually extremely high. In addition to providing an overall legal analysis, some fact-finders may also have to systematise and determine some quantitative information linked, for example, to alleged victims or perpetrators, location of incidents, institutions involved, court cases and proceedings, *et cetera*.

c) The dispensation of conclusions and factual findings – that is, to *present and disseminate* facts that have been determined and findings that have been made. The main output of the fact-finders' work still comes in the form of a traditional report, which contains all the core information, including key factual findings and the main legal argumentation. Communicating, prompting or defending the factual findings and the conclusions of reports often seem to be an essential part of the work process of the fact-finders. In addition, it may also be relevant to preserve, provide or transfer factual information, which may include dispensing original/source documentation, systematised and aggregated qualitative and quantitative information, as well as other relevant data.

## 16.2.2. Information Technology

The explanation of the meaning of information technology can perhaps start with the general definition of this term, that is, the use of computers and telecommunications equipment (with their associated microelectronics) to send, receive, store and manipulate data.[3]

Determining what type of information technology is specifically relevant for fact-finders, as well as if and how it can enhance the quality of their work, is an open issue, as there are no authoritative definitions or clearly agreed standards in the field. As was mentioned above, there are different practical solutions. However, they are not necessarily based on a common theoretical platform. Although these approaches and models are different from each other, there are also some obvious similarities and overlaps.

One of the possible ways to determine the kinds of information technology systems (or simply IT tools) that are relevant for fact-finding work is to map their functionalities against the work processes of the fact-finders:

---

[3] John Daintith (ed.), "IT", *A Dictionary of Physics*, Oxford University Press, 2009.

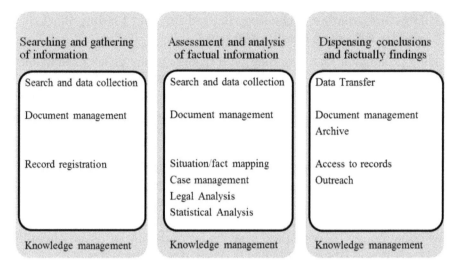

| Searching and gathering of information | Assessment and analysis of factual information | Dispensing conclusions and factually findings |
|---|---|---|
| Search and data collection | Search and data collection | Data Transfer |
| Document management | Document management | Document management<br>Archive |
| Record registration | Situation/fact mapping<br>Case management<br>Legal Analysis<br>Statistical Analysis | Access to records<br>Outreach |
| Knowledge management | Knowledge management | Knowledge management |

The current inventory is primarily focused on the functionalities of IT tools that can be specifically used for fact-finding work. Those elements and functionalities of information technology that are used for general underlying administrative work, data security or infrastructure are not included in the current list.

It is important to highlight that, in practice, such an inventory of functions is rarely provided as one integrated IT tool. Often, these are several tools with parallel and partly overlapping functionalities, commonly referred to as databases, programmes and web sites.

The reasons for this are varied, and both substantive and technical in nature. It is demanding to develop a conceptual basis for such an integrated approach, especially in the absence of a solid and agreed theoretical grounding for it. Additionally, while fact-finding bodies often operate on an *ad hoc* basis, integrated systems require long-term planning and commitment for their development and maintenance. Such an integrated system would also require maximum technical flexibility in order to accommodate the needs of different types of fact-finding missions that may have diverse needs for customisation and adaptation. However, experience shows that the development of such systems is possible.

### 16.3. How Information Technology is Used for Fact-Finding Work and Its Effects on Quality Control

Building a common understanding with regards to the different functionalities of IT tools relevant to fact-finding is instrumental to explaining how information technology can enhance the quality control of fact-finding work. This is described in detail in the following sections.

#### 16.3.1. Search and Data Collection

IT tools can provide different types of capabilities for the search and reception of information. This can be a simple exchange of electronic documentation between different fact-finding missions or, as is often the case, the transfer of documentation from national initiatives to international fact-finding bodies. Automatised systems for data transfer usually help to avoid lengthy and laborious manual transfer of documentation.

Another capability is the search of open sources of information that may be available on web sites of official state institutions, media sources, web sites of civil society groups, as well as other types of video and printed materials accessible through the Internet. Some new technologies even allow the automatic gathering of interesting material linked to a particular situation or issue. However, if the system is not fine-tuned and is not based on a thoroughly planned methodology, fact-finders might face the problem of excessive and/or irrelevant information.

Social media is another technical platform that is increasingly present in the reporting of human rights violations. This new technology has revolutionised the understanding of the victim's right to be heard and seen. Although social media as a technology itself provides immense new opportunities with regards to data collection, it raises a number of methodological dilemmas for fact-finders with regards to the accuracy and reliability of the information, as well as the security and protection of personal data. Moreover, the volume of such information is often so massive that it can cause extra challenges for fact-finders to effectively process this type of data.

#### 16.3.2. Data Transfer

There are different mechanisms, both national and international, which are mandated and have the capacity to observe and/or assess human rights violations and breaches of international humanitarian and criminal law. In some situations, a single file or document can become of interest to fact-finders, judicial bodies and other types of commissions dealing with the consequences of mass atrocities, as well as governmental institutions from the military, to social security and health services, archives, museums, *et cetera*.[4] Well-structured information and the technical capacity to transfer such data could play a vital role in developing practical communication between those institutions, and facilitating their co-operation and co-ordination for the better protection of the rights of the victims.

### 16.3.3. Document Management

One of the essential services that IT tools can provide to fact-finders is the efficient organisation of large amount of documentation (such as text, video, audio and photo). Such systems are particularly relevant for fact-finding missions that are mandated to deal with large and complex investigations that might also last over long periods of time. There is often the potential for such fact-finding missions to be overwhelmed with the large amount of documentation, if there is no appropriate system in place to effectively receive and organise data.

The development of effective document management systems requires careful planning. To save resources, it is vital that the system is properly customised for the individual situation or issue. First of all, it is important to take into consideration the type of documentation fact-finders will be working with. This will help to adapt the logic for the classification of documentation (also known as metadata and keywords) to the individual needs of the fact-finders. For example, in understanding what the main information sources are, different typologies of documents can help to tailor classification systems to individual user needs and make the organisation of data more logical and efficient.

Some of the technical characteristics of the documents can also play an important role in designing the appropriate system. For example, the quality of electronic copies of documents has high relevance for the development of search functions (also referred to as search engines) of the document management system. Poor quality digital copies reduce the pos-

---

[4]   Mechanisms that have been developed both on the international and national levels to deal with the consequences of the mass atrocities that took place in the beginning of 1990s in the former Yugoslavia, including international and national fact-finding bodies and courts, lustration processes, property-restitution arrangements, compensation schemes, documentation initiatives, and archives, have clearly demonstrated a need for better planning and co-operation with regards to factual information.

sibility to use search techniques that are based on text recognition technologies and increase requirements for more advanced systems of classification (metadata and keywords), as well as other technological solutions for file or document recognition.

### 16.3.4. Archive

At the end of the missions, it is often required to preserve all the information that was collected by the fact-finders. The main purpose of electronic archive systems is to serve as the depositary of documentation and to provide the possibility of accessing the documents in the future. The logic of organising the archival system is similar to that of a document management system. The principles differ in that archived documents are no longer actively used by the fact-finders and are not associated with an underlying work process and its requirements.

### 16.3.5. Record Registration

In addition to the information that is received externally, fact-finders produce large amounts of their own documentation. Practices can differ from mission to mission but, most commonly, these include records of victims that would include circumstances of victimisation, personal data of victims as well as subsequent actions undertaken; incident or situation records that could include testimonies and recollection of facts, own observations of incidents or examination of locations in the aftermath of events; and individual complaints or cases that could include short summaries, procedural information as well as notes of trial monitoring.

The main purpose of record registration is to assist fact-finders in gathering and verifying different parcels of information in order to, for example: reconstruct factual circumstances of an alleged atrocity, identify a chain of contextual events; highlight structural problems for systemic human rights violations; or map relevant institutions and regulatory frameworks that might be causes for the structural problems.

At the initial stages of record registration, information is often irregular, random and chaotic. Therefore, it is important that fact-finders have flexibility to follow different methods of identifying and reconstructing facts. It is unrealistic to expect that fact-finders follow a rigid pattern of documentation, for example, structuring information into cases or events. Instead, fact-finders should be able to (a) register essential elements of facts such as: alleged victims, witnesses, protected property, suspects and institutional linkages, incidents and contextual circumstances, classification of crimes and violations; and (b) group these essential elements of fact into different clusters of information as necessary.

Such an approach will allow fact-finders to, for example, group victims into clusters of victims of a given geographical location or type of violation. Some victims from this cluster can be connected to other clusters of information related to a particular incident. The incident can be linked to another cluster of information that is connected to particular institutions or alleged perpetrators.

Even if at the initial stage this might seem to be a random and chaotic set of information, these linkages of data can help to systematise fragmented and irregular information, and facilitate the gradual reconstruction of the factual foundation of the given inquiry.

If an IT tool allows for flexible use of the essential elements of facts (such as victims, suspect and incident), it will be much more convenient to utilise this data for different purposes at the later stages of analysis. For example, the data could be used to build cases and catalogues of victims, as well as map typologies of victimisation, and roles of institutions and individuals involved.

It is particularly useful for fact-finding work if *record registration* and *document management* is integrated in one single system. Such technology will provide the possibility to keep an accurate overview of the fact-finders' records and related original source materials. Hyperlinking fact-finders' records and respective documentation bases help to build a unique network of inter-related facts and sources. This increases the accuracy and reliability of the findings, as well as the overall credibility of final results.

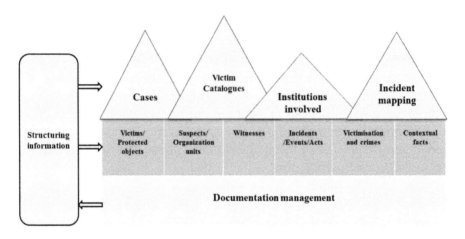

### 16.3.6. Situation or Fact Mapping

Fact-finding missions often target situations of large-scale violations of human rights that affect considerable segments of society. Understanding such complex situations cannot be limited to separate overviews of individual cases or facts. Rather, it requires an overall analysis of the situation that would help to identify repeating patterns of systemic violations of human rights and their root causes. In this regard, IT tools can provide different possibilities for mapping large-scale violations and conducting quantitative and qualitative assessment of collected data.

Very often, fact-finders use geographic mapping of violations in order to analyse territorial and time distribution of the reported atrocities, as well as to visualise different patterns of violations.

More advanced mapping methodology offers a number of qualitative indicators for fact-finding work that could improve the objective systematisation and analysis of information. Using such qualitative indicators can help fact-finders to analyse their findings in a more objective manner, including selecting emblematic cases and prioritising the most pressing human rights issues.

### 16.3.7. Case Management

A fact-finder's work often revolves around individual cases. A case in the context of fact-finding work may be a petition, complaint, communication and/or the report of an individual victim or his or her representative that is submitted to the fact-finders. Furthermore, there are criminal, civil and administrative proceedings that are linked to individual petitions and, as such, are objects of inquiry for fact-finders. For some fact-finding missions, the main mandate is to monitor court cases.

Working with a large amount of cases over long periods of time can require an effective case management system (also referred to as 'CMS'). IT tools that facilitate the effective management of the procedural and factual information of a case can become a vital instrument for organising the work processes of fact-finders. They can help to manage work processes on both: (a) an individual case level – that would be to manage information within a particular case, follow procedural deadlines, and keep an overview of the substantive parts of the case; and (b) on the level of the overall case load – to plan resources for dealing with the case load, to share tasks among colleagues, and to conduct more substantive analyses of the case load. For example, this can include identifying different typology of cases, length of proceedings, main concerns and violations reported, institutions allegedly involved in misconduct, as well as the geographic and time distribution of cases.

### 16.3.8. Legal Analysis

An important, but extremely rare, functionality of IT tools is the provision of support to fact-finders in their legal analysis. It is only logical to expect that legal analysis is a central part of any such system. The purpose of fact-finding work is not only the collection and aggregation of large amounts of quantitative information; it is, first of all, the assessment and analysis of this finding, in accordance to the applicable standards of international criminal, humanitarian and human rights law.

Using right-based (law-driven) systems can contribute to the work of fact-finders. For example, applying the methodology of a legal matrix helps to assess relevant factual findings against applicable legal standards, which comprise the cornerstone of any legal analysis process.

Experience has shown that the absence of legal analysis within IT tools can have demotivating effects on the fact-finder. It is not always easy for a fact-finder to appreciate the laborious task of maintaining electronic records of their work, if the system fails to provide support in their most crucial tasks.

It is important to make a distinction between a legal analysis system and a general classification of types of violation or acts. A legal analysis system is based on a solid understanding of international legal standards, as well as on the application of these norms in practice. It can assist the fact-finder to gather and present an accurate set of facts that are necessary to precisely argue possible violations of international norms.

Such systems also help to secure a consistent quality of work for fact-finders, including the contributions of less experienced members of the team. It enhances possibilities for the transparency and accuracy of the final outcome, by establishing logical chains between factual information, normative frameworks and the conclusions made. A high level of accuracy of factual and legal findings increases the quality of the overall conclusions and recommendations and makes the work more reliable and credible.

### 16.3.9. Statistical Analysis

The use of different types of quantitative data is increasingly applied in fact-finding work. For example, statistical analysis is most frequently used to estimate human losses in situations of gross or systemic violations of human rights. It is a clear and convincing way of showing the scale and consequences of atrocities, and influencing the general public and decision-makers to stop the violence.

IT tools that provide such functionalities require special competence and have to be developed in close co-operation with experts in the field of sociology and statistics.

### 16.3.10. Access to Records and Outreach

The situations that fact-finders study often have high political, social and historical significance. Consequently, there are legitimate expectations from the general public that these findings are accessible to a wider audience. It might also be in the interest of fact-finders to conduct outreach to the wider audience, for example, to challenge the attitudes of the majority group towards vulnerable minority groups in a society.

It might often be relevant to make not only the overall findings and conclusions accessible, but also individual instances of violence and mistreatment. IT tools can play an important role in opening such information to the public, while at the same time ensuring the protection of personal information and other security considerations, as may be required.

### 16.3.11. Knowledge Management

There is always a high expectation from fact-finders that their legal analysis is based on an impeccable understanding of the applicable normative framework. High-profile fact-finding missions are often led by distinguished legal experts who are expected to ensure the quality of the final product. However, legal research is still a very central part of fact-finders' work, irrespective of the profile of its individual members or the complexity of situation or issue.

One of the essential means for legal research in the field of international criminal, humanitarian and human right law is the electronic libraries and databases of main international courts and tribunals. Fact-finding reports often refer to the jurisprudence of these courts, which can be searched and accessed online. There is also an increasing number of electronic legal digests and commenters that provide extremely valuable help to fact-finders in their legal research.

Unfortunately, the majority of information technology systems view knowledge management as a separate tool and work process, which creates an artificial divide between IT tools that help information (fact) management and knowledge management.

IT tools that have overcome this divide and developed an integrated platform for fact-work and legal analysis can better contribute to the quality enhancement of fact-finders' work. Such systems can provide access to substantive legal standards at all stages of the work process (not only the analysis stage), which can secure a consistent and qualitative approach to information gathering and the analysis that follows. An integrated information and knowledge management system can reinforce consistency and quality of work for all members of the team, which is particularly relevant for larger or long-term missions.

## 16.4. Conclusion

The two main areas where information technology can enhance the quality control of fact-finders work are: (a) by supporting effective and accurate information (fact) management at all stages of fact-finding work, and (b) by providing the knowledge-base necessary to secure consistent and high-quality legal analysis.

In general, IT tools can be instrumental in operationalising the mandate and methodology of fact-finders. It can help every stage of the work process, including planning the work, distributing tasks, as well as managing results and outcomes in a highly efficient way.

For the substantive work, IT tools can play an invaluable role in handing large amounts of factual data, especially in complex, large-scale or long-term inquiries. It can make documentation work more precise and reliable and create good preconditions for subsequent systematisation and analysis. If information gathering and analysis is based on an integrated knowledge-base, the efficacy and quality of work is enhanced.

IT tools can open new possibilities for both quantitative and qualitative scrutiny of collected data and give new means for the communication of factual findings to the general public and decision-makers.

# 17

## Human Rights Fact-Finding: Some Legal and Ethical Dilemmas

### Geoffrey Robertson[*]

Human rights fact-finding missions are of increasing importance, especially to the array of war crimes courts that have been established since the 1990s. Their prosecutors draw on the reports of such missions as a basis for initiating investigations, and often seek to call evidence from the fact-finders as part of the prosecution case. A prosecution summons to go into the witness box can cause serious problems for human rights monitors (I would prefer to call them human rights reporters), who must protect their sources and avoid being perceived as partisan. And because the reports of fact-finding missions can now lead to the prosecution of political and military leaders (or at least affect their post-retirement travel plans) some leaders have devised new ways of attacking such reports, by threatening legal actions, usually in England, for libel or breach of confidence.

Academics have generally overlooked the importance of this subject – the most impressive exceptions being a study by Diane Orentlicher[1] back in 1990 and the 2013 first edition of this book. I should also mention the "Guidelines for International Human Rights Fact-Finding Visits and Missions" prepared by the Raoul Wallenberg Institute.[2] It is now time to

---

[*] **Geoffrey Robertson** AO QC is founder and head of Doughty Street Chambers, London's largest human rights practice. He has conducted many human rights fact-finding missions for Amnesty International, the Bar Council and other organisations. He served as the first President of the Special Court in Sierra Leone. He is the author of *Crimes Against Humanity: The Struggle for Global Justice*, Penguin and New Press. This is an edited version of his keynote address at the conference which inaugurated the *Lund-London Guidelines on International Human Rights Fact-Finding Visits and Reports*, prepared by the Raoul Wallenberg Institute. An earlier version was published with the International Bar Association: "Human Rights Fact Finding: Some Legal and Ethical Dilemmas", Human Rights Institute, Thematic Papers No. 1, 2010.

[1] See Diane F Orentlicher, "Bearing Witness: The Art and Science of Human Rights Fact-Finding", in *Harvard Human Rights Journal*, 1990, vol. 3, p. 83.

[2] Raoul Wallenberg Institute, Lund University, *Guidelines on International Human Rights Fact-Finding Visits and Report*, 1 June 2009.

---

take a further look at the ethical and legal dimensions of human rights fact-finding.

There are different kinds of fact-finding exercises. At one level there is the Commission of Inquiry, with statutory powers to summon witnesses and obtain documents. It usually has a counsel to assist, and interested parties are entitled to be represented. Corruption Commissions in the Caribbean, conducted by Sir Louis Blom-Cooper and Sir Robin Auld, are good examples, whilst the Bloody Sunday inquiry, into deaths caused by a demonstration in Belfast in 1971 by British paratroopers, which took years (1998-2010) and cost millions, provides a particularly dreadful example. Statutory commissions into human rights abuses are rare, if only because it usually takes international pressure for a government to set up a commission with the power to examine the misconduct of its own members. The Blom-Cooper Inquiry into the trafficking of arms to the Medellín Cartel, for example, was set up as the result of an international outcry, after guns imported from Israel by an Antiguan government minister on behalf of the Medellín cocaine cartel were used to assassinate presidential candidate in Colombia.[3]

A more common form is an official inquiry by a distinguished personage who lacks legal power, but will obtain some co-operation from the State under scrutiny because of his or her standing. A United Nations ('UN') rapporteur falls into this category – for example, Philip Alston's inquiry into the riots in Kenya and Richard J. Goldstone's inquiry for the Human Rights Council into the Israeli incursion in Gaza. These missions come with the moral force of the UN, although that does not always make them welcome: the Israeli government refused to co-operate with the Goldstone enquiry and the Kenyan government condemned the report of the Alston enquiry.

A third kind of inquiry is one set up by a non-governmental organisation ('NGO'), conducted by an independent person (usually a jurist), who is invited to investigate and then write a report for publication. The International Bar Association tends to send a number of prominent lawyers. Sometimes they are not allowed in, and have to conduct witness interviews outside the country. Even though they can be handicapped by lack of investigative power, the legal conclusions of such an enquiry about facts that are in the public domain, can be of great significance –

---

[3]  See Louis Blom-Cooper, *Guns for Antigua*, Duckworth, 1990.

especially if the conclusion is that such facts give rise to a *prima facie* case of genocide or crime against humanity.

Another kind of inquiry is an independent expert mission which conducts confidential fact-finding for an NGO which will not publish any report directly but will filter its findings into its campaigns and country assessments. Amnesty International missions provide examples. The Commonwealth Secretariat, too, holds inquiries of these kinds. Their advantage is that the fact-finder may obtain important information, and valuable perspective, by speaking confidentially to important government figures – to judges, prosecutors and prison officers who would not be prepared to speak openly. The disadvantage, of course, is that these reports cannot be published and the fact-finder enters into an obligation of confidentiality towards officials who may later become the subject of prosecution. In the case of the Red Cross, confidentiality is absolute and may be enforced under international law.

A fifth kind of human rights fact-finding goes on all the time as a result of the work of human rights monitors working in country, gathering information from local sources. Human Rights Watch calls them 'country representatives' and often gives them awards or asks them to make presentations and certainly makes no secret of their presence within a troubled State. Other NGOs require their reporters to be more low profile. These 'monitors' are on a permanent fact-finding mission and their organisation will from time to time issue reports based on their work. There is a thin line dividing these human rights reporters from newspaper reporters and there is no obvious reason, as a matter of law, why they should not have the same legal protection.

There are other models of human rights fact-finding, but all present similar problems of ensuring accuracy and impartiality, protecting sources, and avoiding being sued for libel, especially in London, the libel capital of the world, if the report makes accusations against identifiable persons. Although a statutory inquiry will generally have absolute privilege from libel action, reports of other inquiries will not have this protection, and this vulnerability is anxious-making for cash-strapped NGOs. Even UN rapporteurs have been sued, although the International Court of Justice in the case of Cumaraswamy has now ruled that rapporteurs have UN immunity. This was a case where the UN's rapporteur on the judiciary made some remarks about judicial corruption in his own country, Malaysia, and was sued by the lawyers and law firm widely accused of corrupting the judges. The Malaysian courts refused to acknowledge his UN immunity, until the Court ruled that he was entitled to it.[4]

*

The cause of human rights has progressed a long way in a very short time. I remember joining Amnesty at university in the early 1970s, when my first task was to compose grovelling letters to General Pinochet, requesting him to abandon the torture of political prisoners. A mere quarter of a century later, I had the pleasure of acting for Human Rights Watch in the House of Lords case that approved his extradition on torture charges. In the intervening period, before international criminal law delivered on the legacy of Nuremberg and before the Internet revolution and satellite television, human rights fact-finding missions were the only way to prise information out of repressive regimes. Today there is more information available, but separating it from rumour and propaganda and blogging fantasies, and analysing its legal significance, is more important than ever.

Trial observation by international monitors is an important aspect of human rights fact-finding. It is usually conducted by lawyers of some distinction who sit in court for as long as they or their supporting NGO afford. They speak to the judge and the prosecutors as well as to the defence counsel, and provide their organisation with some insight into the fairness of the trial. In the case of Amnesty, which conducted many such observations from its inception in the 1960s, the interviewees would be offered a letter from its Secretary-General assuring them that their comments would be treated in utter confidence. The information provided would be factored into the observer's confidential report, which would never see the light of day: it would be considered along with information from other sources by office researchers and editors and find its filtered way into the next Amnesty annual report. The report itself would often be disputed by the government, but Amnesty reports in this period were recognised as fairly accurate and the organisation had a much higher reputation for getting at the truth than the government in question. This was largely as a result of the ability of its observers to speak confidentially to officials of that government. There was no doubt that a binding offer of confidentiality was essential to the success of fact-finding missions.

---

[4]  International Court of Justice, *Differences Relating to Immunity from Legal Process of a Special Rapporteur of the Commission on Human Rights*, Advisory Opinion, ICJ Reports 1999, p. 62.

---

Ethical problems were apt to arise. I remember conducting a mission for Amnesty to South Africa in relation to the 'Sharpeville Six' appeal – a half dozen protestors sentenced to death under a vague 'common purpose' doctrine for participating in a demonstration, in the course of which a 'necklacing' had occurred. I thought it would be useful to meet the trial judge who had convicted them (there was no jury) and sentenced them to death, a judge somewhat inappropriately named Human. I showed him the Secretary-General's letter and promised him confidentiality, and he took me to his club – the Pretoria Club – which he boasted was very progressive, having recently agreed to admit Jews (although it still banned black people and women). He was a lonely old racist, dying of alcohol poisoning, and after a few drinks made a number of admissions to me that might have founded a further appeal. If the men had not been reprieved, would I have broken my undertaking of confidentiality in order to save their necks? I would obviously have had to discuss this course with Amnesty, but ultimately my conscience would probably have made me speak out: after all, as every equity lawyer knows, there can be no confidence in iniquity.

## 17.1. History

Early twentieth-century fact-finding on subjects we would now associate with 'human rights'[5] often had a propagandistic purpose, especially if appointed or backed by governments. At the outset of the First World War, the British government supported 'fact-finding' about the German invasion of Belgium: Wellington House produced stories from unidentified witnesses about German soldiers bayoneting pregnant women and cold-bloodedly murdering children that were later exposed as fraudulent. Lord James Bryce, formerly Oxford Regius Professor of Civil Law, oversaw this blatant propaganda exercise: its subsequent exposure has tainted the excellent work done by Arnold Toynbee on the Armenian Massacre (*The Blue Book*) to which Bryce wrote the introduction.[6] The most satisfactory human rights fact-finding mission in this period was that of Major General Harbord, conducted for the US government in Turkey in September and October 1919: its work was fast and efficient and its report eloquently

---

[5]    The term was not much used until 1939, see Geoffrey Robertson, "The Human Rights Story", in *Crimes Against Humanity*, Penguin, 2006, chap. 1.

[6]    See Phillip Knightly, *The First Casualty*, Andre Deutsch, 1975, pp. 83-84.

described the horrors of what would later, and rightly, be termed "geno-cide".[7]

Fact-finding missions loomed large in the history of the League of Nations. In fact, it was the very failure of its fact-finding missions which contributed to bringing down the League, an organisation based on the notion of 'collective security' – the principle that if one member-State was attacked, the others would declare war on the attacker. This illusion sustained the League's supporters throughout the 1920s. But in September 1931, Japan (a leading member of the league), invaded Manchuria after an incident in which it claimed that its railway there had been sabotaged by Chinese soldiers. China denied playing any part in this provocation and complained to the League about Japanese aggression. What was the League to do? A fact-finding mission was its first response and it sent Lord Lytton – an English notable who apparently disliked air or train travel, as he went by sea. It took him several months to get to Manchuria and several months to sail back and produce his report in September 1932 – a full year since the incident. By this time Japan had already appointed 'the last Emperor' to be puppet governor of Manchukuo, its new name for the conquered territory. Lord Lytton's report – to the effect that the incident did not constitute provocation and Japan had acted unlawfully and should return the province to China – was too late to have any effect other than to undermine the League's credibility. By this time, aggression was a *fait accompli.*

Did the League learn the lesson that fact-finding missions upon which collective security might depend should find their facts quickly? Not at all. In December 1934, Mussolini contrived an incident at Wal-Wal oasis in Abyssinia, as a pretext for his invasion of that country. Emperor Haile Selassie was highly outraged, and complained to the League, which sent a fact-finding committee to investigate. But it still took them nine months to report that the Abyssinians were blameless. By this time, Mussolini had his canisters of poison gas in place on the border and had secured the silence of Britain and France (which wanted to appease Mussolini – so he would not strike-up an alliance with Hitler!). Once again, de-

---

[7]   James G. Harbord, *Conditions in the Near East. Report of the American Military Mission to Armenia*, sixty-sixth Congress, second Session, Dec. No. 266, 13 April 1920. See Peter Balakian, *The Burning Tigris*, Heinemann, 2003.

lay was fatal to the League's pretentions about collective security: Haile Selassie was highly deserted.

This early history emphasises that fact-finding investigations of recent human rights disasters must report as soon as possible after they have set up: the more they delay, the less their impact. This can also apply to inquiries into events long past: judicial fact-finding in the UK has been severely damaged by the incredible delays in the Saville Inquiry into Bloody Sunday: it took 12 years to investigate the events of one day in the life of Belfast, at the cost of millions of pounds – it turned out to be a lawyer's banquet. In 2009, an Iraq War Inquiry was set up by the UK government, run by civil servants and not by judges – a mistaken decision which it justified by reference to the disastrous Bloody Sunday enquiry.

## 17.2. Problems and Principles

### 17.2.1. Funding

NGO fact-finding began in earnest with the launch of Amnesty International in 1959. Early fact-finding missions to Africa, notably conducted by Louis Blom-Cooper QC, were impressive. However, one such mission to Rhodesia was discredited when it leaked out that the money to fund the inquiry had come in secret from the UK Foreign and Commonwealth Office. This taught Amnesty's founder, Peter Berenson, the lesson that he should never again take money from governments, a rule that has been adopted by Human Rights Watch. I am not sure that this need be a universal rule, but there is one fundamental principle here for NGOs and foundations, namely that the funding for fact-finding missions must always be disclosed. The general belief that 'he who pays the piper calls the tune' makes it all too easy to discredit mission reports, even if none of the participants is personally remunerated, if the costs of the hearings or of travel or of printing the report have been secretly paid by an interested party or a government. Fact-finding missions should be entirely transparent about their funding.

### 17.2.2. Composition of the Delegation

The Lund-London guidelines correctly state:

> The mission's delegation must comprise individuals who are
> and are seen to be unbiased. The NGO should be confident
> that the delegation members have the competence, experi-

ence and expertise relevant to the matters pertaining to the
terms of reference.[8]

Compliance with this principle will be crucial to the success of the
mission. When the stakes are high, governments and their unscrupulous
propagandists will not hesitate to defame the authors of critical reports
and the NGOs which have tasked them. Pro-Israeli sources have recently
attempted to discredit a Human Rights Watch fact-finder, who is an histo-
rian of Nazi (and American) war time medals and uniforms. Even Richard
J. Goldstone has been accused of bias, after his investigation for the Human Rights Council concluded that Israeli commanders committed war
crimes in their attack on Gaza. Although the Council itself has displayed
prejudice against Israel, its choice of Goldstone as a fact-finder meant that
his report could not sensibly be assailed for partisanship. There have been
outrageous cases in the past where trial observers have masqueraded as
impartial – most notably the fellow travelling English barristers who
white-washed Stalin's show trials (with dishonest reports entitled "The
Moscow Trials Were Fair").

Expertise in the subject matter of the mission should be carefully
evaluated, because some undoubted experts will already have committed
themselves to an opinion, and could therefore be criticised for pre-
judgment. Very often it will be most appropriate to choose individuals
who have no connection at all with the country or the persons involved in
the mission, but who have a reputation for independence and for good
judgment. For trial observers, some familiarity with the system of law under which trial is held will avoid the ignorance sometimes displayed by
continental observers of adversary trials and by Anglo-American observers of inquisitorial proceedings. The UN Secretary-General appointed, as
one of five Lockerbie trial observers, an obscure Austrian philosopher
who has been condemning the verdict and everyone associated with it ever since, in a way that appears to reveal a lack of understanding of adversary trial procedure and evidence, and a propensity to impugn the integrity
of defence lawyers, prosecutors and judges. The case for re-opening a trial
verdict is not helped by unsupported allegations of this kind.[9]

---

8  Article 8, see *supra* note 2.

9  See Hans Kochler, "I Saw the Trial – And the Verdict Made No Sense", *The Independent*,
   21 August 2009. This, according to Kochler, was because it was "based on circumstantial
   evidence" (which lawyers know is often the best evidence) because the co-defendant was

### 17.2.3. Even-Handedness

American NGOs have learnt to look at life from both sides now. America's Watch and the Lawyer's Committee were precursors of Human Rights Watch: they grew out of the civil disobedience movement of the 1960s and produced tough lawyer-journalists like Michael Posner, Ray Bonner and Reed Brody. They exposed the US government's behaviour in places like El Salvador (where the CIA was secretly supporting army death squads) and Nicaragua (where the CIA was secretly supporting the Contras). The Reagan administration, most notably through the work of Elliot Abrams, an Assistant Secretary of State (ironically for Humanitarian Affairs), went for the jugular and tried to discredit Ray Bonner over his exposure of the El Mazote massacre, and Reed Brody over his report about Contra funding, which Reagan personally condemned as 'bought and paid for by the Sandinistas'. The White House, in McCarthyite mode, enlisted all its tamed media connections: the *New York Times* dispensed with Bonner's services, and *Time* magazine attacked Brody. To their credit, calumny did not stop them and both were in time vindicated – Brody's reports proved accurate, and years later, Bonner's claims about the existence of a mass grave, derided by the Reagan administration, was proved true when the grave, with the bodies of hundreds of women and children, was discovered.

Nonetheless, the criticism served to teach the lesson that human rights reports should be even-handed, should examine and, if appropriate, criticise both sides. Many fact-finding missions will focus upon the government over its oppression of insurgent groups, but the behaviour of these groups should be judged as severely and by the same criteria as government conduct. This has become a counsel not only of fairness but of prudence: it was much in evidence in those commentaries in 2009 on the Sri Lankan army's butchery of Tamils, balanced by references to the terrorist behaviour of the Tamil Tigers.

Amnesty, taking a purist position, has pointed out that its remit is to investigate the conduct of the State rather than the conduct of those op-

---

acquitted (an indication of the fairness of the court), because one witness had been taken fishing by the Scottish police (what else is there to do in Scotland?), and because information about a break-in at Heathrow was withheld (it was fully available to the Appeal Court, where the five judges analysed it carefully and concluded that it gave no possible support to the defence), and because only one person was convicted (which does not mean that the person they did convict was innocent!).

posed to the State. Thus, it made no criticism of ANC guerrilla actions when condemning the apartheid policies of the South African government. However, the legitimacy of State counter-insurgency policies may depend upon the reasonableness of response to the conduct of insurgents. So, it was right to condemn the Tamil Tigers for using their own people as human shields and virtual hostages, whilst criticising the conduct of the Sri Lankan army in putting civilians at risk during the final stages of the war.

One important example of the need for fact-finding missions to assess the behaviour of insurgents as well as governments is provided by Richard J. Goldstone's investigation into the Israeli-Palestinian conflict in Gaza. He had to lobby hard in order to obtain the Human Rights Council's approval to investigate the behaviour of Hamas as well as that of Israel. In such tit-for-tat conflicts, passing judgment on the conduct of *both* sides is inevitable: the whole question of proportionality justification for Israeli conduct is bound up with the degree of provocation constituted by Hamas rocket attacks on Israel. Despite Goldstone's attempt to avoid becoming one-eyed in Gaza, it is regrettable that the Israeli government refused to co-operate with his mission and condemned his report as soon as it was published. His insistence on investigating Hamas underlines the principle of even-handedness: examine the conduct of insurgents as well as the response to that conduct by the government.

### 17.2.4. Obeying Local Laws

Another issue that can bedevil fact-finding missions is the question of whether they should obey the law in countries where nobody else seems to do so. This can be difficult in repressive regimes, where the official exchange rate, for example, bears no relationship to reality and the 'Black Market' rate is that at which money in almost all circumstances changes hands. I am afraid that fact-finding mission members must remain in the minority, and scrupulously obey the local law. The importance of this principle was brought home to me on a pre-Velvet Revolution mission to Stalinist Czechoslovakia, when I invited Václav Havel to lunch. He was understandably nervous, because he was on bail and the authorities could return him to prison at any moment. When I did not have sufficient local currency to pay for our meal, I assumed I could pay the rest in US dollars, accepted with alacrity everywhere in the city. But Havel was horrified, and explained that he would immediately be arrested by the secret police watching us from the far table, as an accomplice in 'black-marketeering'.

"This is the first rule of being a dissident", said Kafka's successor: "You must scrupulously obey the law".

Sometimes, it is difficult to obey the local law, for practical reasons. When I was observing trials for Amnesty in the puppet homeland of Venda, I would arrive at Johannesburg airport from London at about 05:00, hire a car, and drive up an almost continually straight road for several hours before turning off to the court room. Inevitably, on one occasion I fell into a speed trap where an apologetic policeman issued me a ticket which I duly paid. When I mentioned this to Amnesty, they took it very seriously and a top-level meeting was convened on the question of whether they should repay my speeding ticket. They decided to do so – but I would not rely upon the case as a precedent.

Suppose, however, that you are the *victim* of breaches of the law. There is not much point in complaining if the perpetrator is the President. I recall one mission, which I led on behalf of the British Bar and the Law Society, to Hasting Banda's Malawi, to investigate cases where he had ordered opponents to be killed without compunction. We obtained a meeting with the President-for-life, who expressed himself as delighted that one of our number was female – she was a North London solicitor renowned for bringing cases of sexual harassment: "Ah, you have bought with you a Mbumba!" (a woman, in the Chichewa language), he chortled as he greeted our delegation. "I am so pleased you have brought Mbumba. I am a powerful man and I like Mbumba! All Mbumbas in Malawi love me and I love them. They sing and dance for me!". At this point, he began to paw our solicitor delegate, in a manner which would have him arrested for indecent assault in Britain, but would have us all arrested for an attack on the President if our delegate reacted as she would doubtless have done in North London. We would then have had an unrivalled opportunity to find facts about Malawi's prison system, from the inside.

## 17.2.5. Surveillance

A more common problem for members of fact-finding missions is to find themselves followed by secret (and not so secret) police. Here, in such cases, it is important not to lead them to witnesses, and interviews should be cancelled rather than reliance placed upon 'giving them the slip' which may be more difficult than it seems in an unknown or hostile city. In Prague in Stalinist times, I was always followed rather clumsily by ill-paid surveillance operatives; I would head to the city's Jewish cemetery, with its towering forests of tall tombs, and try to lose them: if I failed I would take them behind me to the Terezin Museum, requiring them to pretend an interest in pictures painted by children of the ghetto *en route* to Auschwitz. But I would always avoid leading them to my contacts, unless they were well known dissidents whose meetings were monitored in any event.

### 17.2.6. Interviewing

The same principle of prudence should apply when interviewing people in prison or in any monitored space where guards are nearby, or hidden microphones are possibly present. It is not fair to the prisoner, who either will not tell the truth if aware that his custodians are listening or will be punished if he does tell it. On an Amnesty mission to Vietnamese prisoners in re-education camps, it was very tempting to ask questions of prisoners during an organised visit, but we decided to avoid questioning because guards were invariably within earshot. The prisoners, of course, could volunteer whatever comments they wished, but their opinions were likely tempered by their fear of reprisals.

#### 17.2.6.1. Refugees

Special problems are encountered in refugee camps. There is always a power structure within such camps. They are usually run by a political faction, whose representatives insist on escorting and introducing you to refugees who tend to say the same thing about the conditions from which they have escaped and about their treatment in the camp. The ideal on such missions is to interview new arrivals as they arrive or are being registered and before they come under the sway of local camp leaders who will indoctrinate them with the approved 'line' about political events back home, and will in certain cases coach them as to what to say. It may or may not be the truth, but because it is designed, for instance, to support the political line of the faction, or to support a case for asylum rather than economic migration, such coached stories must be discounted.

#### 17.2.6.2. Victims

Ideally, prisoners and refugees and all persons who may be subject to pressure from custodians or others, should be interviewed alone. This is a counsel of perfection, because investigators will often need an interpreter present and the choice may be problematic, especially if there is no choice and the interpreter is officially imposed. Interviewing prisoners alone does insulate their testimony from influence, although it is important to remember that some victims – especially of sexual crime – may be inhibited by the subject matter and do need support before they can bring themselves to speak freely. Many traumatised victims of rape or torture simply will not divulge their excruciating experience to a stranger. In these circumstances, there can be no hard and fast rules about interviewing witnesses without anyone else present: a friend or counsellor may be a necessary companion.

### 17.2.6.3. Conduct of Interviews

As with other interviews which can have serious consequences, the interviewer has a duty to conduct the discussion as fairly as possible. Leading questions must not put words into the interviewee's mouth. The questions asked must not suggest the answer that is sought or that others have given. (A good reality check in the event of an important allegation is the question "how do you know?"). The way to conduct an interview is to ask "what happened then?" and not to say, for example, "That is when they pulled your fingernails out, didn't they?". Always look for corroboration of serious allegations – ask if there is another prisoner who saw the victim immediately before and after; whether there is an autopsy report that confirms an eye-witness account of a lethal beating; check whether there are newspaper reports that confirm dates and events. Wherever a 'story' is told, there will usually be elements that can be checked with others or with public records.

There is much at stake in how witnesses can be brainwashed, or persuaded (often by money or by threats to relatives) to give false evidence. Human rights fact-finders must develop a degree of cynicism and street wisdom in relation to those who voluntarily testify to them, and be conscious of governments (who may lose aid donors in the event of adverse NGO reports). The more distinguished the fact-finding mission, the more vested interests will try to pull wool over the eyes of its members. Every fact-finder should have well in mind the saga of 'Witness L' in the International Criminal Tribunal for the former Yugoslavia ('ICTY'). He was a witness who was very credible and utterly believed by the prosecutors in the *Tadić* case, and he certainly told them what they wanted to hear. He said that he had been an eye-witness at Omarska camp, who had seen Tadić kill no less than 30 prisoners including Witness L's own father. I suppose he is a wise witness who knows his own father and 'L' was confounded when confronted by his, produced in the courtroom by the defence, alive and well. The trial was halted and the court abandoned all its previous efforts at keeping 'L's' identity a secret. He had been coached, and probably paid, by authorities in Bosnia Herzegovina in order to dishonestly demonise the Serbian defendant.

It is important for NGO fact-finders, and for prosecutors who rely on the facts, to keep in mind the *debacle* that occurred in the very first trial at the ICC, with its very first witness. This child witness not only recanted his testimony, but accused an NGO of fabricating it. It later turned out that he was too terrified by the sight of the defendant to testify against him in his presence (he should have been screened). But the incident showed how vulnerable NGOs are to this sort of allegation. Where witness' evidence is likely to go further – especially to court – the record should be signed, and preferably tape- or video-recorded.

The fact-finder must be astute to detect any personal or political motivations for lying or exaggerating or for blind partisanship. Many witnesses will have an axe to grind: they have undoubtedly suffered and will be anxious to emphasise the guilt of those they believe (or have been made to believe) are to blame. Fact-finders must also factor in the motive that many witnesses have to exaggerate or to emphasise their own innocence: when claiming refugee status, or hoping to claim such status, they will have a motive to exaggerate the extent of their persecution, especially if they think the fact-finders' report may subsequently assist their asylum claim. Always ask: *cui bono* (who benefits)?

### 17.2.7. Admissions Against Interest

In law as in life, an admission by a State can be held against it, and it will be important to examine closely any justification or excuses offered by the regime for attacking its own citizens. One example derives from Singapore in 1988, where Catholics, lawyers and playwrights concerned with the problems of the poor were rounded up and tortured. The government, of course, denied torture, but its relevant minister (and now Prime Minister) LEE Hsien Loong admitted that the secret police used 'psychological pressure'. This was an 'admission against interest', that is, the interest of maintaining the pretence that no pressure at all was used. (The 'psychological pressure' consisted of blasting sub-zero temperature air conditioning at naked detainees in order to force them to confess – without laying a mark upon them.)

## 17.2.8. Should Fact-Finders Have Prior Knowledge?

Amnesty International has a rule that no national of a State under investigation can be part of a fact-finding mission to that State. This is appropriate, since those connected with a nation may have strong feelings for or against its government. But sometimes the alternative of parachuting in an investigator or members of a group who have no experience of a country can be made the butt of State criticism. This was suffered by the UN rapporteur who condemned Kenya after spending 10 days in the country. The government asked how anyone who has been in Kenya for just over a week could begin to understand its complex society. This argument sounds impressive, although there is no reason why an objective and expert observer like Philip Alston could not decide issues relating to public order and policing by extensive reading of source materials and then visiting Kenya and hearing testimony as to how the authorities had behaved. Human rights fact-finding does not require intimate knowledge of local society.

Nonetheless, it does help if fact-finders have experienced guides to the country under investigation. There are some countries where things are seldom what they seem. On my first mission to communist Czechoslovakia, I attended trials of executives of the jazz society. After its leaders were sentenced to prison, I stood on the steps of the court house with Václav Havel while a group of young people in the square in front of us began singing "We shall overcome". I was heartened by the size of the chorus, until Havel turned to me and said: "On these occasions you can always tell who are the secret police. They are the ones who know all the words". I conducted a number of human rights missions to apartheid-era South Africa, but I never knew that beneath the polite veneer of the trials I was observing, there was a sinister sub-culture of State assassination without trial. A friend who was one of the founders of the Black Sash movement was killed in what seemed to be a typical life-wasting South African car accident, and it was only many years later, when the evidence emerged at a Truth and Reconciliation Commission hearing, that I discovered that the brakes of her car had been tampered with in a secret police operation.

### 17.2.9. Should Human Rights Monitors Be Obliged to Testify in International Courts?

It is important to distinguish between three separate issues: (1) the *competence* (or capacity) of a human rights reporter to be a witness; (2) the *compellability* of human rights monitors – that is, whether the court has power to order them to give evidence; and (3) their *right to protect sources* once in the witness box.

### 17.2.9.1. Competence

All human rights monitors are competent to give evidence, except employees or former employees of the Red Cross. They have a special position under the Geneva Conventions, and the ICTY has held, albeit by a majority, that their duty of confidentiality is absolute and that they cannot give evidence, even if they want to and even if they have long left the organisation. An ICTY Trial Chamber decided in *Simić* that the International Committee of the Red Cross ('ICRC') was entitled in customary international law to an absolute privilege, which could be exerted to prevent employees from giving evidence of observations made whilst on Red Cross work. This was a ruling that, in law, Red Cross employees and ex-employees lacked the *capacity* to testify.

Justice Hunt, who dissented, found no warrant in customary international law for such a sweeping and absolute exemption from those dictates of conscience and humanity which will sometimes impel witnesses of crimes against humanity to offer court testimony, irrespective of confidentiality obligations. Of course, the ICRC has a duty to remain neutral, but that does not mean that customary international law should treat its ex-employees as incompetent to testify, certainly if their evidence is indispensable to the determination of guilt or innocence.

A preferable rule would be that the evidence should be excluded unless it is *indispensable* to prove or disprove a crime of the upmost gravity.[10] The Red Cross has long been criticised for choosing to say nothing about the Holocaust, in order that its work in prisoner-of-war camps in

---

[10] This was the ICRC fallback position in argument in *Simić*. See International Criminal Tribunal for the former Yugoslavia ('ICTY'), *Prosecutor v. Simić et al.*, Trial Chamber, Decision on the Prosecution Motion Under Rule 73 for a Ruling Concerning the Testimony of a Witness, 27 July 1999, IT-95-9, para. 19 (https://legal-tools.org/doc/59590d, https://legal-tools.org/doc/777c14).

Nazi Germany might not suffer.[11] Should an ex-employee offer eye-witness evidence that a defendant ordered torture or (even more pointedly) offer conclusive evidence that a defendant was *not* involved in the acts of torture with which he is charged, the majority decision in *Simić* should not, in my view, be followed so as to debar the court from hearing such crucial evidence. The approach of Justice Hunt was to balance the competing interests. His test was "whether the harm which would be done by the allowance of the evidence outweighs the harm done by the frustration or impairment to justice if the evidence is not available".[12] While it would only be in a rare case that a Red Cross employee would be ordered to testify, he identified two such situations: "where the evidence of an official or an employee of the ICRC is vital to establish the innocence of the accused person", and "where the evidence of an official or an employee of the ICRC is vital to establish the guilt of the particular accused in a trial of transcendental importance".[13] He concluded that:

> The correct test is whether the evidence to be given by the witness in breach of the obligations of confidentiality owed by the ICRC is so essential to the case of the relevant party (here the prosecution) as to outweigh the risk of serious consequence of the breach of confidence in the particular case. Both the gravity of the charges and the availability of means to avoid disclosure of the fact that the evidence has been given would be relevant to that determination.[14]

Another court may prefer Judge Hunt's dissent – I certainly do. Red Cross confidentiality can be a Faustian bargain: the organisation kept silent about the torture at Abu Ghraib, for example, and the truth only emerged when a copy of one of its confidential reports, which had gathered dust on the desks of US generals and British bureaucrats, was leaked to the *Wall Street Journal*. And it was infuriating to watch Donald Rumsfeld at press conferences rejecting as ludicrous the idea that torture techniques were being used at Guantanamo; "we have the Red Cross here every day: if there was any torture, they would be the first to complain".

---

[11] See David Rieff, *A Bed For a Night: Humanitarianism in Crisis*, Vintage, 2002, pp. 76-7, 148

[12] *Simić*, Separate opinion of Judge David Hunt, 27 July 1999, para. 27 (https://legal-tools. org/doc/f74214, https://legal-tools.org/doc/c353c9).

[13] *Ibid.*, paras. 29-31.

[14] *Ibid.*, para. 35.

But of course, they could not complain publicly, by virtue of their vow of confidentiality. They are in danger of becoming complicit in the torture and ill treatment that they observe if they can never divulge it to the public. The Red Cross justifies its privilege by pointing out that States would not permit its observers to enter prisoner-of-war camps if they were able to make their findings public. In the recent conflict in Sri Lanka, for example, all NGOs except the Red Cross were prevented from witnessing the army operation. The thinking of the Sri Lankan military, undoubtedly, was that they would be safe with the Red Cross as its employees could never testify.

One way forward would be for the UK or the US to take the lead in disclaiming any right of confidentiality in Red Cross reports, and to promise to disclose them six or nine months after they have been received. This waiver arrangement would ensure that the right to have Red Cross visits would become a meaningful safeguard against torture and abuse in prisoner-of-war camps run by States that were prepared for his degree of transparency.

### 17.2.9.2. Compellability of Human Rights Monitors

Some human rights reporters are only too pleased to give evidence to international courts. But others, especially those still in the field, are horrified at the prospect of losing their perceived neutrality by appearing to endorse the prosecution (if the prosecution asks them to give evidence) or else by appearing to support the defence. Neutrality is vital to war correspondents and to human rights reporters working in war zones and their own and their colleagues' safety may be put at risk if they are perceived to be spies for the prosecutor of an international criminal court.

This was the dilemma that faced Jonathan Randall, a *Washington Post* correspondent who had interviewed a local Serb official named Brđanin, subsequently charged in the ICTY with complicity in war crimes. Randall was still actively engaged in reporting on terrorism, and did not want to be perceived by potential sources as a journalist who co-operated with prosecutors. He and his newspaper believed that his neutrality would be compromised. The ICTY Trial Chamber insisted that he had no testamentary privilege and had to give evidence against Brđanin, even though the quotations in his article had been obtained through the services of an interpreter. The ICTY Appeals Chamber decided, however, that war correspondents could not be compelled to testify in war crimes courts unless the party which subpoenaed them could establish that their evidence would be "really significant", that is, of direct and important value in determining a core issue in the case, and that in any event the evidence could not reasonably be obtained elsewhere. It said:

> In war zones, accurate information is often difficult to obtain and may be difficult to distribute or disseminate as well. The transmission of that information is essential to keeping the international public informed about matters of life and death […] there is the public interest in the work of war correspondents, which requires that the news gathering function be performed without unnecessary constraints so that the international community can receive adequate information on issues of public concern.[15]

The court concluded that compelling war correspondents to testify on a routine basis "may have a significant impact upon their ability to obtain information and thus their ability to inform the public on issues of general concern".[16] In this context, there can be no meaningful distinction between the war correspondent and the human rights reporter or investigator, in terms of the importance of the information they gather or the public interest that its publication will serve. In both cases, there is the danger that information will dry up if the court routinely orders them to identify their sources. *Brđanin* was a case on compellability rather than privilege, but it assumes that on the limited occasions when war correspondents are compelled to testify on core issues, they will be accorded a privilege to withhold the names of their sources.

The appeal court decision that the reporter was only compellable where his information was important and could not be obtained elsewhere was a compromise between the claims of news organisations and human rights NGOs – the latter were initially sceptical about journalists who refused to help war crimes prosecutors. I acted for the *Washington Post*, and recall some anxious discussions with Ken Roth of Human Rights Watch about whether journalists had a duty to their source or to the new war crimes tribunals. Richard J. Goldstone provided expert evidence about the importance of neutrality to those who have a duty objectively to report a

---

[15] ICTY, *Prosecutor v. Brđanin and Tadić*, Decision on Interlocutory Appeal, 11 December 2002, IT-99-36-AR73.9, paras. 36 and 46 (https://legal-tools.org/doc/af7b61).

[16] *Ibid.*, para. 44.s

war, and the appeals chamber decision, largely written by the US judge Theodor Meron, more or less satisfied both sides.

### 17.2.9.3. Source Protection

In the important case of *Goodwin v. UK*, the European Court of Human Rights decided that a qualified privilege to protect journalistic sources followed from the right to freedom of expression. The public right to newsworthy information entails that those who supply information to journalists, frequently in breach of the confidence of their employers or colleagues, should nonetheless be protected because otherwise these sources would 'dry up', that is, stay silent, and much newsworthy material would not be imparted and would not in consequence be published. The European Court of Human Rights held:

> Protection of journalistic sources is one of the basic conditions for press freedom, as is reflected in the laws and the professional codes of conduct in a number of Contracting States and is affirmed in several international instruments on journalistic freedoms [citations omitted]. Without such protection, sources may be deterred from assisting the press in informing the public on matters of public interest. As a result the vital public-watchdog role of the press may be undermined and the ability of the press to provide accurate and reliable information may be adversely affected. Having regard to the importance of the protection of journalistic sources for press freedom in a democratic society and the potentially chilling effect an order of source disclosure has on the exercise of that freedom, such a measure cannot be compatible with Article 10 [...] of the Convention unless it is justified by an overriding requirement in the public interest.[17]

Can this reasoning be applied to protect the sources of human rights reporters and fact-finders, who are tasked with collecting information for public purposes – to inform the reports of the UN Secretary-General or to research for reports issued to the public by NGOs like Amnesty and Human Rights Watch?

The issue arose in the Special Court for Sierra Leone. The prosecution called a UN staff member, who was a human rights monitor, as a wit-

---

[17] European Court of Human Rights, *Goodwin v. UK*, Judgment, 27 March 1996, Application no. 17488/90, para. 39 (https://legal-tools.org/doc/0c5c27).

ness. The UN waived its immunity rights so that he might testify freely, on condition that he be permitted to do so in closed court and that, when giving his evidence, the witness should not be compelled under cross-examination to name any human source from which he had received information. The witness' statement had been disclosed to the defence and consisted both of his direct observations of the war and of what others had told him of the "widespread and systematic" commission of war crimes in some areas. This was relevant but secondary evidence: it was directed to establish an element of the crime charged (namely the widespread and systematic nature of the attacks), but did not directly connect any defendants with an offence. Nonetheless, one Trial Chamber decided that the witness could be compelled to name his sources, and this was the major issue for decision by the Appeal Chamber. We decided it in favour of the witness, primarily on the wording of the Special Court's Rules of Procedure. My concurring judgment considered the broader issue of whether 'human rights reporters' are entitled, in the course of their testimony, to decline to answer questions directed to identifying the source of the information.

The court had *amici* briefs submitted by the UN's Human Rights Commissioner, as well as from Amnesty International and Human Rights Watch, which urged that the public interest requires human rights reporters to possess such a testamentary privilege, either in absolute terms or at least on a qualified basis. But the defence lawyers argued that any such entitlement to resist source disclosure would improperly undermine a defendant's right to challenge the evidence given against him. The competence and compellability of human rights reporters was not in issue: the UN official was perfectly willing to testify and the UN was agreeable so long as he did so without being subjected to cross-examination, in which questions might be asked the honest answer to which would identify a source who had been promised anonymity and who might well be in danger of harsh or even lethal reprisals if publicly named. It was my view that the principle set out in *Goodwin* was equally applicable to human rights monitors giving evidence in war crimes courts:

> There is in my judgement little meaningful difference in this respect between an investigative journalist tracking a story in a war-torn country, a war correspondent reporting on the ebb and flow of the conflict, and a researcher for a human rights organisation filing information for an "in depth" report or for filtered use in an annual report, or for a UN monitor gather-

ing information for a Secretary General's report to the Security Council. All are exercising a right to freedom of expression, (and, more importantly, assisting their source's right of free speech) by extracting information for publication from people who would not give it without an assurance that their names will remain anonymous. The reprisal they often face in such circumstances, unlike the risk run by Mr. Goodwin's source of being sacked or sued for breach of confidence, is of being killed as an "informer" – a traitor to the organisation or the community on whom they are silently squealing. To identify them in court would betray a promise and open them to such reprisals: more importantly, if courts routinely ordered witnesses to name their sources, then information about human rights abuses would diminish because reporters could not in good conscience elicit it by promises to protect their sources. For these reasons, I consider that "human rights monitors", like journalists, have a privilege to refuse to name those sources to whom they have promised anonymity and who are in danger of reprisal if that promise is broken. In practical terms, that means they must not be compelled to do so by threats to invoke the court's power to hold them in contempt and to fine or imprison them. It does not mean, of course, that the evidence that they give, based on information from sources they decline to name, will be accorded normal weight. Their entitlement to protect their source has this downside for the party that calls them: it may lose some and perhaps all of the weight that might otherwise be placed on the evidence that is given based on the anonymous source material.[18]

There is an overriding international public interest in UN human rights reporters being able to give an assurance of confidentiality to those who put their necks on the line to inform on the murderous activities of powerful supporters or figures within their community. Two witnesses who gave evidence to Phillip Alston in Kenya suffered lethal reprisals. The public interest in protecting UN sources applies with the same force to fact-finders engaged by Amnesty and Human Rights Watch who collect and expertly analyse information about human rights abuses, later pub-

---

[18] See Special Court for Sierra Leone, *Prosecutor v. Brima and others*, Appeals Chamber, Judgment, 26 May 2006, SCSL-2004-16-AR73, separate and concurring opinion of Justice Geoffrey Robertson QC, para. 28.

lished in annual or special reports which serve to inform governments and international institutions, as well as the interested public, about such abuses and are used as a basis for campaigns to end them. The public interest in the free flow of information to such publications is at least as great as to other news media. Moreover, the consequences of exposure of sources of this kind can be calamitous. It is apt to recall that the protective rule in *Goodwin* was fashioned in the context of the genteel environment of the city of London, where a business journalist was fined for refusing to name an 'insider' source of information about a company's finances – a source who would face only disciplinary action if exposed. In repressive countries, sources for fact-finding missions who tell of torture, death squads and arbitrary imprisonment, may, if exposed, face these very consequences. Not only may they be brutally treated as punishment for embarrassing the government or other power brokers, but their family and friends may also face reprisals. This fact underlines the need for the protective rule, usually identified as a 'privilege' belonging to the witness, although that 'privilege' is a reflection of the rather weightier 'right' of the source. The privilege is qualified, not absolute, because it must yield in cases where the identification of the source is necessary either to prove guilt or to establish a reasonable doubt about guilt.

There is a problem in the proliferation of 'human rights NGOs', several thousand at last count, with 'monitors' or 'fact-finders' of varying calibre and experience. Some have been accused of sensationalising reports in order to gain support for campaigns or membership subscriptions, whilst others might have a bias derived from political connections or State funding. Certain NGOs with 'human rights' in their title have been credibly accused of undermining human rights causes.[19] Are all these monitors to be accorded a qualified privilege to withhold the names of sources? I do not see how a meaningful distinction can be made, any more than the *Goodwin* privilege can be denied to journalists who have a propaganda agenda or report on wars where they support one side or the other. The reporter's privilege is, after all, the obverse of the right possessed by the source, who may speak low, in fear and trembling, to the first fact-finder who appears in his burnt-out village, completely unaware of any bias and concerned only that their identity be protected if they tell what they know. The prospect that what they say will be 'spun' or exaggerated by partisan

---

[19] See *The Economist*, "Yanukovich's Friends – A Human Rights Group that Defends Dictators", 4 December 2004.

journalists or monitors does not lose the source his or her right to be protected from exposure: but what it does mean is that the court must give the party which cross-examines the reporting witness every opportunity to explore any bias or hidden agenda or other motive for distortion or exaggeration. This is, after all, a set of human rights which belong to defendants and must be upheld to ensure fairness of trial.

Courts must always guard against allowing prosecutors to present evidence which amounts to no more than hearsay demonisation of defendants by human rights groups or by the media. The right of sources to protection is not a charter for lazy prosecutors to make a case based on second-hand reports or investigations. Unchecked hearsay has an inevitable place in the factual matrix upon which expert opinion is based. For example, in *Prosecutor v. Bizimungu*, the late Dr. Alison Des Forges was called as an expert: she based her opinion upon two accounts of a meeting with the ex-president given by confidential sources. Her right to withhold their names was upheld, although the International Criminal Tribunal for Rwanda pointed out that this would be an important factor to consider in evaluating her evidence.[20] Defendants must never be convicted solely on evidence from anonymous accusers: the court effectuates that principle by excluding or else de-valuing hearsay accusations, rather than by compelling a witness who reports them to divulge the identity of the confidential source who made them.

### 17.2.9.4. Summary

Fact-finding missions to repressive or post conflict societies must respect the undertakings they give to sources and must refuse to answer questions that might expose informants when summoned to testify in a war crimes court. Courts should respect that refusal, and decline to make any finding of contempt against a fact-finder, unless the source is crucial to establishing the defendant's guilt or innocence. This approach should be applied pragmatically, by judges who recognise the danger that sources embroiled in armed conflict may be partisan and, in some cases, malicious, even to the extent of inventing or fabricating the information they give to fact-finders. Fabrication may, without identification or cross-examination of its source, fool even the most experienced human rights monitor (it was, after

---

[20] International Criminal Tribunal for Rwanda, *Prosecutor v. Bizimungu*, Trial Chamber, decision on defence motion for exclusion of portions of testimony of expert witness Dr Alison Des Forges, 2 September 2005, ICTR-99-50-T (https://legal-tools.org/doc/8ca7fe).

all, an experienced ex-Amnesty researcher who passed on the notoriously false story about the Kuwaiti babies being thrown out of hospital incubators by Iraqi troops during the first Gulf War). On the other hand, there must be an equal recognition that score settling will continue for long after the conflict and that sources may be assaulted, killed or driven out of their communities as the result of exposure. But testimony based on information from anonymous sources should never to the sole basis for findings of guilt.

### 17.2.10. Reprisals Against Fact-Finders

It is a sad fact of life that those involved in law enforcement in unstable societies will sometimes be the victim of lethal reprisals. A number of prosecutors and journalists have been assassinated for finding out too much, whilst others have been taken hostage and held to ransom. An organisation which sends fact-finders on a mission to a dangerous country will always bear responsibility for their safety and well-being. International law offers no special protection to a member of a fact-finding mission over and above that which the member is entitled by virtue of his or her status as a civilian. Attempts have been made by journalist organisations to encourage the addition to Article 8 of the Rome Statute (which contains an exhaustive definition of war crimes) of a new international crime of killing journalists, to which might be added the intentional killing of human rights monitors and fact-finders. The Red Cross has opposed any extension, on the basis that they are already protected as 'civilians', but obviously armies locked in a civil war do not perceive journalists as civilians, which is why they kill them. The forces of the State (and sometimes insurgents) will threaten human rights investigators precisely because they do not perceive them as civilians, but as persons who are likely to expose their misdeeds to the world.

It is, of course, a war crime to direct attacks against "personnel using the distinctive emblems of the Geneva Conventions in conformity with international law"[21] (so Red Cross personnel are safe) and to attack persons "involved in a humanitarian assistance or peacekeeping mission in accordance with the Charter of the United Nations"[22] – which would cover UN rapporteurs on fact-finding missions, but would not protect

---

[21]   ICC Statute, Article 8(2)(b)(xxiv).

[22]   *Ibid.*, Article 8(2)(b)(iii).

members of human rights missions dispatched by NGOs. There is a powerful case to be made for giving them specific protection.

War correspondents have the inconsequential assistance of Article 79 of the 1977 First Protocol Additional to the Geneva Conventions, which provides that:

> Journalists engaged in dangerous professional missions in areas of armed conflict shall be considered as civilians [...] [and] shall be protected as such under the Conventions and this Protocol, provided that they take no action adversely affecting their status as civilians [...].[23]

This gives journalists, like all civilians, immunity from military discipline and they must not be made specific targets for attack or become the victims of reprisals by any party to the conflict, although their entitlement to civilian status will be jeopardised if they take any action which indicates support for a belligerent – for example, carrying a gun or rendering special assistance to one side or the other. This vague civilian status is unsatisfactory and there needs to be a specific crime to deter attacks on journalists and human rights monitors or fact-finders, for the simple reason that in conflict zones they are not perceived as innocent civilians but as enemies, real or potential, of those whose criminal acts they may expose.

### 17.2.11. Publication of the Report

The fact-finding mission that finds its facts and writes its report may find that its problems are not over. They may be just beginning. English common law regards any slighting criticism liable to lower a person's reputation in the minds of right-thinking people as a defamation which can require recompense of up to GBP 200,000 and – much more crippling – millions of pounds in legal costs. The burden of proving the truth of serious allegations rests on the defendant publisher, and this is virtually impossible when sources must be protected or else refuse to come forward.

London is the libel capital of the world because its law is so plaintiff-friendly, and its courts are the favoured forum for the wealthy of the world to harry their critics. An NGO will not escape by the device of publishing a fact-finding mission's report in America: First Amendment pro-

---

[23] Protocol Additional to the Geneva Conventions 1949 and relating to the protection of victims of international conflict, 1977 (https://legal-tools.org/doc/d9328a).

tection does not cover Internet downloads in the UK. Every human rights report will be accessible in England, either via the Internet or obtainable from Amazon, and English courts welcome forum-shoppers.[24]

Newspapers are sued in London all the time by foreign claimants – most notably Russian oligarchs, and Arab billionaires accused of supporting terrorism. Human rights reporting has so far benefited from the practical consideration that its targets – political and military leaders accused of genocide and torture – are usually reluctant to travel to the UK for fear of a Pinochet style arrest, certainly if their libel action fails. This fear has been reduced by the House of Lords in a libel action brought by Roman Polanski: he was permitted to testify by video-link, safe in a Paris hotel room from the arrest and extradition warrant awaiting him from US law enforcers in London.[25] Some violators are prepared to come to London: the Head of the Ghanaian Secret Police sued *The Independent* when it informed its readers that he had been accused by a judicial inquiry some years before of masterminding the murder of three of that country's judges. This is the kind of allegation which is important for the public to know about, but is virtually impossible to prove without the massive expense of gathering the evidence of the long-disbanded enquiry in a far-off country.[26]

In recent years, the House of Lords (now the Supreme Court) has developed a public interest defence for the media against libel actions, which should cover the publication of most human rights reports. It applies whenever the subject matter is of high public interest and the allegation is made by reputable professionals who honestly and reasonably believe in its truth and who publish it with professional responsibility. This case – *Jameel v. Wall Street Journal* – allowed the newspaper to report what it could not prove, but reasonably and responsibly believed, about Saudi co-operation with the CIA in monitoring a prominent businessman.[27] The *Jameel* case provides a valuable defence, but will not relieve

---

[24] See UK, *Berezovsky v. Forbes.*

[25] See UK, *Polanski v. Conde Nast Publications*, (2000) 1 WLR 1004; *Conde Nast Publications*, (2005) UKHL 10. The film director had jumped bail in California years before, when on trial for child molestation.

[26] See UK, *Tsikata v. Newspaper Publishing Plc*, (1997) 1 All ER 655. The newspaper succeeded in showing that it had qualified privilege to report the inquiry finding, even though it had not led to a prosecution.

[27] UK, *Jameel v. Wall Street Journal* (No 3), (2006) UKHL 44.

---

an NGO from having to spend a considerable amount of money before its defence is upheld, and to cover such costs it may be wise to take out libel insurance, especially where the report criticises powerful officials or wealthy leaders.

Breach of confidence is another legal snare that NGOs must avoid in publishing investigations that have managed to obtain secret documents. Global Witness struck an important blow for human rights reporting when it successfully fought off an injunction from the son of the President of the Republic of the Congo: his credit card statements had been obtained and placed on the Global Witness web site to show that the President's son had secretly been stealing the profits of the State-owned oil company. The court held that the seriousness of the offence justified the breach of confidentiality, as there could be no confidence in iniquity: "the profits of oil sales should go to the people of the Congo, not to those who rule it or their families".[28]

But the anxiety and risk attendant on any such legal action should not be underestimated: Global Witness would have been forced to pay tens of thousands of pounds in legal costs had it lost, and it was fortunate to have *pro bono* representation. The sad fact is that the United Kingdom does not have free speech; it has expensive speech.

## 17.3. Conclusion

The final rule for a human rights report is to make it readable. It will often be written by lawyers, who must remember that it will not be read only by lawyers. To achieve its objective, it must be comprehensible to a wide range of people involved in civil society programmes, to journalists and politicians and diplomats, to victims and even to perpetrators. Some readers will not have English as a first language, and will not have the benefit of translation.

The art is to be simple without becoming simplistic: let the facts speak for themselves, and confine legislation or technical details to appendices. Few reports become bestsellers (one exception is *"Nunca Mas"* – Ernesto Sabato's report that alerted the world to the work of death

---

[28] UK, *LongBeach Ltd and Denis Chrystel Sassou Nguessou v. Global Witness Ltd.*, (2007) EWHC 1980 (QB).

squads in South American dictatorships[29]). Remember that good human rights reporting must stand the test of time and increasingly in war crimes courts, the test of cross-examination.

---

[29] Ernesto Sabato, *Report of the National Commission on the Disappearance of People*, Faber, 1986.

# 18

---

# Finding Facts on Facebook:
# Social Media in the Work of
# Human Rights Fact-Finding Bodies

### Emma Irving[*]

## 18.1. Introduction

In March 2019, a detailed report was published by the United Nations ('UN') Commission of Inquiry on the 2018 Protests in the Occupied Palestinian Territory ('Commission of Inquiry on the GMR').[1] The report itemised the allegedly unlawful killing of Palestinians by Israeli soldiers during the demonstrations that had become known as the 'Great March of Return'. As part of the media outreach that surrounded the release of the report, the Commission put together a video compilation with footage featuring the killing or injuring of eight Palestinians.[2] What is notable about the video compilation is not the use of videos *per se*, but the fact that many of the videos it features were obtained from social media platforms such as Facebook, YouTube and Twitter. By placing content from social media centre stage in the dissemination of its fact-finding work, the Commission of Inquiry highlighted just how central social media has become to accountability efforts.

In today's digital world, social media is key to how people communicate. This remains true for people living through conflict, violence, and insecurity, as social media is a crucial channel for conveying information about events happening on the ground. The widespread availability of smartphones and the Internet means that for some conflicts the

---

[*] **Emma Irving** (M.A. (Cantab), LL.M., Ph.D.) is an Assistant Professor of public international law at the Grotius Centre for International Legal Studies at Leiden University.

[1] Report of the detailed findings of the independent international Commission of inquiry on the protests in the Occupied Palestinian Territory, 18 March 2019, UN Doc. A/HRC/40/CRP.2 (www.legal-tools.org/doc/5912f1/).

[2] OHCHR, "COI on Gaza Protests: Lethal force used against demonstrators not posing imminent threat", 3 April 2019 (available at YouTube).

amount of material shared online is overwhelming: in relation to Syria, there are more hours of footage of the civil war than there have been actual hours of the conflict.[3] Among this deluge of data are videos, photos, and reports that can provide invaluable information about violations of international criminal, humanitarian, and human rights law. Indeed, recent domestic prosecutions are testament to this, with material obtained from social media being used to convict individuals of war crimes committed in Syria and Iraq,[4] and used as key evidence in an International Criminal Court ('ICC') arrest warrant.[5]

Human rights fact-finding bodies, and in particular those established by the UN Office of the High Commissioner for Human Rights ('OHCHR'), have not overlooked the growing importance of social media. From 2015 onwards, we see references to social media content appearing in a number of reports. In the report of the Commission of Inquiry on the 2014 Gaza Conflict, a number of references were made to tweets associated with the Al Qassam Brigades. These tweets concerned the group's targeting practices, as well as attacks purportedly carried out by the group.[6] When the OHCHR conducted its investigation into human rights abuses in Libya between 2014 and 2016, the resulting report made reference to Facebook posts and YouTube videos that showed who may have assassinated a human rights defender,[7] the spreading of hate speech and incitement to violence,[8] and the issuance of orders by military leaders for troops

---

[3] Armin Rosen, "Erasing History: YouTube's Deletion of Syria War Videos Concerns Human Rights Groups", Fast Company, 3 July 2018 (available on Fast Company's web site).

[4] For example: Germany, Higher Regional Court, Frankfurt am Main, *The Prosecutor v. Aria Ladjedvardi*, Judgment, 12 July 2016, 5-3StE2/16-4-1/16; The Netherlands, Rechtbank Den Haag, *Oussama Achraf Akhlafa*, Judgment, 23 July 2019, ECLI:NL:RBDHA:2019: 7430; Sweden, District Court of Stockholm, *The Prosecutor v Haisam Omar Sakhanh*, 16 February 2017, B 3787-16. See also Eurojust, "Prosecuting war crimes of outrage upon personal dignity based on evidence from open sources – Legal framework and recent developments in the Member States of the European Union", February 2018.

[5] International Criminal Court, *The Prosecutor v. Mahmoud Mustafa Busayf Al-Werfalli*, Pre-Trial Chamber I, Arrest Warrant, 15 August 2017, ICC-01/11-01/17-2 (www.legal-tools.org/doc/881fb6/).

[6] For example, Report of the detailed findings of the independent commission of inquiry established pursuant to the Human Rights Council resolution S-21/1, 24 June 2015, UN Doc. A/HR/29/CRP.4, paras. 79, 89, 100 (www.legal-tools.org/doc/a67ee2).

[7] Investigation by the Office of the United Nations High Commissioner for Human Rights on Libya: detailed findings, 23 February 2016, UN Doc. A/HRC/31/CRP.3, para. 224 (www.legal-tools.org/doc/d58b1f).

[8] *Ibid.*, para. 119.

to engage in fighting.[9] The Commission of Inquiry on Burundi also made use of social media – most notably of videos from YouTube – to show the arrest of an anti-corruption campaigner,[10] the humiliating interrogation of a detainee,[11] and speeches designed to incite violence and hatred.[12]

And yet, in these aforementioned reports, the use of social media by the OHCHR fact-finding bodies remained limited. To illustrate, in the report on Burundi, Facebook was mentioned a total of 12 times over the course of 272 pages, and YouTube was mentioned 15 times; in the 95-page report on Libya, Facebook was mentioned four times and YouTube only twice. Social media content remained, therefore, a very minor part of the fact-finding reports, with emphasis being placed on other types of information.

This changed in 2018 with the report of the Fact-Finding Mission on Myanmar. Social media, and Facebook in particular, became a key source of information used throughout the report to support a range of findings on violations of international law. In the 444 pages of the Myanmar report, Facebook is mentioned 289 times. This trend continued in the 2019 report of the Commission of Inquiry on the GMR: Facebook is mentioned 49 times, Twitter 63 times, and there are 138 references to 'videos', many of which were obtained from different social media platforms.

This switch from being a minor, relatively unimportant, source of information, to being a key component of fact-finding reports is one deserving of attention. The quality-control considerations that this development raises are multifaceted. On the one hand, in today's Internet-driven world, to abstain from looking to social media for information would compromise the quality of fact-finding. As the OHCHR notes in its Guidance to Commissions of Inquiry and Fact-Finding Missions on International Human Rights and Humanitarian Law ('OHCHR Guidance'), videos and photos uploaded to social media sites "could provide information on incidents that have not been widely reported" or "several videos could provide different perspectives on incidents" that have been widely report-

---

[9] *Ibid.*, para. 55.
[10] Rapport final détaillé de la Commission d'enquête sur le Burundi, 12 Septembre 2018, UN Doc. A/HRC/39/CRP.1, para. 213 (https://www.legal-tools.org/doc/0efe39/).
[11] *Ibid.*, para. 345.
[12] *Ibid.*, paras. 430-433.

ed.[13] To ignore this trove of online information therefore creates the risk that the record of events will be incomplete or inaccurate.[14] On the other hand, social media poses as many risks to the quality of fact-finding work as it provides opportunities. In the same Guidance, the OHCHR warns of the challenges of veracity, authenticity, and reliability associated with social media content.[15] To overlook these challenges also risks creating an incomplete or inaccurate picture of events.

Balancing these concerns is key to ensuring the quality of human rights fact-finding in the digital age. In these times of 'fake news' and 'deep fakes', when trust in facts is low and falling, maintaining the quality, and thereby the integrity, of UN human rights fact-finding is key to achieving the goals of these missions. For these reasons, the increased use of social media content in human rights fact-finding is a subject worthy of discussion, particularly in a volume concerned with the quality of fact-finding work.

The aim of this chapter is two-fold. First, it aims to shed light on the developing trend of social media use by human rights fact-finding bodies. To do this, the chapter will set out examples of how social media content was used in the reports of the Fact-Finding Mission on Myanmar and the Commission of Inquiry on the GMR. These examples demonstrate the *types* of social media content being used and what *findings* this content is being used to support. The second aim is to draw attention to the quality control considerations raised by the use of social media content. These considerations will be discussed in relation to the examples of social media use selected from the reports.

Section 18.2. below will briefly set out the key characteristics of social media, expand upon why it is key for accountability work, and illustrate the types of authenticity and reliability challenges that always accompany social media content. This is followed by Sections 18.3. and 18.4., which look in detail at the Fact-Finding Mission on Myanmar and Commission of Inquiry on the GMR. It is in these sections that the exam-

---

[13]  Commissions of Inquiry and Fact-Finding Missions on International Human Rights and Humanitarian Law: Guidance and Practice, 2015, UN Doc. HR/PUB/14/7, p. 44.

[14]  On this point, see Fred Abrahams and Daragh Murray, "Open Source Information: Part of the Puzzle", in Sam Dubberley, Alexa Koenig, and Daragh Murray (eds.), *Digital Witness: Using Open Source Information for Human Rights Investigation, Documentation, and Accountability*, Oxford University Press, 2020.

[15]  *Ibid.*

ples will be identified and discussed, and in which the quality-control considerations will be highlighted. Section 18.5., drawing on the discussion in the previous sections, sets out two observations, two points of concern, and two thoughts for the future of social media content in human rights fact-finding. Section 18.6. offers some concluding remarks.

## 18.2. The Opportunities and Challenges of Social Media for Accountability

Social media is the curious product of how the Internet has developed over the past 30 years. From a collection of web pages designed to be passively consumed by users, to a digital ecosystem in which users are constantly shaping and changing the online space, the Internet of today is unrecognisable compared to the Internet of the early 1990s.[16] An important product of, and driver of, this rapid transformation was the introduction and growth of social media platforms.

A precise definition of social media is hard to pin down because of the way in which it evolves and changes on an almost daily basis. However, there are key features that all social media platforms share. First, social media sites allow individual users to upload and share content with other users. As this is content that users themselves create, it is referred to as 'user-generated content'. Other social media users can see and interact with the user-generated content uploaded by others, for example by commenting, sharing, or liking it. Second, nearly all social media platforms have a section that is publicly accessible, in the sense that the content posted there can be accessed by all other users, without needing specific permission from the content uploader. Content of this type is known as 'open source' user-generated content.[17]

In addition to these features, the leading social media platforms – Facebook, YouTube and Twitter[18] – are all designed for general access, meaning that they can be accessed and used by anyone with the necessary

---

[16] For further discussion on this, see Emma Irving and Jolana Makraiova, "Capture, Tweet, Repeat: Social Media and Power in International Criminal Justice", in Morten Bergsmo, Mark Klamberg, Kjersti Lohne and Christopher B. Mahony (eds.), *Power in International Criminal Justice*, Torkel Opsahl Academic EPublisher, Brussels, 2020, chap. 19.

[17] For further detail on the definition of open source information in this context, see Human Rights Center, UC Berkeley School of Law, "The New Forensics: Using Open Source Information to Investigate Grave Crimes", 2017, p. 7.

[18] These were the leading platforms at the time of writing, and given their market dominance, this is unlikely to change in the near future.

hardware (for example, a laptop or smartphone) and an Internet connection.[19] Taken together, these characteristics are what makes social media so well-suited for use by individuals in conflict areas (or areas otherwise experiencing violence and instability) to share their experiences from the ground.

From an accountability perspective, social media is particularly valuable for the way in which it offers a window into areas that are otherwise difficult to gather information about.[20] A notable example of how valuable social media material can be in this regard concerns an incident that took place in a remote area of northern Cameroon in 2015, in which soldiers of the Cameroonian army murdered two women and two children. In 2018, a video of the killings emerged on social media, and experts subsequently analysed the film to determine where it was filmed, when it was filmed, and who the perpetrators were.[21] After the analysis and accompanying investigation were made public, the soldiers in the video were purportedly arrested and proceedings against them instituted.[22] The remoteness of the area where the murders took place means that, without this video, the events may never have come to light and the perpetrators never arrested.

In July 2018, when the video of the murders in Cameroon emerged, its authenticity and reliability were immediately challenged by some social media users and by the Cameroonian authorities. It was argued that the video was shot in Mali, rather than Cameroon; that the people in the video were not who they were described to be; and that the video distorted

---

[19] With the caveat that, according to the respective terms of conditions of these platforms, there are age restrictions for individuals wishing to create an account.

[20] For a detailed discussion of the role that social media – and user-generated content more broadly – can play in human rights investigations, see Jay Aronson, "The Utility of User-Generated Content in Human Rights Investigations", in Molly K. Land and Jay D. Aronson (eds.), *New Technologies for Human Rights Law and Practice*, Cambridge University Press, 2018; for an international criminal law perspective on user-generated content, see Rebecca J. Hamilton, "User-Generated Evidence", in *Columbia Journal of Transnational Law*, 2018, vol. 71, no. 1.

[21] Amnesty International, "Cameroon: Credible evidence that Army personnel responsible for shocking extrajudicial executions caught on video", 12 July 2018; BBC News, "Cameroon atrocity: Finding the soldiers who killed this woman", 24 September 2018. On this incident, see Sam Dubberley, Alexa Koenig, and Daragh Murray, "Introduction", in Dubberley, Koenig, and Murray (eds.), 2020, pp. 1-5, above note 14.

[22] Reuters, "Cameroon probes video showing security forces apparently executing civilians", 10 August 2018; Amnesty International, "Cameroon: Trial of soldiers for killing women and children must lead to justice for victims", 26 August 2019.

the facts.[23] In relation to this particular video, these objections were groundless and convincingly dismissed; however, the objections highlight the authenticity and reliability issues that are ever-present in material obtained from social media.

As social media is built on user-generated content, there is always the possibility that content is inauthentic, either because it was altered before being uploaded, or because it was altered by another user and then re-uploaded. A particular authenticity challenge that has emerged in the past few years is that of identifying 'deep fakes'. Deep fake technology allows for the creation of very convincing fake images and videos, and as this technology develops, fake content will become increasingly difficult to detect.[24]

It is possible for content to be authentic – in that it has not been altered – but still unreliable. For instance, a scene in a video might have been staged,[25] or the footage strategically edited to place emphasis on specific events at the expense of others. An example of such strategic editing was identified by the Commission of Inquiry on the GMR. A video was posted on Twitter by the Israel Defense Forces ('IDF') that appeared to show a medic who was killed by IDF fire admitting to being a human shield for Hamas.[26] The Commission obtained the full footage of the interview, which reportedly shows the medic actually saying that she was acting as a "human shield for injured demonstrators".[27] This editing of the footage by the IDF was noted by the Commission as one of the incidents of misinformation that surrounded the violence.[28]

---

[23] BBC Africa Eye, "Cameroon: Anatomy of a Killing – Documentary – BBC Africa Eye", 23 September 2018 (available at www.youtube.com/watch?v=XbnLkc6r3yc, last accessed 11 November 2019; see specifically the following points in the video: 00:36 mins., 00:55 mins., 05:09 mins.).

[24] See Alexa Koenig, ""Half the Truth is Often a Great Lie": Deep Fakes, Open Source Information, and International Criminal Law", in *AJIL Unbound*, 2019, vol. 113.

[25] For an example of this, see BBC Trending, "#BBCTrending: Syrian "hero boy" video fakes by Norwegian director", 14 November 2014.

[26] Report of the Commission of inquiry on the protests in the Occupied Palestinian Territory, 2019, para. 663, see *supra* note 1.

[27] *Ibid.*, para. 664.

[28] The Report of Commission of inquiry on the protests in the Occupied Palestinian Territory has a six-page section on "Misinformation amid the Great March of Return" in which certain emblematic cases are described. The Commission noted that this created challenges for it during the investigation (*ibid.*).

More could be said about the many ways in which content obtained from social media can offer opportunities and challenges for accountability processes, but this short section suffices to show why the use of social media content by human rights fact-finding bodies requires particular attention. The following sections on Myanmar and the 'Great March of Return' will signal ways in which the fact-finding missions sought to overcome the difficulties and take advantage of the opportunities, and to do so without compromising the quality of their fact-finding.

## 18.3. Myanmar

### 18.3.1. Background

Myanmar has a long history of allegations of human rights abuses, especially with respect to ethnic minorities in the country.[29] The treatment of Rohingyas, a large Muslim minority residing largely in Myanmar's Rakhine State, has attracted particular attention. As far back as 1978, 200,000 Muslims were forced to flee from Myanmar to Bangladesh to escape inter-communal violence and alleged human rights violations,[30] and the trend of repression and persecution has, as noted by the Fact-Finding Mission, continued since then.[31] Rohingyas have in effect been prevented from obtaining citizenship, a large number of their children have not been issued with birth certificates, they have not been recorded in the national census as Rohingyas, and they cannot stand for parliamentary election.[32] Regular outbreaks of violence against the minority have, according to United Nations human rights fact-finders, been characterised by the arbitrary deprivation of life, torture, sexual and gender-based violence, and forced labour.[33]

There was a wave of inter-communal violence in 2012, reportedly involving mobs of Buddhist civilians and the Myanmar security forces attacking Muslims in Rakhine State and elsewhere.[34] This caused the in-

---

[29] Report of the detailed findings of the Independent International Fact-Finding Mission on Myanmar, 17 September 2018, UN Doc. A/HRC/39/CRP.2, paras. 93-104 (www.legal-tools.org/doc/0c0c69/).

[30] *Ibid.*, para. 100.

[31] Report of the Fact-Finding Mission on Myanmar, 2018, paras. 93-103, see *supra* note 29.

[32] Penny Green, Thomas MacManus, and Alicia de la Cour, "Countdown to Annihilation: Genocide in Myanmar", International State Crime Initiative, 2015, p. 19.

[33] Report of the Fact-Finding Mission on Myanmar, 2018, para. 98, see *supra* note 29.

[34] Report of the Fact-Finding Mission on Myanmar, 2018, paras. 624-661, see *supra* note 29.

ternal displacement of tens of thousands. In October 2016 and August 2017, a series of attacks on police and military outposts was undertaken by a Rohingya armed group called the Arakan Rohingya Salvation Army (ARSA). The attacks on 25 August 2017 prompted a military crackdown. In the latter months of 2017, images of fleeing Rohingyas and burning villages following the clearance operations conducted by the Myanmar army – known as the Tatmadaw – in northern Rakhine State were widely publicised in the media. The UN Human Rights Council had already established the Fact-Finding Mission on Myanmar in April 2017, and as such the mission had already begun work when this upswing in violence took place.

The Fact-Finding Mission was mandated to "establish the facts and circumstances of the alleged recent human rights violations by military and security forces, and abuses, in Myanmar, in particular in Rakhine State […] with a view to ensuring full accountability for perpetrators and justice for victims".[35] In order to cover the key events, the mission decided to examine events in Kachin and Shan States as of 2011, and events in Rakhine State as of 2012, as these marked the times when violence resumed or escalated, and when renewed reports of serious human rights violations began to emerge.[36] As such, the report covers not only violence against the Rohingya in Rakhine State, but also against other ethnic minorities in Kachin and Shan States. While the main focus of the report is the allegations of violations committed by the Tatmadaw, reference is also made to alleged violations by ethnic armed groups. Ultimately, the Fact-Finding Mission concluded that crimes against humanity and war crimes had been committed in Kachin, Shan, and Rakhine States;[37] as to genocide, the mission concluded that there was sufficient information to warrant the investigation and prosecution of senior officials of the Tatmadaw for this crime.[38]

---

[35] Situation of human rights in Myanmar, 3 April 2017, UN Doc. A/HRC/RES/34/22, operative para. 11 (www.legal-tools.org/doc/842442/).

[36] Report of the Fact-Finding Mission on Myanmar, 2018, para. 5, see *supra* note 29.

[37] Report of the independent international fact-finding mission on Myanmar, 12 September 2018, UN Doc. A/HRC/39/64, paras. 88-89 (www.legal-tools.org/doc/61cb49/).

[38] *Ibid.*, para. 87.

From the outset, the Fact-Finding Mission was met with a lack of co-operation from the Myanmar authorities.[39] While not unexpected, this meant that it was not possible to conduct investigations on the ground in Myanmar, and requests for information made to representatives of the Myanmar government went unanswered. Because of this lack of access, the Fact-Finding Mission had to find alternative ways of collecting information. In part this was done by interviewing survivors who had fled Myanmar to neighbouring countries.[40] Other methods, such as analysing satellite images to track the destruction of villages, also played a role.[41] A significant source of information, and indeed a very rich one, was content uploaded to social media platforms, in particular Facebook. Facebook has a central place in Myanmar's Internet connectivity: in the words of the Fact-Finding Mission, in Myanmar "Facebook is the Internet".[42]

### 18.3.2. Social Media in the 2018 Fact-Finding Mission Report on Myanmar

Content from social media, and from Facebook in particular, was used to support a range of different factual findings in the report of the Fact-Finding Mission on Myanmar. These factual findings then form part of the body of evidence upon which legal findings of violations are made. This section illustrates the way that social media is used in the report by taking examples from the report itself. Based on these examples, observations are offered on questions of social media and quality control. Some observations are specific to the described example, but a common observational thread that runs throughout this chapter relates to how the social media content used by both the Fact-Finding Mission on Myanmar and the Commission of Inquiry on the GMR fits within the investigative methodologies set out by these bodies.

As such, before proceeding to a discussion of the examples, it is worth examining the methodology section of the report by the Fact-Finding Mission on Myanmar. The report begins by stating that the Mission adhered to the best practices set out in the OHCHR Guidance. As noted in the Introduction to the present chapter, this Guidance makes par-

---

[39]  Report of the Fact-Finding Mission on Myanmar, 2018, para. 3, see *supra* note 29: "the mission deeply regrets the lack of cooperation from the Government of Myanmar".

[40]  *Ibid.*, paras. 19-21 and 23.

[41]  See, for example, *ibid.*, para. 773.

[42]  *Ibid.*, para. 1345.

ticular reference to social media, and highlights its usefulness as a source of information about violations and perpetrators,[43] armed group hierarchies,[44] and timelines for particular events.[45] While it does warn that online content can be hard to verify and authenticate, especially for fact-finding missions facing resource constraints, the Guidance does not offer concrete advice on how these problems can be overcome, other than to stress the importance of corroboration.

After noting the OHCHR Guidance, the Mission set out the standard of proof employed in the report, and detailed the approach taken to meeting this standard. In line with numerous previous OHCHR fact-finding missions,[46] the Fact-Finding Mission on Myanmar adopted the 'reasonable grounds' standard of proof, and considered it to be met when "a sufficient and reliable body of primary information, consistent with other information, would allow an ordinarily prudent person to reasonably conclude that a case, incident, or pattern of conduct" occurred.[47] Included among the class of primary information were authenticated videos and photos, and admissions of relevant facts by Myanmar officials.[48] As will be shown below, a large portion of the social media content used in the report falls within one of these two categories. While it was not set out in detail when photos and videos would be deemed 'authenticated', the following were said to be relevant to the authentication process: secondary information, expert interviews, an organisation's raw notes or data (if the video or photo was obtained in this way), submissions, and open source material.[49]

It was stressed in the methodology section that, unless otherwise stated, nothing in the report was based solely on one source of information.[50] From a quality-control perspective, this is important, and goes a

---

[43] OHCHR Guidance and Practice, 2015, p. 57, see *supra* note 13.

[44] *Ibid.*, p. 49.

[45] *Ibid.*, p. 48.

[46] Including the Investigation by the Office of the United Nations High Commissioner for Human Rights on Libya, 2016, para. 11, see *supra* note 7; Report of the Independent International Commission of Inquiry on the Syrian Arab Republic, 31 January 2019, UN Doc. A/HRC/40/70, para. 3 (https://undocs.org/A/HRC/40/70).

[47] Report of the Fact-Finding Mission on Myanmar, 2018, para. 10, see *supra* note 29.

[48] *Ibid.*, para. 13.

[49] *Ibid.*, para. 22.

[50] With the exception of some instances of sexual or gender-based violence, where additional sources are difficult to come by. This challenge is addressed in *ibid.*, para. 12.

long way to mitigating the challenges that are inherent in social media content in terms of authenticity and reliability. Also significant from a quality perspective is the fact that the Mission sought specialist advice on digital verification,[51] a first for an OHCHR fact-finding mission.

The report offers a great deal of potential examples to discuss, of which only a sample were selected. The examples discussed in this section have been grouped into two categories: findings relating to the military and security forces, and findings relating to the dissemination of hate speech and incitement.

### 18.3.2.1. Findings Relating to the Military and Security Forces

With respect to the military and security forces, this section sets out three examples: 1) the use of social media content for demonstrating the "hallmarks of Tatmadaw operations", 2) the use of this content to establish who the perpetrators of violations were and who was responsible for these violations, and 3) social media content as an indicator of specific intent, relevant to allegations of genocide. For each of these examples, the Fact-Finding Mission drew on the Facebook posts of high-ranking military officials or of individual soldiers.

Starting with the "hallmarks of Tatmadaw operations", the report identified a number of these. One such hallmark was reported to be the targeting of civilians. Among the various different materials discussed by this Mission in this regard was a Facebook post from a soldier. In this post, the soldier is quoted as saying that anyone who remained in a given geographical area after a given deadline would be considered an "accomplice of the KIA", and so would be targeted, including civilians.[52] In the post, the soldier explicitly referred to the 'Four Cuts' policy, a counter-insurgency policy of the Tatmadaw that aims to cut non-State armed groups off from access to resources such as food, financing and recruits.[53] The 'Four Cuts' policy was allegedly implemented through clearance operations that involved destroying villages and killing civilians.[54]

The Fact-Finding Mission discussed the historical use of the 'Four Cuts' policy, but did not find conclusively that the policy was formally in

---

[51]  *Ibid.*, para. 22.

[52]  *Ibid.*, para. 1368.

[53]  *Ibid.*, para. 1367.

[54]  *Ibid.*, para. 1367

effect during the period of time it was examining. Instead, the Facebook posts by soldiers (of which the just-mentioned is one example), along with other indicators of the pattern of military operations, *suggested* that the policy was still in use. Here we see the Mission's caution: the Facebook posts were not enough in and of themselves to justify a finding that the 'Four Cuts' policy was still formally in place, even when placed alongside other information. However, these posts were deemed reliable enough to be included in the report, and to contribute to an overall finding by the Mission, based on a range of information, that the Tatmadaw engaged in the widespread and systematic targeting of civilians.[55]

The second example of social media content in the report was its use to build a picture of who the perpetrators of crimes were and of the chain of command responsible for these perpetrators.[56] With respect to identifying perpetrators, the Mission used Facebook posts to establish when a given military unit arrived in an area and when it left, which is highly relevant if mass killings of civilians not participating in hostilities and other violations are alleged to have taken place within that timeframe.[57] This discussion of perpetrators was carefully phrased, and the Facebook posts about troop movements were not used to draw conclusions about whether a military unit was actually involved in a specific clearance operation. Instead, the posts lent support to other information the Mission had collected about who perpetrated certain atrocities. This approach is in line with standard practices and is not unique to when social media content is used; however, it does demonstrate that this content was treated in a similar way to other types of information, and is neither elevated to a special status nor unduly downplayed.

In addition to helping to identify perpetrators by showing which troops were in a particular area and when, social media was also employed to establish command responsibility on the part of the Tatmadaw leadership. Particular attention was paid to the Commander-in-Chief, Senior-General Min Aung Hlaing. The Mission, referring to Article 28(a) of the Rome Statute of the ICC, set out the requirements for establishing

---

[55] *Ibid.*, para. 1369.

[56] Who's Responsible? Attributing Individual Responsibility for Violations of International Human Rights and Humanitarian Law in United Nations Commissions of Inquiry, Fact-Finding Missions and Other Investigations, 2018, UN Doc. HR/PUB/18/3, p. 65; Aronson, 2018, pp. 136-7, see *supra* note 20.

[57] Report of the Fact-Finding Mission on Myanmar, 2018, para. 1254, see *supra* note 29.

command responsibility;[58] for three out of five of these requirements, social media is used to support the finding of responsibility.

One of the requirements for command responsibility is whether the military commanders, and specifically the Commander-in-Chief, had effective control over the perpetrators of violations. In this respect, the Mission referred to the large-scale and co-ordinated nature of attacks as strong indicators of high-level supervision and planning. In addition, the frequent updates about military operations posted to the Commander-in-Chief's official Facebook page were said to demonstrate his "close involvement" in the actions of his subordinates.[59] Indeed, this Facebook page was very active during the violence, and for this reason was referred to a great deal throughout the report in relation to a variety of different points.[60]

Another requirement of command responsibility is that the Commander-in-Chief and other Tatmadaw leaders knew, or should have known, that the forces under their control were committing crimes. Here, the Mission referred to a number of points, including the allegation that such crimes took place in every operation, and that the issue had been raised multiple times over the years by UN Special Rapporteurs.[61] In ascribing knowledge to the Commander-in-Chief in particular, social media played a key role. Facebook posts were used in the report to allege that the Commander was given detailed on-site briefings, and that in meetings with local commanders he exhibited extensive knowledge of the events transpiring on the ground. Once again, reference was then made to the

---

[58] *Ibid.*, para. 1533: "A commander can be held criminally liable for the crimes committed by subordinates, if he or she is (a) a military commander or person effectively acting as a military commander; (b) who has effective command and control over troops; (c) who knew (or owing to the circumstances at the time should have known) that the forces were committing or about to commit such crimes; (d) who failed to take all necessary and reasonable measures to prevent or repress the commission; and (e) the crimes occurred as a result of the commander's failures".

[59] *Ibid.*, para. 1533.

[60] Posts from the Commander-in-Chief's Facebook page are referred to in relation to alleged attacks by ARSA, including casualty numbers (for example, *ibid.*, paras. 1037, 1040 and 1066), in relation to the spreading of hate speech and incitement (for example, para. 753), and in relation to the weaponry of ARSA (for example, para. 1031).

[61] *Ibid.*, paras. 1537-1538.

"daily" updates on the Commander-in-Chief's Facebook page about how "clearance operations" were progressing.[62]

The final requirement of command responsibility where social media played a role in the Mission's report was in the need to establish a causal link between a failure on the part of the Tatmadaw leadership to prevent and punish crimes, and the alleged criminal actions of their subordinates. Particular attention was paid to a reported climate of impunity and normalisation of violence against civilians. One example noted by the Mission was a Facebook post containing an official statement from the Commander-in-Chief, in which it was stated that the security forces were acting in accordance with the law and were following orders at all times. The Mission pointed out that "when military operations that encompass widespread attacks on civilians are celebrated as an example of soldiers acting in accordance with the law, and when those who direct them are praised and promoted, the scene is set for cycles of violence".[63] In this way, the Mission drew a connection between the Commander-in-Chief's attitude towards the alleged crimes of subordinates, and the climate of impunity which causally led to a continuation of violence.

Moving on to final example to be discussed in this section: the use of social media for establishing genocidal intent. What sets genocide apart from other atrocity crimes is the specific intent requirement. Killing or seriously harming individuals belonging to a particular group will not be characterised as genocide unless there is an intent on the part of the perpetrator to destroy that group in whole or in part.[64] It is this element that makes convicting individuals of genocide particularly difficult. In 2016, Radovan Karadžić was convicted by the International Criminal Tribunal for the former Yugoslavia of crimes against humanity, war crimes, and genocide; however, for one of the counts of genocide, the Trial Chamber held that the *actus reus* of genocide was proven, but that the *mens rea* was not. In other words, while it was established beyond reasonable doubt that

---

62    *Ibid.*, para. 1539.

63    *Ibid.*, para. 1545.

64    Rome Statute of the International Criminal Court, 1998, Article 6 (https://legal-tools.org/doc/e5faa8); Convention on the Prevention and Punishment of the Crime of Genocide, 1948, Article II (https://legal-tools.org/doc/498c38).

Karadžić was responsible for killings[65] and for causing serious harm,[66] it was not proven that these acts were done with the intent to destroy a protected group as such in whole or in part.[67] In order to assess the allegations of genocide against the Tatmadaw, therefore, the Fact-Finding Mission needed to examine the difficult issue of genocidal intent.

The Mission set out different factors that were considered when looking at the question of genocidal intent. Social media content was relevant to one of these, namely the "specific utterances of government officials, politicians, religious authorities and military commanders, as well as of direct perpetrators".[68] In addition to witness statements and other sources, the report mentioned a YouTube video in which a politician chants about shooting and killing Rohingyas,[69] a Facebook post from a police officer in which he discusses killing the 'Kalar' (a derogatory term used also for Muslims in Rakhine),[70] and an inflammatory Facebook post by the Commander-in-Chief.[71] This last Facebook post, which named the unrest in Rakhine State as "the Bengali problem" that the government was working to solve, was afforded much weight by the Mission. In the full report, it is mentioned several times, and it is highlighted as the key piece of evidence of genocidal intent in the abbreviated version of the report, released five days before the full version.[72] Taken together with the other information collated by the Mission, these social media posts contributed to the Mission's conclusion that "the factors allowing for the inference of genocidal intent are present".[73] As to adjudicating the guilt or innocence of particular individuals, this was left to a "competent prosecutorial body".

The use of social media to demonstrate genocidal intent is especially interesting, as it relates to the internal mental state and attitudes of perpetrators. That being said, despite the Facebook posts about the 'Bengali

---

[65] International Criminal Tribunal for the former Yugoslavia, *Prosecutor v Karadžić*, Trial Chamber, Judgment, 24 March 2016, IT-95-5/18-T, para. 2579 (https://legal-tools.org/doc/173e23).

[66] *Ibid.*, para. 2582.

[67] *Ibid.*, para. 2626.

[68] Report of the Fact-Finding Mission on Myanmar, 2018, para. 1422, see *supra* note 29.

[69] *Ibid.*, para. 1423.

[70] *Ibid.*, 2018, para. 1422.

[71] *Ibid.*, 2018, para. 1424, referring to the post that is set out in full at para. 753.

[72] Abbreviated Report on Myanmar, 2018, para. 86, see *supra* note 37.

[73] Report of the Fact-Finding Mission on Myanmar, 2018, para. 1441, see *supra* note 29.

problem' weighing heavily in the report, social media remained only a small part of the overall discussion of genocidal intent, showing how this challenging element of the crime requires a great many sources to substantiate it.

Most of the social media content mentioned in the examples in this section would fall into the category of 'primary information' according to the methodology employed by the Mission. Generally, the information used by the Mission was posted by members of the Tatmadaw, including frequently on the Commander-in-Chief's Facebook page. As such, these posts could be understood as falling under the category of "publicly available admissions of relevant facts by Myanmar officials". Assuming this to be the case, it does not mean that the information was subject to a lower level of scrutiny, or that it was less extensively corroborated, but it does signal that content obtained from social media is no longer only a peripheral source of information for fact-finders such as the Myanmar Mission. Instead, it is a primary source that is central to the investigative work of fact-finding missions. Other information is used to corroborate the social media posts, rather than the social media posts being the corroborating information.

That being said, there remains some ambiguity as to when content of this type would be deemed primary information. Clarity is lacking as to what the Mission considered to be an 'admission of fact', and who qualifies as a 'Myanmar official'. If the publishing of information must be done in an official press release format to be considered an 'admission of fact', then only the Facebook post by the Senior-General Min Aung Hlaing about the 'Bengali problem' would potentially qualify. The others appear to be more informal in nature, or alternatively the report does not provide sufficient information to draw a conclusion. There is also the question of whether a Tatmadaw soldier or a police officer would qualify as a 'Myanmar official', such that their personal Facebook posts could be considered primary information. In addition, one can raise the concern that the Facebook posts of high-ranking officials – such as the Commander-in-Chief – are unlikely to have been drafted and posted by the official themselves; more likely this was done by a member of their staff. These unanswered questions mean that it is not always clear how social media information was classified by the Mission, and therefore what part it played in building the picture of the violence in Myanmar.

## 18.3.2.2.  Findings Relating to Hate Speech and Incitement

In addition to investigating alleged war crimes, crimes against humanity, and genocide in Myanmar, the Fact-Finding Mission examined the situation in the country concerning democratic space and the exercise of fundamental freedoms. Among these freedoms were the right to free speech and opinion, and the right to non-discrimination, both of which were affected by the dissemination of hate speech and incitement to violence.

Monitoring social media was a key part of the Mission's strategy for understanding the issue of hate speech and incitement to violence in Myanmar. Over 150 public social media accounts were examined, with particular attention paid to Facebook accounts deemed influential because of the number of followers, the level of engagement by users, and the frequency of new posts.[74] In the report, the Mission catalogued a number of hateful terms and phrases, using emblematic social media posts to illustrate how the terms were used and how far the hate speech was able to spread. In one instance, the Mission noted that a Facebook post containing hateful language "had 47,000 reactions, over 830 comments, and nearly 10,000 shares".[75]

What is notable about the section of the report on hate speech is the shift away from using social media content posted by individuals affiliated with the military or security forces of Myanmar. Whereas the examples described in the previous section were attributed to either the Commander-in-Chief, individual soldiers, or other public officials, the social media posts referred to in the hate speech and incitement section of the report emanate from an array of different social media users or pages. The common thread between the accounts is that they are influential – in the sense that their posts reach large numbers of people – but otherwise they range from private individuals to organised political or religious groups. As a result of this, it is not clear how the information fits into the Mission's stated methodology, as it does not neatly correspond to either the primary sources of information or the corroborating sources of information. To the extent that the content involves photos or videos, these could be primary sources if authenticated – but given that hate speech and incitement are often bound up with misinformation, we cannot speak of authentication in the same way for content of this type.

---

[74]  *Ibid.*, para. 1310.
[75]  *Ibid.*, para. 1312.

From a quality-control perspective, this lack of clarity about social media and the Mission's methodology makes it harder to scrutinise the approach taken to social media content and to understand the quality processes it was subjected to.

The challenge of understanding how social media posts of different types from different sources fit into fact-finding methodology is also present in the work of the Commission of Inquiry on the GMR. As with the Fact-Finding Mission on Myanmar, some types of social media content correspond to the identified methodological boxes, while others do not. The following section will set out the background of the Commission of Inquiry, will provide examples of how social media was used in the report, and will offer some reflections on quality control. Following from this, observations will be offered on the practices of both the Fact-Finding Mission and the Commission of the Inquiry with respect to social media.

## 18.4. The Occupied Palestinian Territory

### 18.4.1. Background

Since 2010, the UN Human Rights Council has established a number of separate fact-finding missions to investigate alleged violations of international human rights and humanitarian law in the Occupied Palestinian Territory ('OPT'), particularly in the Gaza Strip.[76] These missions were part of the international community's response to the ongoing cycles of violence between Palestine and Palestinian groups, and Israel, with the most recent mission being established in 2018 to examine the border protests in Gaza.

In March 2018, a movement of weekly protests began in Gaza whereby large groups of people would gather at the separation fence between Gaza and Israel. The aim of the protests, which came to be known as the 'Great March of Return', was to draw attention to the dire humani-

---

[76] Resolution S-9/1, "The grave violations of human rights in the Occupied Palestinian Territory, particularly due to the recent Israeli military attacks against the occupied Gaza Strip", 12 January 2009, UN Doc. A.HRC/S-9/L.1 (www.legal-tools.org/doc/27fa66/); resolution S-21/1, "Ensuring respect for international law in the Occupied Palestinian Territory, including East Jerusalem", 24 July 2014, UN Doc. A/HRC/RES/S-21/1 (www.legal-tools.org/doc/70051c/); resolution 28/1, "Violations of international law in the context of large-scale civilian protests in the Occupied Palestinian Territory, including East Jerusalem", 22 May 2018, UN Doc. A/HRC/RES/S-28/1 (https://undocs.org/A/HRC/RES/S-28/1).

tarian situation in Gaza in a non-violent manner,[77] as well as "to achieve the return of the refugees who were displaced in 1948 to their land".[78] Much of the time the protestors simply gathered in camps close to the fence, at other times attempts were made to climb the fence or remove it; some instances involved protestors setting fire to tyres and sending incendiary kites over the border. On the whole, however, the character of the protests was said to be peaceful.[79]

Within the first few weeks, the number of casualties resulting from Israeli fire targeting protestors garnered international attention,[80] and in May 2018 the Human Rights Council established the UN Commission of Inquiry on the GMR.[81] The Commission was specifically mandated to examine alleged violations of international human rights and humanitarian law that occurred within the context of military assaults on the civilian protests.

Social media has been an important component in the cycles of conflict between Israel and Palestine for some time. In the Gaza conflict of 2012 – referred to by some as a "Twitter War"[82] – both Hamas and Israel made extensive use of Twitter to control the narrative of the conflict.[83] The fact that many of the posts were in English shows that the social media fight was also for the benefit of an international audience.[84] As the protests of the 'Great March of Return' gathered momentum in 2018, it became clear that social media would carry on playing a key role.[85] In-

---

[77] Report of the Commission of inquiry on the protests in the Occupied Palestinian Territory, 2019, paras. 195-198, see *supra* note 1.

[78] *Ibid.*, para. 200.

[79] See Section 18.4.2.1.

[80] See, for example, Independent, "Three dead and hundreds injured as protests on Gaza border turn violent", 27 April 2018; BBC News, "Gaza-Israel border: Clashes "leave 16 Palestinians dead and hundreds injured"", 31 March 2018; Aljazeera, "Palestinians' Great March of Return: The human cost", 16 May 2018.

[81] Resolution S-28/1, 2018, see *supra* note 76.

[82] Huffington Post, "Israel, Hamas Fight Twitter War", 15 November 2012; CNN, "Will Twitter war become the new norm?", 19 November 2012.

[83] See Thomas Zeitzoff, "Does Social Media Influence Conflict? Evidence from the 2012 Gaza Conflict", in *Journal of Conflict Resolution*, 2018, vol. 62, no. 1.

[84] *Ibid.*, pp 35-36.

[85] Tablet, "Israel is Losing the Social Media War", 25 June 2018.

deed, the protests were originally sparked by a Facebook post,[86] and were co-ordinated throughout over social media.[87] Social media continued to be used to communicate to domestic and international audiences about events on the ground and to build a narrative of the conflict.

This widespread use of social media surrounding the 'Great March of Return' protests made it inevitable that the Commission of Inquiry would follow the Fact-Finding Mission on Myanmar's lead and turn to social media in its fact-finding. This was particularly so given that, as was the case with Myanmar, the Commission received no co-operation from Israel.[88] Information was sourced from different social media platforms, including Facebook, Twitter and YouTube. At times, the Commission indicated only that the information is from a 'video', without specifying whether the footage was obtained from social media or from another source. However, a member of the Commission's fact-finding team confirmed that, despite the lack of attribution, in approximately 95 per cent of cases the videos mentioned were found on social media platforms. In addition to social media content in Hebrew, Arabic, and English, the Commission of Inquiry reviewed satellite imagery, expert legal opinions, affidavits, and medical reports.[89] The Commission also interviewed 325 individuals, either remotely or in person (including while on mission in Jordan and Turkey).[90]

In its conclusions, the Commission of Inquiry found reasonable grounds to believe that the Israeli Security Forces ('ISF') "killed and gravely injured civilians who were neither participating directly in hostilities nor posing an imminent threat to life".[91] The number killed was listed as 183, with a further 6,106 said to have been wounded by live ammunition. These were found to be violations of international human rights and humanitarian law,[92] and potentially war crimes and crimes against humanity.[93] Findings were also made against Hamas and the Palestinian Authori-

---

[86] Report of the Commission of inquiry on the protests in the Occupied Palestinian Territory, 2019, para. 195, see *supra* note 1.
[87] *Ibid.*, para. 210.
[88] *Ibid.*, para. 30.
[89] *Ibid.*, para. 6.
[90] *Ibid.*, para. 5.
[91] *Ibid.*, p. 1.
[92] *Ibid.*, paras. 691-706.
[93] *Ibid.*, p. 2.

ty, for failing to stop incendiary kites and for failing to uphold the right to peaceful assembly.[94]

### 18.4.2. Social Media in the 2019 Commission of Inquiry Report on the 'Great March of Return'

Material from social media was a crucial part of the information on which the Commission of Inquiry based its findings. Perhaps most importantly, social media was used to ascertain where individuals were standing and what they were doing at the moment they were shot by the ISF, allowing the Commission to form an opinion on whether they posed an imminent threat to life such that their targeting would be justified. In addition to this, information from social media was used to support broader findings about the peaceful (or otherwise) nature of the protests,[95] about injuries to Israeli soldiers,[96] and about the flying of incendiary kites.[97] This section will examine examples in order to show how social media was used in the report and to offer some observations about quality control in the Commission's approach to social media content.

As was the case with the Myanmar Mission's report, the observations in this section relate to the place of social media content within the Commission of Inquiry's methodology, and as such, some introductory remarks about this methodology are in order. The Commission of Inquiry indicated at the outset of its report that it followed the OHCHR Guidance,[98] and as a result, it can be assumed that the points on social media material contained therein (and discussed above in Section 18.3.2.) were taken into account. As was the case for the Myanmar fact-finding, the Commission worked to the 'reasonable grounds to believe' standard of proof for factual findings, and based on these factual findings, came to conclusions about legal violations.[99] To reach a finding under this standard, the Commission required that there be at least one credible 'direct' source of information that was corroborated by one or more additional credible sources.

---

[94]   *Ibid.*, p. 2.
[95]   See Section 18.4.2.1.
[96]   See, for example, Report of the Commission of inquiry on the protests in the Occupied Palestinian Territory, 2019, paras. 618, 620-621, see *supra* note 1.
[97]   See, for example, *ibid.*, paras. 626, 632.
[98]   *Ibid.*, para. 15.
[99]   *Ibid.*, para. 16.

Listed among the 'direct' sources of information were authenticated video and photographic material, and publicly available admissions of relevant facts by representatives of Israel, the Palestinian Authority, Hamas (including its military wing), and Palestinian Islamic Jihad (including its military wing).[100] A significant amount of the social media content mentioned in the report fits into one of these two categories, but as will be discussed in the sections that follow, some of the content does not.

Direct information was corroborated by 'additional' information, whether this be witness testimony, public reports, information from experts, and so forth. Importantly from a quality-control perspective, factual findings were always based on more than one source of information. For example, where a video was obtained from social media, this was corroborated with at least three witness statements, along with other information, including but not limited to posts on other social media accounts, timestamps, and death certificates (where relevant).[101] Also relevant for quality control was the fact that a digital verification expert was hired as part of the investigation team. Although the report does not openly state this (unlike the Myanmar report), this was confirmed to the author by a member of the Commission investigative team.

Social media content is present throughout the Commission of Inquiry's report, and as such there is ample material for discussion. That being said, this section will focus on two types of finding for which social media content proved particularly important: findings about the general character of the protests, and findings about injuries to particular individuals.

### 18.4.2.1. Findings Relating to the General Character of the Protests

A point of contention between Israel and Palestine for the duration of the 'Great March of Return' protests was the character of these protests, namely whether or not they were peaceful in nature.[102] This was important from a legal point of view, as it influenced the legal framework against which Israel's conduct was assessed. If the protests were peaceful, the

---

[100] *Ibid.*, para. 19.

[101] Interview with member of the Commission of Inquiry investigative team.

[102] For an example of how social media was used to spread misinformation about the nature of the protests, see Report of the Commission of inquiry on the protests in the Occupied Palestinian Territory, 2019, paras. 635-8, above note 1.

rules governing Israel's response to them would be different than if the protests were not peaceful.

According to the Commission of Inquiry, civilian protests are governed by the so-called 'law enforcement paradigm', meaning that the applicable legal framework is that of international human rights law. Under this framework, a person can only be targeted with lethal force if they pose an imminent threat of death or serious injury to other people. If, however, civilian protests cease to be peaceful and instead evolve into hostilities, the Commission indicated that the 'conduct of hostilities paradigm' would apply. Under this framework, anyone who is directly participating in the hostilities can be targeted with lethal force, even if they do not pose an imminent threat of death or serious injury. As such, the peaceful or otherwise nature of the protests was important.[103]

In determining whether a protest had escalated into hostilities, one of the relevant factors was whether the protestors were carrying arms, and particularly whether they were firing arms at ISF soldiers. In determining this, social media played a role. For example, the Commission reviewed photos and videos (as well as witness reports) to determine that no arms were present at protest sites.[104] Over the course of the investigation, there was one incident that the Commission found may have amounted to civilians directly participating in hostilities. In this incident, a person in civilian clothes fired a rifle towards the Israeli side of the separation fence while cheered on by the crowd. The Israeli soldiers retaliated with tank and gunfire.[105] The incident was filmed and the Commission based its finding – in part – on this video. As a result of this characterisation as hostilities, the legal assessment of the deaths and injuries at that protest was done in accordance with *both* the conduct of hostilities and the law enforcement paradigms.

A further relevant consideration when painting a picture of the character of the protests was the statements issued by the protest organisers. The Commission noted how, over the period examined, posts on the 'Great March of Return' Facebook page reiterated the need to preserve the peaceful nature of the protests.[106] In relation to a specific incident, prior to

---

[103] *Ibid.*, sect. III.
[104] *Ibid.*, para. 461.
[105] *Ibid.*, para. 467.
[106] *Ibid.*, para. 211.

the large protests that took place on 14 May 2018 (coinciding with the opening of the US embassy in Jerusalem), the organisers posted on Facebook "[a]lways remember that our marches are non-violent and use only non-violent means".[107] While these statements are not definitive, when taken with the other information about the nature of the protests, they were used by the Commission to support the finding that the 'Great March of Return' was a peaceful movement to which the law enforcement paradigm should apply.

In line with the Commission's methodology, the photos and videos would be considered direct information. The Facebook posts of the protest organisers are, however, harder to characterise. Even if the organisers were affiliated with the Palestinian Authority or Hamas (a matter of great contention between the parties), it is not clear that calls for the protests to remain peaceful can be understood as 'admissions of relevant facts'. The precise value of this social media content in the investigation therefore remains ambiguous.

### 18.4.2.2. Findings Relating to Injuries to Particular Individuals

The core of the Commission of Inquiry's findings related to particular individuals whose killing or injuring was deemed to be emblematic of the ISF's conduct on a particular day or at a particular location. The report is therefore principally structured around examining individual cases and determining whether their deaths or injuries were lawfully inflicted. As the protests were found to be peaceful (with the one exception mentioned above), the Commission applied the law enforcement paradigm. Consequently, from a legal perspective, the key inquiry in the context of the 'Great March of Return' protests was whether an individual posed an imminent threat of death or serious injury to the ISF soldiers at the time they were shot. If this was the case, then their targeting would be lawful; if this was not the case, their targeting would be unlawful.[108]

Establishing the facts surrounding the targeting of an individual was assisted in many cases by the use of videos and photos. As mentioned above, in the majority of cases the Commission obtained these videos from social media. One way in which the videos proved useful was by showing where an individual was standing at the time they were shot, par-

---

[107] *Ibid.*, para. 442, fn. 598.
[108] *Ibid.*, paras. 84-93.

ticularly in cases where they were standing at a distance from the separation fence.[109] Such was the case with Ahmed Abu Hussein, who could be seen in video footage standing approximately 250 to 300 metres from the separation fence at the time he was shot.[110] Videos also gave an indication of whether targeted individuals had a special status. For example, an unnamed female journalist was shown in a video wearing a press vest at the time of her injury.[111] This contributed to the Commission's finding that Israeli snipers targeted journalists deliberately, despite them being clearly marked.[112] Health workers are also attributed a special status, and videos played a part in the Commission concluding that Israeli snipers deliberately targeted them during protests.[113] In some cases, videos suggested that the killing or injuring of an individual may have been accidental. Such was the case with a schoolboy who was filmed standing near a man who was exhorting the crowd and who was thought to be the intended target.[114] These different factors were relevant in the individual cases when the Commission determined that the individual did not pose an imminent threat, and that their targeting was therefore unlawful.

In addition to the above, videos were also used for information about what protestors were doing at the time they were shot, whether this be standing calmly,[115] or whether this be burning tyres,[116] cutting or pulling at the barbed wire of the separation fence,[117] or climbing the fence.[118] In each case, even though the protestors were engaging in this behaviour, the Commission concluded that these actions were not sufficient to render the individuals an imminent threat of death or serious injury to ISF soldiers.[119] The threshold for finding that such a threat existed was high,

---

[109] Examples include Mohammad Obeid (*ibid.*, p. 110), Abed El Fatah Nabi (p. 112), Mohammad Ayoub (pp. 145-6), Ahmad Abu Tyoor (p. 147), Ahmed Abu Hussein (p. 157).

[110] *Ibid.*, p. 157.

[111] *Ibid.*, p. 158.

[112] *Ibid.*, para. 536.

[113] *Ibid.*, para. 526.

[114] *Ibid.*, pp. 123-4.

[115] For example, Mohammed Obeid (*ibid.*, p. 110).

[116] Examples include Tahrir Wahba (*ibid.*, pp. 159-160).

[117] For example, Osama Abu Khater and Mohammad El Hamaydah (*ibid.*, p. 135).

[118] For example, Othman Hilles (*ibid.*, pp. 145-6).

[119] For example, in the case of Mohammad Ayoub, the Commission stated that: "Even if Mohammad had been previously trying to damage the security fence, that act alone would not pose an imminent threat to life or serious injury to ISF soldiers", *ibid.*, pp.143-4.

namely that "the attacker should have no remaining preparatory steps and should be in sufficient geographic proximity for the attack to succeed".[120] The defences in place and alternatives available to the ISF soldiers meant that even when protestors were cutting barbed wire or throwing stones, the use of live ammunition was determined by the Commission to be neither necessary nor proportionate.[121]

The extensive use of video and photographic material by the Commission of Inquiry on the GMR is easy to position within the investigative methodology outlined in the report. As mentioned above, authenticated photos and videos are considered to be direct information, which is then to be corroborated by additional information. However, the social media content used was not exclusively of this type. For example, in support of a finding that an individual died shortly after arriving at hospital, reference is made to a tweet from the Twitter account of the European Gaza hospital.[122] This tweet was only text, so there was no video or photo to authenticate, and was issued by a hospital, not a public official. Information such as this does not correspond to either the primary/direct information category, or the 'additional' information category, making it hard to pinpoint the role this information played in reaching a factual (and then legal) conclusion. As will be mentioned in the following section, this concern about methodology is a feature of both reports.

## 18.5. Observations, Concerns and Looking Forward

Drawing comparisons between the use of social media in the Myanmar report and the 'Great March of Return' report is not straightforward. Not only was the approach to the mandates quite different, but the style of report-writing was also contrasting. When approaching its mandate, the Fact-Finding Mission on Myanmar discussed emblematic *situations*, such as alleged violence and oppression in Rakhine State and the violation of particular rights. In the 'Great March of Return' report, focus was placed on emblematic *cases*, covering the alleged injury or death of identifiable individuals. Whereas the former looked more at broad patterns of conduct across time and a geographical area, the latter looked at specific events on specific days. The approach to the collected information was therefore

---

[120] *Ibid.*, para. 91.
[121] *Ibid.*, para. 694.
[122] *Ibid.*, p. 116.

different. As to the style in which the reports were written, in the Myanmar report the Mission very often attributed particular points to particular sources of information, with ample references to, *inter alia*, witness accounts and social media posts to demonstrate what information a statement in the report was based on. In the 'Great March of Return' report, the Commission tended to build narratives of events that were not attributed to particular sources. Reference might be made to a 'video' or a 'witness' without further detail as to *which* video or *which* witness. This information has been held back, likely so it can be passed on to relevant authorities to undertake criminal proceedings.[123] The approach in the Myanmar report allowed for the more granular analysis of social media use that is found in Section 18.3.2. of this chapter, as compared with the more general discussion in Section 18.4.2.

Another point of divergence between the reports is the types of finding social media is used to support. In the 'Great March of Return' report, social media is mostly used to show what happened: where a protestor was standing, when an incendiary kite was launched, when an Israeli soldier was injured, whether a person was wearing a press jacket or a white coat. By contrast, the Myanmar report uses social media predominantly to demonstrate what soldiers and military commanders were allegedly saying about the unfolding events. One of the notable elements in the Myanmar report is the way that the Mission used social media to try to see into the mind of the alleged perpetrators; posts to social media were used to demonstrate genocidal intent and to show that a military leader was aware of the violations committed by soldiers. When it came to establishing the facts – which villages were cleared, what violations took place – more reliance was placed on witness testimony and satellite images.

Given this disparity in approaches, it is too soon to draw broad ranging conclusions on how the quality of human rights fact-finding is affected by the turn to social media. The pool of study, with only two re-

---

[123] The Commission of Inquiry indicated that it compiled files/dossiers with confidential information on the responsibility of military and civilian structures which bear responsibility for the alleged violations. The Commission has authorized the UN High Commissioner for Human Rights to provide access to these files/dossiers to the International Criminal Court and national authorities "conducting credible investigations for the purposes of ensuring accountability for crimes and other serious violations committed in this context", *ibid.*, para. 783.

ports, remains too small. That being said, from reading and analysing the use of social media content in the Myanmar and 'Great March of Return' reports, some general remarks can be made about this trend in fact-finding work. These remarks have been condensed into two observations, two points of concern, and two points for looking to the future.

### 18.5.1. Observations

The first of the two observations about the use of social media in the Myanmar and 'Great March of Return' reports is that, between the two reports, we see a shift in the type of social media content being used. The previous section noted that the type of *finding* that social media was used to support differed between the reports; this difference is reflected in the type of social media *content* being used. Whereas the report on Myanmar mainly uses material from the Facebook pages of Myanmar officials, military leaders, and soldiers, the report on the 'Great March of Return' relies heavily on content from citizens. Instead of press releases by the Commander-in-Chief of the Tatmadaw, we see citizen videos and photos from participants in the protests.

Fact-finding work (as well as criminal investigations) have long relied on public statements from civilian and military officials, such as a speech given at a rally, an interview, or an official press release.[124] These can be used, for example, to show what a commander knew about a given operation, what strategy was in place, or whether an individual showed signs of genocidal intent. The change with the advent of social media is that those press releases and speeches are disseminated online, rather than only on television, radio or newspapers. The online medium may pose challenges regarding verification and authentication, but the nature of the information is the same. By contrast, the use of *citizen*-generated content in fact-finding and international crime investigations is an emerging phenomenon, particularly on the scale that we see in the 'Great March of Return' report.

Photos and videos captured by citizens were not absent from investigations in the past,[125] but they were included on a much smaller scale.

---

[124] Carla del Ponte, "Investigation and Prosecution of Large-scale Crimes at the International Level", in *Journal of International Criminal Justice*, 2006, vol. 4, 539, p. 554.

[125] See, for example, the reference to "private amateur videos" in International Criminal Tribunal for the former Yugoslavia, *Prosecutor v. Zejnil Delalić, Zdravko Mucić, Hazim Delić,*

With the advent of the smartphone and the Internet, our ability to capture and share our own content has exponentially grown, allowing citizen videos and photos to play a central role in the work of fact-finding missions (and in international criminal cases). Between the Myanmar report and the 'Great March of Return' report, we see a shift from the familiar terrain of public statements from officials (but posted on social media instead of in traditional media) to the much less familiar terrain of citizen generated content.

This difference could be down to a range of factors. It might be the case that the type of material that came out of Gaza during the protests was not the same as that which came out of Myanmar. For the 'Great March of Return' there is footage from multiple angles and sources showing the same event, which allows for corroboration and verification.[126] The recorded event was often the shooting itself, and/or its immediate aftermath. For the violence in Myanmar there may be less material of the clearance operations actually taking place, and instead the videos and photos depict the aftermath, possibly hours or days later, and possibly only from one source. This makes the Myanmar material much harder to verify. The quality requirement that videos and photos be authenticated means that this material could therefore not be included in the report.

Alternatively, or in addition to the above explanation, the difference could signal that fact-finding bodies are growing more comfortable with using social media content in their work. Once the Fact-Finding Mission on Myanmar had laid the groundwork for using social media content, the Commission of Inquiry on the GMR had the licence to further explore this source of information, and include a broader range of content. The Commission may have had more confidence in its ability to maintain the quality of its work because of a growing familiarity with social media material.

The second observation, also relevant to quality control, is that the two fact-finding bodies remained duly cautious when it came to social media content, but not substantially more so than with other types of information. Authentication, verification and corroboration are all required,

---

*and Esad Landžo*, Trial Chamber, Judgment, 16 November 1998, IT-96-21-T, para. 716 (https://legal-tools.org/doc/d09556).

[126] For example, an investigation by the *New York Times* into the death of the medic Rouzan al-Najjar noted that "virtually every minute of the day she died was filmed by journalists, medics, and protestors", New York Times, "A Day, a Life: When a Medic Was Killed in Gaza, Was It an Accident?", 30 December 2018 (at 01:30 mins. of video in article).

as they are with any source of information, but the bar does not seem to have been set impossibly high for material obtained from social media. In this way, a balance is struck between the competing concerns of, on the one hand, needing to include social media content because it contains valuable information and insights, and on the other hand, needing to exercise caution because of the challenges inherent in this material. Social media content – whether videos, photos, press releases, personal posts, and so forth – was only ever part of the bigger picture that the fact-finding bodies put together using a range of sources of information.

Maintaining this broad range of sources is as important for upholding the quality and integrity of the report as a whole as it is for controlling the quality of individual pieces of information. This is because while social media provides a window into inaccessible areas, it has significant blind spots when it comes to the types of violations it depicts and the narratives that it emphasises. Certain violations are more visible on social media than others: for example, while many photos have emerged from Syria and Iraq in recent years featuring fighters posing with the severed heads of their enemies,[127] very little content has emerged featuring sexual violence. An over-reliance on social media therefore risks obscuring certain violations and prioritising others, thereby further entrenching the already poor visibility of certain types of violence. Certain communities may also be more visible on social media than others, thereby promoting particular narratives of the violence over others. This may reinforce historical biases and divides.

### 18.5.2. Concerns

The first point of concern has already been noted at several points in this chapter, and stems from the lack of clarity regarding the methodology employed by the Fact-Finding Mission and the Commission of Inquiry when it comes to social media content. In both the Myanmar and 'Great March of Return' reports care has been taken to set out detailed explanations of the methodology used in the investigations, down to the factors that went to the credibility of witnesses. Despite this detail, it is not always clear how social media content fits in.

---

[127] For an overview of cases, see Eurojust, "Prosecuting war crimes of outrage upon personal dignity based on evidence from open sources – Legal framework and recent developments in the Member States of the European Union", February 2018.

If the content used in the report was obtained from the social media page of a government or military official, or if the content was an 'authenticated' photo or video from any social media page, this could be designated as 'primary' or 'direct' information (the terminology differed between the reports). This meant that it could be corroborated with 'additional' information of other types, or with further primary/direct information.

Where the social media content was of another type, it is not clear whether it would be classified as a primary/direct source. Examples of 'other types' of social media content mentioned in Sections 18.3. and 18.4. include the hate speech and misinformation referred to in the Myanmar report, the statements from the 'Great March of Return' organisers about the need to keep the protests peaceful, and the report from the hospital in Gaza about the death of certain individuals. Information such as this does not correspond to either the primary/direct information category, or the 'additional' information category. This issue, while somewhat technical, goes to the question of how information is approached and corroborated, which goes to quality control. Given the attention dedicated to the methodology sections of both reports, and the extensive use of social media in both investigations, it is surprising that there was not a more careful consideration of the place of social media content in the methodology.

Turning to the second point of concern, this relates to the authentication process undertaken by both fact-finding bodies when approaching videos and photos from social media. Neither report explains how this authentication was done, and the OHCHR Guidance to which both reports refer goes no further than posing some questions which fact-finders should ask themselves when faced with any video or photo.[128] Based on a conversation with a member of the Commission of Inquiry's investigative team, it is clear that the authentication of the videos and photos was undertaken thoroughly and with great care, but there is no indication that a consistent and uniform approach has been adopted across different fact-finding bodies.

This problem is common across the broad range of actors working with digitally derived information and evidence, and is not unique to fact-

---

[128] "Were the images altered? Did the incident actually occur? Did the persons in the images actually commit the acts portrayed?": OHCHR Guidance and Practice, 2015, p. 44, see *supra* note 13.

finding bodies. It stems from the newness of the online investigations field, and from the diversity of actors who engage in these investigations and who conduct fact-finding for different ends. Harmonisation efforts are underway, however, with the "International Protocol on Open Source Investigations" expected in 2020.[129] The Protocol is directed at international criminal and human rights investigations, and aims to "set common standards and guidelines for the identification, collection, preservation, verification and analysis of online open source information".[130] Initiatives of this type are an opportunity for actors such as the UN OHCHR to adopt a common approach to working with online content across the different fact-finding bodies. This will promote uniformity and consistency in the quality of online investigations.

### 18.5.3. Looking to the Future

Social media content, and digitally derived information generally, seem set to remain an important component in the investigation of international humanitarian, human rights, and criminal law violations. Looking to the future, there are two points that will be mentioned here as issues to bear in mind.

The first point to mention is the question of funding, and in particular funding for specialised staff members. It is sometimes argued that conducting investigations online, using resources such as social media, will reduce the costs of investigations. This is based on the idea that less time will need to be spent conducting investigations on-site, and so less on-the-ground staff will be required (as well as less travel time). However, this may not be the case. As highlighted in Section 18.5.1., for the quality of fact-finding to be maintained, it is important that social media only ever make up one part of a bigger picture that draws on a range of sources of information. There is still a need for on-site investigations (where possible) and for location visits in order to interview witnesses, gather information, and so on. Social media content can provide useful leads, but will need to be corroborated by other sources, particularly witnesses.

---

[129] Human Rights Center, UC Berkeley School of Law, *International Protocol on Open Source Investigations: A Manual on the Effective Use of Open Source Information for International Criminal and Human Rights Investigations*, 2020.

[130] Human Rights Center, UC Berkeley School of Law, "Open Source Investigations Protocol" (available on its web site).

Rather than being a financial saving, using social media content to its full potential requires funding for specialised staff. There is an ever-growing number of photos, videos and reports being uploaded onto social media platforms: on YouTube alone, 500 hours of video content are uploaded every minute.[131] The issue facing investigators is not that there is not enough information online; it is that the amount of information online is overwhelming. The challenge of sorting through the noise to find information pertinent to an investigation requires expertise. Once relevant information is collected, specialised knowledge is then required to authenticate and verify it. This process is not only technical, but also time-consuming. For example, identifying the precise location where a photo was taken can take anywhere from a few hours to a few weeks (or longer). As the field of open source digital investigation continues to develop, new issues will emerge and require attention and expertise. For example, some time after the publication of the Myanmar report, stories emerged of the automated translation function on Facebook mistranslating the Burmese language.[132] The range of issues that arise when analysing social media content therefore require the hiring of multiple expert staff members with a range of expertise. Providing sufficient funding for this will therefore be crucial going forward.

The second point to note for the future is that fact-finding bodies of different types can learn a great from each other's increasing expertise. As the online investigation field develops, there are lessons that the OHCHR fact-finding bodies can learn from the use of social media content by international criminal courts, domestic criminal courts, and NGOs. Convictions for war crimes have already been obtained using social media content at both the ICC[133] and at the domestic level,[134] with other cases yet to commence.[135] Many NGOs use social media to gather information for their advocacy work, with organisations such as Bellingcat specialising in

---

[131] Figures from Tubefiller, "More Than 500 Hours of Content Are Now Being Uploaded to YouTube Every Minute", 7 May 2019 (available on its web site).

[132] BBC News, "Facebook blames 'technical issue' for offensive Xi Jinping translation", 19 January 2020.

[133] International Criminal Court, *The Prosecutor v. Ahmad Al Faqi Al Mahdi*, Trial Chamber VIII, Judgment and Sentence, 27 September 2016, ICC-01/12-01/15-171 (www.legal-tools.org/doc/042397).

[134] See *supra* note 4.

[135] Al-Werfalli Arrest Warrant, see *supra* note 5.

online open source investigations that draw, at least in part, on social media content. Each actor will develop their own practices and guidelines, and will learn from their respective mistakes.

How different actors approach content obtained from social media will differ depending on their aims and on the standard of proof to which they are working, and this should be borne in mind when examining their work. That being said, there is much that the different actors can learn from each other in terms of best practices for quality control. Furthermore, knowledge of other institutional practices will be important in situations where it is envisaged that one institution will take on and further develop the work of another. On 14 November 2019, judges at the ICC authorised the opening of an investigation into Myanmar/Bangladesh in connection with the violence in Myanmar which led to thousands of Rohingyas and other minorities fleeing across the border into Bangladesh.[136] On 10 December 2019, the International Court of Justice ('ICJ') heard an application by The Gambia for provisional measures to be ordered against Myanmar in connection with an alleged violation by the latter of the Genocide Convention.[137] Four provisional measures were granted by the Court in an Order dated 23 January 2020,[138] pursuant to which Myanmar submitted a comprehensive report to the Court on 22 May 2020. There is scope for material collected by the Fact-Finding Mission to be useful to the ICC and the ICJ, and the use of common standards and practices would facilitate such co-operation.

## 18.6. Conclusion

The reports of the Fact-Finding Mission on Myanmar and the Commission of Inquiry on the GMR are rich reading for those interested in how social media content plays a role in substantiating the findings of human rights fact-finding bodies. This chapter has described some of the highlights of how social media was used in these reports, and particularly the findings it was used to support. For the report on Myanmar, Section 18.3.

---

[136] ICC Press Release, "ICC judges authorise opening of an investigation into the situation in Bangladesh/Myanmar", 14 November 2019.

[137] Application of the Convention on the Prevention and Punishment of the Crime of Genocide (The Gambia v. Myanmar), Request for the Indication of Provisional Measures, The Court to Hold Hearings from Tuesday 10 to Thursday 12 December 2019, International Court of Justice Press Release, 18 November 2019.

[138] Application of the Convention on the Prevention and Punishment of the Crime of Genocide (The Gambia v. Myanmar), Order, 23 January 2020.

above discussed how social media was used to allege that Myanmar's Defence Services targeted civilians, that the military leadership was responsible for such violations, and that there are indications that the violence against Rohingyas was carried out with genocidal intent. Furthermore, social media content provided numerous examples of the types of hate speech that was circulating in Myanmar at the time that the violations took place. For the report on the 'Great March of Return', Section 18.4. above described how social media content was used to support findings that individual protestors had allegedly been unlawfully killed or injured by ISF soldiers, and to show that the majority of the protests were peaceful in nature.

The examples included in this chapter could be easily supplemented by many more. For example, with respect to the 'Great March of Return' report, there is an interesting section on the spread of misinformation during the protests and the complications this created for the Commission in carrying out its work. With respect to the Myanmar report, there is discussion of the alleged violence perpetrated by non-State armed groups such as the Arakan Rohingya Salvation Army as well as patterns of discrimination and persecution of minorities. Each of these sections in the reports feature social media content among the information cited, and could have been included as further examples in this chapter. There is therefore, more that could have been said.

In choosing the examples, focus was directed to those that illustrated the Mission's and the Commission's approach to social media content from a quality-control perspective, and which were representative of the reports as a whole in this respect. The examples, as well as the discussions on methodology in the reports, showed that both the Mission and the Commission were cautious in their approach to social media, and subjected the material to corroboration, authentication, and verification processes.

Those interested in how social media is used in fact-finding work, and in how quality control is incorporated into this work, can look forward to the report of the fact-finding mission on Venezuela, expected in June 2020. Social media has proved to be a significant medium to enable Venezuelans to communicate to the outside world the unrest and violence in their country,[139] and will therefore be an important source of infor-

---

[139] The Washington Post, "Venezuela's crisis shows social media at its worst – but also at its best", 1 May 2019; The Washington Post, "Social media remains key to Venezuela's oppo-

mation for the Venezuela mission as it investigates alleged "extrajudicial executions, enforced disappearances, arbitrary detentions and torture and other cruel, inhumane or degrading treatment".[140] Against this report we can revisit the observations, concerns, and points for the future mentioned above. We can see whether the mission continues to work with citizen-made content, and whether it continues to use a range of information sources to paint a picture of events. We can see whether the concerns relating to methodological clarity and to consistency in authentication methods are allayed or exacerbated. And we can see whether the funding of the mission facilitates the hiring of technical experts, as well as whether the mission draws on the growing expertise being developed by other actors in the field. As the body of 'social media' human rights fact-finding reports grows, it will certainly be worthwhile to revisit discussions about quality control.

---

sition, despite efforts to block it", 1 May 2019; NBC News, "How Venezuela's vice grip on the Internet leaves citizens in the dark during crises", 16 May 2019; Time, "'Venezuelans Are Starving for Information.' The Battle of Get News in a Country in Chaos", 16 April 2019.

[140] "Situation of human rights in the Bolivarian Republic of Venezuela", 24 September 2019, UN Doc. A/HRC/42/L.4/Rev.1, para. 24 (https://undocs.org/A/HRC/42/L.4/Rev.1).

# 19

———

# International(ised) Criminal Justice at a Crossroads: The Role of Civil Society in the Investigation of Core International Crimes and the 'CIJA Model'

**William H. Wiley**[*]

## 19.1. Introduction

International(ised)[1] criminal justice is at a crossroads: State-donor fatigue, driven by dissatisfaction with the financial cost relative to output of international courts and tribunals – mostly the International Criminal Court ('ICC') and the United Nations International Residual Mechanism for Criminal Tribunals ('MICT') – has given rise to a much-reduced preparedness on the part of Western States to agree to the establishment of new international courts and tribunals.[2] As an alternative, the international

---

[*] **William H. Wiley** is the Executive Director and founder of the Commission for International Justice and Accountability; prior service with the Department of Justice of Canada war-crimes section, the United Nations *ad hoc* Tribunals for Rwanda and the former Yugoslavia, the International Criminal Court, and the Iraqi High Tribunal. The views expressed in this chapter are those of the author.

[1] The adjective 'international(ised)' is employed in this chapter to denote purely international bodies, such as the International Criminal Court ('ICC') and the United Nations *ad hoc* Tribunals, hybrid courts, and tribunals as well as domestic courts addressing the alleged perpetration of core international crimes.

[2] 'Hybrid' courts and tribunals are bodies which bring together, in the same institution, domestic and international judicial actors. Such institutions generally apply international criminal and humanitarian law as well as domestic substantive and procedural provisions. Examples of hybrid bodies include the Special Court for Sierra Leone, the Extraordinary Chambers in the Courts of Cambodia, the Court of Bosnia and Herzegovina, and the Special Tribunal for Lebanon. The initial appeal of hybrid bodies, in the minds of the States funding them, was their limited budgets relative to the United Nations *ad hoc* Tribunals as well as the ICC. For its part, civil society champions of the hybrid model have pointed to the transitional-justice benefits ostensibly accruing where adjudicative mechanisms are situated in close physical proximity to the conflict-affected societies.

community would appear to be experimenting with the establishment of *ad hoc* criminal-investigative bodies, with annual budgets in the region of USD 12,000,000 to 20,000,000. Three such institutions were established during 2016–2018.[3] However, the so-called International, Impartial and Independent Mechanism ('IIIM'), the United Nations Investigative Team for Accountability of Da'esh/ISIL ('UNITAD'), and the Independent Investigative Mechanism for Myanmar ('IIMM') have no adjudicative arm nor, for that matter, any prosecutorial role. It remains to be seen how they will entreat in practice with domestic and international courts. It appears unlikely that the world of international(ised) criminal justice is seeing the start of a trend towards the establishment of United Nations-mandated, criminal-investigative bodies in response to each and every situation in which there are credible reports of the widespread perpetration of core international crimes.[4] Amidst all this, groups claiming to speak for victims

---

[3] The IIIM was established by the United Nations General Assembly ('UNGA') through UNGA resolution 71/248 (December 2016), International, Impartial and Independent Mechanism to Assist in the Investigation and Prosecution of Persons Responsible for the Most Serious Crimes under International Law Committed in the Syrian Arab Republic since March 2011, UN Doc. A/RES/71/248, 11 January 2017, para. 4 (https://www.legal-tools.org/doc/fecaf0). It is known formally as the International, Impartial and Independent Mechanism to assist in the investigation and prosecution of persons responsible for the most serious crimes under International Law committed in the Syrian Arab Republic since March 2011. UNITAD (the United Nations Investigative Team for Accountability of Da'esh/ISIL) was created by the United Nations Security Council ('UNSC') through UNSC resolution 2379 (September 2017). Finally, the IIMM (Independent Investigative Mechanism for Myanmar) was called into being by Human Rights Council ('HRC') resolution 39/2 (September 2018).

[4] The limited (that is, Islamic State in Iraq-specific) mandate of UNITAD reflects the fact that it was established by the UNSC, where three of the five Permanent Members (that is, France, the United Kingdom and the United States) were engaged militarily against Da'esh when UNSC resolution 2379 was passed. For its part, a fourth Permanent UNSC Member, the Russian Federation, was concomitantly attacking Islamic State forces in Syria – at least in those operational sectors where Da'esh constituted a military threat to the Government of Syria. The broad mandate of the IIIM to examine allegations of criminal misconduct by all belligerent parties to the war is far more problematical, from a politico-diplomatic point of view, insofar as a number of Western States see the Syria Mechanism as an unwelcome precedent for the establishment, through the UNGA, of further investigative bodies designed to target allied States, in particular, Israel. Other considerations mitigating against the establishment of additional conflict-specific investigative mechanisms include (i) the desire of ICC States Parties to avoid the creation of public bodies whose jurisdiction might overlap with that of the ICC, for fear of undermining the latter, and (ii) the financial cost of these limited initiatives which, whilst modest compared to an entire court or tribunal, is not insignificant. All things considered, the establishment by the HRC of the IIMM in Septem-

---

in conflict-affected societies are increasingly frustrated with the pace at which criminal prosecutions for violations of core international crimes are being brought – where cases are brought at all. By 2025, there is every possibility that the only international court or tribunal will be the ICC. In that event, the well-documented problems which the ICC Office of the Prosecutor ('OTP') has in bringing substantive cases to trial and in securing convictions on a consistent basis threatens to reduce that body to the sort of practical irrelevancy which plagued the International Court of Justice during the Cold War.

The leadership cadres dominating the existing international offices of the prosecutor, including that of the ICC, are collectively a good deal more capable than they have ever been. A wealth of creative thinking is very much in evidence, not least in response to (i) funding constraints and (ii) certain intractable challenges inherent where investigations require forays into high physical-risk environments. The same might be said about the leadership of the IIIM, UNITAD and IIMM[5] as well as the war-crimes programmes situated in key Western States. However, more out-of-the-box thinking shall be required if the system of international(ised) criminal justice is to remain a stalwart in the fight against impunity for core international crimes. For instance, investigations must be more expeditious in order to facilitate timely prosecutions with an eye to meeting the demands of conflict-affected societies as well as donor States. What is more, the sort of enhanced investigative pace posited here in response to outbreaks of egregious violations of international criminal and humanitarian law, such as that witnessed in Syria from 2011, must be realised at a cost much reduced from current expenditures, the latter being clearly unsustainable in the minds of the national governments footing the bills. Aside from donor concerns regarding ICC and MICT expenditures, the cost-to-output ratio of the IIIM was first called into question fewer than two years after it was established.[6]

---

ber 2018 came as something of a surprise insofar as there was only modest political opposition to the IIMM initiative.

[5] At the time of publication, key personnel in all three mandates formerly served at the ICTY.

[6] Since the last quarter of 2018, the author of this chapter has been questioned in increasingly pointed terms by a range of Western diplomats (speaking privately) and non-governmental actors (in public forums) regarding the perceived – by the various interlocutors – insufficiency of output of the IIIM which had begun concomitantly to signal a desire to its donors that its annual budget should rise by not less than 50 per cent in the near term.

The demands of donors for greater efficiency, coupled with the understandably low physical-risk tolerance of public institutions, can be met only through the effective engagement of civil society in criminal-investigative processes, where the development of both crime-bases and linkage-cases is concerned. The system of international(ised) criminal justice might be saved in something like its current form – and indeed strengthened – only through the establishment of effective public–private partnerships at the investigative stage. Recent United Nations tinkering with the architecture of international(ised) criminal investigations, whilst most welcome, will not in and of itself solve all or even most of the challenges plaguing this structure; simply put, the root of the difficulties undermining purely public-sector investigations lies in the general inability of public institutions to collect evidence in high physical-risk situations or otherwise find expeditious routes into operational environments characterised by politico-diplomatic complexity.

Founded as it was with a detailed understanding of the unavoidable limitations of public institutions, the Commission for International Justice and Accountability ('CIJA') constitutes the first meaningful effort on the part of a private institution – in this case, a non-profit foundation – to undertake investigations to criminal-evidentiary standards with the sole objective of rendering support to public investigative and prosecutorial organs, both international and domestic. What is more, since its establishment in 2011, CIJA has demonstrated the immense contribution which a private institution, led by personnel with experience of both the criminal investigation and prosecution of core international crimes, is able to make to the pursuit of criminal justice whilst operating on, by public-sector standards, a modest budget.

It is the practice of CIJA to defer on questions of law to those of its partners with a prosecutorial arm, the primary role of CIJA being to secure evidence for present and future prosecutions within complex operating environments where the public-sector investigative response to the

---

In the event, the objectives of the IIIM are not the business of the CIJA. The fact that senior CIJA personnel are being questioned about such matters is evidently a function of a prevailing understanding amongst Syria observers that the IIIM will assume responsibility not only for the immense volumes of *prima facie* evidence collected by the CIJA in Syria since 2011, but also for the prosecution case-building function of the CIJA, where the Syrian regime and Islamic State operations in Syria are concerned. The IIIM has enjoyed access to all CIJA evidence relevant to the mandate of the IIIM since 2017. CIJA leaves it to others to determine what the CIJA should do with these materials.

---

perpetration of egregious core international crimes is unavoidably weak or non-existent. Whilst not envisioned by the founder of CIJA at its creation, the application of the CIJA model has had the unintended effect of affording to civil society – and especially the conflict-affected populations alongside which CIJA engages – a voice in the application of international criminal justice which has most certainly not been characteristic of the international-adjudicative institutions established since 1993, for instance, the United Nations *ad hoc* Tribunals and the ICC. Where the CIJA model is applied in a conflict zone, decisions on what is investigated and how tend to be taken in part from the hands of public officials and placed into those of civil-society groups with an investigative focus such as CIJA. In turn, such a civil-society actor, required as it is to conform to the evidentiary standards informing criminal investigations and prosecutions, must distribute the responsibility for evidence collection within its own structure between international criminal and humanitarian law specialists and the locally retained personnel who are responsible in the first instance for the collection of *prima facie* evidence. Public–private partnerships operating in the justice space necessarily shift decision-making power to a degree from the public space to the private – and, arguably, from the international level to the domestic.[7]

In CIJA's experience, public-sector investigative and prosecutorial authorities are comfortable with this evolution in the power dynamic in the investigation of core international crimes, if that they give it any thought at all. Where the partial shift of power from the public to the private domain *is* questioned – invariably in the context of a discussion on whether it is desirable that a private organisation should be undertaking complex criminal investigations – such concerns have been put forward, somewhat paradoxically, by international human rights groups which have long been calling for a greater role to be played by conflict-affected societies in criminal justice processes. The view taken here is that the international human-rights community might wish to compare the socio-justice benefits to a conflict-affected population of passive participation in inter-

---

[7] On the question of the ownership, so to speak, of international criminal justice and the CIJA, see Melinda Rankin, "Investigating Crimes Against Humanity in Syria and Iraq: The Commission for International Justice and Accountability", in *Global Responsibility to Protect*, 2017, vol. 9, no. 4, pp. 395–421; Rankin, "The Future of International Criminal Evidence in New Wars? The Evolution of the Commission for International Justice and Accountability (CIJA)", in *Journal of Genocide Research*, 2018, vol. 20, no. 3, pp. 392–411.

national(ised) criminal justice processes, through victim-participation arrangements and the like, with those to be accrued where local civil-society actors have a role in shaping, alongside international experts, the wider criminal justice response to the alleged perpetration of core international crimes.

## 19.2. Current Level of International(ised) Investigative Capacity

The difficult situation in which international(ised) criminal justice finds itself is not immutable. International criminal and humanitarian law has emerged as a field of legal practice in its own right since 1993, with the discipline now populated by a great many more talented practitioners than the current range of international institutions is capable of employing and, as a reasonable body of available literature demonstrates, the last 25 years have witnessed the emergence of coherent investigative methodologies which can be brought to bear in any situation in which core international crimes have been (or are being) perpetrated. What is more, the domestic application of international criminal and humanitarian law is increasingly widespread in the West, and occasionally seen in the developing world, with a case in point being the successful prosecution of the former President of Chad, Hissène Habré before a specially-constituted trial chamber in Senegal.

The domestication of international criminal and humanitarian law is a necessary rejoinder to politico-diplomatic complexity and the cost of organising an international-institutional response to every conflict and disturbance which has given rise to the perpetration of core international crimes. Most European and North American States now have dedicated 'war-crimes' units, and the co-operation of their investigators, analysts and prosecutors is facilitated greatly by the Eurojust Genocide Network[8] (a group which regularly brings together domestic officials from every credible national programme). Likewise, Europol was afforded competence over war-crimes issues in 2017.[9] Suspects identified by war-crimes units operating within national jurisdictions can expect to be investigated

---

[8]  Formally the European Network of contact points in respect of persons responsible for genocide, crimes against humanity and war crimes, situated in The Hague, Netherlands.

[9]  Regulation (EU) 2016/794 of the European Parliament and of the Council of 11 May 2016 on the European Union Agency for Law Enforcement Cooperation (Europol) and replacing and repealing Council decisions 2009/371/JHA, 2009/934/JHA, 2009/935/JHA, 2009/936/JHA and 2009/968/JHA.

and, where the evidence warrants, prosecuted with relative despatch in accordance with fundamental due process guarantees. That noted, there remains very limited capacity outside the West – notwithstanding *Habré* – to investigate and prosecute core international crimes domestically in accordance with the requirements of international criminal and humanitarian law as well as internationally-agreed due process guarantees. The most egregious and widely-known failure in this respect would be the Iraqi High Tribunal which, whilst ostensibly applying international criminal and humanitarian law, had investigations, prosecutions, adjudication and defence advocacy found to be appallingly flawed with near-uniform consistency.[10]

The raw numbers of perpetrators of core international crimes emerging from dictatorships and armed conflicts of any magnitude necessarily render highly symbolic the criminal justice response to each and every situation characterised by a widespread violation of international criminal and humanitarian law. The joint capacity at the present time of international(ised) prosecutorial bodies as well as domestic war-crimes programmes to respond, in even a token manner, to the majority of situations in which international offences are witnessed, is grossly insufficient where the application of international criminal and humanitarian law is seen to be a key tool in the fight against impunity for the perpetrators of egregious crimes. The root of this problem is often the sort of politico-diplomatic resistance to criminal justice accountability which is sometimes evident where efforts are made to bring warring sides to the peace table or otherwise nudge recalcitrant dictators towards retirement. At the same time, the insufficiency of resources referenced here is often a function of the considerable financial cost of undertaking to a criminal law standard of evidence the investigation of high-level perpetrators, that is, suspects who operate at arm's length from the physical acts for which, in law, they might nonetheless be held accountable.

---

[10] See the selected scholarship of two former IHT international legal advisors: Eric H. Blinderman, "The Execution of Saddam Hussein – A Legal Analysis", in Jann K. Kleffner and Timothy McCormack (eds.), *Yearbook of International Humanitarian Law*, Asser Press, 2006, pp. 153–179; William H. Wiley, "The Case of Taha Yaseen Ramadan before the Iraqi High Tribunal: An Insider's Perspective", in Jann K. Kleffner and Timothy McCormack (eds.), *Yearbook of International Humanitarian Law*, Asser Press, 2006, pp. 181–243. A more charitable assessment of the IHT might be found in Michael A. Newton and Michael P. Scharf, *Enemy of the State: The Trial and Execution of Saddam Hussein*, St. Martin's Press, 2008.

## 19.3. Civil Society and Criminal Justice

Civil society groups of many stripes – and those concerned with human rights especially – have long railed against the effective impunity enjoyed by all but the unluckiest perpetrators of core international crimes. Such expressions of disquiet are well placed. However, where those calling for an end to de facto impunity come up short is in demanding a criminal-investigative response to every situation in which core international crimes would appear to be perpetrated. Such calls are invariably made without any evident thought having been given to the question of how such engagement might be staffed and funded, even where there are no jurisdictional hurdles to the engagement of a given public institution such as the ICC.

Demands from civil society for the application of criminal justice are extraordinary by virtue of their volume and geographical breadth. By way of random example, in 2016 Human Rights Watch joined Amnesty International and a handful of other (including African) organisations in informing the United Nations Human Rights Council member States that a referral of North Korea to the ICC "should remain a priority for the international community".[11] The year prior, a coalition of human rights groups, including at least one of the signatories to the aforementioned letter, demanded that the ICC Prosecutor commence a preliminary examination into the conduct of State security forces in Mexico.[12] The civil society coalition calling for the referral of the Syria situation to the ICC in 2014 cobbled together the most impressive numbers, that is, a total of 117 groups from around the world.[13] Every apparent outburst of criminality in Africa gives rise to like demands for international-judicial (usually ICC) intervention, the unrest in Burundi constituting but one exemplar.[14] The calls of non-governmental organisations ('NGOs') for ICC engagement in

---

[11] Human Rights Watch, "Joint Letter to UN Human Rights Council Members, Re: DPRK Resolution – Need for Enhanced focus on Accountability", 15 February 2016 (https://legal-tools.org/doc/87b4qt).

[12] International Federation for Human Rights ('FIDH'), "Human Rights Groups Call on the ICC to Proceed with the Preliminary Examination into the Situation in Mexico", 12 September 2014 (https://legal-tools.org/doc/ghqw0l).

[13] GCHR, "Syria: Groups Call for ICC Referral/Statement by Civil Society Organizations on Need for Justice", 15 May 2014 (available on its web site).

[14] FIDH, "Burundi: NGOs Call for a Special Session of the Human Rights Council", 9 November 2015 (https://legal-tools.org/doc/0g6sjf).

---

response to alleged crimes perpetrated in Myanmar against ethnic Rohingya were at one juncture too numerous to read.[15] The NGO cacophony
clearly caught the attention of policy-political actors, leading indirectly to
the establishment of the IIMM whilst concomitantly facilitating a rather
novel decision by an ICC pre-trial chamber which afforded the OTP at
least partial jurisdiction over *prima facie* crimes perpetrated on the territory of a non-State party to the Rome Statute.[16]

Taken as a whole, demands of the foregoing nature for criminal justice intervention are wildly at odds with the material resources and physical reach of the system of international(ised) criminal justice as it exists
currently. The only extant *public* criminal-investigative body which can in
principle, where it is afforded jurisdiction, engage anywhere in the world
is the ICC-OTP. However, the Investigations Division of the ICC-OTP
employs fewer than 100 investigators and analysts, ostensibly tasked with
covering the globe; and in 2018, the Division expended approximately
EUR 20,000,000 – an impressive figure until one considers that this
budget constituted slightly less than 14 per cent of the overall projected
cost of maintaining the Court as a whole during the course of the same
year.[17] For their part, the IIIM, UNITAD and the IIMM can soon be expected to have similar annual budgets, if they do not already, with which
to address relatively narrowly-defined situations, although only the IIMM
has been afforded temporal and geographical jurisdiction which overlaps
with that of the ICC-OTP. Whereas the ICC and the United Nations criminal-investigative mechanisms are all positioned to support national war-
crimes programmes, informed observers can only question the mid-term
tolerance of the international community for *investigations* expenditures
by the four bodies (that is, the ICC, the IIIM, UNITAD and the IIMM)
which are likely to total USD 80,000,000 annually by 2020 or 2021. The
problem facing the institutions and their donors is that affording more
money to public investigations may not translate readily into more or
stronger cases when the public bodies find themselves unable to secure

---

[15] By way of one example, see Physician for Human Rights, "PHR Joins Call for Myanmar
Referral to ICC", 8 May 2018 (available on its web site).

[16] ICC, Pre-Trial Chamber I, *Decision on the "Prosecution's Request for a Ruling on Jurisdiction under Article 19(3) of the Statute"*, 6 September 2018, ICC-RoC46(3)-01/18-37
(https://www.legal-tools.org/doc/73aeb4).

[17] ICC Assembly of States Parties ('ASP'), "Proposed Programme Budget for 2018 of the
International Criminal Court, 11 September 2018", ICC-ASP/16/10 (https://www.legal-
tools.org/doc/ac4e16).

ready access to evidence situated in locations to which access by public-sector investigators is complicated greatly by politico-diplomatic challenges as well as considerations of physical risk.

To what extent more (or otherwise higher-quality) evidence might be secured by public institutions, acting singly or in concert with one another, is a question which lies at the heart of this chapter and it shall be addressed below at some length. It has already been posited, as part of the introduction to this chapter, that the public sector needs to collaborate with private partners such as CIJA if it is to secure, in a timely manner, evidence sufficient to facilitate successful criminal prosecutions. As such, NGO demands for more money to be shovelled towards public-sector investigative bodies do not constitute a rational response to otherwise well-placed concerns that the overwhelming majority of perpetrators of core international crimes enjoy *de facto* immunity from prosecution, not least where they find discreet sanctuary in Western States.

What the system of international(ised) criminal justice requires is a tangible contribution from the whole NGO community to the *criminal* investigation of core international crimes. International human rights groups, geared as they are towards advocacy rather than criminal-investigative ends, have proven themselves, with occasional exceptions, to be unable or otherwise unwilling to make any substantial input to prosecution case-building processes. This State of affairs is unconscionable to the extent that it is inconsistent with the important contribution made in other respects by international human rights organisations concerned with questions of international(ised) criminal justice. In particular, human rights groups were instrumental in facilitating the re-emergence of international criminal justice from 1993 after its long, post-Nuremberg slumber; this contribution arguably reached its zenith through the advocacy efforts which gave rise to the Rome Statute of the ICC, followed by its remarkably-swift operationalisation. [18] Unsurprisingly, human rights groups consider themselves to be key stakeholders in the system of international criminal justice. However, as it stands, the relative dearth of concrete evidentiary support provided by NGOs to public criminal-investigative bodies serves only to perpetuate the so-called impunity gap which continues to bedevil the system of international(ised) criminal jus-

---

[18] Marlies Glasius, *The International Criminal Court: A Global Civil Society Achievement*, Routledge Taylor & Francis Group, 2006.

tice. What international civil society needs to do with its stake in this field of law is to recognise that successful investors seek constantly to facilitate improvement at those points of a given venture where underperformance threatens the efficiency of the enterprise as a whole. The difficulties plaguing international(ised) criminal justice, which has shifted its focus markedly to ongoing armed conflicts from more accessible post-conflict situations such as Rwanda and the former Yugoslavia, are rooted almost entirely in the challenges arising when seeking to secure evidence sufficient to inform successful prosecutions; the sort of victim participation and witness protection questions so highly valued by international NGOs, whilst of indisputable moral significance, are secondary to the core requirements of successful prosecutions. All this is to argue that until civil society mobilises itself to engage effectively at this core, in a manner and to a degree which has not heretofore been witnessed, the prevalence of *de facto* impunity for the perpetrators of core international crimes, which human rights organisations rightly regret, shall remain unchanged.

## 19.4. Challenges Confronting Public Institutions Operating in the Domain of International(ised) Criminal Justice

If international(ised) criminal justice is to constitute a truly effective response to the prevailing climate of impunity, four interrelated challenges must be addressed: (1) the insufficient evidential quality which has characterised a substantial number of those international investigations that have been subjected to judicial scrutiny; (2) the general absence of any meaningful contribution by civil society to the criminal investigation of core international crimes; (3) the perceived inadequacy of international(ised) criminal justice in the collective minds of conflict-affected societies; and (4) State-donor fatigue, which has its roots in what interested public officials have increasingly come to see as the exorbitant cost relative to output of the international institutions charged with the investigation of core international crimes. Each of these phenomena will be examined in turn.

### 19.4.1. International Criminal Investigations and Physical Risk

From 2003, when the ICC-OTP became operationalised, through 2015, the ICC issued arrest warrants or summonses to appear for 39 individuals. Thirty-two of these suspects were alleged by the chief Prosecutor to have perpetrated core international crimes; the remaining seven suspects were accused of offences against the administration of justice (effectively, witness tampering). Of those persons alleged to have perpetrated core international crimes, at the conclusion of 2015, 18 had appeared voluntarily or otherwise before the Court. Of this number, committal proceedings were concluded in 17 cases during the aforementioned period. In four of those cases,[19] the pre-trial chambers refused to confirm any of the prosecution charges. In five additional cases, pre-trial chambers confirmed some of the prosecution charges, although in two instances[20] the prosecution subsequently withdrew all allegations on the grounds that the OTP lacked sufficient evidence to secure a conviction. In a further eight cases, the pre-trial chambers confirmed all of the charges. In those instances where some or all of the charges were confirmed, leading to the accused being committed to trial, trials were concluded in three instances, resulting in two convictions and one acquittal. Convictions in two cases have been registered since 2018 – in *Al-Mahdi* as a result of a guilty plea and in *Bemba* followed a full trial – although all of the convictions in *Bemba* were subsequently vacated in 2018 by an ICC appellate chamber.[21] In early-2019,

---

[19] ICC, Situation in Darfur, *The Prosecutor v. Bahr Idriss Abu Garda*, Pre-Trial Chamber I, Decision on the Confirmation of Charges, 8 February 2010, ICC-02/05-02/09-243-Red (https://www.legal-tools.org/doc/cb3614); ICC, Situation in the Democratic Republic of the Congo, *The Prosecutor v. Callixte Mbarushimana*, Pre-Trial Chamber I, Decision on the Confirmation of Charges, 16 December 2011, ICC-01/04-01/10-465-Red (https://www.legal-tools.org/doc/63028f); ICC, Situation in the Republic of Kenya, *The Prosecutor v. Francis Kirimi Muthaura, Uhuru Muigai Kenyatta and Mohammed Hussein Ali*, Pre-Trial Chamber II, Decision on the Confirmation of Charges Pursuant to Article 61(7)(a) and (b) of the Rome Statute, 23 January 2012, ICC-01/09-02/11-382-Red (https://www.legal-tools.org/doc/4972c0); ICC, Situation in the Republic of Kenya, *The Prosecutor v. William Samoei Ruto, Henry Kiprono Kosgey and Joshua Arap Sang*, Pre-Trial Chamber II, Decision on the Confirmation of Charges Pursuant to Article 61(7)(a) and (b) of the Rome Statute, 23 January 2012, ICC-01/09-01/11-373 (https://www.legal-tools.org/doc/96c3c2).

[20] ICC, Situation in the Republic of Kenya, *The Prosecutor v. Francis Kirimi Muthaura and Uhuru Muigai Kenyatta*, Trial Chamber, Decision on the withdrawal of charges against Mr. Muthaura, 18 March 2013 (https://www.legal-tools.org/doc/44ecc9); ICC, Situation in the Republic of Kenya, *The Prosecutor v. Uhuru Muigui Kenyatta*, Trial Chamber V(B), Notice of the withdrawal of charges against Uhuru Muigai Kenyatta, 5 December 2014, ICC-01/09-02/11 (https://www.legal-tools.org/doc/b57a97).

[21] ICC, Situation in the Republic of Mali, *The Prosecutor v. Ahmad Al Faqi Al Mahdi*, Trial Chamber VIII, Judgment and Sentence, 27 September 2016, ICC-01/12-01/15-171 (https://www.legal-tools.org/doc/042397) ; ICC, Situation in the Central African Republic, *The Prosecutor v. Jean-Pierre Bemba Gombo*, Trial Chamber III, Judgement pursuant to Article 74 of the Statute, 21 March 2016, ICC-01/05-01/08 (https://www.legal-tools.org/doc/edb0cf); ICC, Situation in the Central African Republic, *The Prosecutor v.*

---

the OTP found itself confronted with a debacle of arguably greater significance than that presented to it by the appellate judgement in *Bemba*: the collapse mid-trial – on the grounds of insufficient prosecution evidence – of the prosecution of Charles Blé Goudé and his co-defendant, Laurent Gbagbo, the former President of Côte d'Ivoire.

In summary, of the 17 OTP cases that made it through the pre-trial and trial phases by 2015, in four instances the prosecution lacked sufficient evidence to warrant the suspects being committed to trial; in two additional cases, the OTP found itself compelled by a lack of evidence to withdraw the allegations, after the accused had been committed to trial. In a seventh case, the accused was acquitted of all charges following a trial. During the period in which these 17 cases were seen through the pre-trial stage, leading to seven of the accused being set free without judicial sanction of any sort, the ICC-OTP expended in excess of EUR 310,000,000. Looking at the 2003-2015 figures, and the trial as well as appellate proceedings since, persons well disposed towards the ICC-OTP might conclude that OTP investigations take some time, incur considerable financial expenditure, and not infrequently experience difficulty in securing sufficient evidence to meet the "substantial grounds to believe" threshold for the committal of accused persons to trial, as well as the "beyond a reasonable doubt" standard set out in the Rome Statute for a conviction of sufficient strength to survive appellate proceedings.[22]

There is widespread consensus amongst practitioners of international criminal and humanitarian law that the performance of the first ICC chief Prosecutor, Mr. Luis Moreno-Ocampo was inadequate in a number of important respects and has caused lasting damage to the Court.[23] His

---

Jean-Pierre *Bemba Gombo*, Appeals Chamber, Judgment on the appeal of Mr Jean Pierre Bemba Gombo against Trial Chamber III's Judgement pursuant to Article 74 of the Statute, 8 June 2018, ICC-01/05-01/08-3636-Red (https://www.legal-tools.org/doc/40d35b).

[22] Rome Statute of the International Criminal Court, 17 July 1998, Articles 61(7), 66(3) ('ICC Statute') (http://www.legal-tools.org/doc/7b9af9/).

[23] The best overview of OTP investigative practices can be found in War Crimes Research Office, American University College of Law, "Investigative Management, Strategies, and Techniques of the International Criminal Court's Office of the Prosecutor", October 2012; On Mr. Moreno-Ocampo, see Julie Flint and Alex de Waal, "Case Closed: A Prosecutor without Borders", in *World Affairs Journal*, 2009, vol. 171, no. 4; and Morten Bergsmo, Wolfgang Kaleck, Sam Muller and William H. Wiley, "A Prosecutor Falls, Time for the Court to Rise", FICHL Policy Brief Series No. 86 (2017), Torkel Opsahl Academic EPublisher, Brussels, 2017 (http://www.toaep.org/pbs-pdf/86-four-directors/).

replacement is a very experienced international jurist and her leadership team, much of which was inherited from the Moreno-Ocampo era (which concluded in 2012), is on the whole strong. However, the post-Moreno-Ocampo record of the ICC-OTP suggests that there remain challenges inherent in seeing suspects committed to trial on a consistent basis and, in turn, prosecuted successfully. It would follow from these observations that the issue bedevilling the ICC-OTP is the collective inability of its relevant staff to secure sufficient evidence and to do so in a timely manner in order to maintain a pace of case-building and successful prosecutions in accordance with the budgetary provisions as well as expectations of the Assembly of States Parties ('ASP'), professional peers around the world, and more widely. Similar challenges plague the Special Tribunal for Lebanon ('STL') and the Kosovo Specialist Chambers and Special Prosecutor's Office (Kosovo Tribunal), neither of which has secured a single conviction, despite having commenced their investigative work, in earlier institutional iterations, a good many years ago. In light of the foregoing, it can be concluded that the key challenge facing public, criminal-investigative bodies – such as the amply-staffed institutions cited here by name – is how they might extend their evidence-gathering reach to areas which pose physical dangers to staff which are not commensurate with the modest risk tolerance of public institutions charged with the investigation of core international crimes.

The general willingness of private bodies such as human rights groups to engage physically in dangerous or otherwise unstable environments for prolonged periods renders such groups potentially valuable partners in criminal-investigative processes. There are two reasons therefore, both of them to be understood in the context of the structural handicaps which justice actors employed by public institutions have a great deal of difficulty transcending. First, public-sector investigative bodies charged with responding to offences perpetrated in a wide array of disparate conflicts will frequently find it difficult to develop sufficient in-house expertise, most especially on the analytical side of their operations, to deal in a nuanced manner with the large volumes of linkage evidence which must be collected in order to tie high-level perpetrators to the underlying criminal acts authored physically by their subordinates. This is particularly the case where relatively small, national war-crimes programmes are concerned. The skill set required to build complex criminal cases in response to core international crimes might be generic, but this generic expertise, if it is to be applied effectively, must be coupled with the sort of situation-specific knowledge which tends to emerge only where investigators, analysts and ideally counsel are assigned to a particular situation over a prolonged time. Such were the staffing practices of the ICTY and the ICTR; both of these institutions, whose investigators operated in post-conflict situations armed with Chapter VII mandates, brought – however slowly and at immense expense – a great number of successful prosecutions. Secondly, the collection of high-quality information which might be transformed into evidence through analytical processes undertaken in the context of the substantive law (for instance, international criminal and humanitarian law), invariably necessitates a degree of physical-risk tolerance. Hazards of this nature are most especially present where investigations are (or ought to be, under ideal circumstances) undertaken in the midst of an ongoing war or otherwise unstable environment. As was noted earlier in this chapter, the prevailing trend in international(ised) criminal justice has seen the investigative focus of the public institutions shift from post-conflict situations to active war zones and other environments unwelcoming to criminal investigators.

Public-international and national institutions charged with the investigation of core international crimes are not structured to engage effectively in geographical locations where there is anything more than a minimal level of physical risk to the public servants whose investigative deployment is ultimately necessary to ensure successful prosecutions in a timely manner. Whilst *domestic* law-enforcement personnel run all manner of physical risks to uphold the law within national borders, and are correspondingly killed on occasion, no such risk tolerance is in evidence where core international crimes have been perpetrated abroad. Less explicably, this aversion to physical risk during the investigation of international criminal and humanitarian law offences has been central to the culture of the international criminal-investigative bodies established since 1993. The upshot of the low physical-risk tolerance evinced by public bodies charged with the investigation of core international crimes is that investigative and prosecutorial organs seeking to build cases against high-level suspects frequently find themselves with a paucity of information of evidential value. In turn, this challenge is coupled frequently with insufficient institutional, conflict-specific expertise of the sort required to analyse whatever information can be acquired within the physical-risk parameters set by the public institutions.[24] The uneven prosecutorial record of the ICC, the STL and the Kosovo Tribunal is not a function of allegedly insufficient budgetary resources nor the quality of their personnel; rather, it reflects a collective inability on the part of these institutions to operate effectively on the ground in their respective situation countries. At the ICC, difficulties arising from the general lack of effective access to situation countries are compounded by uneven levels of situation-specific expertise within an investigation division which is ostensibly responsible for the entire world.

### 19.4.2. Donor Fatigue[25]

International(ised) judicial institutions cost enormous sums of money to establish and maintain. The United Nations *ad hoc* Tribunals for Rwanda and the former Yugoslavia, which have now been rolled into the MICT, expended roughly USD 1,000,000,000 and USD 2,000,000,000 during their respective lifespans.[26] What is more, the States Parties to the Rome Statute have contributed in excess of EUR 1,300,000,000 to the ICC since 2002. The 2018 budget of the STL was set at EUR 58,800,000, with substantial annual expenditures having been witnessed since 2009 – with (as noted above) no convictions having yet been registered; the 2017-2018 budget of the Kosovo Tribunal, which has not issued a single indictment, accounted for EUR 41,314,000.[27] Whether expenditures of this magnitude constitute – in the parlance of modern governmental bureaucracy – value for money, is a question about which reasonable persons might disagree.

Interviewed by a Canadian journalist in early-2015, the ICC chief Prosecutor, Ms. Fatou Bensouda, was adamant that the OTP annual budget, which then stood at EUR 39,612,600, was insufficient. For the same

---

[24] A third challenge, specific to the ICC, is that the Rules of Procedure and Evidence create considerable difficulties for investigators seeking to entreat effectively with insider witnesses who, whilst not targets for prosecution, are likely to have themselves perpetrated offences enumerated in the Rome Statute.

[25] For an examination of the link between State donors and international courts and tribunals, see Sara Kendall, "Donors' Justice: Recasting International Criminal Accountability", in *Leiden Journal of International* Law, 2011, vol. 24, no. 3, pp. 585–606.

[26] These figures are taken from Gordon N. Bardos, "Trials and Tribulations: Politics as Justice at the ICTY", in *World Affairs Journal*, 2013, vol. 179, no. 3.

[27] Special Tribunal for Lebanon, Ninth Annual Report (2017-2018) (https://www.legal-tools.org/doc/1a1fad); Kosovo Specialist Chambers and Specialist Prosecutor's Office, "First Report", 2018 (https://legal-tools.org/doc/wpvp2r).

story in which Ms. Bensouda was cited, the Canadian Department of Foreign Affairs issued a statement noting that "Canada is concerned about the rate of growth of the ICC budget and […] continue[s] to monitor the finances of the ICC".[28] In private conversations, at least with the author of this chapter, public servants in States which have proffered enormous financial as well as moral support to international(ised) criminal justice since 1993 have been scathing in their criticism of the financial cost of both the ICC and the MICT. These same public servants have noted, in more than one instance, that the appetite for the provision of monetary support to new courts and tribunals – including those for which formal provision has already been made (that is, in the Central African Republic and South Sudan) – will remain severely limited for the foreseeable future. It has already been noted elsewhere in this chapter that States well disposed towards the IIIM began to express concerns as early as late-2018 regarding the output of that body relative to its rapidly growing budgetary projections.

Donor fatigue cannot be measured quantitatively until funding to a given institution is cut – although, as noted above, donor-State disquiet with the overall spending levels of the ICC, the MICT and other public-international organisations is becoming more vocal. However, it must be conceded that where there are calls for the establishment of new institutions to uphold international criminal and humanitarian law, the financial cost of such bodies is rarely the only consideration informing decisions regarding the provision of State support. For instance, the insufficiency of State backing for, say, the establishment of a hybrid body to address the egregious core international crimes being perpetrated in Syria must be seen in part in the context of ongoing diplomatic discussions in which peace and justice are not infrequently perceived to be mutually exclusive objectives. What, though, of the proposed judicial institutions to deal with international offences allegedly perpetrated in South Sudan and the Central African Republic during the ongoing conflicts in those States, where the geo-political stakes are minimal from the perspective of Western self-interest? Both of these institutions are largely bereft of funding.

Whilst national interests have always informed the willingness of States to contribute to international(ised) judicial mechanisms, only the

---

28   Mark MacKinnon, "ICC chief prosecutor fights to prove the institution's worth", in *The Globe and Mail*, 6 February 2015 (available on its web site).

most cynical would claim that generous donations to such bodies from, for instance, the Netherlands, Canada, Germany, Japan and Sweden have been driven purely by Machiavellian considerations. The financial support of these particular donors, and a great many others, has clearly been influenced at least in part by a belief in governing circles in the benefits of the rule of international law. That faith is certainly still in evidence if the creation of the IIIM is indicative, if one considers the considerable number of politico-diplomatic reservations wholly unrelated to Syria which were expressed privately by Western diplomats in New York when the idea of establishing a criminal-investigative body through the UNGA was first mooted.[29] Adherence to the principles of international law and international criminal justice remains strong within (most) States, though there are increasing limits to that for which the international community is prepared to pay in light of what is widely perceived by diplomats as excessive spending relative to output by the judicial institutions established since 1993. What the States covering the bulk of the international justice-sector budgets are demanding is not less international(ised) justice. What they want to see is more value for money; and, if the system of international(ised) criminal justice is to survive and concomitantly make a meaningful contribution to the fight against impunity, those charged with the practice and – if one will – management of international criminal and humanitarian law, would do well to grasp with alacrity any and all means of assuaging donor-State financial concerns before international(ised) criminal justice erodes further in the face of donor fatigue.

It is currently fashionable for the friends of international criminal justice to blame certain States (for example, Russia) for the weakening of the mechanisms of accountability for those alleged to have perpetrated core international crimes. Such criticisms are not misplaced. However, it is likewise time that those charged with the day-to-day care of international criminal justice give a good deal more thought to their own role in calling its future into question after a quarter century of profligate spending which has been coupled frequently with an insufficiency of creative thinking by international investigations and prosecutors.

---

[29]  See *supra* note 6.

### 19.4.3. The Impatience of Conflict-Affected Societies

Domestic as well as international prosecutions of alleged perpetrators of core international crimes follow what are invariably drawn-out investigations. The length of international(ised) criminal investigations is invariably a function of resource limitations, the complexity of cases involving high-level suspects and the difficulties which arise where evidence must be secured within physically-dangerous (to the investigators) environments. At the same time, conflict-affected societies show a marked preference for cases to be brought with a despatch that is arguably unrealistic, most especially given the current configuration and practices of the international(ised) criminal-investigative system. In the event, the pace of prosecution case-building must be enhanced significantly, not least to avoid the increasing risk that conflict-affected societies will withdraw their consent for international(ised) criminal justice. On the face of it, such consent is irrelevant to criminal justice where the latter is viewed through a narrow, legal-positivist lens. However, the voices of victim groups have an important bearing upon the policy and funding decisions of the States which push and finance the prosecution of core international crimes. A recent case in point is the exercise of ICC jurisdiction in Myanmar along with the establishment of the IIMM.

Whilst ascertaining the needs of conflict-affected societies, and victims in particular, is a notoriously difficult task – not least as the hopes invested in (and understanding of) criminal justice mechanisms will invariably differ between individuals – there is a growing body of literature which argues that international(ised) criminal justice constitutes a highly-imperfect vehicle for anything beyond the determination of the culpability in law of the accused.[30] To take but one example, the scholarship assessing societal attitudes to international(ised) criminal justice arising out of the conflict in Bosnia-Herzegovina is particularly voluminous. This literature is likewise homogeneous in its finding that Bosnian society, irrespective of the side of the conflict with which any given sub-group identifies, has been disappointed with the outcome of the relevant criminal justice processes, in no small measure because the societal expectations invested in the ICTY, the MICT and the relevant domestic courts have

---

[30] See, for instance, Mina Rauschenbach and Damien Scalia, "Victims and International Criminal Justice: A Vexed Question?", in *International Review of the Red Cross*, 2008, vol. 90, no. 870, pp. 441–459.

proven to be wholly inconsistent with the restorative capability of criminal justice mechanisms.[31]

One of the principal changes in international criminal justice between its post-Second World War and modern (that is, from 1993) applications is the manner in which the emergence of human rights advocacy has sought to place victimisation at the centre of international(ised) criminal justice processes. The place afforded to self-identified victims and their representatives stands in marked contrast to the more immediate post-1945 phase of international criminal justice. More specifically, the post-war experiment focused upon the criminal culpability of individuals accused within the broader context of a principle, held by the States which had prevailed militarily over Germany and Japan, that there should be no impunity for those most responsible for the heinous offences which had offended the conscience of humanity. The belief that the fight against impunity lies at the centre of international(ised) criminal justice in the post-1993 era remains, though in practice a great deal of difficulty has been experienced in reconciling this objective with the desire, championed in the main by civil society groups which profess to speak for wider conflict-affected constituencies, that international(ised) criminal courts should concomitantly afford a voice to the *prima facie* victims of whatever allegations are being considered.

The wisdom and practicality of putting something as difficult to define as the interests of victims at the centre of complex trials concerned with the criminal culpability of alleged high-level perpetrators is best considered in a different forum. The salient point to be made here is that, at the ICC and elsewhere, efforts to incorporate victims into criminal justice processes, in the belief that harnessing criminal justice to these ends will serve broad transitional-justice objectives geared towards the amelioration of social tensions, have proved to be unsatisfactory for a critical majority of victims as well as international criminal and humanitarian law practitioners.[32] In and of itself, victim representation in criminal trials, as it has been exercised to date, would presumably not be a concern were it possi-

---

[31] See, for instance, Diane Orentlicher, *That Someone Guilty be Punished: The Impact of the ICTY in Bosnia*, Open Society Institute, New York, 2010.

[32] For a critical study of victim participation at the ICC, see Stephen Smith Cody, Eric Stover, Mychelle Balthazard and Alexa Koenig, *The Victims' Court? A study of 622 Victim Participants at the International Criminal Court*, Human Rights Center, University of California, Berkeley School of Law, 2015.

ble to characterise the attempts to meld restorative and criminal justice as well-meaning experiments which have come up short. In the event, international-criminal and restorative justice has become confused in the popular mind, not least in conflict-affected societies, thanks in no small measure to human rights advocacy efforts. Civil society arguments to the effect that conflict-affected populations enjoy 'ownership' of, in particular, the ICC – a conceit encouraged by elements of the Court – are ubiquitous. The alleged failure of public institutions to incorporate victim concerns into prosecutorial processes to the satisfaction of victim constituencies is, despite enormous expenditures of resources to this end, serving to call into question the efficient functioning of international(ised) criminal justice as a whole; what ought to be the core purpose of criminal justice – symbolic prosecutions in accordance with the highest standards of due process in order to signal the absence of impunity – is being lost in a cacophony which holds that the system of international(ised) criminal justice is failing because the voices of victims are not being heard. The latter assertion may or may not be true. The problem facing international criminal justice at the present time is that this charge is perceived to be factually correct within important donor States; and, until such time as criminal justice is brought into harmony with broader transitional-justice mechanisms, one of the key (and perfectly legitimate) complaints of victims and their representatives – that the pace at which international criminal justice runs its course is too slow – needs to be addressed. The view taken here that the engagement of civil society in investigative (rather than prosecutorial) processes, through the devolution to the private domain where possible of certain evidence-collection activities, can only help to ameliorate certain of the complaints made by conflict-affected societies to the effect that their voices are not being heard within the criminal justice realm.

### 19.4.4. The Contribution of Civil Society to International Criminal Investigations[33]

The ICC-OTP started to build the Investigations Division in 2003; the first investigator commenced work in October of that year.[34] As hiring continued apace through 2004, Human Rights First, a civil society group based in New York, prepared a discussion paper for the ICC-ASP which examined the contribution which human rights NGOs might make to ICC-OTP investigations.[35] The paper was bold in asserting that there was a role which civil society groups could play in ICC investigations. Particularly novel was the suggestion, advanced somewhat tentatively, that each investigation might see one OTP official designated as a NGO liaison officer, tasked with responsibility for communicating with civil society groups which "have already documented violations". At the same time, the document evinced a degree of naivety with respect to the structure of international criminal investigations and prosecutions, in particular insofar as it focussed exclusively upon how NGOs might assist the OTP in developing crime bases. Nowhere in the paper was there recognition of the fact that the overwhelming bulk of investigative resources available to international criminal and humanitarian law investigations need to be put into the development of linkage evidence with an eye to establishing the individual criminal responsibility of high-level perpetrators.

*Crime base* and *linkage* are terms of art used by investigators and analysts to identify what those with a legal education would term (i) the physical elements of the offences (that is, crime base) and (ii) the mental elements of the offences along with the mental and material elements of the modes of liability (that is, linkage). Owing to the fact that international-criminal investigations rarely concern themselves with the physical au-

---

[33] The first scholarly considerations of the possibility that civil society groups might contribute to international criminal investigations took the form of Morten Bergsmo and William H. Wiley, "Human Rights Professionals and the Criminal Investigation and Prosecution of Core International Crimes", in Siri Skåre, Ingvild Burkey and Hege Mørk (eds.), *Manual on Human Rights Monitoring: An Introduction for Human Rights Field Officers*, Norwegian Centre for Human Rights, 2008 (First Edition, 1997); Elena Baylis, "Outsourcing investigations", in *UCLA Journal of International Law and Foreign Affairs*, 2009, vol. 14, pp. 121–149.

[34] The author of this chapter.

[35] "The Role of Human Rights NGOs in Relation to ICC Investigations, Discussion Paper for the Third Session of the ICC Assembly of States Parties", Human Rights First, September 2004.

thors of crime bases, the collection of linkage information, and its transformation into evidence through analytical processes undertaken in the context of the applicable substantive law, will invariably consume upwards of 90 per cent of the human and material resources expended during a properly-conducted, complex investigation. The principal sources of linkage information of evidential quality are not victims and others drawn from the social milieu of such unfortunates; to suggest otherwise, as remains too often the case in the reports of human rights defenders, is to display considerable ignorance of international-criminal, investigative practice which is rooted in the legal requirements of the modes of liability set out in international criminal and humanitarian law. Far and away the most important form of information and evidence in a complex international case is documentation generated contemporaneously by the party (or parties) to the offences, for instance, the reports, returns and directives of armed groups, security-intelligence agencies and the like. Where witness testimony is required, it ought to be collected to fill gaps in the documentary record – and only after careful analysis of the latter. To build a linkage case upon oral testimony, in particular that taken from crime-base witnesses, is the insufficient response of the inexperienced and unimaginative to the necessity of establishing individual criminal responsibility. Rather, linkage witnesses are invariably drawn from perpetrating organisations and the ranks of the fellow travellers of suspected perpetrators. Unsurprisingly, individuals of such pedigree are almost without exception of the view that there is no benefit to them in offering prosecution investigators full or otherwise truthful disclosure. For these and other reasons, the effective handling of linkage witnesses is a matter of considerable learned skill rarely acquired during the course of a career by anyone save a minority of police and intelligence officers. Unsurprisingly, given their focus on the human rights of victims, expressed through oftentimes very skilful public advocacy, human rights NGOs are not well equipped to deal with the legal requirements of building linkage cases.

Civil society groups made no discernible contribution to the investigations undertaken by the United Nations *ad hoc* tribunals, save where the forensic sciences were applied, although human rights advocates did, on occasion, testify at trial. Likewise, during the formative years of the ICC-OTP, the practical contribution of human rights groups to the building of prosecution cases was limited. Individual (that is, unaffiliated) activists were certainly utilised from time to time with positive effect, most especially in the eastern Democratic Republic of the Congo, where in several cases free agents of this nature, working under the *de facto* direction of experienced ICC investigators who covered out-of-pocket expenses, found caches of documentation generated by individuals and organisations which proved to be of particular lead and, later, evidentiary value. The practical contribution, if any, of international NGOs as well as local groups – the latter being very often regarded by OTP investigators as little more than proxies of the international organisations – did not extend beyond the provision of assistance in establishing *prima facie* crime bases. The view in some quarters of the ICC-OTP Investigation Division – or at any rate, the view of the author of this chapter – was that several international NGOs were demanding swift criminal justice in the service of their fund-raising strategies. In practice, these same groups were providing the OTP with little if anything in the way of useful information, evidently for fear of compromising their neutrality as advocacy groups. A notable exception to the aforementioned approach was that of the International Federation for Human Rights which sought, within the limits of its resources, to provide such crime base support as it could to OTP personnel engaged in a variety of investigations.

The early-DRC and Uganda files were mainly developed during the short tenure of Deputy Prosecutor Dr. Serge Brammertz, who oversaw the ICC Investigations Division until January 2006. They were built in keeping with best investigative practices developed, most especially, at the ICTY, but without meaningful assistance from human rights NGOs. Increasingly from 2006, the then chief Prosecutor sought arrest warrants and the confirmation of charges not on the basis of sound OTP investigative output, but on the basis of inquiries undertaken quite independently of the OTP by third parties, principally NGOs and institutional actors, with the latter generally being linked to the United Nations human-rights infrastructure. The problem with this approach, which has been much remarked upon unfavourably by various chambers of the ICC – and for which the third-party actors were in no way themselves responsible – is that the investigative work of NGOs and UN human-rights offices is undertaken for reasons of advocacy rather than with an eye to the evidentiary standards which inform criminal courts.

It cannot be stated with absolute certainty what motivated Mr. Moreno-Ocampo, given the strength of his Investigations Division, to put his prosecutors at the mercy of the findings of non-criminal investigators working to standards of proof quite different from those of criminal courts. His objective would appear to have been to secure arrest warrants with minimal effort in the belief that, once a suspect had been arrested, sufficient time would become available to the OTP to prepare properly for committal proceedings. In practice, upon the appearance of a given suspect in The Hague, the OTP proved itself to be unable to prepare properly (or at any rate, efficiently) for committal proceedings – let alone trial – owing to the growing cadre of investigators, analysts and prosecutors who were compelled by the then-chief Prosecutor to employ, invariably with considerable professional unease, investigative *modus operandi* and accompanying legal arguments which could be foreseen as being unlikely to produce the sort of evidence and well-reasoned pleadings expected by the ICC pre-trial and trial chambers. Whatever the motivation of the first chief Prosecutor, the vacuity of the arrest-now-investigate-later approach reached its nadir in *Mbarushimana*, where the pre-trial chamber observed, among other things, that certain OTP allegations were unaccompanied by any evidence whatsoever, despite the accused having languished in pre-trial detention for roughly one year.[36] The earlier pre-trial chamber decision in *Abu Garda*, which likewise rejected all of the prosecution charges against the accused, ought to have served notice to the OTP that its reliance upon third-party materials was inadequate for the purposes of committing suspects to trial. Particularly telling in *Abu Garda* was a remark made by Judge Tarfusser in a concurring opinion which noted "the Prosecutor's failure to establish a proper connection between a given event and a given individual".[37] Rephrased using international-investigative vernacular, the case against *Abu Garda* collapsed because the prosecution had failed to present sufficient linkage evidence, that is, evidence tying the accused to the underlying criminal acts. In other cases – most notably *Kenyatta* – the second chief Prosecutor, Ms. Bensouda, took the decision to withdraw all of the OTP allegations at the pre-trial stage, perhaps in part to avoid further humiliation at the hands of ICC judges. One can sympathise with the position in which she found herself placed by her predecessor.

---

[36] *Prosecutor v. Callixte Mbarushimana*, see *supra* note 19.

[37] *Prosecutor v. Bahr Idriss Abu Garda*, p. 101, see *supra* note 19.

### 19.5. A Way Forward for International(ised) Criminal Investigations: The CIJA Model

There are a number of challenges facing public-sector institutions charged with the investigation of core international crimes. Frequently, these obstacles prove to be intractable where public organs are left to rely solely upon their own resources, most especially where there is a need to secure evidence in conflict zones or from otherwise highly-unstable environments. Politico-diplomatic, physical-risk and resource limitations invariably bedevil case building efforts and, where arrests are nonetheless effected, successful prosecutions. CIJA was founded with an intimate understanding of such problems and designed, from the start, to support public authorities in their resolution.

Given that CIJA and its public partners are guided equally by substantive and procedural law, the approach of CIJA to its field collection, analytical and legal work is not extensively different from that which public institutions would take, were they to enjoy the sort of freedom of action available to CIJA. Whilst necessarily adjusted to account for the prevailing logistical and security conditions in any given field environment, CIJA investigations conform to a certain generic standard. Guided by substantive and procedural law, this standard has been designed with an eye to simplicity as well as the prospects for its replication by organisations possessed of limited financial resources though otherwise equipped with the necessary degree of technical expertise and physical-risk tolerance. This methodology is characterised as the CIJA model.

### 19.5.1. Origins and Operational Areas

CIJA was founded in May 2012 as the Syrian Commission for Justice and Accountability ('SCJA'). The SCJA itself grew out of a small project, funded by the United Kingdom Foreign and Commonwealth Office during 2011-2012, in which several dozen Syrian activists were sensitised to the types of information and evidence which inform international-criminal investigations. The undertaking was executed under the tutelage of a handful of mentors with long service in various international prosecution and investigation divisions who would later form the initial international nucleus of the SCJA. Notwithstanding the fact that the personnel receiving the aforementioned training were operating in the midst of a high-intensity armed conflict, they straightaway showed promise as collectors of information with *prima facie* evidentiary value. The recognition by the international mentors of the Syrian potential, coupled with their conclusion that the engagement of an international court or tribunal was unrealistic at that juncture for a range of politico-diplomatic reasons, gave rise to thinking on the part of the project lead – the author of this chapter – that criminal investigations to the highest standards might nonetheless be launched *vis-à-vis* the Syrian regime through a non-public vehicle. This line of thinking gave rise to the SCJA/CIJA in its initial incarnation and built upon an idea explored in a scholarly paper co-authored by the project leader several years earlier.[38]

The initial SCJA concept paper envisioned the establishment of the individual criminal responsibility of high-level perpetrators, the deferral of most crime-base building to a later date and the passage of the resulting case briefs as well as supporting evidence to investigative and prosecutorial authorities in the public domain at such time as the latter found themselves in a position to exercise jurisdiction over persons alleged to have perpetrated offences of international criminal and humanitarian law in Syria. The only checks on the transfer of data from the SCJA to public authorities envisioned at the start were that (i) the justice systems in question would need to offer accused persons due-process guarantees which met international human rights standards and (ii) the SCJA would at no time support criminal prosecutions which might lead to the award of capital sentences. Eight years later, these objectives and principles remain the foundation upon which CIJA stands, notwithstanding the subsequent engagement of CIJA in several conflicts other than the war in Syria and some expansion of what might be termed the service offerings of the organisation.

SCJA fundraising efforts commenced in early-2012; and, whilst donors other than the United Kingdom were initially cool to the concept of a private (albeit not-for-profit) criminal-investigative body (despite the enthusiast support of Mr. Stephen Rapp, the then-United States Ambassador for Global Criminal Justice), from mid-2013 the SCJA started to receive substantial financial support from several Western States, along with the European Union. The SCJA grew quickly from 2013 and, within two years, the SCJA-*cum*-CIJA found itself operating in the midst of two armed conflicts with an annual budget of roughly EUR 6,000,000 – monies sufficient to retain (from 2015) roughly 150 analysts, counsel and field

---

[38] Bergsmo and Wiley, 2008, see *supra* note 33.

investigators to handle all CIJA operations in Syria and Iraq. With the emergence of the IIIM and UNITAD, CIJA envisions scaling down its operations in and around these States as it gravitates towards new situations in North Africa, sub-Saharan Africa and South Asia. As the public-sector response to the perpetration of core international crimes in Syria and Iraq assumes a certain efficiency, CIJA shall redirect its expertise towards new (to CIJA) wars, to which the system of international(ised) criminal justice is not yet sufficiently structured to respond. Indeed, this evolution of the CIJA focus commenced during 2018.

### 19.5.2. Mandate, Objectives and Operational Partners

CIJA undertakes its work independently of the sectarian, ethnic and confessional prejudices which invariably serve to fuel the sorts of conflicts amidst which CIJA engages. Operating as it does with public monies, CIJA sees itself as a servant of those domestic as well as international institutions which, properly and in law, are ultimately responsible for fighting impunity through criminal-prosecutorial processes. The mandate of CIJA is derived from, and its operational plans are agreed annually with, the CIJA donors.[39] Simply, CIJA puts forth a workplan every 12 months and the donors decide, individually, whether they wish to support it. Whereas by convention the donors cannot and do not interfere in either operational or staffing matters, they are perfectly free to cease funding CIJA as they see fit, not least in response to CIJA ineptitude or irrelevance.

The CIJA leadership is aware that it is vulnerable to reproach, which has very occasionally been directed at it by international human rights groups, that it might undertake only the investigations targeting structures (for instance, the Syrian regime) to which its donor States and the European Union are opposed as a matter of policy or otherwise find distasteful. There is certainly some truth to such arguments to the extent that it is inconceivable that CIJA would be funded by a donor to investigate, say, allegations that its State forces, or those of an ally, perpetrated offences of international criminal and humanitarian law during a given military campaign; and, as CIJA does not have a trust fund upon which to draw, nor private monies save, on occasion, a relatively small outlay of Open Society Justice Initiative (that is, Soros) funding, CIJA donors could effectively block any CIJA initiative of which they do not approve simply

---

[39] CIJA has received funding over the years from Canada, Denmark, the European Union, Germany, Norway, Switzerland, the United Kingdom and the United States.

by declining to fund it. The ethical salvation for CIJA, in recognising as much, is that it is committed to never being instrumentalised by donors, that is, taking instruction from a donor or donors regarding which individuals or groups to investigate.[40]

It must also be observed that it is not for CIJA, as but one civil society actor, to take it upon itself to investigate every alleged instance of egregious criminal wrongdoing by the agents of a given State or non-State actor. Where CIJA has not engaged in a particular situation or investigated a given group, for whatever reason, there is nothing stopping an NGO from so doing *to criminal-prosecutorial standards*, where it has the financial means secured from public or non-public sources. For instance, CIJA has never made any secret of the fact that it collaborates to criminal-investigative ends with a number of armed opposition groups in Syria as well as with federal and Kurdistan Region forces in Iraq. The collection in the field of *prima facie* evidence in quantities sufficient to support criminal investigations demands as much. Put another way, these relationships are driven by a pragmatic acceptance on the part of CIJA that, without these partnerships, the investigation of Da'esh and Syrian regime criminality would scarcely be feasible by CIJA or any other body, public or private. However, there is nothing stopping, by way of example, Human Rights Watch or Amnesty International from applying their considerable financial resources to the investigation of these belligerent parties, or any other, in accordance with evidentiary standards consistent with the needs of international(ised) criminal justice. The fact of the matter is that no criminal-investigative body, public or private, is going to find itself in a position to work effectively in the midst of conflict zones where it attempts to take on all, or most, of the belligerent parties. Such an approach is feasible, if only just, where a public institution, ideally armed with a Chapter VII mandate, engages in a post-conflict situation.

Donor criticisms of the performance of CIJA have not been witnessed to date and are not anticipated. There are more checks and balances weighing upon CIJA – not least where the quality of its output is concerned – than there are constraining the senior leadership of an international court or tribunal. That noted, donors do not in every case renew

---

40 CIJA has never opened an investigation at the bequest of a State or the European Union; rather, it is CIJA practice to identify situations in which CIJA engagement would be useful to law-enforcement and prosecutorial authorities with, in turn, CIJA approaching donors for the necessary funds.

their support for CIJA. For instance, in 2016 a theretofore generous donor to CIJA determined – or rather, the then foreign minister decided – that CIJA-led criminal investigations, which by then had come to encompass the uppermost leadership of the Syrian regime, constituted a threat to on-going peace negotiations, taking place in Geneva and elsewhere. CIJA was duly informed that no more monies would be forthcoming from the State in question. As it turned out, a cacophony of media and political pro-test was engendered by this pronouncement – somewhat to the surprise of CIJA, which had made no complaint regarding the political decision – leading to a renewal of the earlier funding arrangement. Similarly, Swit-zerland withdrew its financial support to CIJA several years ago on the grounds that the provision of Swiss public monies to criminal investiga-tions in Syria was incompatible with the role played by Switzerland as a host of the aforementioned peace talks.

Despite the ebb and flow of specific-donor support, CIJA has not to date (that is, early-2019) found itself with insufficient monies to execute its annual operational plans. The initial and overriding objective of CIJA field operations remains the securing of sufficient evidence upon which its analysts and counsel might build case-files for international prosecution. Taking international criminal and humanitarian law as its starting point, CIJA cases are summarised in textual form, encompassing both factual and legal analyses. These documents are known internally as pre-trial briefs and conform, in practice, to the format which prevails in interna-tional offices of the prosecutor. The first CIJA investigative cycle in Syria ran for slightly in excess of one year, leading to the completion of three case files, encompassing 24 high level accused, principally security-intelligence officers and members of the *de facto* Syrian regime war cabi-net, including the President of Syria, Bashar Al Assad. The second Syrian regime investigative cycle, which lasted one year, produced multiple ac-cused cases built upon the conduct of hostilities by the regime in Homs Governorate as well as a file examining the role of economic actors in providing support of a criminal nature to the regime. The Homs investiga-tion served as the foundation for the provision of CIJA evidentiary sup-port to a civil case brought in United States Federal Court by the family of the Anglo-American journalist, Marie Colvin, killed in a targeted rocket attack in Homs in February 2012. The CIJA submissions, including an expert-witness brief, proved decisive in the decision of the presiding judge to award the family of Ms. Colvin in excess of USD 300,000,000 to be recovered from the Syrian State as well as President Al Assad and his brother Maher.[41]

CIJA operations *vis-à-vis* the Islamic State commenced in Syria in early-2014 and were extended to Iraqi territory roughly one year later. Several substantial Da'esh-specific prosecution briefs have been completed in the interim. Since being afforded sufficient monies in mid-2013 to build an analytical capacity atop the field collection operations which commenced in 2011, CIJA has produced a total of 16 substantial cases – 10 Syrian regime and 6 Islamic State files – which, to the extent possible in the absence of a court or tribunal to submit them to, are prosecution-ready. In terms of total volume, the briefs taken together run to several thousand closely-argued pages with supporting evidence and jurisprudence referenced in extensive footnotes. Additionally, the briefs set out the individual criminal responsibility of several dozen members of the high- and highest-ranking Syrian regime and Islamic State political, military and security-intelligence leadership. Overall, CIJA expenditures from 2011 through 2018, during which the aforementioned cases were built and a great deal other work undertaken besides, were roughly EUR 24,000,000. Although this figure constitutes a significant sum in the view of CIJA, its advisors and its donors, it can be viewed favourably in the context of the volume, quality and speed of the output of CIJA.

Whilst to date CIJA has engaged in conflicts where there is an international-jurisdictional vacuum – to whit, neither the ICC nor any other international court or tribunal has yet been afforded jurisdiction over the ongoing perpetration of core international crimes in Syria and Iraq – CIJA began to work closely with a host of domestic law-enforcement institutions from 2015. The logic informing the provision of support to domestic actors was and remains tied to the continuing absence of any near-term prospect for international trials relating to the perpetration of core international crimes in Syria, since 2011, and in Iraq, since 2014. A further explanation for CIJA engagement with domestic authorities has been the significant number of persons of interest who have fled westwards from Iraq and indeed Syria during recent years, for the most part hidden amongst the ranks of asylum seekers moving into the European Union from Turkey.

---

[41] United States District Court for the District of Columbia, *Cathleen Colvin, et al., v. Syrian Arab Republic*, Amended Memorandum Opinion, 30 January 2019.

Domestic actors warmed quickly to the CIJA model, not least because of the high quality of the CIJA evidence holdings but also given the resource and physical-risk limitations faced by national authorities confronted with the need to secure evidence from Syria and Iraq. Likewise, attractive to the domestic partners, was and remains the fact that CIJA, as a non-profit, supports all public authorities at no cost, to the extent that it is funded by its donors sufficiently to do so. What is more, CIJA proffers assistance to public institutions without reference to whether or not those institutions fall under the authority of a State which is providing monies to CIJA.

Since 2014, CIJA has worked with officials in a total of 13 States, principally European and North American; the domestic partners have, for the most part, been national war-crimes programmes and asylum-screening offices. During 2018, domestic law-enforcement partners submitted 128 requests for assistance ('RFAs') to CIJA, involving more than 500 suspects.[42] During the period of October 2016 (when CIJA first began to compile RFA-related statistics) through February 2019, CIJA received a total of 221 RFAs. Further growth in this respect is expected, with delegations of domestic police officers and prosecutors finding their way to CIJA headquarters, on average, every second week. By way of contrast, since its formal establishment in December 2016, the IIIM has received 14 RFAs.[43]

Whilst the number of arrests effected by domestic authorities on the basis, for the most part, of CIJA evidence is not yet commensurate with the volume of RFAs received from its national partners, there have to date been several successes of note. For instance, during 2018 a group of Syrian nationals who had served with Da'esh and were suspected by CIJA of remaining on an operational footing in Europe, were detained by German authorities on the basis of CIJA information and evidence, which the Germans were no doubt careful to corroborate to the greatest extent pos-

---

[42] Of the 128 RFAs received by CIJA from domestic authorities during 2018, 87 constituted new requests and 41 followed upon RFAs submitted (and responded to) prior to that year. Forty of the 2018 requests concerned Islamic State structures and individuals; eighty-eight focused upon the Syrian regime and its alleged adherents.

[43] Report of the International, Impartial and Independent Mechanism to Assist in the Investigation and Prosecution of Persons Responsible for the Most Serious Crimes under International Law Committed in the Syrian Arab Republic since March 2011, UNGA, seventy-third session, 13 February 2019, para. 6 (https://legal-tools.org/doc/8fgco9).

sible before executing the warrants of arrest. In this particular case, a CI-
JA field investigator was identified by the relevant public authorities as
the star witness and this individual has correspondingly been taken into a
witness-protection programme. The testimony of the said star witness,
along with that of the CIJA Executive Director, contributed to a finding of
criminal culpability and the award of a custodial sentence of eight years
for the only accused brought to trial, to date.[44] In a different case supported heavily by CIJA, three Syrian regime security-intelligence officers,
including one of particularly senior rank, were detained during a joint
Franco-German operation executed in February 2019.[45] The increasingly-
focused nature of certain of the RFAs which CIJA is receiving from European authorities as a whole, suggests strongly that additional arrests in
unrelated cases should be anticipated during 2019 and beyond.

Operational relationships have likewise been established with Europol and Interpol, the objectives of these organisations being, broadly
speaking, to populate their systems with primary-source data, most especially those relating to Islamic State structures and personnel. CIJA engagement with the federal authorities in Iraq, which is concerned solely
with the digitalisation and collation of the large volumes of captured
Da'esh materials held in various security-intelligence repositories in
Baghdad, is predicated in the first instance upon the objective of ensuring
the transmission of relevant data to the police-intelligence databases
maintained by these institutions. Secondly, the Baghdad initiative is designed to facilitate the prosecution of Da'esh personnel apprehended in
Europe and North America for (where the evidence warrants) the perpetration of core international crimes. At the present time, there is no jurisdiction anywhere in the world prosecuting Da'esh personnel for anything
other than the provision of material support to a terrorist organisation,
generally for lack of evidence to pursue any other prosecutorial course of
action. It is the view of CIJA that the prosecution of a selection of Da'esh
suspects for core international crimes would serve broader transitional-
justice objectives of interest to victims and, concomitantly, support indi-

---

[44] As of March 2019, the other suspects remain in custody, awaiting trial.

[45] Two of the three suspects in this particular case were known to CIJA, which had tracked
them to Europe from Syria, prior to the receipt of national RFAs concerning the individuals as well as the units in which they served. The Franco-German arrests following closely
upon CIJA disclosure of documentary evidence as well as witness testimony to the requesting authorities.

rectly counter-Da'esh recruitment initiatives by illustrating, through the introduction of crime base evidence, that the overwhelming majority of the victims of Da'esh criminality, most especially in Syria, have been Sunni Muslims. This truism, which is not brought to light through material-support prosecutions, insofar as the latter do not require crime-base evidence, is contrary to the Islamic State narrative that its victims are, in every case, non-believers.

CIJA entered into a Memorandum of Understanding with the IIIM in 2017 in order to facilitate the transfer of completed CIJA case files as well as the relevant CIJA evidentiary holdings to that body. Should it be desirous of so doing, the IIIM shall supplant nearly all CIJA functions relating to the war in Syria. The exception to this handover of responsibility shall be evidence collection in the field which, for politico-diplomatic reasons and owing to the intolerable levels of physical risk involved, the IIIM (nor any other public body) cannot take over. In light of the operationalisation of the IIIM, CIJA ceased case-building activities in Syria relating to the Syrian regime on 31 March 2019, with CIJA to maintain its field-collection capability, as just noted, as well as its ability to answer RFAs into the year 2020, by which time the IIIM should have sufficient analytical strength to handle such requests on its own. UNITAD, which for its part does not expect to be fully operational until the second half of 2019, shall continue to receive case-building and all other forms of CIJA support which it desires for the foreseeable future. Owing to the fact that UNITAD and the IIIM are determining how to divide responsibility for Da'esh criminality, CIJA shall continue to build Islamic State-specific case files relating to Da'esh criminality in Iraq as well as Syria through the first quarter of 2020.

In light of the fact that the international and domestic public sectors are coming to grips with the wars in Syria and Iraq as law-enforcement problems, CIJA has been free for some time to commence engagement in new conflicts where CIJA and its partners concur that the application of its model would be of use, that is, in North Africa, sub-Saharan Africa and South Asia. This evolution of the CIJA focus towards new (to CIJA) wars reflects the fact that the organisation is built upon highly-adaptable staffing and leadership structures; these are designed in no small part to ensure that CIJA engagement in any particular situation shall be of optimal service to the public-sector consumers of the CIJA product. In other words, CIJA is concerned with outcomes. It is the belief of the leadership that placing the emphasis of the organisation upon the efficient provision of services to its public-sector partners shall ensure the perpetuation of the model as long as there is a demonstrable need for the provision of support to public law-enforcement institutions through private means.

### 19.5.3. Investigative *Modus Operandi* and Evidentiary Base

The investigative *modus operandi* of CIJA, directed as it is towards the establishment of the individual criminal responsibility of higher- and highest-level perpetrators in the context of international criminal and humanitarian law, does not differ from the best practices established, through sometimes painful processes of trial and error, by the public institutions within which the senior CIJA leadership served for prolonged periods.[46]

The one area where CIJA investigations tend to differ from those undertaken by international(ised) courts and tribunals is in the width and depth of the crime base. Typically, international investigations, most especially those of the *ad hoc* tribunals, have been characterised by extremely wide crime bases, with a great many distinct incidences of criminality informing most prosecution indictments. If the crime base and linkage components of a typical ICTY case were put into graphic form, the shape would be something akin to a pyramid. For its part, CIJA starts from the premise that accused persons, if convicted at trial, will receive effectively the same sentence for the murder of 20 persons or two thousand. The organisation has always assessed that international as well as domestic prosecutors will, in due course, likely seek to expand the crime base in any given prosecution, where they assume control of a given CIJA case file. For this reason, and cognisant of its resource limitations as well as the need to complete prosecutable cases with relative despatch, CIJA seeks to build the widest possible linkage cases upon very narrow crime bases. Rendered in graphic form, the structure of a CIJA investigation would be something akin to a rhombus: the narrow point at the bottom constituting the crime base, moving upwards to the widest point, this representing

---

[46] Senior CIJA staff have been employed in, amongst other international(ised) institutions, national war-crimes units, the ICTY, the ICTR, the ICC, the UNIIIC-STL, the State Court in Sarajevo, the Special Court for Sierra Leone, the Extraordinary Chambers of the Courts of Cambodia, and the Iraqi High Tribunal. Most of the senior CIJA personnel started their careers in the field of international criminal and humanitarian law in the 1990s or early-2000s.

mid-level perpetrators whose criminal responsibility has been (or can be readily) demonstrated with the available evidence, to the peak of the rhombus, representing those most responsible for the offences. It is the latter category of suspects who receive the most attention from CIJA, once they have been identified through the careful analysis of the command, control and communications arrangements of the units and formations acting under their authority. That is to say, CIJA does not, as a matter of policy, undertake target-driven investigations on the grounds that such an approach raises considerable risks that exculpatory evidence will be overlooked. For their part, mid-level perpetrators are generally ignored by CIJA, save where information presents itself that they have made their way to Europe. In the event, the heavy emphasis which CIJA places upon the building of linkage cases renders the organisation particularly well suited to react quickly when mid-level perpetrators come onto its radar.

The principal form of evidence secured by CIJA constitutes materials – in the main, documentation – generated contemporaneously by the suspected perpetrating institutions, most especially, military and security-intelligence forces, be they allied with State or non-State bodies. Securing such information, rather than the establishment to criminal-law standards of a crime base, is the first priority in every CIJA investigation. For this reason, amongst others, CIJA has extracted from Syria roughly eight hundred thousand original pages of Syrian regime documentation – military, security-intelligence and Ba'ath Party records – through myriad acquisition and movement operations of considerable complexity and concomitant expense, owing not least to the fluidity of the confrontation lines in Syria and the need to move the paper, which together weighs in excess of three metric tons, across international borders. As noted above, CIJA has more recently started a process of digitalisation of what is expected to run to several million pages of Islamic State documents, held by various belligerent parties to the wars in Syria and Iraq. What CIJA will not do, where the Da'esh documentation is concerned, is take ownership of the same, though the organisation has long had its own so-called battlefield evidence collection capability within the Da'esh investigative team. This effort has borne considerable fruit since 2014.

Other forms of information of evidential value collected in large quantities by CIJA include open-source materials generated by perpetrators as well as the organisations in which they serve. Modern social media is a particularly rich seam for exploitation, for instance, YouTube, Twitter, Facebook, and Instagram. CIJA employs several open-source analysts who focus entirely on these platforms; the CIJA cyber team also oversees the extraction of data from captured computer hard drives and smartphones. Whilst information of this nature gives rise to unique authentication challenges, the multi-source collection and analysis effort which the Commission brings to bear when building its case files enables CIJA to authenticate cyber product through comparison with more traditional forms of information-*cum*-evidence, for instance, the several thousand witness interviews recorded to date by CIJA personnel – with a heavy focus upon insider witnesses – and documentation generated by perpetrating institutions.

### 19.5.4. Leadership and Oversight

The CIJA leadership is advised by a panel of independent professionals – the *ad hoc* Advisory Panel – who support CIJA on a *pro bono* basis, in particular, through the undertaking of periodical case-file reviews. Every Advisory Panel member has held a senior position in one or more of the international(ised) courts or tribunals as an investigator, analyst, trial lawyer, clerk in chambers or as defence counsel. Additionally, there is a Board of Commissioners, the establishment of which is mandated by the Dutch law which governs CIJA; it is chaired by Mr. Stephen Rapp, the long-time United States Ambassador for Global Criminal Justice and former chief Prosecutor of the Special Court for Sierra Leone. Additionally, the ranks of this board include Professor Alex Whiting, a former senior official at the ICC-OTP, and Professor Larry Johnson, erstwhile UN Assistant Secretary-General for Legal Affairs who also served as *Chef de cabinet* at the ICTY. Dr. Nawaf Obaid, an Adjunct Professor at Harvard with a specialisation in Middle East matters, and concomitant connections of importance to CIJA garnered during his own service as a diplomat, joined the board in 2018. Similarly serving *pro bono*, the Board of Commissioners along with the Advisory Panel members are the only persons not retained by CIJA, other than law-enforcement and prosecutorial authorities, with access to CIJA pre-trial briefs and related materials, including evidence.

Finally, CIJA has a Board of Directors. Likewise a legal requirement pursuant to Dutch law, this board is chaired by the CIJA Executive Director (the author of this chapter), who takes most decisions on a consensus basis with the two CIJA Directors, Ms. Nerma Jelačić (Management and External Relations) and Mr. Chris Engels (Operations and Investigations), both of whom have brought to CIJA substantial experience of international public service, not least secured through international courts and tribunals. Other senior CIJA personnel are, as noted above, drawn from the ranks of men and women who have served with distinction in the system of international criminal justice.[47]

### 19.5.5. Staffing and Professional Development

The salaries paid to CIJA international staff – analysts and counsel, in particular – are set by the foundation at competitive levels relative to public institutions whilst costing the organisation a fraction of the overall amounts afforded to international public servants of comparable rank and seniority. Cost savings are realised by CIJA through modest administration overheads, amounting to nine per cent of the annual budgets, and the absence of fringe benefits such as education grants for dependent children and pension credits. Field-investigator salaries vary between countries, in accordance with what we might refer to as market conditions, which they anyhow exceed; by way of a guide, Syria-based investigators are paid roughly USD 1,000 per month.[48] Iraqi salaries are somewhat higher, at approximately USD 2,000 per month for each investigator. It is the field-based investigators who absorb the considerable physical risks inherent in securing high-quality information of evidential value, and it hardly needs stating that the success of the CIJA model is, in the first instance, entirely dependent upon the capacity and work ethic of the deployed personnel. As such, a considerable investment is made in training, mentoring and equipping the field-investigative cadres; CIJA having spent several million USD to such ends since 2011.[49] The work of the men and women in Syria

---

[47] See *ibid*.

[48] At February 2018, CIJA retained roughly 40 investigators inside Syria, a number that was more or less consistent with the field complement first reached in 2012. These personnel are divided between a number of operational teams. A further 20 investigators have been operational in Iraq since early-2015.

[49] CIJA is well aware of its considerable moral and ethical responsibilities to its field personnel, most especially at the point that CIJA ceases to engage in a situation in which its investigators, who frequently become politically exposed by virtue of their work, are confronted by an intolerable level of physical risk, such that they cannot realistically be left at the mercy of a deteriorating political-military situation. This has been a recurring problem in Syria since 2014, and CIJA has long had contingency plans for the movement of its personnel out of harm's way in that State, which have been triggered regularly and with suc-

and Iraq is guided by headquarters-based analysts working seamlessly with legal counsel, with forward-deployed teams operating in States bordering Syria under the direction of internationals providing logistical, security and other forms of support. Whereas CIJA senior personnel have in every instance served in one or more of the international courts and tribunals (from which unsolicited *curricula vitae* are received routinely by the CIJA leadership), analysts (save those of more senior rank) are invariably selected on the basis of fluency in both Arabic and English, whereupon they are put through an intensive programme of on-the-job training. The result of this in-house, professional development programme is that the only concentration of Arabic-fluent, war-crimes analysts in the world is retained by CIJA. The language profile of the organisation will evolve as CIJA engages in additional conflicts, although a requirement for a high degree of Arabic fluency within the organisation is likely to last until 2023, if not beyond.

It is the experience of CIJA that it takes approximately one year of intensive training and mentoring to raise a new investigator and inexperienced analyst to a reasonable level of competence. Whilst the junior analysts have the benefit of working alongside senior counsel and seasoned analysts at CIJA headquarters, the field investigators are necessarily controlled from a distance. As such, still more time is generally required to reach the point at which newly-retained investigators can be relied upon to undertake consistently the competent interviewing of crime base and linkage witnesses. Within this context, significant financial and temporal investment has been made by CIJA in preparing, within the broader investigative ranks, specialists who deal with males and females who are believed to have been subjected to sexual offences. All CIJA interviews, whether they are led by Syrians, Iraqis or international personnel, are recorded in the third person, in order not to undermine unwittingly later prosecutorial efforts.[50]

---

cess since 2017. With respect to the broader discussion of the responsibility of international organisations to their local staff in a humanitarian-aid context, see Jonathan Corpus Ong and Pamela Combinido, "Local Aid Workers in the Digital Humanitarian Project: Between 'Second Class Citizens' and 'Entrepreneurial Survivors'", in *Critical Asian Studies*, 2018, vol. 50, no. 1, pp. 86–102.

[50] Recording interviews in the third person will render far more difficult future defence counsel efforts to find inconsistencies between statements taken by public officials and the reports compiled by CIJA personnel. Put another way, inconsistencies between formal state-

## 19.6. Concluding Remarks

International(ised) criminal justice is at a critical juncture: notwithstanding enormous financial expenditures, successful prosecutions are being brought at a pace which is regarded as deleterious by both donor States as well as conflict-affected communities. Whilst the leadership cadres of the remaining international offices of the prosecutor are arguably stronger than they have ever been, and a number of national war-crimes units have been significantly reinforced (for example, in Germany and France), there are limits to what the public institutions can achieve with the resources on hand, not least as these resources are often of limited use where an operational area presents a physical-risk profile to which public institutions alone cannot conform.

Surmounting these inevitable financial and physical-risk limitations requires creative approaches on the part of the public bodies – first and foremost, a willingness to work with private institutions which are agile, cost effective, marked by a high tolerance of physical risk and willing as well as sufficiently skilled to work to strict criminal-evidentiary standards. CIJA is the first (and still the only) organisation to structure itself with the sole objective of closing the gap between the evidence required for successful criminal prosecutions and the limitations weighing upon even the best-resourced public institutions where the latter set out to acquire such evidence without the assistance of external parties. It should be noted in this context that CIJA has not set out to monopolise the private, criminal-investigative sphere and, what is more, its structure and *modus operandi* are not regarded by CIJA as intellectual property. The CIJA model is there for public authorities to draw upon as they see fit and for non-governmental actors to replicate.

It is the experience of the CIJA, based upon its engagement over several years with a wide array of international(ised) law-enforcement and prosecutorial authorities, that its public sector partners are untroubled by the partial shift of responsibility for criminal justice to the private sector which is implied by the CIJA model. The public-sector partners of CIJA have put investigative and prosecutorial pragmatism ahead of the sort of reservations expressed occasionally by international human rights defend-

---

ments taken by public authorities and earlier interview reports compiled in the third person by CIJA personnel can always be ascribed by prosecutors to errors on the part of the CIJA personnel.

---

ers about such arrangements. It is the expectation of CIJA that these concerns will be voiced still less frequently as civil society engagement in the international(ised) criminal-investigative domain becomes more common – giving rise, in turn, to more international(ised) criminal justice. The alternative to private-sector participation is a further loss of the hard-won progress made since 1993 in the fight against impunity for core international crimes as a result of donor concerns regarding allegedly profligate public spending and the disquiet of civil societies with the slow pace of justice.

# INDEX

## A

Abrams, Elliot, 487
absorb facts, xvii
Abyssinia, 484
accountability, 2, 228, 343
actual and perceived independence, 60
*actus reus*, 369, 372, 379, 381, 385
*ad hoc* basis, 19
Additional Protocol I to the Geneva
  Conventions
  Article 79, 504
  Article 90, 3
Admiralty Code, 410
admission against interest, 492
Aeschylus, 444
Africa, 554
African Commission on Human and
  Peoples' Rights, 15
  Fact-Finding Mission to Zimbabwe, 35
African National Congress, 49, 51
African Union Fact-Finding Mission in
  Côte d'Ivoire, 40
African Union fact-finding team for
  Darfur, 38
Albanian National Liberation Army, 326
al-Samouni area of Zeytoun, 58
al-Samouni, Wa'el, 58
Alston, Philip, 244, 480, 493
America's Watch. *See* Human Rights
  Watch
*amicus curiae*, 69, 74
amnesty, 235, 237, 245
Amnesty International, 200, 426, 485, 554
  confidentiality, 482
  mission, 481
  trial observation, 482
ample grounds to conclude, 359
Angola, 16
Annan, Kofi, 53, 225, 389
anonymity, 234, 240, 252, 270, 271
anonymous witness testimony and
  statements, 239

anti-corruption commissions, 379
applicable law, 291, 348, 363
*Application of the Convention on the
  Prevention and Punishment of the
  Crime of Genocide (The Gambia v.
  Myanmar)*, vi, 543
Arab Organization for Human Rights, 16
arbitrary detention, 29
archive, xv
Argentina's Dirty War, 378
*Armed Activities on the Territory of the
  Congo (Democratic Republic of the
  Congo v. Uganda)*, v
Armed Police Force, 234
Armenian massacre, 483
Army of the Serb Republic of the Krajina,
  287
attitude of neutrality, 27
Auld, Robin, 480
authenticity of source, xi

## B

Bahrain, 16
Bahrain Independent Commission of
  Inquiry, 40
balance of probabilities, 432, 436
Banda, Hasting, 489
Bangladesh War of Liberation (1971), 378
Bassiouni, M. Cherif, 204, 223, 302, 410
Bayes, Reverend Thomas, 91
Bayesian epistemology, 85
  Bayes' Rule, 95
  Bayesian Network, 91, 93
  Bayesianism, 96
Becker, Michael A., vi
Beirut, 147
Beit Hanoun, 403
Belgium
  German invasion of, 483
Belgrade, 167
Belgrade Minimal Rules, 167, 209, 210,
  430

# P

# Q

# R

# TOAEP TEAM

# OTHER VOLUMES IN THE PUBLICATION SERIES

Morten Bergsmo, Mads Harlem and Nobuo Hayashi (editors):
Importing Core International Crimes into National Law
Torkel Opsahl Academic EPublisher
Oslo, 2010
FICHL Publication Series No. 1 (Second Edition, 2010)
ISBN: 978-82-93081-00-5

Nobuo Hayashi (editor):
National Military Manuals on the Law of Armed Conflict
Torkel Opsahl Academic EPublisher
Oslo, 2010
FICHL Publication Series No. 2 (Second Edition, 2010)
ISBN: 978-82-93081-02-9

Morten Bergsmo, Kjetil Helvig, Ilia Utmelidze and Gorana Žagovec:
The Backlog of Core International Crimes Case Files in Bosnia and Herzegovina
Torkel Opsahl Academic EPublisher
Oslo, 2010
FICHL Publication Series No. 3 (Second Edition, 2010)
ISBN: 978-82-93081-04-3

Morten Bergsmo (editor):
Criteria for Prioritizing and Selecting Core International Crimes Cases
Torkel Opsahl Academic EPublisher
Oslo, 2010
FICHL Publication Series No. 4 (Second Edition, 2010)
ISBN: 978-82-93081-06-7

Morten Bergsmo and Pablo Kalmanovitz (editors):
Law in Peace Negotiations
Torkel Opsahl Academic EPublisher
Oslo, 2010
FICHL Publication Series No. 5 (Second Edition, 2010)
ISBN: 978-82-93081-08-1

Morten Bergsmo, César Rodríguez Garavito, Pablo Kalmanovitz and Maria Paula Saffon (editors):
Distributive Justice in Transitions
Torkel Opsahl Academic EPublisher
Oslo, 2010
FICHL Publication Series No. 6 (2010)
ISBN: 978-82-93081-12-8

Morten Bergsmo, César Rodriguez-Garavito, Pablo Kalmanovitz and Maria Paula Saffon (editors):
Justicia Distributiva en Sociedades en Transición
Torkel Opsahl Academic EPublisher
Oslo, 2012
FICHL Publication Series No. 6 (2012)
ISBN: 978-82-93081-10-4

Morten Bergsmo (editor):
Complementarity and the Exercise of Universal Jurisdiction for Core International Crimes
Torkel Opsahl Academic EPublisher
Oslo, 2010
FICHL Publication Series No. 7 (2010)
ISBN: 978-82-93081-14-2

Morten Bergsmo (editor):
Active Complementarity: Legal Information Transfer
Torkel Opsahl Academic EPublisher
Oslo, 2011
FICHL Publication Series No. 8 (2011)
ISBN print: 978-82-93081-56-2
ISBN e-book: 978-82-93081-55-5

Morten Bergsmo (editor):
Abbreviated Criminal Procedures for Core International Crimes
Torkel Opsahl Academic EPublisher
Brussels, 2017
FICHL Publication Series No. 9 (2018)
ISBN print: 978-82-93081-20-3
ISBN e-book: 978-82-8348-104-4

Sam Muller, Stavros Zouridis, Morly Frishman and Laura Kistemaker (editors):
The Law of the Future and the Future of Law
Torkel Opsahl Academic EPublisher
Oslo, 2010
FICHL Publication Series No. 11 (2011)
ISBN: 978-82-93081-27-2

Morten Bergsmo, Alf Butenschøn Skre and Elisabeth J. Wood (editors):
Understanding and Proving International Sex Crimes
Torkel Opsahl Academic EPublisher
Beijing, 2012
FICHL Publication Series No. 12 (2012)
ISBN: 978-82-93081-29-6

Morten Bergsmo (editor):
Thematic Prosecution of International Sex Crimes
Torkel Opsahl Academic EPublisher
Beijing, 2012
FICHL Publication Series No. 13 (2012)
ISBN: 978-82-93081-31-9

Terje Einarsen:
The Concept of Universal Crimes in International Law
Torkel Opsahl Academic EPublisher
Oslo, 2012
FICHL Publication Series No. 14 (2012)
ISBN: 978-82-93081-33-3

莫滕·伯格斯默 凌岩(主编):
国家主权与国际刑法
Torkel Opsahl Academic EPublisher
Beijing, 2012
FICHL Publication Series No. 15 (2012)
ISBN: 978-82-93081-58-6

Morten Bergsmo and LING Yan (editors):
State Sovereignty and International Criminal Law
Torkel Opsahl Academic EPublisher
Beijing, 2012
FICHL Publication Series No. 15 (2012)
ISBN: 978-82-93081-35-7

Morten Bergsmo and CHEAH Wui Ling (editors):
Old Evidence and Core International Crimes
Torkel Opsahl Academic EPublisher
Beijing, 2012
FICHL Publication Series No. 16 (2012)
ISBN: 978-82-93081-60-9

YI Ping:
戦争と平和の間——発足期日本国際法学における「正しい戦争」の観念とその帰結
Torkel Opsahl Academic EPublisher
Beijing, 2013
FICHL Publication Series No. 17 (2013)
ISBN: 978-82-93081-66-1

Morten Bergsmo and SONG Tianying (editors):
On the Proposed Crimes Against Humanity Convention
Torkel Opsahl Academic EPublisher
Brussels, 2014
FICHL Publication Series No. 18 (2014)
ISBN: 978-82-93081-96-8

Morten Bergsmo, CHEAH Wui Ling and YI Ping (editors):
Historical Origins of International Criminal Law: Volume 1
Torkel Opsahl Academic EPublisher
Brussels, 2014
FICHL Publication Series No. 20 (2014)
ISBN: 978-82-93081-11-1

Morten Bergsmo, CHEAH Wui Ling and YI Ping (editors):
Historical Origins of International Criminal Law: Volume 2
Torkel Opsahl Academic EPublisher
Brussels, 2014
FICHL Publication Series No. 21 (2014)
ISBN: 978-82-93081-13-5

Morten Bergsmo, CHEAH Wui Ling, SONG Tianying and YI Ping (editors):
Historical Origins of International Criminal Law: Volume 3
Torkel Opsahl Academic EPublisher
Brussels, 2015
FICHL Publication Series No. 22 (2015)
ISBN print: 978-82-8348-015-3
ISBN e-book: 978-82-8348-014-6

Morten Bergsmo, CHEAH Wui Ling, SONG Tianying and YI Ping (editors):
Historical Origins of International Criminal Law: Volume 4
Torkel Opsahl Academic EPublisher
Brussels, 2015
FICHL Publication Series No. 23 (2015)
ISBN print: 978-82-8348-017-7
ISBN e-book: 978-82-8348-016-0

Morten Bergsmo, Klaus Rackwitz and SONG Tianying (editors):
Historical Origins of International Criminal Law: Volume 5
Torkel Opsahl Academic EPublisher
Brussels, 2017
FICHL Publication Series No. 24 (2017)
ISBN print: 978-82-8348-106-8
ISBN e-book: 978-82-8348-107-5

Morten Bergsmo and SONG Tianying (editors):
Military Self-Interest in Accountability for Core International Crimes
Torkel Opsahl Academic EPublisher
Brussels, 2015
FICHL Publication Series No. 25 (2015)
ISBN print: 978-82-93081-61-6
ISBN e-book: 978-82-93081-81-4

Wolfgang Kaleck:
Double Standards: International Criminal Law and the West
Torkel Opsahl Academic EPublisher
Brussels, 2015
FICHL Publication Series No. 26 (2015)
ISBN print: 978-82-93081-67-8
ISBN e-book: 978-82-93081-83-8

LIU Daqun and ZHANG Binxin (editors):
Historical War Crimes Trials in Asia
Torkel Opsahl Academic EPublisher
Brussels, 2016
FICHL Publication Series No. 27 (2015)
ISBN print: 978-82-8348-055-9
ISBN e-book: 978-82-8348-056-6

Mark Klamberg (editor):
Commentary on the Law of the International Criminal Court
Torkel Opsahl Academic EPublisher
Brussels, 2017
FICHL Publication Series No. 29 (2017)
ISBN print: 978-82-8348-100-6
ISBN e-book: 978-82-8348-101-3

Stian Nordengen Christensen:
Counterfactual History and Bosnia-Herzegovina
Torkel Opsahl Academic EPublisher
Brussels, 2018
Publication Series No. 30 (2018)
ISBN print: 978-82-8348-102-0
ISBN e-book: 978-82-8348-103-7

Stian Nordengen Christensen:
Possibilities and Impossibilities in a Contradictory Global Order
Torkel Opsahl Academic EPublisher
Brussels, 2018
Publication Series No. 31 (2018)
ISBN print: 978-82-8348-104-4
ISBN e-book: 978-82-8348-105-1

Morten Bergsmo and Carsten Stahn (editors):
Quality Control in Preliminary Examination: Volume 1
Torkel Opsahl Academic EPublisher
Brussels, 2018
Publication Series No. 32 (2018)
ISBN print: 978-82-8348-123-5
ISBN e-book: 978-82-8348-124-2

Morten Bergsmo and Carsten Stahn (editors):
Quality Control in Preliminary Examination: Volume 2
Torkel Opsahl Academic EPublisher
Brussels, 2018
Publication Series No. 33 (2018)
ISBN print: 978-82-8348-111-2
ISBN e-book: 978-82-8348-112-9

Morten Bergsmo and Emiliano J. Buis (editors):
Philosophical Foundations of International Criminal Law: Correlating Thinkers
Torkel Opsahl Academic EPublisher
Brussels, 2018
Publication Series No. 34 (2018)
ISBN print: 978-82-8348-117-4
ISBN e-book: 978-82-8348-118-1

Morten Bergsmo and Emiliano J. Buis (editors):
Philosophical Foundations of International Criminal Law: Foundational Concepts
Torkel Opsahl Academic EPublisher
Brussels, 2019
Publication Series No. 35 (2019)
ISBN print: 978-82-8348-119-8
ISBN e-book: 978-82-8348-120-4

Terje Einarsen and Joseph Rikhof:
A Theory of Punishable Participation in Universal Crimes
Torkel Opsahl Academic EPublisher
Brussels, 2018
Publication Series No. 37 (2018)
ISBN print: 978-82-8348-127-3
ISBN e-book: 978-82-8348-128-0

All volumes are freely available online at http://www.toaep.org/ps/. For printed copies, see http://www.toaep.org/about/distribution/. For reviews of earlier books in this Series in academic journals and yearbooks, see http://www.toaep.org/reviews/.

Lightning Source UK Ltd.
Milton Keynes UK
UKHW022100140820
368278UK00006B/172/J